PENGUIN CLASSICS

GUYS AND DOLLS AND OTHER WRITINGS

DAMON RUNYON was born in Kansas in 1884 and grew up in Pueblo, Colorado. As a teenager he wrote articles for the local newspapers, and in 1898, at the age of fourteen, he enlisted in the Spanish-American War. He returned to work on various newspapers and became a sportswriter for the *New York American* in 1911. During the First World War he was a war correspondent for the Hearst newspaper chain and after the war continued to work as a Hearst columnist. He died in 1946.

PETE HAMILL is a veteran journalist and novelist. He has written many best-selling books, including *A Drinking Life, Snow in August,* and *Forever.* His most recent book is *Downtown: My Manhattan.* He is a Distinguished Writer in Residence at New York University. He is a past winner of the Damon Runyon Award from the Denver Press Club.

DANIEL R. SCHWARZ is the Frederic J. Whiton Professor of English and the Stephen H. Weiss Presidential Fellow at Cornell University. He is the author of numerous poems, articles, and books, including *Broadway Boogie Woogie: Damon Runyon and the Making of New York City Culture, Imagining the Holocaust, Reading Joyce's* Ulysses, *Reconfiguring Modernism: Explorations in the Relationship Between Modern Art and Modern Literature, Rereading Conrad,* and *Disraeli's Fiction.*

DAMON RUNYON

Guys and Dolls
and Other Writings

Introduction by PETE HAMILL
Essay and Annotations by DANIEL R. SCHWARZ

PENGUIN BOOKS

PENGUIN BOOKS

Published by the Penguin Group

Penguin Group (USA) Inc., 375 Hudson Street, New York, New York 10014, U.S.A.

Penguin Group (Canada), 90 Eglinton Avenue East, Suite 700, Toronto,
Ontario, Canada M4P 2Y3 (a division of Pearson Penguin Canada Inc.)

Penguin Books Ltd, 80 Strand, London WC2R 0RL, England

Penguin Ireland, 25 St Stephen's Green, Dublin 2, Ireland
(a division of Penguin Books Ltd)

Penguin Group (Australia), 250 Camberwell Road, Camberwell,
Victoria 3124, Australia (a division of Pearson Australia Group Pty Ltd)

Penguin Books India Pvt Ltd, 11 Community Centre,
Panchsheel Park, New Delhi–110 017, India

Penguin Group (NZ), 67 Apollo Drive, Rosedale, North Shore 0632,
New Zealand (a division of Pearson New Zealand Ltd)

Penguin Books (South Africa) (Pty) Ltd, 24 Sturdee Avenue,
Rosebank, Johannesburg 2196, South Africa

Penguin Books Ltd, Registered Offices:
80 Strand, London WC2R 0RL, England

This edition first published in Penguin Books 2008

1 3 5 7 9 10 8 6 4 2

Copyright © American Rights Management Co., LLC, 2008
Introduction copyright © Pete Hamill, 2008
Essay and annotations copyright © Daniel R. Schwarz, 2008
All rights reserved

Special acknowledgment is made to Matteo Molinari for his assistance with this book.

The original sources of the selections in this book are cited in
"A Note on the Text" and the annotations section.

Excerpts from *Broadway Boogie Woogie: Damon Runyon and the Making of New York City Culture*
by Daniel R. Schwarz in Mr. Schwarz's essay are reprinted by permission of Palgrave Macmillan.
Copyright © Daniel R. Schwarz, 2003.

LIBRARY OF CONGRESS CATALOGING-IN-PUBLICATION DATA
Runyon, Damon, 1880–1946.
Guys and dolls and other writings / Damon Runyon ; introduction by Pete Hamill ;
essay and annotations by Daniel R. Schwarz.
p. cm.
Includes bibliographical references.
ISBN 978-0-14-118672-6
I. Schwarz, Daniel R. II. Title.
PS3535.U52A6 2008
813'.52—dc22 2007017004

Printed in the United States of America
Set in Sabon

Contents

Introduction

The beautiful thing about Damon Runyon is that he still speaks to us across the decades. He was born in the nineteenth century—fittingly in Manhattan, Kansas—and died in 1946 after a long struggle with cancer. In between, he wrote millions of words of journalism, some poetry, and the wonderful Broadway stories that make up part of this book.

Almost all of them are tales related by an unnamed narrator (who is surely a stand-in for Runyon), and they describe a world that vanished long ago, if indeed it ever existed at all. The world was located in about ten square blocks of midtown Manhattan during the second and third decades of the twentieth century. Usually the area is called Times Square, although Runyon, who worked for Hearst and never *The New York Times,* seldom uses that name. It is a world primarily inhabited by the New York children of Irish, Jewish, and Italian immigrants, although Runyon enjoys describing the collisions of his Broadway people with various outlanders: slumming members of the upper class, greenhorns from way out in America, ambitious grifters in town to make big scores. There are almost no African-Americans (and in the racist argot of the era, Runyon refers to various black porters and waiters as "stove lids"). Harlem in that era was vivid with life and ambition. Runyon, the story writer, never bothered going there, except for glancing visits on the way to and from the Polo Grounds, where a team called the Giants once played baseball, long ago.

The Runyon world appears in these stories to be a male club (one critic describes it as "homoerotic"). His gangsters, gamblers, old bootleggers, prizefighters, waiters, musicians, and newspapermen are triumphantly male. Their language has a male rhythm. So do their lives, where the macho codes often lead them to mayhem. But many of the stories feature women, and the effect they have on men. The women are often tougher than men, and certainly more realistic. Most of them accept the notion of love, but they almost never separate that dangerous and delightful emotion from the hard realities of economics. Runyon's showgirls all seem to understand that their beauty is a transient thing, an accident of genes and luck, but that with clarity and a certain amount of guile, a doll can build a secure future upon that splendid accident. Most of Runyon's females would have agreed with Runyon's advice to young writers: "Get the money."

One result: the men are terminally wary of women and live with them in a state of comical alert. Here is the narrator in the story "Tobias the Terrible" (1937):

> If I have all the tears that are shed on Broadway by guys in love, I will have enough salt water to start an opposition ocean to the Atlantic and Pacific, with enough left over to run the Great Salt Lake out of business. But I wish to say I never shed any of these tears personally, because I am never in love, and furthermore, barring a bad break, I never expect to be in love, for the way I look at it love is strictly the old phedinkus.

Nobody alive knows what a "phedinkus" is, and Runyon's stories are sprinkled with other words whose meanings have vanished into air. But their meanings can almost always be deciphered from context. A phedinkus must be a swindle, a fraud, a sweet lie created to tear down personal defenses. Runyon, of course, was not immune to the old phedinkus. All accounts of his life tell the story of his two failed marriages, his estrangement from his children, his erratic romances, his abiding solitude and loneliness. In the Runyon story, there was another object of his enduring capacity for love: the city of New York.

He started life as Alfred Damon Runyan (with an "a"). The date of birth was October 4, 1880, a year before Doc Holiday and the Earps fought in the Gunfight at the O.K. Corral, while Henry James, in a very different America, published *The Portrait of a Lady*. His father, Alfred Lee Runyan, was a second-generation newspaperman, an itinerant who could set type and write stories and who settled for a long while in Pueblo, Colorado. There the boy was raised and began to learn his trade. The boy's mother died when he was either seven or eleven (the biographical confusion came from Runyon himself, who at the height of his fame shaved four years off his age for an entry in *Who's Who in America*). The best bet is eleven. His widowed father was part of the hard-drinking newspaper tradition, while Damon roamed Pueblo with his school-mates. He went only as far as the sixth grade but would get his most valuable education (about craft and life) from working at newspapers, following the unwritten syllabus of a classical appren-ticeship. At fifteen he was being paid to write for the *Pueblo Evening Press*. In one of his early bylined stories, a typo changed the "a" to an "o," and the young man let it stand, perhaps as a small dec-laration of independence from his father.

In 1898 he enlisted in the army for the Spanish-American War (with the Thirteenth Minnesota volunteers) and was sent to the Philippines. He saw no action but did write stories for papers called *Manila Freedom* and *Soldier's Letter*. When he returned to Col-orado, he moved from paper to paper, constantly developing his craft, before landing at the *Denver Post,* a big-time newspaper. There he became a star sportswriter who could also report fea-tures, politics, and an occasional murder. He began writing short fiction for national magazines, much of it set in the West. At the same time he ached for the East, specifically that other, larger, more glittering Manhattan. In 1910 he got his chance.

He went to work for William Randolph Hearst, another west-erner who had gone east. He started covering baseball and boxing for Hearst's *New York American* (where an editor cut the "Alfred" out of his byline). He gave up drinking for life (but kept smoking heavily), married a newspaperwoman named Ellen Egan, and fa-thered two children. By 1914 he was a star reporter, traveling to the Mexican border to observe Pershing's futile pursuit of Pancho Villa and covering murder trials, eventually the war in France, the first exploits of pilots in the heroic early days of flight, and then the multiple imbecilities of Prohibition. He was earning about $500 a week.

By all accounts, he was a small, quiet man, given to expensive clothes and good food, with a fine eye for detail and an ear for the nuances of human speech. As a newspaperman, in that era before television, he could put the reader in the courtroom or the ballpark or the scene of a murder. His silence was not surly. He was listen-ing. Reporters learn quickly that if they are doing the talking, they can't hear a word from anyone else. The same accounts tell us that Runyon, in the years of his growing fame, was a dreadful husband. (His wife would die in 1931 from the effects of alcoholism while Runyon lived in solitude at the Hotel Forrest.) He was, like many of his characters, a heavy gambler, always in need of money.

In 1929, that year when all the certainties of the Roaring Twenties began to shudder and then disappear into the Great Depression, Runyon found a way to get more money.

The first of Runyon's Broadway stories appeared in Hearst's *Cosmopolitan* two months before the Wall Street crash and was called "Romance in the Roaring Forties." It was about a rough customer called Dave the Dude, his doll, Miss Billy Perry, and a gossip columnist called Waldo Winchester. Like most of the Broadway stories, it's about love and money. Dave the Dude was probably based on real-life gangster Frank Costello (who by mob standards was a pacifist, preferring brains to muscle). The gossip columnist was an obvious version of Walter Winchell, who would soon be the most powerful journalist in America and much later, in the last years of Runyon's life, a close friend. That first Broadway story was something new in American fiction, with its own rhythms and language and a view of human beings that was at once cynical and embracing.

The audience must have loved it, and certainly magazine editors did, in that era when the short story was a major form of American fiction. More than eighty stories would follow, featuring Nathan Detroit, Feet Samuels, Sky Masterson, Big Jule, Nicely-Nicely Jones, Madame La Gimp, Good Time Charley Bernstein, Miss Missouri Martin (based on Texas Guinan), Benny South Street, and scores of others. Many would later appear in the Frank Loesser musical *Guys and Dolls,* which opened on Broadway in 1950. Runyon wouldn't live to see this wonderful show, but I suspect he would have loved it. The lyrics, music, and spoken word were absolutely true to Runyon's stories and his vision of Broadway.

The voice of those stories is usually the "historical present," as in "Butch Minds the Baby":

One evening along about seven o'clock I am sitting in Mindy's restaurant putting on the gefilte fish, when in comes three parties

from Brooklyn wearing caps as follows: Harry the Horse, Little
Isadore and Spanish John.

The narrator is not sitting in Mindy's while he is telling the story;
this unfolding story happened in the past, even though Runyon
uses the present tense. But the simple device gives the stories a
kind of energy that would be absent in most uses of the past tense.
It looks easy, until you try to do it. The voice was above all urban,
drawing on Yiddish, which in the 1920s was New York's second
language, as Spanish is today. Thus, a five-dollar bill is a "finiff"
and various people are "starkers" (tough guys) or "gonophs"
(thieves, cheats, pickpockets). Sometimes we can hear Runyon's
people talking above their station, playing social roles that are lies,
but we certainly don't mistake them for characters out of Edith
Wharton, who do the same thing.

This is, of course, a fictional world. The gangsters don't speak
the way real gangsters spoke in that era, or in ours. There is no
obscenity, for example, no compounding of vile words to express
contempt. And in the tales of romance there are subtle implica-
tions of sexual activity but no clinical details and no eroticism.
Runyon is often accused of sentimentalizing his gangsters, and is
sometimes guilty as charged. But a close reading of most of these
stories shows us a clear darker side. His people often do terrible
things to each other, and out of base motives.

He actually knew many of the people he describes in his fictions. One such character he called Nathan Detroit in some stories and in others, Armand Rosenthal, The Brain. The character was
loosely based on the notorious gambler Arnold Rothstein, who was
said to have fixed the 1919 World Series. In his 1925 masterwork,
The Great Gatsby, F. Scott Fitzgerald presented a minor character
named Meyer Wolfsheim, also based on Rothstein, but alas, he is
a clumsy anti-Semitic caricature. Runyon's version was free of this
virus, for good reason. He knew Rothstein well and often sat with
him for coffee at the Rothstein table near the cashier at Lindy's
restaurant on Broadway (as Mindy's, the location of many of his
stories). Rothstein was no common thug. He was, by most accounts,
articulate, subtle, intelligent. Presumably their conversations were
about gambling, women, and food, and not the meaning of life,
but Runyon never told us. On November 4, 1928, Runyon had one

final whispery conversation with Rothstein at Lindy's before the gambler went off to be shot dead at the Park Central Hotel for welshing on a gigantic gambling debt. He lives on in Runyon's stories.

So does the New York that almost certainly existed only in the imagination of the man who wrote about it. Perhaps it was New York as he wanted it to be, the place he had yearned for when he was young in the West. Perhaps it was a city that was both magical and real. Certainly Runyon loved New York as William Faulkner later said he loved Mississippi: in spite of, not because. These stories were almost all written during the Great Depression, but hard times never overwhelm the players, even the two-dollar horse players. They know that their fate is to die broke. Runyon was free of ideology, generally embracing the principles of the New Deal (although he grew more conservative as he grew older). There are a few ideologues in the stories, usually figures of fun, and at least one story deals with the civil war in Spain, which consumed so much energy among many New Yorkers. But Runyon did not write fiction to change his readers' minds. He wanted them to laugh. And they did, and still do.

Yes, he was an entertainer. So was Mark Twain. He never wrote a novel. Neither did Anton Chekhov. He said he wrote for money, and he made a lot of it at the typewriter, with at least sixteen of his tales becoming movies. "I took one little section of New York," he said once, "and made half a million dollars writing about it." Around 1940 he moved to Hollywood, where he worked for a few years as a producer and made more money. He continued writing his newspaper column. But he was already sick with the cancer that would ultimately kill him.

In 1932, a year after his first wife died, Runyon married a young woman he called Patricia del Grande of Caliditas, Spain. She was, he insisted, "a Spanish countess." Maybe she was, but her story is the stuff of fiction. In one version Runyon met her in Mexico when he was covering the Pershing-Villa events, was touched by her poverty, and offered to pay for her education. She was then simply Patricia Amati. She was also Mexican, not Spanish, and definitely not a countess. In the late 1920s she came to find Runyon in New York, where she hoped to become a dancer. He fell in love with her, in the sudden way so many of his characters did, even though he was twenty-six years her senior. For a while they lived very well indeed, in Beverly Hills, and in a villa on Hibiscus Island in Miami, across from Palm Island, where Al Capone had his mansion.

In 1944 Runyon's cancerous larynx was removed. He continued to write occasional newspaper columns, but the fiction dried up. At some point his wife began to live a separate life and divorced him in early 1946 to marry a younger man. By then he was back in New York, where he had lived most intensely and written his finest work. After his death his ashes were scattered over Manhattan from an airplane flown by the World War I ace Eddie Rickenbacker.

Today not many remember Runyon himself, or the era in which he lived with so much verve and melancholy. But here are the stories. They forever remain part of the long tale of New York.

—Pete Hamill

Suggestions for Further Reading

by Daniel R. Schwarz

I. WORKS BY DAMON RUNYON

My Old Man. New York: Stackpole Sons, 1939.

My Wife Ethel. Philadelphia: David McKay, 1940.

The Damon Runyon Omnibus. Garden City, N.Y.: The Sun Dial Press, 1944.

In Our Town. New York: Creative Age Press, 1946.

Short Takes. New York: Somerset Books, 1946.

Trials and Other Tribulations. Philadelphia: J. B. Lippincott, 1947.

Poems for Men. New York: Duell, Sloan and Pearce, 1947.

More Guys and Dolls. Garden City, N.Y.: Garden City Books, 1951.

Runyon on Broadway. London: Constable, 1951.

The Turps. London: Constable, 1951.

Runyon from First to Last. London: Constable, 1964.

II. ESSENTIAL CRITICAL AND SCHOLARLY MATERIALS

Behn, Noel. *Lindbergh: The Crime.* New York: Atlantic Monthly Press, 1994.

Bender, Thomas. *New York Intellect: A History of Intellectual Life in New York City from 1750 to the Beginnings of Our Own Time.* New York: Alfred A. Knopf, 1987.

Bernhardt, Debra. *Ordinary People, Extraordinary Lives.* New York: New York University Press, 2000.

Breslin, Jimmy. *Damon Runyon.* New York: Ticknor and Fields, 1991.

Burrows, Edwin G., and Mike Wallace. *Gotham: A History of New York City to the 1890s.* New York: Oxford University Press, 1999.

Clark, Tom. *The World of Damon Runyon,* New York: Harper & Row, 1978.

Cooney, Terry A. *The Rise of the New York Intellectuals: Partisan Review and its Circle, 1934–45.* Madison: University of Wisconsin Press, 1986.

D'itri, Patricia Ward. *Damon Runyon.* New York: Twayne, 1982.

Douglas, Anne. *Terrible Honesty: Mongrel Manhattan in the 1920s.* New York: Farrar, Straus and Giroux, 1996.

Erenberg, Lewis. *Steppin' Out: New York Night Life and the Transformation of American Culture, 1890–1930.* Chicago: University of Chicago Press, 1981.

————."Impresarios of Broadway Nightlife." In *Inventing Times Square: Commerce and Culture at the Crossroads of the World,* ed. William Taylor. New York: Russell Sage Foundation, 1991.

Fitzgerald, F. Scott. *The Great Gatsby.* New York: Scribner's, 1925.

Friendly, Albert, and Ronald L. Goldfarb, eds. *Crime and Publicity: The Impact of News on the Administration of Justice.* New York: Twentieth Century Fund, 1967.

Fritzsche, Peter. *Reading Berlin* 1900. Cambridge, Mass.: Harvard University Press, 1996.

Gabler, Neal. *Winchell: Gossip, Power and the Culture of Celebrity.* New York: Alfred A. Knopf, 1994.

Harris, Neil. "Urban Tourism and the Commercial City." In *Inventing Times Square: Commerce and Culture at the Crossroads of the World,* ed. William Taylor. New York: Russell Sage Foundation, 1991.

————. "The View from the City." In *Norman Rockwell: Pictures for the American People,* eds. Maureen Hart Hennessey and Judy L. Larson. Atlanta: High Museum of Art, and New York: Harry N. Abrams, 1999.

Hoyt, Edwin P. *A Gentleman of Broadway.* Boston: Little, Brown, 1964.

Kahn, Bonnie Menes. *Cosmopolitan Culture.* New York: Atheneum, 1987.

Kennedy, David M. *Freedom from Fear: The American People in Depression and War 1929–1945.* New York: Oxford University Press, 1999.

Kennedy, Ludovic. *The Airman and the Carpenter.* New York: Viking Penguin, 1985.

Kennedy, William. *Guys and Dolls: The Stories of Damon Runyon.* New York: Penguin, 1992.

Lampard, Eric. "Introductory Essay." In *Inventing Times Square: Commerce and Culture at the Crossroads of the World,* ed. William Taylor. New York: Russell Sage Foundation, 1991.

Lofton, John. *Justice and the Press.* Boston: Beacon Press, 1966.

Melville, Herman. "Bartleby, the Scrivener." In *The Great Short Works of Herman Melville.* New York: Harper & Row, 1969.

Mosedale, John. *The Men Who Invented Broadway.* New York: Richard Marek, Publisher, 1981.

Mumford, Lewis. *The Culture of Cities.* New York: Harcourt, Brace, 1938.

Nelson, Richard, ed. *Strictly Dishonorable and Other Lost American Plays.* New York: Theatre Communications Group, 1986.

Roberts, C. E. Bechhofer. *The New World of Crime: Famous American Trials.* London: Eyre and Spottiswoode, 1933.

Schwarz, Daniel R. *Broadway Boogie Woogie: Damon Runyon and the Making of New York City Culture.* New York: Palgrave, 2003.

Senelick, Laurence. "Private Parts in Public Places." In *Inventing Times Square: Commerce and Culture at the Crossroads of the World,* ed. William Taylor. New York: Russell Sage Foundation, 1991.

Wagner, Jean. *Runyonese: The Mind and Craft of Damon Runyon.* New York: Stechert Hafner, 1965.

Weber, Max. *The City.* New York: Free Press, 1958.

Weiner, Edward H. *The Damon Runyon Story,* London: Longmans, 1964.

A Note on the Text

The works of Damon Runyon appeared in a great variety of periodicals, books, and newspapers throughout his lifetime, and beyond. The following Broadway stories were taken from the collection *Guys and Dolls: The Stories of Damon Runyon,* published by Penguin Books, 1992: "Madame La Gimp," "Blood Pressure," "The Lily of St. Pierre," "The Bloodhounds of Broadway," "Dream Street Rose," "Tobias the Terrible," "Dancing Dan's Christmas," "It Comes Up Mud," "Broadway Complex," "The Three Wise Guys," "The Lemon Drop Kid," "Sense of Humor," and "Breach of Promise." The following Broadway stories were taken from *Romance in the Roaring Forties and Other Stories,* published by American Play Company, 1986: "Romance in the Roaring Forties," "Butch Minds the Baby," "The Hottest Guy in the World," "The Snatching of Bookie Bob," "Hold 'em Yale!" "For a Pal," "Little Miss Marker," "Earthquake," "The Idyll of Miss Sarah Brown," and "The Old Doll's House." The remaining Broadway stories can be found in *The Damon Runyon Omnibus,* published by The Sun Dial Press, 1944, which features selections from three of Runyon's volumes *(Guys and Dolls, Blue Plate Special,* and *Money from Home)*: "A Very Honorable Guy," "Dark Dolores," "Lillian," "Social Error," "'Gentlemen, the King!'" "The Brain Goes Home," "Broadway Financier," "The Brakeman's Daughter," "Princess O'Hara," "A Nice Price," and "Undertaker Song." The final Broadway story, "A Light in France," was first published in *Collier's,* January 15, 1944. "A Call on the President" first appeared in *The Saturday Evening Post,* August 21, 1937, and "The Defense of Strikerville" in *McClure's,* February 1907. "Two Men Named Collins" was printed in *Reader,* September 1907, and "Lou Louder" in *Collier's,* August 5, 1936. "Mr. 'B' and His Stork Club" was first published in *Cosmopolitan,* May 1947. For the original sources of all remaining inclusions, please refer to "Essay and Annotations" by Daniel R. Schwarz.

Guys and Dolls and Other Writings

THE BROADWAY STORIES

ROMANCE IN
THE ROARING FORTIES

Only a rank sucker will think of taking two peeks at Dave the Dude's doll, because while Dave may stand for the first peek, figuring it is a mistake, it is a sure thing he will get sored up at the second peek, and Dave the Dude is certainly not a man to have sored up at you.

But this Waldo Winchester is one hundred per cent sucker, which is why he takes quite a number of peeks at Dave's doll. And what is more, she takes quite a number of peeks right back at him. And there you are. When a guy and a doll get to taking peeks back and forth at each other, why, there you are indeed.

This Waldo Winchester is a nice-looking young guy who writes pieces about Broadway for the *Morning Item*. He writes about the goings-on in night clubs, such as fights, and one thing and another, and also about who is running around with who, including guys and dolls.

Sometimes this is very embarrassing to people who may be married and are running around with people who are not married, but of course Waldo Winchester cannot be expected to ask one and all for their marriage certificates before he writes his pieces for the paper.

The chances are if Waldo Winchester knows Miss Billy Perry is Dave the Dude's doll, he will never take more than his first peek at her, but nobody tips him off until his second or third peek, and by this time Miss Billy Perry is taking her peeks back at him and Waldo Winchester is hooked.

In fact, he is plumb gone, and being a sucker, like I tell you, he does not care whose doll she is. Personally, I do not blame him much, for Miss Billy Perry is worth a few peeks, especially when she is out on the floor of Miss Missouri Martin's Sixteen Hundred Club doing her tap dance. Still, I do not think the best tap-dancer that ever lives can make me take two peeks at her if I know she is Dave the Dude's doll, for Dave somehow thinks more than somewhat of his dolls.

He especially thinks plenty of Miss Billy Perry, and sends her fur coats, and diamond rings, and one thing and another, which she sends back to him at once, because it seems she does not take presents from guys. This is considered most surprising all along Broadway, but people figure the chances are she has some other angle.

Anyway, this does not keep Dave the Dude from liking her just the same, and so she is considered his doll by one and all, and is respected accordingly until this Waldo Winchester comes along.

It happens that he comes along while Dave the Dude is off in the Modoc on a little run down to the Bahamas to get some goods for his business, such as Scotch and champagne, and by the time Dave gets back Miss Billy Perry and Waldo Winchester are at the stage where they sit in corners between her numbers and hold hands.

Of course nobody tells Dave the Dude about this, because they do not wish to get him excited. Not even Miss Missouri Martin tells him, which is most unusual because Miss Missouri Martin, who is sometimes called "Mizzoo" for short, tells everything she knows as soon as she knows it, which is very often before it happens.

You see, the idea is when Dave the Dude is excited he may blow somebody's brains out, and the chances are it will be nobody's brains but Waldo Winchester's, although some claim that Waldo Winchester has no brains or he will not be hanging around Dave the Dude's doll.

I know Dave is very, very fond of Miss Billy Perry, because I hear him talk to her several times, and he is most polite to her and never gets out of line in her company by using cuss words, or anything like this. Furthermore, one night when One-eyed Solly Abrahams is a little stewed up he refers to Miss Billy Perry as a broad, meaning no harm whatever, for this is the way many of the boys speak of the dolls.

But right away Dave the Dude reaches across the table and bops One-eyed Solly right in the mouth, so everybody knows from then on that Dave thinks well of Miss Billy Perry. Of course Dave is always thinking fairly well of some doll as far as this goes, but it is seldom he gets to bopping guys in the mouth over them.

Well, one night what happens but Dave the Dude walks into the

Sixteen Hundred Club, and there in the entrance, what does he see but this Waldo Winchester and Miss Billy Perry kissing each other back and forth friendly. Right away Dave reaches for the old equalizer to shoot Waldo Winchester, but it seems Dave does not happen to have the old equalizer with him, not expecting to have to shoot anybody this particular evening.

So Dave the Dude walks over and, as Waldo Winchester hears him coming and lets go his strangle-hold on Miss Billy Perry, Dave nails him with a big right hand on the chin. I will say for Dave the Dude that he is a fair puncher with his right hand, though his left is not so good, and he knocks Waldo Winchester bow-legged. In fact, Waldo folds right up on the floor.

Well, Miss Billy Perry lets out a screech you can hear clear to the Battery and runs over to where Waldo Winchester lights, and falls on top of him squalling very loud. All anybody can make out of what she says is that Dave the Dude is a big bum, although Dave is not so big, at that, and that she loves Waldo Winchester.

Dave walks over and starts to give Waldo Winchester the leather, which is considered customary in such cases, but he seems to change his mind, and instead of booting Waldo around, Dave turns and walks out of the joint looking very black and mad, and the next anybody hears of him he is over in the Chicken Club doing plenty of drinking.

This is regarded as a very bad sign indeed, because while everybody goes to the Chicken Club now and then to give Tony Bertazzola, the owner, a friendly play, very few people care to do any drinking there, because Tony's liquor is not meant for anybody to drink except the customers.

Well, Miss Billy Perry gets Waldo Winchester on his pegs again, and wipes his chin off with her handkerchief, and by and by he is all okay except for a big lump on his chin. And all the time she is telling Waldo Winchester what a big bum Dave the Dude is, although afterwards Miss Missouri Martin gets hold of Miss Billy Perry and puts the blast on her plenty for chasing a two-handed spender such as Dave the Dude out of the joint.

"You are nothing but a little sap," Miss Missouri Martin tells Miss Billy Perry. "You cannot get the right time off this newspaper guy, while everybody knows Dave the Dude is a very fast man with a dollar."

"But I love Mr. Winchester," says Miss Billy Perry. "He is so romantic. He is not a bootlegger and a gunman like Dave the Dude. He puts lovely pieces in the paper about me, and he is a gentleman at all times."

Now of course Miss Missouri Martin is not in a position to argue about gentlemen, because she meets very few in the Sixteen Hundred Club and anyway, she does not wish to make Waldo Winchester mad as he is apt to turn around and put pieces in his paper that will be a knock to the joint, so she lets the matter drop.

Miss Billy Perry and Waldo Winchester go on holding hands between her numbers, and maybe kissing each other now and then, as young people are liable to do, and Dave the Dude plays the chill for the Sixteen Hundred Club and everything seems to be all right. Naturally we are all very glad there is no more trouble over the proposition, because the best Dave can get is the worst of it in a jam with a newspaper guy.

Personally, I figure Dave will soon find himself another doll and forget all about Miss Billy Perry, because now that I take another peek at her, I can see where she is just about the same as any other tap-dancer, except that she is red-headed. Tap-dancers are generally blackheads, but I do not know why.

Moosh, the doorman at the Sixteen Hundred Club, tells me Miss Missouri Martin keeps plugging for Dave the Dude with Miss Billy Perry in a quiet way, because he says he hears Miss Missouri Martin make the following crack one night to her: "Well, I do not see any Simple Simon on your lean and linger."

This is Miss Missouri Martin's way of saying she sees no diamond on Miss Billy Perry's finger, for Miss Missouri Martin is an old experienced doll, who figures if a guy loves a doll he will prove it with diamonds. Miss Missouri Martin has many diamonds herself, though how any guy can ever get himself heated up enough about Miss Missouri Martin to give her diamonds is more than I can see.

I am not a guy who goes around much, so I do not see Dave the Dude for a couple of weeks, but late one Sunday afternoon little Johnny McGowan, who is one of Dave's men, comes and says to me like this: "What do you think? Dave grabs the scribe a little while ago and is taking him out for an airing!"

Well, Johnny is so excited it is some time before I can get him cooled out enough to explain. It seems that Dave the Dude gets his biggest car out of the garage and sends his driver, Wop Joe, over to the *Item* office where Waldo Winchester works, with a message that Miss Billy Perry wishes to see Waldo right away at Miss Missouri Martin's apartment on Fifty-ninth Street.

Of course this message is nothing but the phonus bolonus, but Waldo drops in for it and gets in the car. Then Wop Joe drives him up to Miss Missouri Martin's apartment, and who gets in the car there but Dave the Dude. And away they go.

Now this is very bad news indeed, because when Dave the Dude takes a guy out for an airing the guy very often does not come back. What happens to him I never ask, because the best a guy can get by asking questions in this man's town is a bust in the nose.

But I am much worried over this proposition, because I like Dave the Dude, and I know that taking a newspaper guy like Waldo Winchester out for an airing is apt to cause talk, especially if he does not come back. The other guys that Dave the Dude takes out for airings do not mean much in particular, but here is a guy who may produce trouble, even if he is a sucker, on account of being connected with a newspaper.

I know enough about newspapers to know that by and by the editor or somebody will be around wishing to know where Waldo Winchester's pieces about Broadway are, and if there are no pieces from Waldo Winchester, the editor will wish to know why. Finally it will get around to where other people will wish to know, and after a while many people will be running around saying: "Where is Waldo Winchester?"

And if enough people in this town get to running around saying where is So-and-so, it becomes a great mystery and the newspapers hop on the cops and the cops hop on everybody, and by and by there is so much heat in town that it is no place for a guy to be.

But what is to be done about this situation I do not know. Personally, it strikes me as very bad indeed, and while Johnny goes away to do a little telephoning, I am trying to think up someplace to go where people will see me, and remember afterwards that I am there in case it is necessary for them to remember.

Finally Johnny comes back, very excited, and says: "Hey, the Dude is up at the Woodcock Inn on the Pelham Parkway, and he is sending out the word for one and all to come at once. Good Time Charley Bernstein just gets the wire and tells me. Something is doing. The rest of the mob are on their way, so let us be moving."

But here is an invitation which does not strike me as a good

thing at all. The way I look at it, Dave the Dude is no company for
a guy like me at this time. The chances are he either does something to Waldo Winchester already, or is getting ready to do something to him which I wish no part of.

Personally, I have nothing against newspaper guys, not even the
ones who write pieces about Broadway. If Dave the Dude wishes
to do something to Waldo Winchester, all right, but what is the
sense of bringing outsiders into it? But the next thing I know,
I am in Johnny McGowan's roadster, and he is zipping along very
fast indeed, paying practically no attention to traffic lights or anything else.

As we go busting out the Concourse, I get to thinking the situation over, and I figure that Dave the Dude probably keeps thinking about Miss Billy Perry, and drinking liquor such as they sell in
the Chicken Club, until finally he blows his topper. The way I
look at it, only a guy who is off his nut will think of taking a
newspaper guy out for an airing over a doll, when dolls are a dime
a dozen in this man's town.

Still, I remember reading in the papers about a lot of different
guys who are considered very sensible until they get tangled up
with a doll, and maybe loving her, and the first thing anybody
knows they hop out of windows, or shoot themselves, or somebody else, and I can see where even a guy like Dave the Dude may
go daffy over a doll.

I can see that little Johnny McGowan is worried, too, but he
does not say much, and we pull up in front of the Woodcock Inn
in no time whatever, to find a lot of other cars there ahead of us,
some of which I recognize as belonging to different parties.

The Woodcock Inn is what is called a roadhouse, and is run by
Big Nig Skolsky, a very nice man indeed, and a friend of everybody's. It stands back a piece off the Pelham Parkway and is a
very pleasant place to go to, what with Nig having a good band
and a floor show with a lot of fair-looking dolls, and everything
else a man can wish for a good time. It gets a nice play from nice
people, although Nig's liquor is nothing extra.

Personally, I never go there much, because I do not care for
roadhouses, but it is a great spot for Dave the Dude when he is
pitching parties, or even when he is only drinking single-handed.
There is a lot of racket in the joint as we drive up, and who comes
out to meet us but Dave the Dude himself with a big hello. His

face is very red, and he seems heated up no little, but he does not look like a guy who is meaning any harm to anybody, especially a newspaper guy.

"Come in, guys!" Dave the Dude yells. "Come right in!"

So we go in, and the place is full of people sitting at tables, or out on the floor dancing, and I see Miss Missouri Martin with all her diamonds hanging from her in different places, and Good Time Charley Bernstein, and Feet Samuels, and Tony Bertazzola, and Skeets Bolivar, and Nick the Greek, and Rochester Red, and a lot of other guys and dolls from around and about.

In fact, it looks as if everybody from all the joints on Broadway are present, including Miss Billy Perry, who is all dressed up in white and is lugging a big bundle of orchids and so forth, and who is giggling and smiling and shaking hands and going on generally. And finally I see Waldo Winchester, the scribe, sitting at a ringside table all by himself, but there is nothing wrong with him as far as I can see. I mean, he seems to be all in one piece so far.

"Dave," I say to Dave the Dude, very quiet, "what is coming off here? You know a guy cannot be too careful what he does around this town, and I will hate to see you tangled up in anything right now."

"Why," Dave says, "what are you talking about? Nothing is coming off here but a wedding, and it is going to be the best wedding anybody on Broadway ever sees. We are waiting for the preacher now."

"You mean somebody is going to be married?" I ask, being somewhat confused.

"Certainly," Dave the Dude says. "What do you think? What is the idea of a wedding, anyway?"

"Who is going to be married?" I ask.

"Nobody but Billy and the scribe," Dave says. "This is the greatest thing I ever do in my life. I run into Billy the other night and she is crying her eyes out because she loves this scribe and wishes to marry him, but it seems the scribe has nothing he can use for money. So I tell Billy to leave it to me, because you know I love her myself so much I wish to see her happy at all times, even if she has to marry to be that way.

"So I frame this wedding party, and after they are married I am going to stake them to a few G's so they can get a good running start," Dave says. "But I do not tell the scribe and I do not let Billy tell him as I wish it to be a big surprise to him. I kidnap him this afternoon and bring him out here and he is scared half to death thinking I am going to scrag him.

"In fact," Dave says, "I never see a guy so scared. He is still so scared nothing seems to cheer him up. Go over and tell him to shake himself together, because nothing but happiness for him is coming off here."

Well, I wish to say I am greatly relieved to think that Dave intends doing nothing worse to Waldo Winchester than getting him married up, so I go over to where Waldo is sitting. He certainly looks somewhat alarmed. He is all in a huddle with himself, and he has what you call a vacant stare in his eyes. I can see that he is indeed frightened, so I give him a jolly slap on the back and I say: "Congratulations, pal! Cheer up, the worst is yet to come!"

"You bet it is," Waldo Winchester says, his voice so solemn I am greatly surprised.

"You are a fine-looking bridegroom," I say. "You look as if you are at a funeral instead of a wedding. Why do you not laugh ha-ha, and maybe take a dram or two and go to cutting up some?"

"Mister," says Waldo Winchester, "my wife is not going to care for me getting married to Miss Billy Perry."

"Your wife?" I say, much astonished. "What is this you are speaking of? How can you have any wife except Miss Billy Perry? This is great foolishness."

"I know," Waldo says, very sad. "I know. But I got a wife just the same, and she is going to be very nervous when she hears about this. My wife is very strict with me. My wife does not allow me to go around marrying people. My wife is Lola Sapola, of the Rolling Sapolas, the acrobats, and I am married to her for five years. She is the strong lady who juggles the other four people in the act. My wife just gets back from a year's tour of the Interstate time, and she is at the Marx Hotel right this minute. I am upset by this proposition."

"Does Miss Billy Perry know about this wife?" I ask.

"No," he says. "No. She thinks I am single-o."

"But why do you not tell Dave the Dude you are already married when he brings you out here to marry you off to Miss Billy Perry?" I ask. "It seems to me a newspaper guy must know it is against the law for a guy to marry several different dolls unless he is a Turk, or some such."

"Well," Waldo says, "if I tell Dave the Dude I am married after taking his doll away from him, I am quite sure Dave will be very much excited, and maybe do something harmful to my health."

Now there is much in what the guy says, to be sure. I am inclined to think, myself, that Dave will be somewhat disturbed when he learns of this situation, especially when Miss Billy Perry starts in being unhappy about it. But what is to be done I do not know, except maybe to let the wedding go on, and then when Waldo is out of reach of Dave, to put in a claim that he is insane, and that the marriage does not count. It is a sure thing I do not wish to be around when Dave the Dude hears Waldo is already married.

I am thinking that maybe I better take it on the lam out of here, when there is a great row at the door and I hear Dave the Dude yelling that the preacher arrives. He is a very nice-looking preacher, at that, though he seems somewhat surprised by the goings-on, especially when Miss Missouri Martin steps up and takes charge of him. Miss Missouri Martin tells him she is fond of preachers, and is quite used to them, because she is twice married by preachers, and twice by justices of the peace, and once by a ship's captain at sea.

By this time one and all present, except maybe myself and Waldo Winchester, and the preacher and maybe Miss Billy Perry, are somewhat corned. Waldo is still sitting at his table looking very sad and saying "Yes" and "No" to Miss Billy Perry whenever she skips past him, for Miss Billy Perry is too much pleasured up with happiness to stay long in one spot.

Dave the Dude is more corned than anybody else, because he has two or three days' running start on everybody. And when Dave the Dude is corned I wish to say that he is a very unreliable guy as to temper, and he is apt to explode right in your face any minute. But he seems to be getting a great bang out of the doings.

Well, by and by Nig Skolsky has the dance floor cleared, and then he moves out on the floor a sort of arch of very beautiful flowers. The idea seems to be that Miss Billy Perry and Waldo Winchester are to be married under this arch. I can see that Dave the Dude must put in several days planning this whole proposition, and it must cost him plenty of the old do-re-mi, especially as I see him showing Miss Missouri Martin a diamond ring as big as a cough drop.

"It is for the bride," Dave the Dude says. "The poor loogan she is marrying will never have enough dough to buy her such a rock, and she always wishes a big one. I get it off a guy who brings it in from Los Angeles. I am going to give the bride away myself in person, so how do I act, Mizzoo? I want Billy to have everything according to the book."

Well, while Miss Missouri Martin is trying to remember back to one of her weddings to tell him, I take another peek at Waldo Winchester to see how he is making out. I once see two guys go to the old warm squativoo up in Sing Sing, and I wish to say both are laughing heartily compared to Waldo Winchester at this moment.

Miss Billy Perry is sitting with him and the orchestra leader is calling his men dirty names because none of them can think of how "Oh, Promise Me" goes, when Dave the Dude yells: "Well, we are all set! Let the happy couple step forward!"

Miss Billy Perry bounces up and grabs Waldo Winchester by the arm and pulls him up out of his chair. After a peek at his face I am willing to lay six to five he does not make the arch. But he finally gets there with everybody laughing and clapping their hands, and the preacher comes forward, and Dave the Dude looks happier than I ever see him look before in his life as they all get together under the arch of flowers.

Well, all of a sudden there is a terrible racket at the front door of the Woodcock Inn, with some doll doing a lot of hollering in a deep voice that sounds like a man's, and naturally everybody turns and looks that way. The doorman, a guy by the name of Slugsy Sachs, who is a very hard man indeed, seems to be trying to keep somebody out, but pretty soon there is a heavy bump and Slugsy Sachs falls down, and in comes a doll around four feet high and five feet wide.

In fact, I never see such a wide doll. She looks all hammered down. Her face is almost as wide as her shoulders, and makes me think of a great big full moon. She comes in bounding-like, and I can see that she is all churned up about something. As she bounces in, I hear a gurgle, and I look around to see Waldo Winchester slumping down to the floor, almost dragging Miss Billy Perry with him.

Well, the wide doll walks right up to the bunch under the arch and says in a large bass voice: "Which one is Dave the Dude?"

"I am Dave the Dude," says Dave the Dude, stepping up. "What do you mean by busting in here like a walrus and gumming up our wedding?"

"So you are the guy who kidnaps my ever-loving husband to marry him off to this little red-headed pancake here, are you?" the wide doll says, looking at Dave the Dude, but pointing at Miss Billy Perry.

Well now, calling Miss Billy Perry a pancake to Dave the Dude is a very serious proposition, and Dave the Dude gets very angry. He is usually rather polite to dolls, but you can see he does not care for the wide doll's manner whatever.

"Say, listen here," Dave the Dude says, "you better take a walk before somebody clips you. You must be drunk," he says. "Or daffy," he says. "What are you talking about, anyway?"

"You will see what I am talking about," the wide doll yells. "The guy on the floor there is my lawful husband. You probably frighten him to death, the poor dear. You kidnap him to marry this red-headed thing, and I am going to get you arrested as sure as my name is Lola Sapola, you simple-looking tramp!"

Naturally, everybody is greatly horrified at a doll using such language to Dave the Dude, because Dave is known to shoot guys for much less, but instead of doing something to the wide doll at once, Dave says: "What is this talk I hear? Who is married to who? Get out of here!" Dave says, grabbing the wide doll's arm.

Well, she makes out as if she is going to slap Dave in the face with her left hand, and Dave naturally pulls his kisser out of the way. But instead of doing anything with her left, Lola Sapola suddenly drives her right fist smack-dab into Dave the Dude's stomach, which naturally comes forward as his face goes back.

I wish to say I see many a body punch delivered in my life, but I never see a prettier one than this. What is more, Lola Sapola steps in with the punch, so there is plenty on it.

Now a guy who eats and drinks like Dave the Dude does cannot take them so good in the stomach, so Dave goes "oof," and sits down very hard on the dance floor, and as he is sitting there he is fumbling in his pants pocket for the old equalizer, so everybody around tears for cover except Lola Sapola, and Miss Billy Perry, and Waldo Winchester.

But before he can get his pistol out, Lola Sapola reaches down and grabs Dave by the collar and hoists him to his feet. She lets go her hold on him, leaving Dave standing on his pins, but teetering around somewhat, and then she drives her right hand to Dave's stomach a second time.

The punch drops Dave again, and Lola steps up to him as if she is going to give him the foot. But she only gathers up Waldo Winchester from off the floor and slings him across her shoulders like he is a sack of oats, and starts for the door. Dave the Dude sits up on the floor again, and by this time he has the old equalizer in his duke.

"Only for me being a gentleman I will fill you full of slugs," he yells.

Lola Sapola never even looks back, because by this time she is petting Waldo Winchester's head and calling him loving names and saying what a shame it is for bad characters like Dave the Dude to be abusing her precious one. It all sounds to me as if Lola Sapola thinks well of Waldo Winchester.

Well, after she gets out of sight, Dave the Dude gets up off the floor and stands there looking at Miss Billy Perry, who is out to break all crying records. The rest of us come out from under cover, including the preacher, and we are wondering how mad Dave the Dude is going to be about the wedding being ruined. But Dave the Dude seems only disappointed and sad.

"Billy," he says to Miss Billy Perry, "I am mighty sorry you do not get your wedding. All I wish for is your happiness, but I do not believe you can ever be happy with this scribe if he also has to have his lion tamer around. As Cupid I am a total bust. This is the only nice thing I ever try to do in my whole life, and it is too bad it does not come off. Maybe if you wait until we can drown her, or something—"

"Dave," says Miss Billy Perry, dropping so many tears that she seems to finally wash herself right into Dave the Dude's arms, "I will never, never be happy with such a guy as Waldo Winchester. I can see now you are the only man for me."

"Well, well, well," Dave the Dude says, cheering right up. "Where is the preacher? Bring on the preacher and let us have our wedding anyway."

I see Mr. and Mrs. Dave the Dude the other day, and they seem very happy. But you never can tell about married people, so of course I am never going to let on to Dave the Dude that I am the one who telephones Lola Sapola at the Marx Hotel, because maybe I do not do Dave any too much of a favor, at that.

A VERY HONORABLE GUY

Off and on I know Feet Samuels a matter of eight or ten years, up and down Broadway, and in and out, but I never have much truck with him because he is a guy I consider no dice. In fact, he does not mean a thing.

In the first place, Feet Samuels is generally broke, and there is no percentage in hanging around brokers. The way I look at it, you are not going to get anything off a guy who has not got anything. So while I am very sorry for brokers, and am always willing to hope that they get hold of something, I do not like to be around them. Long ago an old-timer who knows what he is talking about says to me:

"My boy," he says, "always try to rub up against money, for if you rub up against money long enough, some of it may rub off on you."

So in all the years I am around this town, I always try to keep in with the high shots and guys who carry these large coarse bank-notes around with them, and I stay away from small operators and chiselers and brokers. And Feet Samuels is one of the worst brokers in this town, and has been such as long as I know him.

He is a big heavy guy with several chins and very funny feet, which is why he is called Feet. These feet are extra large feet, even for a big guy, and Dave the Dude says Feet wears violin-cases for shoes. Of course this is not true, because Feet cannot get either of his feet in a violin-case, unless it is a case for a very large violin, such as a 'cello.

I see Feet one night in the Hot Box, which is a night club, dancing with a doll by the name of Hortense Hathaway, who is in Georgie White's *Scandals,* and what is she doing but standing on Feet's feet as if she is on sled runners, and Feet never knows it. He only thinks the old gondolas are a little extra heavy to shove around this night, because Hortense is no invalid. In fact, she is a good rangy welterweight.

She has blonde hair and plenty to say, and her square monicker is Annie O'Brien, and not Hortense Hathaway at all. Furthermore, she comes from Newark, which is in New Jersey, and her papa is a taxi jockey by the name of Skush O'Brien, and a very rough guy, at that, if anybody asks you. But of course the daughter of a taxi jockey is as good as anybody else for Georgie White's *Scandals* as long as her shape is okay, and nobody ever hears any complaint from the customers about Hortense on this proposition.

She is what is called a show girl, and all she has to do is to walk around and about Georgie White's stage with only a few light bandages on, and everybody considers her very beautiful, especially from the neck down, although personally I never care much for Hortense because she is very fresh to people. I often see her around the night clubs, and when she is in these deadfalls Hortense generally is wearing quite a number of diamond bracelets and fur wraps, and one thing and another, so I judge she is not doing bad for a doll from Newark, New Jersey.

Of course Feet Samuels never knows why so many other dolls besides Hortense are wishing to dance with him, but gets to thinking maybe it is because he has the old sex appeal, and he is very sore indeed when Henri, the head waiter at the Hot Box, asks him to please stay off the floor except for every tenth dance, because Feet's feet take up so much room when he is on the floor that only two other dancers can work out at the same time, it being a very small floor.

I must tell you more about Feet's feet, because they are very remarkable feet indeed. They go off at different directions under him, very sharp, so if you see Feet standing on a corner it is very difficult to tell which way he is going, because one foot will be headed one way, and the other foot the other way. In fact, guys around Mindy's restaurant often make bets on the proposition as to which way Feet is headed when he is standing still.

What Feet Samuels does for a living is the best he can, which is the same thing many other guys in this town do for a living. He hustles some around the race tracks and crap games and prize fights, picking up a few bobs here and there as a runner for the bookmakers, or scalping bets, or steering suckers, but he is never really in the money in his whole life. He is always owing and always paying off, and I never see him but what he is troubled with the shorts as regards to dough.

The only good thing you can say about Feet Samuels is he is very honorable about his debts, and what he owes he pays when he can. Anybody will tell you this about Feet Samuels, although of course it is only what any hustler such as Feet must do if he wishes to protect his credit and keep in action. Still, you will be surprised how many guys forget to pay.

It is because Feet's word is considered good at all times that he is nearly always able to raise a little dough, even off The Brain, and The Brain is not an easy guy for anybody to raise dough off of. In fact, The Brain is very tough about letting people raise dough off of him.

If anybody gets any dough off of The Brain he wishes to know right away what time they are going to pay it back, with certain interest, and if they say at five-thirty Tuesday morning, they better not make it five-thirty-one Tuesday morning, or The Brain will consider them very unreliable and never let them have any money again. And when a guy loses his credit with The Brain he is in a very tough spot indeed in this town, for The Brain is the only man who always has dough.

Furthermore, some very unusual things often happen to guys who get money off The Brain and fail to kick it back just when they promise, such as broken noses and sprained ankles and other injuries, for The Brain has people around him who seem to resent guys getting dough off of him and not kicking it back. Still, I know of The Brain letting some very surprising guys have dough, because he has a bug that he is a wonderful judge of guys' characters, and that he is never wrong on them, although I must say that no guy who gets dough off of The Brain is more surprising than Feet Samuels.

The Brain's right name is Armand Rosenthal, and he is called The Brain because he is so smart. He is well known to one and all in this town as a very large operator in gambling, and one thing and another, and nobody knows how much dough The Brain has, except that he must have plenty, because no matter how much dough is around, The Brain sooner or later gets hold of all of it. Someday I will tell you more about The Brain, but right now I wish to tell you about Feet Samuels.

It comes on a tough winter in New York, what with nearly all hands who have the price going to Miami and Havana and New

Orleans, leaving the brokers behind. There is very little action of any kind in town with the high shots gone, and one night I run into Feet Samuels in Mindy's, and he is very sad indeed. He asks me if I happen to have a finnif on me, but of course I am not giving finnifs to guys like Feet Samuels, and finally he offers to compromise with me for a deuce, so I can see things must be very bad with Feet for him to come down from five dollars to two.

"My rent is away overdue for the shovel and broom," Feet says, "and I have a hard-hearted landlady who will not listen to reason. She says she will give me the wind if I do not lay something on the line at once. Things are never so bad with me," Feet says, "and I am thinking of doing something very desperate."

I cannot think of anything very desperate for Feet Samuels to do, except maybe go to work, and I know he is not going to do such a thing no matter what happens. In fact, in all the years I am around Broadway I never know any broker to get desperate enough to go to work.

I once hear Dave the Dude offer Feet Samuels a job riding rum between here and Philly at good wages, but Feet turns it down because he claims he cannot stand the open air, and anyway Feet says he hears riding rum is illegal and may land a guy in the pokey. So I know whatever Feet is going to do will be nothing difficult.

"The Brain is still in town," I say to Feet. "Why do you not put the lug on him? You stand okay with him."

"There is the big trouble," Feet says. "I owe The Brain a C note already, and I am supposed to pay him back by four o'clock Monday morning, and where I am going to get a hundred dollars I do not know, to say nothing of the other ten I must give him for interest."

"What are you figuring on doing?" I ask, for it is now a Thursday, and I can see Feet has very little time to get together such a sum.

"I am figuring on scragging myself," Feet says, very sad. "What good am I to anybody? I have no family and no friends, and the world is packing enough weight without me. Yes, I think I will scrag myself."

"It is against the law to commit suicide in this man's town," I say, "although what the law can do to a guy who commits suicide I am never able to figure out."

"I do not care," Feet says. "I am sick and tired of it all. I am especially sick and tired of being broke. I never have more than a few quarters to rub together in my pants pocket. Everything I try turns out wrong. The only thing that keeps me from scragging myself at once is the C note I owe The Brain, because I do not wish to have him going around after I am dead and gone saying I am no good. And the toughest thing of all," Feet says, "is I am in love. I am in love with Hortense."

"Hortense?" I say, very much astonished indeed. "Why, Hortense is nothing but a big—"

"Stop!" Feet says. "Stop right here! I will not have her called a big baloney or whatever else big you are going to call her, because I love her. I cannot live without her. In fact," Feet says, "I do not wish to live without her."

"Well," I say, "what does Hortense think about you loving her?"

"She does not know it," Feet says. "I am ashamed to tell her, because naturally if I tell her I love her, Hortense will expect me to buy her some diamond bracelets, and naturally I cannot do this. But I think she likes me more than somewhat, because she looks at me in a certain way. But," Feet says, "there is some other guy who likes her also, and who is buying her diamond bracelets and what goes with them, which makes it very tough on me. I do not know who the guy is, and I do not think Hortense cares for him so much, but naturally any doll must give serious consideration to a guy who can buy her diamond bracelets. So I guess there is nothing for me to do but scrag myself."

Naturally I do not take Feet Samuels serious, and I forget about his troubles at once, because I figure he will wiggle out some way, but the next night he comes into Mindy's all pleasured up, and I figure he must make a scratch somewhere, for he is walking like a man with about sixty-five dollars on him.

But it seems Feet only has an idea, and very few ideas are worth sixty-five dollars.

"I am laying in bed thinking this afternoon," Feet says, "and I get to thinking how I can raise enough dough to pay off The Brain, and maybe a few other guys, and my landlady, and leave a few bobs over to help bury me. I am going to sell my body."

Well, naturally I am somewhat bewildered by this statement, so I ask Feet to explain, and here is his idea: He is going to find some doctor who wishes a dead body and sell his body to this doctor for as much as he can get, his body to be delivered after Feet scrags himself, which is to be within a certain time.

"I understand," Feet says, "that these croakers are always look-ing for bodies to practice on, and that good bodies are not easy to get nowadays."

"How much do you figure your body is worth?" I ask.

"Well," Feet says, "a body as big as mine ought to be worth at least a G."

"Feet," I say, "this all sounds most gruesome to me. Personally I do not know much about such a proposition, but I do not be-lieve if doctors buy bodies at all that they buy them by the pound. And I do not believe you can get a thousand dollars for your body, especially while you are still alive, because how does a doctor know if you will deliver your body to him?"

"Why," Feet says, very indignant, "everybody knows I pay what I owe. I can give The Brain for reference, and he will okay me with anybody for keeping my word."

Well, it seems to me that there is very little sense to what Feet Samuels is talking about, and anyway I figure that maybe he blows his topper, which is what often happens to brokers, so I pay no more attention to him. But on Monday morning, just before four o'clock, I am in Mindy's, and what happens but in walks Feet with a handful of money, looking much pleased.

The Brain is also there at the table where he always sits facing the door so nobody can pop in on him without him seeing them first, because there are many people in this town that The Brain likes to see first if they are coming in where he is. Feet steps up to the table and lays a C note in front of The Brain and also a saw-buck, and The Brain looks up at the clock and smiles and says:

"Okay, Feet, you are on time."

It is very unusual for The Brain to smile about anything, but af-terwards I hear he wins two C's off of Manny Mandelbaum, who bets him Feet will not pay off on time, so The Brain has a smile coming.

"By the way, Feet," The Brain says, "some doctor calls me up today and asks me if your word is good, and you may be glad to know I tell him you are one hundred per cent. I put the okay on you because I know you never fail to deliver on a promise. Are you sick, or something?"

"No," Feet says, "I am not sick. I just have a little business deal on with the guy. Thanks for the okay."

Then he comes over to the table where I am sitting, and I can see he still has money left in his duke. Naturally I am anxious to know where he makes the scratch, and by and by he tells me.

"I put over the proposition I am telling you about," Feet says. "I sell my body to a doctor over on Park Avenue by the name of Bodeeker, but I do not get a G for it as I expect. It seems bodies are not worth much right now because there are so many on the market, but Doc Bodeeker gives me four C's on thirty days' delivery.

"I never know it is so much trouble selling a body before," Feet says. "Three doctors call the cops on me when I proposition them, thinking I am daffy, but Doc Bodeeker is a nice old guy and is glad to do business with me, especially when I give The Brain as reference. Doc Bodeeker says he is looking for a head shaped just like mine for years, because it seems he is a shark on heads. But," Feet says, "I got to figure out some way of scragging myself besides jumping out a window, like I plan, because Doc Bodeeker does not wish my head mussed up."

"Well," I say, "this is certainly most ghastly to me and does not sound legitimate. Does The Brain know you sell your body?"

"No," Feet says, "Doc Bodeeker only asks him over the phone if my word is good, and does not tell him why he wishes to know, but he is satisfied with The Brain's okay. Now I am going to pay my landlady, and take up a few other markers here and there, and feed myself up good until it is time to leave this bad old world behind."

But it seems Feet Samuels does not go to pay his landlady right away. Where he goes is to Johnny Crackow's crap game downtown, which is a crap game with a five-hundred-dollar limit where the high shots seldom go, but where there is always some action for a small operator. And as Feet walks into the joint it seems that Big Nig is trying to make four with the dice, and everybody knows that four is a hard point for Big Nig, or anybody else, to make.

So Feet Samuels looks on a while watching Big Nig trying to make four, and a guy by the name of Whitey offers to take two to one for a C note that Big Nig makes this four, which is certainly more confidence than I will ever have in Big Nig. Naturally Feet hauls out a couple of his C notes at once, as anybody must do who has a couple of C notes, and bets Whitey two hundred to a hundred that Big Nig does not make the four. And right away Big Nig outs with a seven, so Feet wins the bet.

Well, to make a long story short, Feet stands there for some time betting guys that other guys will not make four, or whatever it is they are trying to make with the dice, and the first thing anybody knows Feet Samuels is six G's winner, and has the crap game all crippled up. I see him the next night up in the Hot Box, and this big first baseman, Hortense, is with him, sliding around on Feet's feet, and a blind man can see that she has on at least three more diamond bracelets than ever before.

A night or two later I hear of Feet beating Long George McCormack, a high shot from Los Angeles, out of eighteen G's playing a card game that is called low ball, and Feet Samuels has no more license to beat a guy like Long George playing low ball than I have to lick Jack Dempsey. But when a guy finally gets his rushes in gambling nothing can stop him for a while; and this is the way it is with Feet. Every night you hear of him winning plenty of dough at this or that.

He comes into Mindy's one morning, and naturally I move over to his table at once, because Feet is now in the money and is a guy anybody can associate with freely. I am just about to ask him how things are going with him, although I know they are going pretty good when in pops a fierce-looking old guy with his face all covered with gray whiskers that stick out every which way, and whose eyes peek out of these whiskers very wild indeed. Feet turns pale as he sees the guy, but nods at him, and the guy nods back and goes out.

"Who is the Whiskers?" I ask Feet. "He is in here the other morning looking around, and he makes people very nervous because nobody can figure who he is or what his dodge may be."

"It is old Doc Bodeeker," Feet says. "He is around checking up on me to make sure I am still in town. Say, I am in a very hot spot one way and another."

"What are you worrying about?" I ask. "You got plenty of dough and about two weeks left to enjoy yourself before this Doc Bodeeker forecloses on you."

"I know," Feet says, very sad. "But now I get this dough things do not look as tough to me as formerly, and I am very sorry I make the deal with the doctor. Especially," Feet says, "on account of Hortense."

"What about Hortense?" I ask.

"I think she is commencing to love me since I am able to buy her more diamond bracelets than the other guy," Feet says. "If it is not for this thing hanging over me, I will ask her to marry me, and maybe she will do it, at that."

"Well, then," I say, "why do you not to go old Whiskers and pay him his dough back, and tell him you change your mind about selling your body, although of course if it is not for Whiskers's buying your body you will not have all this dough."

"I do go to him," Feet says, and I can see there are big tears in his eyes. "But he says he will not cancel the deal. He says he will not take the money back; what he wants is my body, because I have such a funny-shaped head. I offer him four times what he pays me, but he will not take it. He says my body must be delivered to him promptly on March first."

"Does Hortense know about this deal?" I ask.

"Oh, no, no!" Feet says. "And I will never tell her, because she will think I am crazy, and Hortense does not care for crazy guys. In fact, she is always complaining about the other guy who buys her the diamond bracelets, claiming he is a little crazy, and if she thinks I am the same way the chances are she will give me the breeze."

Now this is a situation indeed, but what to do about it I do not know. I put the proposition up to a lawyer friend of mine the next day, and he says he does not believe the deal will hold good in court, but of course I know Feet Samuels does not wish to go to court, because the last time Feet goes to court he is held as a material witness and is in the Tombs ten days.

The lawyer says Feet can run away, but personally I consider this a very dishonorable idea after The Brain putting the okay on Feet with old Doc Bodeeker, and anyway I can see Feet is not going to do such a thing as long as Hortense is around. I can see that one hair of her head is stronger than the Atlantic cable with Feet Samuels.

A week slides by, and I do not see so much of Feet, but I hear of him murdering crap games and short card players, and winning plenty, and also going around the night clubs with Hortense, who finally has so many bracelets there is no more room on her arms, and she puts a few of them on her ankles, which are not bad ankles to look at, at that, with or without bracelets.

Then goes another week, and it just happens I am standing in front of Mindy's about four-thirty one morning and thinking that Feet's time must be up and wondering how he makes out with old Doc Bodeeker, when all of a sudden I hear a ploppity-plop coming up Broadway, and what do I see but Feet Samuels running so fast he is passing taxis that are going thirty-five miles an hour like they are standing still. He is certainly stepping along.

There are no traffic lights and not much traffic at such an hour in the morning, and Feet passes me in a terrible hurry. And about twenty yards behind him comes an old guy with gray whiskers, and I can see it is nobody but Doc Bodeeker. What is more, he has a big long knife in one hand, and he seems to be reaching for Feet at every jump with the knife.

Well, this seems to me a most surprising spectacle, and I follow them to see what comes of it, because I can see at once that Doc Bodeeker is trying to collect Feet's body himself. But I am not much of a runner, and they are out of my sight in no time, and only that I am able to follow them by ear through Feet's feet going ploppity-plop I will ever trail them.

They turn east onto Fifty-fourth Street off Broadway, and when I finally reach the corner I see a crowd halfway down the block in front of the Hot Box, and I know this crowd has something to do with Feet and Doc Bodeeker even before I get to the door to find that Feet goes on in while Doc Bodeeker is arguing with Soldier Sweeney, the doorman, because as Feet passes the Soldier he tells the Soldier not to let the guy who is chasing him in. And the Soldier, being a good friend of Feet's, is standing the doc off.

Well, it seems that Hortense is in the Hot Box waiting for Feet, and naturally she is much surprised to see him come in all out of breath, and so is everybody else in the joint, including Henri, the head waiter, who afterwards tells me what comes off there, because you see I am out in front.

"A crazy man is chasing me with a butcher knife," Feet says to Hortense. "If he gets inside I am a goner. He is down at the door trying to get in."

Now I will say one thing for Hortense, and this is she has plenty of nerve, but of course you will expect a daughter of Skush O'Brien to have plenty of nerve. Nobody ever has more moxie than Skush. Henri, the head waiter, tells me that Hortense does not get excited, but says she will just have a little peek at the guy who is chasing Feet.

The Hot Box is over a garage, and the kitchen windows look down onto Fifty-fourth Street, and while Doc Bodeeker is arguing with Soldier Sweeney, I hear a window lift, and who looks out but Hortense. She takes one squint and yanks her head in quick, and Henri tells me afterwards she shrieks:

"My Lord, Feet! This is the same daffy old guy who sends me all the bracelets, and who wishes to marry me!"

"And he is the guy I sell my body to," Feet says, and then he tells Hortense the story of his deal with Doc Bodeeker.

"It is all for you, Horty," Feet says, although of course this is nothing but a big lie, because it is all for The Brain in the beginning. "I love you, and I only wish to get a little dough to show you a good time before I die. If it is not for this deal I will ask you to be my ever-loving wife."

Well, what happens but Hortense plunges right into Feet's arms, and gives him a big kiss on his ugly mush, and says to him like this:

"I love you too, Feet, because nobody ever makes such a sacrifice as to hock their body for me. Never mind the deal. I will marry you at once, only we must first get rid of this daffy old guy downstairs."

Then Hortense peeks out of the window again and hollers down at old Doc Bodeeker. "Go away," she says. "Go away, or I will chuck a moth in your whiskers, you old fool."

But the sight of her only seems to make old Doc Bodeeker a little wilder than somewhat, and he starts struggling with Soldier Sweeney very ferocious, so the Soldier takes the knife away from the doc and throws it away before somebody gets hurt with it.

Now it seems Hortense looks around the kitchen for something to chuck out the window at old Doc Bodeeker, and all she sees is a nice new ham which the chef just lays out on the table to slice up for ham sandwiches. This ham is a very large ham, such as will last the Hot Box a month, for they slice the ham in their ham sandwiches very, very thin up at the Hot Box. Anyway, Hortense grabs up the ham and runs to the window with it and gives it a heave without even stopping to take aim.

Well, this ham hits the poor old Doc Bodeeker kerbowie smack-dab on the noggin. The doc does not fall down, but he commences staggering around with his legs bending under him like he is drunk.

I wish to help him, because I feel sorry for a guy in such a spot as this, and what is more I consider it a dirty trick for a doll such as Hortense to slug anybody with a ham.

Well, I take charge of the old doc and lead him back down Broadway and into Mindy's, where I set him down and get him a cup of coffee and a Bismarck herring to revive him, while quite a number of citizens gather about him very sympathetic.

"My friends," the old doc says finally, looking around, "you see in me a broken-hearted man. I am not a crack-pot, although of course my relatives may give you an argument on this proposition. I am in love with Hortense. I am in love with her from the night I first see her playing the part of a sunflower in *Scandals*. I wish to marry her, as I am a widower of long standing, but somehow the idea of me marrying anybody never appeals to my sons and daughters.

"In fact," the doc says, dropping his voice to a whisper, "sometimes they even talk of locking me up when I wish to marry somebody. So naturally I never tell them about Hortense, because I fear they may try to discourage me. But I am deeply in love with her and send her many beautiful presents, although I am not able to see her often on account of my relatives. Then I find out Hortense is carrying on with this Feet Samuels.

"I am desperately jealous," the doc says, "but I do not know what to do. Finally Fate sends this Feet to me offering to sell his body. Of course, I am not practicing for years, but I keep an office on Park Avenue just for old times' sake, and it is to this office he comes. At first I think he is crazy, but he refers me to Mr. Armand Rosenthal, the big sporting man, who assures me that Feet Samuels is all right.

"The idea strikes me that if I make a deal with Feet Samuels for his body as he proposes, he will wait until the time comes to pay his obligation and run away, and," the doc says, "I will never be troubled by his rivalry for the affections of Hortense again. But he does not depart. I do not reckon on the holding power of love.

"Finally in a jealous frenzy I take after him with a knife, figuring to scare him out of town. But it is too late. I can see how Hortense loves him in return, or she will not drop a scuttle of coal on me in his defense as she does.

"Yes, gentlemen," the old doc says, "I am broken-hearted. I also seem to have a large lump on my head. Besides, Hortense has all my presents, and Feet Samuels has my money, so I get the worst of it all around. I only hope and trust that my daughter Eloise, who is Mrs. Sidney Simmons Bragdon, does not hear of this, or she may be as mad as she is the time I wish to marry the beautiful cigarette girl in Jimmy Kelley's."

Here Doc Bodeeker seems all busted up by his feelings and starts to shed tears, and everybody is feeling very sorry for him indeed, when up steps The Brain, who is taking everything in.

"Do not worry about your presents and your dough," The Brain says. "I will make everything good, because I am the guy who okays Feet Samuels with you. I am wrong on a guy for the first time in my life, and I must pay, but Feet Samuels will be very, very sorry when I find him. Of course, I do not figure on a doll in the case, and this always makes quite a difference, so I am really not a hundred per cent wrong on the guy, at that.

"But," The Brain says, in a very loud voice so everybody can hear, "Feet Samuels is nothing but a dirty welsher for not turning in his body to you as per agreement, and as long as he lives he will never get another dollar or another okay off of me, or anybody I know. His credit is ruined forever on Broadway."

But I judge that Feet and Hortense do not care. The last time I hear of them they are away over in New Jersey where not even The Brain's guys dast to bother them on account of Skush O'Brien, and I understand they are raising chickens and children right and left, and that all of Hortense's bracelets are now in Newark municipal bonds, which I am told are not bad bonds, at that.

MADAME LA GIMP

One night I am passing the corner of Fiftieth Street and Broadway, and what do I see but Dave the Dude standing in a doorway talking to a busted-down old Spanish doll by the name of Madame La Gimp. Or rather Madame La Gimp is talking to Dave the Dude, and what is more he is listening to her, because I can hear him say yes, yes, as he always does when he is really listening to anybody, which is very seldom.

Now this is a most surprising sight to me, because Madame La Gimp is not such an old doll as anybody will wish to listen to, especially Dave the Dude. In fact, she is nothing but an old hay-bag, and generally somewhat ginned up. For fifteen years, or maybe sixteen, I see Madame La Gimp up and down Broadway, or sliding along through the Forties, sometimes selling newspapers, and sometimes selling flowers, and in all these years I seldom see her but what she seems to have about half a heat on from drinking gin.

Of course, nobody ever takes the newspapers she sells, even after they buy them off of her, because they are generally yesterday's papers, and sometimes last week's, and nobody ever wants her flowers, even after they pay her for them, because they are flowers such as she gets off an undertaker over on Tenth Avenue, and they are very tired flowers indeed.

Personally, I consider Madame La Gimp nothing but an old pest, but kind-hearted guys like Dave the Dude always stake her to a few pieces of silver when she comes shuffling along putting on the moan about her tough luck. She walks with a gimp in one leg, which is why she is called Madame La Gimp, and years ago I hear somebody say Madame La Gimp is once a Spanish dancer, and a big shot on Broadway, but that she meets up with an accident which puts her out of the dancing dodge, and that a busted romance makes her become a gin-head.

I remember somebody telling me once that Madame La Gimp is quite a beauty in her day, and has her own servants, and all this and that, but I always hear the same thing about every bum on Broadway, male and female, including some I know are bums, in spades, right from taw, so I do not pay any attention to these stories.

Still, I am willing to allow that maybe Madame La Gimp is once a fair looker, at that, and the chances are has a fair shape, because once or twice I see her when she is not ginned up, and has her hair combed, and she is not so bad-looking, although even then if you put her in a claiming race I do not think there is any danger of anybody claiming her out of it.

Mostly she is wearing raggedy clothes, and busted shoes, and her gray hair is generally hanging down her face, and when I say she is maybe fifty years old I am giving her plenty the best of it. Although she is Spanish, Madame La Gimp talks good English, and in fact she can cuss in English as good as anybody I ever hear, barring Dave the Dude.

Well, anyway, when Dave the Dude sees me as he is listening to Madame La Gimp, he motions me to wait, so I wait until she finally gets through gabbing to him and goes gimping away. Then Dave the Dude comes over to me looking much worried.

"This is quite a situation," Dave says. "The old doll is in a tough spot. It seems that she once has a baby which she calls by the name of Eulalie, being it is a girl baby, and she ships this baby off to her sister in a little town in Spain to raise up, because Madame La Gimp figures a baby is not apt to get much raising-up off of her as long as she is on Broadway. Well, this baby is on her way here. In fact," Dave says, "she will land next Saturday and here it is Wednesday already."

"Where is the baby's papa?" I ask Dave the Dude.

"Well," Dave says, "I do not ask Madame La Gimp this, because I do not consider it a fair question. A guy who goes around this town asking where babies' papas are, or even who they are, is apt to get the name of being nosy. Anyway, this has nothing whatever to do with the proposition, which is that Madame La Gimp's baby, Eulalie, is arriving here.

"Now," Dave says, "it seems that Madame La Gimp's baby, being now eighteen years old, is engaged to marry the son of a very proud old Spanish nobleman who lives in this little town in Spain, and it also seems that the very proud old Spanish nobleman, and his ever-loving wife, and the son, and Madame La Gimp's sister, are all with the baby. They are making a tour of the whole world, and will stop over here a couple of days just to see Madame La Gimp."

"It is commencing to sound to me like a movie such as a guy is apt to see at a midnight show," I say.

"Wait a minute," Dave says, getting impatient. "You are too gabby to suit me. Now it seems that the proud old Spanish nobleman does not wish his son to marry any lob, and one reason he is coming here is to look over Madame La Gimp, and see that she is okay. He thinks that Madame La Gimp's baby's own papa is dead, and that Madame La Gimp is now married to one of the richest and most aristocratic guys in America."

"How does the proud old Spanish nobleman get such an idea as this?" I ask. "It is a sure thing he never sees Madame La Gimp, or even a photograph of her as she is at present."

"I will tell you how," Dave the Dude says. "It seems Madame La Gimp gives her baby the idea that such is the case in her letters to her. It seems Madame La Gimp does a little scrubbing business around a swell apartment hotel on Park Avenue that is called the Marberry, and she cops stationery there and writes her baby in Spain on this stationery, saying this is where she lives, and how rich and aristocratic her husband is. And what is more, Madame La Gimp has letters from her baby sent to her care of the hotel and gets them out of the employees' mail."

"Why," I say, "Madame La Gimp is nothing but an old fraud to deceive people in this manner, especially a proud old Spanish nobleman. And," I say, "this proud old Spanish nobleman must be something of a chump to believe a mother has plenty of dough, although of course I do not know just how smart a proud old Spanish nobleman can be."

"Well," Dave says, "Madame La Gimp tells me the thing that makes the biggest hit of all with the proud old Spanish nobleman is that she keeps her baby in Spain all these years because she wishes her raised up a true Spanish baby in every respect until she is old enough to know what time it is. But I judge the proud old Spanish nobleman is none too bright, at that," Dave says, "because Madame La Gimp tells me he always lives in his little town which does not even have running water in the bathrooms.

"But what I am getting at is this," Dave says. "We must have Madame La Gimp in a swell apartment in the Marberry with a rich and aristocratic guy for a husband by the time her baby gets here, because if the proud old Spanish nobleman finds out Madame La Gimp is nothing but a bum, it is a hundred to one he will cancel his son's engagement to Madame La Gimp's baby and break a lot of people's hearts, including his son's.

"Madame La Gimp tells me her baby is daffy about the young guy, and he is daffy about her, and there are enough broken hearts in this town as it is. I know I will get the apartment, so you go and bring me Judge Henry G. Blake for a rich and aristocratic husband, or anyway for a husband."

Well, I know Dave the Dude to do many a daffy thing, but never a thing as daffy as this. But I know there is no use arguing with him when he gets an idea, because if you argue with Dave the Dude too much he is apt to reach over and lay his Sunday punch on your snoot, and no argument is worth a punch on the snoot, especially from Dave the Dude.

So I go out looking for Judge Henry G. Blake to be Madame La Gimp's husband, although I am not so sure Judge Henry G. Blake will care to be anybody's husband, and especially Madame La Gimp's after he gets a load of her, for Judge Henry G. Blake is kind of a classy old guy.

To look at Judge Henry G. Blake, with his gray hair, and his nose glasses, and his stomach, you will think he is very important people indeed. Of course, Judge Henry G. Blake is not a judge, and never is a judge, but they call him Judge because he looks like a judge, and talks slow, and puts in many long words, which very few people understand.

They tell me Judge Blake once has plenty of dough, and is quite a guy on Wall Street, and a high shot along Broadway, but he misses a few guesses at the market, and winds up without much dough, as guys generally do who miss guesses at the market. What Judge Henry G. Blake does for a living at this time nobody knows, because he does nothing much whatever, and yet he seems to be a producer in a small way at all times.

Now and then he makes a trip across the ocean with such as Little Manuel, and other guys who ride the tubs, and sits in with them on games of bridge, and one thing and another, when they need him. Very often when he is riding the tubs, Little Manuel runs into some guy he cannot cheat, so he has to call in Judge Henry G. Blake to outplay the guy on the level, although of course Little Manuel will much rather get a guy's dough by cheating him than by outplaying him on the level. Why this is, I do not know, but this is the way Little Manuel is.

Anyway, you cannot say Judge Henry G. Blake is a bum, especially as he wears good clothes, with a wing collar, and a derby hat, and most people consider him a very nice old man. Personally I never catch the judge out of line on any proposition whatever, and he always says hello to me, very pleasant.

It takes me several hours to find Judge Henry G. Blake, but finally I locate him in Derle's billiards-room playing a game of pool with a guy from Providence, Rhode Island. It seems the judge is playing the guy from Providence for five cents a ball, and the judge is about thirteen balls behind when I step into the joint, because naturally at five cents a ball the judge wishes the guy from Providence to win, so as to encourage him to play for maybe twenty-five cents a ball, the judge being very cute this way.

Well, when I step in I see the judge miss a shot anybody can make blindfolded, but as soon as I give him the office I wish to speak to him, the judge hauls off and belts in every ball on the table, bingity-bing, the last shot being a bank that will make Al de Oro stop and think, because when it comes to pool, the old judge is just naturally a curly wolf.

Afterwards he tells me he is very sorry I make him hurry up this way, because of course after the last shot he is never going to get the guy from Providence to play him pool even for fun, and the judge tells me the guy sizes up as a right good thing, at that.

Now Judge Henry G. Blake is not so excited when I tell him what Dave the Dude wishes to see him about, but naturally he is willing to do anything for Dave, because he knows that guys who are not willing to do things for Dave the Dude often have bad luck. The judge tells me that he is afraid he will not make much of a husband because he tries it before several times on his own hook and is always a bust, but as long as this time it is not to be anything serious, he will tackle it. Anyway, Judge Henry G. Blake says, being aristocratic will come natural to him.

Well, when Dave the Dude starts out on any proposition, he is a wonder for fast working. The first thing he does is to turn Madame La Gimp over to Miss Billy Perry, who is now Dave's ever-loving wife which he takes out of tap-dancing in Miss Missouri Martin's Sixteen Hundred Club, and Miss Billy Perry calls in Miss Missouri Martin to help.

This is water on Miss Missouri Martin's wheel, because if there is anything she loves it is to stick her nose in other people's business, no matter what it is, but she is quite a help at that, although at first they have a tough time keeping her from telling Waldo Winchester, the scribe, about the whole cat-hop, so he will put a story in the *Morning Item* about it, with Miss Missouri Martin's name in it. Miss Missouri Martin does not believe in ever overlooking any publicity bets on the layout.

Anyway, it seems that between them Miss Billy Perry and Miss Missouri Martin get Madame La Gimp dolled up in a lot of new clothes, and run her through one of these beauty joints until she comes out very much changed indeed. Afterwards I hear Miss Billy Perry and Miss Missouri Martin have quite a few words, because Miss Missouri Martin wishes to paint Madame La Gimp's hair the same color as her own, which is a high yellow, and buy her the same kind of dresses which Miss Missouri Martin wears herself, and Miss Missouri Martin gets much insulted when Miss Billy Perry says no, they are trying to dress Madame La Gimp to look like a lady.

They tell me Miss Missouri Martin thinks some of putting the slug on Miss Billy Perry for this crack, but happens to remember just in time that Miss Billy Perry is now Dave the Dude's ever-loving wife, and that nobody in this town can put the slug on Dave's ever-loving wife, except maybe Dave himself.

Now the next thing anybody knows, Madame La Gimp is in a swell eight- or nine-room apartment in the Marberry, and the way this comes about is as follows: It seems that one of Dave the Dude's most important champagne customers is a guy by the name of Rodney B. Emerson, who owns the apartment, but who is at his summer home in Newport, with his family, or anyway with his ever-loving wife.

This Rodney B. Emerson is quite a guy along Broadway, and a great hand for spending dough and looking for laughs, and he is very popular with the mob. Furthermore, he is obliged to Dave the Dude, because Dave sells him good champagne when most guys are trying to hand him the old phonus bolonus, and naturally Rodney B. Emerson appreciates this kind treatment.

He is a short, fat guy, with a round, red face, and a big laugh, and the kind of a guy Dave the Dude can call up at his home in Newport and explain the situation and ask for the loan of the apartment, which Dave does.

Well, it seems Rodney B. Emerson gets a big bang out of the idea, and he says to Dave the Dude like this:

"You not only can have the apartment, Dave, but I will come over and help you out. It will save a lot of explaining around the Marberry if I am there."

So he hops right over from Newport, and joins in with Dave the Dude, and I wish to say Rodney B. Emerson will always be kindly remembered by one and all for his co-operation, and nobody will ever again try to hand him the phonus bolonus when he is buying champagne, even if he is not buying it off of Dave the Dude.

Well, it is coming on Saturday and the boat from Spain is due, so Dave the Dude hires a big town car, and puts his own driver, Wop Sam, on it, as he does not wish any strange driver tipping off anybody that it is a hired car. Miss Missouri Martin is anxious to go to the boat with Madame La Gimp, and take her jazz band, the Hi Hi Boys, from her Sixteen Hundred Club with her to make it a real welcome, but nobody thinks much of this idea. Only Madame La Gimp and her husband, Judge Henry G. Blake, and Miss Billy Perry go, though the judge holds out for some time for Little Manuel, because Judge Blake says he wishes somebody around to tip him off in case there are any bad cracks made about him as a husband in Spanish, and Little Manuel is very Spanish.

The morning they go to meet the boat is the first time Judge Henry G. Blake gets a load of his ever-loving wife, Madame La Gimp, and by this time Miss Billy Perry and Miss Missouri Martin give Madame La Gimp such a going-over that she is by no means the worst looker in the world. In fact, she looks first-rate, especially as she is off gin and says she is off it for good.

Judge Henry G. Blake is really quite surprised by her looks, as he figures all along she will turn out to be a crow. In fact, Judge Blake hurls a couple of shots into himself to nerve himself for the ordeal, as he explains it, before he appears to go to the boat. Between these shots, and the nice clothes, and the good cleaning-up

Miss Billy Perry and Miss Missouri Martin give Madame La Gimp, she is really a pleasant sight to the judge.

They tell me the meeting at the dock between Madame La Gimp and her baby is very affecting indeed, and when the proud old Spanish nobleman and his wife, and their son, and Madame La Gimp's sister, all go into action, too, there are enough tears around there to float all the battleships we once sink for Spain. Even Miss Billy Perry and Judge Henry G. Blake do some first-class crying, although the chances are the judge is worked up to the crying more by the shots he takes for his courage than by the meeting.

Still, I hear the old judge does himself proud, with his kissing Madame La Gimp's baby plenty, and duking the proud old Spanish nobleman, and his wife, and son, and giving Madame La Gimp's sister a good strong hug that squeezes her tongue out.

It turns out that the proud old Spanish nobleman has white sideburns, and is entitled Conde de Something, so his ever-loving wife is the Condesa, and the son is a very nice-looking quiet young guy any way you take him, who blushes every time anybody looks at him. As for Madame La Gimp's baby, she is as pretty as they come, and many guys are sorry they do not get Judge Henry G. Blake's job as stepfather, because he is able to take a kiss at Madame La Gimp's baby on what seems to be very small excuse. I never see a nicer-looking young couple, and anybody can see they are very fond of each other indeed.

Madame La Gimp's sister is not such a doll as I will wish to have sawed off on me, and is up in the paints as regards to age, but she is also very quiet. None of the bunch talk any English, so Miss Billy Perry and Judge Henry G. Blake are pretty much outsiders on the way uptown. Anyway, the judge takes the wind as soon as they reach the Marberry, because the judge is now getting a little tired of being a husband. He says he has to take a trip out to Pittsburgh to buy four or five coal mines, but will be back the next day.

Well, it seems to me that everything is going perfect so far, and that it is good judgment to let it lay as it is, but nothing will do Dave the Dude but to have a reception the following night. I advise Dave the Dude against this idea, because I am afraid something will happen to spoil the whole cat-hop, but he will not listen to me, especially as Rodney B. Emerson is now in town and is a strong booster for the party, as he wishes to drink of some of the good champagne he has planted in his apartment.

Furthermore, Miss Billy Perry and Miss Missouri Martin are very indignant at me when they hear about my advice, as it seems they both buy new dresses out of Dave the Dude's bank roll when they are dressing up Madame La Gimp, and they wish to spring these dresses somewhere where they can be seen. So the party is on.

I get to the Marberry around nine o'clock and who opens the door of Madame La Gimp's apartment for me but Moosh, the doorman from Miss Missouri Martin's Sixteen Hundred Club. Furthermore, he is in his Sixteen Hundred Club uniform, except he has a clean shave. I wish Moosh a hello, and he never raps to me but only bows, and takes my hat.

The next guy I see is Rodney B. Emerson in evening clothes, and the minute he sees me he yells out, "Mister O. O. McIntyre." Well, of course, I am not Mister O. O. McIntyre, and never put myself away as Mister O. O. McIntyre, and furthermore there is no resemblance whatever between Mister O. O. McIntyre and me, because I am a fairly good-looking guy, and I start to give Rodney B. Emerson an argument, when he whispers to me like this:

"Listen," he whispers, "we must have big names at this affair, so as to impress these people. The chances are they read the newspapers back there in Spain, and we must let them meet the folks they read about, so they will see Madame La Gimp is a real big shot to get such names to a party."

Then he takes me by the arm and leads me to a group of people in a corner of the room, which is about the size of the Grand Central waiting-room.

"Mister O. O. McIntyre, the big writer!" Rodney B. Emerson says, and the next thing I know I am shaking hands with Mr. and Mrs. Conde, and their son, and with Madame La Gimp and her baby, and Madame La Gimp's sister, and finally with Judge Henry G. Blake, who has on a swallowtail coat, and does not give me much of a tumble. I figure the chances are Judge Henry G. Blake is getting a swelled head already, not to tumble up a guy who helps him get his job, but even at that I wish to say the old judge looks immense in his swallowtail coat, bowing and giving one and all the castor-oil smile.

Madame La Gimp is in a low-neck black dress and is wearing a lot of Miss Missouri Martin's diamonds, such as rings and bracelets, which Miss Missouri Martin insists on hanging on her, although I hear afterwards that Miss Missouri Martin has Johnny

Brannigan, the plain-clothes copper, watching these diamonds. I wonder at the time why Johnny is there, but figure it is because he is a friend of Dave the Dude's. Miss Missouri Martin is no sucker, even if she is kind-hearted.

Anybody looking at Madame La Gimp will bet you all the coffee in Java that she never lives in a cellar over on Tenth Avenue, and drinks plenty of gin in her day. She has her gray hair piled up high on her head, with a big Spanish comb in it, and she reminds me of a picture I see somewhere, but I do not remember just where. And her baby, Eulalie, in a white dress is about as pretty a little doll as you will wish to see, and nobody can blame Judge Henry G. Blake for copping a kiss off of her now and then.

Well, pretty soon I hear Rodney B. Emerson bawling, "Mister Willie K. Vanderbilt," and in comes nobody but Big Nig, and Rodney B. Emerson leads him over to the group and introduces him.

Little Manuel is standing alongside Judge Henry G. Blake, and he explains in Spanish to Mr. and Mrs. Conde and the others that "Willie K. Vanderbilt" is a very large millionaire, and Mr. and Mrs. Conde seem much interested, anyway, though naturally Madame La Gimp and Judge Henry G. Blake are jerry to Big Nig, while Madame La Gimp's baby and the young guy are interested in nobody but each other.

Then I hear, "Mister Al Jolson," and in comes nobody but Tony Bertazzola, from the Chicken Club, who looks about as much like Al as I do like O. O. McIntyre, which is not at all. Next comes "the Very Reverend John Roach Straton," who seems to be Skeets Bolivar to me, then "the Honorable Mayor James J. Walker," and who is it but Good Time Charley Bernstein.

"Mister Otto H. Kahn," turns out to be Rochester Red, and "Mister Heywood Broun" is Nick the Greek, who asks me privately who Heywood Broun is, and gets very sore at Rodney B. Emerson when I describe Heywood Broun to him.

Finally there is quite a commotion at the door, and Rodney B. Emerson announces, "Mister Herbert Bayard Swope," in an extra loud voice which makes everybody look around, but it is nobody but the Pale Face Kid. He gets me to one side, too, and wishes to know who Herbert Bayard Swope is, and when I explain to him, the Pale Face Kid gets so swelled up he will not speak to Death House Donegan, who is only "Mister William Muldoon."

Well, it seems to me they are getting too strong when they announce, "Vice-President of the United States, the Honorable Charles Curtis," and in pops Guinea Mike, and I say as much to Dave the Dude, who is running around every which way looking after things, but he only says, "Well, if you do not know it is Guinea Mike, will you know it is not Vice-President Curtis?"

But it seems to me all this is most disrespectful to our leading citizens, especially when Rodney B. Emerson calls, "The Honorable Police Commissioner, Mister Grover A. Whalen," and in pops Wild William Wilkins, who is a very hot man at this time, being wanted in several spots for different raps. Dave the Dude takes personal charge of Wild William and removes a rod from his pants pocket, because none of the guests are supposed to come rodded up, this being strictly a social matter.

I watch Mr. and Mrs. Conde, and I do not see that these names are making any impression on them, and I afterwards find out that they never get any newspapers in their town in Spain except a little local bladder which only prints the home news. In fact, Mr. and Mrs. Conde seem somewhat bored, although Mr. Conde cheers up no little and looks interested when a lot of dolls drift in. They are mainly dolls from Miss Missouri Martin's Sixteen Hundred Club, and the Hot Box, but Rodney B. Emerson introduces them as "Sophie Tucker," and "Theda Bara," and "Jeanne Eagels," and "Helen Morgan," and "Aunt Jemima," and one thing and another.

Well, pretty soon in comes Miss Missouri Martin's jazz band, the Hi Hi Boys, and the party commences getting up steam, especially when Dave the Dude gets Rodney B. Emerson to breaking out the old grape. By and by there is dancing going on, and a good time is being had by one and all, including Mr. and Mrs. Conde. In fact, after Mr. Conde gets a couple of jolts of the old grape, he turns out to be a pretty nice old skate, even if nobody can understand what he is talking about.

As for Judge Henry G. Blake, he is full of speed indeed. By this time anybody can see that the judge is commencing to believe that all this is on the level and that he is really entertaining celebrities in his own home. You put a quart of good grape inside the old judge and he will believe anything. He soon dances himself plumb out of wind, and then I notice he is hanging around Madame La Gimp a lot.

Along about midnight, Dave the Dude has to go out into the kitchen and settle a battle there over a crap game, but otherwise everything is very peaceful. It seems that "Herbert Bayard Swope," "Vice-President Curtis," and "Grover Whalen" get a little game going, when "the Reverend John Roach Straton" steps up and cleans them in four passes, but it seems they soon discover that "the Reverend John Roach Straton" is using tops on them, which are very dishonest dice, and so they put the slug on "the Reverend John Roach Straton" and Dave the Dude has to split them out.

By and by I figure on taking the wind, and I look for Mr. and Mrs. Conde to tell them good night, but Mr. Conde and Miss Missouri Martin are still dancing, and Miss Missouri Martin is pouring conversation into Mr. Conde's ear by the bucketful, and while Mr. Conde does not savvy a word she says, this makes no difference to Miss Missouri Martin. Let Miss Missouri Martin do all the talking, and she does not care a whoop if anybody understands her.

Mrs. Conde is over in a corner with "Herbert Bayard Swope," or the Pale Face Kid, who is trying to find out from her by using hog Latin and signs on her if there is any chance for a good twenty-one dealer in Spain, and of course Mrs. Conde is not able to make heads or tails of what he means, so I hunt up Madame La Gimp.

She is sitting in a darkish corner off by herself and I really do not see Judge Henry G. Blake leaning over her until I am almost on top of them, so I cannot help hearing what the judge is saying.

"I am wondering for two days," he says, "if by any chance you remember me. Do you know who I am?"

"I remember you," Madame La Gimp says. "I remember you—oh, so very well, Henry. How can I forget you? But I have no idea you recognize me after all these years."

"Twenty of them now," Judge Henry G. Blake says. "You are beautiful then. You are still beautiful."

Well, I can see the old grape is working first-class on Judge Henry G. Blake to make such remarks as this, although at that, in the half-light with the smile on her face, Madame La Gimp is not so bad. Still, give me them carrying a little less weight for age.

"Well, it is all your fault," Judge Henry G. Blake says. "You go and marry that chile con carne guy, and look what happens!"

I can see there is no sense in me horning in on Madame La Gimp and Judge Henry G. Blake while they are cutting up old touches in this manner, so I think I will just say good-bye to the young people and let it go at that, but while I am looking for Madame La Gimp's baby, and her guy, I run into Dave the Dude.

"You will not find them here," Dave says. "By this time they are being married over at Saint Malachy's with my ever-loving wife and Big Nig standing up with them. We get the license for them yesterday afternoon. Can you imagine a couple of young saps wishing to wait until they go plumb around the world before getting married?"

Well, of course, this elopement creates much excitement for a few minutes, but by Monday Mr. and Mrs. Conde and the young folks and Madame La Gimp's sister take a train for California to keep on going around the world, leaving us nothing to talk about but about old Judge Henry G. Blake and Madame La Gimp getting themselves married, too, and going to Detroit where Judge Henry G. Blake claims he has a brother in the plumbing business who will give him a job, although personally I think Judge Henry G. Blake figures to do a little booting on his own hook in and out of Canada. It is not like Judge Henry G. Blake to tie himself up to the plumbing business.

So there is nothing more to the story, except that Dave the Dude is around a few days later with a big sheet of paper in his duke and very, very indignant.

"If every single article listed here is not kicked back to the owners of the different joints in the Marberry that they are taken from by next Tuesday night, I will bust a lot of noses around this town," Dave says. "I am greatly mortified by such happenings at my social affairs, and everything must be returned at once. Especially," Dave says, "the baby grand piano that is removed from Apartment 9-D."

DARK DOLORES

Waldo Winchester, the newspaper scribe, is saying to me the other night up in the Hot Box that it is a very great shame that there are no dolls around such as in the old days to make good stories for the newspapers by knocking off guys right and left, because it seems that newspaper scribes consider a doll knocking off a guy very fine news indeed, especially if the doll or the guy belongs to the best people.

Then Waldo Winchester tells me about a doll by the name of Lorelei who hangs out in the Rhine River some time ago and stools sailors up to the rocks to get them wrecked, which I consider a dirty trick, although Waldo does not seem to make so much of it. Furthermore, he speaks of another doll by the name of Circe, who is quite a hand for luring guys to destruction, and by the time Waldo gets to Circe he is crying because there are no more dolls like her around to furnish news for the papers.

But of course the real reason Waldo is crying is not because he is so sorry about Circe. It is because he is full of the liquor they sell in the Hot Box, which is liquor that is apt to make anybody bust out crying on a very short notice. In fact, they sell the cryingest liquor in town up in the Hot Box.

Well, I get to thinking over these dolls Waldo Winchester speaks of, and, thinks I, the chances are Dolores Dark connects up with one of them away back yonder, and maybe with all of them for all I know, Dolores Dark being the name of a doll I meet when I am in Atlantic City with Dave the Dude the time of the big peace conference.

Afterwards I hear she is called Dark Dolores in some spots on account of her complexion, but her name is really the other way around. But first I will explain how it is I am in Atlantic City with Dave the Dude the time of the big peace conference as follows:

One afternoon I am walking along Broadway thinking of not much, when I come on Dave the Dude just getting in a taxicab with a suitcase in his duke, and the next thing I know Dave is jerking me into the cab and telling the jockey to go to the Penn Station. This is how I come to be in Atlantic City the time of the big peace conference, although, of course, I have nothing to do with the peace conference, and am only with Dave the Dude to keep him company.

I am a guy who is never too busy to keep people company, and Dave the Dude is a guy who just naturally loves company. In fact, he hates to go anywhere, or be anywhere, by himself, and the reason is because when he is by himself Dave the Dude has nobody to nod him yes, and if there is one thing Dave is very, very fond of, it is to have somebody to nod him yes. Why it is that Dave the Dude does not have Big Nig with him I do not know, for Big Nig is Dave's regular nod-guy.

But I am better than a raw hand myself at nodding. In fact, I am probably as good a nod-guy as there is in this town, where there must be three million nod-guys, and why not, because the way I look at it, it is no bother whatever to nod a guy. In fact, it saves a lot of conversation.

Anyway, there I am in Atlantic City the time of the big peace conference, although I wish to say right now that if I know in advance who is going to be at this peace conference, or that there is going to be any peace conference, I will never be anywhere near Atlantic City, because the parties mixed up in it are no kind of associates for a nervous guy like me.

It seems this peace conference is between certain citizens of St. Louis, such as Black Mike Marrio, Benny the Blond Jew, and Scoodles Shea, who all have different mobs in St. Louis, and who are all ripping and tearing each other for a couple of years over such provisions as to who shall have what in the way of business privileges of one kind and another, including alky, and liquor, and gambling.

From what I hear there is plenty of shooting going on between these mobs, and guys getting topped right and left. Also there is much heaving of bombs, and all this and that, until finally the only people making any dough in the town are the undertakers, and it seems there is no chance of anybody cutting in on the undertakers, though Scoodles Shea tries.

Well, Scoodles, who is a pretty smart guy, and who is once in the war in France, finally remembers that when all the big nations get broke, and sick and tired of fighting, they hold a peace conference and straighten things out, so he sends word to Black Mike and Benny the Blond Jew that maybe it will be a good idea if they do the same thing, because half their guys are killed anyway, and trade is strictly on the bum.

It seems Black Mike and Benny think very well of this proposition, and are willing to meet Scoodles in a peace conference, but Scoodles, who is a very suspicious character, asks where they will hold this conference. He says he does not wish to hold any conference with Black Mike and Benny in St. Louis, except maybe in his own cellar, because he does not know of any other place in St. Louis where he will be safe from being guzzled by some of Black Mike's or Benny's guys, and he says he does not suppose Black Mike and Benny will care to go into his cellar with him.

So Scoodles Shea finally asks how about Atlantic City, and it seems this is agreeable to Black Mike because he has a cousin in Atlantic City by the name of Pisano that he does not see since they leave the old country.

Benny the Blond Jew says any place is okay with him as long as it is not in the State of Missouri, because he says, he does not care to be seen anywhere in the State of Missouri with Black Mike and Scoodles, as it will be a knock to his reputation.

This seems to sound somewhat insulting, and almost busts up the peace conference before it starts, but finally Benny withdraws the bad crack, and says he does not mean the State of Missouri, but only St. Louis, so the negotiations proceed, and they settle on Atlantic City as the spot.

Then Black Mike says some outside guy must sit in with them as a sort of umpire, and help them iron out their arguments, and Benny says he will take President Hoover, Colonel Lindbergh, or Chief Justice Taft. Now of course this is great foolishness to think they can get any one of these parties, because the chances are President Hoover, Colonel Lindbergh, and Chief Justice Taft are too busy with other things to bother about ironing out a mob war in St. Louis.

So finally Scoodles Shea suggests Dave the Dude. Both Black Mike and Benny say Dave is okay, though Benny holds out for some time for at least Chief Justice Taft. So Dave the Dude is asked to act as umpire for the St. Louis guys, and he is glad to do same, for Dave often steps into towns where guys are battling and straightens them out, and sometimes they do not start battling again for several weeks after he leaves town.

You see, Dave the Dude is friendly with everybody everywhere, and is known to one and all as a right guy, and one who always gives everybody a square rattle in propositions of this kind. Furthermore, it is a pleasure for Dave to straighten guys out in other towns, because the battling tangles up his own business interests in spots such as St. Louis.

Now it seems that on their way to the station to catch a train for Atlantic City, Scoodles Shea and Black Mike and Benny decide to call on a young guy by the name of Frankie Farrone, who bobs up all of a sudden in St. Louis with plenty of nerve, and who is causing them no little bother one way and another.

In fact, it seems that this Frankie Farrone is as good a reason as any other why Scoodles and Black Mike and Benny are willing to hold a peace conference, because Frankie Farrone is nobody's friend in particular and he is biting into all three wherever he can, showing no respect whatever to old-established guys.

It looks as if Frankie Farrone will sooner or later take the town away from them if they let him go far enough, and while each one of the three tries at different times to make a connection with him, it seems he is just naturally a lone wolf, and wishes no part of any of them. In fact, somebody hears Frankie Farrone say he expects to make Scoodles Shea and Black Mike and Benny jump out of a window before he is through with them, but whether he means one window or three different windows he does not say.

So there is really nothing to be done about Frankie Farrone but to call on him, especially as the three are now together, because the police pay no attention to his threats and make no move to protect Scoodles and Black Mike and Benny, the law being very careless in St. Louis at this time.

Of course, Frankie Farrone has no idea Scoodles and Black Mike and Benny are friendly with each other, and he is probably very much surprised when they drop in on him on their way to the station. In fact, I hear there is a surprised look still on his face when they pick him up later.

He is sitting in a speakeasy reading about the Cardinals losing another game to the Giants when Scoodles Shea comes in the front door, and Black Mike comes in the back door, and Benny the Blond Jew slides in through a side entrance, it being claimed afterwards that they know the owner of the joint and get him to fix it for them so they will have no bother about dropping in on Frankie Farrone sort of unexpected like.

Well, anyway the next thing Frankie Farrone knows he has four slugs in him, one from Scoodles Shea, one from Benny, and two from Black Mike, who seems to be more liberal than the others. The chances are they will put more slugs in him, only they leave their taxi a block away with the engine running and they know the St. Louis taxi jockeys are terrible for jumping the meter on guys who keep them waiting.

So they go on to catch their train, and they are all at the Ritz Hotel in Atlantic City when Dave the Dude and I get there, and they have a nice lay-out of rooms looking out over the ocean, for these are high-class guys in every respect, and very good spenders.

They are sitting around a table with their coats off playing pinocle and drinking liquor when Dave and I show up, and right away Black Mike says: "Hello, Dave! Where do we find the tomatoes?"

I can see at once that this Black Mike is a guy who has little bringing up, or he will not speak of dolls as tomatoes, although, of course, different guys have different names for dolls, such as broads, and pancakes, and cookies, and tomatoes, which I claim are not respectful.

This Black Mike is a Guinea, and not a bad-looking Guinea at that, except for a big scar on one cheek.

Benny the Blond Jew is a tall, pale guy, with soft, light-colored hair and blue eyes, and if I do not happen to know that he personally knocks off about nine guys I will consider him as harmless a looking guy as I ever see. Scoodles Shea is a big, red-headed muzzler with a lot of freckles and a big grin all over his kisser.

They are all maybe thirty-odd, and wear colored silk shirts with soft collars fastened with gold pins, and Black Mike and Scoodles Shea are wearing diamond rings and wrist-watches. Unless you know who they are, you will never figure them to be gorills, even from St. Louis, although at the same time the chances are you will not figure them to be altar boys unless you are very simpleminded.

They seem to be getting along first-rate together, which is not surprising, because it will be considered very bad taste indeed for guys such as these from one town to go into another town and start up any heat. It will be regarded as showing no respect whatever for the local citizens.

Anyway, Atlantic City is never considered a spot for anything but pleasure, and even guys from Philly who may be mad at each other, and who meet up in Atlantic City, generally wait until they get outside the city limits before taking up any arguments.

Well, it seems that not only Black Mike wishes to meet up with some dolls, but Scoodles Shea and Benny are also thinking of such, because the first two things guys away from home think of are liquor and dolls, although personally I never give these matters much of a tumble.

Furthermore, I can see that Dave the Dude is not so anxious about them as you will expect, because Dave is now married to Miss Billy Perry, and if Miss Billy Perry hears that Dave is having any truck with liquor and dolls, especially dolls, it is apt to cause gossip around his house.

But Dave figures he is a sort of host in this territory, because the others are strangers to Atlantic City, and important people where they come from, so we go down to Joe Goss's joint, which is a big cabaret just off the Boardwalk, and in no time there are half a dozen dolls of different shapes and sizes from Joe Goss's chorus, and also several of Joe Goss's hostesses, for Joe Goss gets many tired business men from New York among his customers, and there is nothing a tired business man from New York appreciates more than a lively hostess. Furthermore, Joe Goss himself is sitting with us as a mark of respect to Dave the Dude.

Black Mike and Scoodles and Benny are talking with the dolls and dancing with them now and then, and a good time is being had by one and all, as far as I can see, including Dave the Dude after he gets a couple of slams of Joe Goss's liquor in him and commences to forget about Miss Billy Perry. In fact, Dave so far forgets about Miss Billy Perry that he gets out on the floor with one of the dolls, and dances some, which shows you what a couple of slams of Joe Goss's liquor will do to a guy.

Most of the dolls are just such dolls as you will find in a cabaret, but there is one among them who seems to be a hostess, and whose name seems to be Dolores, and who is a lily for looks. It is afterwards that I find out her other name is Dark, and it is Dave the Dude who afterwards finds out that she is called Dark Dolores in spots.

She is about as good a looker as a guy will wish to clap an eye on. She's tall and limber, like a buggy whip, and she has hair as black as the ace of spades, and maybe blacker, and all smooth and shiny. Her eyes are black and as big as doughnuts, and she has a look in them that somehow makes me think she may know more than she lets on, which I afterwards find out is very true indeed.

She does not have much to say, and I notice she does not drink, and does not seem to be so friendly with the other dolls, so I figure her a fresh-laid one around there, especially as Joe Goss himself does not act as familiar towards her as he does towards most of his dolls, although I can see him give her many a nasty look on account of her passing up drinks.

In fact, nobody gives her much of a tumble at all at first, because guys generally like gabby dolls in situations such as this. But finally I notice that Benny the Blond Jew is taking his peeks at her, and I figure it is because he has better judgment than the others, although I do not understand how Dave the Dude can overlook such a bet, because no better judge of dolls ever lives than Dave the Dude.

But even Benny does not talk to Dolores or offer to dance with her, and at one time when Joe Goss is in another part of the joint chilling a beef from some customer about a check, or maybe about the liquor, which calls for at least a mild beef, and the others are out on the floor dancing, Dolores and I are left alone at the table.

We sit there quite a spell with plenty of silence between us, because I am never much of a hand to chew the fat with dolls, but finally, not because I wish to know or care a whoop, but just to make small talk, I ask her how long she is in Atlantic City.

"I get here this afternoon, and go to work for Mr. Goss just this very night," she says. "I am from Detroit."

Now I do not ask her where she is from, and her sticking in this information makes me commence to think that maybe she is a gabby doll after all, but she dries up and does not say anything else until the others come back to the table.

Now Benny the Blond Jew moves into a chair alongside Dolores, and I hear him say:

"Are you ever in St. Louis? Your face is very familiar to me."

"No," she says. "I am from Cleveland. I am never in St. Louis in my life."

"Well," Benny says, "you look like somebody I see before in St. Louis. It is very strange, because I cannot believe it possible for there to be more than one wonderful beautiful doll like you."

I can see Benny is there with the old stuff when it comes to carrying on a social conversation, but I am wondering how it comes this Dolores is from Detroit with me and from Cleveland with him. Still, I know a thousand dolls who cannot remember offhand where they are from if you ask them quick.

By and by Scoodles Shea and Black Mike notice Benny is all tangled in conversation with Dolores, which makes them take a second peek at her, and by this time they are peeking through plenty of Joe Goss's liquor, which probably makes her look ten times more beautiful than she really is. And I wish to say that any doll ten times more beautiful than Dolores is nothing but a dream.

Anyway, before long Dolores is getting much attention from Black Mike and Scoodles, as well as Benny, and the rest of the dolls finally take the wind, because nobody is giving them a tumble anymore. And even Dave the Dude begins taking dead aim at Dolores until I remind him that he must call up Miss Billy Perry, so he spends the next half-hour in a phone booth explaining to Miss Billy Perry that he is in his hotel in the hay, and that he loves her very dearly.

Well, we are in Joe Goss's joint until five o'clock a.m., with Black Mike and Scoodles and Benny talking to Dolores and taking turns dancing with her, and Dave the Dude is plumb wore out, especially as Miss Billy Perry tells him she knows he is a liar and a bum, as she can hear an orchestra playing "I Get So Blue When It Rains," and for him to just wait until she sees him. Then we take Dolores and go to Childs's restaurant on the Boardwalk and have some coffee, and finally all hands escort her to a little fleabag on North Carolina Avenue where she says she is stopping.

"What are you doing this afternoon, beautiful one?" asks Benny the Blond Jew as we are telling her good night, even though it is morning, and at this crack Black Mike and Scoodles Shea look at Benny, very, very cross.

"I am going bathing in front of the Ritz," she says. "Do some of you boys wish to come along with me?"

Well, it seems that Black Mike and Scoodles and Benny all think this is a wonderful idea, but it does not go so big with Dave the Dude or me. In fact, by this time, Dave the Dude and me are pretty sick of Dolores.

"Anyway," Dave says, "we must start our conference this afternoon and get through with it, because my ever-loving doll is already steaming, and I have plenty of business to look after in New York."

But the conference does not start this afternoon, or the next night, or the next day, or the next day following, because in the afternoons Black Mike and Scoodles and Benny are in the ocean with Dolores and at night they are in Joe Goss's joint, and in between they are taking her riding in rolling chairs on the Boardwalk, or feeding her around the different hotels.

No one guy is ever alone with her as far as I can see, except when she is dancing with one in Joe Goss's joint, and about the third night they are so jealous of each other they all try to dance with her at once.

Well, naturally even Joe Goss complains about this because it makes confusion on his dance floor, and looks unusual. So Dolores settles the proposition, by not dancing with anybody, and I figure this is a good break for her, as no doll's dogs can stand all the dancing Black Mike and Scoodles and Benny wish to do.

The biggest rolling chair on the Boardwalk only takes in three guys or two guys and one doll, or, what is much better, one guy and two dolls, so when Dolores is in a rolling chair with a guy sitting on each side of her the other walks alongside the chair, which is a peculiar sight indeed.

How they decide the guy who walks I never know, but I suppose Dolores fixes it. When she is in bathing in the ocean, Black Mike and Scoodles and Benny all stick so close to her that she is really quite crowded at times.

I doubt if even Waldo Winchester, the scribe, who hears of a lot of things, ever hears of such a situation as this with three guys all daffy over the same doll, and guys who do not think any too well of each other to begin with. I can see they are getting more and more hostile towards each other over her, but when they are not with Dolores they stick close to each other for fear one will cop a sneak, and get her to himself.

I am very puzzled, because Black Mike and Scoodles and Benny do not get their rods out and start a shooting match among themselves over her, but I find that Dave the Dude makes them turn in their rods to him the second day because he does not care to have them doing any target practice around Atlantic City.

So they cannot start a shooting match among themselves if they wish, and the reason they do not put the slug on each other is because Dolores tells them she hates tough guys who go around putting the slug on people. So they are gentlemen, bar a few bad cracks passing among them now and then.

Well, it comes on a Friday, and there we are in Atlantic City since a Monday and nothing stirring on the peace conference as yet, and Dave the Dude is very much disgusted indeed.

All night Friday and into Saturday morning we are in Joe Goss's, and personally I can think of many other places I will rather be. To begin with, I never care to be around gorills when they are drinking, and when you take gorills who are drinking and get them all crazy about the same doll, they are apt to turn out to be no gentlemen any minute.

I do not know who it is who suggests a daybreak swimming party, because I am half asleep, and so is Dave the Dude, but I hear afterwards it is Dolores. Anyway, the next thing anybody knows we are out on the beach, and Dolores and Black Mike and Scoodles Shea and Benny the Blond Jew are in their bathing suits and the dawn is touching up the old ocean very beautiful.

Of course, Dave the Dude and me are not in bathing suits, because in the first place neither of us is any hand for going in bathing, and in the second place, if we are going in bathing, we will not go in bathing at such an hour. Furthermore, as far as I am personally concerned, I hope I am never in a bathing suit if I will look no better in it than Black Mike, while Scoodles Shea is no Gene Tunney in regards to shape. Benny the Blond Jew is the only one who looks human, and I do not give him more than sixty-five points.

Dave the Dude and me stand around watching them, and mostly we are watching Dolores. She is in a red bathing suit with a red rubber cap over her black hair, and while most dolls in bathing suits hurt my eyes, she is still beautiful. I will always claim she is the most beautiful thing I ever see, bar Blue Larkspur, and of course Blue Larkspur is a racehorse and not a doll. I am very glad that Miss Billy Perry is not present to see the look in Dave the Dude's eyes as he watches Dolores in her bathing suit, for Miss Billy Perry is quick to take offense.

When she is in the water Dolores slides around like a big beautiful red fish. You can see she loves it. The chances are I can swim better on my back than Black Mike or Scoodles Shea can on their stomachs, and Benny the Blond Jew is no Gertrude Ederle, but of course, I am allowing for them being well loaded with Joe Goss's liquor, and a load of Joe Goss's liquor is not apt to float well anywhere.

Well, after they paddle around in the ocean awhile, Dolores and her three Romeos lay out on the sand, and Dave the Dude and me are just figuring on going to bed, when all of a sudden we see Dolores jump up and start running for the ocean with Black Mike and Benny head-and-head just behind her, and Scoodles Shea half a length back.

She tears into the water, kicking it every which way until she gets to where it is deep, when she starts to swim, heading for the open sea. Black Mike and Scoodles Shea and Benny the Blond Jew are paddling after her like blazes. We can see it is some kind of a chase, and we stand watching it. We can see Dolores's little red cap bouncing along over the water like a rubber ball on a sidewalk, with Black Mike and Scoodles and Benny staggering along behind her, for Joe Goss's liquor will make a guy stagger on land or sea.

She is away ahead of them at first, but then she seems to pull up and let them get closer to her. When Black Mike, who is leading the other two, gets within maybe fifty yards of her, the red cap bounces away again, always going farther out. It strikes me that Dolores is sort of swimming in wide circles, now half turning as if coming back to the beach, and then taking a swing that carries her seaward again.

When I come to think it over afterwards, I can see that when you are watching her it does not look as if she is swimming away from the beach, and yet all the time she is getting away from it.

One of her circles takes her almost back to Benny, who is a bad last to Black Mike and Scoodles Shea, and in fact she gets so close to Benny that he is lunging for her, when she slides away again, and is off faster than any fish I ever see afloat. Then she does the same to Black Mike and Scoodles. I figure they are playing tag in the water, or some such, and while this may be all right for guys who are full of liquor, and a light-headed doll, I do not consider it a proper amusement at such an hour for guys in their right senses, like Dave the Dude and me.

So I am pleased when he says we better go to bed because by this time Dolores and Black Mike and Scoodles Shea and Benny seem to be very far out in the water indeed. As we are strolling along the Boardwalk, I look back again and there they are, no bigger than pin points on the water, and it seems to me that I can see only three pin points, at that, but I figure Dolores is so far out I cannot see her through the haze.

"They will be good and tuckered out by the time they get back," I say to Dave the Dude.

"I hope they drown," Dave says, but a few days later he apologizes for this crack and explains he makes it only because he is tired and disgusted.

Well, I often think now that it is strange neither Dave the Dude or me see anything unnatural in the whole play, but we do not even mention Dolores or Black Mike or Scoodles Shea or Benny the Blond Jew until late in the afternoon when we are putting on the old grapefruit and ham and eggs in Dave's room and Dave is looking out over the ocean.

"Say," he says, as if he just happens to remember it, "do you know those guys are away out yonder the last we see of them? I wonder if they get back okay?"

And as if answering his question there is a knock on the door, and who walks in but Dolores. She looks all fagged out, but she is so beautiful I will say she seems to light up the room, only I do not wish anybody to think I am getting romantic. Anyway, she is beautiful, but her voice is very tired as she says to Dave the Dude:

"Your friends from St. Louis will not return, Mister Dave the Dude. They do not swim so well, but better than I thought. The one that is called Black Mike and Scoodles Shea turn back when we are about three miles out, but they never reach the shore. I see them both go down for the last time. I make sure of this, Mister Dave the Dude. The pale one, Benny, lasts a little farther, although he is the worst swimmer of them all, and he never turns back. He is still trying to follow me when a cramp gets him and he sinks. I guess he loves me the most at that as he always claims."

Well, naturally I am greatly horrified by this news, especially as she tells it without batting one of her beautiful eyes.

"Do you mean to tell us you let these poor guys drown out there in all this salt water?" I say, very indignant. "Why, you are nothing but a cad."

But Dave the Dude makes a sign for me to shut up, and Dolores says:

"I come within a quarter of a mile of swimming the English Channel in 1927, as you will see by looking up the records," she says, "and I can swim the Mississippi one handed, but I cannot pack three big guys such as these on my back. Even," she says, "if I care to, which I do not. Benny is the only one who speak to me before he goes. The last time I circle back to him he waves his hand and says, 'I know all along I see you somewhere before. I remember now. You are Frankie Farrone's doll.'"

"And you are?" asks Dave the Dude.

"His widow," says Dolores. "I promise him as he lays in his coffin that these men will die, and they are dead. I spent my last dollar getting to this town by airplane, but I get there, and I get them. Only it is more the hand of Providence," she says. "Now I will not need this."

And she tosses out on the table among our breakfast dishes a little bottle that we find out afterwards is full of enough cyanide to kill forty mules, which always makes me think that this Dolores is a doll who means business.

"There is only one thing I wish to know," Dave the Dude says. "Only one thing. How do you coax these fatheads to follow you out in the water?"

"This is the easiest thing of all," Dolores says. "It is an inspiration to me as we lay out on the beach. I tell them I will marry the first one who reaches me in the water. I do not wish to seem hard-hearted, but it is a relief to me when I see Black Mike sink. Can you imagine being married to such a bum?"

It is not until we are going home that Dave the Dude has anything to say about the proposition, and then he speaks to me as follows:

"You know," Dave says, "I will always consider I get a very lucky break that Dolores does not include me in her offer, or the chances are I will be swimming yet."

LILLIAN

What I always say is that Wilbur Willard is nothing but a very lucky guy, because what is it but luck that has been teetering along Forty-ninth Street one cold snowy morning when Lillian is merowing around the sidewalk looking for her mamma?

And what is it but luck that has Wilbur Willard all mulled up to a million, what with him having been sitting out a few seidels of Scotch with a friend by the name of Haggerty in an apartment over on Fifty-ninth Street? Because if Wilbur Willard is not mulled up, he will see Lillian as nothing but a little black cat, and give her plenty of room, for everybody knows that black cats are terribly bad luck, even when they are only kittens.

But being mulled up like I tell you, things look very different to Wilbur Willard, and he does not see Lillian as a little black kitten scrabbling around in the snow. He sees a beautiful leopard, because a copper by the name of O'Hara, who is walking past about then, and who knows Wilbur Willard, hears him say:

"Oh, you beautiful leopard!"

The copper takes a quick peek himself, because he does not wish any leopards running around his beat, it being against the law, but all he sees, as he tells me afterwards, is this rumpot ham, Wilbur Willard, picking up a scrawny little black kitten and shoving it in his overcoat pocket, and he also hears Wilbur say:

"Your name is Lillian."

Then Wilbur teeters on up to his room on the top floor of an old fleabag on Eighth Avenue that is called the Hotel de Brussels, where he lives quite a while, because the management does not mind actors, the management of the Hotel de Brussels being very broad-minded indeed.

There is some complaint this same morning from one of Wilbur's neighbors, an old burlesque doll by the name of Minnie

Madigan, who is not working since Abraham Lincoln is assassinated, because she hears Wilbur going on in his room about a
beautiful leopard, and calls up the clerk to say that an hotel which
allows wild animals is not respectable. But the clerk looks in on Wilbur and finds him playing with nothing but a harmless-looking little black kitten, and nothing comes of the old doll's beef, especially
as nobody ever claims the Hotel de Brussels is respectable anyway,
or at least not much.

Of course when Wilbur comes out from under the ether next afternoon he can see Lillian is not a leopard, and in fact Wilbur is
quite astonished to find himself in bed with a little black kitten,
because it seems Lillian is sleeping on Wilbur's chest to keep warm.
At first Wilbur does not believe what he sees, and puts it down to
Haggerty's Scotch, but finally he is convinced, and so he puts Lillian in his pocket, and takes her over to the Hot Box night club
and gives her some milk, of which is seems Lillian is very fond.

Now where Lillian comes from in the first place of course nobody knows. The chances are somebody chucks her out of a window into the snow, because people are always chucking kittens,
and one thing and another, out of windows in New York. In fact,
if there is one thing this town has plenty of, it is kittens, which finally grow up to be cats, and go snooping around ash cans, and
mer-owing on roofs, and keeping people from sleeping good.

Personally, I have no use for cats, including kittens, because I
never see one that has any too much sense, although I know a guy
by the name of Pussy McGuire who makes a first-rate living doing
nothing but stealing cats, and sometimes dogs, and selling them to
old dolls who like such things for company. But Pussy only steals
Persian and Angora cats, which are very fine cats, and of course
Lillian is no such cat as this. Lillian is nothing but a black cat, and
nobody will give you a dime a dozen for black cats in this town,
as they are generally regarded as very bad jinxes.

Furthermore, it comes out in a few weeks that Wilbur Willard
can just as well name her Herman, or Sidney, as not, but Wilbur
sticks to Lillian, because this is the name of his partner when he is
in vaudeville years ago. He often tells me about Lillian Withington when he is mulled up, which is more often than somewhat, for
Wilbur is a great hand for drinking Scotch, or rye, or bourbon, or
gin, or whatever else there is around for drinking, except water. In
fact, Wilbur Willard is a high-class drinking man, and it does no

good to tell him it is against the law to drink in this country, because it only makes him mad, and he says to the dickens with the law, only Wilbur Willard uses a much rougher word than dickens.

"She is like a beautiful leopard," Wilbur says to me about Lillian Withington. "Black-haired, and black-eyed, and all ripply, like a leopard I see in an animal act on the same bill at the Palace with us once. We are headliners then," he says, "Willard and Withington, the best singing and dancing act in the country.

"I pick her up in San Antonia, which is a spot in Texas," Wilbur says. "She is not long out of a convent, and I just lose my old partner, Mary McGee, who ups and dies on me of pneumonia down there. Lillian wishes to go on the stage, and joins out with me. A natural-born actress with a great voice. But like a leopard," Wilbur says. "Like a leopard. There is cat in her, no doubt of this, and cats and women are both ungrateful. I love Lillian Withington. I wish to marry her. But she is cold to me. She says she is not going to follow the stage all her life. She says she wishes money, and luxury, and a fine home and of course a guy like me cannot give a doll such things.

"I wait on her hand and foot," Wilbur says. "I am her slave. There is nothing I will not do for her. Then one day she walks in on me in Boston very cool and says she is quitting me. She says she is marrying a rich guy there. Well, naturally it busts up the act and I never have the heart to look for another partner, and then I get to belting that old black bottle around, and now what am I but a cabaret performer?"

Then sometimes he will bust out crying, and sometimes I will cry with him, although the way I look at it, Wilbur gets a pretty fair break, at that, in getting rid of a doll who wishes things he cannot give her. Many a guy in this town is tangled up with a doll who wishes things he cannot give her, but who keeps him tangled up just the same and busting himself trying to keep her quiet.

Wilbur makes pretty fair money as an entertainer in the Hot Box, though he spends most of it for Scotch, and he is not a bad entertainer, either. I often go to the Hot Box when I am feeling blue to hear him sing "Melancholy Baby" and "Moonshine Valley" and other sad songs which break my heart. Personally, I do not see why any doll cannot love Wilbur, especially if they listen to him sing such songs as "Melancholy Baby" when he is mulled up good, because he is a tall, nice-looking guy with long eyelashes, and sleepy brown eyes, and his voice has a low moaning sound that usually goes very big with the dolls. In fact, many a doll does do some pitching to Wilbur when he is singing in the Hot Box, but somehow Wilbur never gives them a tumble, which I suppose is because he is thinking of Lillian Withington.

Well, after he gets Lillian, the black kitten, Wilbur seems to find a new interest in life, and Lillian turns out to be right cute, and not bad-looking after Wilbur gets her fed up good. She is blacker than a yard up a chimney, with not a white spot on her, and she grows so fast that by and by Wilbur cannot carry her in his pocket anymore, so he puts a collar on her and leads her round. So Lillian becomes very well known on Broadway, what with Wilbur taking her many places, and finally she does not even have to be led around by Wilbur, but follows him like a pooch. And in all the Roaring Forties there is no pooch that cares to have any truck with Lillian, for she will leap aboard them quicker than you can say scat, and scratch and bite them until they are very glad indeed to get away from her.

But of course the pooches in the Forties are mainly nothing but Chows, and Pekes, and Poms, or little woolly white poodles, which are led around by blonde dolls, and are not fit to take their own part against a smart cat. In fact, Wilbur Willard is finally not on speaking terms with any doll that owns a pooch between Times Square and Columbus Circle, and they are all hoping that both Wilbur and Lillian will go lay down and die somewhere. Furthermore, Wilbur has a couple of battles with guys who also belong to the dolls, but Wilbur is no sucker in a battle if he is not mulled up too much and leg-weary.

After he is through entertaining people in the Hot Box, Wilbur generally goes around to any speakeasies which may still be open, and does a little off-hand drinking on top of what he already drinks down in the Hot Box, which is plenty, and although it is considered very risky in this town to mix Hot Box liquor with any other, it never seems to bother Wilbur. Along towards daylight he takes a couple of bottles of Scotch over to his room in the Hotel de Brussels and uses them for a nightcap, so by the time Wilbur Willard is ready to slide off to sleep he has plenty of liquor of one kind and another inside him, and he sleeps pretty.

Of course nobody on Broadway blames Wilbur so very much for being such a rumpot, because they know about him loving Lillian Withington, and losing her, and it is considered a reasonable excuse in this town for a guy to do some drinking when he loses a doll, which is why there is so much drinking here, but it is a mystery to one and all how Wilbur stands off all this liquor without croaking. The cemeteries are full of guys who do a lot less drinking than Wilbur, but he never even seems to feel extra tough, or if he does he keeps it to himself and does not go around saying it is the kind of liquor you get nowadays.

He costs some of the boys around Mindy's plenty of dough one winter, because he starts in doing most of his drinking after hours in Good Time Charley's speakeasy, and the boys lay a price of four to one against him lasting until spring, never figuring a guy can drink very much of Good Time Charley's liquor and keep on living. But Wilbur Willard does it just the same, so everybody says the guy is naturally superhuman, and lets it go at that.

Sometimes Wilbur drops into Mindy's with Lillian following him on the look-out for pooches, or riding on his shoulder if the weather is bad, and the two of them will sit with us for hours chewing the rag about one thing and another. At such times Wilbur generally has a bottle on his hip and takes a shot now and then, but of course this does not come under the head of serious drinking with him. When Lillian is with Wilbur she always lays as close to him as she can get and anybody can see that she seems to be very fond of Wilbur, and that he is very fond of her, although he sometimes forgets himself and speaks of her as a beautiful leopard. But of course this is only a slip of the tongue, and anyway if Wilbur gets any pleasure out of thinking Lillian is a leopard, it is nobody's business but his own.

"I suppose she will run away from me someday," Wilbur says, running his hand over Lillian's back until her fur crackles. "Yes, although I give her plenty of liver and catnip, and one thing and another, and all my affection, she will probably give me the shake. Cats are like women, and women are like cats. They are both very ungrateful."

"They are both generally bad luck," Big Nig, the crap shooter, says. "Especially cats, and most especially black cats."

Many other guys tell Wilbur about black cats being bad luck, and advise him to slip Lillian into the North River some night with a sinker on her, but Wilbur claims he already has all the bad luck in the world when he loses Lillian Withington, and that Lillian, the cat, cannot make it any worse, so he goes on taking extra good care of her, and Lillian goes on getting bigger and bigger, until I commence thinking maybe there is some St. Bernard in her.

Finally I commence to notice something funny about Lillian. Sometimes she will be acting very loving towards Wilbur, and then again she will be very unfriendly to him, and will spit at him, and snatch at him with her claws, very hostile. It seems to me that she is all right when Willard is mulled up, but is as sad and fretful as he is himself when he is only a little bit mulled. And when Lillian is sad and fretful she makes it very tough indeed on the pooches in the neighborhood of the Brussels.

In fact, Lillian takes to pooch-hunting, sneaking off when Wilbur is getting his rest, and running pooches bow-legged, especially when she finds one that is not on a leash. A loose pooch is just naturally cherry pie for Lillian.

Well, of course, this causes great indignation among the dolls who own the pooches, particularly when Lillian comes home one day carrying a Peke as big as she is herself by the scruff of the neck, and with a very excited blonde doll following her and yelling bloody murder outside Wilbur Willard's door when Lillian pops into Wilbur's room through a hole he cuts in the door for her, still lugging the Peke. But it seems that instead of being mad at Lillian and giving her a pasting for such goings-on, Wilbur is somewhat pleased, because he happens to be still in a fog when Lillian arrives with the Peke, and is thinking of Lillian as a beautiful leopard.

"Why," Wilbur says, "this is devotion indeed. My beautiful leopard goes off into the jungle and fetches me an antelope for dinner."

Now of course there is no sense whatever to this, because a Peke is certainly not anything like an antelope, but the blonde doll outside Wilbur's door hears Wilbur mumble, and gets the idea that he is going to eat her Peke for dinner and the squawk she puts up is very terrible. There is plenty of trouble around the Brussels in chilling the blonde doll's beef over Lillian snagging her Peke, and what is more the blonde doll's ever-loving guy, who turns out to be a tough Ginney bootlegger by the name of Gregorio, shows up at the Hot Box the next night and wishes to put the slug on Wilbur Willard.

But Wilbur rounds him up with a few drinks and by singing "Melancholy Baby" to him, and before he leaves the Ginney gets very sentimental towards Wilbur, and Lillian, too, and wishes to give Wilbur five bucks to let Lillian grab the Peke again, if Lillian will promise not to bring it back. It seems Gregorio does not really care for the Peke, and is only acting quarrelsome to please the blonde doll and make her think he loves her dearly.

But I can see Lillian is having different moods, and finally I ask Wilbur if he notices it.

"Yes," he says, very sad, "I do not seem to be holding her love. She is getting very fickle. A guy moves on to my floor at the Brussels the other day with a little boy, and Lillian becomes very fond of this kid at once. In fact, they are great friends. Ah, well," Wilbur says, "cats are like women. Their affection does not last."

I happen to go over to the Brussels a few days later to explain to a guy by the name of Crutchy, who lives on the same floor as Wilbur Willard, that some of our citizens do not like his face and that it may be a good idea for him to leave town, especially if he insists on bringing ale into their territory, and I see Lillian out in the hall with a youngster which I judge is the kid Wilbur is talking about. This kid is maybe three years old, and very cute, what with black hair, and black eyes, and he is wooling Lillian around the hall in a way that is most surprising, for Lillian is not such a cat as will stand for much wooling around, not even from Wilbur Willard.

I am wondering how anybody comes to take such a kid to a joint like the Brussels, but I figure it is some actor's kid, and that maybe there is no mamma for it. Later I am talking to Wilbur about this, and he says:

"Well, if the kid's old man is an actor, he is not working at it. He sticks close to his room all the time, and he does not allow the kid to go anywhere but in the hall, and I feel sorry for the little guy, which is why I allow Lillian to play with him."

Now it comes on a very cold spell, and a bunch of us are sitting in Mindy's along towards five o'clock in the morning when we hear fire engines going past. By and by in comes a guy by the name of Kansas, who is named Kansas because he comes from Kansas, and who is a crap shooter by trade.

"The old Brussels is on fire," this guy Kansas says.

"She is always on fire," Big Nig says, meaning there is always plenty of hot stuff going on around the Brussels.

About this time who walks in but Wilbur Willard, and anybody can see he is just naturally floating. The chances are he comes from Good Time Charley's, and he is certainly carrying plenty of pressure. I never see Wilbur Willard mulled up more. He does not have Lillian with him, but then he never takes Lillian to Good Time Charley's, because Charley hates cats.

"Hey, Wilbur," Big Nig says, "your joint, the Brussels, is on fire."

"Well," Wilbur says, "I am a little firefly, and I need a light. Let us go where there is fire."

The Brussels is only a few blocks from Mindy's, and there is nothing else to do just then, so some of us walk over to Eighth Avenue with Wilbur teetering along ahead of us. The old shack is certainly roaring good when we get in sight of it, and the firemen are tossing water into it, and the coppers have the fire lines out to keep the crowd back, although there is not much of a crowd at such an hour in the morning.

"Is it not beautiful?" Wilbur Willard says, looking up at the flames. "Is it not like a fairy palace all lighted up this way?"

You see, Wilbur does not realize the joint is on fire, although guys and dolls are running out of it every which way, most of them half dressed, or not dressed at all, and the firemen are getting out the life nets in case anybody wishes to hop out of the windows.

"It is certainly beautiful," Wilbur says. "I must get Lillian so she can see this."

And before anybody has time to think, there is Wilbur Willard walking into the front door of the Brussels as if nothing happens. The firemen and the coppers are so astonished all they can do is holler at Wilbur, but he pays no attention whatever. Well, naturally everybody figures Wilbur is a gone gosling, but in about ten minutes he comes walking out of this same door through the fire and smoke as cool as you please, and he has Lillian in his arms.

"You know," Wilbur says, coming over to where we are standing with our eyes popping out, "I have to walk all the way up to my floor because the elevators seem to be out of commission. The service is getting terrible in this hotel. I will certainly make a strong beef to the management about it as soon as I pay something on my account."

Then what happens but Lillian lets out a big mer-ow, and hops out of Wilbur's arms and skips past the coppers and the firemen with her back all humped up and the next thing anybody knows she is tearing through the front door of the old hotel and making plenty of speed.

"Well, well," Wilbur says, looking much surprised, "there goes Lillian."

And what does this daffy Wilbur Willard do but turn and go marching back into the Brussels again, and by this time the smoke is pouring out of the front doors so thick he is out of sight in a second. Naturally he takes the coppers and firemen by surprise, because they are not used to guys walking in and out of fires on them.

This time anybody standing around will lay you plenty of odds—two and a half and maybe three to one—that Wilbur never shows up again, because the old Brussels is now just popping with fire and smoke from the lower windows, although there does not seem to be quite so much fire in the upper story. Everybody seems to be out of the joint, and even the firemen are fighting the blaze from the outside because the Brussels is so old and ramshackly there is no sense in them risking the floors.

I mean everybody is out of the joint except Wilbur Willard and Lillian, and we figure they are getting a good frying somewhere inside, although Feet Samuels is around offering to take thirteen to five for a few small bets that Lillian comes out okay, because Feet claims that a cat has nine lives and that is a fair bet at the price.

Well, up comes a swell-looking doll all heated up about something and pushing and clawing her way through the crowd up to the ropes and screaming until you can hardly hear yourself think, and about this same minute everybody hears a voice going ai-lee-hi-hee-hoo, like a Swiss yodeler, which comes from the roof of the Brussels, and looking up what do we see but Wilbur Willard standing up there on the edge of the roof, high above the fire and smoke, and yodeling very loud.

Under one arm he has a big bundle of some kind, and under the other he has the little kid I see playing in the hall with Lillian. As he stands up there going ai-lee-hi-hee-hoo, the swell-dressed doll near us begins yipping louder than Wilbur is yodeling, and the firemen rush over under him with a life net.

Wilbur lets go another ai-lee-hi-hee-hoo, and down he comes all spraddled out, with the bundle and the kid, but he hits the net sitting down and bounces up and back again for a couple of minutes before he finally settles. In fact, Wilbur is enjoying the bouncing, and the chances are he will be bouncing yet if the firemen do not drop their hold on the net and let him fall to the ground.

Then Wilbur steps out of the net, and I can see the bundle is a rolled-up blanket with Lillian's eyes peeking out of one end. He still has the kid under the other arm with his head stuck out in front, and his legs stuck out behind, and it does not seem to me that Wilbur is handling the kid as careful as he is handling Lillian. He stands there looking at the firemen with a very sneering look, and finally he says:

"Do not think you can catch me in your net unless I wish to be caught. I am a butterfly, and very hard to overtake."

Then all of a sudden the swell-dressed doll who is doing so much hollering, piles on top of Wilbur and grabs the kid from him and begins hugging and kissing it.

"Wilbur," she says, "God bless you, Wilbur, for saving my baby! Oh, thank you, Wilbur, thank you! My wretched husband kidnaps and runs away with him, and it is only a few hours ago that my detectives find out where he is."

Wilbur gives the doll a funny look for about half a minute and starts to walk away, but Lillian comes wiggling out of the blanket, looking and smelling pretty much singed up, and the kid sees Lillian and begins hollering for her, so Wilbur finally hands Lillian over to the kid. And not wishing to leave Lillian, Wilbur stands around somewhat confused, and the doll gets talking to him, and finally they go away together, and as they go Wilbur is carrying the kid, and the kid is carrying Lillian, and Lillian is not feeling so good from her burns.

Furthermore, Wilbur is probably more sober than he ever is before in years at this hour in the morning, but before they go I get a chance to talk some to Wilbur when he is still rambling somewhat, and I make out from what he says that the first time he goes to get Lillian he finds her in his room and does not see hide or hair of the little kid and does not even think of him, because he does not know what room the kid is in, anyway, having never noticed such a thing.

But the second time he goes up, Lillian is sniffing at the crack under the door of a room down the hall from Wilbur's and Wilbur says he seems to remember seeing a trickle of something like water coming out of the crack.

"And," Wilbur says, "as I am looking for a blanket for Lillian, and it will be a bother to go back to my room, I figure I will get one out of this room. I try the knob but the door is locked, so I kick it in, and walk in to find the room full of smoke, and fire is shooting through the windows very lovely, and when I grab a blanket off the bed for Lillian, what is under the blanket but the kid?

"Well," Wilbur says, "the kid is squawking, and Lillian is mer-owing, and there is so much confusion generally that it makes me nervous, so I figure we better go up on the roof and let the stink blow off us, and look at the fire from there. It seems there is a guy stretched out on the floor of the room alongside an upset table be-tween the door and the bed. He has a bottle in one hand, and he is dead. Well, naturally there is no percentage in lugging a dead guy along, so I take Lillian and the kid and go up on the roof, and we just naturally fly off like humming birds. Now I must get a drink," Wilbur says. "I wonder if anybody has anything on their hip?"

Well, the papers are certainly full of Wilbur and Lillian the next day, especially Lillian, and they are both great heroes.

But Wilbur cannot stand the publicity very long, because he never has any time to himself for his drinking, what with the scribes and the photographers hopping on him every few minutes wish-ing to hear his story, and to take more pictures of him and Lillian, so one night he disappears, and Lillian disappears with him.

About a year later it comes out that he marries his old doll, Lil-lian Withington-Harmon, and falls into a log of dough, and what is more he cuts out the liquor and becomes quite a useful citizen one way and another. So everybody has to admit that black cats are not always bad luck, although I say Wilbur's case is a little ex-ceptional because he does not start out knowing Lillian is a black cat, but thinking she is a leopard.

I happen to run into Wilbur one day all dressed up in good clothes and jewelry and chucking quite a swell.

"Wilbur," I say to him, "I often think how remarkable it is the way Lillian suddenly gets such an attachment for the little kid and remembers about him being in the hotel and leads you back there a second time to the right room. If I do not see this come off with my own eyes, I will never believe a cat has brains enough to do such a thing, because I consider cats extra dumb."

"Brains nothing," Wilbur says. "Lillian does not have brains enough to grease a gimlet. And what is more, she has no more at-tachment for the kid than a jack rabbit. The time has come," Wilbur says, "to expose Lillian. She gets a lot of credit which is never coming to her. I will now tell you about Lillian, and nobody knows this but me.

"You see," Wilbur says, "when Lillian is a little kitten I always put a little Scotch in her milk, partly to help make her good and strong, and partly because I am never no hand to drink alone, unless there is nobody with me. Well, at first Lillian does not care so much for this Scotch in her milk, but finally she takes a liking to it, and I keep making her toddy stronger until in the end she will lap up a good big snort without any milk for a chaser, and yell for more. In fact, I suddenly realize that Lillian becomes a rumpot, just like I am in those days, and simply must have her grog, and it is when she is good and rummed up that Lillian goes off snatching Pekes, and acting tough generally.

"Now," Wilbur says, "the time of the fire is about the time I get home every morning and give Lillian her schnapps. But when I go into the hotel and get her the first time I forget to Scotch her up, and the reason she runs back into the hotel is because she is looking for her shot. And the reason she is sniffing at the kid's door is not because the kid is in there but because the trickle that is coming through the crack under the door is nothing but Scotch that is running out of the bottle in the dead guy's hand. I never mention this before because I figure it may be a knock to a dead guy's memory," Wilbur says. "Drinking is certainly a disgusting thing, especially secret drinking."

"But how is Lillian getting along these days?" I ask Wilbur Willard.

"I am greatly disappointed in Lillian," he says. "She refuses to reform when I do, and the last I hear of her she takes up with Gregorio, the Ginney bootlegger, who keeps her well Scotched up all the time so she will lead his blonde doll's Peke a dog's life."

SOCIAL ERROR

When Mr. Ziegfeld picks a doll, she is apt to be above the average when it comes to looks, for Mr. Ziegfeld is by no means a chump at picking dolls. But when Mr. Ziegfeld picks Miss Midgie Muldoon, he beats his own best record, or anyway ties it. I never see a better-looking doll in my life, although she is somewhat smaller than I like them. I like my dolls big enough to take a good hold on, and Miss Midgie Muldoon is only about knee-high to a Pomeranian. But she is very cute, and I do not blame Handsome Jack Maddigan for going daffy about her.

Now most any doll on Broadway will be very glad indeed to have Handsome Jack Maddigan give her a tumble, so it is very surprising to one and all when Miss Midgie Muldoon plays the chill for Handsome Jack, especially when you figure that Miss Midgie Muldoon is nothing but a chorus doll, while Handsome Jack is quite a high shot in this town. But one night in the Hot Box when Handsome Jack sends word to Miss Midgie Muldoon, by Miss Billy Perry, who is Dave the Dude's wife, that he will like to meet up with her, Miss Midgie Muldoon sends word back to Handsome Jack that she is not meeting up with tough guys.

Well, naturally this crack burns Handsome Jack up quite some. But Dave the Dude says never mind, and furthermore Dave says Miss Midgie Muldoon's crack serves Handsome Jack right for sitting around shooting off his mouth, and putting himself away as a tough guy, because if there is anything Dave hates it is a guy letting on he is tough, no matter how tough he really is, and Handsome Jack is certainly such a guy.

He is a big tall blond guy who comes up out of what they call Hell's Kitchen over on the West Side, and if he has a little more sense the chances are he will be as important a guy as Dave the Dude himself in time, instead of generally working for Dave, but

Handsome Jack likes to wear very good clothes, and drink, and sit around a lot, and also do plenty of talking, and no matter how much dough he makes he never seems able to hold much of anything.

Personally, I never care to have any truck with Handsome Jack because he always strikes me as a guy who is a little too quick on the trigger to suit me, and I always figure the best you are going to get out of being around guys who are quick on the trigger is the worst of it, and so any time I see Handsome Jack I give him the back of my neck. But there are many people in this world such as Basil Valentine who love to be around these characters.

This Basil Valentine is a little guy who wears horn cheaters and writes articles for the magazines, and is personally a very nice little guy, and as harmless as a water snake, but he cannot have a whole lot of sense, or he will not be hanging out with Handsome Jack and other such characters.

If a guy hangs out with tough guys long enough he is apt to get to thinking maybe he is tough himself, and by and by other people may get the idea he is tough, and the first thing you know along comes some copper in plain clothes, such as Johnny Brannigan, of the strong-arm squad, and biffs him on the noggin with a blackjack just to see how tough he is. As I say, Basil Valentine is a very harmless guy, but after he is hanging out with Handsome Jack a while, I hear Basil talking very tough to a bus boy, and the chances are he is building himself up to talk tough to a waiter, and then maybe to a head waiter, and finally he may consider himself tough enough to talk tough to anybody.

I can show you many a guy who is supposed to be strictly legitimate sitting around with guys who are figured as tough guys, and why this is I do not know, but I am speaking to Waldo Winchester, the newspaper scribe, about the proposition one night, and Waldo Winchester, who is a half-smart guy in many respects, says it is what is called an underworld complex. Waldo Winchester says many legitimate people are much interested in the doings of tough guys, and consider them very romantic, and he says if I do not believe it look at all the junk the newspapers print making heroes out of tough guys.

Waldo Winchester says the underworld complex is a very common complex and that Basil Valentine has it, and so has Miss Harriet Mackyle, or she will not be all the time sticking her snoot into joints where tough guys hang out. This Miss Harriet Mackyle is one of these rich dolls who wears snaky-looking evening clothes, and has her hair cut like a boy's, with her ears sticking out, and is always around the night traps, generally with some guy with a little moustache, and a way of talking like an Englishman, and come to think of it I do see her in tough joints more than somewhat, saying hello to different parties such as nobody in their right minds will say hello to, including such as Red Henry, who is just back from Dannemora, after being away for quite a spell for taking things out of somebody's safe and blowing the safe open to take these things.

In fact, I see Miss Harriet Mackyle dancing one night in the Hearts and Flowers Club, which is a very tough joint indeed, and who is she dancing with but Red Henry, and when I ask Waldo Winchester what he makes of this proposition, he says it is part of the underworld complex he is talking about. He says Miss Harriet Mackyle probably thinks it smart to tell her swell friends she dances with a safe-blower, although personally if I am going to dance with a safe-blower at all, which does not seem likely, I will pick me out a nicer safe-blower than Red Henry, because he is such a guy as does not take a bath since he leaves Dannemora, and he is back from Dannemora for several months.

One party who does not seem to have much of Waldo Winchester's underworld complex as far as I can see is Miss Midgie Muldoon, because I never see her around any night traps except such as the Hot Box and the Sixteen Hundred Club, which are considered very nice places, and reasonably safe for anybody who does not get too far out of line, and Miss Midgie Muldoon is always with very legitimate guys such as Buddy Donaldson, the song writer, or Walter Gumble, who plays the trombone in Paul Whiteman's band, or maybe sometimes with Paul Hawley, the actor.

Furthermore, when she is around such places, Miss Midgie Muldoon minds her own business quite a bit, and always looks right past Handsome Jack Maddigan, which burns Jack up all the more. It is the first time Handsome Jack ever runs into a doll who does not seem excited about him, and he does not know what to make of such a situation.

Well, what happens but Dave the Dude comes to me one day and says to me like this: "Listen," Dave says, "this doll Miss Harriet Mackyle is one of my best customers for high-grade merchandise, and is as good as wheat in the bin, and she is asking a favor of me.

She is giving a party Sunday night in her joint over on Park Avenue, and she wishes me to invite some of the mob, so go around and tell about a dozen guys to be there all dressed, and not get too fresh, because a big order of Scotch and champagne goes with the favor."

Now such a party is by no means unusual, although generally it is some swell guy who gives it rather than a doll, and he gets Broadway guys to be there to show his pals what a mixer he is. Waldo Winchester says it is to give color to things, though where the color comes in I do not know, for Broadway guys, such as will go to a party like this, are apt to just sit around and say nothing, and act very gentlemanly, because they figure they are on exhibition like freaks, and the only way you can get them to such parties in the first place is through some such connection as Miss Harriet Mackyle has with Dave the Dude.

Anyway, I go around and about and tell a lot of guys what Dave the Dude wishes them to do, and among others I tell Handsome Jack, who is tickled to death by the invitation, because if there is anything Jack loves more than anything else it is to be in a spot where he can show off some. Furthermore, Handsome Jack has a sneaking idea Miss Harriet Mackyle is red hot for him because she sometimes gives him the old eye when she sees him around the Sixteen Hundred Club, and other spots, but then she does the same thing to Big Nig, and a lot of other guys I can mention, because that is just naturally the way Miss Harriet Mackyle is. But of course I do not speak of this to Handsome Jack. Basil Valentine is with Jack when I invite him, so I tell Basil to come along, too, because I do not wish him to think I am a snob.

It turns out that Basil is one of the very first guys to show up Sunday night at Miss Harriet Mackyle's apartment, where I am already on hand to help get in the Scotch and champagne, and to make Miss Harriet Mackyle acquainted with such of the mob as I invite, although I find we are about lost in the shuffle of guys with little moustaches, and dolls in evening clothes that leave plenty of them sticking out here and there. It seems everybody on Broadway is there, as well as a lot of Park Avenue, and Mr. Ziegfeld is especially well represented, and among his people I see Miss Midgie Muldoon, although I have to stand on tiptoe to see her on account of the guys with little moustaches around her, and their interest in Miss Midgie Muldoon proves that they are not such saps as they look, even if they do wear little moustaches.

It is a very large apartment, and the first thing I notice is a big green parrot swinging in the ring hung from the ceiling in a corner of what seems to be the main room, and the reason I notice this parrot is because it is letting out a squawk now and then, and yelling different words, such as Polly wants a cracker. There are also a lot of canary birds hung around the joint, so I judge Miss Harriet Mackyle loves animals, as well as peculiar people; such as she has for guests.

I am somewhat surprised to see Red Henry all dressed up in evening clothes moving around among the guests. I do not invite Red Henry, so I suppose Miss Harriet Mackyle invites him, or he hears rumors of the party, and just crashes in, but personally I consider it very bad taste on Red Henry's part to show himself in such a spot, and so does everybody else that knows him, although he seems to be minding his own business pretty well.

Finally when the serious drinking is under way, and a good time is being had by one and all, Miss Harriet Mackyle comes over to me and says to me like this: "Now tell me about your different friends, so I can tell my other guests. They will be thrilled to death meeting these bad characters."

"Well," I say, "you see the little guy over there staring at you as if you are a ghost, or some such? Well, he is nobody but Bad Basil Valentine, who will kill you as quick as you can say scat, and maybe quicker. He is undoubtedly the toughest guy here tonight, or anywhere else in this man's town for that matter. Yes, ma'am, Bad Basil Valentine is one dead tough mug," I say, "although he is harmless-looking at this time. Bad Basil kills many a guy in his day. In fact, Miss Mackyle," I say, "Bad Basil can scarcely sleep good any night he does not kill some guy."

"My goodness!" Miss Harriet Mackyle says, looking Basil over very carefully. "He does not look so bad at first glance, although now that I examine him closely I believe I do detect a sinister gleam in his eye."

Well, Miss Harriet Mackyle can hardly wait until she gets away from me, and the next I see of her she has Basil Valentine surrounded and is almost chewing his ear off as she gabs to him, and anybody can see that Basil is all pleasured up by this attention. In fact, Basil is snagged if ever I see a guy snagged, and personally I do not blame him, because Miss Harriet Mackyle may not look a million, but she has a couple, and you can see enough of her in her evening clothes to know that nothing about her is phony.

The party is going big along towards one o'clock when all of a sudden in comes Handsome Jack Maddigan with half a heat on, and in five minutes he is all over the joint, drinking everything that is offered him, and making a fast play for all the dolls, and talking very loud. He is sored up more than somewhat when he finds Miss Harriet Mackyle does not give him much of a tumble, because he figures she will be calling him on top the minute he blows in, but Miss Harriet Mackyle is too busy with Basil Valentine finding out from Basil how he knocks off six of Al Capone's mob out in Chicago one time when he is out there on a pleasure trip.

Well, while feeling sored up about Miss Harriet Mackyle passing him up for Basil Valentine, and not knowing how it comes Basil is in so stout with her, Handsome Jack bumps into Red Henry, and Red Henry makes some fresh crack to Jack about Basil moving in on him, which causes Handsome Jack to hit Red Henry on the chin, and knock him half into the lap of Miss Midgie Muldoon, who is sitting in a chair with a lot of little moustaches around her.

Naturally this incident causes some excitement for a moment. But the way Miss Midgie Muldoon takes it is very surprising. She just sort of dusts Red Henry off her, and stands up no bigger than a demi-tasse, and looks Handsome Jack right in the eye very cool, and says: "Ah, a parlor tough guy." Then she walks away, leaving Handsome Jack with his mouth open, because he does not know up to this moment that Miss Midgie Muldoon is present.

Well, somebody heaves Red Henry out of the joint, and the party continues, but I see Handsome Jack wandering around looking very lonesome, and with not much speed left compared to what he brings in. Somehow I figure Handsome Jack is looking for Miss Midgie Muldoon, but she keeps off among the little moustaches, and finally Handsome Jack takes to belting the old grape right freely to get his zing back. He gets himself pretty well organized, and when he suddenly comes upon Miss Midgie Muldoon standing by herself for a moment, he is feeling very brisk indeed, and he says to her like this: "Hello, Beautiful, are you playing the hard-to-get for me?" But Miss Midgie Muldoon only looks him in the eye again and says: "Ah, the parlor tough guy! Go away, tough guy. I do not like tough guys."

Well, this is not so encouraging when you come to think of it, but Handsome Jack is a guy who will never be ruled off for not trying with the dolls, and he is just about to begin giving her a little more work, when all of a sudden a voice goes "Ha-ha-ha," and then it says: "Hello, you fool!"

Now of course it is nothing but the parrot talking, and it says again: "Ha-ha-ha. Hello, you fool!" Of course, the parrot, whose name turns out to be Polly, does not mean Handsome Jack, but of course Handsome Jack does not know the parrot does not mean him, and naturally he feels very much insulted. Furthermore, he has plenty of champagne inside him. So all of a sudden he outs with the old equalizer and lets go at Polly, and the next minute there are green feathers flying all over the joint, and poor old Mister, or maybe Missus, Polly is stretched out as dead as a doornail, and maybe deader.

Well, I never see a doll carry on like Miss Harriet Mackyle does when she finds out her Polly is a goner, and what she says to Handsome Jack is really very cutting, and quite extensive, and the chances are Handsome Jack will finally haul off and smack Miss Harriet Mackyle in the snoot, only he realizes he is already guilty of a very grave social error in shooting the parrot, and he does not wish to make it any worse.

Anyway, Miss Midgie Muldoon is standing looking at Handsome Jack out of her great big round beautiful eyes with what Waldo Winchester, the scribe, afterwards tells me is plenty of scorn, and it looks to me as if Handsome Jack feels worse about Miss Midgie Muldoon's looks than he does about what Miss Harriet Mackyle is saying to him. But Miss Midgie Muldoon never opens her mouth. She just keeps looking at him for quite a spell, and then finally walks away, and it looks to me as if she is ready to bust out crying any minute, maybe because she feels sorry for Polly.

Well, naturally Handsome Jack's error busts up the party, because Miss Harriet Mackyle does not wish to take any chances on Handsome Jack starting in to pot her canaries, so we all go away leaving Miss Harriet Mackyle weeping over what she can find of Polly, and Basil Valentine crying with her, which I consider very chummy of Basil, at that.

A couple of nights later Basil comes into Mindy's restaurant, where I happen to be sitting with Handsome Jack, and anybody can tell that Basil is much worried about something.

"Jack," he says, "Miss Harriet Mackyle is very, very, very angry about you shooting Polly. In fact, she hates you, because Polly is a family heirloom."

"Well," Jack says, "tell her I apologize, and will get her a new parrot as soon as I get the price. You know I am broke now. Tell her I am very sorry, although," Jack says, "her parrot has no right to call me a fool, and I leave this to everybody."

"Miss Harriet Mackyle is after me every day to shoot you, Jack," Basil says. "She thinks I am a very tough guy, and that I will shoot anybody on short notice, and she wishes me to shoot you. In fact, she is somewhat displeased because I do not shoot you when you shoot poor Polly, but of course I explain to her I do not have a gun at the moment. Now Miss Harriet Mackyle says if I do not shoot you she will not love me, and I greatly wish to have Miss Harriet Mackyle love me, because I am practically daffy about her. So," Basil says, "I am wondering how much you will take to hold still and let me shoot you, Jack?"

"Why," Handsome Jack says, very much astonished, "you must be screwy."

"Of course I do not mean to really shoot you, Jack," Basil says. "I mean to maybe shoot you with a blank cartridge, so Miss Harriet Mackyle will think I am shooting you sure enough, which will make her very grateful to me. I am thinking that maybe I can pay you one thousand five hundred dollars for such a job, although this sum represents nearly my life savings."

"Why," Handsome Jack says, "your proposition sounds very reasonable, at that. I am just wondering where I can get hold of a few bobs to send Miss Midgie Muldoon a bar pin, or some such, and see if I cannot round myself up with her. She is still playing plenty of chill for me. You better make it two grand while you are about it."

Well, Basil Valentine finally agrees to pay the two grand. Furthermore, Basil promises to put the dough up in advance with Dave the Dude, or some other reliable party, as this is rather an unusual business deal, and naturally Handsome Jack wishes to have his interests fully protected.

Well, the thing comes off a few nights later in the Hot Box, and it is all pretty well laid out in advance. It is understood that Basil

is to bring Miss Harriet Mackyle into the Hot Box after regular
hours when there are not apt to be any too many people around,
and to find Handsome Jack there. Basil is to out with a gun and
take a crack at Handsome Jack, and Handsome Jack is to let on
he is hit, and Basil is to get Miss Harriet Mackyle out of the joint
in the confusion.

Handsome Jack promises to lay low a few weeks afterwards so
it will look as if he is dead, and Basil figures that in the meantime
Miss Harriet Mackyle will be so grateful to him that she will love
him very much indeed, and maybe marry him, which is really the
big idea with Basil.

It is pretty generally known to one and all what is coming off,
and quite a number of guys drift into the Hot Box during the night,
including Dave the Dude, who seems to be getting quite a bang
out of the situation. But who also bobs up very unexpectedly but
Miss Midgie Muldoon with Buddy Donaldson, the song writer.

Handsome Jack is all upset by Miss Midgie Muldoon being
there, but she never as much as looks at him. So Handsome Jack
takes to drinking Scotch more than somewhat, and everybody
commences to worry about whether he will hold still for Basil
Valentine to shoot him, even with a blank cartridge. The Hot Box
closes at three o'clock in the morning, and everybody is always
turned out except the regulars. So by three-thirty there are only
about a dozen guys and dolls in the joint when in comes Basil
Valentine and Miss Harriet Mackyle.

Handsome Jack happens to be standing with his back to the
door and not far from the table where Miss Midgie Muldoon and
this Buddy Donaldson are sitting when Basil and Miss Harriet
Mackyle come in, and right away Basil sings out, his voice wobbling no little: "Handsome Jack Maddigan, your time has come!"
At this Handsome Jack turns around, and there is Basil Valentine
tugging a big rod out of the hind pocket of his pants.

The next thing anybody knows, there is a scream, and a doll's
voice cries: "Jack! Look out, Jack!" and out of her seat and over
to Handsome Jack Maddigan bounces Miss Midgie Muldoon,
and just as Basil finally raises the rod and turns it on, Miss Midgie
Muldoon plants herself right in front of Jack and stretches out her
arms on either side of her as if to shield him.

Well, the gun goes bingo in Basil's hand, but instead of falling
like he is supposed to do, Handsome Jack stands there with his

mouth open looking at Miss Midgie Muldoon, not knowing what to make of her jumping between him and the gun, and it is a good thing he does not fall, at that, because he is able to catch Miss Midgie Muldoon as she starts to keel over. At first we think maybe it is only a faint, but she has on a low-neck dress, and across her left shoulder there slowly spreads a red smear, and what is this red smear but blood, and as Handsome Jack grabs her she says to him like this: "Hold me, dear, I am hurt."

Now this is most unexpected indeed, and is by no means a part of the play. Basil Valentine is standing by the door with the rod in his duke looking quite astonished, and making no move to get Miss Harriet Mackyle out of the joint as he is supposed to the minute he fires, and Miss Harriet Mackyle is letting out a few off-hand screams which are very piercing, and saying she never thinks that Basil will take her seriously and really plug anybody for her, although she also says she appreciates his thoughtfulness, at that.

You can see Basil is standing there wondering what goes wrong, when Dave the Dude, who is a fast thinker under all circumstances, takes a quick peek at Miss Midgie Muldoon, and then jumps across the room and nails Basil. "Why," Dave says to Basil, "you are nothing but a rascal. You mean to kill him after all. You do not shoot a blank, you throw a slug, and you get Miss Midgie Muldoon with it in the shoulder."

Well, Basil is a pretty sick-looking toad as Dave the Dude takes hold of him, and Miss Harriet Mackyle is putting on a few extra yips when Basil says: "My goodness, Dave," he says. "I never know this gun is really loaded. In fact, I forget all about getting a gun of my own until the last minute, and am looking around for one when Red Henry comes along and says he will lend me his. I explain to him how the whole proposition is a joke, and tell him I must have blanks, and he kindly takes the lead out of the cartridges in front of my own eyes and makes them blank."

"The chances are Red Henry works a quick change on you," Dave the Dude says. "Red Henry is very angry at Jack for hitting him on the chin."

Then Dave takes the rod out of Basil's hand and breaks it open, and sure enough there are enough real slugs in it to sink a rowboat and no blanks whatever, which surprises Basil Valentine no little.

"Now," Dave says, "get away from here before Jack realizes what happens, and keep out of sight until you hear from me, because if Miss Midgie Muldoon croaks it may cause some gossip. Furthermore," Dave says, "take this squawking doll with you."

Well, you can see that Dave the Dude is pretty much steamed up, and he remains steamed up until it comes out that Miss Midgie Muldoon is only a little bit shot, and is by no means in danger of dying. We take her over to the Polyclinic Hospital, and a guy there digs the bullet out of her shoulder, and we leave her there with Handsome Jack holding her tight in his arms, and swearing he will never be tough again, but will get her a nice little home on Basil Valentine's two grand, and find himself a job, and take no more part in his old life, all of which seems to sound fair enough.

It is a couple of years before we hear of Miss Harriet Mackyle again, and then she is Mrs. Basil Valentine, and is living in Naples over in Italy, and the people there are very much surprised because Mrs. Basil Valentine never lets Mr. Basil Valentine associate with guys over ten years old, and never lets him handle anything more dangerous than a niblick.

So this is about all there is to the story, except that when Handsome Jack Maddigan and Miss Midgie Muldoon stand up to be married by Father Leonard, Dave the Dude sizes them up for a minute, and then turns to me and says like this:

"Look," Dave says, "and tell me where does Miss Midgie Muldoon's shoulder come up to on Jack's left side."

"Well," I say, "her shoulder comes just up to Jack's heart."

"So you see," Dave says, "it is just as well for Jack she stops Basil's bullet, at that."

BLOOD PRESSURE

It is maybe eleven-thirty of a Wednesday night, and I am standing at the corner of Forty-eighth Street and Seventh Avenue, thinking about my blood pressure, which is a proposition I never before think much about.

In fact, I never hear of my blood pressure before this Wednesday afternoon when I go around to see Doc Brennan about my stomach, and he puts a gag on my arm and tells me that my blood pressure is higher than a cat's back, and the idea is for me to be careful about what I eat, and to avoid excitement, or I may pop off all of a sudden when I am least expecting it.

"A nervous man such as you with a blood pressure away up in the paint cards must live quietly," Doc Brennan says. "Ten bucks, please," he says.

Well, I am standing there thinking it is not going to be so tough to avoid excitement the way things are around this town right now, and wishing I have my ten bucks back to bet it on Sun Beau in the fourth race at Pimlico the next day, when all of a sudden I look up, and who is in front of me but Rusty Charley.

Now if I have any idea Rusty Charley is coming my way, you can go and bet all the coffee in Java I will be somewhere else at once, for Rusty Charley is not a guy I wish to have any truck with whatever. In fact, I wish no part of him. Furthermore, nobody else in this town wishes to have any part of Rusty Charley, for he is a hard guy indeed. In fact, there is no harder guy anywhere in the world. He is a big wide guy with two large hard hands and a great deal of very bad disposition, and he thinks nothing of knocking people down and stepping on their kissers if he feels like it.

In fact, this Rusty Charley is what is called a gorill, because he is known to often carry a gun in his pants pocket, and sometimes to shoot people down as dead as door-nails with it if he does not like the way they wear their hats—and Rusty Charley is very crit-ical of hats. The chances are Rusty Charley shoots many a guy in this man's town, and those he does not shoot he sticks with his shiv—which is a knife—and the only reason he is not in jail is be-cause he just gets out of it, and the law does not have time to think up something to put him back in again for.

Anyway, the first thing I know about Rusty Charley being in my neighborhood is when I hear him saying: "Well, well, well, here we are!"

Then he grabs me by the collar, so it is no use of me thinking of taking it on the lam away from there, although I greatly wish to do so.

"Hello, Rusty," I say, very pleasant. "What is the score?"

"Everything is about even," Rusty says. "I am glad to see you, because I am looking for company. I am over in Philadelphia for three days on business."

"I hope and trust that you do all right for yourself in Philly, Rusty," I say; but his news makes me very nervous, because I am a great hand for reading the papers and I have a pretty good idea what Rusty's business in Philly is. It is only the day before that I see a little item from Philly in the papers about how Gloomy Gus Smallwood, who is a very large operator in the alcohol business there, is guzzled right at his front door.

Of course, I do not know that Rusty Charley is the party who guzzles Gloomy Gus Smallwood, but Rusty Charley is in Philly when Gus is guzzled, and I can put two and two together as well as anybody. It is the same thing as if there is a bank robbery in Cleveland, Ohio, and Rusty Charley is in Cleveland, Ohio, or near there. So I am very nervous, and I figure it is a sure thing my blood pressure is going up every second.

"How much dough do you have on you?" Rusty says. "I am plumb broke."

"I do not have more than a couple of bobs, Rusty," I say. "I pay a doctor ten bucks to-day to find out my blood pressure is very bad. But of course you are welcome to what I have."

"Well, a couple of bobs is no good to high-class guys like you and me," Rusty says. "Let us go to Nathan Detroit's crap game and win some money."

Now, of course, I do not wish to go to Nathan Detroit's crap game; and if I do wish to go there I do not wish to go with Rusty

Charley, because a guy is sometimes judged by the company he keeps, especially around crap games, and Rusty Charley is apt to be considered bad company. Anyway, I do not have any dough to shoot craps with, and if I do have dough to shoot craps with, I will not shoot craps with it at all, but will bet it on Sun Beau, or maybe take it home and pay off some of the overhead around my joint, such as rent.

Furthermore, I remember what Doc Brennan tells me about avoiding excitement, and I know there is apt to be excitement around Nathan Detroit's crap game if Rusty Charley goes there, and maybe run my blood pressure up and cause me to pop off very unexpected. In fact, I already feel my blood jumping more than somewhat inside me, but naturally I am not going to give Rusty Charley any argument, so we go to Nathan Detroit's crap game.

This crap game is over a garage on Fifty-second Street this particular night, though sometimes it is over a restaurant on Forty-seventh Street, or in back of a cigar store on Forty-fourth Street. In fact, Nathan Detroit's crap game is apt to be anywhere, because it moves around every night, as there is no sense in a crap game staying on one spot until the coppers find out where it is.

So Nathan Detroit moves his crap game from spot to spot, and citizens wishing to do business with him have to ask where he is every night; and of course almost everybody on Broadway knows this, as Nathan Detroit has guys walking up and down, and around and about, telling the public his address, and giving out the password for the evening.

Well, Jack the Beefer is sitting in an automobile outside the garage on Fifty-second Street when Rusty Charley and I come along, and he says "Kansas City," very low, as we pass, this being the password for the evening; but we do not have to use any password whatever when we climb the stairs over the garage, because the minute Solid John, the doorman, peeks out through his peephole when we knock, and sees Rusty Charley with me, he opens up very quick indeed, and gives us a big castor-oil smile, for nobody in this town is keeping doors shut on Rusty Charley very long.

It is a very dirty room over the garage, and full of smoke, and the crap game is on an old pool table; and around the table, and packed in so close you cannot get a knitting-needle between any two guys with a mawl, are all the high shots in town, for there is plenty of money around at this time, and many citizens are very prosperous. Furthermore, I wish to say there are some very tough guys around the table, too, including guys who will shoot you in the head, or maybe the stomach, and think nothing whatever about the matter.

In fact, when I see such guys as Harry the Horse, from Brooklyn, and Sleepout Sam Levinsky, and Lone Louie, from Harlem, I know this is a bad place for my blood pressure, for these are very tough guys indeed, and are known as such to one and all in this town.

But there they are wedged up against the table with Nick the Greek, Big Nig, Gray John, Okay Okun, and many other high shots, and they all have big coarse G notes in their hands which they are tossing back and forth as if these G notes are nothing but pieces of waste paper.

On the outside of the mob at the table are a lot of small operators who are trying to cram their fists in between the high shots now and then to get down a bet, and there are also guys present who are called Shylocks, because they will lend you dough when you go broke at the table, on watches or rings, or maybe cufflinks, at very good interest.

Well, as I say, there is no room at the table for as many as one more very thin guy when we walk into the joint, but Rusty Charley lets out a big hello as we enter, and the guys all look around, and the next minute there is space at the table big enough not only for Rusty Charley but for me, too. It really is quite magical the way there is suddenly room for us when there is no room whatever for anybody when we come in.

"Who is the gunner?" Rusty Charley asks, looking all around.

"Why, you are, Charley," Big Nig, the stick man in the game, says very quick, handing Charley a pair of dice, although afterward I hear that his pal is right in the middle of a roll trying to make nine when we step up to the table. Everybody is very quiet, just looking at Charley. Nobody pays any attention to me, because I am known to one and all as a guy who is just around, and nobody figures me in on any part of Charley, although Harry the Horse looks at me once in a way that I know is no good for my blood pressure, or for anybody else's blood pressure as far as this goes.

Well, Charley takes the dice and turns to a little guy in a derby hat who is standing next to him, scrooching back so Charley will not notice him, and Charley lifts the derby hat off the little guy's head, and rattles the dice in his hand and chucks them into the hat and goes "Hah!" like crap shooters always do when they are rolling the dice. Then Charley peeks into the hat and says "Ten," although he does not let anybody else look in the hat, not even me, so nobody knows if Charley throws a ten, or what.

But, of course, nobody around is going to up and doubt that Rusty Charley throws a ten, because Charley may figure it is the same thing as calling him a liar, and Charley is such a guy as is apt to hate being called a liar.

Now Nathan Detroit's crap game is what is called a head-and-head game, although some guys call it a fading game, because the guys bet against each other rather than against the bank, or house. It is just the same kind of game as when two guys get together and start shooting craps against each other, and Nathan Detroit does not have to bother with a regular crap table and layout such as they have in gambling houses. In fact, about all Nathan Detroit has to do with the game is to find a spot, furnish the dice, and take his percentage, which is by no means bad.

In such a game as this there is no real action until a guy is out on a point, and then the guys around commence to bet he makes this point, or that he does not make this point, and the odds in any country in the world that a guy does not make a ten with a pair of dice before he rolls seven, is two to one.

Well, when Charley says he rolls a ten in the derby hat, nobody opens their trap, and Charley looks all around the table, and all of a sudden he sees Jew Louie at one end, although Jew Louie seems to be trying to shrink himself up when Charley's eyes light on him.

"I will take the odds for five C's," Charley says, "and Louie, you get it"—meaning he is letting Louie bet him $1000 to $500 that he does not make his ten.

Now Jew Louie is a small operator at all times and more of a Shylock than he is a player, and the only reason he is up there against the table at all at this moment is because he moves up to lend Nick the Greek some dough; and ordinarily there is no more chance of Jew Louie betting a thousand to five hundred on any proposition whatever than there is of him giving his dough to the Salvation Army, which is no chance at all. It is a sure thing he will never think of betting a thousand to five hundred a guy will not make ten with the dice, and when Rusty Charley tells Louie he has such a bet, Louie starts trembling all over.

The others around the table do not say a word, and so Charley rattles the dice again in his duke, blows on them, and chucks them into the derby hat and says "Hah!" But, of course, nobody can see in the derby hat except Charley, and he peeks in at the dice and says "Five." He rattles the dice once more and chucks them into the derby and says "Hat!" and then after peeking into the hat at the dice he says "Eight." I am commencing to sweat for fear he may heave a seven in the hat and blow his bet, and I know Charley has no five C's to pay off with, although, of course, I also know Charley has no idea of paying off, no matter what he heaves.

On the next chuck, Charley yells "Money!"—meaning he finally makes his ten, although nobody sees it but him; and he reaches out his hand to Jew Louie, and Jew Louie hands him a big fat G note, very, very slow. In all my life I never see a sadder-looking guy than Louie when he is parting with his dough. If Louie has any idea of asking Charley to let him see the dice in the hat to make sure about the ten, he does not speak about the matter, and as Charley does not seem to wish to show the ten around, nobody else says anything either, probably figuring Rusty Charley isn't a guy who is apt to let anybody question his word, especially over such a small matter as a ten.

"Well," Charley says, putting Louie's G note in his pocket, "I think this is enough for me to-night," and he hands the derby hat back to the little guy who owns it and motions me to come on, which I am glad to do, as the silence in the joint is making my stomach go up and down inside me, and I know this is bad for my blood pressure. Nobody as much as opens his face from the time we go in until we start out, and you will be surprised how nervous it makes you to be in a big crowd with everybody dead still, especially when you figure it a spot that is liable to get hot any minute. It is only just as we get to the door that anybody speaks, and who is it but Jew Louie, who pipes up and says to Rusty Charley like this:

"Charley," he says, "do you make it the hard way?"

Well, everybody laughs, and we go on out, but I never hear myself whether Charley makes his ten with a six and a four, or with two fives—which is the hard way to make a ten with the dice—although I often wonder about the matter afterward.

I am hoping that I can now get away from Rusty Charley and go on home, because I can see he is the last guy in the world to have around a blood pressure, and, furthermore, that people may get the wrong idea of me if I stick around with him, but when I suggest going to Charley, he seems to be hurt.

"Why," Charley says, "you are a fine guy to be talking of quitting a pal just as we are starting out. You will certainly stay with me because I like company, and we will go down to Ikey the Pig's and play stuss. Ikey is an old friend of mine, and I owe him a complimentary play."

Now, of course, I do not wish to go to Ikey the Pig's, because it is a place away downtown, and I do not wish to play stuss, because this is a game which I am never able to figure out myself, and, furthermore, I remember Doc Brennan says I ought to get a little sleep now and then; but I see no use in hurting Charley's feelings, especially as he is apt to do something drastic to me if I do not go.

So he calls a taxi, and we start downtown for Ikey the Pig's, and the jockey who is driving the short goes so fast that it makes my blood pressure go up a foot to a foot and a half from the way I feel inside, although Rusty Charley pays no attention to the speed. Finally I stick my head out of the window and ask the jockey to please take it a little easy, as I wish to get where I am going all in one piece, but the guy only keeps busting along.

We are at the corner of Nineteenth and Broadway when all of a sudden Rusty Charley yells at the jockey to pull up a minute, which the guys does. Then Charley steps out of the cab and says to the jockey like this:

"When a customer asks you to take it easy, why do you not be nice and take it easy? Now see what you get."

And Rusty Charley hauls off and clips the jockey a punch on the chin that knocks the poor guy right off the seat into the street, and then Charley climbs into the seat himself and away we go with Charley driving, leaving the guy stretched out as stiff as a board. Now Rusty Charley once drives a short for a living himself, until the coppers get an idea that he is not always delivering his customers to the right address, especially such as may happen to be drunk when he gets them, and he is a pretty fair driver, but he only looks one way, which is straight ahead.

Personally, I never wish to ride with Charley in a taxicab under any circumstances, especially if he is driving, because he certainly drives very fast. He pulls up a block from Ikey the Pig's, and says we will leave the short there until somebody finds it and turns it in, but just as we are walking away from the short up steps a copper in uniform and claims we cannot park the short in this spot without a driver.

Well, Rusty Charley just naturally hates to have coppers give him any advice, so what does he do but peek up and down the street to see if anybody is looking, and then haul off and clout the copper on the chin, knocking him bow-legged. I wish to say I never see a more accurate puncher than Rusty Charley, because he always connects with that old button. As the copper tumbles, Rusty Charley grabs me by the arm and starts me running up a side street, and after we go about a block we dodge into Ikey the Pig's.

It is what is called a stuss house, and many prominent citizens of the neighborhood are present playing stuss. Nobody seems any too glad to see Rusty Charley, although Ikey the Pig lets on he is tickled half to death. This Ikey the Pig is a short fat-necked guy who will look very natural at New Year's, undressed, and with an apple in his mouth, but it seems he and Rusty Charley are really old-time friends, and think fairly well of each other in spots.

But I can see that Ikey the Pig is not so tickled when he finds Charley is there to gamble, although Charley flashes his G note at once, and says he does not mind losing a little dough to Ikey just for old times' sake. But I judge Ikey the Pig knows he is never going to handle Charley's G note, because Charley puts it back in his pocket and it never comes out again even though Charley gets off loser playing stuss right away.

Well, at five o'clock in the morning, Charley is stuck one hundred and thirty G's, which is plenty of money even when a guy is playing on his muscle, and of course Ikey the Pig knows there is no chance of getting one hundred and thirty cents off of Rusty Charley, let alone that many thousands. Everybody else is gone by this time and Ikey wishes to close up. He is willing to take Charley's marker for a million if necessary to get Charley out, but the trouble is in stuss a guy is entitled to get back a percentage of what he loses, and Ikey figures Charley is sure to wish this percentage even if he gives a marker, and the percentage will wreck Ikey's joint.

Furthermore, Rusty Charley says he will not quit loser under such circumstances because Ikey is his friend, so what happens but Ikey finally sends out and hires a cheater by the name of Dopey Goldberg, who takes to dealing the game and in no time he has Rusty Charley even by cheating in Rusty Charley's favor.

Personally, I do not pay much attention to the play, but grab myself a few winks of sleep in a chair in a corner, and the rest seems to help my blood pressure no little. In fact, I am not noticing my blood pressure at all when Rusty Charley and I get out of Ikey the Pig's, because I figure Charley will let me go home and I can go to bed. But although it is six o'clock, and coming on broad daylight when we leave Ikey's, Charley is still full of zing, and nothing will do him but we must go to a joint that is called the Bohemian Club.

Well, this idea starts my blood pressure going again, because the Bohemian Club is nothing but a deadfall where guys and dolls go when there is positively no other place in town open, and it is run by a guy by the name of Knife O'Halloran, who comes from down around Greenwich Village and is considered a very bad character. It is well known to one and all that a guy is apt to lose his life in Knife O'Halloran's any night, even if he does nothing more than drink Knife O'Halloran's liquor.

But Rusty Charley insists on going there, so naturally I go with him; and at first everything is very quiet and peaceful, except that a lot of guys and dolls in evening clothes, who wind up there after being in night clubs all night, are yelling in one corner of the joint. Rusty Charley and Knife O'Halloran are having a drink together out of a bottle which Knife carries in his pocket, so as not to get it mixed up with the liquor he sells his customers, and are cutting up old touches of the time when they run with the Hudson Dusters together, when all of a sudden in comes four coppers in plain clothes.

Now these coppers are off duty and are meaning no harm to anybody, and are only wishing to have a dram or two before going home, and the chances are they will pay no attention to Rusty Charley if he minds his own business, although of course they know who he is very well indeed and will take great pleasure in putting the old sleeve on him if they only have a few charges against him, which they do not. So they do not give him a tumble. But if there is one thing Rusty Charley hates it is a copper, and he starts eyeing them from the minute they sit down at a table, and by and by I hear him say to Knife O'Halloran like this:

"Knife," Charley says, "what is the most beautiful sight in the world?"

"I do not know, Charley," Knife says. "What is the most beautiful sight in the world?"

"Four dead coppers in a row," Charley says.

Well, at this I personally ease myself over toward the door, because I never wish to have any trouble with coppers and especially with four coppers, so I do not see everything that comes off. All I see is Rusty Charley grabbing at the big foot which one of the coppers kicks at him, and then everybody seems to go into a huddle, and the guys and dolls in evening dress start squawking, and my blood pressure goes up to maybe a million.

I get outside the door, but I do not go away at once as anybody with any sense will do, but stand there listening to what is going on inside, which seems to be nothing more than a loud noise like ker-bump, ker-bump, ker-bump. I am not afraid there will be any shooting, because as far as Rusty Charley is concerned he is too smart to shoot any coppers, which is the worst thing a guy can do in this town, and the coppers are not likely to start any blasting because they will not wish it to come out that they are in a joint such as the Bohemian Club off duty. So I figure they will all just take it out in pulling and hauling.

Finally the noise inside dies down, and by and by the door opens and out comes Rusty Charley, dusting himself off here and there with his hands and looking very much pleased indeed, and through the door before it flies shut again I catch a glimpse of a lot of guys stretched out on the floor. Furthermore, I can still hear guys and dolls hollering.

"Well, well," Rusty Charley says, "I am commencing to think you take the wind on me, and am just about to get mad at you, but here you are. Let us go away from this joint, because they are making so much noise inside you cannot hear yourself think. Let us go to my joint and make my old woman cook us up some breakfast, and then we can catch some sleep. A little ham and eggs will not be bad to take right now."

Well, naturally ham and eggs are appealing to me no little at this time, but I do not care to go to Rusty Charley's joint. As far as I am personally concerned, I have enough of Rusty Charley to do me a long, long time, and I do not care to enter into his home life to any extent whatever, although to tell the truth I am somewhat surprised to learn he has any such life. I believe I do once hear that Rusty Charley marries one of the neighbors' children, and that he lives somewhere over on Tenth Avenue in the Forties, but nobody really knows much about this, and everybody figures if it is true his wife must lead a terrible dog's life.

But while I do not wish to go to Charley's joint, I cannot very well refuse a civil invitation to eat ham and eggs, especially as Charley is looking at me in a very much surprised way because I do not seem so glad, and I can see that it is not everyone that he invites to his joint. So I thank him, and say there is nothing I will enjoy more than ham and eggs such as his old woman will cook for us, and by and by we are walking along Tenth Avenue up around Forty-fifth Street.

It is still fairly early in the morning, and business guys are opening up their joints for the day, and little children are skipping along the sidewalks going to school and laughing tee-hee, and old dolls are shaking bedclothes and one thing and another out of the windows of the tenement houses, but when they spot Rusty Charley and me everybody becomes very quiet indeed, and I can see that Charley is great respected in his own neighborhood. The business guys hurry into their joints, and the little children stop skipping and tee-heeing and go tiptoeing along, and the old dolls yank in their noodles, and a great quiet comes to the street. In fact, about all you can hear is the heels of Rusty Charley and me hitting on the sidewalk.

There is an ice wagon with a couple of horses hitched to it standing in front of a store, and when he sees the horses Rusty Charley seems to get a big idea. He stops and looks the horses over very carefully, although as far as I can see they are nothing but horses, and big and fat, and sleepy-looking horses, at that. Finally Rusty Charley says to me like this:

"When I am a young guy," he says, "I am a very good puncher with my right hand, and I often hit a horse on the skull with my fist and knock it down. I wonder," he says, "if I lose my punch. The last copper I hit back there gets up twice on me."

Then he steps up to one of the ice-wagon horses and hauls off and biffs it right between the eyes with a right-hand smack that does not travel more than four inches, and down goes old Mister Horse to his knees looking very much surprised indeed. I see many a hard puncher in my day including Dempsey when he really can punch, but I never see a harder punch than Rusty Charley gives this horse.

Well, the ice-wagon driver comes busting out of the store all heated up over what happens to his horse, but he cools out the minute he sees Rusty Charley, and goes on back into the store leaving the horse still taking a count, while Rusty Charley and I keep walking. Finally we come to the entrance of a tenement house that Rusty Charley says is where he lives, and in front of this house is a wop with a push-cart loaded with fruit and vegetables and one thing and another, which Rusty Charley tips over as we go into the house, leaving the wop yelling very loud, and maybe cussing us in wop for all I know. I am very glad, personally, we finally get somewhere, because I can feel that my blood pressure is getting worse every minute I am with Rusty Charley.

We climb two flights of stairs, and then Charley opens a door and we step into a room where there is a pretty little red-headed doll about knee high to a flivver, who looks as if she may just get out of the hay, because her red hair is flying around every which way on her head, and her eyes seem still gummed up with sleep. At first I think she is a very cute sight indeed, and then I see something in her eyes that tells me this doll, whoever she is, is feeling very hostile to one and all.

"Hello, tootsie," Rusty Charley says. "How about some ham and eggs for me and my pal here? We are all tired out going around and about."

Well, the little red-headed doll just looks at him without saying a word. She is standing in the middle of the floor with one hand behind her, and all of a sudden she brings this hand around, and what does she have in it but a young baseball bat, such as kids play ball with, and which cost maybe two bits; and the next thing I know I hear something go ker-bap, and I can see she smacks Rusty Charley on the side of the noggin with the bat.

Naturally I am greatly horrified at this business, and figure Rusty Charley will kill her at once, and then I will be in a jam for witnessing the murder and will be held in jail several years like all witnesses to anything in this man's town; but Rusty Charley only falls into a big rocking-chair in a corner of the room and sits there with one hand to his head, saying, "Now hold on, tootsie," and "Wait a minute there, honey." I recollect hearing him say, "We have company for breakfast," and then the little red-headed doll turns on me and gives me a look such as I will always remember, although I smile at her very pleasant and mention it is a nice morning.

Finally she says to me like this:

"So you are the trambo who keeps my husband out all night, are you, you trambo?" she says, and with this she starts for me, and I start for the door; and by this time my blood pressure is all out of whack, because I can see Mrs. Rusty Charley is excited more than somewhat. I get my hand on the knob and just then something hits me alongside the noggin, which I afterwards figure must be the baseball bat, although I remember having a sneaking idea the roof caves in on me.

How I get the door open I do not know, because I am very dizzy in the head and my legs are wobbling, but when I think back over the situation I remember going down a lot of steps very fast, and by and by the fresh air strikes me, and I figure I am in the clear. But all of a sudden I feel another strange sensation back of my head and something goes plop against my noggin, and I figure at first that maybe my blood pressure runs up so high that it squirts out the top of my bean. Then I peek around over my shoulder just once to see that Mrs. Rusty Charley is standing beside the wop peddler's cart snatching fruit and vegetables of one kind and another off the cart and chucking them at me.

But what she hits me with back of the head is not an apple, or a peach, or a rutabaga, or a cabbage, or even a casaba melon, but a brickbat that the wop has on his cart to weight down the paper sacks in which he sells his goods. It is this brickbat which makes a lump on the back of my head so big that Doc Brennan thinks it is a tumor when I go to him the next day about my stomach, and I never tell him any different.

"But," Doc Brennan says, when he takes my blood pressure again, "your pressure is down below normal now, and as far as it is concerned you are in no danger whatever. It only goes to show what just a little bit of quiet living will do for a guy," Doc Brennan says. "Ten bucks, please," he says.

BUTCH MINDS THE BABY

One evening along about seven o'clock I am sitting in Mindy's restaurant putting on the gefilte fish, which is a dish I am very fond of, when in come three parties from Brooklyn wearing caps as follows: Harry the Horse, Little Isadore, and Spanish John.

Now these parties are not such parties as I will care to have much truck with, because I often hear rumors about them that are very discreditable, even if the rumors are not true. In fact, I hear that many citizens of Brooklyn will be very glad indeed to see Harry the Horse, Little Isadore, and Spanish John move away from there, as they are always doing something that is considered a knock to the community, such as robbing people, or maybe shooting or stabbing them, and throwing pineapples, and carrying on generally.

I am really much surprised to see these parties on Broadway, as it is well known that the Broadway coppers just naturally love to shove such parties around, but there they are in Mindy's, and there I am, so of course I give them a very large hello, as I never wish to seem inhospitable, even to Brooklyn parties. Right away they come over to my table and sit down, and Little Isadore reaches out and spears himself a big hunk of my gefilte fish with his fingers, but I overlook this, as I am using the only knife on the table.

Then they all sit there looking at me without saying anything, and the way they look at me makes me very nervous indeed. Finally I figure that maybe they are a little embarrassed being in a high-class spot such as Mindy's, with legitimate people around and about, so I say to them, very polite:

"It is a nice night."

"What is nice about it?" asks Harry the Horse, who is a thin man with a sharp face and sharp eyes.

Well, now that it is put up to me in this way, I can see there is nothing so nice about the night, at that, so I try to think of something else jolly to say, while Little Isadore keeps spearing at my gefilte fish with his fingers, and Spanish John nabs one of my potatoes.

"Where does Big Butch live?" Harry the Horse asks.

"Big Butch?" I say, as if I never hear the name before in my life, because in this man's town, it is never a good idea to answer any question without thinking it over, as some time you may give the right answer to the wrong guy, or the wrong answer to the right guy. "Where does Big Butch live?" I ask them again.

"Yes, where does he live?" Harry the Horse says, very impatient. "We wish you to take us to him."

"Now wait a minute, Harry," I say, and I am now more nervous than somewhat. "I am not sure I remember the exact house Big Butch lives in, and furthermore I am not sure Big Butch will care to have me bringing people to see him, especially three at a time, and especially from Brooklyn. You know Big Butch has a very bad disposition, and there is no telling what he may say to me if he does not like the idea of me taking you to him."

"Everything is very kosher," Harry the Horse says. "You need not be afraid of anything whatever. We have a business proposition for Big Butch. It means a nice score for him, so you take us to him at once, or the chances are I will have to put the arm on somebody around here."

Well, as the only one around there for him to put the arm on at this time seems to be me, I can see where it will be good policy for me to take these parties to Big Butch, especially as the last of my gefilte fish is just going down Little Isadore's gullet, and Spanish John is finishing up my potatoes, and is donking a piece of ryebread in my coffee, so there is nothing more for me to eat.

So I lead them over onto West Forty-ninth Street, near Tenth Avenue, where Big Butch lives on the ground floor of an old brownstone-front house, and who is sitting out on the stoop but Big Butch himself. In fact, everybody in the neighborhood is sitting out on the front stoops over there, including women and children, because sitting out on the front stoops is quite a custom in this section.

Big Butch is peeled down to his undershirt and pants, and he has no shoes on his feet, as Big Butch is a guy who loves his comfort.

Furthermore, he is smoking a cigar, and laid out on the stoop beside him on a blanket is a little baby with not much clothes on. This baby seems to be asleep, and every now and then Big Butch fans it with a folded newspaper to shoo away the mosquitoes that wish to nibble on the baby. These mosquitoes come across the river from the Jersey side on hot nights and they seem to be very fond of babies.

"Hello, Butch," I say, as we stop in front of the stoop.

"Sh-h-h-h!" Butch says, pointing at the baby, and making more noise with his shush than an engine blowing off steam. Then he gets up and tiptoes down to the sidewalk where we are standing, and I am hoping that Butch feels all right, because when Butch does not feel so good he is apt to be very short with one and all. He is a guy of maybe six foot two and a couple of feet wide, and he has big hairy hands and a mean look.

In fact, Big Butch is known all over this man's town as a guy you must not monkey with in any respect, so it takes plenty of weight off me when I see that he seems to know the parties from Brooklyn, and nods at them very friendly, especially at Harry the Horse. And right away Harry states a most surprising proposition to Big Butch.

It seems that there is a big coal company which has an office in an old building down on West Eighteenth Street, and in this office is a safe, and in this safe is the company pay roll of twenty thousand dollars cash money. Harry the Horse knows the money is there because a personal friend of his who is the paymaster for the company puts it there late this very afternoon.

It seems that the paymaster enters into a dicker with Harry the Horse and Little Isadore and Spanish John for them to slug him while he is carrying the pay roll from the bank to the office in the afternoon, but something happens that they miss connections on the exact spot, so the paymaster has to carry the sugar on to the office without being slugged, and there it is now in two fat bundles.

Personally it seems to me as I listen to Harry's story that the paymaster must be a very dishonest character to be making deals to hold still while he is being slugged and the company's sugar taken away from him, but of course it is none of my business, so I take no part in the conversation.

Well, it seems that Harry the Horse and Little Isadore and Spanish John wish to get the money out of the safe, but none of them knows anything about opening safes, and while they are standing around over in Brooklyn talking over what is to be done in this emergency Harry suddenly remembers that Big Butch is once in the business of opening safes for a living.

In fact, I hear afterwards that Big Butch is considered the best safe-opener east of the Mississippi River in his day, but the law finally takes to sending him to Sing Sing for opening these safes, and after he is in and out of Sing Sing three different times for opening safes Butch gets sick and tired of the place, especially as they pass what is called the Baumes Law in New York, which is a law that says if a guy is sent to Sing Sing four times hand running, he must stay there the rest of his life, without any argument about it.

So Big Butch gives up opening safes for a living, and goes into business in a small way, such as running beer, and handling a little Scotch now and then, and becomes an honest citizen. Furthermore, he marries one of the neighbors' children over on the West Side by the name of Mary Murphy, and I judge the baby on this stoop comes of this marriage between Big Butch and Mary because I can see that it is a very homely baby indeed. Still, I never see many babies that I consider rose geraniums for looks, anyway.

Well, it finally comes out that the idea of Harry the Horse and Little Isadore and Spanish John is to get Big Butch to open the coal company's safe and take the pay-roll money out, and they are willing to give him fifty per cent of the money for his bother, taking fifty per cent for themselves for finding the plant, and paying all the overhead, such as the paymaster, out of their bit, which strikes me as a pretty fair sort of deal for Big Butch. But Butch only shakes his head.

"It is old-fashioned stuff," Butch says. "Nobody opens pete boxes for a living anymore. They make the boxes too good, and they are all wired up with alarms and are a lot of trouble generally. I am in a legitimate business now and going along. You boys know I cannot stand another fall, what with being away three times already, and in addition to this I must mind the baby. My old lady goes to Mrs. Clancy's wake to-night up in the Bronx, and the chances are she will be there all night, as she is very fond of wakes, so I must mind little John Ignatius Junior."

"Listen, Butch," Harry the Horse says, "this is a very soft pete. It is old-fashioned, and you can open it with a toothpick. There are no wires on it, because they never put more than a dime in it before in years. It just happens they have to put the twenty G's in it tonight because my pal the paymaster makes it a point not to get back from the jug with the scratch in time to pay off to-day, especially after he sees we miss out on him. It is the softest touch you will ever know, and where can a guy pick up ten G's like this?"

I can see that Big Butch is thinking the ten G's over very seriously, at that, because in these times nobody can afford to pass up ten G's, especially a guy in the beer business, which is very, very tough just now. But finally he shakes his head again and says like this:

"No," he says, "I must let it go, because I must mind the baby. My old lady is very, very particular about this, and I dast not leave little John Ignatius Junior for a minute. If Mary comes home and finds I am not minding the baby she will put the blast on me plenty. I like to turn a few honest bobs now and then as well as anybody, but," Butch says, "John Ignatius Junior comes first with me."

Then he turns away and goes back to the stoop as much as to say he is through arguing, and sits down beside John Ignatius Junior again just in time to keep a mosquito from carrying off one of John's legs. Anybody can see that Big Butch is very fond of this baby, though personally I will not give you a dime for a dozen babies, male and female.

Well, Harry the Horse and Little Isadore and Spanish John are very much disappointed, and stand around talking among themselves, and paying no attention to me, when all of a sudden Spanish John, who never has much to say up to this time, seems to have a bright idea. He talks to Harry and Isadore, and they get all pleasured up over what he has to say, and finally Harry goes to Big Butch.

"Sh-h-h-h!" Big Butch says, pointing to the baby as Harry opens his mouth.

"Listen, Butch," Harry says in a whisper, "we can take the baby with us, and you can mind it and work, too."

"Why," Big Butch whispers back, "this is quite an idea indeed. Let us go into the house and talk things over."

So he picks up the baby and leads us into his joint, and gets out some pretty fair beer, though it is needled a little, at that, and we sit around the kitchen chewing the fat in whispers. There is a crib in the kitchen, and Butch puts the baby in this crib, and it keeps on snoozing away first rate while we are talking. In fact, it is sleeping so sound that I am commencing to figure that Butch must give it some of the needled beer he is feeding us, because I am feeling a little dopey myself.

Finally Butch says that as long as he can take John Ignatius Junior with him, he sees no reason why he shall not go and open the safe for them, only he says he must have five per cent more to put in the baby's bank when he gets back, so as to round himself up with his ever-loving wife in case of a beef from her over keeping the baby out in the night air. Harry the Horse says he considers this extra five per cent a little strong, but Spanish John, who seems to be a very square guy, says that after all it is only fair to cut the baby in if it is to be with them when making the score, and Little Isadore seems to think this is all right, too. So Harry the Horse gives in, and says five per cent it is.

Well, as they do not wish to start out until after midnight, and as there is plenty of time, Big Butch gets out some more needled beer, and then he goes looking for the tools with which he opens safes, and which he says he does not see since the day John Ignatius Junior is born and he gets them out to build the crib.

Now this is a good time for me to bid one and all farewell, and what keeps me there is something I cannot tell you to this day, because personally I never before have any idea of taking part in a safe opening, especially with a baby, as I consider such actions very dishonorable. When I come to think over things afterwards, the only thing I can figure is the needled beer, but I wish to say I am really very much surprised at myself when I find myself in a taxicab along about one o'clock in the morning with these Brooklyn parties and Big Butch and the baby.

Butch has John Ignatius Junior rolled up in a blanket, and John is still pounding his ear. Butch has a satchel of tools, and what looks to me like a big flat book, and just before we leave the house Butch hands me a package and tells me to be very careful with it. He gives Little Isadore a smaller package, which Isadore shoves into his pistol pocket, and when Isadore sits down in the taxi something goes wa-wa, like a sheep, and Big Butch becomes very indignant because it seems Isadore is sitting on John Ignatius Junior's doll, which says "Mamma" when you squeeze it.

It seems Big Butch figures that John Ignatius Junior may wish something to play with in case he wakes up, and it is a good thing for Little Isadore that the mamma doll is not squashed so it cannot say "Mamma" anymore, or the chances are Little Isadore will get a good bust in the snoot.

We let the taxicab go a block away from the spot we are headed for on West Eighteenth Street, between Seventh and Eighth Avenues, and walk the rest of the way two by two. I walk with Big Butch carrying my package, and Butch is lugging the baby and his satchel and the flat thing that looks like a book. It is so quiet down on West Eighteenth Street at such an hour that you can hear yourself think, and in fact I hear myself thinking very plain that I am a big sap to be on a job like this, especially with a baby, but I keep going just the same, which shows you what a very big sap I am, indeed.

There are very few people on West Eighteenth Street when we get there, and one of them is a fat guy who is leaning against a building almost in the center of the block, and who takes a walk for himself as soon as he sees us. It seems that this fat guy is the watchman at the coal company's office and is also a personal friend of Harry the Horse, which is why he takes the walk when he sees us coming.

It is agreed before we leave Big Butch's house that Harry the Horse and Spanish John are to stay outside the place as lookouts, while Big Butch is inside opening the safe, and that Little Isadore is to go with Butch. Nothing whatever is said by anybody about where I am to be at any time, and I can see that, no matter where I am, I will still be an outsider, but, as Butch gives me the package to carry, I figure he wishes me to remain with him.

It is no bother at all getting into the office of the coal company, which is on the ground floor, because it seems the watchman leaves the front door open, this watchman being a most obliging guy indeed. In fact, he is so obliging that by and by he comes back and lets Harry the Horse and Spanish John tie him up good and tight, and stick a handkerchief in his mouth and chuck him in an areaway next to the office, so nobody will think he has anything to do with opening the safe in case anybody comes around asking.

The office looks out on the street, and the safe that Harry the Horse and Little Isadore and Spanish John wish Big Butch to open is standing up against the rear wall of the office facing the street windows. There is one little electric light burning very dim over the safe so that when anybody walks past the place outside, such as a watchman, they can look in through the window and see the safe at all times, unless they are blind. It is not a tall safe, and it is not a big safe, and I can see Big Butch grin when he sees it, so I figure this safe is not much of a safe, just as Harry the Horse claims.

Well, as soon as Big Butch and the baby and Little Isadore and me get into the office, Big Butch steps over to the safe and unfolds what I think is the big flat book, and what is it but a sort of screen painted on one side to look exactly like the front of a safe. Big Butch stands this screen up on the floor in front of the real safe, leaving plenty of space in between, the idea being that the screen will keep anyone passing in the street outside from seeing Butch while he is opening the safe, because when a man is opening a safe he needs all the privacy he can get.

Big Butch lays John Ignatius Junior down on the floor on the blanket behind the phony safe front and takes his tools out of the satchel and starts to work opening the safe, while Little Isadore and me get back in a corner where it is dark, because there is not room for all of us back of the screen. However, we can see what Big Butch is doing, and I wish to say while I never before see a professional safe-opener at work, and never wish to see another, this Butch handles himself like a real artist.

He starts drilling into the safe around the combination lock, working very fast and very quiet, when all of a sudden what happens but John Ignatius Junior sits up on the blanket and lets out a squall. Naturally this is most disquieting to me, and personally I am in favor of beaning John Ignatius Junior with something to make him keep still, because I am nervous enough as it is. But the squalling does not seem to bother Big Butch. He lays down his tools and picks up John Ignatius Junior and starts whispering, "There, there, there, my itty oddleums. Da-dad is here."

Well, this sounds very nonsensical to me in such a situation, and it makes no impression whatever on John Ignatius Junior. He keeps on squalling, and I judge he is squalling pretty loud because I see Harry the Horse and Spanish John both walk past the window and look in very anxious. Big Butch jiggles John Ignatius Junior up and down and keeps whispering baby talk to him, which sounds very undignified coming from a high-class safe-opener, and finally Butch whispers to me to hand him the package I am carrying.

He opens the package, and what is in it but a baby's nursing bottle full of milk. Moreover, there is a little tin stew pan, and

Butch hands the pan to me and whispers to me to find a water tap somewhere in the joint and fill the pan with water. So I go stumbling around in the dark in a room behind the office and bark my shins several times before I find a tap and fill the pan. I take it back to Big Butch, and he squats there with the baby on one arm, and gets a tin of what is called canned heat out of the package, and lights this canned heat with his cigar lighter, and starts heating the pan of water with the nursing bottle in it.

Big Butch keeps sticking his finger in the pan of water while it is heating, and by and by he puts the rubber nipple of the nursing bottle in his mouth and takes a pull at it to see if the milk is warm enough, just like I see dolls who have babies do. Apparently the milk is okay, as Butch hands the bottle to John Ignatius Junior, who grabs hold of it with both hands, and starts sucking on the business end. Naturally he has to stop squalling, and Big Butch goes to work on the safe again, with John Ignatius Junior sitting on the blanket, pulling on the bottle and looking wiser than a treeful of owls.

It seems the safe is either a tougher job than anybody figures, or Big Butch's tools are not so good, what with being old and rusty and used for building baby cribs, because he breaks a couple of drills and works himself up into quite a sweat without getting anywhere. Butch afterwards explains to me that he is one of the first guys in this country to open safes without explosives, but he says to do this work properly you have to know the safes so as to drill to the tumblers of the lock right, and it seems that this particular safe is a new type to him, even if it is old, and he is out of practice.

Well, in the meantime, John Ignatius Junior finishes his bottle and starts mumbling again, and Big Butch gives him a tool to play with, and finally Butch needs this tool and tries to take it away from John Ignatius Junior, and the baby lets out such a squawk that Butch has to let him keep it until he can sneak it away from him, and this causes more delay.

Finally Big Butch gives up trying to drill the safe open, and he whispers to us that he will have to put a little shot in it to loosen up the lock, which is all right with us, because we are getting tired of hanging around and listening to John Ignatius Junior's glug-glugging. As far as I am personally concerned, I am wishing I am home in bed.

Well, Butch starts pawing through his satchel looking for something, and it seems that what he is looking for is a little bottle of some kind of explosive with which to shake the lock on the safe up some, and at first he cannot find this bottle, but finally he discovers that John Ignatius Junior has it and is gnawing at the cork, and Butch has quite a battle making John Ignatius Junior give it up.

Anyway, he fixes the explosive in one of the holes he drills near the combination lock on the safe, and then he puts in a fuse, and just before he touches off the fuse Butch picks up John Ignatius Junior and hands him to Little Isadore, and tells us to go into the room behind the office. John Ignatius Junior does not seem to care for Little Isadore, and I do not blame him, at that, because he starts to squirm around quite some in Isadore's arms and lets out a squall, but all of a sudden he becomes very quiet indeed, and, while I am not able to prove it, something tells me that Little Isadore has his hand over John Ignatius Junior's mouth.

Well, Big Butch joins us right away in the back room, and sound comes out of John Ignatius Junior again as Butch takes him from Little Isadore, and I am thinking that it is a good thing for Isadore that the baby cannot tell Big Butch what Isadore does to him.

"I put in just a little bit of a shot," Big Butch says, "and it will not make any more noise than snapping your fingers."

But a second later there is a big whoom from the office, and the whole joint shakes, and John Ignatius laughs right out loud. The chances are he thinks it is the Fourth of July.

"I guess maybe I put in too big a charge," Big Butch says, and then he rushes into the office with Little Isadore and me after him, and John Ignatius Junior still laughing very heartily for a small baby. The door of the safe is swinging loose, and the whole joint looks somewhat wrecked, but Big Butch loses no time in getting his dukes into the safe and grabbing out two big bundles of cash money, which he sticks inside his shirt.

As we go into the street Harry the Horse and Spanish John come running up much excited, and Harry says to Big Butch like this:

"What are you trying to do," he says, "wake up the whole town?"

"Well," Butch says, "I guess maybe the charge is too strong, at that, but nobody seems to be coming, so you and Spanish John walk over to Eighth Avenue, and the rest of us will walk to Seventh, and if you go along quiet, like people minding their own business, it will be all right."

But I judge Little Isadore is tired of John Ignatius Junior's company by this time, because he says he will go with Harry the Horse and Spanish John, and this leaves Big Butch and John Ignatius Junior and me to go the other way. So we start moving, and all of a sudden two cops come tearing around the corner toward which Harry and Isadore and Spanish John are going. The chances are the cops hear the earthquake Big Butch lets off and are coming to investigate.

But the chances are, too, that if Harry the Horse and the other two keep on walking along very quietly like Butch tells them to, the coppers will pass them up entirely, because it is not likely that coppers will figure anybody to be opening safes with explosives in this neighborhood. But the minute Harry the Horse sees the coppers he loses his nut, and he outs with the old equalizer and starts blasting away, and what does Spanish John do but get his out, too, and open up.

The next thing anybody knows, the two coppers are down on the ground with slugs in them, but other coppers are coming from every which direction, blowing whistles and doing a little blasting themselves, and there is plenty of excitement, especially when the coppers who are not chasing Harry the Horse and Little Isadore and Spanish John start poking around the neighborhood and find Harry's pal, the watchman, all tied up nice and tight where Harry leaves him, and the watchman explains that some scoundrels blow open the safe he is watching.

All this time Big Butch and me are walking in the other direction toward Seventh Avenue and Big Butch has John Ignatius in his arms, and John Ignatius is now squalling very loud indeed. The chances are he is still thinking of the big whoom back there which tickles him so and is wishing to hear some more whooms. Anyway, he is beating his own best record for squalling, and as we go walking along Big Butch says to me like this:

"I dast not run," he says, "because if any coppers see me running they will start popping at me and maybe hit John Ignatius Junior, and besides running will joggle the milk up in him and make him sick. My old lady always warns me never to joggle John Ignatius Junior when he is full of milk."

"Well, Butch," I say, "there is no milk in me, and I do not care if I am joggled up, so if you do not mind, I will start doing a piece of running at the next corner."

But just then around the corner of Seventh Avenue toward which we are headed comes two or three coppers with a big fat sergeant with them, and one of the coppers, who is half-out of breath as if he has been doing plenty of sprinting, is explaining to the sergeant that somebody blows a safe down the street and shoots a couple of coppers in the getaway.

And there is Big Butch, with John Ignatius Junior in his arms and twenty G's in his shirt front and a tough record behind him, walking right up to them.

I am feeling very sorry indeed for Big Butch, and very sorry for myself, too, and I am saying to myself that if I get out of this I will never associate with anyone but ministers of the gospel as long as I live. I can remember thinking that I am getting a better break than Butch, at that, because I will not have to go to Sing Sing for the rest of my life, like him, and I also remember wondering what they will give John Ignatius Junior, who is still tearing off these squalls, with Big Butch saying, "There, there, there, Daddy's itty woogle-ums." Then I hear one of the coppers say to the fat sergeant:

"We better nail these guys. They may be in on this."

Well, I can see it is good-bye to Butch and John Ignatius Junior and me, as the fat sergeant steps up to Big Butch, but instead of putting the arm on Butch, the fat sergeant only points at John Ignatius Junior and asks very sympathetic:

"Teeth?"

"No," Big Butch says. "Not teeth. Colic. I just get the doctor here out of bed to do something for him, and we are going to a drug store to get some medicine."

Well, naturally I am very much surprised at this statement, because of course I am not a doctor, and if John Ignatius Junior has colic it serves him right, but I am only hoping they do not ask for my degree, when the fat sergeant says:

"Too bad. I know what it is. I got three of them at home. But," he says, "it acts more like it is teeth than colic."

Then as Big Butch and John Ignatius Junior and me go on about our business, I hear the fat sergeant say to the copper, very sarcastic:

"Yes, of course a guy is out blowing safes with a baby in his arms! You will make a great detective, you will!"

I do not see Big Butch for several days after I learn that Harry the Horse and Little Isadore and Spanish John get back to Brooklyn all right, except they are a little nicked up here and there from the slugs the coppers toss at them, while the coppers they clip are not damaged so very much. Furthermore, the chances are I will not see Big Butch for several years, if it is left to me, but he comes looking for me one night, and he seems to be all pleasured up about something.

"Say," Big Butch says to me, "you know I never give a copper credit for knowing any too much about anything, but I wish to say that this fat sergeant we run into the other night is a very, very smart duck. He is right about it being teeth that is ailing John Ignatius Junior, for what happens yesterday but John cuts his first tooth."

THE HOTTEST GUY
IN THE WORLD

I wish to say I am very nervous indeed when Big Jule pops into my hotel room one afternoon, because anybody will tell you that Big Jule is the hottest guy in the whole world at the time I am speaking about.

In fact, it is really surprising how hot he is. They wish to see him in Pittsburgh, Pa., about a matter of a mail truck being robbed, and there is gossip about him in Minneapolis, Minn., where somebody takes a fifty-G pay roll off a messenger in cash money, and slugs the messenger around somewhat for not holding still.

Furthermore, the Bankers' Association is willing to pay good dough to talk to Big Jule out in Kansas City, Mo., where a jug is knocked off by a stranger, and in the confusion the paying teller and the cashier, and the second vice-president are clouted about, and the day watchman is hurt, and two coppers are badly bruised, and over fifteen G's is removed from the counters, and never returned.

Then there is something about a department store in Canton, O., and a flour-mill safe in Toledo, and a grocery in Spokane, Wash., and a branch post office in San Francisco, and also something about a shooting match in Chicago, but of course this does not count so much, as only one party is fatally injured. However, you can see that Big Jule is really very hot, what with the coppers all over the country looking for him high and low. In fact, he is practically on fire.

Of course I do not believe Big Jule does all the things the coppers say, because coppers always blame everything no matter where it happens on the most prominent guy they can think of, and Big Jule is quite prominent all over the U.S.A. The chances are he does not do more than half these things, and he probably has a good alibi for the half he does do, at that, but he is certainly hot, and I do not care to have hot guys around me, or even guys who are only just a little bit warm.

But naturally I am not going to say this to Big Jule when he pops in on me, because he may think I am inhospitable, and I do not care to have such a rap going around and about on me, and furthermore, Jule may become indignant if he thinks I am inhospitable, and knock me on my potato, because Big Jule is quick to take offense.

So I say hello to Big Jule, very pleasant, and ask him to have a chair by the window where he can see the citizens walking to and fro down on Eighth Avenue and watch the circus wagons moving into Madison Square Garden by way of the Forty-ninth Street side, for the circus always shows in the Garden in the spring before going out on the road. It is a little warm, and Big Jule takes off his coat, and I can see he has one automatic slung under his arm, and another sticking down in the waistband of his pants, and I hope and trust that no copper steps into the room while Big Jule is there because it is very much against the law for guys to go around rodded up this way in New York City.

"Well, Jule," I say, "this is indeed a very large surprise to me, and I am glad to see you, but I am thinking maybe it is very foolish for you to be popping into New York just now, what with all the heat around here, and the coppers looking to arrest people for very little."

"I know," Jule says. "I know. But they do not have so very much on me around here, no matter what people say, and a guy gets homesick for his old home town, especially a guy who is stuck away where I am for the past few months. I get homesick for the lights and the crowds on Broadway, and for the old neighborhood. Furthermore, I wish to see my maw. I hear she is sick and may not live, and I wish to see her before she goes."

Well, naturally anybody will wish to see their maw under such circumstances, but Big Jule's maw lives over on West Forty-ninth Street near Eleventh Avenue, and who is living in the very same block but Johnny Brannigan, the strong-arm copper, and it is a hundred to one if Big Jule goes nosing around his old neighborhood, Johnny Brannigan will hear of it, and if there is one guy Johnny Brannigan does not care for, it is Big Jule, although they are kids together.

But it seems that even when they are kids they have very little use for each other, and after they grow up and Johnny gets on the strong-arm squad, he never misses a chance to push Big Jule around, and sometimes trying to boff Big Jule with his blackjack, and it is well known to one and all that before Big Jule leaves town the last time, he takes a punch at Johnny Brannigan, and Johnny swears he will never rest until he puts Big Jule where he belongs, although where Big Jule belongs, Johnny does not say.

So I speak of Johnny living in the same block with Big Jule's maw to Big Jule, but it only makes him mad.

"I am not afraid of Johnny Brannigan," he says. "In fact," he says, "I am thinking for some time lately that maybe I will clip Johnny Brannigan good while I am here. I owe Johnny Brannigan a clipping. But I wish to see my maw first, and then I will go around and see Miss Kitty Clancy. I guess maybe she will be much surprised to see me, and no doubt very glad."

Well, I figure it is a sure thing Miss Kitty Clancy will be surprised to see Big Jule, but I am not so sure about her being glad, because very often when a guy is away from a doll for a year or more, no matter how ever-loving she may be, she may get to thinking of someone else, for this is the way dolls are, whether they live on Eleventh Avenue or over on Park. Still, I remember hearing that this Miss Kitty Clancy once thinks very well of Big Jule, although her old man, Jack Clancy, who runs a speakeasy, always claims it is a big knock to the Clancy family to have such a character as Big Jule hanging around.

"I often think of Miss Kitty Clancy the past year or so," Big Jule says, as he sits there by the window, watching the circus wagons, and the crowds. "I especially think of her the past few months. In fact," he says, "thinking of Miss Kitty Clancy is about all I have to do where I am at, which is in an old warehouse on the Bay of Fundy outside of a town that is called St. John's, or some such, up in Canada, and thinking of Miss Kitty Clancy all this time, I find out I love her very much indeed.

"I go to this warehouse," Big Jule says, "after somebody takes a jewelry store in the town, and the coppers start in blaming me. This warehouse is not such a place as I will choose myself if I am doing the choosing, because it is an old fur warehouse, and full of strange smells, but in the excitement around the jewelry store, somebody puts a slug in my hip, and Leon Pierre carries me to the old warehouse, and there I am until I get well.

"It is very lonesome," Big Jule says. "In fact, you will be surprised how lonesome it is, and it is very, very cold, and all I have for company is a lot of rats. Personally, I never care for rats under any circumstances because they carry disease germs, and are apt to bite a guy when he is asleep, if they are hungry, which is what these rats try to do to me.

"The warehouse is away off by itself," Jule says, "and nobody ever comes around there except Leon Pierre to bring me grub and dress my hip, and at night it is very still, and all you can hear is the wind howling around outside, and the rats running here and there. Some of them are very, very large rats. In fact, some of them seem about the size of rabbits, and they are pretty fresh, at that. At first I am willing to make friends with these rats, but they seem very hostile, and after they take a few nips at me, I can see there is no use trying to be nice to them, so I have Leon Pierre bring me a lot of ammunition for my rods every day and I practice shooting at the rats.

"The warehouse is so far off there is no danger of anybody hearing the shooting," Big Jule says, "and it helps me pass the time away. I get so I can hit a rat sitting, or running, or even flying through the air, because these warehouse rats often leap from place to place like mountain sheep, their idea being generally to take a good nab at me as they fly past.

"Well, sir," Jule says, "I keep score on myself one day, and I hit fifty rats hand running without a miss, which I claim makes me the champion rat shooter of the world with a forty-five automatic, although of course," he says, "if anybody wishes to challenge me to a rat shooting match I am willing to take them on for a side bet. I get so I can call my shots on the rats, and in fact several times I say to myself, I will hit this one in the right eye, and this one in the left eye, and it always turns out just as I say, although sometimes when you hit a rat with a forty-five up close it is not always possible to tell afterwards just where you hit him, because you seem to hit him all over.

"By and by," Jule says, "I seem to discourage the rats somewhat, and they get so they play the chill for me, and do not try to nab me even when I am asleep. They find out that no rat dast poke

his whiskers out at me or he will get a very close shave. So I have
to look around for other amusement, but there is not much doing
in such a place, although I finally find a bunch of doctor's books
which turn out to be very interesting reading. It seems these books
are left there by some croaker who retires there to think things
over after experimenting on his ever-loving wife with a knife. In
fact, it seems he cuts his ever-loving wife's head off, and she does
not continue living, so he takes his books and goes to the warehouse and remains there until the law finds him, and hangs him
up very high indeed.

"Well the books are a great comfort to me, and I learn many astonishing things about surgery, but after I read all the books there is
nothing for me to do but think, and what I think about is Miss
Kitty Clancy, and how much pleasure we have together walking
around and about and seeing movie shows, and all this and that,
until her old man gets so tough with me. Yes, I will be very glad to
see Miss Kitty Clancy, and the old neighborhood, and my maw
again."

Well, finally nothing will do Big Jule but he must take a stroll
over into his old neighborhood, and see if he cannot see Miss Kitty
Clancy, and also drop in on his maw, and he asks me to go along
with him. I can think of a million things I will rather do than take
a stroll with Big Jule, but I do not wish him to think I am snob-
bish, because as I say, Big Jule is quick to take offense. Furthermore, I figure that at such an hour of the day he is less likely to
run into Johnny Brannigan or any other coppers who know him
than at any other time, so I say I will go with him, but as we start
out, Big Jule puts on his rods.

"Jule," I say, "do not take any rods with you on a stroll, because somebody may happen to see them, such as a copper, and
you know they will pick you up for carrying a rod in this town
quicker than you can say Jack Robinson, whether they know who
you are or not. You know the Sullivan law is very strong against
guys carrying rods in this town."

But Big Jule says he is afraid he will catch cold if he goes out
without his rods, so we go down onto Forty-ninth Street and start
west toward Madison Square Garden, and just as we reach Eighth
Avenue and are standing there waiting for the traffic to stop, so
we can cross the street, I see there is quite some excitement
around the Garden on the Forty-ninth Street side, with people

running every which way, and yelling no little, and looking up in the air.

So I look up myself, and what do I see sitting up there on the edge of the Garden roof but a big ugly-faced monkey. At first I do not recognize it as a monkey, because it is so big I figure maybe it is just one of the prize-fight managers who stand around on this side of the Garden all afternoon waiting to get a match for their fighters, and while I am somewhat astonished to see a prize-fight manager in such a position, I figure maybe he is doing it on a bet. But when I take a second look I see that it is indeed a big monk, and an exceptionally homely monk at that, although personally I never see any monks I consider so very handsome, anyway.

Well, this big monk is holding something in its arms, and what it is I am not able to make out at first, but then Big Jule and I cross the street to the side opposite the Garden, and now I can see that the monk has a baby in its arms. Naturally I figure it is some kind of advertising dodge put on by the Garden to ballyhoo the circus, or maybe the fight between Sharkey and Risko which is coming off after the circus, but guys are still yelling and running up and down, and dolls are screaming until finally I realize that a most surprising situation prevails.

It seems that the big monk up on the roof is nobody but Bongo, who is a gorilla belonging to the circus, and one of the very few gorillas of any account in this country, or anywhere else, as far as this goes, because good gorillas are very scarce indeed. Well, it seems that while they are shoving Bongo's cage into the Garden, the door becomes unfastened, and the first thing anybody knows, out pops Bongo, and goes bouncing along the street where a lot of the neighbors' children are playing games on the sidewalk, and a lot of mammas are sitting out in the sun alongside baby buggies containing their young. This is a very common sight in side streets such as West Forty-ninth on nice days, and by no means unpleasant, if you like mammas and their young.

Now what does this Bongo do but reach into a baby buggy which a mamma is pushing past on the sidewalk on the Garden side of the street, and snatch out a baby, though what Bongo wants with this baby nobody knows to this day. It is a very young baby, and not such a baby as is fit to give a gorilla the size of Bongo any kind of struggle, so Bongo has no trouble whatever in handling it. Anyway, I always hear a gorilla will make a sucker out of a grown man in a battle, though I wish to say I never see a battle between a gorilla and a grown man. It ought to be a first-class drawing card, at that.

Well, naturally the baby's mamma puts up quite a squawk about Bongo grabbing her baby, because no mamma wishes her baby to keep company with a gorilla, and this mamma starts in screaming very loud, and trying to take the baby away from Bongo, so what does Bongo do but run right up on the roof of the Garden by way of a big electric sign which hangs down on the Forty-ninth Street side. And there old Bongo sits on the edge of the roof with the baby in his arms, and the baby is squalling quite some, and Bongo is making funny noises, and showing his teeth as the folks commence gathering in the street below.

There is a big guy in his shirtsleeves running through the crowd waving his hands, and trying to shush everybody, and saying "Quiet, please" over and over, but nobody pays any attention to him. I figure this guy has something to do with the circus, and maybe with Bongo, too. A traffic copper takes a peek at the situation, and calls for the reserves from the Forty-seventh Street station, and somebody else sends for the fire truck down the street, and pretty soon cops are running from every direction, and the fire engines are coming, and the big guy in his shirtsleeves is more excited than ever.

"Quiet, please," he says. "Everybody keep quiet, because if Bongo becomes disturbed by the noise he will throw the baby down in the street. He throws everything he gets his hands on," the guy says. "He acquires this habit from throwing coconuts back in his old home country. Let us get a life net, and if you all keep quiet we may be able to save the baby before Bongo starts heaving it like a coconut."

Well, Bongo is sitting up there on the edge of the roof about seven stories above the ground peeking down with the baby in his arms, and he is holding this baby just like a mamma would, but anybody can see that Bongo does not care for the row below, and once he lifts the baby high above his head as if to bean somebody with it. I see Big Nig, the crap shooter, in the mob, and afterwards I hear he is around offering to lay seven to five against the baby, but everybody is too excited to bet on such a proposition, although it is not a bad price, at that.

I see one doll in the crowd on the sidewalk on the side of the street opposite the Garden who is standing perfectly still staring up at the monk and the baby with a very strange expression on her face, and the way she is looking makes me take a second gander at her, and who is it but Miss Kitty Clancy. Her lips are moving as she stands there staring up, and something tells me Miss Kitty Clancy is saying prayers to herself, because she is such a doll as will know how to say prayers on an occasion like this.

Big Jule sees her about the same time I do, and Big Jule steps up beside Miss Kitty Clancy, and says hello to her, and though it is over a year since Miss Kitty Clancy sees Big Jule she turns to him and speaks to him as if she is talking to him just a minute before. It is very strange indeed the way Miss Kitty Clancy speaks to Big Jule as if he has never been away at all.

"Do something, Julie," she says. "You are always the one to do something. Oh, please do something, Julie."

Well, Big Jule never answers a word, but steps back in the clear of the crowd and reaches for the waistband of his pants, when I grab him by the arm and say to him like this:

"My goodness, Jule," I say, "what are you going to do?"

"Why," Jule says, "I am going to shoot this thieving monk before he takes a notion to heave the baby on somebody down here. For all I know," Jule says, "he may hit me with it, and I do not care to be hit with anybody's baby."

"Jule," I say, very earnestly, "do not pull a rod in front of all these coppers, because if you do they will nail you sure, if only for having the rod, and if you are nailed you are in a very tough spot indeed what with being wanted here and there. Jule," I say, "you are hotter than a forty-five all over this country, and I do not wish to see you nailed. Anyway," I say, "you may shoot the baby instead of the monk, because anybody can see it will be very difficult to hit the monk up there without hitting the baby. Furthermore, even if you do hit the monk it will fall into the street and bring the baby with it."

"You speak great foolishness," Jule says. "I never miss what I shoot at. I will shoot the monk right between the eyes, and this will make him fall backwards, not forwards, and the baby will not be hurt because anybody can see it is no fall at all from the ledge to the roof behind. I make a study of such propositions,"

Jule says, "and I know if a guy is in such a position as this monk sitting on a ledge looking down from a high spot, his defensive reflexes tend backwards, so this is the way he is bound to fall if anything unexpected comes up on him, such as a bullet between the eyes. I read all about it in the doctor's books," Jule says.

Then all of a sudden up comes his hand, and in his hand is one of his rods, and I hear a sound like ker-bap. When I come to think about it afterwards, I do not remember Big Jule even taking aim like a guy will generally do if he is shooting at something sitting, but old Bongo seems to lift up a little bit off the ledge at the crack of the gun, and then he keels over backwards, the baby still in his arms, and squalling more than somewhat, and Big Jule says to me like this:

"Right between the eyes, and I will bet on it," he says, "although it is not much of a target, at that."

Well, nobody can figure what happens for a minute, and there is much silence except from the guy in his shirtsleeves who is expressing much indignation with Big Jule and saying the circus people will sue him for damages sure if he has hurt Bongo, because the monk is worth $100,000, or some such. I see Miss Kitty Clancy kneeling on the sidewalk with her hands clasped, and looking upwards, and Big Jule is sticking his rod back in his waistband again.

By this time some guys are out on the roof getting through from the inside of the building with the idea of heading Bongo off from that direction, and they let out a yell, and pretty soon I see one of them holding the baby up so everyone in the street can see it. A couple of other guys get down near the edge of the roof and pick up Bongo and show him to the crowd, as dead as a mackerel, and one of the guys puts a finger between Bongo's eyes to show where the bullet hits the monk, and Miss Kitty Clancy walks over to Big Jule and tries to say something to him, but only busts out crying very loud.

Well, I figure this is a good time for Big Jule and me to take a walk, because everybody is interested in what is going on up on the roof, and I do not wish the circus people to get a chance to serve a summons in a damage suit on Big Jule for shooting the valuable monk. Furthermore, a couple of coppers in harness are looking Big Jule over very critically, and I figure they are apt to put the old sleeve on Jule any second.

All of a sudden a slim young guy steps up to Big Jule and says to him like this:

"Jule," he says, "I want to see you," and who is it but Johnny Brannigan. Naturally Big Jule starts reaching for a rod, but Johnny starts him walking down the street so fast Big Jule does not have time to get in action just then.

"No use getting it out, Jule," Johnny Brannigan says. "No use, and no need. Come with me, and hurry."

Well, Big Jule is somewhat puzzled because Johnny Brannigan is not acting like a copper making a collar, so he goes along with Johnny, and I follow after him, and half-way down the block Johnny stops a Yellow short, and hustles us into it and tells the driver to keep shoving down Eighth Avenue.

"I am trailing you ever since you get in town, Jule," Johnny Brannigan says. "You never have a chance around here. I am going over to your maw's house to put the arm on you, figuring you are sure to go there, when the thing over by the Garden comes off. Now I am getting out of this cab at the next corner, and you go on and see your maw, and then screw out of town as quick as you can, because you are red hot around here, Jule.

"By the way," Johnny Brannigan says, "do you know it is my kid you save, Jule? Mine and Kitty Clancy's? We are married a year ago to-day."

Well, Big Jule looks very much surprised for a moment, and then he laughs, and says like this: "Well, I never know it is Kitty Clancy's, but I figure it for yours the minute I see it because it looks like you."

"Yes," Johnny Brannigan says, very proud, "everybody says he does."

"I can see the resemblance even from a distance," Big Jule says. "In fact," he says, "it is remarkable how much you look alike. But," he says, "for a minute, Johnny, I am afraid I will not be able to pick out the right face between the two on the roof, because it is very hard to tell the monk and your baby apart."

THE LILY OF ST. PIERRE

There are four of us sitting in Good Time Charley Bernstein's little joint on Forty-eighth Street one Tuesday morning about four o'clock, doing a bit of quartet singing, very low, so as not to disturb the copper on the beat outside, a very good guy by the name of Carrigan, who likes to get his rest at such an hour.

Good Time Charley's little joint is called the Crystal Room, although of course there is no crystal whatever in the room, but only twelve tables, and twelve hostesses, because Good Time Charley believes in his customers having plenty of social life.

So he has one hostess to a table, and if there are twelve different customers, which is very seldom, each customer has a hostess to talk with. And if there is only one customer, he has all twelve hostesses to gab with and buy drinks for, and no customer can ever go away claiming he is lonesome in Good Time Charley's.

Personally, I will not give you a nickel to talk with Good Time Charley's hostesses, one at a time or all together, because none of them are anything much to look at, and I figure they must all be pretty dumb or they will not be working as hostesses in Good Time Charley's little joint. I happen to speak of this to Good Time Charley, and he admits that I may be right, but he says it is very difficult to get any Peggy Joyces for twenty-five bobs per week.

Of course I never buy any drinks in Good Time Charley's for hostesses, or anybody else, and especially for myself, because I am a personal friend of Good Time Charley's, and he will not sell me any drinks even if I wish to buy any, which is unlikely, as Good Time Charley figures that anybody who buys drinks in his place is apt to drink these drinks, and Charley does not care to see any of his personal friends drinking drinks at his place. If one of his personal friends wishes to buy a drink, Charley always sends him to

Jack Fogarty's little speak down the street, and in fact Charley will generally go with him.

So I only go to Good Time Charley's to talk with him, and to sing in quartet with him. There are very seldom any customers in Good Time Charley's until along about five o'clock in the morning after all the other places are closed, and then it is sometimes a very hot spot indeed, and it is no place to sing in quartet at such hours, because everybody around always wishes to join in, and it ruins the harmony. But just before five o'clock it is okay, as only the hostesses are there, and of course none of them dast to join in our singing, or Good Time Charley will run them plumb out of the joint.

If there is one thing I love to do more than anything else, it is to sing in quartet. I sing baritone, and I wish to say I sing a very fine baritone, at that. And what we are singing—this morning I am talking about—is a lot of songs such as "Little White Lies," and "The Old Oaken Bucket," and "My Dad's Dinner Pail," and "Chloe," and "Melancholy Baby," and I do not know what else, including "Home, Sweet Home," although we do not go so good on this because nobody remembers all the words, and half the time we are all just going ho-hum-hum-ho-hum-hum, like guys nearly always do when they are singing "Home, Sweet Home."

Also we sing "I Can't Give You Anything but Love, Baby," which is a very fine song for quartet singing, especially when you have a guy singing a nice bass, such as Good Time Charley, who can come in on every line with a big bum-bum like this:

> I can't give you anything but luh-luh-vuh,
> Bay-hay-bee!
> BUM-BUM!

I am the one who holds these last words, such as love, and baby, and you can hear my fine baritone very far indeed, especially when I give a little extra roll like bay-hay-ay-ay-BEE! Then when Good Time Charley comes in with his old bum-bum, it is worth going a long way to hear.

Well, naturally, we finally get around to torch songs, as guys who are singing in quartet are bound to do, especially at four o'clock in the morning, a torch song being a song which guys sing when they have the big burnt-up feeling inside themselves over a battle with their dolls.

When a guy has a battle with his doll, such as his sweetheart, or even his ever-loving wife, he certainly feels burnt up inside himself, and can scarcely think of anything much. In fact, I know guys who are carrying the torch to walk ten miles and never know they go an inch. It is surprising how much ground a guy can cover just walking around and about, wondering if his doll is out with some other guy, and everybody knows that at four o'clock in the morning the torch is hotter than at any other time of the day.

Good Time Charley, who is carrying a torch longer than anybody else on Broadway, which is nearly a year, or even since his doll, Big Marge, gives him the wind for a rich Cuban, starts up a torch song by Tommy Lyman, which goes as follows, very, very slow, and sad:

> Gee, but it's tough
> When the gang's gone home.
> Out on the corner
> You stand alone.

Of course there is no spot in this song for Good Time Charley's bum-bum, but it gives me a great chance with my fine baritone, especially when I come to the line that says Gee, I wish I had my old gal back again.

I do not say I can make people bust out crying and give me money with this song like I see Tommy Lyman do in night clubs, but then Tommy is a professional singer, besides writing this song for himself, so naturally he figures to do a little better with it than me. But I wish to say it is nothing for me to make five or six of the hostesses in Good Time Charley's cry all over the joint when I hit this line about Gee, I wish I had my old gal back again, and making five or six hostesses out of twelve cry is a fair average anywhere, and especially Good Time Charley's hostesses.

Well, all of a sudden who comes popping into Good Time Charley's by way of the front door, looking here and there, and around and about, but Jack O'Hearts, and he no sooner pokes his snozzle into the joint than a guy by the name of Louie the Lug, who is singing a very fair tenor with us, jumps up and heads for the back door.

But just at he gets to the door, Jack O'Hearts outs with the old equalizer and goes whangity-whang-whang at Louie the Lug. As a general proposition, Jack O'Hearts is a fair kind of a shot, but all he does to Louie the Lug is to knock his right ear off. Then Louie gets the back door open and takes it on the lam through an area-way, but not before Jack O'Hearts gets one more crack at him, and it is this last crack which brings Louie down half an hour later on Broadway, where a copper finds him and sends him to the Polyclinic.

Personally, I do not see Louie's ear knocked off, because by the second shot I am out the front door, and on my way down Forty-eighth Street, but they tell me about it afterwards.

I never know Jack O'Hearts is even mad at Louie, and I am wondering why he takes these shots at him, but I do not ask any questions, because when a guy goes around asking questions in this town people may get the idea he is such a guy as wishes to find things out.

Then the next night I run into Jack O'Hearts in Bobby's Chop House, putting on the hot meat, and he asks me to sit down and eat with him, so I sit down and order a hamburger steak, with plenty of onions, and while I am sitting there waiting for my hamburger, Jack O'Hearts says to me like this:

"I suppose," he says, "I owe you guys an apology for busting up your quartet when I toss those slugs at Louie the Lug?"

"Well," I say, "some considers it a dirty trick at that, Jack, but I figure you have a good reason, although I am wondering what it is."

"Louie the Lug is no good," Jack says.

Well, of course I know this much already, and so does everybody else in town for that matter, but I cannot figure what it has to do with Jack shooting off ears in this town for such a reason, or by and by there will be very few people left with ears.

"Let me tell you about Louie the Lug," Jack O'Hearts says. "You will see at once that my only mistake is I do not get my shots an inch to the left. I do not know what is the matter with me lately."

"Maybe you are letting go too quick," I say, very sympathetic, because I know how it annoys him to blow easy shots.

"Maybe," he says. "Anyway, the light in Charley's dump is no good. It is only an accident I get Louie with the last shot, and it is very sloppy work all around. But now I tell you about Louie the Lug."

It is back in 1924 (Jack O'Hearts says) that I go to St. Pierre for the first time to look after some business matters for John the Boss, rest his soul, who is at this time one of the largest operators in high-grade merchandise in the United States, especially when it comes to Scotch. Maybe you remember John the Boss, and the heat which develops around and about when he is scragged in Detroit? John the Boss is a very fine character, and it is a terrible blow to many citizens when he is scragged.

Now if you are never in St. Pierre, I wish to say you miss nothing much, because what is it but a little squirt of a burg sort of huddled up alongside some big rocks off Newfoundland, and very hard to get to, any way you go. Mostly you go there from Halifax by boat; though personally I go there in 1924 in John the Boss's schooner by the name of the *Maude*, in which we load a thousand cases of very nice merchandise for the Christmas trade.

The first time I see St. Pierre I will not give you eight cents for the whole lay-out, although of course it is very useful to parties in our line of business. It does not look like much, and it belongs to France, and nearly all the citizens speak French, because most of them are French, and it seems it is the custom of the French people to speak French no matter where they are, even away off up yonder among the fish.

Well, anyway, it is on this trip to St. Pierre in 1924 that I meet an old guy by the name of Doctor Armand Dorval, for what happens to me but I catch pneumonia, and it looks as if maybe I am a gone gosling, especially as there is no place in St. Pierre where a guy can have pneumonia with any comfort. But this Doctor Armand Dorval is a friend of John the Boss, and he takes me into his house and lets me be as sick there as I please, while he does his best to doctor me up.

Now this Doctor Armand Dorval is an old Frenchman with whiskers, and he has a little granddaughter by the name of Lily, who is maybe twelve years old at the time I am talking about, with her hair hanging down her back in two braids. It seems her papa, who is Doctor Armand's son, goes out one day looking for cod on the Grand Banks when Lily is nothing but a baby, and never comes back, and then her mamma dies, so old Doc raises up Lily and is very fond of her indeed.

They live alone in the house where I am sick with this pneumonia, and it is a nice, quiet little house and very old fashioned, with a good view of the fishing boats, if you care for fishing boats. In fact, it is the quietest place I am ever in in my life, and the only place I ever know any real peace. A big fat old doll who does not talk English comes in every day to look after things for Doctor Armand and Lily, because it seems Lily is not old enough to keep house as yet, although she makes quite a nurse for me.

Lily talks English very good, and she is always bringing me things, and sitting by my bed and chewing the rag with me about this and that, and sometimes she reads to me out of a book which is called *Alice in Wonderland,* and which is nothing but a pack of lies, but very interesting in spots. Furthermore, Lily has a big, blonde, dumb-looking doll by the name of Yvonne, which she makes me hold while she is reading to me, and I am very glad indeed that the *Maude* goes on back to the United States and there is no danger of any of the guys walking in on me while I am holding this doll, or they will think I blow my topper.

Finally, when I am able to sit up around the house of an evening, I play checkers with Lily, while old Doctor Armand Dorval sits back in a rocking-chair, smoking a pipe and watching us, and sometimes I sing for her. I wish to say I sing a first-class tenor, and when I am in the war business in France with the Seventy-seventh Division I am always in great demand for singing a quartet. So I sing such songs to Lily as "There's a Long, Long Trail," and "Mademoiselle from Armentières," although of course when it comes to certain spots in this song I just go dum-dum-dee-dum and do not say the words right out.

By and by Lily gets to singing with me, and we sound very good together, especially when we sing the "Long, Long Trail," which Lily likes very much, and even old Doctor Armand joins in now and then, although his voice is very terrible. Anyway, Lily and me and Doctor Armand become very good pals indeed, and what is more I meet up with other citizens of St. Pierre and become friends with them, and they are by no means bad people to know, and it is certainly nice to be able to walk up and down without being afraid every other guy you meet is going to chuck a slug at you, or a copper put the old sleeve on you and say that they wish to see you at headquarters.

Finally I get rid of this pneumonia and take the boat to Halifax, and I am greatly surprised to find that Doctor Armand and Lily are very sorry to see me go, because never before in my life do I leave a place where anybody is sorry to see me go.

But Doctor Armand seems very sad and shakes me by the hand over and over again, and what does Lily do but bust out crying, and the first thing I know I am feeling sad myself and wishing that I am not going. So I promise Doctor Armand I will come back someday to see him, and then Lily hauls off and gives me a big kiss right in the smush, and this astonishes me so much that it is half an hour afterwards before I think to wipe it off.

Well, for the next few months I find myself pretty busy back in New York, what with one thing and another, and I do not have time to think much of Doctor Armand Dorval and Lily, and St. Pierre, but it comes along the summer of 1925, and I am all tired out from getting a slug in my chest in the run-in with Jerk Donovan's mob in Jersey, for I am now in beer and have no more truck with the boats.

But I get to thinking of St. Pierre and the quiet little house of Doctor Armand Dorval again, and how peaceful it is up there, and nothing will do but I must pop off to Halifax, and pretty soon I am in St. Pierre once more. I take a raft of things for Lily with me, such as dolls, and handkerchiefs, and perfume, and a phonograph, and also a set of razors for Doctor Armand, although afterwards I am sorry I take these razors because I remember the old Doc does not shave and may take them as a hint I do not care for his whiskers. But as it turns out the Doc finds them very useful in operations, so the razors are a nice gift after all.

Well, I spend two peaceful weeks there again, walking up and down in the daytime and playing checkers and singing with Lily in the evening, and it is tough tearing myself away, especially as Doctor Armand Dorval looks very sad again and Lily busts out crying, louder than before. So nearly every year after this I can hardly wait until I can get to St. Pierre for a vacation, and Doctor Armand Dorval's house is like my home, only more peaceful.

Now in the summer of 1928 I am in Halifax on my way to St. Pierre, when I run across Louie the Lug, and it seems Louie is a lammister out of Detroit on account of some job or other, and is broke, and does not know which way to turn. Personally, I always figure Louie a petty-larceny kind of guy, with no more moxie than a canary bird, but he always dresses well, and always has a fair line of guff, and some guys stand for him. Anyway, here he is in trouble, so what happens but I take him with me to St. Pierre, figuring he can lay dead there until things blow over.

Well, Lily and old Doctor Armand Dorval are certainly glad to see me, and I am just as glad to see them, especially Lily, for she is now maybe sixteen years old and as pretty a doll as ever steps in shoe leather, what with her long black hair, and her big black eyes, and a million dollars' worth of personality. Furthermore, by this time she swings a very mean skillet indeed and gets me up some very tasty fodder out of fish and one thing and another.

But somehow things are not like they used to be at St. Pierre with this guy Louie the Lug around, because he does not care for the place whatever, and goes roaming about very restless, and making cracks about the citizens, and especially the dolls, until one night I am compelled to tell him to keep his trap closed, although, at that, the dolls in St. Pierre, outside of Lily are no such lookers as will get Ziegfeld heated up.

But even in the time when St. Pierre is headquarters for many citizens of the United States who are in the business of handling merchandise out of there, it is always sort of underhand that such citizens will never have any truck with the dolls at St. Pierre. This is partly because the dolls at St. Pierre never give the citizens of the United States a tumble, but more because we do not wish to get in any trouble around there, and if there is anything apt to cause trouble it is dolls.

Now I suppose if I have any brains I will see that Louie is playing the warm for Lily, but I never think of Lily as anything but a little doll with her hair in braids, and certainly not a doll such as a guy will start pitching to, especially a guy who calls himself one of the mob.

I notice Louie is always talking to Lily when he gets a chance, and sometimes he goes walking up and down with her, but I see nothing in this, because after all any guy is apt to get lonesome at St. Pierre and go walking up and down with anybody, even a little young doll. In fact, I never see Louie do anything that strikes me as out of line, except he tries to cut in on the singing between Lily and me, until I tell him one tenor at a time is enough in any singing combination. Personally, I consider Louie the Lug's tenor very flat indeed.

Well, it comes time for me to go away, and I take Louie with me, because I do not wish him hanging around St. Pierre alone, especially as old Doctor Armand Dorval does not seem to care for him whatever, and while Lily seems as sad as ever to see me go I notice that for the first time she does not kiss me good-bye. But I figure this is fair enough, as she is now quite a young lady, and the chances are a little particular about who she kisses.

I leave Louie in Halifax and give him enough dough to go on to Denver, which is where he says he wishes to go, and I never see him again until the other night in Good Time Charley's. But almost a year later, when I happen to be in Montreal, I hear of him. I am standing in the lobby of the Mount Royal Hotel thinking of not much, when a guy by the name of Bob the Bookie, who is a hustler around the race tracks, gets to talking to me and mentions Louie's name. It brings back to me a memory of my last trip to St. Pierre, and I get to thinking that this is the longest stretch I ever go in several years without a visit there and of the different things that keep me from going.

I am not paying much attention to what Bob says, because he is putting the blast on Louie for running away from an ever-loving wife and a couple of kids in Cleveland several years before, which is something I do not know about Louie, at that. Then I hear Bob saying like this:

"He is an awful rat any way you take him. Why, when he hops out of here two weeks ago, he leaves a little doll he brings with him from St. Pierre dying in a hospital without a nickel to her name. It is a sin and a shame."

"Wait a minute, Bob," I say, waking up all of a sudden. "Do you say a doll from St. Pierre? What-for looking kind of a doll, Bob?" I say.

"Why," Bob says, "she is black-haired, and very young, and he calls her Lily, or some such. He is knocking around Canada with her for quite a spell. She strikes me as a t.b., but Louie's dolls always look this way after he has them a while. I judge," Bob says, "that Louie does not feed them any too good."

Well, it is Lily Dorval, all right, but never do I see such a change in anybody as there is in the poor little doll I find lying on a bed in a charity ward in a Montreal hospital. She does not look to weigh more than fifty pounds, and her black eyes are sunk away back in her head, and she is in tough shape generally. But she knows me right off the bat and tries to smile at me.

I am in the money very good at this time, and I have Lily moved into a private room, and get her all the nurses the law allows, and the best croakers in Montreal, and flowers, and one thing and another, but one of the medicos tells me it is even money she will not last three weeks, and seven to five she does not go a month. Finally Lily tells me what happens, which is the same thing that happens to a million dolls before and will happen to a million dolls again. Louie never leaves Halifax, but cons her into coming over there to him, and she goes because she loves him, for this is the way dolls are, and personally I will never have them any other way.

"But," Lily whispers to me, "the bad, bad thing I do is to tell poor old Grandfather I am going to meet you, Jack O'Hearts, and marry you, because I know he does not like Louie and will never allow me to go to him. But he loves you, Jack O'Hearts, and he is so pleased in thinking you are to be his son. It is wrong to tell Grandfather this story, and wrong to use your name, and to keep writing him all this time making him think I am your wife, and with you, but I love Louie, and I wish Grandfather to be happy because he is very, very old. Do you understand, Jack O'Hearts?"

Now of course all this is very surprising news to me indeed, and in fact I am quite flabbergasted, and as for understanding it, all I understand is she gets a rotten deal from Louie the Lug and that old Doctor Armand Dorval is going to be all busted up if he hears what really happens. And thinking about this nice old man, and thinking of how the only place I ever know peace and quiet is now ruined, I am very angry with Louie the Lug.

But this is something to be taken up later, so I dismiss him from my mind, and go out and get me a marriage license and a priest, and have this priest marry me to Lily Dorval just two days before she looks up at me for the last time, and smiles a little smile, and then closes her eyes for good and all. I wish to say, however, that up to this time I have no more idea of getting myself a wife than I have of jumping out the window, which is practically no idea at all.

I take her body back to St. Pierre myself in person, and we bury her in a little cemetery there, with a big fog around and about, and the siren moaning away very sad, and old Doctor Armand Dorval whispers to me like this:

"You will please sing the song about the long trail, Jack O'Hearts."

So I stand there in the fog, the chances are looking like a big sap, and I sing as follows:

> There's a long, long trail a-winding
> Into the land of my dreams,
> Where the nightingale is singing,
> And the white moon beams.

But I can get no farther than this, for something comes up in my throat, and I sit down by the grave of Mrs. Jack O'Hearts, who was Lily Dorval, and for the first time I remember I bust out crying.

So (he says) this is why I say Louie the Lug is no good.

Well, I am sitting there thinking that Jack O'Hearts is right about Louie, at that, when in comes Jack's chauffeur, a guy by the name of Fingers, and he steps up to Jack and says, very low:

"Louie dies half an hour ago at the Polyclinic."

"What does he say before he goes?" Jack asks.

"Not a peep," Fingers says.

"Well," Jack O'Hearts says, "it is sloppy work, at that. I ought to get him the first crack. But maybe he had a chance to think a little of Lily Dorval."

Then he turns to me and says like this:

"You guys need not feel bad about losing your tenor, because," he says, "I will be glad to fill in for him at all times."

Personally I do not think Jack's tenor is as good as Louie the Lug's especially when it comes to hitting the very high notes in such songs as "Sweet Adeline," because he does not hold them long enough to let Good Time Charley in with his bum-bum.

But of course this does not go if Jack O'Hearts hears it, as I am never sure he does not clip Louie the Lug just to get a place in our quartet, at that.

THE BLOODHOUNDS
OF BROADWAY

One morning along about four bells, I am standing in front of Mindy's restaurant on Broadway with a guy by the name of Regret, who has this name because it seems he wins a very large bet the year the Whitney filly, Regret, grabs the Kentucky Derby, and can never forget it, which is maybe because it is the only very large bet he ever wins in his life.

What this guy's real name is I never hear, and anyway names make no difference to me, especially on Broadway, because the chances are that no matter what name a guy has, it is not his square name. So, as far as I am concerned, Regret is as good a name as any other for this guy I am talking about, who is a fat guy, and very gabby, though generally he is talking about nothing but horses, and how he gets beat three dirty noses the day before at Belmont, or wherever the horses are running.

In all the years I know Regret he must get beat ten thousand noses, and always they are dirty noses, to hear him tell it. In fact, I never once hear him say he is beat a clean nose, but of course this is only the way horse-racing guys talk. What Regret does for a living besides betting on horses I do not know, but he seems to do pretty well at it, because he is always around and about, and generally well dressed, and with a lot of big cigars sticking up out of his vest pocket.

It is generally pretty quiet on Broadway along about four bells in the morning, because at such an hour the citizens are mostly in speakeasies, and night clubs, and on this morning I am talking about it is very quiet indeed except for a guy by the name of Marvin Clay hollering at a young doll because she will not get into a taxicab with him to go to his apartment. But of course Regret and I do not pay much attention to such a scene, except that Regret remarks that the young doll seems to have more sense than you will expect to see in a doll loose on Broadway at four bells in the morning, because it is well known to one and all that any doll who goes to Marvin Clay's apartment, either has no brains whatever, or wishes to go there.

This Marvin Clay is a very prominent society guy, who is a great hand for hanging out in night clubs, and he has plenty of scratch which comes down to him from his old man, who makes it out of railroads and one thing and another. But Marvin Clay is a most obnoxious character, being loud and ungentlemanly at all times, on account of having all this scratch, and being always very rough and abusive with young dolls such as work in nightclubs, and who have to stand for such treatment from Marvin Clay because he is a very good customer.

He is generally in evening clothes, as he is seldom around and about except in the evening, and he is maybe fifty years old, and has a very ugly mug, which is covered with blotches, and pimples, but of course a guy who has so much scratch as Marvin Clay does not have to be so very handsome, at that, and he is very welcome indeed wherever he goes on Broadway. Personally, I wish no part of such a guy as Marvin Clay, although I suppose in my time on Broadway I must see a thousand guys like him, and there will always be guys like Marvin Clay on Broadway as long as they have old men to make plenty of scratch out of railroads to keep them going.

Well, by and by Marvin Clay gets the doll in the taxicab, and away they go, and it is all quiet again on Broadway, and Regret and I stand there speaking of this and that, and one thing and another, when along comes a very strange-looking guy leading two very strange-looking dogs. The guy is so thin I figure he must be about two pounds lighter than a stack of wheats. He has a long nose, and a sad face, and he is wearing a floppy old black felt hat, and he has on a flannel shirt, and baggy corduroy pants, and a see-more coat, which is a coat that lets you see more hip pockets than coat.

Personally, I never see a stranger-looking guy on Broadway, and I wish to say I see some very strange-looking guys on Broadway in my day. But if the guy is strange-looking, the dogs are even stranger-looking because they have big heads, and jowls that hang down like an old-time faro bank dealer's, and long ears the size of bed sheets. Furthermore, they have wrinkled faces, and big, round eyes that seem so sad I half expect to see them bust out crying.

The dogs are a sort of black and yellow in color, and have long tails, and they are so thin you can see their ribs sticking out of their hides. I can see at once that the dogs and the guy leading them can use a few hamburgers very nicely, but then so can a lot of other guys on Broadway at this time, leaving out the dogs.

Well, Regret is much interested in the dogs right away, because he is a guy who is very fond of animals of all kinds, and nothing will do but he must stop the guy and start asking questions about what sort of dogs they are, and in fact I am also anxious to hear myself, because while I see many a pooch in my time I never see anything like these.

"They is bloodhounds," the sad-looking guy says in a very sad voice, and with one of these accents such as Southern guys always have. "They is man-tracking bloodhounds from Georgia."

Now of course both Regret and me know what bloodhounds are because we see such animals chasing Eliza across the ice in *Uncle Tom's Cabin* when we are young squirts, but this is the first time either of us meet up with any bloodhounds personally, especially on Broadway. So we get to talking quite a bit to the guy, and his story is as sad as his face, and makes us both feel very sorry for him.

In fact, the first thing we know we have him and the bloodhounds in Mindy's and are feeding one and all big steaks, although Mindy puts up an awful squawk about us bringing the dogs in, and asks us what we think he is running, anyway. When Regret starts to tell him, Mindy says never mind, but not to bring any more Shetland ponies into his joint again as long as we live.

Well, it seems that the sad-looking guy's name is John Wangle, and he comes from a town down in Georgia where his uncle is the high sheriff, and one of the bloodhounds' name is Nip, and the other Tuck, and they are both trained from infancy to track down guys such as lags who escape from the county pokey, and bad niggers, and one thing and another, and after John Wangle gets the kinks out of his belly on Mindy's steaks, and starts talking good, you must either figure him a high-class liar, or the hounds the greatest man-trackers the world ever sees.

Now, looking at the dogs after they swallow six big sirloins apiece, and a lot of matzohs, which Mindy has left over from the Jewish holidays, and a job lot of goulash from the dinner bill, and some other odds and ends, the best I can figure them is hearty eaters, because they are now lying down on the floor with their faces hidden behind their ears, and are snoring so loud you can scarcely hear yourself think.

How John Wangle comes to be in New York with these bloodhounds is quite a story indeed. It seems that a New York guy drifts into John's old home town in Georgia when the bloodhounds are tracking down a bad nigger, and this guy figures it will be a wonderful idea to take John Wangle and the dogs to New York and hire them out to the movies to track down the villains in the pictures. But when they get to New York, it seems the movies have other arrangements for tracking down their villains, and the guy runs out of scratch and blows away, leaving John Wangle and the bloodhounds stranded.

So here John Wangle is with Nip and Tuck in New York, and they are all living together in one room in a tenement house over on West Forty-ninth Street, and things are pretty tough with them, because John does not know how to get back to Georgia unless he walks, and he hears the walking is no good south of Roanoke. When I ask him why he does not write to his uncle, the high sheriff down there in Georgia, John Wangle says, there are two reasons, one being that he cannot write, and the other that his uncle cannot read.

Then I ask him why he does not sell the bloodhounds, and he says it is because the market for bloodhounds is very quiet in New York, and furthermore if he goes back to Georgia without the bloodhounds his uncle is apt to knock his ears down. Anyway, John Wangle says he personally loves Nip and Tuck very dearly, and in fact he says it is only his great love for them that keeps him from eating one or the other and maybe both, the past week, when his hunger is very great indeed.

Well, I never before see Regret so much interested in any situation as he is in John Wangle and the bloodhounds, but personally I am getting very tired of them, because the one that is called Nip finally wakes up and starts chewing on my leg, thinking it is maybe more steak, and when I kick him in the snoot, John Wangle scowls at me, and Regret says only very mean guys are unkind to dumb animals.

But to show you that John Wangle and his bloodhounds are not so dumb, they come moseying along past Mindy's every morning after this at about the same time, and Regret is always there ready to feed them, although he now has to take the grub out on the sidewalk, as Mindy will not allow the hounds in the joint again. Naturally Nip and Tuck become very fond of Regret, but they are by no means as fond of him as John Wangle, because John is commencing to fat up very nicely, and the bloodhounds are also taking on weight.

Now what happens but Regret does not show up in front of Mindy's for several mornings hand running, because it seems that Regret makes a very nice score for himself one day against the horses, and buys himself a brand-new tuxedo, and starts stepping out around the night clubs, and especially around Miss Missouri Martin's Three Hundred Club, where there are many beautiful young dolls who dance around with no more clothes on them than will make a pad for a crutch, and it is well known that Regret dearly loves such scenes.

Furthermore, I hear reports around and about of Regret becoming very fond of a doll by the name of Miss Lovey Lou, who works in Miss Missouri Martin's Three Hundred Club, and of him getting in some kind of a jam with Marvin Clay over this doll, and smacking Marvin Clay in the kisser, so I figure Regret is getting a little simple, as guys who hang around Broadway long enough are bound to do. Now, when John Wangle and Nip and Tuck come around looking for a hand-out, there is nothing much doing for them, as nobody else around Mindy's feels any great interest in bloodhounds, especially such interest as will cause them to buy steaks, and soon Nip and Tuck are commencing to look very sad again, and John Wangle is downcast more than somewhat.

It is early morning again, and warm, and a number of citizens are out in front of Mindy's as usual, breathing the fresh air, when along comes a police inspector by the name of McNamara, who is a friend of mine, with a bunch of plain-clothes coppers with him, and Inspector McNamara tells me he is on his way to investigate a situation in an apartment house over on West Fifty-fourth Street, about three blocks away, where it seems a guy is shot; and not having anything else to do, I go with them, although as a rule I do not care to associate with coppers, because it arouses criticism from other citizens.

Well, who is the guy who is shot but Marvin Clay, and he is stretched out on the floor of the living-room of his apartment in evening clothes, with his shirt front covered with blood, and after

Inspector McNamara takes a close peek at him, he sees that Marvin Clay is plugged smack dab in the chest, and that he seems to be fairly dead. Furthermore, there seems to be no clue whatever to who does the shooting, and Inspector McNamara says it is undoubtedly a very great mystery, and will be duck soup for the newspapers, especially as they do not have a good shooting mystery for several days.

Well, of course all this is none of my business, but all of a sudden I happen to think of John Wangle and his bloodhounds, and it seems to me it will be a great opportunity for them, so I say to the Inspector as follows:

"Listen, Mac," I say, "there is a guy here with a pair of man-tracking bloodhounds from Georgia, who are very expert in tracking down matters such as this, and," I say, "maybe they can track down the rascal who shoots Marvin Clay, because the trail must be hotter than mustard right now."

Well, afterwards I hear there is much indignation over my suggestion, because many citizens feel that the party who shoots Marvin Clay is entitled to more consideration than being tracked with bloodhounds. In fact, some think the party is entitled to a medal, but this discussion does not come up until later.

Anyway, at first the Inspector does not think much of my idea, and the other coppers are very skeptical, and claim that the best way to do under the circumstances is to arrest everybody in sight and hold them as material witnesses for a month or so, but the trouble is there is nobody in sight to arrest at this time, except maybe me, and the Inspector is a broad-minded guy, and finally he says all right, bring on the bloodhounds.

So I hasten back to Mindy's, and sure enough John Wangle and Nip and Tuck are out on the sidewalk peering at every passing face in the hope that maybe one of these faces will belong to Regret. It is a very pathetic sight indeed but John Wangle cheers up when I explain about Marvin Clay to him, and hurries back to the apartment house with me so fast that he stretches Nip's neck a foot, and is pulling Tuck along on his stomach half the time.

Well, when we get back to the apartment, John Wangle leads Nip and Tuck up to Marvin Clay, and they snuffle him all over, because it seems bloodhounds are quite accustomed to dead guys. Then John Wangle unhooks their leashes, and yells something at them, and the hounds begin snuffing all around and about the joint, with Inspector McNamara and the other coppers watching with great interest. All of a sudden Nip and Tuck go busting out of the apartment and into the street, with John Wangle after them, and all the rest of us after John Wangle. They head across Fifty-fourth Street back to Broadway, and the next thing anybody knows they are doing plenty of snuffling around in front of Mindy's.

By and by they take off up Broadway with their snozzles to the sidewalk, and we follow them very excited, because even the coppers now admit that it seems to be a sure thing they are red hot on the trail of the party who shoots Marvin Clay. At first Nip and Tuck are walking, but pretty soon they break into a lope, and there we are loping after them, John Wangle, the Inspector, and me, and the coppers.

Naturally, such a sight as this attracts quite some attention as we go along from any citizens stirring at this hour, and by and by milkmen are climbing down off their wagons, and scavenger guys are leaving their trucks standing where they are, and newsboys are dropping everything, and one and all joining in the chase, so by the time we hit Broadway and Fifty-sixth there is quite a delegation following the hounds with John Wangle in front, just behind Nip and Tuck, and yelling at them now and then as follows:

"Hold to it, boys!"

At Fifty-sixth the hounds turn east off Broadway and stop at the door of what seems to be an old garage, this door being closed very tight, and Nip and Tuck seem to wish to get through this door, so the Inspector and the coppers kick the door open, and who is in the garage having a big crap game but many prominent citizens of Broadway. Naturally, these citizens are greatly astonished at seeing the bloodhounds, and the rest of us, especially the coppers, and they start running every which way trying to get out of the joint, because crap shooting is quite illegal in these parts.

But the Inspector only says Ah-ha, and starts jotting down names in a notebook as if it is something he will refer to later, and Nip and Tuck are out of the joint almost as soon as they get in and are snuffling on down Fifty-sixth. They stop at four more doors on Fifty-sixth Street along, and when the coppers kick open these doors they find they are nothing but speakeasies, although one is a hop joint, and the citizens in these places are greatly put out by the excitement, especially as Inspector McNamara keeps jotting down things in his notebook.

Finally the Inspector starts glaring very fiercely at the coppers with us, and anybody can see that he is much displeased to find so much illegality going on in this district, and the coppers are starting in to hate Nip and Tuck quite freely, and one copper says to me like this:

"Why," he says, "these mutts are nothing but stool pigeons."

Well, naturally, the noise of John Wangle's yelling, and the gabble of the mob following the hounds makes quite a disturbance, and arouses many of the neighbors in the apartment houses and hotels in the side streets, especially as this is summer, and most everybody has their windows open.

In fact, we see many tousled heads poked out of windows, and hear guys and dolls inquiring as follows:

"What is going on?"

It seems that when word gets about that bloodhounds are tracking down a wrongdoer it causes great uneasiness all through the Fifties, and in fact I afterwards hear that three guys are taken to the Polyclinic suffering with broken ankles and several bruises from hopping out of windows in the hotels we pass in the chase, or from falling off of fire-escapes.

Well, all of a sudden Nip and Tuck swing back onto Seventh Avenue, and pop into the entrance of a small apartment house, and go tearing up the stairs to the first floor, and when we get there these bloodhounds are scratching vigorously at the door of Apartment B-2, and going woofle-woofle, and we are all greatly excited indeed, but the door opens, and who is standing there but a doll by the name of Maud Milligan, who is well known to one and all as the ever-loving doll of Big Nig, the crap shooter, who is down in Hot Springs at this time taking the waters, or whatever it is guys take in Hot Springs.

Now, Maude Milligan is not such a doll as I will care to have any part of, being red-headed, and very stern, and I am glad Nip and Tuck do not waste any more time in her apartment than it takes for them to run through her living-room and across her bed, because Maud is commencing to put the old eye on such of us present as she happens to know. But Nip and Tuck are in and out of the joint before you can say scat, because it is only a two-room apartment, at that, and we are on our way down the stairs and back onto Seventh Avenue again while Inspector McNamara is still jotting down something in his notebook.

Finally, where do these hounds wind up, with about four hundred citizens behind them, and everybody perspiring quite freely indeed from the exercise, but at the door of Miss Missouri Martin's Three Hundred Club, and the doorman, who is a guy by the name of Soldier Sweeney, tries to shoo them away, but Nip runs between the Soldier's legs and upsets him, and Tuck steps in the Soldier's eye in trotting over him, and most of the crowd behind the hounds tread on him in passing, so the old Soldier is pretty well flattened out at the finish.

Nip and Tuck are now more excited than somewhat, and are going zoople-zoople in loud voices as they bust into the Three Hundred Club with John Wangle and the law, and all these citizens behind them. There is a very large crowd present and Miss Missouri Martin is squatted on the back of a chair in the middle of the dance floor when we enter, and is about to start her show when she sees the mob surge in, and at first she is greatly pleased because she thinks new business arrives, and if there is anything Miss Missouri Martin dearly loves, it is new business.

But before she can say hello, sucker, or anything else whatever, Nip runs under her chair, thinking maybe he is a dachshund, and dumps Miss Missouri Martin on the dance floor, and she lays there squawking no little, while the next thing anybody knows, Nip and Tuck are over in one corner of the joint, and are eagerly crawling up and down a fat guy who is sitting there with a doll alongside of him, and who is the fat buy but Regret!

Well, as Nip and Tuck rush at Regret he naturally gets up to defend himself, but they both hit him at the same time, and over he goes on top of the doll who is with him, and who seems to be nobody but Miss Lovey Lou. She is getting quite a squashing with Regret's heft spread out over her, and she is screaming quite some, especially when Nip lets out a foot of tongue and washes her make-up off her face, reaching for Regret. In fact, Miss Lovey Lou seems to be more afraid of the bloodhounds than she does of being squashed to death, for when John Wangle and I hasten to her rescue and pull her out from under Regret she is moaning as follows:

"Oh, do not let them devour me—I will confess."

Well, as nobody but me and John Wangle seem to hear this crack, because everybody else is busy trying to split out Regret and the bloodhounds, and as John Wangle does not seem to understand what Miss Lovey Lou is mumbling about, I shove her off into the crowd, and on back into the kitchen, which is now quite deserted, what with all the help being out watching the muss in the corner, and I say to her like this:

"What is it you confess?" I say. "Is it about Marvin Clay?"

"Yes," she says. "It is about him. He is a pig," she says. "I shoot him, and I am glad of it. He is not satisfied with what he does to me two years ago, but he tries his deviltry on my baby sister. He has her in his apartment and when I find it out and go to get her, he says he will not let her go. So I shoot him. With my brother's pistol," she says, "and I take my baby sister home with me, and I hope he is dead, and gone where he belongs."

"Well, now," I say, "I am not going to give you any argument as to where Marvin Clay belongs, but," I say, "you skip out of here and go on home, and wait until we can do something about this situation, while I go back and help Regret, who seems to be in a tough spot."

"Oh, do not let these terrible dogs eat him up," she says, and with this she takes the breeze and I return to the other room to find there is much confusion indeed, because it seems that Regret is now very indignant at Nip and Tuck, especially when he discovers that one of them plants a big old paw right on the front of Regret's shirt bosom, leaving a dirty mark. So when he struggles to his feet, Regret starts letting go with both hands, and he is by no means a bad puncher for a guy who does not do much punching as a rule. In fact, he flattens Nip with a right-hand to the jaw, and knocks Tuck plumb across the room with a left hook.

Well, poor Tuck slides over the slick dance floor into Miss Missouri Martin just as she is getting to her feet again, and bowls her over once more, but Miss Missouri Martin is also indignant by this time, and she gets up and kicks Tuck in a most unladylike manner. Of course, Tuck does not know so much about Miss Martin, but he is pretty sure his old friend Regret is only playing with him, so back he goes to Regret with his tongue out, and his tail wagging, and there is no telling how long this may go on if John Wangle does not step in and grab both hounds, while Inspector McNamara puts the arm on Regret and tells him he is under arrest for shooting Marvin Clay.

Well, of course everybody can see at once that Regret must be the guilty party all right, especially when it is remembered that he once had trouble with Marvin Clay, and one and all present are looking at Regret in great disgust, and saying you can see by his face that he is nothing but a degenerate type.

Furthermore, Inspector McNamara makes a speech to Miss Missouri Martin's customers in which he congratulates John Wangle and Nip and Tuck on their wonderful work in tracking down this terrible criminal and at the same time putting in a few boosts for the police department, while Regret stands there paying very little attention to what the Inspector is saying, but trying to edge himself over close enough to Nip and Tuck to give them the old foot.

Well, the customers applaud what Inspector McNamara says, and Miss Missouri Martin gets up a collection of over two C's for John Wangle and his hounds, not counting what she holds out for herself. Also the chef comes forward and takes John Wangle and Nip and Tuck back into the kitchen and stuffs them full of food, although personally I will just as soon not have any of the food they serve in the Three Hundred Club.

They take Regret to the jail house, and he does not seem to understand why he is under arrest, but he knows it has something to do with Nip and Tuck and he tries to bribe one of the coppers to put the bloodhounds in the same cell with him for a while, though naturally the copper will not consider such a proposition. While Regret is being booked at the jail house, word comes around that Marvin Clay is not only not dead, but the chances are he will get well, which he finally does, at that.

Moreover, he finally bails Regret out, and not only refuses to prosecute him but skips the country as soon as he is able to move, although Regret lays in the sneezer for several weeks, at that, never letting on after he learns the real situation that he is not the party who plugs Marvin Clay. Naturally, Miss Lovey Lou is very grateful to Regret for his wonderful sacrifice, and will no doubt become his ever-loving wife in a minute, if Regret thinks to ask her, but it seems Regret finds himself brooding so much over the idea of an ever-loving wife who is so handy with a Roscoe that he never really asks.

In the meantime, John Wangle and Nip and Tuck go back to Georgia on the dough collected by Miss Missouri Martin, and with a big reputation as man-trackers. So this is all there is to the story, except that one night I run into Regret with a suitcase in his hand, and he is perspiring very freely, although it is not so hot, at that, and when I ask him if he is going away, he says this is indeed his general idea. Moreover, he says he is going very far away. Naturally, I ask him why this is, and Regret says to me as follows:

"Well," he says, "ever since Big Nig, the crap shooter, comes back from Hot Springs, and hears how the bloodhounds track the shooter of Marvin Clay, he is walking up and down looking at me out of the corner of his eyes. In fact," Regret says, "I can see that Big Nig is studying something over in his mind, and while Big Nig is a guy who is not such a fast thinker as others, I am afraid he may finally think himself to a bad conclusion.

"I am afraid," Regret says, "that Big Nig will think himself to the conclusion that Nip and Tuck are tracking me instead of the shooter, as many evil-minded guys are already whispering around and about, and that he may get the wrong idea about the trail leading to Maud Milligan's door."

"GENTLEMEN, THE KING!"

On Tuesday evening I always go to Bobby's Chop House to get myself a beef stew, the beef stews in Bobby's being very nourishing indeed and quite reasonable. In fact, the beef stews in Bobby's are considered a most fashionable dish by one and all on Broadway on Tuesday evenings.

So on this Tuesday evening I am talking about, I am in Bobby's wrapping myself around a beef stew and reading the race results in the *Journal,* when who comes into the joint but two old friends of mine from Philly, and a third guy I never see before in my life, but who seems to be an old sort of guy, and very fierce-looking.

One of these old friends of mine from Philly is a guy by the name of Izzy Cheesecake, who is called Izzy Cheesecake because he is all the time eating cheesecake around delicatessen joints, although of course this is nothing against him, as cheesecake is very popular in some circles, and goes very good with java. Anyway, this Izzy Cheesecake has another name, which is Morris something, and he is slightly Jewish, and has a large beezer, and is considered a handy man in many respects.

The other old friend of mine from Philly is a guy by the name of Kitty Quick, who is maybe thirty-two or -three years old, and who is a lively guy in every way. He is a great hand for wearing good clothes, and he is mobbed up with some very good people in Philly in his day, and at one time has plenty of dough, although I hear that lately things are not going so good for Kitty Quick, or for anybody else in Philly, as far as that is concerned.

Now of course I do not rap to these old friends of mine from Philly at once, and in fact I put the *Journal* up in front of my face, because it is never good policy to rap to visitors in this town, especially visitors from Philly, until you know why they are visiting. But it seems that Kitty Quick spies me before I can get the *Journal* up high enough, and he comes over to my table at once, bringing Izzy Cheesecake and the other guy with him, so naturally I give them a big hello, very cordial, and ask them to sit down and have a few beef stews with me, and as they pull up chairs, Kitty Quick says to me like this:

"Do you know Jo-jo from Chicago?" he says, pointing his thumb at the third guy.

Well, of course I know Jo-jo by his reputation, which is very alarming, but I never meet up with him before, and if it is left to me, I will never meet up with him at all, because Jo-jo is considered a very uncouth character, even in Chicago.

He is an Italian, and a short wide guy, very heavy set, and slow moving, and with jowls you can cut steaks off of, and sleepy eyes, and he somehow reminds me of an old lion I once see in a cage in Ringling's circus. He has a black moustache, and he is an old-timer out in Chicago, and is pointed out to visitors to the city as a very remarkable guy because he lives as long as he does, which is maybe forty years.

His right name is Antonio something, and why he is called Jo-jo I never hear, but I suppose it is because Jo-jo is handier than Antonio. He shakes hands with me, and says he is pleased to meet me, and then he sits down and begins taking on beef stew very rapidly while Kitty Quick says to me as follows:

"Listen," he says, "do you know anybody in Europe?"

Well, this is a most unexpected question, and naturally I am not going to reply to unexpected questions by guys from Philly without thinking them over very carefully, so to gain time while I think, I say to Kitty Quick:

"Which Europe do you mean?"

"Why," Kitty says, greatly surprised, "is there more than one Europe? I mean the big Europe on the Atlantic Ocean. This is the Europe where we are going, and if you know anybody there we will be glad to go around and say hello to them for you. We are going to Europe on the biggest proposition anybody ever hears of," he says. "In fact," he says, "it is a proposition which will make us all rich. We are sailing to-night."

Well, off hand I cannot think of anybody I know in Europe, and if I do know anybody there I will certainly not wish such parties as Kitty Quick, and Izzy Cheesecake, and Jo-jo going around saying hello to them, but of course I do not mention such a thought out loud. I only say I hope and trust that they have a very good *bon voyage* and do not suffer too much from seasickness. Naturally I do not ask what their proposition is, because if I ask such a question they may think I wish to find out, and will consider me a very nosy guy, but I figure the chances are they are going to look after come commercial matter, such as Scotch, or maybe cordials.

Anyway, Kitty Quick and Izzy Cheesecake and Jo-jo eat up quite a few beef stews, and leave me to pay the check, and this is the last I see or hear of any of them for several months. Then one day I am in Philly to see a prize fight, and I run into Kitty Quick on Broad Street, looking pretty much the same as usual, and I ask him how he comes out in Europe.

"It is no good," Kitty says. "The trip is something of a bust, although we see many interesting sights, and have quite a few experiences. Maybe," Kitty says, "you will like to hear why we go to Europe? It is a very unusual story indeed, and is by no means a lie, and I will be pleased to tell it to someone I think will believe it."

So we go into Walter's restaurant, and sit down in a corner, and order up a little java, and Kitty Quick tells me the story as follows:

It all begins (Kitty says) with a certain big lawyer coming to me here in Philly, and wishing to know if I care to take up a proposition which will make me rich, and naturally I say I can think of nothing that will please me more, because at this time things are very bad indeed in Philly, what with investigations going on here and there, and plenty of heat around and about, and I do not have more than a few bobs in my pants pocket, and can think of no way to get any more.

So this lawyer takes me to the Ritz-Carlton hotel, and there he introduces me to a guy by the name of Count Saro, and the lawyer says he will okay anything Saro has to say to me one hundred per cent, and then he immediately takes the wind as if he does not care to hear what Saro has to say. But I know this mouthpiece is not putting any proposition away as okay unless he knows it is pretty much okay, because he is a smart guy at his own dodge, and everything else, and has plenty of coconuts.

Now this Count Saro is a little guy with an eyebrow moustache, and he wears striped pants, and white spats, and a cutaway coat, and a monocle in one eye, and he seems to be a foreign nobleman, although he talks English first rate. I do not care much for Count

Saro's looks, but I will say one thing for him, he is very businesslike, and gets down to cases at once.

He tells me that he is the representative of a political party in his home country in Europe which has a King, and this country wishes to get rid of the King, because Count Saro says Kings are out of style in Europe, and that no country can get anywhere with a King these days. His proposition is for me to take any assistants I figure I may need and go over and get rid of this King, and Count Saro says he will pay two hundred G's for the job in good old American scratch, and will lay twenty-five G's on the line at once, leaving the balance with the lawyer to be paid to me when everything is finished.

Well, this is a most astonishing proposition indeed, because while I often hear of propositions to get rid of other guys, I never before hear of a proposition to get rid of a King. Furthermore, it does not sound reasonable to me, as getting rid of a King is apt to attract plenty of attention, and criticism, but Count Saro explains to me that his country is a small, out-of-the-way country, and that his political party will take control of the telegraph wires and everything else as soon as I get rid of the King, so nobody will give the news much of a tumble outside the country.

"Everything will be done very quietly, and in good order," Count Saro says, "and there will be no danger to you whatever."

Well, naturally I wish to know from Count Saro why he does not get somebody in his own country to do such a job, especially if he can pay so well for it, and he says to me like this:

"Well," he says, "in the first place there is no one in our country with enough experience in such matters to be trusted, and in the second place we do not wish anyone in our country to seem to be tangled up with getting rid of the King. It will cause internal complications," he says. "An outsider is more logical," he says, "because it is quite well known that in the palace of the King there are many valuable jewels, and it will seem a natural play for outsiders, especially Americans, to break into the palace to get these jewels, and if they happen to get rid of the King while getting the jewels, no one will think it is anything more than an accident, such as often occurs in your country."

Furthermore, Count Saro tells me that everything will be laid out for me in advance by his people, so I will have no great bother getting into the palace to get rid of the King, but he says of course I must not really take the valuable jewels, because his political party wishes to keep them for itself.

Well, I do not care much for the general idea at all, but Count Saro whips out a bundle of scratch, and weeds off twenty-five large coarse notes of a G apiece, and there it is in front of me, and looking at all this dough, and thinking how tough times are, what with banks busting here and there, I am very much tempted indeed, especially as I am commencing to think this Count Saro is some kind of a nut, and is only speaking through his hat about getting rid of a King.

"Listen," I say to Count Saro, as he sits there watching me, "how do you know I will not take this dough off of you and then never do anything whatever for it?"

"Why," he says, much surprised, "you are recommended to me as an honest man, and I accept your references. Anyway," he says, "if you do not carry out your agreement with me, you will only hurt yourself, because you will lose a hundred and seventy-five G's more and the lawyer will make you very hard to catch."

Well, the upshot of it is I shake hands with Count Saro, and then go out to find Izzy Cheesecake, although I am still thinking Count Saro is a little daffy, and while I am looking for Izzy, who do I see but Jo-jo, and Jo-jo tells me that he is on vacation from Chicago for a while, because it seems somebody out there claims he is a public enemy, which Jo-jo says is nothing but a big lie, as he is really very fond of the public at all times.

Naturally I am glad to come across a guy such as Jo-jo, because he is most trustworthy, and naturally Jo-jo is very glad to hear of a proposition that will turn him an honest dollar while he is on his vacation. So Jo-jo and Izzy and I have a meeting, and we agree that I am to have a hundred G's for finding the plant, while Izzy and Jo-jo are to get fifty G's apiece, and this is how we come to go to Europe.

Well, we land at a certain spot in Europe, and who is there to meet us but another guy with a monocle, who states that his name is Baron von Terp, or some such, and who says he is representing Count Saro, and I am commencing to wonder if Count Saro's country is filled with one-eyed guys. Anyway, this Baron von Terp takes us traveling by trains and automobiles for several days, until finally after an extra long hop in an automobile we come to the outskirts of a nice-looking little burg, which seems to be the place we are headed for.

Now Baron von Terp drops us in a little hotel on the outskirts of the town, and says he must leave us because he cannot afford to be seen with us, although he explains he does not mean this as a knock to us. In fact, Baron von Terp says he finds us very nice traveling companions indeed, except for Jo-jo wishing to engage in target practice along the route with his automatic Roscoe, and using such animals as stray dogs and chickens for his targets. He says he does not even mind Izzy Cheesecake's singing, although personally I will always consider this one of the big drawbacks to the journey.

Before he goes, Baron von Terp draws me a rough diagram of the inside of the palace where we are to get rid of the King, giving me a lay-out of all the rooms and doors. He says usually there are guards in and about this palace, but that his people arrange it so these guards will not be present around nine o'clock this night, except one guy who may be on guard at the door of the King's bedroom, and Baron von Terp says if we guzzle this guy it will be all right with him, because he does not like the guy, anyway.

But the general idea, he says, is for us to work fast and quietly, so as to be in and out of there inside of an hour or so, leaving no trail behind us, and I say this will suit me and Izzy Cheesecake and Jo-jo very well indeed as we are getting tired of traveling, and wish to go somewhere and take a long rest.

Well, after explaining all this, Baron von Terp takes the wind, leaving us a big fast car with an ugly-looking guy driving it who does not talk much English, but he is supposed to know all the routes, and it is in this car that we leave the little hotel just before nine o'clock as per instructions, and head for the palace, which turns out to be nothing but a large square old building in the middle of a sort of park, with the town around and about, but some distance off.

Ugly-face drives right into this park and up to what seems to be the front door of the building, and the three of us get out of the car, and Ugly-face pulls the car off into the shadow of some trees to wait for us.

Personally, I am looking for plenty of heat when we start to go into the palace, and I have the old equalizer where I can get at it without too much trouble, while Jo-jo and Izzy Cheesecake also have their rods handy. But just as Baron von Terp tells us, there are no guards around, and in fact there is not a soul in sight as we walk into the palace door, and find ourselves in a big hall with paintings, and armor, and old swords, and one thing and another hanging around and about, and I can see that this is a perfect plant indeed.

I out with my diagram and see where the King's bedroom is located on the second floor, and when we get there, walking very easy and ready to start blasting away if necessary, who is at the door but a big tall guy in a uniform, who is very much surprised at seeing us, and who starts to holler something or other, but what it is nobody will ever know, because just as he opens his mouth, Izzy Cheesecake taps him on the noggin with the butt of a forty-five, and knocks him cock-eyed.

Then Jo-jo grabs some cord off a heavy silk curtain which is hanging across the door, and ties the guy up good and tight, and wads a handkerchief into his kisser in case the guy comes to, and wishes to start hollering again, and when all this is done, I quietly turn the knob of the door to the King's bedroom, and we step into a room that looks more like a young convention hall than it does a bedroom, except that it is hung around and about with silk drapes, and there is much gilt furniture here and there.

Well, who is in this room but a nice-looking doll, and a little kid of maybe eight or nine years old, and the kid is in a big bed with a canopy over it like the entrance to a night club, only silk, and the doll is sitting alongside the bed reading to the kid out of a book. It is a very homelike scene indeed and causes us to stop and look around in great surprise, for we are certainly not expecting such a scene at all.

As we stand there in the middle of the room somewhat confused the doll turns and looks at us, and the little kid sits up in bed. He is a fat little guy with a chubby face, and a lot of curly hair, and eyes as big as pancakes, and maybe bigger. The doll turns very pale when she sees us, and shakes so the book she is reading falls to the floor, but the kid does not seem scared, and he says to us in very good English like this:

"Who are you?" he says.

Well, this is a fair questions, at that, but naturally we do not wish to state who we are at this time, so I say:

"Never mind who we are, where is the King?"

"The King?" the kid says, sitting up straight in the bed, "why, I am the King."

Now of course this seems a very nonsensical crack to us, because we have brains enough to know that Kings do not come as small as this little squirt, and anyway we are in no mood to dicker with him, so I say to the doll as follows:

"Listen," I say, "we do not care for any kidding at his time, because we are in a great hurry. Where is the King?"

"Why," she says, her voice trembling quite some, "this is indeed the King, and I am his governess. Who are you, and what do you want? How do you get in here?" she says. "Where are the guards?"

"Lady," I say, and I am greatly surprised at myself for being so patient with her, "this kid may be a King, but we want the big King. We want the head King himself," I say.

"There is no other," she says, and the little kid chips in like this:

"My father dies two years ago, and I am the King in his place," he says. "Are you English like Miss Peabody here?" he says. "Who is the funny-looking man back there?"

Well, of course Jo-jo is funny-looking, at that, but no one ever before is impolite enough to speak of it to his face, and Jo-jo begins growling quite some, while Izzy Cheesecake speaks as follows:

"Why," Izzy says, "this is a very great outrage. We are sent to get rid of a King, and here the King is nothing but a little punk. Personally," Izzy says, "I am not in favor of getting rid of punks, male or female."

"Well," Jo-jo says, "I am against it myself as a rule, but this is a pretty fresh punk."

"Now," I say, "there seems to be some mistake around here, at that. Let us sit down and talk things over quietly, and see if we cannot get this matter straightened out. It looks to me," I say, "as if this Count Saro is nothing but a swindler."

"Count Saro," the doll says, getting up and coming over to me, and looking very much alarmed. "Count Saro, do you say? Oh, sir, Count Saro is a very bad man. He is the tool of the Grand Duke Gino of this country, who is this little boy's uncle. The Grand Duke will be King himself if it is not for this boy, and we suspect many plots against the little chap's safety. Oh, gentlemen," she says, "you surely do not mean any harm to this poor orphan child?"

Well, this is about the first time in their lives that Jo-jo and Izzy Cheesecake are ever mentioned by anybody as gentlemen, and I can see that it softens them up quite some, especially as the little kid is grinning at them very cheerful, although of course he will not be so cheerful if he knows who he is grinning at.

"Why," Jo-jo says, "the Grand Duke is nothing but a rascal for wishing harm to such a little guy as this, although of course," Jo-jo says, "if he is a grown-up King it will be a different matter."

"Who are you?" the little kid says again.

"We are Americans," I say, very proud to mention my home country. "We are from Philly and Chicago, two very good towns, at that."

Well, the little kid's eyes get bigger than ever, and he climbs right out of bed and walks over to us looking very cute in his blue silk pajamas, and his bare feet.

"Chicago?" he says. "Do you know Mr. Capone?"

"Al?" says Jo-jo. "Do I know Al? Why, Al and me are just like this," he says, although personally I do not believe Al Capone will know Jo-jo if he meets him in broad daylight. "Where do you know Al from?" he asks.

"Oh, I do not know him," the kid says. "But I read about him in the magazines, and about the machine guns, and the pineapples. Do you know about the pineapples?" he says.

"Do I know about the pineapples?" Jo-jo says, as if his feelings are hurt by the question. "He asks me do I know about the pineapples. Why," he says, "look here."

And what does Jo-jo do but out with a little round gadget which I recognize at once as a bomb such as these Guineas like to chuck at people they do not like, especially Guineas from Chicago. Of course I never know Jo-jo is packing this article around and about with him, and Jo-jo can see I am much astonished, and by no means pleased, because he says to me like this:

"I bring this along in case of a bear fight," he says. "They are very handy in a bear fight."

Well, the next thing anybody knows we are all talking about this and that very pleasant, especially the little kid and Jo-jo, who is telling lies faster than a horse can trot, about Chicago and Mr. Capone, and I hope and trust that Al never hears some of the lies Jo-jo tells, or he may hold it against me for being with Jo-jo when these lies come off.

I am talking to the doll, whose name seems to be Miss Peabody, and who is not so hard to take, at that, and at the same time I am keeping an eye on Izzy Cheesecake, who is wandering around the room looking things over. The chances are Izzy is trying to find a few of the valuable jewels such as I mention to him when telling him about the proposition of getting rid of the King, and in fact I am taking a stray peek here and there myself, but I do not see anything worthwhile.

This Miss Peabody is explaining to me about the politics of the country, and it seems the reason the Grand Duke wishes to get rid of the little kid King and be King himself is because he has a business deal on with a big nation nearby which wishes to control the kid King's country. I judge from what Miss Peabody tells me that this country is no bigger than Delaware County, Pa., and it seems to be a lot of bother about no more country than this, but Miss Peabody says it is a very nice little country, at that.

She says it will be very lovely indeed if it is not for the Grand Duke Gino, because the little kid King stands okay with the people, but it seems the old Grand Duke is pretty much boss of everything, and Miss Peabody says she is personally long afraid that he will finally try to do something very drastic indeed to get rid of the kid King on account of the kid seeming so healthy. Well, naturally I do not state to her that our middle name is drastic, because I do not wish Miss Peabody to have a bad opinion of us.

Now nothing will do but Jo-jo must show the kid his automatic, which is as long as your arm, and maybe longer, and the kid is greatly delighted, and takes the rod and starts pointing it here and there and saying boom-boom, as kids will do. But what happens but he pulls the trigger, and it seems that Jo-jo does not have the safety on, so the Roscoe really goes boom-boom twice before the kid can take his finger off the trigger.

Well, the first shot smashes a big jar over in one corner of the room, which Miss Peabody afterwards tells me is worth fifteen G's if it is worth a dime, and the second slug knocks off Izzy Cheesecake's derby hat, which serves Izzy right, at that, as he is keeping his hat on in the presence of a lady. Naturally these shots are very disturbing to me at the moment, but afterwards I learn they are a very good thing indeed, because it seems a lot of guys who are hanging around outside, including Baron von Terp, and several prominent politicians of the country, watching and listening to see what comes off, hurry right home to bed, figuring the King is got rid of as per contract, and wishing to be found in bed if anybody comes around asking questions.

Well, Jo-jo is finally out of lies about Chicago and Mr. Capone, when the little kid seems to get a new idea and goes rummaging around the room looking for something, and just as I am hoping he is about to donate the valuable jewels to us he comes up with a box, and what is in this box is a baseball bat, and a catcher's mitt, and a baseball, and it is very strange indeed to find such homelike articles so far away from home, especially as Babe Ruth's name is on the bat.

"Do you know about these things?" the little kid asks Jo-jo. "They are from America, and they are sent to me by one of our people when he is visiting there, but nobody here seems to know what they are for."

"Do I know about them?" Jo-jo says, fondling them very tenderly indeed. "He asks me do I know about them. Why," he says, "in my time I am the greatest hitter on the West Side Blues back in dear old Chi."

Well, now nothing will do the kid but we must show him how these baseball articles work, so Izzy Cheesecake, who claims he is once a star back-stopper with the Vine Streets back in Philly, puts on a pad and mask, and Jo-jo takes the bat and lays a small sofa pillow down on the floor for home plate, and insists that I pitch to him. Now it is years since I handle a baseball, although I wish to say that in my day I am as good an amateur pitcher as there is around Gray's Ferry in Philly, and the chances are I will be with the A's if I do not have other things to do.

So I take off my coat, and get down to the far end of the room, while Jo-jo squares away at the plate, with Izzy Cheesecake behind it. I can see by the way he stands that Jo-jo is bound to be a sucker for a curve, so I take a good windup, and cut loose with the old fadeaway, but of course my arm is not what it used to be, and the ball does not break as I expect, so what happens but Jo-jo belts the old apple right through a high window in what will be right field if the room is laid off like Shibe Park.

Well Jo-jo starts running as if he is going to first, but of course there is no place in particular for him to run, and he almost knocks his brains out against a wall, and the ball is lost, and the game winds up right there, but the little kid is tickled silly over this business, and even Miss Peabody laughs, and she does not look to me like a doll who gets many laughs out of life, at that.

It is now nearly ten o'clock, and Miss Peabody says if she can find anybody around she will get us something to eat, and this sounds very reasonable indeed, so I step outside the door and bring in the guy we tie up there, who seems to be wide awake by now and very much surprised, and quite indignant, and Miss Peabody says something to him in a language which I do not understand. When I come to think it all over afterwards, I am greatly astonished at the way I trust Miss Peabody, because there is no reason why she shall not tell the guy to get the law, but I suppose I trust her because she seems to have an honest face.

Anyway, the guy in the uniform goes away rubbing his noggin, and pretty soon in comes another guy who seems to be a butler, or some such, and who is also greatly surprised at seeing us, and Miss Peabody rattles off something to him and he starts hustling in tables, and dishes, and sandwiches, and coffee, and one thing and another in no time at all.

Well, there we are, the five of us sitting around the table eating and drinking, because what does the butler do but bring in a couple of bottles of good old pre-war champagne, which is very pleasant to the taste, although Izzy Cheesecake embarrasses me no little by telling Miss Peabody that if she can dig up any considerable quantity of this stuff he will make her plenty of bobs by peddling it in our country, and will also cut the King in.

When the butler fills the wine-glasses the first time, Miss Peabody picks hers up, and looks at us, and naturally we have sense enough to pick ours up, too, and then she stands up on her feet and raises her glass high above her head, and says like this:

"Gentlemen, the King!"

Well, I stand up at this, and Jo-jo and Izzy Cheesecake stand up with me, and we say, all together:

"The King!"

And then we swig our champagne, and sit down again and the little kid laughs all over and claps his hands and seems to think it is plenty of fun, which it is, at that, although Miss Peabody does not let him have any wine, and is somewhat indignant when she catches Jo-jo trying to slip him a snort under the table.

Well, finally the kid does not wish us to leave him at all, especially Jo-jo, but Miss Peabody says he must get some sleep, so we tell him we will be back someday, and we take our hats and say good-bye, and leave him standing in the bedroom door with Miss Peabody at his side, and the little kid's arm is around her waist, and I find myself wishing it is my arm, at that.

Of course we never go back again, and in fact we get out of the country this very night, and take the first boat out of the first seaport we hit and return to the United States of America, and the gladdest guy in all the world to see us go is Ugly-face, because he has to drive us about a thousand miles with the muzzle of a rod digging into his ribs.

So (Kitty Quick says) now you know why we go to Europe.

Well, naturally, I am greatly interested in his story, and especially in what Kitty says about the pre-war champagne, because I can see that there may be great business opportunities in such a place if a guy can get in with the right people, but one thing Kitty will never tell me is where the country is located, except that it is located in Europe.

"You see," Kitty says, "we are all strong Republicans here in Philly, and I will not get the Republican administration of this country tangled up in any international squabble for the world. You see," he says, "when we land back home I find a little item of cable news in a paper which says the Grand Duke Gino dies as a result of injuries received in an accident in his home some weeks before.

"And," Kitty says, "I am never sure but what these injuries may be caused by Jo-jo insisting on Ugly-face driving us around to the Grand Duke's house the night we leave and popping his pineapple into the Grand Duke's bedroom window."

THE BRAIN GOES HOME

One night The Brain is walking me up and down Broadway in front of Mindy's restaurant, and speaking of this and that, when along comes a red-headed raggedy doll selling apples at five cents per copy, and The Brain, being very fond of apples, grabs one out of her basket and hands her a five-dollar bill.

The red-headed raggedy doll, who is maybe thirty-odd and is nothing but a crow as far as looks are concerned, squints at the finnif, and says to The Brain like this:

"I do not have change for so much money," she says, "but I will go and get it in a minute."

"You keep the change," The Brain says, biting a big hunk out of the apple and taking my arm to start me walking again.

Well, the raggedy doll looks at The Brain again, and it seems to me that all of a sudden there are large tears in her eyes as she says:

"Oh, thank you, sir! Thank you, thank you, and God bless you, sir!"

And then she goes on up the street in a hurry, with her hands over her eyes and her shoulders shaking, and The Brain turns around very much astonished, and watches her until she is out of sight.

"Why, my goodness!" The Brain says. "I give Doris Clare ten G's last night, and she does not make half as much fuss over it as this doll does over a pound note."

"Well," I say, "maybe the apple doll needs a pound note more than Doris needs ten G's."

"Maybe so," The Brain says. "And of course, Doris gives me much more in return than just an apple and a God bless me. Doris gives me her love. I guess," The Brain says, "that love costs me about as much dough as any guy that ever lives."

"I guess it does," I say, and the chances are we both guess right, because off-hand I figure that if The Brain gets out on three hun-

dred G's per year for love, he is running his love business very eco-
nomically indeed, because it is well known to one and all that The
Brain has three different dolls, besides an ever-loving wife.

In fact, The Brain is sometimes spoken of by many citizens as
the "Love King," but only behind his back, because The Brain
likes to think his love affairs are a great secret to all but maybe a
few, although the only guy I ever see in this town who does not
know all about them is a guy who is deaf, dumb, and blind.

I once read a story about a guy by the name of King Solomon
who lives a long time ago and who has a thousand dolls all at once,
which is going in for dolls on a very large scale indeed, but I guarantee that all of King Solomon's dolls put together are not as expensive as any one of The Brain's dolls. The overhead on Doris Clare
alone will drive an ordinary guy daffy, and Doris is practically fru-
gal compared to Cynthia Harris and Bobby Baker.

Then there is Charlotte, who is The Brain's ever-loving wife and
who has a society bug and needs plenty of coconuts at all times to
keep her a going concern. I once hear The Brain tell Bobby Baker
that his ever-loving wife is a bit of an invalid, but as a matter of
fact there is never anything the matter with Charlotte that a few
bobs will not cure, although of course this goes for nearly every
doll in this world who is an invalid.

When a guy is knocking around Broadway as long as The
Brain, he is bound to accumulate dolls here and there, but most
guys accumulate one at a time, and when this one runs out on him,
as Broadway dolls will do, he accumulates another, and so on,
and so on, until he is too old to care about such matters as dolls,
which is when he is maybe a hundred and four years old, although
I hear of several guys who beat even this record.

But when The Brain accumulates a doll he seems to keep her accumulated, and none of them ever run out on him, and while this
will be a very great nuisance to the average guy, it pleases The Brain
no little because it makes him think he has a very great power
over dolls.

"They are not to blame if they fall in love with me," The Brain
says to me one night. "I will not cause one of them any sorrow for
all the world."

Well, of course, it is most astonishing to me to hear a guy as
smart as The Brain using such language, but I figure he may really
believe it, because The Brain thinks very good of himself at all

times. However, some guys claim that the real reason The Brain keeps all his dolls is because he is too selfish to give them away, although personally I will not take any of them if The Brain throws in a cash bonus, except maybe Bobby Baker.

Anyway, The Brain keeps his dolls accumulated, and furthermore he spend plenty of dough on them, what with buying them automobiles and furs and diamonds and swell places to live in—especially swell places to live in. One time I tell The Brain he will save himself plenty if he hires a house and bunches his dolls together in one big happy family, instead of having them scattered all over town, but The Brain says this idea is no good.

"In the first place," he says, "they do not know about each other, except Doris and Cynthia and Bobby know about Charlotte, although she does not know about them. They each think they are the only one with me. So if I corral them all together they will be jealous of each other over my love. Anyway," The Brain says, "such an arrangement will be very immoral and against the law. No," he says, "it is better to have them in different spots, because think of the many homes it gives me to go to in case I wish to go home. In fact," The Brain says, "I guess I have more homes to go to than any other guy on Broadway."

Well, this may be true, but what The Brain wants with a lot of different homes is a very great mystery on Broadway, because he seldom goes home, anyway, his idea in not going home being that something may happen in this town while he is at home that he is not in on. The Brain seldom goes anywhere in particular. He never goes out in public with any one of his dolls, except maybe once or twice a year with Charlotte, his ever-loving wife, and finally he even stops going with her because Doris Clare says it does not look good to Doris's personal friends.

The Brain marries Charlotte long before he becomes the biggest guy in gambling operations in the East, and a millionaire two or three times over, but he is never much of a hand to sit around home and chew the fat with his ever-loving wife, as husbands often do. Furthermore, when he is poor he has to live in a neighborhood which is too far away for it to be convenient for him to go home, so finally he gets out of the habit of going there.

But Charlotte is not such a doll as cares to spend more than one or two years looking at the pictures on the wall, because it seems the pictures on the wall are nothing but pictures of cows in the meadows and houses covered with snow, so she does not go home any more than necessary, either, and has her own friends and is very happy indeed, especially after The Brain gets so he can send in right along.

I will say one thing about The Brain and his dolls: he never picks a crow. He has a very good eye for faces and shapes, and even Charlotte, his ever-loving wife, is not a crow, although she is not as young as she used to be. As for Doris Clare, she is one of the great beauties on the Ziegfeld roof in her day, and while her day is by no means yesterday, or even the day before, Doris holds on pretty well in the matter of looks. Giving her a shade the best of it, I will say that Doris is thirty-two or -three, but she has plenty of zing left in her, at that, and her hair remains very blonde, no matter what.

In fact, The Brain does not care much if his dolls are blonde or brunette, because Cynthia Harris's hair is as black as the inside of a wolf, while Bobby Baker is betwixt and between, her hair being a light brown. Cynthia Harris is more of a Johnny-come-lately than Doris, being out of Mr. Earl Carroll's *Vanities*, and I hear she first comes to New York as Miss Somebody in one of these beauty contests which she will win hands down if one of the judges does not get a big wink from a Miss Somebody Else.

Of course, Cynthia is doing some winking herself at this time, but it seems that she picks a guy to wink at thinking he is one of the judges, when he is nothing but a newspaperman and has no say whatever about the decision.

Well, Mr. Earl Carroll feels sorry for Cynthia, so he puts her in the *Vanities* and lets her walk around raw, and The Brain sees her, and the next thing anybody knows she is riding in a big foreign automobile the size of a rum chaser, and is chucking a terrible swell.

Personally, I always consider Bobby Baker the smartest of all The Brain's dolls, because she is just middling as to looks and she does not have any of the advantages of life like Doris Clare and Cynthia Harris, such as jobs on the stage where they can walk around showing off their shapes to guys such as The Brain. Bobby Baker starts off as nothing but a private secretary to a guy in Wall Street, and naturally she is always wearing clothes, or anyway, as many clothes as an ordinary doll wears nowadays, which is not so many, at that.

It seems that The Brain once has some business with the guy Bobby works for and happens to get talking to Bobby, and she tells him how she always wishes to meet him, what with hearing and reading about him, and how he is just as handsome and romantic-looking as she always pictures him to herself.

Now I wish to say I will never call any doll a liar, being at all times a gentleman, and for all I know, Bobby Baker may really think The Brain is handsome and romantic-looking, but personally I figure if she is not lying to him, she is at least a little excited when she makes such a statement to The Brain. The best you can give The Brain at this time is that he is very well dressed.

He is maybe forty years old, give or take a couple of years, and he is commencing to get a little bunchy about the middle, what with sitting down at card-tables so much and never taking any exercise outside of walking guys such as me up and down in front of Mindy's for a few hours every night. He has a clean-looking face, always very white around the gills, and he has nice teeth and a nice smile when he wishes to smile, which is never at guys who owe him dough.

And I will say for The Brain he has what is called personality. He tells a story well, although he is always the hero of any story he tells, and he knows how to make himself agreeable to dolls in many ways. He has a pretty fair sort of education, and while dolls such as Cynthia and Doris and maybe Charlotte, too, will rather have a charge account at Cartier's than all the education in Yale and Harvard put together, it seems that Bobby Baker likes highbrow gab, so naturally she gets plenty of same from The Brain.

Well, pretty soon Bobby is riding around in a car bigger than Cynthia's, though neither is as big as Doris's car, and all the neighbors' children over in Flatbush, which is where Bobby hails from, are very jealous of her and running around spreading gossip about her, but keeping their eyes open for big cars themselves. Personally, I always figure The Brain lowers himself socially by taking up with a doll from Flatbush, especially as Bobby Baker soon goes in for literary guys, such as newspaper scribes and similar characters around Greenwich Village.

But there is no denying Bobby Baker is a very smart little doll, and in the four or five years she is one of The Brain's dolls, she gets more dough out of him than all the others put together, because she is always telling him how much she loves him, and saying she cannot do without him, while Doris Clare and Cynthia Harris sometimes forget to mention this more than once or twice a month.

Now what happens early one morning but a guy by the name of Daffy Jack hauls off and sticks a shiv in The Brain's left side. It seems that this is done at the request of a certain party by the name of Homer Swing, who owes The Brain plenty of dough in a gambling transaction, and who becomes very indignant when The Brain presses him somewhat for payment. It seems that Daffy Jack, who is considered a very good shiv artist, aims at The Brain's heart, but misses it by a couple of inches, leaving The Brain with a very bad cut in his side which calls for some stitching.

Big Nig, the crap shooter, and I are standing at Fifty-second Street and Seventh Avenue along about 2 a.m. speaking of not much, when The Brain comes stumbling out of Fifty-second Street, and falls in Big Nig's arms, practically ruining a brand-new top-coat which Big Nig pays sixty bucks for a few days back with the blood that is coming out of the cut. Naturally, Big Nig is indignant about this, but we can see that it is no time to be speaking to The Brain about such matters. We can see that The Brain is carved up quite some, and is in a bad way.

Of course, we are not greatly surprised at seeing The Brain in this condition, because for years he is practically no price around this town, what with this guy and that being anxious to do something or other to him, but we are never expecting to see him carved up like a turkey. We are expecting to see him with a few slugs in him, and both Big Nig and me are very angry to think that there are guys around who will use such instruments as a knife on anybody.

But while we are thinking it over, The Brain says to me like this:

"Call Hymie Weissberger, and Doc Frisch," he says, "and take me home."

Naturally, a guy such as The Brain wishes his lawyer before he wishes his doctor, and Hymie Weissberger is The Brain's mouth-piece, and a very sure-footed guy, at that.

"Well," I say, "we better take you to a hospital where you can get good attention at once."

"No," The Brain says. "I wish to keep this secret. It will be a bad thing for me right now to have this get out, and if you take me to a hospital they must report it to the coppers. Take me home."

Naturally, I say which home, being somewhat confused about The Brain's homes, and he seems to study a minute as if this is a question to be well thought out.

"Park Avenue," The Brain says finally, so Big Nig stops a taxi-cab, and we help The Brain into the cab and tell the jockey to take us to the apartment house on Park Avenue near Sixty-fourth where The Brain's ever-loving wife Charlotte lives.

When we get there, I figure it is best for me to go up first and break the news gently to Charlotte, because I can see what a shock it is bound to be to any ever-loving wife to have her husband brought home in the early hours of the morning all shivved up.

Well, the doorman and the elevator guy in the apartment house give me an argument about going up to The Brain's apartment, saying a blow-out of some kind is going on there, but after I explain to them that The Brain is sick, they let me go. A big fat butler comes to the door of the apartment when I ring, and I can see there are many dolls and guys in evening clothes in the apartment, and somebody is singing very loud.

The butler tries to tell me I cannot see Charlotte, but I finally convince him it is best, so by and by she comes to the door, and a very pleasant sight she is, at that, with jewelry all over her. I stall around awhile, so as not to alarm her too much, and then I tell her The Brain meets with an accident and that we have him outside in a cab, and ask her where we shall put him.

"Why," she says, "put him in a hospital, of course. I am entertaining some very important people to-night, and I cannot have them disturbed by bringing in a hospital patient. Take him to a hospital, and tell him I will come and see him to-morrow and bring him some broth."

I try to explain to her that The Brain does not need any broth, but a nice place to lie down in, but finally she gets very testy with me and shuts the door in my face, saying as follows:

"Take him to a hospital, I tell you. This is a ridiculous hour for him to be coming home, anyway. It is twenty years since he comes home so early."

Then as I am waiting for the elevator, she opens the door again just a little bit and says:

"By the way, is he hurt bad?"

I say we do not know how bad he is hurt, and she shuts the door again, and I go back to the cab again, thinking what a heartless doll she is, although I can see where it will be very inconvenient for her to bust up her party, at that.

The Brain is lying back in the corner of the cab, his eyes half-closed, and by this time it seems that Big Nig stops the blood somewhat with a handkerchief, but The Brain acts somewhat weak to me. He sort of rouses himself when I climb in the cab, and when I tell him his ever-loving wife is not home he smiles a bit and whispers:

"Take me to Doris."

Now Doris lives in a big apartment house away over on West Seventy-second Street near the Drive, and I tell the taxi jockey to go there while The Brain seems to slide off into a doze. Then Big Nig leans over to me and says to me like this:

"No use taking him there," Big Nig says. "I see Doris going out to-night all dressed up in her ermine coat with this actor guy, Jack Walen, she is struck on. It is a very great scandal around and about the way they carry on. Let us take him to Cynthia," Nig says. "She is a very large-hearted doll who will be very glad to take him in."

Now Cynthia Harris has a big suite of rooms that cost fifteen G's a year in a big hotel just off Fifth Avenue, Cynthia being a doll who likes to be downtown so if she hears of anything coming off anywhere she can get there very rapidly. When we arrive at the hotel I call her on the house 'phone and tell her I must see her about something very important, so Cynthia says for me to come up.

It is now maybe three-fifteen, and I am somewhat surprised to find Cynthia home, at that, but there she is, and looking very beautiful indeed in a négligée with her hair hanging down, and I can see that The Brain is no chump when it comes to picking them. She gives me a hello pleasant enough, but as soon as I explain what I am there for, her kisser gets very stern and she says to me like this:

"Listen," she says, "I got trouble enough around this joint, what with two guys getting in a fight over me at a little gathering I have here last night and the house copper coming to split them out, and I do not care to have any more. Suppose it gets out that The Brain is here? What will the newspapers print about me? Think of my reputation!"

Well, in about ten minutes I can see there is no use arguing with her, because she can talk faster than I can, and mostly she talks about what a knock it will be to her reputation if she takes The

Brain in, so I leave her standing at the door in her négligée, still looking very beautiful, at that.

There is now nothing for us to do but take The Brain to Bobby Baker, who lives in a duplex apartment in Sutton Place over by the East River, where the swells set up a colony of nice apartments in the heart of an old tenement-house neighborhood, and as we are on our way there with The Brain lying back in the cab just barely breathing, I say to Big Nig like this:

"Nig," I say, "when we get to Bobby's, we will carry The Brain in without asking her first and just dump him on her so she cannot refuse to take him in, although," I say, "Bobby Baker is a nice little doll, and I am pretty sure she will do anything she can for him, especially," I say, "since he pays fifty G's for this apartment we are going to."

So when the taxicab stops in front of Bobby's house, Nig and I take The Brain out of the cab and lug him between us up to the door of Bobby's apartment, where I ring the bell. Bobby opens the door herself, and I happen to see a guy's legs zip into a room in the apartment behind her, although of course there is nothing wrong in such a sight, even though the guy's legs are in pink pajamas.

Naturally, Bobby is greatly astonished to see us with The Brain dangling between us, but she does not invite us in as I explain to her that The Brain is stabbed and that his last words are for us to take him to his Bobby. Furthermore, she does not let me finish my story which will be very sad indeed, if she keeps on listening.

"If you do not take him away from here at once," Bobby says, before I am down to the pathetic part, "I will call the cops and you guys will be arrested on suspicion that you know something about how he gets hurt."

Then she slams the door on us, and we lug The Brain back down the stairs into the street, because all of a sudden it strikes us that Bobby is right, and if The Brain is found in our possession all stabbed up, and he happens to croak, we are in a very tough spot, because the cops just naturally love to refuse to believe guys like Big Nig and me, no matter what we say.

Furthermore, the same idea must hit the taxicab jockey after we lift The Brain out of the cab, because he is nowhere to be seen, and there we are away over by the East River in the early morning, with no other taxis in sight, and a cop liable to happen along any minute.

Well, there is nothing for us to do but get away from there, so Big Nig and I start moving, with me carrying The Brain's feet, and Big Nig his head. We get several blocks away from Sutton Place, going very slow and hiding in dark doorways when we hear anybody coming, and now we are in a section of tenement houses, when all of a sudden up out of the basement of one of these tenements pops a doll.

She sees us before we can get in a dark place, and she seems to have plenty of nerve for a doll, because she comes right over to us and looks at Big Nig and me, and then looks at The Brain, who loses his hat somewhere along the line, so his pale face is plain to be seen by even the dim street light.

"Why," the doll says, "it is the kind gentleman who give me the five dollars for the apple—the money that buys the medicine that saves my Joey's life. What is the matter?"

"Well," I say to the doll, who is still raggedy and still red-headed, "there is nothing much the matter except if we do not get him somewhere soon, this guy will up and croak on us."

"Bring him into my house," she says, pointing to the joint she just comes out of. "It is not much of a place, but you can let him rest there until you get help. I am just going over here to a drug store to get some more medicine for Joey, although he is out of danger now, thanks to this gentleman."

So we lug The Brain down the basement steps with the doll leading the way, and we follow her into a room that smells like a Chinese laundry and seems to be full of kids sleeping on the floor. There is only one bed in the room, and it is not much of a bed any way you take it, and there seems to be a kid in this bed, too, but the red-headed doll rolls this kid over to one side of the bed and motions us to lay The Brain alongside of the kid. Then she gets a wet rag and starts bathing The Brain's noggin.

He finally opens his eyes and looks at the red-headed raggedy doll, and she grins at him very pleasant. When I think things over afterwards, I figure The Brain is conscious of much of what is going on when we are packing him around, although he does not say anything, maybe because he is too weak. Anyway, he turns his head to Big Nig, and says to him like this:

"Bring Weissberger and Frisch as quick as you can," he says. "Anyway, get Weissberger. I do not know how bad I am hurt, and I must tell him some things."

Well, The Brain is hurt pretty bad, as it turns out, and in fact he never gets well, but he stays in the basement dump until he dies three days later, with the red-headed raggedy doll nursing him alongside her sick kid Joey, because the croaker, old Doc Frisch, says it is no good moving The Brain, and may only make him pop off sooner. In fact, Doc Frisch is much astonished that The Brain lives at all, considering the way we lug him around.

I am present at The Brain's funeral at Wiggins's Funeral Parlors, like everybody else on Broadway, and I wish to say I never see more flowers in all my life. They are all over the casket and kneedeep on the floor, and some of the pieces must cost plenty, the price of flowers being what they are in this town nowadays. In fact, I judge it is the size and cost of the different pieces that makes me notice a little bundle of faded red carnations not much bigger than your fist that is laying alongside a pillow of violets the size of a horse blanket.

There is a small card tied to the carnations, and it says on this card, as follows: "To a kind gentleman," and it comes to my mind that out of all the thousands of dollars' worth of flowers there, these faded carnations represent the only true sincerity. I mention this to Big Nig, and he says the chances are I am right, but that even true sincerity is not going to do The Brain any good where he is going.

Anybody will tell you that for off-hand weeping at a funeral The Brain's ever-loving wife Charlotte does herself very proud indeed, but she is not one-two-seven with Doris Clare, Cynthia Harris, and Bobby Baker. In fact, Bobby Baker weeps so loud that there is some talk of heaving her out of the funeral altogether.

However, I afterwards hear that loud as they are at the funeral, it is nothing to the weep they all put on when it comes out that The Brain has Hymie Weissberger draw up a new will while he is dying and leaves all his dough to the red-headed raggedy doll, whose name seems to be O'Halloran, and who is the widow of a bricklayer and has five kids.

Well, at first all the citizens along Broadway say it is a wonderful thing for The Brain to do, and serves his ever-loving wife and Doris and Cynthia and Bobby just right; and from the way one and all speaks you will think they are going to build a monument to The Brain for his generosity to the red-headed raggedy doll.

But about two weeks after he is dead, I hear citizens saying the chances are the red-headed raggedy doll is nothing but one of The

Brain's old-time dolls, and that maybe the kids are his and that he leaves them the dough because his conscience hurts him at the finish, for this is the way Broadway is. But personally I know it cannot be true, for if there is one thing The Brain never has it is a conscience.

THE SNATCHING OF
BOOKIE BOB

Now it comes on the spring of 1931, after a long hard winter, and times are very tough indeed, what with the stock market going all to pieces, and banks busting right and left, and the law getting very nasty about this and that, and one thing and another, and many citizens of this town are compelled to do the best they can.

There is very little scratch anywhere and along Broadway many citizens are wearing their last year's clothes and have practically nothing to bet on the races or anything else, and it is a condition that will touch anybody's heart.

So I am not surprised to hear rumors that the snatching of certain parties is going on in spots, because while snatching is by no means a high-class business, and is even considered somewhat illegal, it is something to tide over the hard times.

Furthermore, I am not surprised to hear that this snatching is being done by a character by the name of Harry the Horse, who comes from Brooklyn, and who is a character who does not care much what sort of business he is in, and who is mobbed up with other characters from Brooklyn such as Spanish John and Little Isadore, who do not care what sort of business they are in, either.

In fact, Harry the Horse and Spanish John and Little Isadore are very hard characters in every respect, and there is considerable indignation expressed around and about when they move over from Brooklyn into Manhattan and start snatching, because the citizens of Manhattan feel that if there is any snatching done in their territory, they are entitled to do it themselves.

But Harry the Horse and Spanish John and Little Isadore pay no attention whatever to local sentiment and go on the snatch on a pretty fair scale, and by and by I am hearing rumors of some very nice scores. These scores are not extra large scores, to be sure, but they are enough to keep the wolf from the door, and in fact from three different doors, and before long Harry the Horse and Spanish John and Little Isadore are around the race tracks betting on the horses, because if there is one thing they are all very fond of, it is betting on the horses.

Now many citizens have the wrong idea entirely of the snatching business. Many citizens think that all there is to snatching is to round up the party who is to be snatched, and then just snatch him, putting him away somewhere until his family or friends dig up enough scratch to pay whatever price the snatchers are asking. Very few citizens understand that the snatching business must be well organized and very systematic.

In the first place, if you are going to do any snatching, you cannot snatch just anybody. You must know who you are snatching, because naturally it is no good snatching somebody who does not have any scratch to settle with. And you cannot tell by the way a party looks or how he lives in this town if he has any scratch, because many a party who is around in automobiles, and wearing good clothes, and chucking quite a swell is nothing but the phonus bolonus and does not have any real scratch whatever.

So of course such a party is no good for snatching, and of course guys who are on the snatch cannot go around inquiring into bank accounts, or asking how much this and that party has in a safe-deposit vault, because such questions are apt to make citizens wonder why, and it is very dangerous to get citizens to wondering why about anything. So the only way guys who are on the snatch can find out about parties worth snatching is to make a connection with some guy who can put the finger on the right party.

The finger guy must know the party he fingers has plenty of ready scratch to begin with, and he must also know that this party is such a party as is not apt to make too much disturbance about being snatched, such as telling the gendarmes. The party may be a legitimate party, such as a business guy, but he will have reasons why he does not wish it to get out that he is snatched, and the finger must know the reasons. Maybe the party is not leading the right sort of life, such as running around with blondes when he has an ever-loving wife and seven children in Mamaroneck, but does not care to have his habits known, as is apt to happen if he is snatched, especially if he is snatched when he is with a blonde.

And sometimes the party is such a party as does not care to have matches run up and down the bottom of his feet, which often happens to parties who are snatched and who do not seem to wish to settle their bill promptly, because many parties are very ticklish on the bottom of the feet, especially if the matches are lit. On the other hand maybe the party is not a legitimate guy, such as a party who is running a crap game or a swell speakeasy, or who has some other dodge he does not care to have come out, and who also does not care about having his feet tickled.

Such a party is very good indeed for the snatching business, because he is pretty apt to settle without any argument. And after a party settles one snatching, it will be considered very unethical for anybody else to snatch him again very soon, so he is not likely to make any fuss about the matter. The finger guy gets a commission of twenty-five per cent of the settlement, and one and all are satisfied and much fresh scratch comes into circulation, which is very good for the merchants. And while the party who is snatched may know who snatches him, one thing he never knows is who puts the finger on him, this being considered a trade secret.

I am talking to Waldo Winchester, the newspaper scribe, one night and something about the snatching business comes up, and Waldo Winchester is trying to tell me that it is one of the oldest dodges in the world, only Waldo calls it kidnapping, which is a title that will be very repulsive to guys who are on the snatch nowadays. Waldo Winchester claims that hundreds of years ago guys are around snatching parties, male and female, and holding them for ransom, and furthermore Waldo Winchester says they even snatch very little children and Waldo states that it is all a very, very wicked proposition.

Well, I can see where Waldo is right about it being wicked to snatch dolls and little children, but of course no guys who are on the snatch nowadays will ever think of such a thing, because who is going to settle for a doll in these times when you can scarcely even give them away? As for little children, they are apt to be a great nuisance, because their mammas are sure to go running around hollering bloody murder about them, and furthermore little children are very dangerous indeed, what with being apt to break out with measles and mumps and one thing and another any minute and give it to everybody in the neighborhood.

Well, anyway, knowing that Harry the Horse and Spanish John

and Little Isadore are now on the snatch, I am by no means pleased to see them come along one Tuesday evening when I am standing at the corner of Fiftieth and Broadway, although of course I give them a very jolly hello, and say I hope and trust they are feeling nicely.

They stand there talking to me a few minutes, and I am very glad indeed that Johnny Brannigan, the strong-arm cop, does not happen along and see us, because it will give Johnny a very bad impression of me to see me in such company, even though I am not responsible for the company. But naturally I cannot haul off and walk away from this company at once, because Harry the Horse and Spanish John and Little Isadore may get the idea that I am playing the chill for them, and will feel hurt.

"Well," I say to Harry the Horse, "how are things going, Harry?"

"They are going no good," Harry says. "We do not beat a race in four days. In fact," he says, "we go overboard to-day. We are washed out. We owe every bookmaker at the track that will trust us, and now we are out trying to raise some scratch to pay off. A guy must pay his bookmaker no matter what."

Well, of course this is very true indeed, because if a guy does not pay his bookmaker it will lower his business standing quite some, as the bookmaker is sure to go around putting the blast on him, so I am pleased to hear Harry the Horse mention such honorable principles.

"By the way," Harry says, "do you know a guy by the name of Bookie Bob?"

Now I do not know Bookie Bob personally, but of course I know who Bookie Bob is, and so does everybody else in this town that ever goes to a race track, because Bookie Bob is the biggest bookmaker around and about, and has plenty of scratch. Furthermore, it is the opinion of one and all that Bookie Bob will die with this scratch, because he is considered a very close guy with his scratch. In fact, Bookie Bob is considered closer than a dead heat.

He is a short fat guy with a bald head, and his head is always shaking a little from side to side, which some say is a touch of palsy, but which most citizens believe comes of Bookie Bob shaking his head "No" to guys asking for credit in betting on the races. He has an ever-loving wife, who is a very quiet little old doll with gray hair and a very sad look in her eyes, but nobody can blame her for this when they figure that she lives with Bookie Bob for many years.

I often see Bookie Bob and his ever-loving wife eating in different joints along in the Forties, because they seem to have no home except an hotel, and many a time I hear Bookie Bob giving her a going-over about something or other, and generally it is about the price of something she orders to eat, so I judge Bookie Bob is as tough with his ever-loving wife about scratch as he is with everybody else. In fact, I hear him bawling her out one night because she has on a new hat which she says cost her six bucks, and Bookie Bob wishes to know if she is trying to ruin him with her extravagances.

But of course I am not criticizing Bookie Bob for squawking about the hat, because for all I know six bucks may be too much for a doll to pay for a hat, at that. And furthermore, maybe Bookie Bob has the right idea about keeping down his ever-loving wife's appetite, because I know many a guy in this town who is practically ruined by dolls eating too much on him.

"Well," I say to Harry the Horse, "if Bookie Bob is one of the bookmakers you owe, I am greatly surprised to see that you seem to have both eyes in your head, because I never before hear of Bookie Bob letting anybody owe him without giving him at least one of their eyes for security. In fact," I say, "Bookie Bob is such a guy as will not give you the right time if he has two watches."

"No," Harry the Horse says, "we do not owe Bookie Bob. But," he says, "he will be owing us before long. We are going to put the snatch on Bookie Bob."

Well, this is most disquieting news to me, not because I care if they snatch Bookie Bob or not, but because somebody may see me talking to them who will remember about it when Bookie Bob is snatched. But of course it will not be good policy for me to show Harry the Horse and Spanish John and Little Isadore that I am nervous, so I only speak as follows:

"Harry," I say, "every man knows his own business best, and I judge you know what you are doing. But," I say, "you are snatching a hard guy when you snatch Bookie Bob. A very hard guy indeed. In fact," I say, "I hear the softest thing about him is his front teeth, so it may be very difficult for you to get him to settle after you snatch him."

"No," Harry the Horse says, "we will have no trouble about it. Our finger gives us Bookie Bob's hole card, and it is a most surprising thing indeed. But," Harry the Horse says, "you come upon many surprising things in human nature when you are on the snatch. Bookie Bob's hole card is his ever-loving wife's opinion of him.

"You see," Harry the Horse says, "Bookie Bob has been putting himself away with his ever-loving wife for years as a very important guy in this town, with much power and influence, although of course Bookie Bob knows very well he stands about as good as a broken leg. In fact," Harry the Horse says, "Bookie Bob figures that his ever-loving wife is the only one in the world who looks on him as a big guy, and he will sacrifice even his scratch, or anyway some of it, rather than let her know that guys have such little respect for him as to put the snatch on him. It is what you call psychology," Harry the Horse says.

Well, this does not make good sense to me, and I am thinking to myself that the psychology that Harry the Horse really figures to work out nice on Bookie Bob is tickling his feet with matches, but I am not anxious to stand there arguing about it, and pretty soon I bid them all good evening, very polite, and take the wind and I do not see Harry the Horse or Spanish John or Little Isadore again for a month.

In the meantime, I hear gossip here and there that Bookie Bob is missing for several days, and when he finally shows up again he gives it out that he is very sick during his absence, but I can put two and two together as well as anybody in this town and I figure that Bookie Bob is snatched by Harry the Horse and Spanish John and Little Isadore, and the chances are it costs him plenty.

So I am looking for Harry the Horse and Spanish John and Little Isadore to be around the race track with plenty of scratch and betting them higher than a cat's back, but they never show up, and what is more I hear they leave Manhattan and are back in Brooklyn working every day handling beer. Naturally this is very surprising to me, because the way things are running beer is a tough dodge just now, and there is very little profit in same, and I figure that with the scratch they must make off Bookie Bob, Harry the Horse and Spanish John and Little Isadore have a right to be taking things easy.

Now one night I am in Good Time Charley Bernstein's little speak on Forty-eighth Street, speaking of this and that with Charley, when in comes Harry the Horse, looking very weary and by no means prosperous. Naturally I gave him a large hello, and by and by we get to gabbing together and I ask him whatever becomes of the Bookie Bob matter, and Harry the Horse tells me as follows:

Yes (Harry the Horse says), we snatch Bookie Bob all right. In fact, we snatch him the very next night after we are talking to you, or on a Wednesday night. Our finger tells us Bookie Bob is going to a wake over in his old neighborhood on Tenth Avenue, near Thirty-eighth Street, and this is where we pick him up.

He is leaving the place in his car along about midnight, and of course Bookie Bob is alone as he seldom lets anybody ride with him because of the wear and tear on his car cushions, and Little Isadore swings our flivver in front of him and makes him stop. Naturally Bookie Bob is greatly surprised when I poke my head into his car and tell him I wish the pleasure of his company for a short time, and at first he is inclined to argue the matter, saying I must make a mistake, but I put the old convincer on him by letting him peek down the snozzle of my John Roscoe.

We lock his car and throw the keys away, and then we take Bookie Bob in our car and go to a certain spot on Eighth Avenue where we have a nice little apartment all ready. When we get there I tell Bookie Bob that he can call up anybody he wishes and state that the snatch is on him and that it will require twenty-five G's, cash money, to take it off, but of course I also tell Bookie Bob that he is not to mention where he is or something may happen to him.

Well, I will say one thing for Bookie Bob, although everybody is always weighing in the sacks on him and saying he is no good—he takes it like a gentleman, and very calm and businesslike.

Furthermore, he does not seem alarmed, as many citizens are when they find themselves in such a situation. He recognizes the justice of our claim at once, saying as follows:

"I will telephone my partner, Sam Salt," he says. "He is the only one I can think of who is apt to have such a sum as twenty-five G's cash money. But," he says, "if you gentlemen will pardon the question, because this is a new experience to me, how do I know everything will be okay for me after you get the scratch?"

"Why," I say to Bookie Bob, somewhat indignant, "it is well known to one and all in this town that my word is my bond. There are two things I am bound to do," I say, "and one is to keep my word in such a situation as this, and the other is to pay anything I owe a bookmaker, no matter what, for these are obligations of honor with me."

"Well," Bookie Bob says, "of course I do not know you gentlemen, and, in fact, I do not remember ever seeing any of you, although your face is somewhat familiar, but if you pay your bookmaker you are an honest guy, and one in a million. In fact," Bookie Bob says, "if I have all the scratch that is owing to me around this town, I will not be telephoning anybody for such a sum as twenty-five G's. I will have such a sum in my pants pocket for change."

Now Bookie Bob calls a certain number and talks to somebody there but he does not get Sam Salt, and he seems much disappointed when he hangs up the receiver again.

"This is a very tough break for me," he says. "Sam Salt goes to Atlantic City an hour ago on very important business and will not be back until to-morrow evening, and they do not know where he is to stay in Atlantic City. And," Bookie Bob says, "I cannot think of anybody else to call up to get this scratch, especially anybody I will care to have know I am in this situation."

"Why not call your ever-loving wife?" I say. "Maybe she can dig up this kind of scratch."

"Say," Bookie Bob says, "you do not suppose I am chump enough to give my ever-loving wife twenty-five G's, or even let her know where she can get her dukes on twenty-five G's belonging to me, do you? I give my ever-loving wife ten bucks per week for spending money," Bookie Bob says, "and this is enough scratch for any doll, especially when you figure I pay for her meals."

Well, there seems to be nothing we can do except wait until Sam Salt gets back, but we let Bookie Bob call his ever-loving wife, as Bookie Bob says he does not wish to have her worrying about his absence, and tells her a big lie about having to go to Jersey City to sit up with a sick Brother Elk.

Well, it is now nearly four o'clock in the morning, so we put Bookie Bob in a room with Little Isadore to sleep, although, personally, I consider making a guy sleep with Little Isadore very cruel treatment, and Spanish John and I take turns keeping awake and watching out that Bookie Bob does not take the air on us before paying us off. To tell the truth, Little Isadore and Spanish

John are somewhat disappointed that Bookie Bob agreed to settle so promptly, because they are looking forward to tickling his feet with great relish.

Now Bookie Bob turns out to be very good company when he wakes up the next morning, because he knows a lot of race-track stories and plenty of scandal, and he keeps us much interested at breakfast. He talks along with us as if he knows us all his life, and he seems very nonchalant indeed, but the chances are he will not be so nonchalant if I tell him about Spanish John's thought.

Well, about noon Spanish John goes out of the apartment and comes back with a racing sheet, because he knows Little Isadore and I will be wishing to know what is running in different spots although we do not have anything to bet on these races, or any way of betting on them, because we are overboard with every book-maker we know.

Now Bookie Bob is also much interested in the matter of what is running, especially at Belmont, and he is bending over the table with me and Spanish John and Little Isadore, looking at the sheet, when Spanish John speaks as follows:

"My goodness," Spanish John says, "a spot such as this fifth race with Questionnaire at four to five is like finding money in the street. I only wish I have a few bobs to bet on him at such a price," Spanish John says.

"Why," Bookie Bob says, very polite, "if you gentlemen wish to bet on these races I will gladly book to you. It is a good way to pass away the time while we are waiting for Sam Salt, unless you will rather play pinochle?"

"But," I say, "we have no scratch to play the races, at least not much."

"Well," Bookie Bob says, "I will take your markers, because I hear what you say about always paying your bookmaker, and you put yourself away with me as an honest guy, and these other gentlemen also impress me as honest guys."

Now what happens but we begin betting Bookie Bob on the different races, not only at Belmont, but at all the other tracks in the country, for Little Isadore and Spanish John and I are guys who like plenty of action when we start betting on the horses. We write out markers for whatever we wish to bet and hand them to Bookie Bob, and Bookie Bob sticks these markers in an inside pocket, and along in the late afternoon it looks as if he has a tumor on his chest.

We get the race results by phone off a poolroom downtown as fast as they come off, and also the prices, and it is a lot of fun, and Little Isadore and Spanish John and Bookie Bob and I are all little pals together until all the races are over and Bookie Bob takes out the markers and starts counting himself up.

It comes out then that I owe Bookie Bob ten G's, and Spanish John owes him six G's, and Little Isadore owes him four G's, as Little Isadore beats him a couple of races out west.

Well, about this time, Bookie Bob manages to get Sam Salt on the phone, and explains to Sam that he is to go to a certain safe-deposit box and get out twenty-five G's, and then wait until midnight and hire himself a taxicab and start riding around the block between Fifty-first and Fifty-second, from Eighth to Ninth avenues, and to keep riding until somebody flags the cab and takes the scratch off of him.

Naturally Sam Salt understands right away that the snatch is on Bookie Bob, and he agrees to do as he is told, but he says he cannot do it until the following night because he knows there is not twenty-five G's in the box and he will have to get the difference at the track the next day. So there we are with another day in the apartment and Spanish John and Little Isadore and I are just as well pleased because Bookie Bob has us hooked and we naturally wish to wiggle off.

But the next day is worse than ever. In all the years I am playing the horses I never have such a tough day, and Spanish John and Little Isadore are just as bad. In fact, we are all going so bad that Bookie Bob seems to feel sorry for us and often lays us a couple of points above the track prices, but it does no good. At the end of the day, I am in a total of twenty G's, while Spanish John owes fifteen, and Little Isadore fifteen, a total of fifty G's among the three of us. But we are never any hands to hold post-mortems on bad days, so Little Isadore goes out to a delicatessen store and lugs in a lot of nice things to eat, and we have a fine dinner, and then we sit around with Bookie Bob telling stories, and even singing a few songs together until time to meet Sam Salt.

When it comes on midnight Spanish John goes out and lays for Sam, and gets a little valise off of Sam Salt. Then Spanish John comes back to the apartment and we open the valise and the twenty-five G's are there okay, and we cut this scratch three ways.

Then I tell Bookie Bob he is free to go on about his business, and good luck to him, at that, but Bookie Bob looks at me as if he is very much surprised, and hurt, and says to me like this:

"Well, gentlemen, thank you for your courtesy, but what about the scratch you owe me? What about these markers? Surely, gentlemen, you will pay your bookmaker?"

Well, of course we owe Bookie Bob these markers, all right, and of course a man must pay his bookmaker, no matter what, so I hand over my bit and Bookie Bob puts down something in a little notebook that he takes out of his kick.

Then Spanish John and Little Isadore hand over their dough, too, and Bookie Bob puts down something more in the little notebook.

"Now," Bookie Bob says, "I credit each of your accounts with these payments, but you gentlemen still owe me a matter of twenty-five G's over and above the twenty-five I credit you with, and I hope and trust you will make arrangements to settle this at once, because," he says, "I do not care to extend such accommodations over any considerable period."

"But," I say, "we do not have any more scratch after paying you the twenty-five G's on account."

"Listen," Bookie Bob says, dropping his voice down to a whisper, "what about putting the snatch on my partner, Sam Salt, and I will wait over a couple of days with you and keep booking to you, and maybe you can pull yourselves out. But of course," Bookie Bob whispers, "I will be entitled to twenty-five per cent of the snatch for putting the finger on Sam for you."

But Spanish John and Little Isadore are sick and tired of Bookie Bob and will not listen to staying in the apartment any longer, because they say he is a jinx to them and they cannot beat him in any manner, shape, or form. Furthermore, I am personally anxious to get away because something Bookie Bob says reminds me of something.

It reminds me that besides the scratch we owe him, we forget to take out six G's two-fifty for the party who puts the finger on Bookie Bob for us, and this is a very serious matter indeed, because anybody will tell you that failing to pay a finger is considered a very dirty trick. Furthermore, if it gets around that you fail to pay a finger, nobody else will ever finger for you.

So (Harry the Horse says) we quit the snatching business because there is no use continuing while this obligation is outstanding against us, and we go back to Brooklyn to earn enough scratch to pay our just debts.

We are paying off Bookie Bob's I O U a little at a time, because we do not wish to ever have anybody say we welsh on a book-maker, and furthermore we are paying off the six G's two-fifty commission we owe our finger.

And while it is tough going, I am glad to say our honest effort is doing somebody a little good, because I see Bookie Bob's ever-loving wife the other night all dressed up in new clothes and look-ing very happy indeed.

And while a guy is telling me she is looking so happy because she gets a large legacy from an uncle who dies in Switzerland, and is now independent of Bookie Bob, I only hope and trust (Harry the Horse says) that it never get out that our finger in this case is nobody but Bookie Bob's ever-loving wife.

HOLD 'EM, YALE!

What I am doing in New Haven on the day of a very large football game between the Harvards and the Yales is something which calls for quite a little explanation, because I am not such a guy as you will expect to find in New Haven at any time, and especially on the day of a large football game.

But there I am, and the reason I am there goes back to a Friday night when I am sitting in Mindy's restaurant on Broadway thinking of very little except how I can get hold of a few potatoes to take care of the old overhead. And while I am sitting there, who comes in but Sam the Gonoph, who is a ticket speculator by trade, and who seems to be looking all around and about.

Well, Sam the Gonoph gets to talking to me, and it turns out that he is looking for a guy by the name of Gigolo Georgie, who is called Gigolo Georgie because he is always hanging around night clubs wearing a little moustache and white spats, and dancing with old dolls. In fact, Gigolo Georgie is nothing but a gentleman bum, and I am surprised that Sam the Gonoph is looking for him.

But it seems that the reason Sam the Gonoph wishes to find Gigolo Georgie is to give him a good punch in the snoot, because it seems that Gigolo Georgie promotes Sam for several duckets to the large football game between the Harvards and the Yales to sell on commission, and never kicks back anything whatever to Sam. Naturally Sam considers Gigolo Georgie nothing but a rascal for doing such a thing to him, and Sam says he will find Gigolo Georgie and give him a going-over if it is the last act of his life.

Well, then, Sam explains to me that he has quite a few nice duckets for the large football game between the Harvards and the Yales and that he is taking a crew of guys with him to New Haven the next day to hustle these duckets, and what about me going along and helping to hustle these duckets and making a few bobs for myself, which is an invitation that sounds very pleasant to me indeed.

Now of course it is very difficult for anybody to get nice duckets to a large football game between the Harvards and the Yales unless they are personally college guys, and Sam the Gonoph is by no means a college guy. In fact, the nearest Sam ever comes to a college is once when he is passing through the yard belonging to the Princetons, but Sam is on the fly at the time as a gendarme is after him, so he does not really see much of the college.

But every college guy is entitled to duckets to a large football game with which his college is connected, and it is really surprising how many college guys do not care to see large football games even after they get their duckets, especially if a ticket spec such as Sam the Gonoph comes along offering them a few bobs more than the duckets are worth. I suppose this is because a college guy figures he can see a large football game when he is old, while many things are taking place around and about that is necessary for him to see while he is young enough to really enjoy them, such as the *Follies*.

Anyway, many college guys are always willing to listen to reason when Sam the Gonoph comes around offering to buy their duckets, and then Sam takes these duckets and sells them to customers for maybe ten times the price the duckets call for, and in this way Sam does very good for himself.

I know Sam the Gonoph for maybe twenty years, and always he is speculating in duckets of one kind and another. Sometimes it is duckets for the World Series, and sometimes for big fights, and sometimes it is duckets for nothing but lawn-tennis games, although why anybody wishes to see such a thing as lawn tennis is always a very great mystery to Sam the Gonoph and everybody else.

But in all those years I see Sam dodging around under the feet of the crowds at these large events, or running through the special trains offering to buy or sell duckets, I never hear of Sam personally attending any of these events except maybe a baseball game, or a fight, for Sam has practically no interest in anything but a little profit on his duckets.

He is a short, chunky, black-looking guy with a big beezer, and he is always sweating even on a cold day, and he comes from down around Essex Street, on the Lower East Side. Moreover, Sam the Gonoph's crew generally comes from the Lower East Side, too, for as Sam goes along he makes plenty of potatoes for himself and

branches out quite some, and has a lot of assistants hustling duckets around these different events.

When Sam is younger the cops consider him hard to get along
with, and in fact his monicker, the Gonoph, comes from his young
days down on the Lower East Side, and I hear it is Yiddish for
thief, but of course as Sam gets older and starts gathering plenty
of potatoes, he will not think of stealing anything. At least not
much, and especially if it is anything that is nailed down.

Well, anyway, I meet Sam the Gonoph and his crew at the information desk in Grand Central the next morning, and this is
how I come to be in New Haven on the day of the large football
game between the Harvards and the Yales.

For such a game as this, Sam has all his best hustlers, including
such as Jew Louie, Nubbsy Taylor, Benny South Street, and old
Liverlips, and to look at these parties you will never suspect that
they are top-notch ducket hustlers. The best you will figure them
is a lot of guys who are not to be met up with in a dark alley, but
then ducket-hustling is a rough-and-tumble dodge and it will
scarcely be good policy to hire female impersonators.

Now while we are hustling these duckets out around the main
gates of the Yale Bowl I notice a very beautiful little doll of maybe
sixteen or seventeen standing around watching the crowd, and I
can see she is waiting for somebody, as many dolls often do at football games. But I can also see that this little doll is very much worried as the crowd keeps going in, and it is getting on toward game
time. In fact, by and by I can see this little doll has tears in her eyes
and if there is anything I hate to see it is tears in a doll's eyes.

So finally I go over to her, and I say as follows: "What is eating
you, little Miss?"

"Oh," she says, "I am waiting for Elliot. He is to come up from
New York and meet me here to take me to the game, but he is not
here yet, and I am afraid something happens to him. Furthermore,"
she says, the tears in her eyes getting very large indeed, "I am
afraid I will miss the game because he has my ticket."

"Why," I say, "this is a very simple proposition. I will sell you a
choice ducket for only a sawbuck, which is ten dollars in your language, and you are getting such a bargain only because the game
is about to begin, and the market is going down."

"But," she says, "I do not have ten dollars. In fact, I have only
fifty cents left in my purse, and this is worrying me very much, for

what will I do if Elliot does not meet me? You see," she says, "I come from Miss Peevy's school at Worcester, and I only have enough money to pay my railroad fare here, and of course I cannot ask Miss Peevy for any money as I do not wish her to know I am going away."

Well, naturally all this is commencing to sound to me like a hard-luck story such as any doll is apt to tell, so I go on about my business because I figure she will next be trying to put the lug on me for a ducket, or maybe for her railroad fare back to Worcester, although generally dolls with hard-luck stories live in San Francisco.

She keeps on standing there, and I notice she is now crying more than somewhat, and I get to thinking to myself that she is about as cute a little doll as I ever see, although too young for anybody to be bothering much about. Furthermore, I get to thinking that maybe she is on the level, at that, with her story.

Well, by this time the crowd is nearly all in the Bowl, and only a few parties such as coppers and hustlers of one kind and another are left standing outside, and there is much cheering going on inside, when Sam the Gonoph comes up looking very much disgusted, and speaks as follows:

"What do you think?" Sam says. "I am left with seven duckets on my hands, and these guys around here will not pay as much as face value for them, and they stand me better than three bucks over that. Well," Sam says, "I am certainly not going to let them go for less than they call for if I have to eat them. What do you guys say we use these duckets ourselves and go in and see the game? Personally," Sam says, "I often wish to see one of these large football games just to find out what makes suckers willing to pay so much for duckets."

Well, this seems to strike one and all, including myself, as a great idea, because none of the rest of us ever see a large football game either, so we start for the gate, and as we pass the little doll who is still crying, I say to Sam the Gonoph like this:

"Listen, Sam," I say, "you have seven duckets, and we are only six, and here is a little doll who is stood up by her guy, and has no ducket, and no potatoes to buy one with, so what about taking her with us?"

Well, this is all right with Sam the Gonoph, and none of the others object, so I step up to the little doll and invite her to go with us, and right away she stops crying and begins smiling, and saying we are very kind indeed. She gives Sam the Gonoph an extra big smile, and right away Sam is saying she is very cute indeed, and then she gives old Liverlips an even bigger smile, and what is more she takes old Liverlips by the arm and walks with him, and old Liverlips is not only very much astonished, but very much pleased. In fact, old Liverlips begins stepping out very spry, and Liverlips is not such a guy as cares to have any part of dolls, young or old.

But while walking with old Liverlips, the little doll talks very friendly to Jew Louie and to Nubbsy Taylor and Benny South Street, and even to me, and by and by you will think to see us that we are all her uncles, although of course if this little doll really knows who she is with, the chances are she will start chucking faints one after the other.

Anybody can see that she has very little experience in this wicked old world, and in fact is somewhat rattleheaded, because she gabs away very freely about her personal business. In fact, before we are in the Bowl she lets it out that she runs away from Miss Peevy's school to elope with this Elliot, and she says the idea is they are to be married in Hartford after the game. In fact, she says Elliot wishes to go to Hartford and be married before the game.

"But," she says, "my brother John is playing substitute with the Yales today, and I cannot think of getting married to anybody before I see him play, although I am much in love with Elliot. He is a wonderful dancer," she says, "and very romantic. I meet him in Atlantic City last summer. Now we are eloping," she says, "because my father does not care for Elliot whatever. In fact, my father hates Elliot, although he only sees him once, and it is because he hates Elliot so that my father sends me to Miss Peevy's school in Worcester. She is an old pill. Do you not think my father is unreasonable?" she says.

Well, of course none of us have any ideas on such propositions as this, although old Liverlips tells the little doll he is with her right or wrong, and pretty soon we are inside the Bowl and sitting in seats as good as any in the joint. It seems we are on the Harvards' side of the field, although of course I will never know this if the little doll does not mention it.

She seems to know everything about this football business, and as soon as we sit down she tries to point out her brother playing substitute for the Yales, saying he is the fifth guy from the end among a bunch of guys sitting on a bench on the other side of the field all wrapped in blankets. But we cannot make much of him from where we sit, and anyway it does not look to me as if he has much of a job.

It seems we are right in the middle of all the Harvards and they are making an awful racket, what with yelling, and singing, and one thing and another, because it seems the game is going on when we get in, and that the Harvards are shoving the Yales around more than somewhat. So our little doll lets everybody know she is in favor of the Yales by yelling, "Hold 'em, Yale!"

Personally, I cannot tell which are the Harvards and which are the Yales at first, and Sam the Gonoph and the others are as dumb as I am, but she explains the Harvards are wearing the red shirts and the Yales the blue shirts, and by and by we are yelling for the Yales to hold 'em, too, although of course it is only on account of our little doll wishing the Yales to hold 'em, and not because any of us care one way or the other.

Well, it seems that the idea of a lot of guys and a little doll getting right among them and yelling for the Yales to hold 'em is very repulsive to the Harvards around us, although any of them must admit it is very good advice to the Yales, at that, and some of them start making cracks of one kind and another, especially at our little doll. The chances are they are very jealous because she is outyelling them, because I will say one thing for our little doll, she can yell about as loud as anybody I ever hear, male or female.

A couple of Harvards sitting in front of old Liverlips are imitating our little doll's voice, and making guys around them laugh very heartily, but all of a sudden these parties leave their seats and go away in great haste, their faces very pale indeed, and I figure maybe they are both taken sick at the same moment, but afterwards I learn that Liverlips takes a big shiv out of his pocket and opens it and tells them very confidentially that he is going to carve their ears off.

Naturally, I do not blame the Harvards for going away in great haste, for Liverlips is such a looking guy as you will figure to take great delight in carving off ears. Furthermore, Nubbsy Taylor and Benny South Street and Jew Louie and even Sam the Gonoph commence exchanging such glances with other Harvards around us who are making cracks at our little doll that presently there is almost a dead silence in our neighborhood, except for our little doll yelling, "Hold 'em, Yale!" You see by this time we are all very fond of our little doll because she is so cute-looking and has so much zing in her, and we do not wish anybody making cracks at her or at us either, and especially at us.

In fact, we are so fond of her that when she happens to mention that she is a little chilly, Jew Louie and Nubbsy Taylor slip around among the Harvards and come back with four steamer rugs, six mufflers, two pairs of gloves and a thermos bottle full of hot coffee for her, and Jew Louie says if she wishes a mink coat to just say the word. But she already has a mink coat. Furthermore, Jew Louie brings her a big bunch of red flowers that he finds on a doll with one of the Harvards, and he is much disappointed when she says it is the wrong color for her.

Well, finally the game is over, and I do not remember much about it, although afterwards I hear that our little doll's brother John plays substitute for the Yales very good. But it seems that the Harvards win, and our little doll is very sad indeed about this, and is sitting there looking out over the field, which is now covered with guys dancing around as if they all suddenly go daffy, and it seems they are all Harvards, because there is really no reason for the Yales to do any dancing.

All of a sudden our little doll looks toward one end of the field, and says as follows:

"Oh, they are going to take our goalposts!"

Sure enough, a lot of Harvards are gathering around the posts at this end of the field, and are pulling and hauling at the posts, which seem to be very stout posts indeed. Personally, I will not give you eight cents for these posts, but afterwards one of the Yales tells me that when a football team wins a game it is considered the proper caper for this team's boosters to grab the other guys' goalposts. But he is not able to tell me what good the posts are after they get them, and this is one thing that will always be a mystery to me.

Anyway, while we are watching the goings-on around the goalposts, our little doll says come on and jumps up and runs down an aisle and out onto the field, and into the crowd around the goalposts, so naturally we follow her. Somehow she manages to wiggle through the crowd of Harvards around the posts, and the next thing anybody knows she shins up one of the posts faster than you can say scat, and pretty soon is roosting out on the crossbar between the posts like a chipmunk.

Afterwards she explains that her idea is the Harvards will not be ungentlemanly enough to pull down the goalposts with a lady roosting on them, but it seems these Harvards are no gentlemen, and keep on pulling, and the posts commence to teeter, and our little doll is teetering with them, although of course she is in no danger if she falls because she is sure to fall on the Harvards' noggins, and the way I look at it, the noggin of anybody who will be found giving any time to pulling down goalposts is apt to be soft enough to break a very long fall.

Now Sam the Gonoph and old Liverlips and Nubbsy Taylor and Benny South Street and Jew Louie and I reach the crowd around the goalposts at about the same time, and our little doll sees us from her roost and yells to us as follows:

"Do not let them take our posts!"

Well, about this time one of the Harvards who seems to be about nine feet high reaches over six other guys and hits me on the chin and knocks me so far that when I pick myself up I am pretty well out of the way of everybody and have a chance to see what is going on.

Afterwards somebody tells me that the guy probably thinks I am one of the Yales coming to the rescue of the goalposts, but I wish to say I will always have a very low opinion of college guys, because I remember two other guys punch me as I am going through the air, unable to defend myself.

Now Sam the Gonoph and Nubbsy Taylor and Jew Louie and Benny South Street and old Liverlips somehow manage to ease their way through the crowd until they are under the goalposts, and our little doll is much pleased to see them, because the Harvards are now making the posts teeter more than somewhat with their pulling, and it looks as if the posts will go any minute.

Of course Sam the Gonoph does not wish any trouble with these parties, and he tries to speak nicely to the guys who are pulling at the posts, saying as follows:

"Listen," Sam says, "the little doll up there does not wish you to take these posts."

Well, maybe they do not hear Sam's words in the confusion, or if they do hear them they do not wish to pay any attention to them, for one of the Harvards mashes Sam's derby hat down over his eyes, and another smacks old Liverlips on the left ear, while Jew Louie and Nubbsy Taylor and Benny South Street are shoved around quite some.

"All right," Sam the Gonoph says, as soon as he can pull his hat off his eyes, "all right, gentlemen, if you wish to play this way. Now, boys, let them have it!"

So Sam the Gonoph and Nubbsy Taylor and Jew Louie and Benny South Street and old Liverlips begin letting them have it, and what they let them have it with is not only their dukes, but with the good old difference in their dukes, because these guys are by no means suckers when it comes to a battle, and they all carry something in their pockets to put in their dukes in case of a fight, such as a dollar's worth of nickels rolled up tight.

Furthermore, they are using the old leather, kicking guys in the stomach when they are not able to hit them on the chin, and Liverlips is also using his noodle to good advantage, grabbing guys by their coat lapels and yanking them into him so he can butt them between the eyes with his noggin, and I wish to say that old Liverlips' noggin is a very dangerous weapon at all times.

Well, the ground around them is soon covered with Harvards, and it seems that some Yales are also mixed up with them, being Yales who think Sam the Gonoph and his guys are other Yales defending the goalposts, and wishing to help out. But of course Sam the Gonoph and his guys cannot tell the Yales from the Harvards, and do not have time to ask which is which, so they are just letting everybody have it who comes along. And while all this is going on our little doll is sitting up on the crossbar and yelling plenty of encouragement to Sam and his guys.

Now it turns out that these Harvards are by no means soft touches in a scrabble such as this, and as fast as they are flattened they get up and keep belting away, and while the old experience is running for Sam the Gonoph and Jew Louie and Nubbsy Taylor and Benny South Street and old Liverlips early in the fight, the Harvards have youth in their favor.

Pretty soon the Harvards are knocking down Sam the Gonoph, then they start knocking down Nubbsy Taylor, and by and by they are knocking down Benny South Street and Jew Louie and Liverlips, and it is so much fun that the Harvards forget all about the goalposts. Of course as fast as Sam the Gonoph and his guys are knocked down they also get up, but the Harvards are too many for them, and they are getting an awful shellacking when the nine-foot guy who flattens me, and who is knocking down Sam the Gonoph so often he is becoming a great nuisance to Sam, sings out:

"Listen," he says, "these are game guys, even if they do go to Yale. Let us cease knocking them down," he says, "and give them a cheer."

So the Harvards knock down Sam the Gonoph and Nubbsy Taylor and Jew Louie and Benny South Street and Old Liverlips just once more and then all the Harvards put their heads together and say rah-rah-rah, very loud, and go away, leaving the goalposts still standing, with our little doll still roosting on the crossbar, although afterwards I hear some Harvards who are not in the fight get the posts at the other end of the field and sneak away with them. But I always claim these posts do not count.

Well, sitting there on the ground because he is too tired to get up from the last knockdown, and holding one hand to his right eye, which is closed tight, Sam the Gonoph is by no means a well guy, and all around and about him is much suffering among his crew. But our little doll is hopping up and down chattering like a jaybird and running between old Liverlips, who is stretched out against one goalpost, and Nubbsy Taylor, who is leaning up against the other, and she is trying to mop the blood off their kissers with a handkerchief the size of a postage stamp.

Benny South Street is laying across Jew Louie and both are still snoring from the last knockdown, and the Bowl is now pretty much deserted except for the newspaper scribes away up in the press box, who do not seem to realize that the Battle of the Century just comes off in front of them. It is coming on dark, when all of a sudden a guy pops up out of the dusk wearing white spats and an overcoat with a fur collar, and he rushes up to our little doll.

"Clarice," he says, "I am looking for you high and low. My train is stalled for hours behind a wreck the other side of Bridgeport, and I get here just after the game is over. But," he says, "I figure you will be waiting somewhere for me. Let us hurry on to Hartford, darling," he says.

Well, when he hears this voice, Sam the Gonoph opens his good eye wide and takes a peek at the guy. Then all of a sudden Sam jumps up and wobbles over to the guy and hits him a smack between the eyes. Sam is wobbling because his legs are not so good from the shellacking he takes off the Harvards, and furthermore he is away off in his punching as the guy only goes to his knees and comes right up standing again as our little doll lets out a screech and speaks as follows:

"Oo-oo!" she says. "Do not hit Elliot! He is not after our goalposts!"

"Elliot?" Sam the Gonoph says. "This is no Elliot. This is nobody but Gigolo Georgie. I can tell him by his white spats," Sam says, "and I am now going to get even for the pasting I take from the Harvards."

Then he nails the guy again and this time he seems to have a little more on his punch, for the guy goes down and Sam the Gonoph gives him the leather very good, although our little doll is still screeching, and begging Sam not to hurt Elliot. But of course the rest of us know it is not Elliot, no matter what he may tell her, but only Gigolo Georgie.

Well, the rest of us figure we may as well take a little something out of Georgie's hide, too, but as we start for him he gives a quick wiggle and hops to his feet and tears across the field, and the last we see of him is his white spats flying through one of the portals.

Now a couple of other guys come up out of the dusk, and one of them is a tall, fine-looking guy with a white moustache and anybody can see that he is somebody, and what happens but our little doll runs right into his arms and kisses him on the white moustache and calls him daddy and starts to cry more than somewhat, so I can see we lose our little doll then and there. And now the guy with the white moustache walks up to Sam the Gonoph and sticks out his duke and says as follows:

"Sir," he says, "permit me the honor of shaking the hand which does me the very signal service of chastising the scoundrel who just escapes from the field. And," he says, "permit me to introduce myself to you. I am J. Hildreth Van Cleve, president of the Van Cleve Trust. I am notified early to-day by Miss Peevy of my daughter's sudden departure from school, and we learn she purchases a ticket for New Haven. I at once suspect this fellow has something to do with it. Fortunately," he says, "I have these private detectives here keeping tab on him for some time, knowing my child's schoolgirl infatuation for him, so we easily trail him here. We are on the train with him, and arrive in time for your last little scene with him. Sit," he says, "again I thank you."

"I know who you are, Mr. Van Cleve," Sam the Gonoph says. "You are the Van Cleve who is down to his last forty million. But," he says, "do not thank me for putting the slug on Gigolo Georgie. He is a bum in spades, and I am only sorry he fools your nice little kid even for a minute, although," Sam says, "I figure she must be dumber than she looks to be fooled by such a guy as Gigolo Georgie."

"I hate him," the little doll says. "I hate him because he is a coward. He does not stand up and fight when he is hit like you and Liverlips and the others. I never wish to see him again."

"Do not worry," Sam the Gonoph says. "I will be too close to Gigolo Georgie as soon as I recover from my wounds for him to stay in this part of the country."

Well, I do not see Sam the Gonoph or Nubbsy Taylor or Benny South Street or Jew Louie or Liverlips for nearly a year after this, and then it comes on fall again and one day I get to thinking that here it is Friday and the next day the Harvards are playing the Yales a large football game in Boston.

I figure it is a great chance for me to join up with Sam the Gonoph again to hustle duckets for him for this game, and I know Sam will be leaving along about midnight with his crew. So I go over to the Grand Central station at such a time, and sure enough he comes along by and by, busting through the crowd in the station with Nubbsy Taylor and Benny South Street and Jew Louie and old Liverlips at his heels, and they seem very much excited.

"Well, Sam," I say, as I hurry along with them, "here I am ready to hustle duckets for you again, and I hope and trust we do a nice business."

"Duckets!" Sam the Gonoph says. "We are not hustling duckets for this game, although you can go with us, and welcome. We are going to Boston," he says, "to root for the Yales to kick hell out of the Harvards and we are going as the personal guest of Miss Clarice Van Cleve and her old man."

"Hold 'em, Yale!" old Liverlips says, as he pushes me to one side and the whole bunch goes trotting through the gate to catch their train, and then I notice they are all wearing blue feathers in their hats with a little white Y on these feathers such as college guys always wear at football games, and that moreover Sam the Gonoph is carrying a Yale pennant.

FOR A PAL

For a matter of maybe fifteen years or more, Little Yid and Blind Benny are pals, and this is considered a very good thing for Benny because he is as blind as a bat, and maybe blinder, while Yid can see as good as anybody and sometimes better.

So Little Yid does the seeing for Benny, explaining in his own way to Benny just what he sees, such as a horse race or a baseball game or a prize fight or a play or a moving picture or anything else, for Yid and Blind Benny are great hands for going around and about wherever anything is coming off, no matter what, and up to the time this doll Mary Marble comes into their lives they are as happy as two pups in a basket.

How Benny comes to go blind I do not know, and nobody else along Broadway seems to know either, and in fact nobody cares, although I once hear Regret, the horse player, say it is probably in sympathy with the judges at the race track, Regret being such a guy as claims all these judges are very blind indeed. But of course Regret is sore at these race-track judges because they always call the wrong horse for him in the close finishes.

Little Yid tells me that Blind Benny is once a stick man in a gambling joint in Denver, and a very good stick man, at that, and one night a fire comes off in a flop house on Larimer Street, and Blind Benny, who is not blind at this time, runs into the fire to haul out an old guy who has more smoke in him than somewhat, and a rush of flames burns Benny's eyes so bad he loses his sight.

Well, this may be the true story of how Benny comes to go blind, but I know Little Yid likes Benny so much that he is not going to give Benny the worst of any story he tells about him, and for all anybody knows maybe Benny really goes into the fire to search for the old guy. Personally, I do not believe in taking too much stock in any story you hear on Broadway about anything.

But there is no doubt about Blind Benny being blind. His eye-lids are tacked down tight over his eyes, and there is no chance that he is faking, because many guys keep close tab on him for years and never catch him peeping once.

Furthermore, several guys send Benny to eye specialists at different times to see if they can do anything about his eyes, and all these specialists say he is one of the blindest guys they ever examine. Regret says maybe it is a good thing, at that, because Benny is so smart as a blind guy that the chances are if he can see he will be too smart to live.

He is especially smart when it comes to playing such games as pinochle. In fact, Benny is about as good a single-handed pinochle player as there is in this town, and there are many first-rate pinochle players in this town, if anybody asks you.

Benny punches little holes in the cards so he can tell which is which by feeling them, and the only way anybody can beat him is to cheat him, and it is considered most discourteous to cheat a blind guy, especially as Benny is always apt to catch a guy at cheating and put up an awful beef.

He is a tall, skinny guy with a thin face, and is by no means bad-looking, while Little Yid is about knee high to a snake, and they look like a father and his little boy as they go along the street with Little Yid hanging on to Blind Benny's arm and giving him the right steer.

Of course it is by no means an uncommon thing on Broadway for citizens to steer these blind guys across the street, although if the blind guys have any sense they will keep their dukes on their tin cups while they are being steered, but it is a most unusual proposition in this town for anybody to go steering a blind guy around for fifteen years the way Little Yid steers Blind Benny, as Blind Benny is a guy who takes plenty of steering.

In fact, one time Yid has to be away from business for a week and he leaves Blind Benny with a committee of guys, and every day one of these guys has to steer Benny around wherever he wishes to go, which is wherever there is anything going on, and Benny wears the whole committee plumb out before Yid gets back, as Benny is certainly a guy who likes to go around and about. Furthermore, he is so unhappy while Yid is away that he becomes a great nuisance, because it seems that none of the committee can see things as good as Yid for him, or explain them so he can understand them.

Personally, I will not care to have Little Yid do my seeing for me, even if I am blind, because I listen to him telling what he sees to Blind Benny many times, and it seems to me Little Yid is often somewhat cock-eyed in his explanations.

Furthermore, I will hate to be explaining things to Blind Benny, because he is always arguing about what is taking place, and giving you his opinions of it, even though he cannot see. In fact, although he cannot see a lick, Blind Benny is freer with his opinions than guys who can see from here to Europe.

It is a very interesting sight to watch Little Yid and Blind Benny at the race track, for they are both great hands for playing the horses and, in fact, Benny is a better handicapper than a lot of guys who have two good eyes and a pair of spectacles to do their handicapping with.

At night when they get the form sheet and sit up in their room with Yid reading off the past performances and the time trials, and all this and that, and with Blind Benny doping the horses from what Yid reads, and picking the ones he figures ought to win the next day. They always have a big argument over each horse, and Yid will tell Blind Benny he is daffy to be picking whatever horse it is he picks, and Benny will tell Yid he is out of his mind to think anything else can beat this horse, and they will holler and yell at each other for hours.

But they always wind up very friendly, and they always play the horse Benny picks, for Yid has much confidence in Benny's judgment, although he hollers and yells at him more than somewhat when one of his picks loses. They sit up in the grandstand during every race and Yid will explain to Benny what is doing in the race, and generally he manages to mention that the horse they are betting on is right up there and going easy, even though it may be laying back of the nine ball, for Yid believes in making Blind Benny feel good at all times.

But when a horse they are betting on is really in the running, especially in the stretch, Yid starts to root him home, and Benny roots right along with him as if he can see, and rocks back and forth in his seat, and pounds with his cane, and yells, "Come on with him, Jock," the same as anybody with two good eyes.

I am telling you all this about Little Yid and Benny to show you that they are very close friends indeed. They live together and eat together and argue together, and nobody ever hears of a nicer friendship on Broadway, although naturally some citizens figure for a while that one or the other must have some angle in this friendship, as it is practically uncanny for a friendship to last all these years on Broadway.

Blind Benny has some kind of an income from his people out West who are sorry about him being blind, and Little Yid has a piece of a small factory run by a couple of his brothers over in Hoboken where they make caps such as some citizens wear on their heads, and it seems this factory does very well, and the brothers are willing to send Little Yid his piece without him being around the factory very much, as they do not seem to consider him any boost to a cap factory.

So Yid and Blind Benny have all the money they need to go along, what with making a little scratch now and then on the races, and they never seem to care for any company but their own and are very happy and contented with each other. In all the years they are together Yid is never known to more than say hello to a doll, and of course Blind Benny cannot see dolls, anyway, which many citizens claim is a great break for Benny, so Yid and Benny are carrying no weight in this respect.

Now one night it seems that Ike Jacobs, the ticket spec, has a pair of Chinese duckets on the opening of a new play by the name of *Red Hot Love,* a Chinese ducket being a complimentary ducket that is punched full of holes like Chinese money, and which you do not have to pay for, and Ike gives these duckets to Little Yid and Blind Benny, which is considered very large-hearted of Ike, at that.

So when the curtain goes up on *Red Hot Love,* Yid and Benny are squatted right down in front among many well-known citizens who are all dressed up in evening clothes, because this *Red Hot Love* has a bunch of swell actors in it, and is expected to be first class.

Naturally, when the play begins, Yid has to give Blind Benny a little information about what is doing, otherwise Benny cannot appreciate the thing. So Yid starts off in a whisper, but anytime Yid starts explaining anything to Benny he always winds up getting excited, and talking so loud you can hear him down at the Battery.

Of course Blind Benny can follow the play as good as anybody if there is plenty of gab on the stage, but he likes to know what actors are doing the gabbing, and what they look like, and what the scenery looks like, and other details that he cannot see, and Little Yid is telling him in such a voice as causes some of the citizens around to say shush-shush. But Little Yid and Blind Benny are accustomed to being shushed in theaters, so they do not pay much attention.

Well, *Red Hot Love* is one of these problem plays, and neither Little Yid nor Blind Benny can make much of it, although they are no worse off any anybody else around them, at that. But Little Yid tries to explain to Blind Benny what it is all about, and Benny speaks out loud as follows:

"It sounds to me like a rotten play."

"Well," Little Yid says, "maybe the play is not so rotten, but the acting is."

There is much shushing from one and all around them, and the actors are giving them the bad eye from the stage, because the actors can hear what they say, and are very indignant, especially over this crack about acting.

Well, the next thing anybody knows down the aisle come a couple of big guys who put the arm on Little Yid and Blind Benny and give them the old heave-o out of the joint, as you are not supposed to speak out loud in a theater about any bad acting that is going on there, no matter how bad it is.

Anyway, as Little Yid and Blind Benny are being prodded up the aisle by the big guys, Blind Benny states as follows:

"I still claim," he says, "that it sounds like a rotten play."

"Well," Little Yid says, "the acting certainly is."

There is much applause as Yid and Benny are getting the heave-o, and many citizens claim it is because the customers are glad to see them heaved, but afterwards it comes out that what many of the customers are really applauding is the statements by Little Yid and Benny.

Well, Yid and Benny do not mind getting the heave-o so much, as they are heaved out of many better theaters than this in their time, but they are very indignant when the box office refuses to give them back the admission price, although of course their duckets do not cost them anything in the first place and they are a little out of line in trying to collect.

They are standing on the sidewalk saying what an outrage it is when all of a sudden out of the theater pops this doll by the name of Mary Marble, and her face is very red, and she is also very indignant, because it seems that in the second act of the play there are some very coarse cracks let out on the stage, and it seems that Mary Marble is such a doll as believes that cracks of this nature are only fit for married people to hear, and she is by no means married.

Of course Little Yid and Blind Benny do not know at the time that she is Mary Marble, and in fact they do not know her from Adam's off ox as she marches up to them and speaks as follows:

"Gentlemen," she says, "I wish to compliment you on your judgment of the affair inside. I hear what you say as you are getting ejected," she says, "and I wish to state that you are both right. It is a rotten play, and the acting is rotten."

Now off this meeting, what happens but Mary Marble gets to going around with Little Yid and Blind Benny wherever she can spare time from her job, which is managing a little joint on Broadway where they sell stockings such as dolls wear on their legs, except in summer-time, although even when they wear these stockings you cannot tell if a doll has anything on her legs unless you pinch them, the stockings that dolls wear nowadays being very thin indeed.

Furthermore, whenever she is with them, it is now Mary Marble who does most of the explaining to Blind Benny of what is going on, because Mary Marble is such a doll as is just naturally bound to do all the explaining necessary when she is around.

When it comes to looks, Mary Marble is practically no dice.

In fact, if she is not the homeliest doll on Broadway, I will guarantee she is no worse than a dead-heat with the homeliest. She has a large beezer and large feet, and her shape is nothing whatever to speak of, and Regret, the horse player, says they never need to be afraid of entering Mary Marble in a claiming race at any price. But of course Regret is such a guy as will not give you a counterfeit dime for any doll, no matter what she looks like.

Mary Marble is maybe twenty-five years old—although Regret says he will lay six to five against her being any better than twenty-eight—and about all she has running for her, any way you take her, is a voice that is soft and gentle and very nice indeed, except that she is fond of using it more than somewhat.

She comes from a little town over in Pennsylvania, and is pretty well educated, and there is no doubt whatever that she is unusually respectable, because such a looking doll as Mary Marble has no excuse for being anything but respectable on Broadway. In fact,

Mary Marble is so respectable that many citizens figure there must be an angle, but it is agreed by one and all that she is perfectly safe with Little Yid and Blind Benny, no matter what.

And now at night instead of always doping the horse, Little Yid and Blind Benny will often sit up in their room talking about nothing much but Mary Marble, and Benny asks Yid a million questions over and over again.

"Tell me, Yid," Blind Benny will say, "what does Mary look like?"

"She is beautiful," Yid always says.

Well, of course, this is practically perjury, and many citizens figure that Yid tells Blind Benny this very large lie because he has an idea Benny wishes to hear only the best about Mary Marble, although it comes out afterwards that Little Yid thinks Mary Marble beautiful, at that.

"She is like an angel," he says.

"Yes, yes," Blind Benny says, "tell me more."

And Little Yid keeps on telling him, and if Mary Marble is only one-eighth as good-looking as Yid tells, Ziegfeld and Georgie White and Earl Carroll will be breaking each other's legs trying to get to her first.

"Well," Blind Benny often says, after Little Yid gets through telling him about Mary Marble, she is just as I picture her to myself, Yid," he says. "I never care so much about not being able to see until now, and even now all I wish to see is Mary."

The idea seems to be that Blind Benny is in love with Mary Marble, and the way Little Yid is always boosting her it is no wonder. In fact, the chances are a lot of other citizens will be in love with Mary Marble if they listen to Yid telling Blind Benny about her, and never get a gander at her personally.

But Blind Benny does not mention right out that he is in love with Mary Marble, and it may be that he does not really know what is eating him, which is often the case with guys who are in love. All Blind Benny knows is that he likes to be with Mary Marble and to listen to her explaining things to him, and, what is more, Mary Marble seems to like to be with Blind Benny, and to explain things to him, although as far as this goes Mary Marble is such a doll as likes to be explaining things to anybody anytime she gets a chance.

Now Little Yid and Blind Benny are still an entry at all times, even when Mary Marble is with them, but many citizens see that

Little Yid is getting all sorrowed up, and they figure it is because he feels Blind Benny is gradually drifting away from him after all these years, and everybody sympathizes with Little Yid no little, and there is some talk of getting him another blind guy to steer around in case Blind Benny finally leaves him for good.

Then it comes on a Saturday night when Little Yid says he must go over to Hoboken to see his brothers about the cap business and, as Mary Marble has to work in the stocking joint Saturday nights, Little Yid asks Blind Benny to go with him.

Of course Blind Benny does not care two cents about the cap business, but Little Yid explains to him that he knows a Dutchman's in Hoboken where there is some very nice real beer, and if there is one thing Blind Benny likes more than somewhat it is nice real beer, especially as it seems that since they become acquainted with Mary Marble he seldom gets nice real beer, as Mary Marble is a terrible knocker against such matters as nice real beer.

So they start for Hoboken, and Little Yid sees his brothers about the cap business, and then he takes Blind Benny to a Dutchman's to get the nice real beer, only it turns out that the beer is not real, and by no means nice, being all needled up with alky, and full of headaches, and one thing and another. But of course Little Yid and Blind Benny are not going around complaining about beer even if it is needled, as, after all, needled beer is better than no beer whatever.

They sit around the Dutchman's quite a while, although it turns out that the Dutchman is nothing but a Polack, and then they nab a late ferryboat for home, as Little Yid says he wishes to ride on a ferryboat to get the breeze. As far as Blind Benny is concerned, he does not care how they go as long as he can get back to New York to meet up with Mary Marble when she is through work.

There are not many citizens on the ferryboat with them, because it is getting on towards midnight, and at such an hour anybody who lives in Jersey is home in bed. In fact, there are not over four or five other passengers on the ferryboat with Little Yid and Blind Benny, and these passengers are all dozing on the benches in the smoking-room with their legs stuck out in front of them.

Now if you know anything about a ferryboat you know that they always hook big gates across each end of such a boat to keep automobiles and trucks and citizens and one thing and another from going off these ends into the water when the ferryboat is traveling back and forth, as naturally it will be a great nuisance to other boats in the river to have things falling off the ferryboats and clogging up the stream.

Well, Little Yid is away out on the end of the ferryboat up against the gate enjoying the breeze, and Blind Benny is leaning against the rail just outside the smoking-room door where Little Yid plants him when they get on the boat, and Blind Benny is smoking a big heater that he gets at the Dutchman's and maybe thinking of Mary Marble, when all of a sudden Little Yid yells like this:

"Oh, Benny," he yells, "come here."

Naturally Benny turns and goes in the direction of the voice and Little Yid's voice comes from the stern, and Blind Benny keeps following his beezer in the direction of the voice, expecting to feel Little Yid's hand stopping him any minute, and the next thing he knows he is walking right off the ferryboat into the river.

Of course Blind Benny cannot continue walking after he hits the water, so he sinks at once, making a sound like glug-glug as he goes down. It is in the fall of the year, and the water is by no means warm, so as Benny comes up for air he naturally lets out a loud squawk, but by this time the ferryboat is quite some jumps away from him, and nobody seems to see him, or even hear him.

Now Blind Benny cannot swim a lick so he sinks again with a glug-glug. He comes up once more, and this time he does not squawk so loud, but he sings out, very distinct, as follows: "Good-bye, Pal Yid."

All of a sudden there is quite a splash in the water near the ferryboat, and Little Yid is swimming for Blind Benny so fast the chances are he will make a sucker of Johnny Weissmuller if Johnny happens to be around, for Little Yid is a regular goldfish when it comes to water, although he is not much of a hand for going swimming without provocation.

He has to dive for Blind Benny, for by this time Blind Benny is going down for the third time, and everybody knows that a guy is only allowed three downs when he is drowning. In fact, Blind Benny is almost down where the crabs live before Little Yid can get a fistful of his collar. At first Little Yid's idea is to take Blind Benny by the hair, but he remembers in time that Benny does not have much hair, so he compromises on the collar.

And being a little guy, Yid has quite a job getting Benny to the top and keeping him there. By this time the ferryboat is almost at its dock on the New York side, and nobody on board seems to realize that it is shy a couple of passengers, although of course the ferryboat company is not going to worry about that as it collects the fares in advance.

But it is a pretty lucky break for Little Yid and Blind Benny that a tugboat happens along and picks them up, or Yid may be swimming around the North River to this day with Blind Benny by the nape of the neck going glug-glug.

The captain of the tugboat is a kind old guy with whiskers by the name of Deusenberg, and he is very sorry indeed to see them in such a situation, so after he hauls them on board the tugboat, and spreads them out on bunks to let them dry, he throws a couple of slugs of gin into Little Yid and Blind Benny, it being gin of such a nature that they are half sorry they do not go ahead and drown before they meet up with it.

Then the captain unloads them at Forty-second Street on the New York side, and by this time, between the water and the gin, Blind Benny is very much fagged out indeed and in bad shape generally, so Little Yid puts him in a cab and takes him to a hospital.

Well, for several days Blind Benny is not better than even money to get well, because after they get the water out of him they still have to contend with the gin, and Mary Marble is around carrying on quite some, and saying she does not see how Little Yid can be so careless as to let Benny walk off the end of a ferryboat when there are gates to prevent such a thing, or how he can let Benny drink tugboat gin, and many citizens do not see either, especially about the gin.

As for Little Yid, he is looking very sad, and is at the hospital at all times, and finally, one day when Blind Benny is feeling all right again, Little Yid sits down beside his bed, and speaks to him as follows:

"Benny," Little Yid says, "I will now make a confession to you and I will then go away somewhere and knock myself off. Benny," he says, "I let you fall into the river on purpose. In fact," Little Yid says, "I unhook the gate across the passageway and call you, figuring you will follow the sound of my voice and walk on off the boat into the water.

"I am very sorry about this," Little Yid says, "but, Benny," he says, "I love Mary Marble more than somewhat, although I never before mention this to a soul. Not even to Mary Marble, because,"

Little Yid says, "I know she loves you, as you love her. I love her," Little Yid says, "from the night we first meet, and this love winds up by making me a little daffy.

"I get to thinking," Little Yid says, "that with you out of the way Mary Marble will turn to me and love me instead. But," he says, starting to shed large tears, "when I hear your voice from the water saying "Good-bye, Pal Yid," my heart begins to break, and I must jump in after you. So now you know, and I will go away and shoot myself through the head if I can find somebody to lend me a Roscoe, because I am no good."

"Why," Blind Benny says, "Pal Yid, what you tell me about leading me into the river is no news to me. In fact," he says, "I know it the minute I hit the water because, although I am blind, I see many things as I am going down, and I see very plain that you must do this thing on purpose, because I know you are close enough around to grab me if you wish.

"I know, of course," Blind Benny says, "that there is bound to be a gate across the end of the boat because I often fix this gate when we are leaving Hoboken. So," he says, "I see that you must unhook this gate. I see that for some reason you wish to knock me off although I do not see the reason, and the chances are I will never see it unless you tell me now, so I do not put up more of a holler and maybe attract the attention of the other guys on the boat. I am willing to let it all go as it lays."

"My goodness," Little Yid says, "this is most surprising to me indeed. In fact," he says, "I scarcely know what to say, Benny. In fact," he says, "I cannot figure out why you are willing to go without putting up a very large beef."

"Well, Pal Yid," Benny says, reaching out and taking Little Yid by the hand, "I am so fond of you that I figure if my being dead is going to do you any good, I am willing to die, even though I do not know why. Although," Benny says, "it seems to me you can think up a nicer way of scragging me than by drowning, because you know I loathe and despise water. Now then," he says, "as for Mary Marble, if you—"

But Little Yid never lets Blind Benny finish this, because he cuts in and speaks as follows:

"Benny," he says, "if you are willing to die for me, I can certainly afford to give up a doll for you, especially," he says, "as my people tell me only yesterday that if I marry anybody who is not of my religion, which is slightly Jewish, they will chop me off at the pants' pocket. You take Mary Marble," he says, "and I will stake you to my blessing, and maybe a wedding present."

So the upshot of the whole business is Mary Marble is now Mrs. Blind Benny, and Blind Benny seems to be very happy indeed, although some citizens claim the explanations he gets nowadays of whatever is going on are much shorter than when he is with Little Yid, while Little Yid is over in Hoboken in the cap racket with his brothers, and he never sees Blind Benny anymore, as Mary Marble still holds the gin against him.

Personally, I always consider Little Yid's conduct in this matter very self-sacrificing, and furthermore I consider him a very great hero for rescuing Blind Benny from the river, and I am saying as much only the other day to Regret the horse player.

"Yes," Regret says, "it sounds very self-sacrificing, indeed, and maybe Little Yid is a hero, at that, but," Regret says, "many citizens are criticizing him no little for sawing off such a crow as Mary Marble on a poor blind guy."

BROADWAY FINANCIER

Of all the scores made by dolls on Broadway the past twenty-five years, there is no doubt but what the very largest score is made by a doll who is called Silk, when she knocks off a banker by the name of Israel Ib, for the size of Silk's score is three million one hundred bobs and a few odd cents.

It is admitted by one and all who know about these matters that the record up to this time is held by a doll by the name of Irma Teak, who knocks off a Russian duke back in 1911 when Russian dukes are considered very useful by dolls, although of course in these days Russian dukes are about as useful as dandruff. Anyway, Irma Teak's score off this Russian duke is up around a million, and she moves to London with her duke and chucks quite a swell around there for a time. But finally Irma Teak goes blind, which is a tough break for her as she can no longer see how jealous she is making other dolls with her diamonds and sables and one thing and another, so what good are they to her, after all?

I know Irma Teak when she is a show doll at the old Winter Garden, an I also know the doll by the name of Mazie Mitz, who is a Florodora revival, and who makes a score of maybe three hundred G's off a guy who has a string of ten-cent stores, and three hundred G's is by no means hay. But Mazie Mitz finally hauls off and runs away with a saxophone player she is in love with and so winds up back of the fifteen ball.

Furthermore, I know Clara Simmons, the model from Rickson's, who gets a five-story town house and a country place on Long Island off a guy on Wall Street for birthday presents, and while I never meet this guy personally, I always figure he must be very dumb because anybody who knows Clara Simmons knows she will be just as well satisfied with a bottle of perfume for a birthday present. For all I know, Clara Simmons may still own the town house and the country place, but she must be shoving on toward forty now, so naturally nobody on Broadway cares what becomes of her.

I know a hundred other dolls who run up different scores, and some of them are very fair scores indeed, but none of these scores are anything much alongside Silk's score off Israel Ib, and this score is all the more surprising because Silk starts out being greatly prejudiced against bankers. I am no booster for bankers myself, as I consider them very stony-hearted guys, but I am not prejudiced against them. In fact, I consider bankers very necessary, because if we do not have bankers many citizens will not be able to think of anybody to give a check on.

It is quite a while before she meets Israel Ib that Silk explains to me why she is prejudiced against bankers. It is when she is nothing but a chorus doll in Johnny Oakley's joint on Fifty-third Street, and comes into Mindy's after she gets through work, which is generally along about four o'clock in the morning.

At such an hour many citizens are sitting around Mindy's resting from the crap games and one thing and another, and dolls from the different joints around and about, including chorus dolls and hostesses, drop in for something to eat before going home, and generally these dolls are still in their make-up and very tired.

Naturally they come to know the citizens who are sitting around, and say hello, and maybe accept the hospitality of these citizens, such as java and Danish pastry, or maybe a few scrambled eggs, and it is all very pleasant and harmless, because a citizen who is all tuckered out from shooting craps is not going to get any high blood pressure over a tired chorus doll or a hostess, and especially a hostess.

Well, one morning Silk is sitting at my table guzzling a cup of java and a piece of apple pie, when in comes The Greek looking very weary, The Greek being a high shot who is well known far and wide. He drops into a chair alongside me and orders a Bismarck herring with sliced onions to come along, which is a dish that is considered most invigorating, and then The Greek mentions that he is playing the bank for twenty-four hours hand running, so right away Silk speaks up as follows:

"I hate banks," she says. "Furthermore," she says, "I hate bankers. If it is not for a banker maybe I will not be slaving in Johnny Oakley's dirty little drum for thirty bobs per week. Maybe my mamma will still be alive, and I will be living at home with her instead of in a fleabag on Forty-seventh Street.

"My mamma once saves up three hundred bobs from scrubbing floors in an office building to send me to school," Silk says, "and a banker in one of the buildings where she does this scrubbing tells her to put her dough in this bank, and what happens but the bank busts and it is such a terrible blow to my mamma that she ups and dies. I am very small at the time," Silk says, "but I can remember standing in front of the busted bank with my mamma, and my mamma crying her eyes out."

Well, personally, I consider Silk's crack about Johnny Oakley's joint uncalled for, as it is by no means little, but I explain to her that what The Greek is talking about is a faro bank, and not a bank you put your money in, as such a bank is called a jug, and not a bank at all, while faro bank is a gambling game, and the reason I explain this to Silk is because everybody always explains things to her.

The idea is everybody wishes Silk to be well smartened up, especially everybody who hangs out around Mindy's because she is an orphan and never has a chance to go to school, and we do not wish her to grow up dumb like the average doll, as one and all are very fond of Silk from the first minute she bobs up around Mindy's.

Now at this time Silk is maybe seventeen years old and weighs maybe ninety pounds, sopping wet, and she is straight up and down like a boy. She has soft brown hair and brown eyes that seem too big for her face, and she looks right at you when she talks to you and she talks to you like one guy to another guy. In fact, I always claim there is more guy in Silk than there is doll, as she finally gets so she thinks like a guy, which is maybe because she associates more with guys than she does with other dolls and gets a guy's slant on things in general.

She loves to sit around Mindy's in the early morning gabbing with different citizens, although she does more listening than gabbing herself, and she loves to listen to gab about horse-racing and baseball and fights and crap-shooting and to guys cutting up old touches and whatever else is worth gabbing about, and she seldom sticks in her oar, except maybe to ask a question. Naturally a doll who is willing to listen instead of wishing to gab herself is bound to be popular because if there is anything most citizens hate and despise it is a gabby doll.

So then many citizens take a real interest in Silk's education, including Regret, the horse player, who explains to her how to build up a sucker to betting on a hot horse, although personally I do not consider such knowledge of any more value to a young doll just starting out in the world than the lesson Big Nig, the crap shooter, gives her one night on how to switch in a pair of tops on a craps game.

Then there is Doc Daro, who is considered one of the highest-class operators that ever rides the tubs in his day, being a great hand for traveling back and forth across the ocean and outplaying other passengers at bridge and poker and one thing and another, but who finally gets rheumatism in his hands so bad he can no longer shuffle the cards. And of course if Doc Daro cannot shuffle the cards there is no sense whatever in trying to play games of skill anymore.

Doc Daro is always telling Silk what rascals guys are and explaining to her the different kinds of business they will try to give her, this being the same kind of business the Doc gives dolls himself in his time. The Doc has an idea that a young doll who is battling Broadway needs plenty of education along such lines, but Silk tells me privately that she is jerry to the stuff Doc is telling her when she is five years old.

The guy I figure does Silk the most good is an old pappy guy by the name of Professor D, who is always reading books when he is not busy doping the horses. In fact, Professor D is considered somewhat daffy on the subject of reading books, but it seems he gets the habit from being a teacher in a college out in Ohio before he becomes a horse player. Anyway, Professor D takes to giving Silk books to read, and what is more she reads them and talks them over afterwards with the professor, who is greatly pleased by this.

"She is a bight little doll," Professor D says to me one day. "Furthermore," the professor says, "she has soul."

"Well," I say, "Big Nig claims she can palm a pair of dice as good as anybody he ever sees."

But the professor only says heigh-ho, and goes along, and I can see he does not consider me a character worth having much truck with, even though I am as much interested in Silk's education as anybody else.

Well, what happens one night but the regular singer in Johnny Oakley's joint, a doll by the name of Myrtle Marigold, hauls off and catches the measles from her twelve-year-old son, and as Johnny has enough trouble getting customers into his joint without giving them the measles after getting them there he gives Myrtle Marigold plenty of wind at once.

But there he is without anybody to sing "Stacker Lee" to his customers, "Stacker Lee" being a ditty with which Myrtle Marigold panics the customers, so Johnny looks his chorus over and finally asks Silk if she can sing "Stacker Lee," because she considers it a low-down lullaby, at best. She says she will sing something classical and, being desperate for singing, Johnny Oakley says go ahead. So what does Silk do but sing a very old song called "Annie Laurie," which she learns from her mamma, and she sings this song so loud that sobs are heard all over the joint.

Of course if anybody investigates they will learn that the sobbing is being done by Professor D and Big Nig and The Greek, who happen to be in the joint at the time, and what they are sobbing about is the idea of Silk singing at all, but Johnny Oakley considers her a big hit and keeps her singing "Annie Laurie" right along, and one night Harry Fitz, the booking agent, drops in and hears her singing and tells Ziegfeld he discovers a doll with a brand-new style.

Naturally Ziggie signs her up at once for the *Follies*, because he has great faith in Harry Fitz's judgment but after Ziggie hears Silk sing he asks her if she can do anything else, and is greatly relieved when he learns she can dance.

So Silk becomes a Ziegfeld dancer, and she is quite a sensation with the dramatic critics on the night she opens because she dances with all her clothes on, which is considered a very great novelty indeed. The citizens around Mindy's chip in and send Silk a taxicab full of orchids, and a floral pillow, and Professor D contributes a book called *The Outline of History*, and Silk is the happiest doll in town.

A year goes by, and what a year in the *Follies* does for Silk is most astonishing. Personally, I never see a lot of change in her looks, except her figure fills out so it has bumps here and there where a doll is entitled to have bumps, and her face grows to fit her eyes more, but everybody else claims she becomes beautiful, and her picture is always in the papers and dozens of guys are always hanging around after her and sending her flowers and one thing and another.

One guy in particular starts sending her jewelry, which Silk always brings around to Mindy's for Jewelry Joe to look at, this Jewelry Joe being a guy who peddles jewelry along Broadway for years, and who can tell you in a second what a piece of jewelry is worth.

Jewelry Joe finds that the jewelry Silk brings around is nothing much but slum, and naturally he advises her to have no further truck with any party who cannot send in anything better than this, but one morning she shows up in Mindy's with an emerald ring the size of a cake of soap, and the minute Jewelry Joe sees the emerald he tells Silk that whoever donates this is worthy of very careful consideration.

Now it seems that the party who sends the emerald is nobody but Israel Ib, the banker who owns the jug down on the Lower East Side that is called the Bank of the Bridges, and the way Silk comes to connect with him is most unusual. It is through a young guy by the name of Simeon Slotsky, who is a teller in Israel Ib's jug, and who sees Silk dancing one night in the *Follies* and goes right off his ka-zip about her.

It is this Simeon Slotsky who is sending the jewelry that Silk first brings around, and the way he is buying this jewelry is by copping a little dough out of the jug now and then which does not belong to him. Naturally this is a most dishonest action, and by and by they catch up with Simeon Slotsky in the jug, and Israel Ib is going to place him in the pokey.

Well, Simeon Slotsky does not wish to be placed in the pokey and not knowing what else to do, what does he do but go to Silk and tell her his story, explaining that he commits his dishonest business only because he is daffy about her, even though Silk never gives him a tumble, and in fact never says as much as two words to him before.

He tells her that he comes of respectable old parents down on the Lower East Side, who will be very sad if he is placed in the pokey, especially his mamma, but Israel Ib is bound and determined to put him away, because Israel Ib is greatly opposed to anybody copping dough out of his jug. Simeon Slotsky says his mamma cries all over Israel Ib's vest trying to cry him out of the idea of placing her son in the pokey, but that Israel Ib is a very hard-hearted guy and will not give in no matter what, and furthermore he is very indignant because Simeon's mamma's tears spot up his vest. So Simeon says it looks as if he must go to the pokey unless Silk can think of something.

Now Silk is very young herself and very tender-hearted and she is sorry for Simeon Slotsky, because she can see he is nothing but a hundred-per-cent chump, so she sits down and writes a letter to Israel Ib asking him to call on her backstage at the *Follies* on a matter of great importance. Of course Silk does not know that it is not the proper caper to be writing a banker such a letter, and ordinarily it is a thousand to one, according to the way The Greek figures the odds, that a banker will pay no attention to such a letter except maybe to notify his lawyer.

But it seems that the letter tickles Israel Ib, as he always secretly wishes to get a peek backstage at the *Follies* to see if the dolls back there wear as few clothes as he hears, so he shows up the very same night, and in five minutes Silk has him all rounded up as far as Simeon Slotsky is concerned. Israel Ib says he will straighten out everything and send Simeon to a job in a jug out West.

So the next day Simeon Slotsky comes around and thanks Silk for all she does for him, and bawls quite some, and gets a photograph off her with her name signed to it which he says he will give to his mamma so she can stick it up on her wall on the East Side to always remember the doll who saves her son, and then Simeon Slotsky goes on about his business, and for all I know becomes a very honest and useful citizen. And forty-eight hours later, Silk is wearing the emerald from Israel Ib.

Now this Israel Ib is by no means a Broadway character, and in fact few ever hear of him before he bobs up sending Silk an emerald ring. In fact, it seems that Israel Ib is a quiet, industrious guy, who has nothing on his mind but running his jug and making plenty of scratch until the night he goes to see Silk.

He is a little short fat guy of maybe forty-odd at this time with a little round stomach sticking out in front of him and he always wears a white vest on his stomach, with a pair of gold-rimmed cheaters hanging on a black ribbon across the vest. He has a large snozzle and is as homely as a mud fence, any way you take him, but it is well known to one and all that he is a coming guy in the banking dodge.

Silk is always making jokes about Israel Ib, because naturally she cannot see much to such a looking guy, but every morning she comes into Mindy's with all kinds of swag, such as bracelets and rings and brooches, and Jewelry Joe finally speaks to her very severely and tells her that a guy who can send her such merchandise is no joking matter.

There is no doubt that Israel Ib is dizzy about her, and personally I consider it very sad that a guy as smart as he must be lets himself get tangled up in such a situation. But then I remember that guys ten thousand times smarter than Israel Ib let themselves get tangled up the same way, so it is all even.

The upshot of the whole business is that Silk begins to pay a little serious attention to Israel Ib, and the next thing anybody knows she quits the *Follies* and takes to living in a large apartment on Park Avenue and riding around in a big car with a guy in uniform driving her, and she has enough fur coats for a tribe of Eskimos, including a chinchilla flogger that moves Israel back thirty G's.

Furthermore, it comes out that the apartment house she is living in is in her own name, and some citizens are greatly surprised, as they do not figure a doll just off Broadway smart enough to get anything in her own name, except maybe a traffic summons. But Professor D says he is not surprised because he once makes Silk read a book entitled *The Importance of Property*.

We do not see much of Silk anymore these days, but every now and then we hear rumors of her getting more apartment houses and business buildings in her own name, and the citizens around Mindy's are greatly pleased because they figure it proves that the trouble they take educating Silk is by no means wasted. Finally we hear Silk goes to Europe, and for nearly two years she is living in Paris and other spots, and some say the reason she sticks around Europe is because she finds out all of a sudden that Israel Ib is a married guy, although personally I figure Silk must know this all along, because it certainly is no mystery. In fact, Israel Ib is very much married indeed, and his ever-loving wife is a big fat old doll whose family has plenty of potatoes.

The chances are Silk is sick and tired of looking at Israel Ib, and stays abroad so she will not have to look at his ugly kisser more than two or three times a year, which is about as often as Israel Ib can think up excuses to go over and see her. Then one winter we hear that Silk is coming home to stay, and it is the winter of 1930 when things are very tough indeed.

It is close to Christmas when Silk lands one morning around eleven o'clock from the steamship, and it seems she is expecting

Israel Ib to meet her at the dock, but Israel Ib is not present, and nobody else is there to tell her why Israel Ib is absent.

It seems that some of Silk's luggage is being held up by the customs guys, as she brings over enough merchandise of one kind and another to stock a department store, and she wishes to see Israel Ib to get this matter straightened out, so she hires a taxi and tells the jockey to take her to Israel Ib's jug, figuring to stop in a minute and give Israel Ib his instructions, and maybe a good rousting around for not meeting her.

Now Silk never before goes to Israel Ib's jug, which is deep down on the Lower East Side where many citizens wear long whiskers and do not speak much English, and where there always seems to be a smell of herring around and about, and she is greatly surprised and much disgusted by her surroundings as she approaches the corner where Israel Ib's jug stands.

Furthermore, she is much surprised to find a big crowd in front of the jug, and this crowd is made up of many whiskers and old dolls wearing shawls over their heads, and kids of all sizes and shapes, and everybody in the crowd seems much excited, and there is plenty of moaning and groaning from one and all, and especially from an old doll who is standing in the doorway of a little store a couple of doors from the jug.

In fact, this old doll is making more racket than all the rest of the crowd put together, and at times is raising her voice to a scream and crying out in a strange language words that sound quite hostile.

Silk's taxi cannot get through the mob and a copper steps up and tells the driver he better make a detour, so Silk asks the copper why these people are raising such a rumpus in the street, instead of being home keeping warm, for it is colder than a blonde's heart, and there is plenty of ice around about.

"Why," the copper says, "do you not hear? This jug busts this morning and the guy who runs it, Israel Ib, is over in the Tombs, and the people are nervous because many of them have their potatoes in the jug. In fact," the copper says, "some of them, including the old doll over there in front of the store who is doing all the screeching, have their lifetime savings in this jug, and it looks as if they are ruined. It is very sad," he says, "because they are very, very poor people."

And then tears come to his eyes, and he boffs an old guy with whiskers over the skull with his club because the old guy is moaning so loud the copper can scarcely make himself heard.

Now naturally all this is most surprising news to Silk, and while she is pretty much sored up because she cannot see Israel Ib to get her merchandise out of the customs, she has the taxi jockey take her away from these scenes right away, and up to her apartment on Park Avenue, which she has ready for her coming home. Then she sends out for the early editions of the evening papers and reads all about what a rapscallion Israel Ib is for letting his jug bust right in the poor people's faces.

It seems that Israel Ib is placed in the Tombs because somebody suspects something illegal about the busting, but of course nobody figures Israel Ib will be kept in the Tombs long on account of being a banker, and in fact there is already some talk that the parties who placed him there in the first place may find themselves in plenty of heat later on, because it is considered most discourteous to a banker to place him in the Tombs where the accommodations are by no means first class.

One of the papers has a story about Israel Ib's ever-loving wife taking it on the lam as soon as the news gets out about the jug busting and Israel Ib being in the Tombs, and about her saying he can get out of this predicament the best way he can, but that she will never help with as much as a thin dime of her dough and hinting pretty strong that Israel Ib's trouble is on account of him squandering the jug's scratch on a doll.

The story says she is going back to her people, and from the way the story reads it sounds as if the scribe who writes it figures this is one good break, at least, for Israel Ib.

Now these hints let out by Israel Ib's ever-loving wife about him squandering the jug's scratch on a doll are printed as facts in the morning papers the next morning, and maybe if Silk bothers to read these morning sheets she will think better of going down to Israel Ib's jug again, because her name is mentioned right out, and there are big pictures of her in the papers from her old days in the *Follies*.

But there Silk is in a taxi in front of the Bank of the Bridges at nine o'clock the next morning, and it seems her brain is buzzing with quite a large idea, although this idea does not come out until later.

There is already quite a crowd around the jug again, as it is always very difficult to make people who live on the Lower East Side and wear whiskers and shawls understand about such matters as busted jugs. They are apt to hang around a busted jug for days at a time with their bank-books in their hands, and sometimes it takes as much as a week to convince such people that their potatoes are gone for good, and make them disperse to their homes and start saving more.

There is still much moaning and groaning, though not as much as the day before, and every now and then the old doll pops out of the little store and stands in the doorway and shakes her fist at the busted jug and hollers in a strange language. A short, greasy-looking guy with bristly whiskers and an old black derby hat jammed down over his ears is standing with a morning paper spread out in his hands, and a bunch of other guys are around him listening to him read what the paper has to say about the situation.

Just one copper is walking up and down now, and it is the copper who speaks to Silk the day before, and he seems to remember her as she gets out of the taxi and he walks over to her, while a lot of people stop moaning and groaning to take a gander at her, for it is by no means a common sight to see such a looking doll in this neighborhood.

The copper no more than says good morning to Silk when the guy who is reading the paper stops reading and takes a peek at her, and then at her picture which is on the page in front of him. Then he points at the picture and points at Silk, and begins jabbering a blue streak to the guys around him. About this time the old doll peeps out of the store to shake her fist at Israel Ib's jug again and, hearing the jabbering, she joins the bunch around the guy with the paper.

She listens to the jabbering awhile, peeking over the guy's shoulder at the picture, and then taking a good long look at Silk, and then all of a sudden the old doll turns and pops back into the store.

Now all the shawls and whiskers start gathering around Silk and the copper, and anybody can tell from the way they are looking that they are all sored up, and what they are sored up at is Silk, because naturally they figure out that she is the doll whose picture is in the morning paper and is therefore the doll who is responsible for Israel Ib's jug busting.

But of course the copper does not know that they are sored up at Silk, and figures they are gathering around just out of curiosity, as people will do when they see a copper talking to anybody. He is a young copper and naturally he does not wish to have an audience when he is speaking to such a looking doll as Silk, even if most of the audience cannot understand English, so as the crowd nudges closer he gets his club ready to boff a few skulls.

Just about then half a brickbat hits him under the right ear, and he begins wobbling about very loose at the hinges, and at the same minute all the shawls and whiskers take to pulling and hauling at Silk. There are about a hundred of the shawls and whiskers to begin with and more are coming up from every-which direction, and they are all yelling and screaming and punching and scratching at Silk.

She is knocked down two or three times, and many shawls and whiskers are walking up and down her person while she is on the ground, and she is bleeding here and there, and the chances are they will kill her as dead as a door-nail in their excitement if the old doll from the little store near the jug does not bob up all of a sudden with a mop handle in her duke and starts boffing the shawls and whiskers on their noggins.

In fact, the old doll plays a regular tune on these noggins with the mop handle, sometimes knocking a shawl or whiskers quite bow-legged, and soon clearing a path through the crowd to Silk and taking hold of Silk and dragging her off into the store just as the reserves and an ambulance arrive.

The young copper is still wobbling about from the brickbat and speaking of how he hears the birdies singing in the trees, although of course there are no birdies in this neighborhood at such a time of year, and no trees either, and there are maybe half a dozen shawls and whiskers sitting on the pavement rubbing their noggins, and others are diving into doorways here and there, and there is much confusion generally.

So the ambulance takes Silk and some of the shawls and whiskers to a hospital and Professor D and Doc Daro visit her there a couple of hours later, finding her in bed somewhat plastered up in spots but in no danger, and naturally Professor D and Doc Daro wish to know what she is doing around Israel Ib's jug, anyway.

"Why," Silk says, "I am not able to sleep a wink all last night thinking of these poor people suffering on account of me taking

Israel Ib's dough, although," Silk says, "of course I do not know it is wrong dough when I receive it. I do not know Israel Ib is clipping these poor people. But seeing them around the jug yesterday morning, I remember what happens to my poor mamma when the jug busts on her. I see her standing in front of the busted jug with me beside her, crying her eyes out, and my heart is very heavy," Silk says. "So I get to thinking," she says, "that it will be a very nice thing indeed if I am first to tell the poor souls who have their dough in Israel Ib's jug that they are going to get it back."

"Wait a minute," Doc Daro says. "What do you mean—they are going to get their dough back?"

"Why," Silk says, "I consult with Judge Goldstein, who is my tongue, and a very good guy, at that, and fairly honest, last night, and Judge Goldstein tells me that I am worth in negotiable securities and real estate and jewelry, and one thing and another, about three million one hundred bobs, and a few odd cents.

"Judge Goldstein tells me," Silk says, "that such a sum will more than pay off all the depositors in Israel Ib's jug. In fact, Judge Goldstein tells me that what I have probably represents most of the deposits in the jug, and," she says, "I sign everything I own in this world over to Judge Goldstein to do this, although Judge Goldstein says there is no doubt I can beat any attempt to take my dough away from me if I wish to keep it.

"So," Silk says, "I am so happy to think these poor people will get their dough back that I cannot wait for Judge Goldstein to let it out. I wish to break the news to them myself, but," Silk says, "before I can say a word they hop on me and start giving me a pasting, and if it is not for the old doll with the mop handle maybe you will have to chip in to bury me, because I certainly do not have enough dough left to bury myself."

Well, this is about all there is to this story, except that the Bank of the Bridges pays off one hundred per cent on the dollar, and what is more Israel Ib is running it again, and doing very well indeed, and his ever-loving wife returns to him, and everything is hotsy-totsy between them.

As for Silk, she is back on Broadway, and the last time I see her she is in love with a very legitimate guy who is in the hotel business, and while he does not strike me as having much brains, he has plenty of youth running for him, and Silk says it is the best break she ever gets in her life when Israel Ib's jug busts.

But anybody will tell you that the best break Silk ever gets is when the old doll on the Lower East Side recognizes her from the photograph she has stuck up on the wall in the little store near Israel Ib's jug as the doll who once saves her son, Simeon Slotsky, from being placed in the pokey.

LITTLE MISS MARKER

One evening along toward seven o'clock, many citizens are standing out on Broadway in front of Mindy's restaurant, speaking of one thing and another, and particularly about the tough luck they have playing the races in the afternoon, when who comes up the street with a little doll hanging on to his right thumb but a guy by the name of Sorrowful.

This guy is called Sorrowful because this is the way he always is about no matter what, and especially about the way things are with him when anybody tries to put the bite on him. In fact, if anybody who tries to put the bite on Sorrowful can listen to him for two minutes about how things are with him and not bust into tears, they must be very hard-hearted indeed.

Regret, the horse player, is telling me that he once tries to put the bite on Sorrowful for a sawbuck, and by the time Sorrowful gets through explaining how things are with him, Regret feels so sorry for him that he goes out and puts the bite on somebody else for the saw and gives it to Sorrowful, although it is well known to one and all that Sorrowful has plenty of potatoes hid away somewhere.

He is a tall, skinny guy with a long, sad, mean-looking kisser, and a mournful voice. He is maybe sixty years old, give or take a couple of years, and for as long as I can remember he is running a hand-book over on Forty-ninth Street next door to a chop-suey joint. In fact, Sorrowful is one of the largest handbook makers in this town.

Anytime you see him he is generally by himself, because being by himself is not apt to cost him anything, and it is therefore a most surprising scene when he comes along Broadway with a little doll.

And there is much speculation among the citizens as to how this comes about, for no one ever hears of Sorrowful having any family, or relations of any kind, or even any friends.

The little doll is a very little doll indeed, the top of her noggin only coming up to Sorrowful's knee, although of course Sorrowful has very high knees, at that. Moreover, she is a very pretty little doll, with big blue eyes and fat pink cheeks, and a lot of yellow curls hanging down her back, and she has fat little legs and quite a large smile, although Sorrowful is lugging her along the street so fast that half the time her feet are dragging the sidewalk and she has a license to be bawling instead of smiling.

Sorrowful is looking sadder than somewhat, which makes his face practically heart-rending, so he pulls up in front of Mindy's and motions us to follow him in. Anybody can see that he is worried about something very serious, and many citizens are figuring that maybe he suddenly discovers all his potatoes are counterfeit, because nobody can think of anything that will worry Sorrowful except money.

Anyway, four or five of us gather around the table where Sorrowful sits down with the little doll beside him, and he states a most surprising situation to us.

It seems that early in the afternoon a young guy who is playing the races with Sorrowful for several days pops into his place of business next door to the chop-suey joint, leading the little doll, and this guy wishes to know how much time he has before post in the first race at Empire.

Well, he only has about twenty-five minutes, and he seems very down-hearted about this, because he explains to Sorrowful that he has a sure thing in this race, which he gets the night before off a guy who is a pal of a close friend of Jockey Workman's valet.

The young guy says he is figuring to be himself about a deuce on this sure thing, but he does not have such a sum as a deuce on him when he goes to bed, so he plans to get up bright and early in the morning and hop down to a spot on Fourteenth Street where he knows a guy who will let him have the deuce.

But it seems he oversleeps, and here it is almost post time, and it is too late for him to get to Fourteenth Street and back before the race is run off, and it is all quite a sad story indeed, although of course it does not make much impression on Sorrowful, as he is already sadder than somewhat himself just from thinking that somebody may beat him for a bet during the day, even though the races do not start anywhere as yet.

Well, the young guy tells Sorrowful he is going to try to get to Fourteenth Street and back in time to bet on the sure thing, because he says it will be nothing short of a crime if he has to miss such a wonderful opportunity.

"But," he says to Sorrowful, "to make sure I do not miss, you take my marker for a deuce, and I will leave the kid here with you as security until I get back."

Now, ordinarily, asking Sorrowful to take a marker will be considered great foolishness, as it is well known to one and all that Sorrowful will not take a marker from Andrew Mellon. In fact, Sorrowful can almost break your heart telling you about the poorhouses that are full of bookmakers who take markers in their time.

But it happens that business is just opening up for the day, and Sorrowful is pretty busy, and besides the young guy is a steady customer for several days, and has an honest pan, and Sorrowful figures a guy is bound to take a little doll out of hock for a deuce. Furthermore, while Sorrowful does not know much about kids, he can see the little doll must be worth a deuce, at least, and maybe more.

So he nods his head, and the young guy puts the little doll on a chair and goes tearing out of the joint to get the dough, while Sorrowful marks down a deuce bet on Cold Cuts, which is the name of the sure thing. Then he forgets all about the proposition for a while, and all the time the little doll is sitting on the chair as quiet as a mouse, smiling at Sorrowful's customers, including the Chinks from the chop-suey joint who come in now and then to play the races.

Well, Cold Cuts blows, and in fact is not even fifth, and along late in the afternoon Sorrowful suddenly realizes that the young guy never shows up again, and that the little doll is still sitting in the chair, although she is now playing with a butcher knife which one of the Chinks from the chop-suey joint gives her to keep her amused.

Finally it comes on Sorrowful's closing time, and the little doll is still there, so he can think of nothing else to do in this situation, but to bring her around to Mindy's and get a little advice from different citizens, as he does not care to leave her in his place of business alone, as Sorrowful will not trust anybody in there alone, not even himself.

"Now," Sorrowful says, after giving us this long spiel, "what are we to do about this proposition?"

Well, of course, up to this minute none of the rest of us know we are being cut in on any proposition, and personally I do not care for any part of it, but Big Nig, the crap shooter, speaks up as follows:

"If this little doll is sitting in your joint all afternoon," Nig says, "the best thing to do right now is to throw a feed into her, as the chances are her stomach thinks her throat is cut."

Now this seems to be a fair sort of an idea, so Sorrowful orders up a couple of portions of ham hocks and sauerkraut, which is a very tasty dish in Mindy's at all times, and the little doll tears into it very enthusiastically, using both hands, although a fat old doll who is sitting at the next table speaks up and says this is terrible fodder to be tossing into a child at such an hour, and where is her mamma?

"Well," Big Nig says to the old doll, "I hear of many people getting a bust in the snoot for not minding their own business in this town, but you give off an idea, at that. Listen," Big Nig says to the little doll, "where is your mamma?"

But the little doll does not seem to know, or maybe she does not wish to make this information public, because she only shakes her head and smiles at Big Nig, as her mouth is too full of ham hocks and sauerkraut for her to talk.

"What is your name?" Big Nig asks, and she says something that Big Nig claims sounds like Marky, although personally I think she is trying to say Martha. Anyway it is from this that she gets the name we always call her afterwards, which is Marky.

"It is a good monicker," Big Nig says. "It is short for marker, and she is certainly a marker unless Sorrowful is telling us a large lie. Why," Big Nig says, "this is a very cute little doll, at that, and pretty smart. How old are you, Marky?"

She only shakes her head again, so Regret, the horse player, who claims he can tell how old a horse is by its teeth, reaches over and sticks his finger in her mouth to get a peek at her crockery, but she seems to think Regret's finger is a hunk of ham hock and shuts down on it so hard Regret lets out an awful squawk. But he says that before she tries to cripple him for life he sees enough of her teeth to convince him she is maybe three, rising four, and this seems reasonable, at that. Anyway, she cannot be much older.

Well, about this time a Guinea with a hand organ stops out in front of Mindy's and begins grinding out a tune while his ever-loving wife is passing a tambourine around among the citizens on the sidewalk and, on hearing this music, Marky slides off of her chair with her mouth still full of ham hock and sauerkraut, which she swallows so fast she almost chokes, and then she speaks as follows:

"Marky dance," she says.

Then she begins hopping and skipping around among the tables, holding her little short skirt up in her hands and showing a pair of white panties underneath. Pretty soon Mindy himself comes along and starts putting up a beef about making a dance hall of his joint, but a guy by the name of Sleep-out, who is watching Marky with much interest, offers to bounce a sugar bowl off of Mindy's sconce if he does not mind his own business.

So Mindy goes away, but he keeps muttering about the white panties being a most immodest spectacle, which of course is great nonsense, as many dolls older than Marky are known to do dances in Mindy's, especially on the late watch, when they stop by for a snack on their way home from the night clubs and the speaks, and I hear some of them do not always wear white panties, either.

Personally, I like Marky's dancing very much, although of course she is no Pavlova, and finally she trips over her own feet and falls on her snoot. But she gets up smiling and climbs back on her chair and pretty soon she is sound asleep with her head against Sorrowful.

Well, now there is much discussion about what Sorrowful ought to do with her. Some claim he ought to take her to a police station, and others say the best thing to do is to put an ad in the Lost and Found columns of the morning bladders, the same as people do when they find Angora cats, and Pekes, and other animals which they do not wish to keep, but none of these ideas seems to appeal to Sorrowful.

Finally he says he will take her to his own home and let her sleep there while he is deciding what is to be done about her, so Sorrowful takes Marky in his arms and lugs her over to a fleabag on West Forty-ninth Street where he has a room for many years, and afterwards a bell hop tells me Sorrowful sits up all night watching her while she is sleeping.

Now what happens but Sorrowful takes on a great fondness for the little doll, which is most surprising, as Sorrowful is never before fond of anybody or anything, and after he has her overnight he cannot bear the idea of giving her up.

Personally, I will just as soon have a three-year-old baby wolf around me as a little doll such as this, but Sorrowful thinks she is the greatest thing that ever happens. He has a few inquiries made around and about to see if he can find out who she belongs to, and he is tickled silly when nothing comes of these inquiries, although nobody else figures anything will come of them anyway, as it is by no means uncommon in this town for little kids to be left sitting in chairs, or on doorsteps, to be chucked into orphan asylums by whoever finds them.

Anyway, Sorrowful says he is going to keep Marky, and his attitude causes great surprise, as keeping Marky is bound to be an expense, and it does not seem reasonable that Sorrowful will go to any expense for anything. When it commences to look as if he means what he says, many citizens naturally figure there must be an angle, and soon there are a great many rumors on the subject.

Of course one of these rumors is that the chances are Marky is Sorrowful's own offspring which is tossed back on him by the wronged mamma, but this rumor is started by a guy who does not know Sorrowful, and after he gets a gander at Sorrowful, the guy apologizes, saying he realizes that no wronged mamma will be daffy enough to permit herself to be wronged by Sorrowful. Personally, I always say that if Sorrowful wishes to keep Marky it is his own business, and most of the citizens around Mindy's agree with me.

But the trouble is Sorrowful at once cuts everybody else in on the management of Marky, and the way he talks to the citizens around Mindy's about her, you will think we are all personally responsible for her. As most of the citizens around Mindy's are bachelors, or are wishing they are bachelors, it is most inconvenient to them to suddenly find themselves with a family.

Some of us try to explain to Sorrowful that if he is going to keep Marky it is up to him to handle all her play, but right away Sorrowful starts talking so sad about all his pals deserting him and Marky just when they need them most that it softens all hearts, although up to this time we are about as pally with Sorrowful as a burglar with a copper. Finally every night in Mindy's is meeting night for a committee to decide something or other about Marky.

The first thing we decide is that the fleabag where Sorrowful lives is no place for Marky, so Sorrowful hires a big apartment in one of the swellest joints on West Fifty-ninth Street, overlooking Central Park, and spends plenty of potatoes furnishing it, although up to this time Sorrowful never sets himself back more than about ten bobs per week for a place to live and considers it extravagance, at that. I hear it costs him five G's to fix up Marky's bedroom alone, not counting the solid gold toilet set that he buys for her.

Then he gets her an automobile and he has to hire a guy to drive it for her, and finally when we explain to Sorrowful that it does not look right for Marky to be living with nobody but him and a chauffeur, Sorrowful hires a French doll with bobbed hair and red cheeks by the name of Mam'selle Fifi as a nurse for Marky, and this seems to be quite a sensible move, as it insures Marky plenty of company.

In fact, up to the time that Sorrowful hires Mam'selle Fifi, many citizens are commencing to consider Marky something of a nuisance and are playing the duck for her and Sorrowful, but after Mam'selle Fifi comes along you can scarcely get in Sorrowful's joint on Fifty-ninth Street, or around his table in Mindy's when he brings Marky and Mam'selle Fifi in to eat. But one night Sorrowful goes home early and catches Sleep-out guzzling Mam'selle Fifi, and Sorrowful makes Mam'selle Fifi take plenty of breeze, claiming she will set a bad example to Marky.

Then he gets an old tomato by the name of Mrs. Clancy to be Marky's nurse, and while there is no doubt Mrs. Clancy is a better nurse than Mam'selle Fifi and there is practically no danger of her setting Marky a bad example, the play at Sorrowful's joint is by no means as brisk as formerly.

You can see that from being closer than a dead heat with his potatoes, Sorrowful becomes as loose as ashes. He not only spends plenty on Marky, but he starts picking up checks in Mindy's and other spots, although up to this time picking up checks is something that is most repulsive to Sorrowful.

He gets so he will hold still for a bite, if the bite is not too savage and, what is more, a great change comes over his kisser. It is no longer so sad and mean-looking, and in fact it is almost a pleasant sight at times, especially as Sorrowful gets so he smiles now and then, and has a big hello for one and all, and everybody says the Mayor ought to give Marky a medal for bringing about such a wonderful change.

Now Sorrowful is so fond of Marky that he wants her with him all the time, and by and by there is much criticism of him for having her around his handbook joint among the Chinks and the horse players, and especially the horse players, and for taking her around night clubs and keeping her out at all hours, as some people do not consider this a proper bringing-up for a little doll.

We hold a meeting in Mindy's on this proposition one night, and we get Sorrowful to agree to keep Marky out of his joint, but we know Marky is so fond of night clubs, especially where there is music, that it seems a sin and a shame to deprive her of this pleasure altogether, so we finally compromise by letting Sorrowful take her out one night a week to the Hot Box on Fifty-fourth Street, which is only a few blocks from where Marky lives, and Sorrowful can get her home fairly early. In fact, after this Sorrowful seldom keeps her out any later than 2 a.m.

The reason Marky likes night clubs where there is music is because she can do her dance there, as Marky is practically daffy on the subject of dancing, especially by herself, even though she never seems to be able to get over winding up by falling on her snoot, which many citizens consider a very artistic finish, at that.

The Choo-Choo Boys' band in the Hot Box always play a special number for Marky in between the regular dances, and she gets plenty of applause, especially from the Broadway citizens who know her, although Henri, the manager of the Hot Box, once tells me he will just as soon Marky does not do her dancing there, because one night several of his best customers from Park Avenue, including two millionaires and two old dolls, who do not understand Marky's dancing, bust out laughing when she falls on her snoot, and Big Nig puts the slug on the guys, and is trying to put the slug on the old dolls, too, when he is finally headed off.

Now one cold, snowy night, many citizens are sitting around the tables in the Hot Box, speaking of one thing and another and having a few drams, when Sorrowful drops in on his way home, for Sorrowful has now become a guy who is around and about, and in and out. He does not have Marky with him, as it is not her night out and she is home with Mrs. Clancy.

A few minutes after Sorrowful arrives, a party by the name of Milk Ear Willie from the West Side comes in, this Milk Ear Willie being a party who is once a prize fighter and who has a milk ear, which is the reason he is called Milk Ear Willie, and who is known to carry a John Roscoe in his pants pocket. Furthermore, it is well known that he knocks off several guys in his time, so he is considered rather a suspicious character.

It seems that the reason he comes into the Hot Box is to shoot Sorrowful full of little holes, because he has a dispute with Sorrowful about a parlay on the races the day before, and the chances are Sorrowful will now be very dead if it does not happen that, just as Milk Ear outs with the old equalizer and starts taking dead aim at Sorrowful from a table across the room, who pops into the joint but Marky.

She is in a long nightgown that keeps getting tangled up in her bare feet as she runs across the dance floor and jumps into Sorrowful's arms, so if Milk Ear Willie lets go at this time he is apt to put a slug in Marky, and this is by no means Willie's intentions. So Willie puts his rod back in his kick, but he is greatly disgusted and stops as he is going out and makes a large complaint to Henri about allowing children in a night club.

Well, Sorrowful does not learn until afterwards how Marky saves his life, as he is too much horrified over her coming four or five blocks through the snow bare-footed to think of anything else, and everybody present is also horrified and wondering how Marky finds her way there. But Marky does not seem to have any good explanation for her conduct, except that she wakes up and discovers Mrs. Clancy asleep and gets to feeling lonesome for Sorrowful.

About this time, the Choo-Choo Boys start playing Marky's tune, and she slips out of Sorrowful's arms and runs out on the dance floor.

"Marky dance," she says.

Then she lifts her nightgown in her hands and starts hopping and skipping about the floor until Sorrowful collects her in his arms again, and wraps her in an overcoat and takes her home.

Now what happens but the next day Marky is sick from being out in the snow bare-footed and with nothing on but her nightgown, and by night she is very sick indeed, and it seems that she has pneumonia, so Sorrowful takes her to the Clinic hospital, and hires two nurses and two croakers, and wishes to hire more, only they tell him these will do for the present.

The next day Marky is no better, and the next night she is worse, and the management of the Clinic is very much upset because it has no place to put the baskets of fruit and candy and floral horseshoes and crates of dolls and toys that keep arriving every few minutes. Furthermore, the management by no means approves of the citizens who are tiptoeing along the hall on the floor where Marky has her room, especially such as Big Nig, and Sleep-out, and Wop Joey, and the Pale Face Kid and Guinea Mike and many other prominent characters, especially as these characters keep trying to date up the nurses.

Of course I can see the management's point of view, but I wish to say that no visitor to the Clinic ever brings more joy and cheer to the patients than Sleep-out, as he goes calling in all the private rooms and wards to say a pleasant word or two to the inmates, and I never take any stock in the rumor that he is looking around to see if there is anything worth picking up. In fact, an old doll from Rockville Centre, who is suffering with yellow jaundice, puts up an awful holler when Sleep-out is heaved from her room, because she says he is right in the middle of a story about a traveling salesman and she wishes to learn what happens.

There are so many prominent characters in and around the Clinic that the morning bladders finally get the idea that some well-known mob guy must be in the hospital full of slugs, and by and by the reporters come buzzing around to see what is what. Naturally they find out that all this interest is in nothing but a little doll, and while you will naturally think that such a little doll as Marky can scarcely be worth the attention of the reporters, it seems they get more heated up over her when they hear the story than if she is Jack Diamond.

In fact, the next day all the bladders have large stories about Marky, and also about Sorrowful and about how all these prominent characters of Broadway are hanging around the Clinic on her account. Moreover, one story tells about Sleep-out entertaining the other patients in the hospital, and it makes Sleep-out sound like a very large-hearted guy.

It is maybe three o'clock on the morning of the fourth day Marky is in the hospital that Sorrowful comes into Mindy's looking very sad indeed. He orders a sturgeon sandwich on pumpernickel, and then he explains that Marky seems to be getting worse by the minute and that he does not think his doctors are doing her any good, and at this Big Nig, the crap shooter, speaks up and states as follows:

"Well," Big Nig says, "if we are only able to get Doc Beerfeldt, the great pneumonia specialist, the chances are he will cure Marky like breaking sticks. But of course," Nig says, "it is impossible to get Doc Beerfeldt unless you are somebody like John D. Rockefeller, or maybe the President."

Naturally, everybody knows that what Big Nig says is very true, for Doc Beerfeldt is the biggest croaker in this town, but no ordinary guy can get close enough to Doc Beerfeldt to hand him a ripe peach, let alone get him to go out on a case. He is an old guy, and he does not practice much anymore, and then only among a few very rich and influential people. Furthermore, he has plenty of potatoes himself, so money does not interest him whatever, and anyway it is great foolishness to be talking of getting Doc Beerfeldt out at such an hour as this.

"Who do we know who knows Doc Beerfeldt?" Sorrowful says. "Who can we call up who may have influence enough with him to get him to just look at Marky? I will pay any price," he says. "Think of somebody," he says.

Well, while we are all trying to think, who comes in but Milk Ear Willie, and he comes in to toss a few slugs at Sorrowful, but before Milk Ear can start blasting Sleep-out sees him and jumps up and takes him off to a corner table, and starts whispering in Milk Ear's good ear.

As Sleep-out talks to him Milk Ear looks at Sorrowful in great surprise, and finally he begins nodding his head, and by and by he gets up and goes out of the joint in a hurry, while Sleep-out comes back to our table and says like this:

"Well," Sleep-out says, "let us stroll over to the Clinic. I just send Milk Ear Willie up to Doc Beerfeldt's house on Park Avenue to get the old Doc and bring him to the hospital. But, Sorrowful," Sleep-out says, "if he gets him, you must pay Willie the parlay you dispute with him, whatever it is. The chances are," Sleep-out says, "Willie is right. I remember once you out-argue me on a parlay when I know I am right."

Personally, I consider Sleep-out's talk about sending Milk Ear Willie after Doc Beerfeldt just so much nonsense, and so does everybody else, but we figure maybe Sleep-out is trying to raise Sorrowful's hopes, and anyway he keeps Milk Ear from tossing these slugs at Sorrowful, which everybody considers very thoughtful of Sleep-out, at least, especially as Sorrowful is under too great a strain to be dodging slugs just now.

About a dozen of us walk over to the Clinic, and most of us stand around the lobby on the ground floor, although Sorrowful goes up to Marky's floor to wait outside her door. He is waiting there from the time she is first taken to the hospital, never leaving except to go over to Mindy's once in a while to get something to eat, and occasionally they open the door a little to let him get a peek at Marky.

Well, it is maybe six o'clock when we hear a taxi stop outside the hospital and pretty soon in comes Milk Ear Willie with another character from West Side by the name of Fats Finstein, who is well known to one and all as a great friend of Willie's, and in between them they have a little old guy with a Vandyke beard, who does not seem to have on anything much but a silk dressing-gown and who seems somewhat agitated, especially as Milk Ear Willie and Fats Finstein keep prodding him from behind.

Now it comes out that this little old guy is nobody but Doc Beerfeldt, the great pneumonia specialist, and personally I never see a madder guy, although I wish to say I never blame him much for being mad when I learn how Milk Ear Willie and Fats Finstein boff his butler over the noggin when he answers their ring, and how they walk right into old Doc Beerfeldt's bedroom and haul him out of the hay at the point of their Roscoes and make him go with them.

In fact, I consider such treatment most discourteous to a prominent croaker, and if I am Doc Beerfeldt I will start hollering copper as soon as I hit the hospital, and for all I know maybe Doc Beerfeldt has such an idea, but as Milk Ear Willie and Fats Finstein haul him into the lobby who comes downstairs but Sorrowful. And the minute Sorrowful sees Doc Beerfeldt he rushes up to him and says like this:

"Oh Doc," Sorrowful says, "do something for my little girl. She is dying, Doc," Sorrowful says. "Just a little bit of a girl, Doc. Her name is Marky. I am only a gambler, Doc, and I do not mean anything to you or to anybody else, but please save the little girl."

Well, old Doc Beerfeldt sticks out his Vandyke beard and looks at Sorrowful a minute, and he can see there are large tears in old Sorrowful's eyes, and for all I know maybe the Doc knows it has been many and many a year since there are tears in these eyes, at that. Then the Doc looks at Milk Ear Willie and Fats Finstein and the rest of us, and at the nurses and interns who are commencing to come running up from every which way. Finally, he speaks as follows:

"What is this?" he says. "A child? A little child? Why," he says, "I am under the impression that these gorillas are kidnapping me to attend to some other sick or wounded gorilla. A child? This is quite different. Why do you not say so in the first place? Where is the child?" Doc Beerfeldt says, "and," he says, "somebody get me some pants."

We all follow him upstairs to the door of Marky's room and we wait outside when he goes in, and we wait there for hours, because it seems that even old Doc Beerfeldt cannot think of anything to do in this situation no matter how he tries. And along toward ten-thirty in the morning he opens the door very quietly and motions Sorrowful to come in, and then he motions all the rest of us to follow, shaking his head very sad.

There are so many of us that we fill the room around a little high narrow bed on which Marky is lying like a flower against a white wall, her yellow curls spread out over her pillow. Old Sorrowful drops on his knees beside the bed and his shoulders heave quite some as he kneels there, and I hear Sleep-out sniffing as if he has a cold in his head. Marky seems to be asleep when we go in, but while we are standing around the bed looking down at her, she opens her eyes and seems to see us and, what is more, she seems to know us, because she smiles at each guy in turn and then tries to hold out one of her little hands to Sorrowful.

Now very faint, like from far away, comes a sound of music through a half-open window in the room, from a jazz band that is rehearsing in a hall just up the street from the hospital, and Marky hears this music because she holds her head in such a way that anybody can see she is listening, and then she smiles again at us and whispers very plain, as follows:

"Marky dance."

And she tries to reach down as if to pick up her skirt as she always does when she dances, but her hands fall across her breast as soft and white and light as snowflakes, and Marky never again dances in this world.

Well, old Doc Beerfeldt and the nurses make us go outside at once, and while we are standing there in the hall outside the door, saying nothing whatever, a young guy and two dolls, one of them old, and the other not so old, come along the hall much excited.

The young guy seems to know Sorrowful, who is sitting down again in his chair just outside the door, because he rushes up to Sorrowful and says to him like this:

"Where is she?" he says. "Where is my darling child? You remember me?" he says. "I leave my little girl with you one day while I go on an errand, and while I am on this errand everything goes blank, and I wind up back in my home in Indianapolis with my mother and sister here, and recall nothing about where I leave my child, or anything else."

"The poor boy has amnesia," the old doll says. "The stories that he deliberately abandons his wife in Paris and his child in New York are untrue."

"Yes," the doll who is not old puts in. "If we do not see the stories in the newspapers about how you have the child in this hospital we may never learn where she is. But everything is all right now. Of course we never approve of Harold's marriage to a person of the stage, and we only recently learn of her death in Paris soon after their separation there and are very sorry. But everything is all right now. We will take full charge of the child."

Now while all this gab is going on, Sorrowful never glances at them. He is just sitting there looking at Marky's door. And now as he is looking at the door a very strange thing seems to happen to his kisser, for all of a sudden it becomes the sad, mean-looking kisser that it is in the days before he ever sees Marky, and furthermore it is never again anything else.

"We will be rich," the young guy says. "We just learn that my darling child will be sole heiress to her maternal grandpapa's fortune, and the old guy is only a hop ahead of the undertaker right now. I suppose," he says, "I owe you something?"

And then Sorrowful gets up off his chair, and looks at the young guy and at the two dolls, and speaks as follows:

"Yes," he says, "you owe me a two-dollar marker for the bet you blow on Cold Cuts, and," he says, "I will trouble you to send it to me at once, so I can wipe you off my books."

Now he walks down the hall and out of the hospital, never looking back again, and there is a very great silence behind him that is broken only by the sniffing of Sleep-out, and by some first-class sobbing from some of the rest of us, and I remember now that the guy who is doing the best job of sobbing of all is nobody but Milk Ear Willie.

DREAM STREET ROSE

Of an early evening when there is nothing much doing anywhere else, I go around to Good Time Charley's little speak on West Forty-seventh Street that he calls the Gingham Shoppe, and play a little klob with Charley, because business is quiet in the Gingham Shoppe at such an hour, and Charley gets very lonesome.

He once has a much livelier spot on Forty-eighth Street that he calls the Crystal Room, but one night a bunch of G-guys step into the joint and bust it wide open, besides confiscating all of Charley's stock of merchandise. It seems that these G-guys are members of a squad that comes on from Washington, and being strangers in the city they do not know that Good Time Charley's joint is not supposed to be busted up, so they go ahead and bust it, just the same as if it is any other joint.

Well, this action causes great indignation in many quarters, and a lot of citizens advise Charley to see somebody about it. But Charley says no. Charley says if this is the way the government is going to treat him after the way he walks himself bow-legged over in France with the Rainbow Division, making the Germans hard to catch, why, all right. But he is not going to holler copper about it, although Charley says he has his own opinion of Mr. Hoover, at that.

Personally, I greatly admire Charley for taking the disaster so calmly, especially as it catches him with very few potatoes. Charley is a great hand for playing the horses with any dough he makes out of the Crystal Room, and this particular season the guys who play the horses are being murdered by the bookies all over the country, and are in terrible distress.

So I know if Charley is not plumb broke that he has a terrible crack across his belly, and I am not surprised that I do not see him for a couple of weeks after the government guys knock off the

Crystal Room. I hear rumors that he is at home reading the newspapers very carefully every day, especially the obituary notices, for it seems that Charley figures that some of the G-guys may be tempted to take a belt or two at the merchandise they confiscate, and Charley says if they do, he is even for life.

Finally I hear that Charley is seen buying a bolt of gingham in Bloomington's one day, so I know he will be in action again very soon, for all Charley needs to go into action is a bolt of gingham and a few bottles of Golden Wedding. In fact, I know Charley to go into action without the gingham, but as a rule he likes to drape a place of business with gingham to make it seem more homelike to his customers, and I wish to say that when it comes to draping gingham, Charley can make a sucker of Joseph Urban, or anybody else.

Well, when I arrive at the Gingham Shoppe this night I am talking about, which is around ten o'clock, I find Charley in a very indignant state of mind, because an old tomato by the name of Dream Street Rose comes in and tracks up his floor, just after Charley gets through mopping it up, for Charley does his mopping in person, not being able as yet to afford any help.

Rose is sitting at a table in a corner, paying no attention to Charley's remarks about wiping her feet on the Welcome mat at the door before she comes in, because Rose knows there is no Welcome mat at Charley's door, anyway, but I can see where Charley has a right to a few beefs, at that, as she leaves a trail of black hoofprints across the clean floor as if she is walking around in mud somewhere before she comes in, although I do not seem to remember that it is raining when I arrive.

Now this Dream Street Rose is an old doll of maybe fifty-odd, and is a very well-known character around and about, as she is wandering through the Forties for many a year, and especially through West Forty-seventh Street between Sixth and Seventh Avenues, and this block is called Dream Street. And the reason it is called Dream Street is because on this block are many characters of one kind and another who always seem to be dreaming of different matters.

On Dream Street there are many theatrical hotels, and rooming houses, and restaurants, and speaks, including Good Time Charley's Gingham Shoppe, and in the summer-time the characters I mention sit on the stoops or lean against the railings along Dream

Street, and the gab you hear sometimes sounds very dreamy indeed. In fact, it sometimes sounds very pipe-dreamy.

Many actors, male and female, and especially vaudeville actors,
live in the hotels and rooming houses, and vaudeville actors, both
male and female, are great hands for sitting around dreaming out
loud about how they will practically assassinate the public in the
Palace if ever they get a chance.

Furthermore, on Dream Street are always many hand-bookies
and horse players, who sit on the church steps on the cool side of
Dream Street in the summer and dream about big killings on the
races, and there are also nearly always many fight managers, and
sometimes fighters, hanging out in front of the restaurants, picking their teeth and dreaming about winning championships of the
world, although up to this time no champion of the world has yet
come out of Dream Street.

On this street you see burlesque dolls, and hoofers, and guys
who write songs, and saxophone players, and newsboys, and newspaper scribes, and taxi drivers, and blind guys, and midgets, and
blondes with Pomeranian pooches, or maybe French poodles, and
guys with whiskers, and night-club entertainers, and I do not know
what all else. And all of these characters are interesting to look at,
and some of them are very interesting to talk to, although if you
listen to several I know long enough, you may get the idea that
they are somewhat daffy, especially the horse players.

But personally I consider all horse players more or less daffy
anyway. In fact, the way I look at it, if a guy is not daffy he will
not be playing the horses.

Now this Dream Street Rose is a short, thick-set, square-looking
old doll, with a square pan, and square shoulders, and she has
heavy iron-gray hair that she wears in a square bob, and she stands
very square on her feet. In fact, Rose is the squarest-looking doll I
ever see, and she is as strong and lively as Jim Londos, the wrestler.
In fact, Jim Londos will never be any better than six to five in my
line over Dream Street Rose, if she is in any kind of shape.

Nobody in this town wishes any truck with Rose if she has a
few shots of grog in her, and especially Good Time Charley's grog,
for she can fight like the chickens when she is grogged up. In fact,
Rose holds many a decision in this town, especially over coppers,
because if there is one thing she hates and despises more than
somewhat it is a copper, as coppers are always heaving her into

the old can when they find her jerking citizens around and cutting up other didoes.

For many years Rose works in the different hotels along Dream Street as a chambermaid. She never works in any one hotel very long, because the minute she gets a few bobs together she likes to go out and enjoy a little recreation, such as visiting around the speaks, although she is about as welcome in most speaks as a G-guy with a search warrant. You see, nobody can ever tell when Rose may feel like taking the speak apart, and also the customers.

She never has any trouble getting a job back in any hotel she ever works in, for Rose is a wonderful hand for making up beds, although several times, when she is in a hurry to get off, I hear she makes up beds with guests still in them, which causes a few mild beefs to the management, but does not bother Rose. I speak of this matter only to show you that she is a very quaint character indeed, and full of zest.

Well, I sit down to play klob with Good Time Charley, but about this time several customers come into the Gingham Shoppe, so Charley has to go and take care of them, leaving me alone. And while I am sitting there alone I hear Dream Street Rose mumbling to herself over in the corner, but I pay no attention to her, although I wish to say I am by no means unfriendly with Rose.

In fact, I say hello to her at all times, and am always very courteous to her, as I do not wish to have her bawling me out in public, and maybe circulating rumors about me, as she is apt to do, if she feels I am snubbing her.

Finally I notice her motioning to me to come over to her table, and I go over at once and sit down, because I can see that Rose is well grogged up at this time, and I do not care to have her attracting my attention by chucking a cuspidor at me. She offers me a drink when I sit down, but of course I never drink anything that is sold in Good Time Charley's, as a personal favor to Charley. He says he wishes to retain my friendship.

So I just sit there saying nothing much whatever, and Rose keeps on mumbling to herself, and I am not able to make much of her mumbling, until finally she looks at me and says to me like this:

"I am now going to tell you about my friend," Rose says.

"Well, Rose," I say, "personally I do not care to hear about your friend, although," I say, "I have no doubt that what you wish to tell me about this friend is very interesting. But I am here to

play a little klob with Good Time Charley, and I do not have time
to hear about your friend."

"Charley is busy selling his poison to the suckers," Rose says.
"I am now going to tell you about my friend. It is quite a story,"
she says. "You will listen."

So I listen.

It is a matter of thirty-five years ago (Dream Street Rose says)
and the spot is a town in Colorado by the name of Pueblo, where
there are smelters and one thing and another. My friend is at this
time maybe sixteen or seventeen years old, and a first-class looker
in every respect. Her papa is dead, and her mamma runs a boarding-
house for the guys who work in the smelters, and who are very
hearty eaters. My friend deals them off the arm for the guys in her
mamma's boarding-house to save her mamma the expense of a
waitress.

Now among the boarders in this boarding-house are many guys
who are always doing a little pitching to my friend, and trying to
make dates with her to take her places, but my friend never gives
them much of a tumble, because after she gets through dealing
them off the arm all day her feet generally pain her too much to
go anywhere on them except to the hay.

Finally, however, along comes a tall, skinny young guy from the
East by the name of Frank something, who has things to say to my
friend that are much more interesting than anything that has been
said to her by a guy before, including such things as love and marriage, which are always very interesting subjects to any young doll.

This Frank is maybe twenty-five years old, and he comes from
the East with the idea of making his fortune in the West, and while
it is true that fortunes are being made in the West at this time,
there is little chance that Frank is going to make any part of a fortune, as he does not care to work very hard. In fact, he does not
care to work at all, being much more partial to playing a little
poker, or shooting a few craps, or maybe hustling a sucker around
Mike's pool room on Santa Fe Avenue, for Frank is an excellent
pool player, especially when he is playing a sucker.

Now my friend is at this time a very innocent young doll, and a
good doll in every respect, and her idea of love includes a nice little home, and children running here and there and around and
about, and she never has a wrong thought in her life, and believes
that everybody else in the world is like herself. And the chances

are if this Frank does not happen along, my friend will marry a young guy in Pueblo by the name of Higginbottom, who is very fond of her indeed, and who is a decent young guy and afterwards makes plenty of potatoes in the grocery dodge.

But my friend goes very daffy over Frank and cannot see anybody but him, and the upshot of it all is she runs away with him one day to Denver, being dumb enough to believe that he means it when he tells her that he loves her and is going to marry her. Why Frank ever bothers with such a doll as my friend in the first place is always a great mystery to one and all, and the only way anybody can explain it is that she is young and fresh, and he is a heel at heart.

"Well, Rose," I say, "I am now commencing to see the finish of this story about your friend, and," I say, "it is such a story as anybody can hear in a speak at any time in this town, except," I say, "maybe your story is longer than somewhat. So I will now thank you, and excuse myself, and play a little klob with Good Time Charley."

"You will listen," Dream Street Rose says, looking me slap-dab in the eye.

So I listen.

Moreover, I notice now that Good Time Charley is standing behind me, bending in an ear, as it seems that his customers take the wind after a couple of slams of Good Time Charley's merchandise, a couple of slams being about all that even a very hardy customer can stand at one session.

Of course (Rose goes on) the chances are Frank never intends marrying my friend at all, and she never knows until long afterwards that the reason he leads her to the parson is that the young guy from Pueblo by the name of Higginbottom catches up with them at the old Windsor Hotel where they are stopping and privately pokes a six-pistol against Frank's ribs and promises faithfully to come back and blow a hole in Frank you can throw a watermelon through if Frank tries any phenagling around with my friend.

Well, in practically no time whatever, love's young dream is over as far as my friend is concerned. This Frank turns out to be a most repulsive character indeed, especially if you are figuring him as an ever-loving husband. In fact, he is no good. He mistreats my friend in every way any guy ever thought of mistreating a doll, and besides the old established ways of mistreating a doll, Frank thinks up quite a number of new ways, being really quite ingenious in this respect.

Yes, this Frank is one hundred per cent heel.

It is not so much that he gives her a thumping now and then, because, after all, a thumping wears off, and hurts heal up, even when they are such hurts as a broken nose and fractured ribs, and once an ankle cracked by a kick. It is what he does to her heart, and to her innocence. He is by no means a good husband, and does not know how to treat an ever-loving wife with any respect, especially as he winds up by taking my friend to San Francisco and hiring her out to a very loose character there by the name of Black Emanuel, who has a dance joint on the Barbary Coast, which, at the time I am talking about, is hotter than a stove. In this joint my friend has to dance with the customers, and get them to buy beer for her and one thing and another, and this occupation is most distasteful to my friend, as she never cares for beer.

It is there Frank leaves her for good after giving her an extra big thumping for a keepsake, and when my friend tries to leave Black Emanuel's to go looking for her ever-loving husband, she is somewhat surprised to hear Black Emanuel state that he pays Frank three C's for her to remain there and continue working. Furthermore, Black Emanuel resumes the thumpings where Frank leaves off, and by and by my friend is much bewildered and down-hearted and does not care what happens to her.

Well, there is nothing much of interest in my friend's life for the next thirty-odd years, except that she finally gets so she does not mind the beer so much, and, in fact, takes quite a fondness for it, and also for light wines and Bourbon whisky, and that she comes to realize that Frank does not love her after all, in spite of what he says. Furthermore, in later years, after she drifts around the country quite some, in and out of different joints, she realizes that the chances are she will never have a nice little home, with children running here and there, and she often thinks of what a disagreeable influence Frank has on her life.

In fact, this Frank is always on her mind more than somewhat. In fact, she thinks of him night and day, and says many a prayer that he will do well. She manages to keep track of him, which is not hard to do, at that, as Frank is in New York, and is becoming quite a guy in business, and is often in the newspapers. Maybe his success is due to my friend's prayers, but the chances are it is more because he connects up with some guy who has an invention for doing something very interesting in steel, and by grabbing an interest in this invention Frank gets a shove toward plenty of potatoes. Furthermore, he is married, and is raising up a family.

About ten or twelve years ago my friend comes to New York, and by this time she is getting a little faded around the edges. She is not so old, at that, but the air of the Western and Southern joints is bad on the complexion, and beer is no good for the figure. In fact, my friend is now quite a haybag, and she does not get any better-looking in the years she spends in New York as she is practically all out of the old sex appeal, and has to do a little heavy lifting to keep eating. But she never forgets to keep praying that Frank will continue to do well, and Frank certainly does this, as he is finally spoken of everywhere very respectfully as a millionaire and a high-class guy.

In all the years she is in New York my friend never runs into Frank, as Frank is by no means accustomed to visiting the spots where my friend hangs out, but my friend goes to a lot of bother to get acquainted with a doll who is a maid for some time in Frank's town house on East Seventy-fourth Street, and through this doll my friend keeps a pretty fair line on the way Frank lives. In fact, one day when Frank and his family are absent, my friend goes to Frank's house with her friend, just to see what it looks like, and after an hour there my friend has the joint pretty well cased.

So now my friend knows through her friend that on very hot nights such as to-night Frank's family is bound to be at their country place at Port Washington, but that Frank himself is spending the night at his town house, because he wishes to work on a lot of papers of some kind. My friend knows through her friend that all of Frank's servants are at Port Washington, too, except my friend's friend, who is in charge of the town house, and Frank's valet, a guy by the name of Sloggins.

Furthermore, my friend knows through her friend that both her friend and Sloggins have a date to go to a movie at eight-thirty o'clock, to be gone a couple of hours, as it seems Frank is very big-hearted about giving his servants time off for such a purpose when he is at home alone; although one night he squawks no little when my friend is out with her friend drinking a little beer, and my friend's friend loses her door key and has to ring the bell to the servants' entrance, and rousts Frank out of a sound sleep.

Naturally, my friend's friend will be greatly astonished if she ever learns that it is with this key that my friend steps into Frank's house along about nine o'clock to-night. An electric light hangs over the servants' entrance, and my friend locates the button that controls this light just inside the door and turns it off, as my friend figures that maybe Frank and his family will not care to have any of their high-class neighbors, or anyone else, see an old doll who has no better hat than she is wearing, entering or leaving their house at such an hour.

It is an old-fashioned sort of house, four or five stories high, with the library on the third floor in the rear, looking out through French windows over a nice little garden, and my friend finds Frank in the library where she expects to find him, because she is smart enough to figure that a guy who is working on papers is not apt to be doing his work in the cellar.

But Frank is not working on anything when my friend moves in on him. He is dozing in a chair by the window, and, looking at him, after all these years, she finds something of a change indeed. He is much heavier than he is thirty-five years back, and his hair is white, but he looks pretty well to my friend, at that, as she stands there for maybe five minutes watching him. Then he seems to realize somebody is in the room, as sleeping guys will do, for his regular breathing stops with a snort, and he opens his eyes, and looks into my friend's eyes, but without hardly stirring. And finally my friend speaks to Frank as follows:

"Well, Frank," she says, "do you know me?"

"Yes," he says, after a while, "I know you. At first I think maybe you are a ghost, as I once hear something about your being dead. But," he says, "I see now the report is a canard. You are too fat to be a ghost."

Well, of course, this is a most insulting crack indeed, but my friend passes it off as she does not wish to get in any arguments with Frank at this time. She can see that he is upset more than somewhat and he keeps looking around the room as if he hopes he can see somebody else he can cut in on the conversation. In fact, he acts as if my friend is by no means a welcome visitor.

"Well, Frank," my friend says, very pleasant, "there you are, and here I am. I understand you are now a wealthy and prominent citizen of this town. I am glad to know this, Frank," she says. "You will be surprised to hear that for years and years I pray that you will do well for yourself and become a big guy in every respect, with a nice family, and everything else. I judge my prayers are answered," she says. "I see by the papers that you have two sons at Yale, and a daughter in Vassar, and that your ever-loving wife is getting to be very high mucky-mucky in society. Well, Frank," she says, "I am very glad. I pray something like all this will happen to you."

Now, at such a speech, Frank naturally figures that my friend is all right, at that, and the chances are he also figures that she still has a mighty soft spot in her heart for him, just as she has in the days when she deals them off the arm to keep him in gambling and drinking money. In fact, Frank brightens somewhat, and he says to my friend like this:

"You pray for my success?" he says. "Why, this is very thoughtful of you indeed. Well," he says, "I am sitting on top of the world. I have everything to live for."

"Yes," my friend says, "and this is exactly where I pray I will find you. On top of the world," she says, "and with everything to live for. It is where I am when you take my life. It is where I am when you kill me as surely as if you strangle me with your hands. I always pray you will not become a bum," my friend says, "because a bum has nothing to live for, anyway. I want to find you liking to live, so you will hate so much to die."

Naturally, this does not sound so good to Frank, and he begins all of a sudden to shake and shiver and to stutter somewhat.

"Why," he says, "what do you mean? Are you going to kill me?"

"Well," my friend says, "that remains to be seen. Personally," she says, "I will be much obliged if you will kill yourself, but it can be arranged one way or the other. However, I will explain the disadvantages of me killing you.

"The chances are," my friend says, "if I kill you I will be caught and a very great scandal will result, because," she says, "I have on my person the certificate of my marriage to you in Denver, and something tells me you never think to get a divorce. So," she says, "you are a bigamist."

"I can pay," Frank says. "I can pay plenty."

"Furthermore," my friend says, paying no attention to his remark, "I have a sworn statement from Black Emanuel about your transaction with him, for Black Emanuel gets religion before he dies from being shivved by Johnny Mizzoo, and he tries to round himself up by confessing all the sins he can think of, which are quite a lot. It is a very interesting statement," my friend says.

"Now then," she says, "if you knock yourself off you will leave an unsullied, respected name. If I kill you, all the years and effort you have devoted to building up your reputation will go for nothing. You are past sixty," my friend says, "and any way you figure it, you do not have so very far to go. If I kill you," she says, "you will go in horrible disgrace, and everybody around you will feel the disgrace, no matter how much dough you leave them. Your children will hang their heads in shame. Your ever-loving wife will not like it," my friend says.

"I wait on you a long time, Frank," my friend says. "A dozen times in the past twenty years I figure I may as well call on you and close up my case with you, but," she says, "then I always persuade myself to wait a little longer so you would rise higher and higher and life will be a bit sweeter to you. And there you are, Frank," she says, "and here I am."

Well, Frank sits there as if he is knocked plumb out, and he does not answer a word; so finally my friend outs with a large John Roscoe which she is packing in the bosom of her dress, and tosses it in his lap, and speaks as follows:

"Frank," she says, "do not think it will do you any good to pot me in the back when I turn around, because," she says, "you will be worse off than ever. I leave plenty of letters scattered around in case anything happens to me. And remember," she says, "if you do not do this job yourself, I will be back. Sooner or later, I will be back."

So (Dream Street Rose says) my friend goes out of the library and down the stairs, leaving Frank sprawled out in his chair, and when she reaches the first floor she hears what may be a shot in the upper part of the house, and then again maybe only a door slamming. My friend never knows for sure what it is, because a little later as she nears the servants' entrance she hears quite a commotion outside, and a guy cussing a blue streak, and a doll tee-heeing, and pretty soon my friend's friend, the maid, and Sloggins, the valet, come walking in.

Well, my friend just has time to scroonch herself back in a dark corner, and they go upstairs, the guy still cussing and the doll still giggling, and my friend cannot make out what it is all about except that they come home earlier than she figures. So my friend goes tippy-toe out of the servants' entrance, to grab a taxi not far from the house and get away from this neighborhood, and now you will soon hear of the suicide of a guy who is a millionaire, and it will be all even with my friend.

"Well, Rose," I say, "it is a nice long story, and full of romance and all this and that, and," I say, "of course I will never be ungentlemanly enough to call a lady a liar, but," I say, "if it is not a lie, it will do until a lie comes along."

"All right," Rose says. "Anyway, I tell you about my friend. Now," she says, "I am going where the liquor is better, which can be any other place in town, because," she says, "there is no chance of liquor anywhere being any worse."

So she goes out, making more tracks on Good Time Charley's floor, and Charley speaks most impolitely of her after she goes, and gets out his mop to clean the floor, for one thing about Charley, he is as neat as a pin, and maybe neater.

Well, along toward one o'clock I hear a newsboy in the street outside yelling something I cannot make out, because he is yelling as if he has a mouthful of mush, as newsboys are bound to do. But I am anxious to see what goes in the first race at Belmont, on account of having a first-class tip, so I poke my noggin outside Good Time Charley's and buy a paper, and across the front page, in large letters, it states that the wealthy Mr. Frank Billingsworth McQuiggan knocks himself off by putting a slug through his own noggin.

It says Mr. McQuiggan is found in a chair in his library as dead as a door-nail with the pistol in his lap with which he knocks himself off, and the paper states that nobody can figure what causes Mr. McQuiggan to do such a thing to himself as he is in good health and has plenty of potatoes and is at the peak of his career. Then there is a lot about his history.

When Mr. McQuiggan is a young fellow returning from a visit to the Pacific Coast with about two hundred dollars in his pocket after paying his railroad fare, he meets in the train Jonas Calloway, famous inventor of the Calloway steel process. Calloway, also then young, is desperately in need of funds and he offers Mr.

McQuiggan a third interest in his invention for what now seems the paltry sum of one hundred dollars. Mr. McQuiggan accepts the offer and thus paves the way to his own fortune.

I am telling all this to Good Time Charley while he is mopping away at the floor, and finally I come on a paragraph down near the finish which goes like this: "The body was discovered by Mr. McQuiggan's faithful valet, Thomas Sloggins, at eleven o'clock. Mr. McQuiggan was then apparently dead a couple of hours. Sloggins returned home shortly before ten o'clock with another servant after changing his mind about going to a movie. Instead of going to see his employer at once, as is his usual custom, Sloggins went to his own quarters and changed his clothes.

"'The light over the servants' entrance was out when I returned home,' the valet said, 'and in the darkness I stumbled over some scaffolding and other material left near this entrance by workmen who are to regravel the roof of the house tomorrow, upsetting all over the entranceway a large bucket of tar, much of which got on my apparel when I fell, making a change necessary before going to see Mr. McQuiggan.'"

Well, Good Time Charley keeps on mopping harder than ever, though finally he stops a minute and speaks to me as follows:

"Listen," Charley says, "understand I do not say the guy does not deserve what he gets, and I am by no means hollering copper, but," Charley says, "if he knocks himself off, how does it come the rod is still in his lap where Dream Street Rose says her friend tosses it? Well, never mind," Charley says, "but can you think of something that will remove tar from a wood floor? It positively will not mop off."

TOBIAS THE TERRIBLE

One night I am sitting in Mindy's restaurant on Broadway par-taking heartily of some Hungarian goulash which comes very nice in Mindy's, what with the chef being personally somewhat Hun-garian himself, when in pops a guy who is a stranger to me and sits down at my table.

I do not pay any attention to the guy at first as I am busy look-ing over the entries for the next day at Laurel, but I hear him tell the waiter to bring him some goulash, too. By and by I hear the guy making a strange noise and I look at him over my paper and see that he is crying. In fact, large tears are rolling down his face into his goulash and going plop-plop as they fall.

Now it is by no means usual to see guys crying in Mindy's restaurant, though thousands of guys come in there who often feel like crying, especially after a tough day at the track, so I commence weighing the guy up with great interest. I can see he is a very little guy, maybe a shade over five feet high and weighing maybe as much as a dime's worth of liver, and he has a moustache like a mosquito's whiskers across his upper lip, and pale blond hair and a very sad look in his eyes.

Furthermore, he is a young guy and he is wearing a suit of clothes the color of French mustard, with slanting pockets, and I notice when he comes in that he has a brown hat sitting jack-deuce on his noggin. Anybody can see that this guy does not be-long in these parts, with such a sad look and especially with such a hat.

Naturally, I figure his crying is some kind of a dodge. In fact, I figure that maybe the guy is trying to cry me out of the price of his Hungarian goulash, although if he takes the trouble to ask any-body before he comes in, he will learn that he may just as well try to cry Al Smith out of the Empire State Building.

But the guy does not say anything whatever to me but just goes on shedding tears into his goulash, and finally I get very curious about this proposition, and I speak to him as follows:

"Listen, pally," I say, "if you are crying about the goulash, you better dry your tears before the chef sees you, because," I say, "the chef is very sensitive about his goulash, and may take your tears as criticism."

"The goulash seems all right," the guy says in a voice that is just about his size. "Anyway, I am not crying about the goulash. I am crying about my sad life. Friend," the guy says, "are you ever in love?"

Well, of course, at this crack I know what is eating the guy. If I have all the tears that are shed on Broadway by guys in love, I will have enough salt water to start an opposition ocean to the Atlantic and Pacific, with enough left over to run the Great Salt Lake out of business. But I wish to say I never shed any of these tears personally, because I am never in love, and furthermore, barring a bad break, I never expect to be in love, for the way I look at it love is strictly the old phedinkus, and I tell the little guy as much.

"Well," he says, "you will not speak so harshly of love if you are acquainted with Miss Deborah Weems."

With this he starts crying more than somewhat, and his grief is such that it touches my heart and I have half a notion to start crying with him as I am now convinced that the guy is leveling with his tears.

Finally the guy slacks up a little in his crying, and begins eating his goulash, and by and by he seems more cheerful, but then it is well known to one and all that a fair dose of Mindy's goulash will cheer up anybody no matter how sad they feel. Pretty soon the guy starts talking to me, and I make out that his name is Tobias Tweeney, and that he comes from a spot over in Bucks County, Pennsylvania, by the name of Erasmus, or some such.

Furthermore, I judge that this Erasmus is not such a large city, but very pleasant, and that Tobias Tweeney is born and raised there and is never much of anyplace else in his life, although he is now rising twenty-five.

Well, it seems that Tobias Tweeney has a fine position in a shoe store selling shoes and is going along all right when he happens to fall in love with a doll by the name of Miss Deborah Weems, whose papa owns a gas station in Erasmus and is a very prominent citizen. I judge from what Tobias tells me that this Miss Deborah Weems tosses him around quite some, which proves to me that dolls in small towns are just the same as they are on Broadway.

"She is beautiful," Tobias Tweeney says, speaking of Miss Deborah Weems. "I do not think I can live without her. But," he says, "Miss Deborah Weems will have no part of me because she is daffy over desperate characters of the underworld such as she sees in the movies at the Model Theater in Erasmus.

"She wishes to know," Tobias Tweeney says, "why I cannot be a big gunman and go around plugging people here and there and talking up to politicians and policemen, and maybe looking picturesque and romantic like Edward G. Robinson or James Cagney or even Georgie Raft. But, of course," Tobias says, "I am not the type for such a character. Anyway," he says, "Constable Wendell will never permit me to be such a character in Erasmus.

"So Miss Deborah Weems says I have no more nerve than a catfish," Tobias says, "and she goes around with a guy by the name of Joe Trivett, who runs the Smoke Shop, and bootlegs ginger extract to the boys in his back room and claims Al Capone once says 'Hello' to him, although," Tobias says, "personally, I think Joe Trivett is nothing but a great big liar."

At this, Tobias Tweeney starts crying again, and I feel very sorry for him indeed, because I can see he is a friendly, harmless little fellow, and by no means accustomed to being tossed around by a doll, and a guy who is not accustomed to being tossed around by a doll always finds it most painful the first time.

"Why," I say, very indignant, "this Miss Deborah Weems talks great foolishness, because big gunmen always wind up nowadays with the score nine to nought against them, even in the movies. In fact," I say, "if they do not wind up this way in the movies, the censors will not permit the movies to be displayed. Why do you not hit this guy Trivett a punch in the snoot," I say, "and tell him to go on about his business?"

"Well," Tobias says, "the reason I do not him a punch in the snoot is because he has the idea of punching snoots first, and whose snoot does he punch but mine. Furthermore," Tobias says, "he makes my snoot bleed with the punch, and he says he will do it again if I keep hanging around Miss Deborah Weems. And,"

Tobias says, "it is mainly because I do not return the punch, being too busy stopping my snoot from bleeding, that Miss Deborah Weems renounces me forever.

"She says she can never stand for a guy who has no more nerve than me," Tobias says, "but," he says, "I ask you if I am to blame if my mother is frightened by a rabbit a few weeks before I am born, and marks me for life?

"So I leave town," Tobias says. "I take my savings of two hundred dollars out of the Erasmus bank, and I come here, figuring maybe I will meet up with some big gunmen and other desperate characters of the underworld, and get to know them, and then I can go back to Erasmus and make Joe Trivett look sick. By the way," he says, "do you know any desperate characters of the underworld?"

Well, of course I do not know any such characters, and if I do know them I am not going to speak about it, because the best a guy can get in this town if he goes around speaking of these matters is a nice kick in the pants. So I say no to Tobias Tweeney, and tell him I am more or less of a stranger myself, and then he wishes to know if I can show him a tough joint, such as he sees in the movies.

Naturally, I do not know of such a joint, but then I get to thinking about Good Time Charley's little Gingham Shoppe over on Forty-seventh Street, and how Charley is not going so good the last time I am in there, and here is maybe a chance for me to steer a little trade his way, because, after all, guys with two yards in their pocket are by no means common nowadays.

So I take Tobias Tweeney around to Good Time Charley's, but the moment we get in there I am sorry we go, because who is present but a dozen parties from different parts of the city, and none of these parties are any bargain at any time. Some of these parties, such as Harry the Horse and Angie the Ox, are from Brooklyn, and three are from Harlem, including Little Mitzi and Germany Schwartz, and several are from the Bronx, because I recognize Joey Uptown, and Joey never goes around without a few intimate friends from his own neighborhood with him.

Afterwards I learn that these parties are to a meeting on business matters at a spot near Good Time Charley's, and when they get through with their business they drop in to give Charley a little complimentary play, for Charley stands very good with one and all in this town. Anyway, they are sitting around a table when Tobias Tweeney and I arrive, and I give them all a big hello, and they hello me back, and ask me and my friend to sit down as it seems they are in a most hospitable frame of mind.

Naturally I sit down because it is never good policy to decline an invitation from parties such as these, and I motion Tobias to sit down, too, and I introduce Tobias all around, and we all have a couple of drinks, and then I explain to those present just who Tobias is, and how his ever-loving doll tosses him around, and how Joe Trivett punches him in the snoot.

Well, Tobias begins crying again, because no inexperienced guy can take a couple of drinks of Good Time Charley's liquor and not bust out crying, even if it is Charley's company liquor, and one and all are at once very sympathetic with Tobias, especially Little Mitzi, who is just tossed around himself more than somewhat by a doll. In fact, Little Mitzi starts crying with him.

"Why," Joey Uptown says, "I never hear of a greater outrage in my life, although," he says, "I can see there is some puppy in you at that, when you do not return this Trivett's punch. But even so," Joey says, "if I have time I will go back to this town you speak of with you and make the guy hard to catch. Furthermore," he says, "I will give this Miss Deborah Weems a piece of my mind."

Then I tell them how Tobias Tweeney comes to New York figuring he may meet up with some desperate characters of the underworld, and they hear this with great interest, and Angie the Ox speaks as follows:

"I wonder," Angie says, "if we can get in touch with anybody who knows such characters and arrange to have Mr. Tweeney meet them, although personally," Angie says, "I loathe and despise characters of this nature."

Well, while Angie is wondering this there comes a large knock at the front door, and it is such a knock as only the gendarmes can knock, and everybody at the table jumps up. Good Time Charley goes to the door and takes a quiet gander through his peephole and we hear a loud, coarse voice speaking as follows:

"Open up, Charley," the voice says. "We wish to look over your guests. Furthermore," the voice says, "tell them not to try the back door, because we are there, too."

"It is Lieutenant Harrigan and his squad," Charley says as he comes back to the table where we are all standing. "Someone must tip him off you are here. Well," Charley says, "those who have rods to shed will shed them now."

At this, Joey Uptown steps up to Tobias Tweeney and hands him a large Betsy and says to Tobias like this:

"Put this away on you somewhere," Joey says, "and then sit down and be quiet. These coppers are not apt to bother with you," Joey says, "if you sit still and mind your own business, but," Joey says, "it will be very tough on any of us they find with a rod, especially any of us who owe the state any time, and," Joey says, "I seem to remember I owe some."

Now of course what Joey says is very true, because he is only walking around and about on parole, and some of the others present are walking around the same way, and it is a very serious matter for a guy who is walking around on parole to be caught with a John Roscoe in his pocket. So it is a very ticklish situation, and somewhat embarrassing.

Well, Tobias Tweeney is somewhat dazed by his couple of drinks of Good Time Charley's liquor and the chances are he does not realize what is coming off, so he takes Joey's rod and puts it in his hip kick. Then all of a sudden Harry the Horse and Angie the Ox and Little Mitzi, and all the others step up to him and hand him their Roscoes and Tobias Tweeney somehow manages to stow the guns away on himself and sit down before Good Time Charley opens the door and in come the gendarmes.

By this time Joey Uptown and all the others are scattered at different tables around the room, with no more than three at any one table, leaving Tobias Tweeney and me alone at the table where we are first sitting. Furthermore, everybody is looking very innocent indeed, and all hands seem somewhat surprised at the intrusion of the gendarmes, who are all young guys belonging to Harrigan's Broadway squad, and very rude.

I know Harrigan by sight, and I know most of his men, and they know there is no more harm in me than there is in a two-year-old baby, so they pay no attention to me whatever, or to Tobias Tweeney, either, but go around making Joey Uptown, and Angie the Ox, and all the others stand up while the gendarmes fan them to see if they have any rods on them, because these gendarmes are always laying for parties such as these hoping to catch them rodded up.

Naturally the gendarmes do not find any rods on anybody, because the rods are all on Tobias Tweeney, and no gendarme is going to fan Tobias Tweeney looking for a rod after one gander at Tobias, especially at this particular moment, as Tobias is now half-asleep from Good Time Charley's liquor, and has no interest whatever in anything that is going on. In fact, Tobias is nodding in his chair.

Of course the gendarmes are greatly disgusted at not finding any rods, and Angie the Ox and Joey Uptown are telling them that they are going to see their aldermen and find out if law-abiding citizens can be stood up and fanned for rods, and put in a very undignified position like this, but the gendarmes do not seem disturbed by these threats, and Lieutenant Harrigan states as follows:

"Well," he says, "I guess maybe I get a bum steer, but," he says, "for two cents I will give all you wrong gees a good going-over just for luck."

Of course this is no way to speak to parties such as these, as they are all very prominent in their different parts of the city, but Lieutenant Harrigan is a guy who seldom cares how he talks to anybody. In fact, Lieutenant Harrigan is a very tough copper.

But he is just about to take his gendarmes out of the joint when Tobias Tweeney nods a little too far forward in his chair, and then all of a sudden topples over on the floor, and five large rods pop out of his pockets and go sliding every which way around the floor, and the next thing anybody knows there is Tobias Tweeney under arrest with all the gendarmes holding on to some part of him.

Well, the next day the newspapers are plumb full of the capture of a guy they call Twelve-Gun Tweeney, and the papers say the police state that this is undoubtedly the toughest guy the world ever sees, because while they hear of two-gun guys, and even three-gun guys, they never before hear of a guy going around rodded up with twelve guns.

The gendarmes say they can tell by the way he acts that Twelve-Gun Tweeney is a mighty bloodthirsty guy, because he says nothing whatever but only glares at them with a steely glint in his eyes, although of course the reason Tobias stares at him is because he is still too dumbfounded to think of anything to say.

Naturally, I figure that when Tobias comes up for air he is a sure thing to spill the whole business, and all the parties who are in Good Time Charley's when he is arrested figure the same way, and go into retirement for a time. But it seems that when Tobias finally realizes what time it is, he is getting so much attention that it swells him all up and he decides to keep on being Twelve-Gun Tweeney as long as he can, which is a decision that is a very nice break for all parties concerned.

I sneak down to Judge Rascover's court the day Tobias is arraigned on a charge of violation of the Sullivan law, which is a law against carrying rods, and the courtroom is packed with citizens eager to see a character desperate enough to lug twelve rods, and among these citizens are many dolls, pulling and hauling for position, and some of these dolls are by no means crows. Many photographers are hanging around to take pictures of Twelve-Gun Tweeney as he is led in handcuffed to gendarmes on either side of him, and with other gendarmes in front and behind him.

But one and all are greatly surprised and somewhat disappointed when they see what a little squirt Tobias is, and Judge Rascover looks down at him once, and then puts on his specs and takes another gander as if he does not believe what he sees in the first place. After looking at Tobias awhile through his specs, and shaking his head as if he is greatly puzzled, Judge Rascover speaks to Lieutenant Harrigan as follows:

"Do you mean to tell this court," Judge Rascover says, "that this half-portion here is the desperate Twelve-Gun Tweeney?"

Well, Lieutenant Harrigan says there is no doubt whatever about it, and Judge Rascover wishes to know how Tobias carries all these rods, and whereabouts, so Lieutenant Harrigan collects twelve rods from the gendarmes around the courtroom, unloads these rods, and starts in putting the guns here and there on Tobias as near as he can remember where they are found on him in the first place, with Tobias giving him a little friendly assistance.

Lieutenant Harrigan puts two guns in each of the side pockets of Tobias's coat, one in each hip pocket, one in the waistband of Tobias's pants, one in each side pocket of the pants, one up each of Tobias's sleeves, and one in the inside pocket of Tobias's coat. Then Lieutenant Harrigan states to the court that he is all finished, and that Tobias is rodded up in every respect as when they put the arm on him in Good Time Charley's joint, and Judge Rascover speaks to Tobias as follows:

"Step closer to the bench," Judge Rascover says. "I wish to see for myself just what kind of a villain you are."

Well, Tobias takes a step forward, and over he goes on his

snoot, so I see right away what it is makes him keel over in Good Time Charley's joint, not figuring in Charley's liquor. The little guy is naturally top-heavy from the rods.

Now there is much confusion as he falls and a young doll who seems to be fatter than somewhat comes shoving through the crowd in the courtroom yelling and crying, and though the gendarmes try to stop her she gets to Tobias and kneels at his side, and speaks as follows:

"Toby, darling," she says, "it is nobody but Deborah who loves you dearly, and who always knows you will turn out to be the greatest gunman of them all. Look at me, Toby," she says, "and tell me you love me, too. We never realize what a hero you are until we get the New York papers in Erasmus last night, and I hurry to you as quickly as possible. Kiss me, Toby," the fat young doll says, and Tobias raises up on one elbow and does same, and it makes a very pleasing scene indeed, although the gendarmes try to pull them apart, having no patience whatever with such matters.

Now Judge Rascover is watching all this business through his specs, and Judge Rascover is no sucker, but a pretty slick old codger for a judge, and he can see that there is something wrong somewhere about Tobias Tweeney being a character as desperate as the gendarmes make him out, especially when he sees that Tobias cannot pack all these rods on a bet.

So when the gendarmes pick the fat young doll off of Tobias and take a few pounds of rods off of Tobias, too, so he is finally able to get back on his pins and stand there, Judge Rascover adjourns court, and takes Tobias into his private room and has a talk with him, and the chances are Tobias tells him the truth, for the next thing anybody knows Tobias is walking away as free as the little birdies in the trees, except that he has the fat young doll clinging to him like a porous plaster, so maybe Tobias is not so free, at that.

Well, this is about all there is to the story, except that there is afterwards plenty of heat between the parties who are present in Good Time Charley's joint when Tobias is collared, because it seems that the meeting they all attend before going to Charley's is supposed to be a peace meeting of some kind and nobody is supposed to carry any rods to this meeting just to prove their confidence in each other, so everybody is very indignant when it comes out that nobody has any confidence in anybody else at the meeting.

I never hear of Tobias Tweeney but once after all this, and it is some months afterwards when Joey Uptown and Little Mitzi are over in Pennsylvania inspecting a brewery proposition and finding themselves near the town that is called Erasmus, they decide it will be a nice thing to drop in on Tobias Tweeney and see how he is getting along.

Well, it seems Tobias is all married up to Miss Deborah Weems, and is getting along first-class, as it seems the town elects him constable, because it feels that a guy with such a desperate reputation as Tobias Tweeney's is bound to make wrongdoers keep away from Erasmus if he is an officer of the law, and Tobias's first official act is to chase Joe Trivett out of town.

But along Broadway Tobias Tweeney will always be considered nothing but an ingrate for heaving Joey Uptown and Little Mitzi into the town sneezer and getting them fined fifty bobs apiece for carrying concealed weapons.

DANCING DAN'S
CHRISTMAS

Now one time it comes on Christmas, and in fact it is the evening before Christmas, and I am on Good Time Charley Bernstein's little speakeasy on West Forty-seventh Street, wishing Charley a Merry Christmas and having a few hot Tom and Jerrys with him.

This hot Tom and Jerry is an old-time drink that is once used by one and all in this country to celebrate Christmas with, and in fact it is once so popular that many people think Christmas is invented only to furnish an excuse for hot Tom and Jerry, although of course this is by no means true.

But anybody will tell you that there is nothing that brings out the true holiday spirit like hot Tom and Jerry, and I hear that since Tom and Jerry goes out of style in the United States, the holiday spirit is never quite the same.

The reason hot Tom and Jerry goes out of style is because it is necessary to use rum and one thing and another in making Tom and Jerry, and naturally when rum becomes illegal in this country Tom and Jerry is also against the law, because rum is something that is very hard to get around town these days.

For a while some people try making Tom and Jerry without putting rum in it, but somehow it never has the same old holiday spirit, so nearly everybody finally gives up in disgust, and this is not surprising, as making Tom and Jerry is by no means child's play. In fact, it takes quite an expert to make good Tom and Jerry, and in the days when it is not illegal a good hot Tom and Jerry maker commands good wages and many friends.

Now of course Good Time Charley and I are not using rum in the Tom and Jerry we are making, as we do not wish to do anything illegal. What we are using is rye whisky that Good Time Charley gets on a doctor's prescription from a drug store, as we are personally drinking this hot Tom and Jerry and naturally we are not foolish enough to use any of Good Time Charley's own rye in it.

The prescription for the rye whiskey comes from old Doc Moggs, who prescribes it for Good Time Charley's rheumatism in case Charley happens to get rheumatism, as Doc Moggs says there is nothing better for rheumatism than rye whisky, especially if it is made up in a hot Tom and Jerry. In fact, old Doc Moggs comes around and has a few seidels of hot Tom and Jerry with us for his own rheumatism.

He comes around during the afternoon, for Good Time Charley and I start making this Tom and Jerry early in the day, so as to be sure to have enough to last us over Christmas, and it is now along towards six o'clock, and our holiday spirit is practically one hundred per cent.

Well, as Good Time Charley and I are expressing our holiday sentiments to each other over our hot Tom and Jerry, and I am trying to think up the poem about the night before Christmas and all through the house, which I know will interest Charley no little, all of a sudden there is a big knock at the front door, and when Charley opens the door, who comes in carrying a large package under one arm but a guy by the name of Dancing Dan.

This Dancing Dan is a good-looking young guy, who always seems well-dressed, and he is called by the name of Dancing Dan because he is a great hand for dancing around and about with dolls in night clubs, and other spots where there is any dancing. In fact, Dan never seems to be doing anything else, although I hear rumors that when he is not dancing he is carrying on in a most illegal manner at one thing and another. But of course you can always hear rumors in this town about anybody, and personally I am rather fond of Dancing Dan as he always seems to be getting a great belt out of life.

Anybody in town will tell you that Dancing Dan is a guy with no Barnaby whatever in him, and in fact he has about as much gizzard as anybody around, although I wish to say I always question his judgment in dancing so much with Miss Muriel O'Neill, who works in the Half Moon night club. And the reason I question his judgment in this respect is because everybody knows that Miss Muriel O'Neill is a doll who is very well thought of by Heine Schmitz, and Heine Schmitz is not such a guy as will take kindly to anybody dancing more than once and a half with a doll that he thinks well of.

This Heine Schmitz is a very influential citizen of Harlem, where he has large interests in beer, and other business enterprises, and it is by no means violating any confidence to tell you that Heine Schmitz will just as soon blow your brains out as look at you. In fact, I hear, sooner. Anyway, he is not a guy to monkey with and many citizens take the trouble to advise Dancing Dan that he is not only away out of line in dancing with Miss Muriel O'Neill, but that he is knocking his own price down to where he is no price at all.

But Dancing Dan only laughs ha-ha, and goes on dancing with Miss Muriel O'Neill anytime he gets the chance, and Good Time Charley says he does not blame him, at that, as Miss Muriel O'Neill is so beautiful that he will be dancing with her himself no matter what, if he is five years younger and can get a Roscoe out as fast as in the days when he runs with Paddy the Link and other fast guys.

Well, anyway, as Dancing Dan comes in, he weighs up the joint in one quick peek, and then he tosses the package he is carrying into a corner where it goes plunk, as if there is something very heavy in it, and then he steps up to the bar alongside of Charley and me and wishes to know what we are drinking.

Naturally we start boosting hot Tom and Jerry to Dancing Dan, and he says he will take a crack at it with us, and after one crack, Dancing Dan says he will have another crack, and Merry Christmas to us with it, and the first thing anybody knows it is a couple of hours later and we still are still having cracks at the hot Tom and Jerry with Dancing Dan, and Dan says he never drinks anything so soothing in his life. In fact, Dancing Dan says he will recommend Tom and Jerry to everybody he knows, only he does not know anybody good enough for Tom and Jerry, except maybe Miss Muriel O'Neill, and she does not drink anything with drugstore rye in it.

Well, several times while we are drinking this Tom and Jerry, customers come to the door of Good Time Charley's little speakeasy and knock, but by now Charley is commencing to be afraid they will wish Tom and Jerry, too, and he does not feel we will have enough for ourselves, so he hangs out a sign which says "Closed on Account of Christmas," and the only one he will let in is a guy by the name of Ooky, who is nothing but an old rumdum, and who is going around all week dressed like Santa Claus and carrying a sign advertising Moe Lewinsky's clothing joint around on Sixth Avenue.

This Ooky is still wearing his Santa Claus outfit when Charley lets him in, and the reason Charley permits such a character as Ooky in his joint is because Ooky does the porter work for Charley when he is not Santa Claus for Moe Lewinsky, such as sweeping out, and washing the glasses, and one thing and another.

Well, it is about nine-thirty when Ooky comes in, and his puppies are aching, and he is all petered out generally from walking up and down and here and there with his sign, for any time a guy is Santa Claus for Moe Lewinsky he must earn his dough. In fact, Ooky is so fatigued, and his puppies hurt him so much that Dancing Dan and Good Time Charley and I all feel very sorry for him, and invite him to have a few mugs of hot Tom and Jerry with us, and wish him plenty of Merry Christmas.

But old Ooky is not accustomed to Tom and Jerry and after about the fifth mug he folds up in a chair, and goes right to sleep on us. He is wearing a pretty good Santa Claus make-up, what with a nice red suit trimmed with white cotton, and a wig, and false nose, and long white whiskers, and a big sack stuffed with excelsior on his back, and if I do not know Santa Claus is not apt to be such a guy as will snore loud enough to rattle the windows, I will think Ooky is Santa Claus sure enough.

Well, we forget Ooky and let him sleep, and go on with our hot Tom and Jerry, and in the meantime we try to think up a few songs appropriate to Christmas, and Dancing Dan finally renders "My Dad's Dinner Pail" in a nice baritone and very loud, while I do first rate with "Will You Love Me in December—As You Do in May?" But personally I always think Good Time Charley Bernstein is a little out of line trying to sing a hymn in Jewish on such an occasion, and it causes words between us.

While we are singing many customers come to the door and knock, and then read Charley's sign, and this seems to cause some unrest among them, and some of them stand outside saying it is a great outrage, until Charley sticks his noggin out the door and threatens to bust somebody's beezer if they do not go about their business and stop disturbing peaceful citizens.

Naturally the customers go away, as they do not wish their beezers busted, and Dancing Dan and Charley and I continue drinking our hot Tom and Jerry, and with each Tom and Jerry we are wishing one another a very Merry Christmas, and sometimes a very Happy New Year, although of course this does not go for Good Time Charley as yet, because Charley has his New Year separate from Dancing Dan and me.

By and by we take to waking Ooky up in his Santa Claus outfit and offering him more hot Tom and Jerry, and wishing him Merry Christmas, but Ooky only gets sore and calls us names, so we can see he does not have the right holiday spirit in him, and let him alone until along about midnight when Dancing Dan wishes to see how he looks as Santa Claus.

So Good Time Charley and I help Dancing Dan pull off Ooky's outfit and put it on Dan, and this is easy as Ooky only has this Santa Claus outfit on over his ordinary clothes, and he does not even wake up when we are undressing him of the Santa Claus uniform.

Well, I wish to say I see many a Santa Claus in my time, but I never see a better-looking Santa Claus than Dancing Dan, especially after he gets the wig and white whiskers fixed just right, and we put a sofa pillow that Good Time Charley happens to have around the joint for the cat to sleep on down his pants to give Dancing Dan a nice fat stomach such as Santa Claus is bound to have.

"Well," Charley finally says, "it is a great pity we do not know where there are some stockings hung up somewhere, because then," he says, "you can go around and stuff things in these stockings, as I always hear this is the main idea of a Santa Claus. But," Charley says, "I do not suppose anybody in this section has any stockings hung up, or if they have," he says "the chances are they are so full of holes they will not hold anything. Anyway," Charley says, "even if there are any stockings hung up we do not have anything to stuff in them, although personally," he says, "I will gladly donate a few pints of Scotch."

Well, I am pointing out that we have no reindeer and that a Santa Claus is bound to look like a terrible sap if he goes around without any reindeer, but Charley's remarks seem to give Dancing Dan an idea, for all of a sudden he speaks as follows:

"Why," Dancing Dan says, "I know where a stocking is hung up. It is hung up at Miss Muriel O'Neill's flat over here on West Forty-ninth Street. This stocking is hung up by nobody but a party by the name of Gammer O'Neill, who is Miss Muriel O'Neill's grandmamma," Dancing Dan says. "Gammer O'Neill is going on ninety-odd," he says, "and Miss Muriel O'Neill told me she cannot hold out much longer, what with one thing and another, including being a little childish in spots.

"Now," Dancing Dan says, "I remember Miss Muriel O'Neill is telling me just the other night how Gammer O'Neill hangs up her stocking on Christmas Eve all her life, and," he says, "I judge from what Miss Muriel O'Neill says that the old doll always believes Santa Claus will come along one Christmas and fill the stocking full of beautiful gifts. But," Dancing Dan says, "Miss Muriel O'Neill tells me Santa Claus never does this, though Miss Muriel O'Neill personally always takes a few gifts home and puts them into the stocking to make Gammer O'Neill feel better.

"But, of course," Dancing Dan says, "these gifts are nothing much because Miss Muriel O'Neill is very poor, and proud, and also good, and will not take a dime off of anybody and I can lick the guy who says she will.

"Now," Dancing Dan goes on, "it seems that while Gammer O'Neill is very happy to get whatever she finds in her stocking on Christmas morning, she does not understand why Santa Claus is not more liberal, and," he says, "Miss Muriel O'Neill is saying to me that she only wishes she can give Gammer O'Neill one real big Christmas before the old doll puts her checks back in the rack.

"So," Dancing Dan states, "here is a job for us. Miss Muriel O'Neill and her grandmamma live all alone in this flat over on West Forty-ninth Street, and," he says, "at such an hour as this Miss Muriel O'Neill is bound to be working, and the chances are Gammer O'Neill is sound asleep, and we will just hop over there and Santa Claus will fill up her stocking with beautiful gifts.

"Well," I say, "I do not see where we are going to get any beautiful gifts at this time of night, what with all the stores being closed, unless we dash into an all-night drug store and buy a few bottles of perfume and a bum toilet set as guys always do when they forget about their ever-loving wives until after store hours on Christmas Eve," but Dancing Dan says never mind about this, but let us have a few more Tom and Jerrys first.

So we have a few more Tom and Jerrys and then Dancing Dan picks up the package he heaves into the corner, and dumps most of the excelsior out of Ooky's Santa Claus sack, and puts the bundle in, and Good Time Charley turns out all the lights, but one, and leaves a bottle of Scotch on the table in front of Ooky for a Christmas gift, and away we go.

Personally, I regret very much leaving the hot Tom and Jerry, but then I'm also very enthusiastic about going along to help Dancing Dan play Santa Claus, while Good Time Charley is practically overjoyed, as it is the first time in his life Charley is ever mixed up in so much holiday spirit.

As we go up Broadway, headed for Forty-ninth Street, Charley and I see many citizens we know and give them a large hello, and wish them Merry Christmas, and some of these citizens shake hands with Santa Claus, not knowing he is nobody but Dancing Dan, although later I understand there's some gossip among these citizens because they claim a Santa Claus with such a breath on him as our Santa Claus has is a little out of line.

And once we are somewhat embarrassed when a lot of little kids going home with their parents from a late Christmas party somewhere gather about Santa Claus with shouts of childish glee, and some of them wish to climb up Santa Claus' legs. Naturally, Santa Claus gets a little peevish, and calls them a few names, and one of the parents comes up and wishes to know what is the idea of Santa Claus using such language, and Santa Claus takes a punch at the parent, all of which is no doubt astonishing to the little kids who have an idea of Santa Claus as a very kindly old guy.

Well, finally we arrive in front of the place where Dancing Dan says Miss Muriel O'Neill and her grandmamma live, and it is nothing but a tenement house not far back off Madison Square Garden, and furthermore it is a walk-up, and at this time there are no lights burning in the joint except a gas jet in the main hall, and by the light of this jet we look at the names on the letter boxes, such as you always find in the hall of these joints, and we see that Miss Muriel O'Neill and her grandmamma live on the fifth floor.

This is the top floor, and personally I do not like the idea of walking up five flights of stairs, and I am willing to let Dancing Dan and Good Time Charley go, but Dancing Dan insists we must all go, and finally I agree with him because Charley is commencing to argue that the right way for us to do is to get on the roof and let Santa Claus go down a chimney, and is making so much noise I am afraid he will wake somebody up.

So up the stairs we climb and finally we come to a door on the top floor that has a little card in a slot that says O'Neill, so we know we reach our destination. Dancing Dan first tries the knob, and right away the door opens, and we are in a little two- or three-room flat, with not much furniture in it, and what furniture there is, is very poor. One single gas jet is burning near a bed in a room just off the one the door opens into, and by this light we see a very old doll is sleeping on the bed, so we judge this is nobody but Gammer O'Neill.

On her face is a large smile, as if she is dreaming of something very pleasant. On a chair at the head of the bed is hung a long black stocking, and it seems to be such a stocking as is often patched and mended, so I can see that what Miss Muriel O'Neill tells Dancing Dan about her grandmamma hanging up her stocking is really true, although up to this time I have my doubts. Finally Dancing Dan unslings the sack on his back, and takes out his package, and unties this package, and all of a sudden out pops a raft of big diamond bracelets, and diamond rings, and diamond brooches, and diamond necklaces, and I do not know what else in the way of diamonds, and Dancing Dan and I begin stuffing these diamonds into the stocking and Good Time Charley pitches in and helps us. There are enough diamonds to fill the stocking to the muzzle, and it is no small stocking, at that, and I judge that Gammer O'Neill has a pretty fair set of bunting sticks when she is young. In fact, there are so many diamonds that we have enough left over to make a nice little pile on the chair after we fill the stocking plumb up, leaving a nice diamond-studded vanity case sticking out the top where we figure it will hit Gammer O'Neill's eye when she wakes up. And it is not until I get out in the fresh air again that all of a sudden I remember seeing large headlines in the afternoon papers about a five-hundred-G's stickup in the afternoon of one of the biggest diamond merchants on Maiden Lane while he is sitting in his office, and I also recall once hearing rumors that Dancing Dan is one of the best lone-hand git-'em-up guys in the world. Naturally, I commence to wonder if I am in the proper company when I am with Dancing Dan, even if he is Santa Claus. So I leave him on the next corner arguing with Good Time Charley about whether they ought to go and find some more presents somewhere, and look for other stockings to stuff, and I hasten on home and go to bed. The next day I find I have such a noggin that I do not care to stir around, and in fact I do not stir around much for a couple of weeks. Then one night I drop around to Good Time Charley's little speakeasy, and ask Charley what is doing.

"Well," Charley says, "many things are doing, and personally," he says, "I'm greatly surprised I do not see you at Gammer O'Neill's wake. You know Gammer O'Neill leaves this wicked old world a couple of days after Christmas," Good Time Charley says, "and," he says, "Miss Muriel O'Neill states that Doc Moggs claims it is at least a day after she is entitled to go, but she is sustained," Charley says, "by great happiness in finding her stocking filled with beautiful gifts on Christmas morning.

"According to Miss Muriel O'Neill," Charley says, "Gammer O'Neill dies practically convinced that there is a Santa Claus, although of course," he says, "Miss Muriel O'Neill does not tell her the real owner of the gifts, an all-right guy by the name of Shapiro, leaves the gifts with her after Miss Muriel O'Neill notifies him of finding of same.

"It seems," Charley says, "this Shapiro is a tender-hearted guy, who is willing to help keep Gammer O'Neill with us a little longer when Doc Moggs says leaving the gifts with her will do it.

"So," Charley says, "everything is quite all right, as the coppers cannot figure anything except that maybe the rascal who takes the gifts from Shapiro gets conscience-stricken, and leaves them the first place he can, and Miss Muriel O'Neill receives a ten-G's reward for finding the gifts and returning them. And," Charley says, "I hear Dancing Dan is in San Francisco and is figuring on reforming and becoming a dancing teacher, so he can marry Miss Muriel O'Neill, and of course," he says, "we all hope and trust she never learns any details of Dancing Dan's career."

Well, it is Christmas Eve a year later that I run into a guy by the name of Shotgun Sam, who is mobbed up with Heine Schmitz in Harlem, and who is a very, very obnoxious character indeed.

"Well, well, well," Shotgun says, "the last time I see you is another Christmas like this, and you are coming out of Good Time Charley's joint, and," he says, "you certainly have your pots on."

"Well, Shotgun," I says, "I am sorry you get such a wrong impression of me, but the truth is," I say, "on the occasion you speak of, I am suffering from a dizzy feeling in my head."

"It is all right with me," Shotgun says. "I have a tip this guy Dancing Dan is in Good Time Charley's the night I see you, and Mockie Morgan, and Gunnerjack and me are casing the joint, because," he says, "Heine Schmitz is all sored up at Dan over some doll, although of course," Shotgun says, "it is all right now, as Heine has another doll.

"Anyway," he says, "we never get to see Dancing Dan. We watch the joint from six-thirty in the evening until daylight Christmas morning, and nobody goes in all night but old Ooky the Santa Claus guy in his Santa Claus make-up, and," Shotgun says, "nobody comes out except you and Good Time Charley and Ooky.

"Well," Shotgun says, "it is a great break for Dancing Dan he never goes in or comes out of Good Time Charley's, at that, because," he says, "we are waiting for him on the second-floor front of the building across the way with some nice little sawed-offs, and are under orders from Heine not to miss."

"Well, Shotgun," I say, "Merry Christmas."

"Well, all right," Shotgun says, "Merry Christmas."

EARTHQUAKE

Personally, I do not care for coppers, but I believe in being courteous to them at all times, so when Johnny Brannigan comes into Mindy's restaurant one Friday evening and sits down in the same booth with me, because there are no other vacant seats in the joint, I give him a huge hello.

Furthermore, I offer him a cigarette and say how pleased I am to see how well he is looking, although as a matter of fact Johnny Brannigan looks very terrible, what with big black circles under his eyes and his face thinner than somewhat.

In fact, Johnny Brannigan looks as if he is sick, and I am secretly hoping that it is something fatal, because the way I figure it there are a great many coppers in this world, and a few less may be a good thing for one and all concerned.

But naturally I do not mention this hope to Johnny Brannigan, as Johnny Brannigan belongs to what is called the gunman squad and is known to carry a blackjack in his pants pocket and furthermore he is known to boff guys on their noggins with this jack if they get too fresh with him, and for all I know Johnny Brannigan may consider such a hope about his health very fresh indeed.

Now the last time I see Johnny Brannigan before this is in Good Time Charley Bernstein's little joint on Forty-eighth Street with three other coppers, and what Johnny is there for is to put the arm on a guy by the name of Earthquake, who is called Earthquake because he is so fond of shaking things up.

In fact, at the time I am speaking of, Earthquake has this whole town shaken up, what with shooting and stabbing and robbing different citizens, and otherwise misconducting himself, and the law wishes to place Earthquake in the electric chair, as he is considered a great knock to the community.

Now the only reason Brannigan does not put the arm on Earthquake at this time is because Earthquake picks up one of Good Time Charley Bernstein's tables and kisses Johnny Brannigan with same, and furthermore, Earthquake outs with the old equalizer and starts blasting away at the coppers who are with Johnny Brannigan, and he keeps them so busy dodging slugs that they do not have any leisure to put the arm on him, and the next thing anybody knows, Earthquake takes it on the lam out of there.

Well, personally, I also take it on the lam myself, as I do not wish to be around when Johnny Brannigan comes to, as I figure Johnny may be somewhat bewildered and will start boffing people over the noggin with his jack thinking they are all Earthquake, no matter who they are, and I do not see Johnny again until this evening in Mindy's.

But in the meantime I hear rumors that Johnny Brannigan is out of town looking for Earthquake, because it seems that while misconducting himself Earthquake severely injures a copper by the name of Mulcahy. In fact, it seems that Earthquake injures him so severely that Mulcahy hauls off and dies, and if there is one thing that is against the law in this town it is injuring a copper in such a manner. In fact, it is apt to cause great indignation among other coppers.

It is considered very illegal to severely injure any citizen in this town in such a way as to make him haul off and die, but naturally it is not apt to cause any such indignation as injuring a copper, as this town has more citizens to spare than coppers.

Well, sitting there with Johnny Brannigan, I get to wondering if he ever meets up with Earthquake while he is looking for him, and if so how he comes out, for Earthquake is certainly not such a guy as I will care to meet up with, even if I am a copper.

Earthquake is a guy of maybe six foot three, and weighing a matter of two hundred and twenty pounds, and all these pounds are nothing but muscle. Anybody will tell you that Earthquake is one of the strongest guys in this town, because it seems he once works in a foundry and picks up much of his muscle there. In fact, Earthquake likes to show how strong he is at all times, and one of his ways of showing this is to grab a full-sized guy in either duke and hold them straight up in the air over his head.

Sometimes after he gets tired of holding these guys over his head, he will throw them plumb away, especially if they are coppers, or maybe knock their noggins together and leave them with their noggins very sore indeed. When he is in real good humor, Earthquake does not think anything of going into a night club and taking it apart and chucking the pieces out into the street, along with the owner and the waiters and maybe some of the customers, so you can see Earthquake is a very high-spirited guy, and full of fun.

Personally, I do not see why Earthquake does not get a job in a circus as a strong guy, because there is no percentage in wasting all this strength for nothing, but when I mention this idea to Earthquake one time, he says he cannot bear to think of keeping regular hours such as a circus might wish.

Well, Johnny Brannigan does not have anything to say to me at first as we sit there in Mindy's, but by and by he looks at me and speaks as follows:

"You remember Earthquake?" he says. "You remember he is very strong?"

"Strong?" I say to Johnny Brannigan. "Why, there is nobody stronger than Earthquake. Why," I say, "Earthquake is strong enough to hold up a building."

"Yes," Johnny Brannigan says, "what you say is very true. He is strong enough to hold up a building. Yes," he says, "Earthquake is very strong indeed. Now I will tell you about Earthquake."

It is maybe three months after Earthquake knocks off Mulcahy (Johnny Brannigan says) that we get a tip he is in a town by the name of New Orleans, and because I am personally acquainted with him, I am sent there to put the arm on him. But when I get to this New Orleans, I find Earthquake blows out of there and does not leave any forwarding address.

Well, I am unable to get any trace of him for some days, and it looks as if I am on a bust, when I happen to run into a guy by the name of Saul the Soldier, from Greenwich Village. Saul the Soldier winds up in New Orleans following the horse races, and he is very glad indeed to meet a friend from his old home town, and I am also glad to meet Saul, because I am getting very lonesome in New Orleans. Well, Saul knows New Orleans pretty well, and he takes me around and about, and finally I ask him if he can tell me where Earthquake is, and Saul speaks as follows:

"Why," Saul says, "Earthquake sails away on a ship for Central America not long ago with a lot of guys that are going to join a revolution there. I think," Saul says, "they are going to a place by the name of Nicaragua."

Well, I wire my headquarters and they tell me to go after Earth-quake no matter where he is, because it seems the bladders back home are asking what kind of a police force do we have, anyway, and why is somebody not arrested for something.

I sail on a fruit steamer, and finally I get to this Nicaragua, and to a town that is called Managua.

Well, for a week or so I knock around here and there looking for Earthquake, but I cannot find hide or hair of him, and I am commencing to think that Saul the Soldier gives me a bum steer.

It is pretty hot in this town of Managua, and of an afternoon when I get tired of looking for Earthquake I go to a little park in the center of the town where there are many shade trees. It is a pretty park, although down there they call it a plaza, and across from this plaza there is a big old two-story stone building that seems to be a convent, because I see many nuns and small female kids popping in and out of a door on one side of the building, which seems to be the main entrance.

One afternoon I am sitting in the little plaza when a big guy in sloppy white clothes comes up and sits down on another bench near me, and I am greatly surprised to see that this guy is nobody but Earthquake.

He does not see me at first, and in fact he does not know I am present until I step over to him and out with my jack and knock him bow-legged; because, knowing Earthquake, I know there is no use starting out with him by shaking hands. I do not boff him so very hard, at that, but just hard enough to make him slightly insensible for a minute, while I put the handcuffs on him.

Well, when he opens his eyes, Earthquake looks up at the trees, as if he thinks maybe a coconut drops down and beans him, and it is several minutes before he sees me, and then he leaps up and roars, and acts as if he is greatly displeased. But then he dis-covers that he is handcuffed, and he sits down again and speaks as follows:

"Hello, copper," Earthquake says. "When do you get in?"

I tell him how long I am there, and how much inconvenience he causes me by not being more prominent, and Earthquake says the fact of the matter is he is out in the jungles with a lot of guys try-ing to rig up a revolution, but they are so slow getting started they finally exasperate him, and he comes into town.

Well, finally we get to chatting along very pleasant about this and that, and although he is away only a few months, Earthquake is much interested in what is going on in New York and asks me many questions, and I tell him that the liquor around town is getting better.

"Furthermore, Earthquake," I say, "they are holding a nice warm seat for you up at Ossining."

"Well, copper," Earthquake says, "I am sorry I scrag Mulcahy, at that. In fact," he says, "it really is an accident. I do not mean to scrag him. I am aiming at another guy, copper," he says. "In fact," he says, "I am aiming at you."

Now about this time the bench seems to move from under me, and I find myself sitting on the ground, and the ground also seems to be trying to get from under me, and I hear loud crashing noises here and there, and a great roaring, and at first I think maybe Earthquake takes to shaking things up, when I see him laid out on the ground about fifty feet from me.

I get to my pins, but the ground is still wobbling somewhat and I can scarcely walk over to Earthquake, who is now sitting up very indignant, and when he sees me he says to me like this:

"Personally," he says, "I consider it a very dirty trick for you to boff me again when I am not looking."

Well, I explain to Earthquake that I do not boff him again, and that as near as I can figure out what happens is that we are overtaken by what he is named for, which is an earthquake, and looking around and about, anybody can see that this is very true, as great clouds of dust are rising from piles of stone and timber where fair-sized buildings stand a few minutes before, and guys and dolls are running every which way.

Now I happen to look across at the convent, and I can see that it is something of a wreck and is very likely to be more so any minute, as the walls are teetering this way and that, and mostly they are teetering inward. Furthermore, I can hear much screeching from inside the old building.

Then I notice the door in the side of the building that seems to be the main entrance to the convent is gone, leaving the doorway open, and now I must explain to you about this doorway, as it figures quite some in what later comes off. It is a fairly wide doorway in the beginning with a frame of heavy timber set in the side of the stone building, with a timber arch at the top, and the wall around this doorway seems to be caving in from the top and sides, so that the doorway is now shaped like the letter V upside down, with the timber framework bending, instead of breaking.

As near as I can make out, this doorway is the only entrance to the convent that is not closed up by falling stone and timber, and it is a sure thing that pretty soon this opening will be plugged up, too, so I speak to Earthquake as follows:

"Earthquake," I say, "there are a lot of nuns and kids in this joint over here, and I judge from the screeching going on inside that some of them are very much alive. But," I say, "they will not be alive in a few minutes, because the walls are going to tip over and make jelly of them."

"Why, yes," Earthquake says, taking a peek at the convent, "what you say seems reasonable. Well, copper," he says, "what is to be done in this situation?"

"Well," I say, "I see a chance to snatch a few of them out of there if you will help me. Earthquake," I say, "I understand you are a very strong guy?"

"Strong?" Earthquake says. "Why," he says, "you know I am maybe the strongest guy in the world."

"Earthquake," I say, "you see the doorway yonder? Well, Earthquake, if you are strong enough to hold this doorway apart and keep it from caving in, I will slip in through it and pass out any nuns and kids that may be alive."

"Why," Earthquake says, "this is as bright an idea as I ever hear from a copper. Why," he says, "I will hold this doorway apart until next Pancake Tuesday."

Then Earthquake holds out his dukes and I unlock the cuffs. Then he runs over to the doorway of the convent, and I run after him.

This doorway is now closing in very fast indeed, from the weight of tons of stones pressing against the timber frame, and by the time we get there the letter V upside down is so very narrow from top to bottom that Earthquake has a tough time wedging himself into what little opening is left.

But old Earthquake gets in, facing inward, and once in, he begins pushing against the door-frame on either side of him, and I can see at once how he gets his reputation as a strong guy. The doorway commences to widen, and as it widens Earthquake keeps spraddling his legs apart, so that pretty soon there is quite a space between his legs. His head is bent forward so far his chin is resting on his wishbone, as there is plenty of weight on Earthquake's neck and shoulders, and in fact he reminds me of pictures I see of a guy by the name of Atlas holding up the world.

It is through the opening between his spraddled-out legs that I pop, looking for the nuns and the kids. Most of them are in a big room on the ground floor of the building, and they are all huddled up close together screeching in chorus.

I motion them to follow me, and I lead them back over the wreckage, and along the hall to the spot where Earthquake is holding the doorway apart, and I wish to state at this time he is doing a very nice job of same.

But the weight on Earthquake's shoulders must be getting very hefty indeed, because his shoulders are commencing to stoop under it, and his chin is now almost down to his stomach, and his face is purple.

Now through Earthquake's spraddled-out legs, and into the street outside the convent wall, I push five nuns and fifteen female kids. One old nun refused to be pushed through Earthquake's legs, and I finally make out from the way she is waving her hands around and about that there are other kids in the convent, and she wishes me to get them, too.

Well, I can see that any more delay is going to be something of a strain on Earthquake, and maybe a little irritating to him, so I speak to him as follows:

"Earthquake," I say, "you are looking somewhat peaked to me, and plumb tired out. Now then," I say, "if you will step aside, I will hold the doorway apart awhile, and you can go with this old nun and find the rest of the kids."

"Copper," Earthquake says, speaking from off his chest because he cannot get his head up very high, "I can hold this doorway apart with my little fingers if one of them is not sprained, so go ahead and round up the rest."

So I let the old nun lead me back to another part of the building, where I judge she knows there are more kids, and in fact the old nun is right, but it only takes one look to show me there is no use taking these kids out of the place.

Then we go back to Earthquake, and he hears us coming across the rubbish and half-raises his head from off his chest and looks at me, and I can see the sweat is dribbling down his kisser and his eyes are bugging out, and anybody can see that he is quite upset. As I get close to him he speaks to me as follows:

"Get her out quick," he says. "Get the old doll out."

So I push the old nun through Earthquake's spraddled-out legs into the open, and I notice there is not as much space between these legs as formerly, so I judge the old mumblety-pegs are giving out. Then I say to Earthquake like this:

"Well, Earthquake," I say, "it is now time for you and me to be going. I will go outside first," I say, "and then you can ease yourself out, and we will look around for a means of getting back to New York, as headquarters will be getting worried."

"Listen, copper," Earthquake says, "I am never going to get out of this spot. If I move an inch forward or an inch backward, down comes this whole shebang. But, copper," he says, "I see before I get in there that it is a hundred to one against me getting out again, so do not think I am trapped without knowing it. The way I look at it," Earthquake says, "it is better than the chair, at that. I can last a few minutes longer," he says, "and you better get outside."

Well, I pop out between Earthquake's spraddled-out legs, because I figure I am better off outside than in, no matter what, and when I am outside I stand there looking at Earthquake and wondering what I can do about him. But I can see that he is right when he tells me that if he moves one way or another the cave-in will come, so there seems to be nothing much I can do.

Then I hear Earthquake calling me, and I step up close enough to hear him speak as follows:

"Copper," he says, "tell Mulcahy's people I am sorry. And do not forget that you owe old Earthquake whatever you figure your life is worth. I do not know yet why I do not carry out my idea of letting go all holds the minute you push the old nun out of here, and taking you with me wherever I am going. Maybe," he says, "I am getting soft-hearted. Well, good-bye, copper," he says.

"Good-bye, Earthquake," I say, and I walk away.

So (Johnny Brannigan says), now you know about Earthquake.

"Well," I say, "this is indeed a harrowing story, Johnny. But," I say, "if you leave Earthquake holding up anything maybe he is still holding it up, because Earthquake is certainly a very strong guy."

"Yes," Johnny Brannigan says, "he is very strong indeed. But," he says, "as I am walking away another shock hits, and when I get off the ground again and look at the convent, I can see that not even Earthquake is strong enough to stand off this one."

THE IDYLL OF
MISS SARAH BROWN

Of all the high players this country ever sees, there is no doubt but that the guy they call The Sky is the highest. In fact, the reason he is called The Sky is because he goes so high when it comes to betting on any proposition whatever. He will bet all he has, and nobody can bet any more than this.

His right name is Obadiah Masterson, and he is originally out of a little town in southern Colorado where he learns to shoot craps, and play cards, and one thing and another, and where his old man is a very well-known citizen, and something of a sport himself. In fact, The Sky tells me that when he finally cleans up all the loose scratch around his home town and decides he needs more room, his old man has a little private talk with him and says to him like this:

"Son," the old guy says, "you are now going out into the wide, wide world to make your own way, and it is a very good thing to do, as there are no more opportunities for you in this burg. I am only sorry," he says, "that I am not able to bank-roll you to a very large start, but," he says, "not having any potatoes to give you, I am now going to stake you to some very valuable advice, which I personally collect in my years of experience around and about, and I hope and trust you will always bear this advice in mind.

"Son," the old guy says, "no matter how far you travel, or how smart you get, always remember this: Someday, somewhere," he says, "a guy is going to come to you and show you a nice brand-new deck of cards on which the seal is never broken, and this guy is going to offer to bet you that the jack of spades will jump out of this deck and squirt cider in your ear. But, son," the old guy says, "do not bet him, for as sure as you do you are going to get an ear full of cider."

Well, The Sky remembers what his old man says, and he is always very cautious about betting on such propositions as the jack of spades jumping out of a sealed deck of cards and squirting cider in his ear, and so he makes few mistakes as he goes along. In fact, the only real mistake The Sky makes is when he hits St. Louis after leaving his old home town, and loses all his potatoes betting a guy St. Louis is the biggest town in the world.

Now of course this is before The Sky ever sees any bigger towns, and he is never much of a hand for reading up on matters such as this. In fact, the only reading The Sky ever does as he goes along through life is in these Gideon Bibles such as he finds in the hotel rooms where he lives, for The Sky never lives anywhere else but in hotel rooms for years.

He tells me that he reads many items of great interest in these Gideon Bibles, and furthermore The Sky says that several times these Gideon Bibles keep him from getting out of line, such as the time he finds himself pretty much frozen-in over in Cincinnati, what with owing everybody in town except maybe the mayor from playing games of chance of one kind and another.

Well, The Sky says he sees no way of meeting these obligations and he is figuring the only thing he can do is to take a run-out powder, when he happens to read in one of these Gideon Bibles where it says like this:

"Better is it," the Gideon Bible says, "that thou shouldest not vow, than that thou shouldest vow and not pay."

Well, The Sky says he can see that there is no doubt whatever but that this means a guy shall not welsh, so he remains in Cincinnati until he manages to wiggle himself out of the situation, and from that day to this, The Sky never thinks of welshing.

He is maybe thirty years old, and is a tall guy with a round kisser, and big blue eyes, and he always looks as innocent as a little baby. But The Sky is by no means as innocent as he looks. In fact, The Sky is smarter than three Philadelphia lawyers, which makes him very smart indeed, and he is well established as a high player in New Orleans, and Chicago, and Los Angeles, and wherever else there is any action in the way of card-playing, or crapshooting, or horse-racing, or betting on the baseball games, for The Sky is always moving around the country following the action.

But while The Sky will bet on anything whatever, he is more of a short-card player and a crap shooter than anything else, and furthermore he is a great hand for propositions, such as are always coming up among citizens who follow games of chance for a living.

Many citizens prefer betting on propositions to anything you can think of, because they figure a proposition gives them a chance to out-smart somebody, and in fact I know citizens who will sit up all night making propositions to offer other citizens the next day.

A proposition may be only a problem in cards, such as what is the price against a guy getting aces back-to-back, or how often a pair of deuces will win a hand in stud, and then again it may be some very daffy proposition indeed, although the daffier any proposition seems to be, the more some citizens like it. And no one ever sees The Sky when he does not have some proposition of his own.

The first time he ever shows up around this town, he goes to a baseball game at the Polo Grounds with several prominent citizens, and while he is at the ball game, he buys himself a sack of Harry Stevens' peanuts, which he dumps in a side pocket of his coat. He is eating these peanuts all through the game, and after the game is over and he is walking across the field with the citizens, he says to them like this:

"What price," The Sky says, "I cannot throw a peanut from second base to the home plate?"

Well, everybody knows that a peanut is too light for anybody to throw it this far, so Big Nig, the crap shooter, who always likes to have a little the best of it running for him, speaks as follows:

"You can have three to one from me, stranger," Big Nig says.

"Two C's against six," The Sky says, and then he stands on second base, and takes a peanut out of his pocket, and not only whips it to the home plate, but on into the lap of a fat guy who is still sitting in the grandstand putting the zing on Bill Terry for not taking Walker out of the box when Walker is getting a pasting from the other club.

Well, naturally, this is a most astonishing throw indeed, but afterwards it comes out that The Sky throws a peanut loaded with lead, and of course it is not one of Harry Stevens' peanuts, either, as Harry is not selling peanuts full of lead at a dime a bag, with the price of lead what it is.

It is only a few nights after this that The Sky states another most unusual proposition to a group of citizens sitting in Mindy's restaurant when he offers to bet a C note that he can go down into Mindy's cellar and catch a live rat with his bare hands and everybody is greatly astonished when Mindy himself steps up and takes the bet, for ordinarily Mindy will not bet you a nickel he is alive.

But it seems that Mindy knows that The Sky plants a tame rat in the cellar, and this rat knows The Sky and loves him dearly, and will let him catch it anytime he wishes, and it also seems that Mindy knows that one of his dish washers happens upon this rat and not knowing it is tame, knocks it flatter than a pancake. So when The Sky goes down into the cellar and starts trying to catch a rat with his bare hands he is greatly surprised how inhospitable the rat turns out to be, because it is one of Mindy's personal rats, and Mindy is around afterwards saying he will lay plenty of seven to five against even Strangler Lewis being able to catch one of his rats with his bare hands, or with boxing gloves on.

I am only telling you all this to show you what a smart guy The Sky is, and I am only sorry I do not have time to tell you about many other very remarkable propositions that he thinks up outside of his regular business.

It is well-known to one and all that he is very honest in every respect, and that he hates and despises cheaters at cards, or dice and furthermore The Sky never wishes to play with any the best of it himself, or anyway not much. He will never take the inside of any situation, as many gamblers love to do, such as owning a gambling house, and having the percentage run for him instead of against him, for always The Sky is strictly a player, because he says he will never care to settle down in one spot long enough to become the owner of anything.

In fact, in all the years The Sky is drifting around the country nobody ever knows him to own anything except maybe a bank roll and when he comes to Broadway the last time, which is the time I am now speaking of, he has a hundred G's in cash money, and an extra suit of clothes, and this is all he has in the world. He never owns such a thing as a house, or an automobile, or a piece of jewelry. He never owns a watch, because The Sky says time means nothing to him.

Of course some guys will figure a hundred G's comes under the head of owning something, but as far as The Sky is concerned, money is nothing but just something for him to play with and the dollars may as well be doughnuts as far as value goes with him.

The only time The Sky ever thinks of money as money is when he is broke, and the only way he can tell he is broke is when he reaches into his pocket and finds nothing there but his fingers.

Then it is necessary for The Sky to go out and dig up some fresh scratch somewhere, and when it comes to digging up scratch, The Sky is practically supernatural. He can get more potatoes on the strength of a telegram to some place or other than John D. Rockefeller can get on collateral, for everybody knows The Sky's word is as good as wheat in the bin.

Now one Sunday evening The Sky is walking along Broadway, and at the corner of Forty-ninth Street he comes upon a little bunch of mission workers who are holding a religious meeting, such as mission workers love to do of a Sunday evening, the idea being that they may round up a few sinners here and there, although personally I always claim the mission workers come out too early to catch any sinners on this part of Broadway. At such an hour the sinners are still in bed resting up from their sinning of the night before, so they will be in good shape for more sinning a little later on.

There are only four of these mission workers, and two of them are old guys, and one is an old doll, while the other is a young doll who is tootling on a cornet. And after a couple of ganders at this young doll, The Sky is a goner, for this is one of the most beautiful young dolls anybody ever sees on Broadway, and especially as a mission worker. Her name is Miss Sarah Brown.

She is tall, and thin, and has a first-class shape, and her hair is a light brown, going on blonde, and her eyes are like I do not know what, except that they are one-hundred-per-cent eyes in every respect. Furthermore, she is not a bad cornet player, if you like cornet players, although at this spot on Broadway she has to play against a scat band in a chop-suey joint nearby, and this is tough competition, although at that many citizens believe Miss Sarah Brown will win by a large score if she only gets a little more support from one of the old guys with her who has a big bass drum, but does not pound it hearty enough.

Well, The Sky stands there listening to Miss Sarah Brown tootling on the cornet for quite a spell, and then he hears her make a speech in which she puts the blast on sin very good, and boosts religion quite some, and says if there are any souls around that need saving the owners of same may step forward at once. But no one steps forward, so The Sky comes over to Mindy's restaurant where many citizens are congregated and starts telling us about Miss Sarah Brown. But of course we already know about Miss Sarah Brown, because she is so beautiful, and so good.

.Furthermore, everybody feels somewhat sorry for Miss Sarah Brown, for while she is always tootling the cornet, and making speeches, and looking to save any souls that need saving, she never seems to find any souls to save, or at least her bunch of mission workers never gets any bigger. In fact, it gets smaller, as she starts out with a guy who plays a very fair sort of trombone, but this guy takes it on the lam one night with the trombone, which one and all consider a dirty trick.

Now from this time on, The Sky does not take any interest in anything but Miss Sarah Brown, and any night she is out on the corner with the other mission workers, you will see The Sky standing around looking at her, and naturally after a few weeks of this, Miss Sarah Brown must know The Sky is looking at her, or she is dumber than seems possible. And nobody ever figures Miss Sarah Brown dumb, as she is always on her toes, and seems plenty able to take care of herself, even on Broadway.

Sometimes after the street meeting is over, The Sky follows the mission workers to their headquarters in an old storeroom around on Forty-eighth Street where they generally hold an indoor session and I hear The Sky drops many a large coarse note in the collection box while looking at Miss Sarah Brown, and there is no doubt these notes come in handy around the mission, as I hear business is by no means so good there.

It is called the Save-a-Soul Mission, and it is run mainly by Miss Sarah Brown's grandfather, an old guy with whiskers, by the name of Arvide Abernathy, but Miss Sarah Brown seems to do most of the work, including tootling the cornet, and visiting the poor people around and about, and all this and that, and many citizens claim it is a great shame that such a beautiful doll is wasting her time being good.

How The Sky ever becomes acquainted with Miss Sarah Brown is a very great mystery, but the next thing anybody knows, he is saying hello to her, and she is smiling at him out of her one-hundred-per-cent eyes, and one evening when I happen to be with The Sky we run into her walking along Forty-ninth Street, and The Sky hauls off and stops her, and says it is a nice evening which it is, at that. Then The Sky says to Miss Sarah Brown like this:

"Well," The Sky says, "how is the mission dodge going these days? Are you saving any souls?" he says.

Well, it seems from what Miss Sarah Brown says the soul-saving is very slow indeed these days.

"In fact," Miss Sarah Brown says, "I worry greatly about how few souls we seem to save. Sometimes I wonder if we are lacking in grace."

She goes on up the street, and The Sky stands looking after her, and he says to me like this:

"I wish I can think of some way to help this little doll," he says, "especially," he says, "in saving a few souls to build up her mob at the mission. I must speak to her again, and see if I can figure something out."

But The Sky does not get to speak to Miss Sarah Brown again, because somebody weighs in the sacks on him by telling her he is nothing but a professional gambler, and that he is a very undesirable character, and that his only interest in hanging around the mission is because she is a good-looking doll. So all of a sudden Miss Sarah Brown plays a plenty of chill for The Sky. Furthermore, she sends him word that she does not care to accept any more of his potatoes in the collection box, because his potatoes are nothing but ill-gotten gains.

Well, naturally, this hurts The Sky's feelings no little, so he quits standing around looking at Miss Sarah Brown, and going to the mission, and takes to mingling again with the citizens in Mindy's, and showing some interest in the affairs of the community, especially the crap games.

Of course the crap games that are going on at this time are nothing much, because practically everybody in the world is broke, but there is a head-and-head game run by Nathan Detroit over a garage on Fifty-second Street where there is occasionally some action, and who shows up at this crap game early one evening but The Sky, although it seems he shows up there more to find company than anything else.

In fact, he only stands around watching the play, and talking with other guys who are also standing around and watching, and many of these guys are very high shots during the gold rush, although most of them are now as clean as a jaybird, and maybe cleaner. One of these guys is a guy by the name of Brandy Bottle Bates, who is known from coast to coast as a high player when he has anything to play with, and who is called Brandy Bottle Bates because it seems that years ago he is a great hand for belting a brandy bottle around.

This Brandy Bottle Bates is a big, black-looking guy, with a large beezer, and a head shaped like a pear, and he is considered a very immoral and wicked character, but he is a pretty slick gambler, and a fast man with a dollar when he is in the money.

Well, finally The Sky asks Brandy Bottle why he is not playing and Brandy laughs, and states as follows:

"Why," he says, "in the first place I have no potatoes, and in the second place I doubt if it will do me much good if I do have any potatoes the way I am going the past year. Why," Brandy Bottle says, "I cannot win a bet to save my soul."

Now this crack seems to give The Sky an idea, as he stands looking at Brandy Bottle very strangely, and while he is looking, Big Nig, the crap shooter, picks up the dice and hits three times hard-running, bing, bing, bing. Then Big Nig comes out on a six and Brandy Bottle Bates speaks as follows:

"You see how my luck is," he says. "Here is Big Nig hotter than a stove, and here I am without a bob to follow him with, especially," Brandy says, "when he is looking for nothing but a six. Why," he says, "Nig can make sixes all night when he is hot. If he does not make this six, the way he is, I will be willing to turn square and quit gambling forever."

"Well, Brandy," The Sky says, "I will make you a proposition. I will lay you a G note Big Nig does not get his six. I will lay you a G note against nothing but your soul," he says. "I mean if Big Nig does not get his six, you are to turn square and join Miss Sarah Brown's mission for six months."

"Bet!" Brandy Bottle Bates says right away, meaning the proposition is on, although the chances are he does not quite understand the proposition. All Brandy understands is The Sky wishes to wager that Big Nig does not make his six, and Brandy Bottle Bates will be willing to bet his soul a couple of times over on Big Nig making his six, and figure he is getting the best of it, at that, as Brandy has great confidence in Nig.

Well, sure enough, Big Nig makes the six, so The Sky weeds

Brandy Bottle Bates a G note, although everybody is saying The Sky makes a terrible over-lay of the natural price in giving Brandy Bottle a G against his soul. Furthermore, everybody around figures the chances are The Sky only wishes to give Brandy an opportunity to get in action, and nobody figures The Sky is on the level about trying to win Brandy Bottle Bates' soul, especially as The Sky does not seem to wish to go any further after paying the bet.

He only stands there looking on and seeming somewhat depressed as Brandy Bottle goes into action on his own account with the G note, fading other guys around the table with cash money. But Brandy Bottle Bates seems to figure what is in The Sky's mind pretty well, because Brandy Bottle is a crafty old guy.

It finally comes his turn to handle the dice, and he hits a couple of times, and then he comes out on a four, and anybody will tell you that a four is a very tough point to make, even with a lead pencil. Then Brandy Bottle turns to The Sky and speaks to him as follows:

"Well, Sky," he says, "I will take the odds off you on this one. I know you do not want my dough," he says. "I know you only want my soul for Miss Sarah Brown, and," he says, "without wishing to be fresh about it, I know why you want it for her. I am young once myself," Brandy Bottle says. "And you know if I lose to you, I will be over there on Forty-eighth Street in an hour pounding on the door, for Brandy always settles.

"But, Sky," he says, "now I am in the money, and my price goes up. Will you lay me ten G's against my soul I do not make this four?"

"Bet!" The Sky says, and right away Brandy Bottle hits with a four.

Well, when word goes around that The Sky is up at Nathan Detroit's crap game trying to win Brandy Bottle Bates' soul for Miss Sarah Brown, the excitement is practically intense. Somebody telephones Mindy's, where a large number of citizens are sitting around arguing about this and that, and telling one another how much they will bet in support of their arguments, if only they have something to bet, and Mindy himself is almost killed in the rush for the door.

One of the first guys out of Mindy's and up to the crap game is Regret, the horse player, and as he comes in Brandy Bottle is looking for a nine, and The Sky is laying him twelve G's against his soul that he does not make this nine, for it seems Brandy Bottle's soul keeps getting more and more expensive.

Well, Regret wishes to bet his soul against a G that Brandy Bottle gets his nine, and is greatly insulted when The Sky cannot figure his price any better than a double saw, but finally Regret accepts this price, and Brandy Bottle hits again.

Now many other citizens request a little action from The Sky and if there is one thing The Sky cannot deny a citizen it is action, so he says he will lay them according to how he figures their word to join Miss Sarah Brown's mission if Brandy Bottle misses out, but about this time The Sky finds he has no more potatoes on him, being now around thirty-five G's loser, and he wishes to give markers.

But Brandy Bottle says that while ordinarily he will be pleased to extend The Sky this accommodation, he does not care to accept markers against his soul, so then The Sky has to leave the joint and go over to his hotel two or three blocks away, and get the night clerk to open his damper so The Sky can get the rest of his bank roll. In the meantime the crap game continues at Nathan Detroit's among the small operators, while the other citizens stand around and say that while they hear of many a daffy proposition in their time, this is the daffiest that ever comes to their attention, although Big Nig claims he hears of a daffier one, but cannot think what it is.

Big Nig claims that all gamblers are daffy anyway, and in fact he says if they are not daffy they will not be gamblers, and while he is arguing this matter back comes The Sky with fresh scratch, and Brandy Bottle Bates takes up where he leaves off, although Brandy says he is accepting the worst of it, as the dice have a chance to cool off.

Now the upshot of the whole business is that Brandy Bottle hits thirteen licks in a row, and the last lick he makes is on a ten, and it is for twenty G's against his soul, with about a dozen other citizens getting anywhere from one to five C's against their souls, and complaining bitterly of the price.

And as Brandy Bottle makes his ten, I happen to look at The Sky and I see him watching Brandy with a very peculiar expression on his face, and furthermore I see The Sky's right hand creeping inside his coat where I know he always packs a Betsy in a shoulder holster, so I can see something is wrong somewhere.

But before I can figure out what it is, there is quite a fuss at the door, and loud talking, and a doll's voice, and all of a sudden in bobs nobody else but Miss Sarah Brown. It is plain to be seen that she is all steamed up about something.

She marches right up to the crap table where Brandy Bottle Bates and The Sky and the other citizens are standing, and one and all are feeling sorry for Dobber, the doorman, thinking of what Nathan Detroit is bound to say to him for letting her in. The dice are still lying on the table showing Brandy Bottle Bates' last throw, which cleans The Sky and gives many citizens the first means they enjoy in several months.

Well, Miss Sarah Brown looks at The Sky, and The Sky looks at Miss Sarah Brown, and Miss Sarah Brown looks at the citizens around and about, and one and all are somewhat dumbfounded, and nobody seems to be able to think of much to say, although The Sky finally speaks up as follows:

"Good evening," The Sky says. "It is a nice evening," he says. "I am trying to win a few souls for you around here, but," he says, "I seem to be about half out of luck."

"Well," Miss Sarah Brown says, looking at The Sky most severely out of her hundred-per-cent eyes, "you are taking too much upon yourself. I can win any souls I need myself. You better be thinking of your own soul. By the way," she says, "are you risking your own soul, or just your money?"

Well, of course up to this time The Sky is not risking anything but his potatoes, so he only shakes his head to Miss Sarah Brown's question, and looks somewhat disorganized.

"I know something about gambling," Miss Sarah Brown says, "especially about crap games. I ought to," she says. "It ruins my poor papa and my brother Joe. If you wish to gamble for souls, Mister Sky, gamble for your own soul."

Now Miss Sarah Brown opens a small black leather pocketbook she is carrying in one hand, and pulls out a two-dollar bill, and it is such a two-dollar bill as seems to have seen much service in its time, and holding up this deuce, Miss Sarah Brown speaks as follows:

"I will gamble with you, Mister Sky," she says. "I will gamble with you," she says, "on the same terms you gamble with these parties here. This two dollars against your soul, Mister Sky. It is all I have, but," she says, "it is more than your soul is worth."

Well, of course anybody can see that Miss Sarah Brown is doing this because she is very angry, and wishes to make The Sky look small, but right away The Sky's duke comes from inside his coat, and he picks up the dice and hands them to her and speaks as follows:

"Roll them," The Sky says, and Miss Sarah Brown snatches the dice out of his hand and gives them a quick sling on the table in such a way that anybody can see she is not a professional crap shooter, and not even an amateur crap shooter, for all amateur crap shooters first breathe on the dice, and rattle them good, and make remarks to them, such as "Come on, baby!"

In fact, there is some criticism of Miss Sarah Brown afterwards on account of her haste, as many citizens are eager to string with her to hit, while others are just as anxious to bet she misses, and she does not give them a chance to get down.

Well, Scranton Slim is the stick guy, and he takes a gander at the dice as they hit up against the side of the table and bounce back, and then Slim hollers, "Winner, winner, winner," as stick guys love to do, and what is showing on the dice as big as life, but a six and a five, which makes eleven, no matter how you figure, so The Sky's soul belongs to Miss Sarah Brown.

She turns at once and pushes through the citizens around the table without even waiting to pick up the deuce she lays down when she grabs the dice. Afterwards a most obnoxious character by the name of Red Nose Regan tries to claim the deuce as a sleeper and gets the heave-o from Nathan Detroit, who becomes very indignant about this, stating that Red Nose is trying to give his joint a wrong rap.

Naturally, The Sky follows Miss Brown, and Dobber, the doorman, tells me that as they are waiting for him to unlock the door and let them out, Miss Sarah Brown turns on The Sky and speaks to him as follows:

"You are a fool," Miss Sarah Brown says.

Well, at this Dobber figures The Sky is bound to let one go, as this seems to be most insulting language, but instead of letting one go, The Sky only smiles at Miss Sarah Brown and says to her like this:

"Why," The Sky says, "Paul says 'If any man among you seemeth to be wise in this world, let him become a fool, that he may be wise.' I love you, Miss Sarah Brown," The Sky says.

Well now, Dobber has a pretty fair sort of memory, and he says that Miss Sarah Brown tells The Sky that since he seems to know so much about the Bible, maybe he remembers the second verse of the Song of Solomon, but the chances are Dobber muffs the number of the verse, because I look the matter up in one of these Gideon Bibles, and the verse seems a little too much for Miss Sarah Brown, although of course you never can tell.

Anyway, this is about all there is to the story, except that Brandy Bottle Bates slides out during the confusion so quietly even Dobber scarcely remembers letting him out, and he takes most of The Sky's potatoes with him, but he soon gets batted in against the faro bank out in Chicago, and the last anybody hears of him he gets religion all over again, and is preaching out in San Jose, so The Sky always claims he beats Brandy for his soul, at that.

I see The Sky the other night at Forty-ninth Street and Broadway, and he is with quite a raft of mission workers, including Mrs. Sky, for it seems that the soul-saving business picks up wonderfully, and The Sky is giving a big bass drum such a first-class whacking that the scat band in the chop-suey joint can scarcely be heard. Furthermore, The Sky is hollering between whacks, and I never see a guy look happier, especially when Mrs. Sky smiles at him out of her hundred-per-cent eyes. But I do not linger long, because The Sky gets a gander at me, and right away he begins hollering:

"I see before me a sinner of the deepest dye," he hollers. "Oh, sinner, repent before it is too late. Join with us, sinner," he hollers, "and let us save your soul."

Naturally, this crack about me being a sinner embarrasses me no little, as it is by no means true, and it is a good thing for The Sky there is no copper in me, or I will go to Mrs. Sky, who is always bragging about how she wins The Sky's soul by outplaying him at his own game, and tell her the truth.

And the truth is that the dice with which she wins The Sky's soul, and which are the same dice with which Brandy Bottle Bates wins all his potatoes, are strictly phony, and that she gets into Nathan Detroit's just in time to keep The Sky from killing old Brandy Bottle.

THE OLD DOLL'S HOUSE

Now it seems that one cold winter night, a party of residents of Brooklyn comes across the Manhattan Bridge in an automobile wishing to pay a call on a guy by the name of Lance McGowan, who is well known to one and all along Broadway as a coming guy in the business world.

In fact, it is generally conceded that, barring accident, Lance will someday be one of the biggest guys in this country as an importer, and especially as an importer of such merchandise as fine liquors, because he is very bright, and has many good connections throughout the United States and Canada.

Furthermore, Lance McGowan is a nice-looking young guy and he has plenty of ticker, although some citizens say he does not show very sound business judgment in trying to move in on Angie the Ox over in Brooklyn, as Angie the Ox is an importer himself, besides enjoying a splendid trade in other lines, including artichokes and extortion.

Of course Lance McGowan is not interested in artichokes at all, and very little in extortion, but he does not see any reason why he shall not place his imports in a thriving territory such as Brooklyn, especially as his line of merchandise is much superior to anything handled by Angie the Ox.

Anyway, Angie is one of the residents of Brooklyn in the party that wishes to call on Lance McGowan, and besides Angie the party includes a guy by the name of Mockie Max, who is a very prominent character in Brooklyn, and another guy by the name of The Louse Kid, who is not so prominent, but who is considered a very promising young guy in many respects, although personally I think The Louse Kid has a very weak face.

He is supposed to be a wonderful hand with a burlap bag when anybody wishes to put somebody in such a bag, which is considered a great practical joke in Brooklyn, and in fact The Louse Kid has a burlap bag with him on the night in question, and they are figuring on putting Lance McGowan in the bag when they call on him, just for the laugh. Personally, I consider this a very crude form of humor, but then Angie the Ox and the other members of his party are very crude characters, anyway.

Well, it seems they have Lance McGowan pretty well cased, and they know that of an evening along toward ten o'clock he nearly always strolls through West Fifty-fourth Street on his way to a certain spot on Park Avenue that is called the Humming Bird Club, which has a very high-toned clientele, and the reason Lance goes there is because he has a piece of the joint, and furthermore he loves to show off his shape in a tuxedo to the swell dolls.

So these residents of Brooklyn drive in their automobile along this route, and as they roll past Lance McGowan, Angie the Ox and Mockie Max let fly at Lance with a couple of sawed-offs, while The Louse Kid holds the burlap bag, figuring for all I know that Lance will be startled by the sawed-offs and will hop into the bag like a rabbit.

But Lance is by no means a sucker, and when the first blast of slugs from the sawed-offs breezes past him without hitting him, what does he do but hop over a brick wall alongside him and drop into a yard on the other side. So Angie the Ox and Mockie Max and The Louse Kid get out of their automobile and run up close to the wall themselves because they commence figuring that if Lance McGowan starts popping at them from behind this wall, they will be taking plenty the worst of it, for of course they cannot figure Lance to be strolling about without being rodded up somewhat.

But Lance is by no means rodded up, because a rod is apt to create a bump in his shape when he has his tuxedo on, so the story really begins with Lance McGowan behind the brick wall, practically defenseless, and the reason I know this story is because Lance McGowan tells most of it to me, as Lance knows that I know his real name is Lancelot, and he feels under great obligation to me because I never mention the matter publicly.

Now, the brick wall Lance hops over is a wall around a pretty fair-sized yard, and the yard belongs to an old two-story stone house, and this house is well known to one and all in this man's town as a house of great mystery, and it is pointed out as such by the drivers of sightseeing buses.

This house belongs to an old doll by the name of Miss Abigail Ardsley, and anybody who ever reads the newspapers will tell you that Miss Abigail Ardsley has so many potatoes that it is really painful to think of, especially to people who have no potatoes whatever. In fact, Miss Abigail Ardsley has practically all the potatoes in the world, except maybe a few left over for general circulation.

These potatoes are left to her by her papa, old Waldo Ardsley, who accumulates same in the early days of this town by buying corner real estate very cheap before people realize this real estate will be quite valuable later on for fruit-juice stands and cigar stores.

It seems that Waldo is a most eccentric old bloke, and is very strict with his daughter, and will never let her marry, or even as much as look as if she wishes to marry, until finally she is so old she does not care a cuss about marrying, or anything else, and becomes very eccentric herself.

In fact, Miss Abigail Ardsley becomes so eccentric that she cuts herself off from everybody, and especially from a lot of relatives who are wishing to live off her, and anytime anybody cuts themselves off from such characters they are considered very eccentric indeed, especially by the relatives. She lives in the big house all alone, except for a couple of old servants, and it is very seldom that anybody sees her around and about, and many strange stories are told of her.

Well, no sooner is he in the yard than Lance McGowan begins looking for a way to get out, and one way he does not wish to get out is over the wall again, because he figures Angie the Ox and his sawed-offs are bound to be waiting for him on Fifty-fourth Street. So Lance looks around to see if there is some way out of the yard in another direction, but it seems there is no such way, and pretty soon he sees the snozzle of a sawed-off come poking over the wall, with the ugly kisser of Angie the Ox behind it, looking for him, and there is Lance McGowan all cornered up in the yard, and not feeling so good, at that.

Then Lance happens to try a door on one side of the house, and the door opens at once and Lance McGowan hastens in to find himself in the living-room of the house. It is a very large living-room with very nice furniture standing around and about, and oil paintings on the walls, and a big old grandfather's clock as high as the ceiling, and statuary here and there. In fact, it is such a nice, comfortable-looking room that Lance McGowan is greatly surprised, as he is expecting to find a regular mystery-house room such as you see in the movies, with cobwebs here and there, and everything all rotted up, and maybe Boris Karloff wandering about making strange noises.

But the only person in this room seems to be a little old doll all dressed in soft white, who is sitting in a low rocking-chair by an open fireplace in which a bright fire is going, doing some tatting.

Well, naturally Lance McGowan is somewhat startled by this scene, and he is figuring that the best thing he can do is to guzzle the old doll before she can commence yelling for the gendarmes, when she looks up at him and gives him a soft smile, and speaks to him in a soft voice, as follows:

"Good evening," the old doll says.

Well, Lance cannot think of any reply to make to this at once, as it is certainly not a good evening for him, and he stands there looking at the old doll, somewhat dazed, when she smiles again and tells him to sit down.

So the next thing Lance knows, he is sitting there in a chair in front of the fireplace chewing the fat with the old doll as pleasant as you please, and of course the old doll is nobody but Miss Abigail Ardsley. Furthermore, she does not seem at all alarmed, or even much surprised, at seeing Lance in her house, but then Lance is never such a looking guy as is apt to scare old dolls, or young dolls either, especially when he is all slicked up.

Of course Lance knows who Miss Abigail Ardsley is, because he often reads stories in the newspapers about her the same as everybody else, and he always figures such a character must be slightly daffy to cut herself off from everybody when she has all the potatoes in the world, and there is so much fun going on, but he is very courteous to her, because after all he is a guest in her home.

"You are young," the old doll says to Lance McGowan, looking him in the kisser. "It is many years since a young man comes through yonder door. Ah, yes," she says, "so many years."

And with this she lets out a big sigh, and looks so very sad that Lance McGowan's heart is touched.

"Forty-five years now," the old doll says in a low voice, as if she is talking to herself. "So young, so handsome, and so good."

And although Lance is in no mood to listen to reminiscences at this time, the next thing he knows he is hearing a very pathetic love story, because it seems that Miss Abigail Ardsley is once all hotted up over a young guy who is nothing but a clerk in her papa's office.

It seems from what Lance McGowan gathers that there is nothing wrong with the young guy that a million bobs will not cure, but Miss Abigail Ardsley's papa is a mean old waffle, and he will never listen to her having any truck with a poor guy, so they dast not let him know how much they love each other.

But it seems that Miss Abigail Ardsley's ever-loving young guy has plenty of moxie, and every night he comes to see her after her papa goes to the hay, and she lets him in through the same side-door Lance McGowan comes through, and they sit by the fire and hold hands, and talk in low tones, and plan what they will do when the young guy makes a scratch.

Then one night it seems Miss Abigail Ardsley's papa has the stomach ache, or some such, and cannot sleep a wink, so he comes wandering downstairs looking for the Jamaica ginger, and catches Miss Abigail Ardsley and her ever-loving guy in a clutch that will win the title for any wrestler that can ever learn it.

Well, this scene is so repulsive to Miss Abigail Ardsley's papa that he is practically speechless for a minute, and then he orders the young guy out of his life in every respect, and tells him never to darken his door again, especially the side-door.

But it seems that by this time a great storm is raging outside, and Miss Abigail Ardsley begs and pleads with her papa to let the young guy at least remain until the storm subsides, but between being all sored up at the clutching scene he witnesses, and his stomach ache, Mr. Ardsley is very hard-hearted indeed, and he makes the young guy take the wind.

The next morning the poor young guy is found at the side-door frozen as stiff as a board, because it seems that the storm that is raging is the blizzard of 1888, which is a very famous event in the history of New York, although up to this time Lance McGowan never hears of it before, and does not believe it until he looks the matter up afterwards. It seems from what Miss Abigail Ardsley says that as near as anyone can make out, the young guy must return to the door seeking shelter after wandering about in the storm awhile, but of course by this time her papa has the door all bolted up, and nobody hears the young guy.

"And," Miss Abigail Ardsley says to Lance McGowan, after giving him all these details, "I never speak to my papa again as long as he lives, and no other man ever comes in or out of yonder door, or any other door of this house, until your appearance to-night, although," she says, "this side-door is never locked in case such a young man comes seeking shelter."

Then she looks at Lance McGowan in such a way that he wonders if Miss Abigail Ardsley hears the sawed-offs going when Angie the Ox and Mockie Max are tossing slugs at him, but he is too polite to ask.

Well, all these old-time memories seem to make Miss Abigail Ardsley feel very tough, and by and by she starts to weep, and if there is one thing Lance McGowan cannot stand it is a doll weeping, even if she is nothing but an old doll. So he starts in to cheer Miss Abigail Ardsley up, and he pats her on the arm, and says to her like this:

"Why," Lance says, "I am greatly surprised to hear your statement about the doors around here being so little used. Why, Sweetheart," Lance says, "if I know there is a doll as good-looking as you in the neighborhood, and a door unlocked, I will be busting in myself every night. Come, come, come," Lance says, "let us talk things over and maybe have a few laughs, because I may have to stick around here awhile. Listen, Sweetheart," he says, "do you happen to have a drink in the joint?"

Well, at this Miss Abigail Ardsley dries her eyes, and smiles again, and then she pulls a sort of rope near her, and in comes a guy who seems about ninety years old, and who seems greatly surprised to see Lance there. In fact, he is so surprised that he is practically tottering when he leaves the room after hearing Miss Abigail Ardsley tell him to bring some wine and sandwiches.

And the wine he brings is such wine that Lance McGowan has half a mind to send some of the lads around afterwards to see if there is any more of it in the joint, especially when he thinks of the unlocked side-door, because he can sell this kind of wine by the carat.

Well, Lance sits there with Miss Abigail Ardsley sipping wine and eating sandwiches, and all the time he is telling her stories of one kind and another, some of which he cleans up a little when he figures they may be a little too snappy for her, and by and by he has her laughing quite heartily indeed.

Finally he figures there is no chance of Angie and his sawed-offs being outside waiting for him, so he says he guesses he will be going, and Miss Abigail Ardsley personally sees him to the door, and this time it is the front door, and as Lance is leaving he thinks of something he once sees a guy do on the stage, and he takes Miss Abigail Ardsley's hand and raises it to his lips and gives it a large kiss, all of which is very surprising to Miss Abigail Ardsley, but more so to Lance McGowan when he gets to thinking about it afterwards.

Just as he figures, there is no one in sight when he gets out in the street, so he goes on over to the Humming Bird Club, where he learns that many citizens are greatly disturbed by his absence, and are wondering if he is in The Louse Kid's burlap bag, for by this time it is pretty well known that Angie the Ox and his fellow citizens of Brooklyn are around and about.

In fact, somebody tells Lance that Angie is at the moment over in Good Time Charley's little speak on West Forty-ninth Street, buying drinks for one and all, and telling how he makes Lance McGowan hop a brick wall, which of course sounds most disparaging of Lance.

Well, while Angie is still buying these drinks, and still speaking of making Lance a brick-wall hopper, all of a sudden the door of Good Time Charley's speak opens and in comes a guy with a Betsy in his hand and this guy throws four slugs into Angie the Ox before anybody can say hello.

Furthermore, the guy throws one slug into Mockie Max, and one slug into The Louse Kid, who are still with Angie the Ox, so the next thing anybody knows there is Angie as dead as a doornail, and there is Mockie Max even deader than Angie, and there is The Louse making a terrible fuss over a slug in his leg, and nobody can remember what the guy who plugs them looks like, except a couple of stool pigeons who state that the guy looks very much like Lance McGowan.

So what happens but early the next morning Johnny Brannigan, the plain-clothes copper, puts the arm on Lance McGowan for plugging Angie the Ox and Mockie Max and The Louse Kid, and there is great rejoicing in copper circles generally because at this time the newspapers are weighing in the sacks on the coppers quite some, claiming there is too much lawlessness going on around and about and asking why somebody is not arrested for something.

So the collar of Lance McGowan is water on the wheel of one and all because Lance is so prominent, and anybody will tell you that it looks as if it is a sure thing that Lance will be very severely punished, and maybe sent to the electric chair, although he hires Judge Goldstein, who is one of the surest-footed lawyers in this town, to defend him. But even Judge Goldstein admits that Lance is in a tough spot, especially as the newspapers are demanding justice, and printing long stories about Lance, and pictures of him, and calling him some very uncouth names.

Finally Lance himself commences to worry about his predicament, although up to this time a little thing like being charged with murder in the first degree never bothers Lance very much. And in fact he will not be bothering very much about this particular charge if he does not find the D.A. very fussy about letting him out on bail. In fact, it is nearly two weeks before he lets Lance out on bail, and all this time Lance is in the sneezer, which is a most mortifying situation to a guy as sensitive as Lance.

Well, by the time Lance's trial comes up, you can get three to one anywhere that he will be convicted, and the price goes up to five when the prosecution gets through with its case, and proves by the stool pigeons that at exactly twelve o'clock on the night of January 5th, Lance McGowan steps into Good Time Charley's little speak and plugs Angie the Ox, Mockie Max, and The Louse Kid.

Furthermore, several other witnesses who claim they know Lance McGowan by sight testify that they see Lance in the neighborhood of Good Time Charley's around twelve o'clock, so by the time it comes Judge Goldstein's turn to put on the defense, many citizens are saying that if he can do no more than beat the chair for Lance he will be doing a wonderful job.

Well, it is late in the afternoon when Judge Goldstein gets up and looks all around the courtroom, and without making any opening statement to the jury for the defense, as these mouthpieces usually do, he says like this:

"Call Miss Abigail Ardsley," he says.

At first nobody quite realizes just who Judge Goldstein is calling for, although the name sounds familiar to one and all present who read the newspapers, when in comes a little old doll in a black silk dress that almost reaches the floor, and a black bonnet that makes a sort of a frame for her white hair and face.

Afterwards I read in one of the newspapers that she looks like she steps down out of an old-fashioned ivory miniature and that she is practically beautiful, but of course Miss Abigail Ardsley has so many potatoes that no newspaper dast to say she looks like an old chromo.

Anyway, she comes into the courtroom surrounded by so many old guys you will think it must be recess at the Old Men's Home, except they are all dressed up in claw-hammer coat tails, and high collars, and afterwards it turns out that they are the biggest law-yers in this town, and they all represent Miss Abigail Ardsley one way or another, and they are present to see that her interests are protected, especially from each other.

Nobody ever sees so much bowing and scraping before in a court-room. In fact, even the judge bows, and although I am only a spec-tator I find myself bowing too, because the way I look at it, anybody with as many potatoes as Miss Abigail Ardsley is entitled to a gen-eral bowing. When she takes the witness-stand, her lawyers grab chairs and move up as close to her as possible, and in the street outside there is practically a riot as word goes around that Miss Abigail Ardsley is in the court, and citizens come running from every which way, hoping to get a peek at the richest old doll in the world.

Well, when all hands finally get settled down a little, Judge Goldstein speaks to Miss Abigail Ardsley as follows:

"Miss Ardsley," he says, "I am going to ask you just two or three questions. Kindly look at this defendant," Judge Goldstein says, pointing at Lance McGowan, and giving Lance the office to stand up. "Do you recognize him?"

Well, the little old doll takes a gander at Lance, and nods her head yes, and Lance gives her a large smile, and Judge Goldstein says:

"Is he a caller in your home on the night of January fifth?" Judge Goldstein asks.

"He is," Miss Abigail Ardsley says.

"Is there a clock in the living-room in which you receive this de-fendant?" Judge Goldstein says.

"There is," Miss Abigail Ardsley says. "A large clock," she says. "A grandfather's clock."

"Do you happen to notice," Judge Goldstein says, "and do you now recall the hour indicated by this clock when the defendant leaves your home?"

"Yes," Miss Abigail Ardsley says, "I do happen to notice. It is just twelve o'clock by my clock," she says. "Exactly twelve o'clock," she says.

Well, this statement creates a large sensation in the courtroom, because if it is twelve o'clock when Lance McGowan leaves Miss Abigail Ardsley's house on West Fifty-fourth Street, anybody can see that there is no way he can be in Good Time Charley's little speak over five blocks away at the same minute unless he is a magician, and the judge begins peeking over his specs at the coppers in the courtroom very severe, and the cops begin scowling at the stool pigeons, and I am willing to lay plenty of six to five that the stools will wish they are never born before they hear the last of this matter from the gendarmes.

Furthermore, the guys from the D.A.'s office who are handling the prosecution are looking much embarrassed, and the jurors are muttering to each other, and right away Judge Goldstein says he moves that the case against his client be dismissed, and the judge says he is in favor of the motion, and he also says he thinks it is high time the gendarmes in this town learn to be a little careful who they are arresting for murder, and the guys from the D.A.'s office do not seem to be able to think of anything whatever to say.

So there is Lance as free as anybody, and as he starts to leave the courtroom he stops by Miss Abigail Ardsley, who is still sitting in the witness-chair surrounded by her mouthpieces, and he shakes her hand and thanks her, and while I do not hear it myself, somebody tells me afterwards that Miss Abigail Ardsley says to Lance in a low voice, like this:

"I will be expecting you again some night, young man," she says.

"Some night, Sweetheart," Lance says, "at twelve o'clock."

And then he goes on about his business, and Miss Abigail Ardsley goes on about hers, and everybody says it is certainly a wonderful thing that a doll as rich as Miss Abigail Ardsley comes forward in the interests of justice to save a guy like Lance McGowan from a wrong rap.

But of course it is just as well for Lance that Miss Abigail Ardsley does not explain to the court that when she recovers from the shock of the finding of her ever-loving young guy frozen to death, she stops all the clocks in her house at the hour she sees him last, so for forty-five years it is always twelve o'clock in her house.

IT COMES UP MUD

Personally, I never criticize Miss Beulah Beauregard for breaking her engagement to Little Alfie, because from what she tells me she becomes engaged to him under false pretenses, and I do not approve of guys using false pretenses on dolls, except, of course, when nothing else will do.

It seems that Little Alfie promises to show Miss Beulah Beauregard the life of Riley following the races with him when he gets her to give up a first-class job displaying her shape to the customers in the 900 Club, although Miss Beulah Beauregard frankly admits that Little Alfie does not say what Riley, and afterward Little Alfie states that he must be thinking of Four-eyes Riley when he makes the promise, and everybody knows that Four-eyes Riley is nothing but a bum, in spades.

Anyway, the life Little Alfie shows Miss Beulah Beauregard after they become engaged is by no means exciting, according to what she tells me, as Little Alfie is always going around the race tracks with one or two crocodiles that he calls race horses, trying to win a few bobs for himself, and generally Little Alfie is broke and struggling, and Miss Beulah Beauregard says this is no existence for a member of a proud old Southern family such as the Beauregards.

In fact, Miss Beulah Beauregard often tells me that she has half a mind to leave Little Alfie and return to her ancestral home in Georgia, only she can never think of any way of getting there without walking, and Miss Beulah Beauregard says it always makes her feet sore to walk very far, although the only time anybody ever hears of Miss Beulah Beauregard doing much walking is the time she is shell-roaded on the Pelham Parkway by some Yale guys when she gets cross with them.

It seems that when Little Alfie is first canvassing Miss Beulah Beauregard to be his fiancée he builds her up to expect diamonds and furs and limousines and one thing and another, but the only diamond she ever sees is an engagement hoop that Little Alfie gives her as the old convincer when he happens to be in the money for a moment, and it is a very small diamond, at that, and needs a high north light when you look at it.

But Miss Beulah Beauregard treasures this diamond very highly just the same, and one reason she finally breaks off her engagement to Little Alfie is because he borrows the diamond one day during the Hialeah meeting at Miami without mentioning the matter to her, and hocks if for five bobs which he bets on an old caterpillar of his by the name of Governor Hicks to show.

Well, the chances are Miss Beulah Beauregard will not mind Little Alfie's borrowing the diamond so much if he does not take the twenty-five bobs he wins when Governor Hicks drops in there in the third hole and sends it to Colonel Matt Winn in Louisville to enter a three-year-old of his by the name of Last Hope in the Kentucky Derby, this Last Hope being the only other horse Little Alfie owns at this time.

Such an action makes Miss Beulah Beauregard very indignant indeed, because she says a babe in arms will know Last Hope cannot walk a mile and a quarter, which is the Derby distance, let alone run so far, and that even if Last Hope can run a mile and a quarter, he cannot run it fast enough to get up a sweat.

In fact, Miss Beulah Beauregard and Little Alfie have words over this proposition, because Little Alfie is very high on Last Hope and will not stand for anybody insulting this particular horse, not even his fiancée, although he never seems to mind what anybody says about Governor Hicks, and, in fact, he often says it himself.

Personally, I do not understand what Little Alfie sees in Last Hope, because the horse never starts more than once or twice since it is born, and then has a tough time finishing last, but Little Alfie says the fifty G's that Colonel Winn gives to the winner of the Kentucky Derby is just the same as in the jug in his name, especially if it comes up mud on Derby Day, for Little Alfie claims that Last Hope is bred to just naturally eat mud.

Well, Miss Beulah Beauregard says there is no doubt Little Alfie blows his topper, and that there is no percentage in her remaining engaged to a crack-pot, and many citizens put in with her on her statement because they consider entering Last Hope in the Derby very great foolishness, no matter if it comes up mud or what, and right away Tom Shaw offers a thousand to one against the horse in the future book, and everybody says Tom is underlaying the price at that.

Miss Beulah Beauregard states that she is very discouraged by the way things turn out, and that she scarcely knows what to do, because she fears her shape changes so much in the four or five years she is engaged to Little Alfie that the customers at the 900 Club may not care to look at it anymore, especially if they have to pay for this privilege, although personally I will pay any reasonable cover charge to look at Miss Beulah Beauregard's shape anytime, if it is all I suspect. As far as I can see it is still a very nice shape indeed, if you care for shapes.

Miss Beulah Beauregard is at this time maybe twenty-five or twenty-six, and is built like a first baseman, being tall and rangy. She has hay-colored hair, and blue eyes, and lots of health, and a very good appetite. In fact, I once see Miss Beulah Beauregard putting on the fried chicken in the Seven Seas restaurant in a way that greatly astonishes me, because I never knew before that members of proud old Southern families are such hearty eaters. Furthermore, Miss Beulah Beauregard has a very Southern accent, which makes her sound quite cute, except maybe when she is a little excited and is putting the zing on somebody, such as Little Alfie.

Well, Little Alfie says he regrets exceedingly that Miss Beulah Beauregard sees fit to break their engagement, and will not be with him when he cuts up the Derby dough, as he is planning a swell wedding for her at French Lick after the race, and even has a list all made out of the presents he is going to buy her, including another diamond, and now he has all this bother of writing out the list for nothing.

Furthermore, Little Alfie says he is so accustomed to having Miss Beulah Beauregard as his fiancée that he scarcely knows what to do without her, and he goes around with a very sad puss, and is generally quite low in his mind, because there is no doubt that Little Alfie loves Miss Beulah Beauregard more than somewhat.

But other citizens are around stating that the real reason Miss Beulah Beauregard breaks her engagement to Little Alfie is because a guy by the name of Mr. Paul D. Veere is making a powerful play for her, and she does not wish him to know that she has any truck with a character such as Little Alfie, for of course Little Alfie is by no means anything much to look at, and, furthermore, what with hanging out with his horses most of the time, he never smells like any rose geranium.

It seems that this Mr. Paul D. Veere is a New York banker, and he has a little moustache, and plenty of coconuts, and Miss Beulah Beauregard meets up with him one morning when she is displaying her shape on the beach at the Roney Plaza for nothing, and it also seems that there is enough of her shape left to interest Mr. Paul D. Veere no little.

In fact, the next thing anybody knows, Mr. Paul D. Veere is taking Miss Beulah Beauregard here and there, and around and about, although at this time Miss Beulah Beauregard is still engaged to Little Alfie, and the only reason Little Alfie does not notice Mr. Paul D. Veere at first is because he is busy training Last Hope to win the Kentucky Derby, and hustling around trying to get a few bobs together every day to stand off the overhead, including Miss Beulah Beauregard, because naturally Miss Beulah Beauregard cannot bear the idea of living in a fleabag, such as the place where Little Alfie resides, but has to have a nice room at the Roney Plaza.

Well, personally, I have nothing against bankers as a class, and in fact I never meet up with many bankers in my life, but somehow I do not care for Mr. Paul D. Veere's looks. He looks to me like a stony-hearted guy, although, of course, nobody ever sees any banker who does not look stony-hearted, because it seems that being bankers just naturally makes them look this way.

But Mr. Paul D. Veere is by no means an old guy, and the chances are he speaks of something else besides horses to Miss Beulah Beauregard, and furthermore he probably does not smell like horses all the time, so nobody can blame Miss Beulah Beauregard for going around and about with him, although many citizens claim she is a little out of line in accepting Mr. Paul D. Veere's play while she is still engaged to Little Alfie. In fact, there is great indignation in some circles about this, as many citizens feel that Miss Beulah Beauregard is setting a bad example to other fiancées.

But after Miss Beulah Beauregard formally announces that their engagement is off, it is agreed by one and all that she has a right to do as she pleases, and that Little Alfie himself gets out of line in what happens at Hialeah a few days later when he finally notices that Miss Beulah Beauregard seems to be with Mr. Paul D. Veere, and on very friendly terms with him, at that. In fact, Little Alfie comes upon Mr. Paul D. Veere in the act of kissing Miss Beulah Beauregard behind a hibiscus bush out near the paddock, and this scene is most revolting to Little Alfie as he never cares for hibiscus, anyway.

He forgets that Miss Beulah Beauregard is no longer his fiancée, and tries to take a punch at Mr. Paul D. Veere, but he is stopped by a number of detectives, who are greatly horrified at the idea of anybody taking a punch at a guy who has as many coconuts as Mr. Paul D. Veere, and while they are expostulating with Little Alfie, Miss Beulah Beauregard disappears from the scene and is observed no more in Miami. Furthermore, Mr. Paul D. Veere also disappears, but of course nobody minds this very much, and, in fact, his disappearance is a great relief to all citizens who have fiancées in Miami at this time.

But it seems that before he disappears Mr. Paul D. Veere calls on certain officials of the Jockey Club and weighs in the sacks on Little Alfie, stating that he is a most dangerous character to have loose around a race track, and naturally the officials are bound to listen to a guy who has as many coconuts as Mr. Paul D. Veere.

So a day or two later old Cap Duhaine, the head detective around the race track, sends for Little Alfie and asks him what he thinks will become of all the prominent citizens such as bankers if guys go around taking punches at them and scaring them half to death, and Little Alfie cannot think of any answer to this conundrum off-hand, especially as Cap Duhaine then asks Little Alfie if it will be convenient for him to take his two horses elsewhere.

Well, Little Alfie can see that Cap Duhaine is hinting in a polite way that he is not wanted around Hialeah anymore, and Little Alfie is a guy who can take a hint as well as the next guy, especially when Cap Duhaine tells him in confidence that the racing stewards do not seem able to get over the idea that some scalawag slips a firecracker into Governor Hicks the day old Governor Hicks runs third, because it seems from what Cap Duhaine says that the stewards consider it practically supernatural for Governor Hicks to run third anywhere, anytime.

So there Little Alfie is in Miami, as clean as a jaybird, with two horses on his hands, and no way to ship them to any place where horses are of any account, and it is quite a predicament indeed, and causes Little Alfie to ponder quite some. And the upshot of his pondering is that Little Alfie scrapes up a few bobs here and there, and a few oats, and climbs on Governor Hicks one day and boots him in the slats and tells him to giddyup, and away he goes out of Miami, headed north, riding Governor Hicks and leading Last Hope behind him on a rope.

Naturally, this is considered a most unusual spectacle by one and all who witness it and, in fact, it is the first time anybody can remember a horse owner such as Little Alfie riding one of his own horses off in this way, and Gloomy Gus is offering to lay plenty of five to one that Governor Hicks never makes Palm Beach with Little Alfie up, as it is well known that the old Governor has bum legs and is half out of wind and is apt to pig it anytime.

But it seems that Governor Hicks makes Palm Beach all right with Little Alfie up and going so easy that many citizens are around asking Gloomy for a price against Jacksonville. Furthermore, many citizens are now saying that Little Alfie is a pretty smart guy, at that, to think of such an economical idea, and numerous other horse owners are looking their stock over to see if they have anything to ride up north themselves.

Many citizens are also saying that Little Alfie gets a great break when Miss Beulah Beauregard runs out on him, because it takes plenty of weight off him in the way of railroad fare and one thing and another; but it seems Little Alfie does not feel this way about the matter at all.

It seems that Little Alfie often thinks about Miss Beulah Beauregard as he goes jogging along to the north, and sometimes he talks to Governor Hicks and Last Hope about her, and especially to Last Hope, as Little Alfie always considers Governor Hicks somewhat dumb. Also Little Alfie sometimes sings sad love songs right out loud as he is riding along, although the first time he starts to sing he frightens Last Hope and causes him to break loose from the lead rope and run away, and Little Alfie is an hour catching him. But after this Last Hope gets so he does not mind Little Alfie's voice so much, except when Little Alfie tries to hit high C.

Well, Little Alfie has a very nice ride, at that, because the weather is fine and the farmers along the road feed him and his horses, and he has nothing whatever to worry about except a few saddle galls, and about getting to Kentucky for the Derby in May, and here it is only late in February, and anyway Little Alfie does not figure to ride any farther than maybe Maryland where he is bound to make a scratch so he can ship from there.

Now, one day Little Alfie is riding along a road through a stretch of piney woods, a matter of maybe ninety-odd miles north of Jacksonville, which puts him in the State of Georgia, when he passes a half-plowed field on one side of the road near a ramshackly old house and beholds a most unusual scene:

A large white mule hitched to a plow is sitting down in the field and a tall doll in a sunbonnet and a gingham dress is standing beside the mule crying very heartily.

Naturally, the spectacle of a doll in distress, or even a doll who is not in distress, is bound to attract Little Alfie's attention, so he tells Governor Hicks and Last Hope to whoa, and then he asks the doll what is eating her, and the doll looks up at him out of her sunbonnet, and who is this doll but Miss Beulah Beauregard.

Of course Little Alfie is somewhat surprised to see Miss Beulah Beauregard crying over a mule, and especially in a sunbonnet, so he climbs down off of Governor Hicks to inquire into this situation, and right away Miss Beulah Beauregard rushes up to Little Alfie and chucks herself into his arms and speaks as follows:

"Oh, Alfie," Miss Beulah Beauregard says, "I am so glad you find me. I am thinking of you day and night, and wondering if you forgive me. Oh, Alfie, I love, you," she says. "I am very sorry I go away with Mr. Paul D. Veere. He is nothing but a great rapscallion," she says. "He promises to make me his ever-loving wife when he gets me to accompany him from Miami to his shooting-lodge on the Altamaha River, twenty-five miles from here, although," she says, "I never know before he has such a lodge in these parts.

"And," Miss Beulah Beauregard says, "the very first day I have to pop him with a pot of cold cream and render him half unconscious to escape his advances. Oh, Alfie," she says, "Mr. Paul D. Veere's intentions towards me are by no means honorable. Furthermore," she says, "I learn he already has an ever-loving wife and three children in New York."

Well, of course Little Alfie is slightly perplexed by this matter and can scarcely think of anything much to say, but finally he says to Miss Beulah Beauregard like this:

"Well," he says, "but what about the mule?"

"Oh," Miss Beulah Beauregard says, "his name is Abimelech, and I am plowing with him when he hauls off and sits down and refuses to budge. He is the only mule we own," she says, "and he is old and ornery, and nobody can do anything whatever with him when he wishes to sit down. But," she says, "my papa will be very angry because he expects me to get this field all plowed up by supper-time. In fact," Miss Beulah Beauregard says, "I am afraid my papa will be so angry he will give me a whopping, because he by no means forgives me as yet for coming home, and this is why I am shedding tears when you come along."

Then Miss Beulah Beauregard begins crying again as if her heart will break, and if there is one thing Little Alfie hates and despises it is to see a doll crying, and especially Miss Beulah Beauregard, for Miss Beulah Beauregard can cry in a way to wake the dead when she is going good, so Little Alfie holds her so close to his chest he ruins four cigars in his vest pocket, and speaks to her as follows:

"Tut, tut," Little Alfie says. "Tut, tut, tut, tut, tut," he says. "Dry your eyes and we will just hitch old Governor Hicks here to the plow and get this field plowed quicker than you can say scat, because," Little Alfie says, "when I am a young squirt, I am the best plower in Columbia County, New York."

Well, this idea cheers Miss Beulah Beauregard up no little, and so Little Alfie ties Last Hope to a tree and takes the harness off Abimelech, the mule, who keeps right on sitting down as if he does not care what happens, and puts the harness on Governor Hicks and hitches Governor Hicks to the plow, and the way the old Governor carries on when he finds out they wish him to pull a plow is really most surprising. In fact, Little Alfie has to get a club and reason with Governor Hicks before he will settle down and start pulling the plow.

It turns out that Little Alfie is a first-class plower, at that, and while he is plowing, Miss Beulah Beauregard walks along with him and talks a blue streak, and Little Alfie learns more things from her in half an hour than he ever before suspects in some years, and especially about Miss Beulah Beauregard herself.

It seems that the ramshackly old house is Miss Beulah Beauregard's ancestral home, and that her people are very poor, and live in these piney woods for generations, and that their name is Benson and not Beauregard at all, this being nothing but a name that Miss Beulah Beauregard herself thinks up out of her own head when she goes to New York to display her shape.

Furthermore, when they go to the house it comes out that Miss Beulah Beauregard's papa is a tall, skinny old guy with a goatee, who can lie faster than Little Alfie claims Last Hope can run. But it seems that the old skeezicks takes quite an interest in Last Hope when Little Alfie begins telling him what a great horse this horse is, especially in the mud, and how he is going to win the Kentucky Derby.

In fact, Miss Beulah Beauregard's papa seems to believe everything Little Alfie tells him, and as he is the first guy Little Alfie ever meets up with who believes anything he tells about anything whatever, it is a privilege and a pleasure for Little Alfie to talk to him. Miss Beulah Beauregard also has a mamma who turns out to be very fat, and full of Southern hospitality, and quite handy with a skillet.

Then there is a grown brother by the name of Jeff, who is practically a genius, as he knows how to disguise skimmin's so it makes a person only a little sick when they drink it, this skimmin's being a drink which is made from skimmings that come to the top on boiling sugar cane, and generally it tastes like gasoline, and is very fatal indeed.

Now, the consequences are Little Alfie finds this place very pleasant, and he decides to spend a few weeks there, paying for his keep with the services of Governor Hicks as a plow horse, especially as he is now practically engaged to Miss Beulah Beauregard all over again and she will not listen to him leaving without her. But they have no money for her railroad fare, and Little Alfie becomes very indignant when she suggests she can ride Last Hope on north while he is riding Governor Hicks, and wishes to know if she thinks a Derby candidate can be used for a truck horse.

Well, this almost causes Miss Beulah Beauregard to start breaking the engagement all over again, as she figures it is a dirty crack about her heft, but her papa steps in and says they must remain until Governor Hicks get through with the plowing anyway, or he will know the reason why. So Little Alfie stays and he puts in all his spare time training Last Hope and wondering who he can write to for enough dough to send Miss Beulah Beauregard north when the time comes.

He trains Last Hope by walking him and galloping him along the country roads in person, and taking care of him as if he is a baby, and what with this work, and the jog up from Miami, Last

Hope fills out very strong and hearty, and anybody must admit that he is not a bad-looking beetle, though maybe a little more leggy than some like to see.

Now, it comes a Sunday, and all day long there is a very large storm with rain and wind that takes to knocking over big trees, and one thing and another, and no one is able to go outdoors much. So late in the evening Little Alfie and Miss Beulah Beauregard and all the Bensons are gathered about the stove in the kitchen drinking skimmin's, and Little Alfie is telling them all over again about how Last Hope will win the Kentucky Derby, especially if it comes up mud, when they hear a hammering at the door.

When the door is opened, who comes in but Mr. Paul D. Veere, sopping wet from head to foot, including his little moustache, and limping so he can scarcely walk, and naturally his appearance nonplusses Miss Beulah Beauregard and Little Alfie, who can never forget that Mr. Paul D. Veere is largely responsible for the saddle galls he gets riding up from Miami.

In fact, several times since he stops at Miss Beulah Beauregard's ancestral home, Little Alfie thinks of Mr. Paul D. Veere, and every time he thinks of him he is in favor of going over to Mr. Paul D. Veere's shooting-lodge on the Altamaha and speaking to him severely.

But Miss Beulah Beauregard always stops him, stating that the proud old Southern families in this vicinity are somewhat partial to the bankers and other rich guys from the North who have shooting-lodges around and about in the piney woods, and especially on the Altamaha, because these guys furnish a market to the local citizens for hunting guides, and corn liquor, and one thing and another.

Miss Beulah Beauregard says if a guest of the Bensons speaks to Mr. Paul D. Veere severely, it may be held against the family, and it seems that the Benson family cannot stand any more beefs against it just at this particular time. So Little Alfie never goes, and here all of a sudden is Mr. Paul D. Veere right in his lap.

Naturally, Little Alfie steps forward and starts winding up a large right hand with the idea of parking it on Mr. Paul D. Veere's chin, but Mr. Paul D. Veere seems to see that there is hostility afoot, and he backs up against the wall, and raises his hand, and speaks as follows:

"Folks," Mr. Paul D. Veere says, "I just go into a ditch in my automobile half a mile up the road. My car is a wreck," he says, "and my right leg seems so badly hurt I am just barely able to drag myself here. Now, folks," he says, "it is almost a matter of life and death with me to get to the station at Tillinghast in time to flag the Orange Blossom Special. It is the last train to-night to Jacksonville, and I must be in Jacksonville before midnight so I can hire an airplane and get to New York by the time my bank opens at ten o'clock in the morning. It is about ten hours by plane from Jacksonville to New York," Mr. Paul D. Veere says, "so if I can catch the Orange Blossom, I will be able to just about make it!"

Then he goes on speaking in a low voice and states that he receives a telephone message from New York an hour or so before at his lodge telling him he must hurry home, and right away afterwards, while he is trying to telephone the station at Tillinghast to make sure they will hold the Orange Blossom until he gets there, no matter what, all the telephone and telegraph wires around and about go down in the storm.

So he starts for the station in his car, and just as it looks as if he may make it, his car runs smack-dab into a ditch and Mr. Paul D. Veere's leg is hurt so there is no chance he can walk the rest of the way to the station, and there Mr. Paul D. Veere is.

"It is a very desperate case, folks," Mr. Paul D. Veere says. "Let me take your automobile, and I will reward you liberally."

Well, at this Miss Beulah Beauregard's papa looks at a clock on the kitchen wall and states as follows:

"We do not keep an automobile, neighbor," he says, "and anyway," he says, "it is quite a piece from here to Tillinghast and the Orange Blossom is due in ten minutes, so I do not see how you can possibly make it. Rest your hat, neighbor," Miss Beulah Beauregard's papa says, "and have some skimmin's, and take things easy, and I will look at your leg and see how bad you are bunged up."

Well, Mr. Paul D. Veere seems to turn as pale as a pillow as he hears this about the time, and then he says:

"Lend me a horse and buggy," he says. "I must be in New York in person in the morning. No one else will do but me," he says, and as he speaks these words he looks at Miss Beulah Beauregard and then at Little Alfie as if he is speaking to them personally, although up to this time he does not look at either of them after he comes into the kitchen.

"Why, neighbor," Miss Beulah Beauregard's papa says, "we do not keep a buggy, and even if we do keep a buggy we do not have time to hitch up anything to a buggy. Neighbor," he says, "you are certainly on a bust if you think you can catch the Orange Blossom now."

"Well, then," Mr. Paul D. Veere says, very sorrowful, "I will have to go to jail."

Then he flops himself down in a chair and covers his face with his hands, and he is a spectacle such as is bound to touch almost any heart, and when she sees him in this state Miss Beulah Beauregard begins crying because she hates to see anybody as sorrowed up as Mr. Paul D. Veere, and between sobs she asks Little Alfie to think of something to do about the situation.

"Let Mr. Paul D. Veere ride Governor Hicks to the station," Miss Beauregard says. "After all," she says, "I cannot forget his courtesy in sending me half-way here in his car from his shooting-lodge after I pop him with the pot of cold cream, instead of making me walk as those Yale guys do the time they red-light me."

"Why," Little Alfie says, "it is a mile and a quarter from the gate out here to the station. I know," he says, "because I get a guy in an automobile to clock it on his meter one day last week, figuring to give Last Hope a workout over the full Derby route pretty soon. The road must be fetlock deep in mud at this time, and," Little Alfie says, "Governor Hicks cannot as much as stand up in the mud. The only horse in the world that can run fast enough through this mud to make the Orange Blossom is Last Hope, but," Little Alfie says, "of course I'm not letting anybody ride a horse as valuable as Last Hope to catch trains."

Well, at this Mr. Paul D. Veere lifts his head and looks at Little Alfie with great interest and speaks as follows:

"How much is this valuable horse worth?" Mr. Paul D. Veere says.

"Why," Little Alfie says, "he is worth anyway fifty G's to me, because," he says, "this is the sum Colonel Winn is giving to the winner of the Kentucky Derby, and there is no doubt whatever that Last Hope will be this winner, especially," Little Alfie says, "if it comes up mud."

"I do not carry any such large sum of money as you mention on my person," Mr. Paul D. Veere says, "but," he says, "if you are willing to trust me, I will give you my I O U for same, just to let me ride your horse to the station. I am once the best amateur steeplechase rider in the Hunts Club," Mr. Paul D. Veere says, "and if your horse can run at all there is still a chance for me to keep out of jail."

Well, the chances are Little Alfie will by no means consider extending a loan of credit for fifty G's to Mr. Paul D. Veere or any other banker, and especially a banker who is once an amateur steeplechase jock, because if there is one thing Little Alfie does not trust it is an amateur steeplechase jock, and furthermore Little Alfie is somewhat offended because Mr. Paul D. Veere seems to think he is running a livery stable.

But Miss Beulah Beauregard is now crying so loud nobody can scarcely hear themselves think, and Little Alfie gets to figuring what she may say to him if he does not rent Last Hope to Mr. Paul D. Veere at this time and it comes out later that Last Hope does not happen to win the Kentucky Derby after all. So he finally says all right, and Mr. Paul D. Veere at once outs with a little gold pencil and a notebook, and scribbles off a marker for fifty G's to Little Alfie.

And the next thing anybody knows, Little Alfie is leading Last Hope out of the barn and up to the gate with nothing on him but a bridle as Little Alfie does not wish to waste time saddling, and as he is boosting Mr. Paul D. Veere on to Last Hope Little Alfie speaks as follows:

"You have three minutes left," Little Alfie says. "It is almost a straight course, except for a long turn going into the last quarter. Let this fellow run," he says. "You will find plenty of mud all the way, but," Little Alfie says, "this is a mud-running fool. In fact," Little Alfie says, "you are pretty lucky it comes up mud."

Then he gives Last Hope a smack on the hip and away goes Last Hope lickity-split through the mud and anybody can see from the way Mr. Paul D. Veere is sitting on him that Mr. Paul D. Veere knows what time it is when it comes to riding. In fact, Little Alfie himself says he never sees a better seat anywhere in his life, especially for a guy who is riding bareback.

Well, Little Alfie watches them go down the road in a gob of mud, and it will always be one of the large regrets of Little Alfie's life that he leaves his split-second super in hock in Miami, because he says he is sure Last Hope runs the first quarter through the mud faster than any quarter is ever run before in this world. But of course Little Alfie is more excited than somewhat at this moment, and the chances are he exaggerates Last Hope's speed.

However, there is no doubt that Last Hope goes over the road very rapidly indeed, as a colored party who is out squirrel hunting comes along a few minutes afterwards and tells Little Alfie that something goes past him on the road so fast he cannot tell exactly what it is, but he states that he is pretty sure it is old Henry Devil himself, because he smells smoke as it passes him, and hears a voice yelling hi-yah. But of course the chances are this voice is nothing but the voice of Mr. Paul D. Veere yelling words of encouragement to Last Hope.

It is not until the station-master at Tillinghast, a guy by the name of Asbury Potts, drives over to Miss Beulah Beauregard's ancestral home an hour later that Little Alfie hears that as Last Hope pulls up at the station and Mr. Paul D. Veere dismounts with so much mud on him that nobody can tell if he is a plaster cast or what, the horse is gimping as bad as Mr. Paul D. Veere himself, and Asbury Potts says there is no doubt Last Hope bows a tendon, or some such, and that if they are able to get him to the races again he will eat his old wool hat.

"But, personally," Asbury Potts says as he mentions this sad news, "I do not see what Mr. Paul D. Veere's hurry is, at that, to be pushing a horse so hard. He has fifty-seven seconds left by my watch when the Orange Blossom pulls in right on time to the dot," Asbury Potts says.

Well, at this Little Alfie sits down and starts figuring, and finally he figures that Last Hope runs the mile and a quarter in around 2.03 in the mud, with maybe one hundred and sixty pounds up, for Mr. Paul D. Veere is no feather duster, and no horse ever runs a mile and a quarter in the mud in the Kentucky Derby as fast as this, or anywhere else as far as anybody knows, so Little Alfie claims that this is practically flying.

But of course few citizens ever accept Little Alfie's figures as strictly official, because they do not know if Asbury Pott's watch is properly regulated for timing race horses, even though Asbury Potts is one-hundred-per-cent right when he says they will never be able to get Last Hope to the races again.

Well, I meet up with Little Alfie one night this summer in Mindy's restaurant on Broadway, and it is the first time he is observed in these parts in some time, and he seems to be looking very prosperous indeed, and after we get to cutting up old touches, he tells me the reason for this prosperity.

It seems that after Mr. Paul D. Veere returns to New York and puts back in his bank whatever it is that it is advisable for him to put back, or takes out whatever it is that seems best to take out, and gets himself all rounded up so there is no chance of his going to jail, he remembers that there is a slight difference between him and Little Alfie, so what does Mr. Paul D. Veere do but sit down and write out a check for fifty G's to Little Alfie to take up his I O U, so Little Alfie is nothing out on account of losing the Kentucky Derby, and, in fact, he is stone rich, and I am glad to hear of it, because I always sympathize deeply with him in his bereavement over the loss of Last Hope. Then I ask Little Alfie what he is doing in New York at this time, and he states to me as follows:

"Well," Little Alfie says, "I will tell you. The other day," he says, "I get to thinking things over, and among other things I get to thinking that after Last Hope wins the Kentucky Derby, he is a sure thing to go on and also win the Maryland Preakness, because," Little Alfie says, "the Preakness is a sixteenth of a mile shorter than the Derby, and a horse that can run a mile and a quarter in the mud in around 2.03 with a brick house on his back is bound to make anything that wears hair look silly at a mile and three-sixteenths, especially," Little Alfie says, "if it comes up mud."

"So," Little Alfie says, "I am going to call on Mr. Paul D. Veere and see if he does not wish to pay me the Preakness stake, too, because," he says, "I am building the finest house in South Georgia at Last Hope, which is my stock farm where Last Hope himself is on public exhibition, and I can always use a few bobs here and there."

"Well, Alfie," I say, "this seems to me to be a very fair proposition indeed and," I say, "I am sure Mr. Paul D. Veere will take care of it as soon as it is called to his attention, as there is no doubt you and Last Hope are of great service to Mr. Paul D. Veere. By the way, Alfie," I say, "whatever becomes of Governor Hicks?"

"Why," Little Alfie says, "do you know Governor Hicks turns out to be a terrible disappointment to me as a plow horse? He learns how to sit down from Abimelech, the mule, and nothing will make him stir, not even the same encouragement I give him the day he drops down there third at Hialeah.

"But," Little Alfie says, "my ever-loving wife is figuring on using the old Governor as a saddle-horse for our twins, Beulah and Little Alfie, Junior, when they get old enough, although," he says, "I tell her the Governor will never be worth a dime in such a way especially," Little Alfie says, "if it comes up mud."

THE BRAKEMAN'S
DAUGHTER

It is coming on spring in Newark, New Jersey, and one nice afternoon I am standing on Broad Street with a guy from Cleveland, Ohio, by the name of The Humming Bird, speaking of this and that, and one thing and another, when along comes a very tasty-looking young doll.

In fact, she is a doll with black hair, and personally I claim there is nothing more restful to the eye than a doll with black hair, because it is even money, or anyway nine to ten, that it is the natural color of the hair, as it seems that dolls will change the color of their hair to any color but black, and why this is nobody knows, except that it is just the way dolls are.

Well, besides black hair, this doll has a complexion like I do not know what, and little feet and ankles, and a way of walking that is very pleasant to behold. Personally, I always take a gander at a doll's feet and ankles before I start handicapping her, because the way I look at it, the feet and ankles are the big tell in the matter of class, although I wish to state that I see some dolls in my time who have large feet and big ankles, but who are by no means bad.

But this doll I am speaking of is one hundred per cent in every respect, and as she passes, The Humming Bird looks at her, and she looks at The Humming Bird, and it is just the same as if they hold a two hours' conversation on the telephone, for they are both young, and it is spring, and the way language can pass between young guys and young dolls in the spring without them saying a word is really most surprising, and, in fact, it is practically uncanny.

Well, I can see that The Humming Bird is somewhat confused for a minute, while the young doll seems to go right off into a trance, and she starts crossing the street against the lights, which is not only unlawful in Newark, New Jersey, but most indiscreet, and she is about to be run down and mashed like a turnip by one of Big False Face's beer trucks when The Humming Bird hops out into the street and yanks her out of danger, while the jockey is looking back and yelling words you will scarcely believe are known to anybody in Newark, New Jersey.

Then The Humming Bird and the young doll stand on the sidewalk chewing the fat for a minute or two, and it is plain to be seen that the doll is very much obliged to The Humming Bird, and it is also plain to be seen that The Humming Bird will give anyway four bobs to have the jockey of the beer truck where he can talk to him quietly.

Finally the doll goes on across the street, but this time she keeps her head up and watches where she is going, and The Humming Bird comes back to me, and I ask him if he finds out who she is, and does he date her up, or what? But in answer to my questions, The Humming Bird states to me as follows:

"To tell the truth," The Humming Bird says, "I neglect these details, because," he says, "I am already dated up to go out with Big False Face to-night to call on a doll who is daffy to meet me. Otherwise," he says, "I will undoubtedly make arrangements to see more of this pancake I just save from rack and ruin.

"But," The Humming Bird says, "Big Falsy tells me I am going to meet the most wonderful doll in the world, and one that is very difficult to meet, so I cannot be picking up any excess at this time. In fact," he says, "Big Falsy tells me that every guy in this town will give his right leg for the privilege of meeting the doll in question but she will have no part of them. But it seems that she sees me talking to Big Falsy on the street yesterday, and now nothing will do but she must meet up with me personally. Is it not remarkable," The Humming Bird says, "the way dolls go for me?"

Well, I say it is, for I can see that The Humming Bird is such a guy as thinks he has something on the dolls, and for all I know maybe he has, at that, for he has plenty of youth, and good looks, and good clothes, and a nice line of gab, and all these matters are given serious consideration by the dolls, especially the youth.

But I cannot figure any doll that Big False Face knows being such a doll as the one The Humming Bird just yanks out the way of the beer truck, and in fact I do not see how any doll whatever can have any truck with a guy as ugly as Big False Face. But then of course Big False Face is now an important guy in the business world, and has plenty of potatoes, and of course potatoes are also something that is taken into consideration by the dolls.

Big False Face is in the brewery business, and he controls a number of breweries in different spots on the Atlantic seaboard, and especially in New Jersey, and the reason The Humming Bird is in Newark, New Jersey, at this time, is because Big False Face gets a very huge idea in connection with these breweries.

It seems that they are breweries that Big False Face takes over during the past ten years when the country is trying to get along without beer, and the plants are laying idle, and Big False Face opens up these plants and puts many guys to work, and turns out plenty of beer, and thus becomes quite a philanthropist in his way, especially to citizens who like their beer, although up to the time he gets going good as a brewer, Big False Face is considered a very humble character indeed.

He comes from the Lower East Side of New York, and he is called Big False Face from the time he is very young, because he has a very large and a very homely kisser, and on this kisser there is always a castor-oil smile that looks as if it is painted on. But this smile is strictly a throw-off, and Big False Face is often smiling when he is by no means amused at anything, though I must say for him that he is generally a very light-hearted guy.

In his early youth, it is Big False Face's custom to stand chatting with strangers to the city around the railroad stations and ferry-boat landings, and smiling very genially at them, and in this way Big False Face learns much about other parts of the country. But it seems that while he is chatting with these strangers, friends of Big False Face search the strangers' pockets, sometimes removing articles from these pockets such as watches, and lucky pieces, and keepsakes of one kind and another, including money.

Of course it is all in fun, but it seems that some of the strangers become greatly annoyed when they find their pockets empty, and go out of their way to mention the matter to the gendarmes. Well, after the gendarmes hear some little mention from strangers about their pockets being searched while they are chatting with a guy with a large, smiling kisser, the gendarmes take to looking around for such a guy.

Naturally, they finally come upon Big False Face, for at the time I am speaking of, it is by no means common to find guys with smiles on their kissers on the Lower East Side, and, especially, large smiles. So what happens but Big False Face is sent to college in his youth by the gendarmes, and the place where the college is located is Auburn, New York, where they teach him that it is very, very wrong to smile at strangers while their pockets are being searched.

After Big False Face is in college for several years, the warden sends for him one day and gives him a new suit of clothes, and a railroad ticket, and a few bobs, and plenty of sound advice, and tells him to go back home again, and afterward Big False Face says he is only sorry he can never remember the advice, as he has no doubt it will be of great value to him in his subsequent career.

Well, later on, Big False Face takes a post-graduate course at Ossining, and also at Dannemora, and by the time he is through with all this, he finds that conditions change throughout the country, and that his former occupation is old-fashioned, and by no means genteel, so Big False Face has to think up something else to do. And while he is thinking, he drives a taxicab and has his station in front of the Pekin restaurant on Broadway, which is a real hot spot at this time.

Then one night a sailor off a U.S. battleship hires Big False Face to take him riding in Central Park, and it seems that somewhere on this ride the sailor loses his leather containing a month's salary, and he hops out of the taxicab and starts complaining to a gendarme making quite a mountain out of nothing but a molehill, for anybody knows that if the sailor does not lose his leather in the taxicab he is bound to spend it at ten cents a clip dancing with the dolls in the Flowerland dance hall, or maybe taking boat rides on the lagoon in the park.

Well, Big False Face can see an argument coming up, and rather than argue, he retires from the taxicab business at once, leaving his taxicab right there in the park, and going over into New Jersey, and Big False Face always says that one of the regrets of his life is he never collects the taxi fare off the sailor.

In New Jersey, Big False Face secures a position with the late Crowbar Connolly, riding loads down out of Canada, and then he is with the late Hands McGovern, and the late Dark Tony de More, and also the late Lanky-lank Watson, and all this time Big False Face is advancing step by step in the business world, for he has a great personality and is well liked by one and all.

Naturally, many citizens are jealous of Big False Face, and sometimes when they are speaking of him they speak of the days of his youth when he is on the whiz, as if this is something against him, but I always say it is very creditable of Big False Face to rise from such a humble beginning to a position of affluence in the business world.

Personally, I consider Big False Face a remarkable character, especially when he takes over the idle breweries, because it is at a time when everybody is going around saying that if they can only have beer everything will be all right. So Big False Face starts turning out beer that tastes very good indeed, and if everything is not all right, it is by no means his fault.

You must remember that at the time he starts turning out his beer, and for years afterward, Big False Face is being most illegal and quite against the law, and I claim that the way he is able to hide several breweries, each covering maybe half a block of ground, from the gendarmes all these years is practically magical, and proves that what I say about Big False Face being a remarkable character is very true.

Well, when Congress finally gets around to saying that beer is all right again, Big False Face is a well-established, going concern, and has a fair head-start on the old-fashioned brewers who come back into the business again, but Big False Face is smart enough to know that he will be able to keep ahead of them only by great enterprise and industry, because it seems that certain parties are bound and determined to make it tough on the brewers who supply this nation with beer when beer is illegal, such as Big False Face, forgetting all the hardships and dangers that these brewers face through the years to give the American people their beer, and all the bother they are put to in hiding breweries from the gendarmes.

In fact, these certain parties are making it so tough that Big False Face himself has to write twice before he can get permits for his breweries, and naturally this annoys Big False Face no little, as he hates to write letters.

Furthermore, he hears this condition prevails all over the country, so Big False Face gets to thinking things over, and he decides that the thing to do is to organize the independent brewers like himself into an association to protect their interests.

So he calls a meeting in Newark, New Jersey, of all these brewers and this is how it comes that The Humming Bird is present, for The Humming Bird represents certain interests around Cleveland,

Ohio, and furthermore The Humming Bird is personally regarded as a very able young guy when it comes to breweries.

Well, the only reason I am in Newark, New Jersey, at this time is because a guy by the name of Abie Schumtzenheimer is a delegate representing a New York brewery, and this Abie is a friend of mine, and after the meeting lasts three days he sends for me to come over and play pinochle with him because he cannot make heads or tails of what they are all talking about.

And anyway Abie does not care much, because the brewery he represents is going along for nearly twelve years, and is doing all the business it can handle, and anytime it fails to do all the business it can handle, Abie will be around asking a lot of people why.

So Abie's brewery does not care if it enters any association or not, but of course Abie cannot disregard an invitation from such a guy as Big False Face. So there he is, and by and by there I am, and in this way I meet up with The Humming Bird, and, after watching the way he goes darting around and about, especially if a doll happens to pop up in his neighborhood, I can understand why they call him The Humming Bird.

But, personally, I do not mind seeing a young guy displaying an interest in dolls, and, in fact, if a young guy does not display such an interest in dolls, I am apt to figure there is something wrong with him. And anyway what is the use of being young if a guy does not display an interest in dolls?

Well, there are delegates to the meeting from as far west as Chicago, and most of them seem to be greatly interested in Big False Face's proposition, especially a delegate from South Chicago who keeps trying to introduce a resolution to sue the government for libel for speaking of brewers who supply the nation with beer after Prohibition sets in as racket guys and wildcatters.

The reason the meeting lasts so long is partly because Big False Face keeps making motions for recesses so he can do a little entertaining, for if there is one thing Big False Face loves, it is to entertain, but another reason is that not all the delegates are willing to join Big False Face's association, especially certain delegates who are operating in Pennsylvania.

These delegates say it is nothing but a scheme on the part of Big False Face to nab the business on them, and in fact it seems that there is much resentment among these delegates against Big False

Face, and especially on the part of a guy by the name of Cheeks Sheracki, who comes from Philadelphia, Pennsylvania, and I wish to state that if there is one guy in the United States I will not care to have around resenting me it is Cheeks Sheracki, for nobody knows how many guys Cheeks cools off in his time, not even himself.

But Big False Face does not seem to notice anybody resenting him and he is putting on entertainment for the delegates right and left, including a nice steak dinner on the evening of the day I am speaking of, and it is at this dinner that I state to Big False Face that I hear he is taking The Humming Bird out in society.

"Yes," Big False Face says, "I am going to take The Humming Bird to call on the brakeman's daughter."

Well, when I hear this, I wish to say I am somewhat surprised because the brakeman's daughter is nothing but a practical joke and, furthermore, it is a practical joke that is only for rank suckers, and The Humming Bird does not look to be such a sucker to me.

In fact, when Big False Face speaks of the brakeman's daughter I take a gander at The Humming Bird figuring to see some expression on his kisser that will show he knows what the brakeman's daughter is, but instead The Humming Bird is only looking quite eager, and then I get to thinking about what he tells me in the afternoon about Big False Face taking him to see a doll who is daffy to meet him, and I can see that Big False Face is working on him with the brakeman's daughter for some time.

And I also get to thinking that a lot of smarter guys than The Humming Bird will ever be, no matter how smart he gets, fall for the brakeman's daughter joke, including Big False Face himself. In fact, Big False Face falls for it in the spring of 1928 at Hot Springs, Arkansas, and ever since it is his favorite joke, and it becomes part of his entertainment of all visitors to Newark, New Jersey, unless of course they happen to be visitors who are jerry to the brakeman's daughter into quite a well-known institution in Newark, New Jersey, and the way the brakeman's daughter joke goes is as follows:

The idea is Big False Face picks out some guy that he figures is a little doll-dizzy, and the way Big False Face can rap to a doll-dizzy guy is really quite remarkable.

Then he starts telling this guy about the brakeman's daughter, who is the most beautiful doll that ever steps in shoe leather, to hear Big False Face tell it. In fact, I once hear Big False Face telling a sucker about how beautiful the brakeman's daughter is, and I find myself wishing to see her, although of course I know there is no such thing as the brakeman's daughter.

Furthermore, everybody around Big False Face starts putting in a boost for the brakeman's daughter, stating to the sucker that she is so lovely that guys are apt to go silly just looking at her. But it seems that the brakeman's daughter has a papa who is a brakeman on the Central, and who is the orneriest guy in the world when it comes to his daughter, and who will not let anybody get close enough to her to hand her a slice of fruit cake.

In fact, this brakeman is so ornery he will shoot you setting if he catches you fooling around his daughter, the way Big False Face and other citizens of Newark, New Jersey, state the situation to the sucker, and everybody is afraid of the brakeman, including guys who are not supposed to be afraid of anything in this world.

But it seems that Big False Face is acquainted with the brakeman's daughter, and knows the nights the brakeman has to be out on his run, and on these nights the brakeman's daughter is home alone, and on such a night Big False Face occasionally calls on her, and sometimes takes a friend. But Big False Face and everybody else says that it is a dangerous proposition, because if the brakeman ever happens to come home unexpectedly and find callers with his daughter, he is pretty sure to hurt somebody.

Well, the chances are the sucker wishes to call on the brakeman's daughter, no matter what, especially as Big False Face generally lets on that the brakeman's daughter sees the sucker somewhere and is very anxious to meet him, just as he lets on to The Humming Bird, so finally some night Big Falsy takes the sucker to the house where the brakeman's daughter lives, making their approach to the house very roundabout, and mysterious, and sneaky.

Then the minute Big Falsy knocks on the door, out pops a guy from somewhere roaring at them in a large voice, and Big False Face yells that it is the brakeman's daughter's papa himself, and starts running, telling the sucker to follow, although as a rule this is by no means necessary. And when the sucker starts running, he commences to hear shots, and naturally he figures that the old brakeman is popping at him with a Betsy, but what he really hears is incandescent light bulbs going off around him and sometimes they hit him if the bulb-thrower has good control.

Now, the house Big False Face generally uses is an old empty residence pretty well out in a suburb of Newark, New Jersey, and it sits away off by itself in a big yard near a piece of woods, and when he starts running, Big False Face always runs into this woods, and naturally the sucker follows him. And pretty soon Big False Face loses the sucker in the woods, and doubles back and goes on downtown and leaves the sucker wandering around in the woods for maybe hours.

Then when the sucker finally makes his way back to his hotel, he always finds many citizens gathered to give him the ha-ha, and to make him buy refreshments for one and all, and the sucker tries to make out that he is greatly amused himself, although the chances are he is so hot you can fry an egg on any part of him.

The biggest laugh that Big False Face ever gets out of the brakeman's daughter joke is the time he leaves a guy from Brooklyn by the name of Rocco Scarpati in the woods one cold winter night, and Rocco never does find his way out, and freezes as stiff as a starched shirt. And of course Big False Face has quite a time explaining to Rocco's Brooklyn friends that Rocco is not cooled off by other means than freezing.

Well, now the way I tell it, you say to yourself how can anybody be sucker enough to fall for such a plant as this? But Big False Face's record with the brakeman's daughter joke in Newark, New Jersey, includes a congressman, a justice of the peace, three G-guys, eighteen newspaper scribes, five prize fighters, and a raft of guys from different parts of the country, who are such guys as the ordinary citizen will hesitate about making merry with.

In fact, I hear Big False Face is putting the feel on Cheeks Sheracki with reference to the brakeman's daughter until he finds out Cheeks knows this joke as well as he does himself, and then Big False Face discovers The Humming Bird, and no one is talking stronger for the brakeman's daughter with The Humming Bird than Cheeks.

Well, anyway, along about nine o'clock on the night in question, Big False Face tells The Humming Bird that the brakeman is now well out on his run on the Central so they get in Big False Face's car and start out, and I notice that, as they get in the car, Big False Face gives The Humming Bird a quick fanning, as Big False Face does not care to take chances on a sucker having that certain business on him.

The Humming Bird is all sharpened up for this occasion, and furthermore he is quite excited, and one and all are telling him what a lucky guy he is to get to call on the brakeman's daughter, but anybody can see from the way The Humming Bird acts that he feels that it is really the brakeman's daughter who is having the luck.

It seems that Cheeks Sheracki and a couple of his guys from Philadelphia go out to the house in advance to heave the incandescent bulbs and do the yelling, and personally I sit up playing pinochle with Abie Schumtzenheimer waiting to hear what comes off, although Abie says it is all great foolishness, and by no means worthy of grown guys. But Abie admits he will be glad to see the brakeman's daughter himself, if she is as beautiful as Big False Face claims.

Well, when they come within a couple of blocks of the empty house in the suburbs of Newark, New Jersey, Big False Face tells his driver, a guy by the name of Ears Acosta, who afterwards informs me on several points in this transaction, to pull up and wait there, and then Big False Face and The Humming Bird get out of the car and Big False Face leads the way up the street and into the yard.

This yard is filled with big trees and shrubbery, but the moon is shining somewhat, and it is easy enough to make out objects around and about, but there are no lights in the house, and it is so quiet you can hear your watch tick in your pocket, if you happen to have a watch.

Well, Big False Face has The Humming Bird by the coat sleeve, and he tiptoes through the gate and up a pathway, and The Humming Bird tiptoes right with him, and every now and then Big False Face stops and listens, and the way Big False Face puts this on is really wonderful, because he does it so often he can get a little soul into his work.

Now, The Humming Bird has plenty of moxie from all I hear, but naturally seeing the way Big False Face is acting makes him feel a little nervous, because The Humming Bird knows that Big False Face is as game as they come, and he figures that any situation that makes Big False Face act as careful as all this must be a very dangerous situation indeed.

When they finally get up close to the house, The Humming Bird sees there is a porch, and Big False Face tiptoes up on this porch, still leading The Humming Bird by the coat sleeve, and then Big False Face knocks softly on the door, and lets out a little low whistle, and, just as The Humming Bird is commencing to notice that this place seems to be somewhat deserted, all of a sudden a guy comes busting around the corner of the house.

This guy is making a terrible racket, what with yelling and swearing, and among other things he yells as follows:

"Ah-ha!" the guy yells, "now I have you dead to rights!"

And with this, something goes pop, and then something goes pop-pop, and Big False Face says to The Humming Bird like this:

"My goodness," Big False Face says, "it is the brakeman! Run!" he says. "Run for your life!"

Then Big False Face turns and runs, and The Humming Bird is about to turn and run with him because The Humming Bird figures if a guy like Big False Face can afford to run there can be no percentage in standing still himself, but before he can move the door of the house flies open and The Humming Bird feels himself being yanked inside the joint, and he puts up his dukes and gets ready to do the best he can until he is overpowered. Then he hears a doll's voice going like this:

"Sh-h-h-h!" the doll's voice goes. "Sh-h-h-h!"

So The Humming Bird sh-h-h-h's, and the racket goes on outside awhile with a guy still yelling, and much pop-pop-popping away. Then the noise dies out, and all is still, and by the moonlight that is coming through a window on which there is no curtain, The Humming Bird can see a lot of furniture scattered around and about the room, but some of it is upside-down and none of it is arranged in any order.

Furthermore, The Humming Bird can now also see that the doll who pulls him into the house and gives him the sh-h-h-h is nobody but the black-haired doll he hauls out of the way of the beer truck in the afternoon, and naturally The Humming Bird is somewhat surprised to see her at this time.

Well, the black-haired doll smiles at The Humming Bird and finally he forgets his nervousness to some extent, and in fact drops his dukes which he still has up ready to sell his life dearly, and by and by the black-haired doll says to him like this:

"I recognize you through the window in the moonlight," she says. "As I see you coming up on the porch, I also see some parties lurking in the shrubbery, and," she says, "I have a feeling they are seeking to do you harm, so I pull you inside the house. I am glad to see you again," she says.

Well, Big False Face does not show up in his accustomed haunts to laugh at the joke on The Humming Bird, but Ears Acosta returns with disquieting news such as causes many citizens to go looking for Big False Face, and they find him face downward on the path just inside the gateway, and when they turn him over the old castor-oil smile is still on his kisser, and even larger than ever, as if Big False Face is greatly amused by some thought that hits him all of a sudden.

And Big False Face is extremely dead when they find him, as it seems that some of the incandescent bulbs that go pop-popping around him are really sawed-off shotguns, and it also seems that Cheeks Sheracki and his guys from Philadelphia are such careless shots that they tear off half the gate with their slugs, so it is pretty lucky for The Humming Bird that he is not running with Big False Face for this gate at the moment, or in fact anywhere near him.

And back in the house, while they are lugging Big False Face away, The Humming Bird and the black-haired doll are sitting on an overturned sofa in the parlor with the moonlight streaming through the window on which there is no curtain and spilling all over them as The Humming Bird is telling her how much he loves her, and how he hopes and trusts she feels the same towards him, for they are young, and it is spring in Newark, New Jersey.

"Well," The Humming Bird says, "so you are the brakeman's daughter, are you? Well," he says, "I wish to state that they do not overboost you a nickel's worth when they tell me you are the most beautiful doll in all this world, and I am certainly tickled to find you."

"But how do you learn my new address so soon?" the black-haired doll says. "We just move in here this morning, although," she says, "I guess it is a good thing for you we do not have time to put up any window shades. And what do you mean," the black-haired doll says, "by calling me the brakeman's daughter? My papa is one of the oldest and best-known conductors anywhere on the Erie," she says.

WHAT, NO BUTLER?

To look at Ambrose Hammer, the newspaper scribe, you will never suspect that he has sense enough to pound sand in a rat hole, but Ambrose is really a pretty slick guy. In fact, Ambrose is a great hand for thinking, and the way I find this out makes quite a story.

It begins about seven o'clock one May morning when I am standing at the corner of Fiftieth Street and Broadway, and along comes Ambrose with his neck all tied up as if he has a sore throat, and he gives me a large hello in a hoarse tone of voice.

Then we stand there together, speaking of the beautiful sunrise, and one thing and another, and of how we wish we have jobs that will let us enjoy the daylight more, although personally I do not have any job to begin with, and if there is one thing I hate and despise it is the daylight, and the chances are this goes for Ambrose, too.

In fact, in all the years I know Ambrose, I never catch him out in the daylight more than two or three times, and then it is when we are both on our way home and happen to meet up as we do this morning I am talking about. And always Ambrose is telling me what a tough life he leads, and how his nerves are all shot to pieces, although I hear the only time Ambrose's nerves really bother him is once when he goes to Florida for a vacation, and has a nervous breakdown from the quiet that is around and about those parts.

This Ambrose Hammer is a short, chubby guy, with big, round, googly eyes, and a very innocent expression, and in fact it is this innocent expression that causes many guys to put Ambrose away as slightly dumb, because it does not seem possible that a guy who is around Broadway as long as Ambrose can look so innocent unless he is dumb.

He is what is called a dramatic critic by trade, and his job is to write pieces for the paper about the new plays that somebody is always producing on Broadway, and Ambrose's pieces are very interesting indeed, as he loves to heave the old harpoon into actors if they do not act to suit him, and as it will take a combination of Katherine Cornell, Jimmy Durante, and Lillian Gish to really suit Ambrose, he is generally in there harpooning away very good.

Well, while we are standing on the corner boosting the daylight, who comes along but a plain-clothes copper by the name of Marty Kerle, and he stops to give us a big good morning. Personally, I have no use for coppers, even if they are in plain clothes, but I believe in being courteous to them at all times, so I give Marty a big good morning right back at him, and ask him what he is doing out and about at such an hour, and Marty states as follows:

"Why," Marty says, "some doll who claims she is housekeeper for Mr. Justin Veezee just telephones the station that she finds Mr. Justin Veezee looking as if he is very dead in his house over here on West Fifty-sixth Street, and I am going there to investigate this rumor. Maybe," Marty says, "you will wish to come along with me."

"Mr. Justin Veezee?" Ambrose Hammer says. "Why, my goodness gracious, this cannot be true, because I hear he is in the Club Soudan only a few hours ago watching the Arabian acrobatic dancer turn flip-flops, and one thing and another, although personally," Ambrose says, "I do not think she is any more Arabian than Miss Ethel Barrymore."

But of course if Mr. Justin Veezee is dead, it is a nice item of news for Ambrose Hammer to telephone in to his paper, so he tells Marty he will be delighted to go with him, for one, and I decide to go too, as I will rather be looking at a dead guy than at guys hurrying to work at such an hour.

Furthermore, I am secretly hoping that the housekeeper does not make any mistake, as I can think of nothing nicer than seeing Mr. Justin Veezee dead, unless maybe it is two or three Mr. Justin Veezees dead, for personally I consider Mr. Justin Veezee nothing but an old stinker.

In fact, everybody in this town considers Mr. Justin Veezee nothing but an old stinker, because for many years he is along Broadway, in and out, and up and down, and always he is on the grab for young dolls such as work in night clubs and shows, and especially young dolls who do not have brains enough to realize that Mr. Justin Veezee is nothing but an old stinker. And of course there is always a fresh crop of such dolls coming to Broadway every year, and in fact it is getting so nowadays that there are several crops per year.

But although it is well known to one and all that Mr. Justin Veezee is nothing but an old stinker, nobody ever dasts speak of this matter out loud, as Mr. Justin Veezee has plenty of potatoes, which come down to him from his papa, and it is considered very disrespectful along Broadway to speak of a guy with plenty of potatoes as an old stinker, even if he is as tight with his potatoes as Mr. Justin Veezee, which is very, very, very, very tight indeed.

Now, the house on West Fifty-sixth Street where Mr. Justin Veezee lives in between Fifth and Sixth Avenues, and is once the private home of the Veezee family when there is quite a raft of Veezees around, but it seems that these Veezees all die off one by one, except Mr. Justin Veezee, and so he finally turns the old home into an apartment house.

It is a very nice-looking building, maybe four or five stories high, with apartments on each floor, and Mr. Justin Veezee's apartment is on the first floor above the street, and takes in the whole floor, although this does not mean so much space at that, as the house is very narrow.

It is one of these apartment houses where you push a button at the front door on the street floor, and this push rings a bell in the apartment you are after, and then somebody in the apartment pushes a button up there, and this unlocks the front door, and you walk up the stairs to where you are going, as there is no elevator, and no doorman, either.

Well, anyway, it is in the front room of Mr. Justin Veezee's apartment that we see Mr. Justin Veezee himself. He is sitting straight up in a big easy-chair beside a table on which there is a stack of these pictures called etchings, and he has on evening clothes, and his eyes are wide open and bugging out of his head, as if he is totally amazed at something he sees, and the chances are he is, at that.

There is no doubt whatever but that Mr. Justin Veezee is very dead indeed, and Marty Kerle says we are not to touch anything until the medical examiner has a peek, although by the time he says this, Ambrose Hammer is looking the etchings over with great interest, as Ambrose is such a guy as dearly loves to look at works of art.

The housekeeper who calls up the station is present when we arrive, but she turns out to be nothing but an old tomato by the name of Mrs. Swanson, who does not live in Mr. Justin Veezee's house, but who comes every morning at an early hour to clean up the joint. And this Mrs. Swanson states that she finds Mr. Justin Veezee just as he is when she comes in on this particular morning, although she says that usually he is in the hay pounding his ear at such an hour.

She thinks maybe he falls asleep in the chair, and tries to roust him out, but as Mr. Justin Veezee does not say aye, yes, or no, she figures the chances are he is dead, and so she gives the gendarmes a buzz.

"Well," I say to Ambrose Hammer, "this is a most ghastly scene indeed. In fact, Mr. Justin Veezee looks worse dead than he does alive, which I will never consider possible. The chances are this guy dies of old age. He must be fifty, if he is a day," I say.

"No," Ambrose says, "he does not die of old age. The way I look at it, this is a case of homicide. Somebody gets in here and cools off Mr. Justin Veezee, and it is a very dirty trick if you ask me, because," Ambrose says, "they do not give Mr. Justin Veezee a chance to change into something more comfortable than a dinner jacket."

Well, Ambrose says he will look around and see if he can locate any clues, and while he is snooping around the joint in comes a guy from the medical examiner's office and takes a gander at Mr. Justin Veezee. And the guy states at once that Mr. Justin Veezee is positively dead, although nobody is giving him any argument on this point, and he further states that what kills Mr. Justin Veezee is nothing but a broken neck.

Right away this broken neck becomes a very great mystery, because it does not stand to reason that a guy can break his own neck sitting down, unless maybe he is practicing to be a contortionist, and nobody figures it possible that Mr. Justin Veezee is practicing to be a contortionist at his age.

Furthermore, the medical guy finds certain marks on Mr. Justin Veezee's neck which he claims show that somebody grabs Mr. Justin Veezee by the guzzle and cracks his neck for him as if he is nothing but a goose, and the medical guy says it must be somebody with very strong dukes to play such a prank on Mr. Justin Veezee.

Well, Ambrose Hammer seems to be all heated up about this

whole matter, although personally I cannot see where it is any of his put-in. The way I look at it, Mr. Justin Veezee is no prize any way you take him when he is alive and kicking, and his death does not change the betting any as far as I am concerned, because I know from the things I see of Mr. Justin Veezee, and the things I hear of him, that he is still an old stinker, in spades.

Ambrose tells me that he is certainly going to solve this mystery in the interests of justice, and I tell him that the only way to solve a murder mystery is to suspect everybody in town, beginning with the old tomato who discovers the remains of Mr. Justin Veezee, and winding up with the gendarmes who investigate the case.

"But," I say to Ambrose Hammer, "you do not pin the foul deed on any of these parties, but on the butler, because this is the way these things are done in all the murder-mystery movies and plays I ever see, and also in all the murder-mystery books I ever read."

Well, at this Marty Kerle, the plain-clothes copper, states that the only trouble with my idea is that there is no butler connected with Mr. Justin Veezee's establishment in any way, shape, manner, or form, and when I tell Ambrose that maybe we can hire a butler to double in murder for us, Ambrose becomes very indignant, and speaks to me as follows:

"No butler commits this murder," Ambrose says, "and, further-more, I do not consider your remarks in good taste, no matter if you are joking, or what. I am convinced that this crime is the work of nobody but a doll, because of certain clues I encounter in my survey of the premises."

But Ambrose will not tell me what these clues are, and person-ally I do not care, because the way I look at it, even if some doll does give Mr. Justin Veezee the business, it is only retribution for what Mr. Justin Veezee does to other dolls in his time.

Well, the scragging of Mr. Justin Veezee is a very great sensa-tion, and the newspapers make quite a lot of it, because there is no doubt but what it is the greatest mystery in this town in several weeks. Furthermore, anybody that ever as much as speaks to Mr. Justin Veezee in the past twenty years becomes very sorry for it when the newspapers commence printing their names and pic-tures, and especially any dolls who have any truck with Mr. Justin Veezee in the past, for naturally the newspaper scribes and the gendarmes are around asking them where they are at such and such an hour on such and such a date, and it is quite amazing how few guys and dolls can remember this off-hand, especially dolls.

In fact, pretty soon the scragging of Mr. Justin Veezee becomes one of the most embarrassing propositions that ever comes off east of the Mississippi River, and many citizens are thinking of going out and scragging somebody else just to take the attention of the scribes and the gendarmes away from Mr. Justin Veezee.

As near as anybody can find out, the last party to see Mr. Justin Veezee alive the morning he is scragged is a red-headed doll at the Club Soudan by the name of Sorrel-top, and who is by no means a bad-looking doll, if you like them red-headed. This Sorrel-top is in charge of the check-room where one and all are supposed to check their hats and coats on entering the Club Soudan, and to tip Sorrel-top a shilling or two when they go out for keeping cases on these articles.

It seems that Sorrel-top always remembers when Mr. Justin Veezee leaves the Club Soudan, because he never stakes her to as much as a thin dime when he calls for his kady, and naturally Sorrel-top is bound to remember such a guy, especially as he is the only guy in the United States of America who dasts pass up Sorrel-top in this manner.

So she remembers that Mr. Justin Veezee leaves the Club Soudan on the morning in question around three bells, and the chances are he walks home, as none of the taxi jockeys who hang out in front of the Club Soudan remember seeing him, and, anyway, it is only a few blocks from the club to Mr. Justin Veezee's house, and it is a cinch he is never going to pay money to ride in a taxi just a few blocks.

Now it comes out that there are only two entrances to Mr. Justin Veezee's apartment, and one entrance is the front door, but the other entrance is a back door, but the back door is locked and barred on the inside when Mr. Justin Veezee is found, while the front door is locked with a patent snap lock, and Mrs. Swanson, the old tomato who does the housekeeping for Mr. Justin Veezee, states that she and Mr. Justin Veezee have the only two keys in the world to this lock that she knows of, although of course the parties who live in the other apartments in the house have keys to the street door, and so has the old tomato.

Furthermore, the windows of Mr. Justin Veezee's apartment are all locked on the inside, and there seems to be no way whatever that anybody except Mr. Justin Veezee and the old tomato can get in this apartment, and the gendarmes begin looking at the old tomato very suspiciously indeed until she digs up a milkman by the name of Schmalz, who sees her going into the apartment house about six-thirty in the morning, and then sees her a few minutes later come tearing out of the joint yelling watch, murder, police, and the medical guys say there is no chance she can guzzle Mr. Justin Veezee in this time, unless she is a faster worker than anybody they ever hear of in all their days.

Anyway, nobody can figure a motive for the old tomato to guzzle Mr. Justin Veezee, although a couple of the newspaper scribes try to make out that maybe she is an ever-loving sweetheart of Mr. Justin Veezee in the long ago, and that he does her dirt. Personally, I consider this proposition reasonable enough, because it is a sure thing that if the old tomato is ever Mr. Justin Veezee's sweetheart, he is just naturally bound to do her dirt. But the old tomato seems so depressed over losing a customer for her housekeeping that finally nobody pays any more attention to her, and one and all go looking around for someone else who may have a motive for giving Mr. Justin Veezee the business.

Well, it comes out that there are a large number of parties, including both male and female, in this part of the country who figure to have a motive for giving Mr. Justin Veezee the business, but they are all able to prove they are someplace else when this matter comes off, so the mystery keeps getting more mysterious by the minute, especially as the gendarmes say there is no chance that robbery is the motive, because Mr. Justin Veezee has all his jewelry on him and plenty of potatoes in his pockets when he is found, and nothing in the apartment seems disturbed.

Furthermore, they find no finger-prints around and about, except some that turn out to belong to Ambrose Hammer, and at that Ambrose has a tough time explaining that he makes these finger-prints after Mr. Justin Veezee is found, and not before. They find most of Ambrose's finger-prints on the etchings, and personally I am glad I am not around fingering anything while I am in the joint, as the gendarmes may not listen to my explanations as easy as they listen to Ambrose.

Well, I do not see Ambrose for several nights, but it seems that this is because there are some shows opening around town and

Ambrose is busy harpooning the actors. Finally one night he comes looking for me, and he states that as I am with him when he starts working on the mystery of who gives Mr. Justin Veezee the business, it is only fair that I be present when he exposes the party who commits this dastardly deed. And, Ambrose says, the hour now arrives, and although I do my best to show Ambrose that there can be no percentage for him in hollering copper on anybody in this matter, nothing will do but I must go with him.

And where does he take me but to the Club Soudan, and as it is early in the evening there are very few customers in the joint when we arrive, as the Club Soudan does not heat up good until along about midnight. Furthermore, I judge that the customers are strangers in the city, as they seem to be partaking of food, and nobody who is not a stranger in the city will think of partaking of food in the Club Soudan, although the liquor there is by no means bad.

Well, Ambrose and I get to talking to a character by the name of Flat-wheel Walter, who has a small piece of the joint, and who is called by this name because he walks with a gimp on one side, and by and by Ambrose asks for the Arabian acrobatic dancer, and Flat-wheel says she is at this time in her dressing-room making up for her dance. So Ambrose takes me up a flight of stairs to a little room, which is one of several little rooms along a hallway, and sure enough, there is this Arabian acrobatic dancer making up.

And the way she is making up is by taking off her clothes, because it seems that an Arabian acrobatic dancer cannot dance with anything on except maybe a veil or two, and personally I am somewhat embarrassed by the spectacle of a doll taking off her clothes to make up, especially an Arabian. But Ambrose Hammer does not seem to mind, as he is greatly calloused to such scenes because of his experience with the modern stage, and, anyway, the Arabian manages to get a few veils around her before I can really find any grounds for complaint. But I wish to say that I am greatly surprised when I hear this Arabian dancer speak in very good English, and in fact with a Brooklyn accent, and as follows:

"Oh, Ambrose," she says, "I am so glad to see you again."

With this she makes out as if to put her arms around Ambrose Hammer, but then she remembers just in time that if she does this she will have to let go her hold of the veils and, anyway, Ambrose pulls away from her and stands looking at her with a very strange expression on his kisser.

Well, I will say one thing for Ambrose Hammer, and this is that he is at all times very gentlemanly, and he introduces me to the Arabian acrobatic dancer, and I notice that he speaks of her as Miss Cleghorn, although I remember that they bill her in lights in front of the Club Soudan as Illah-Illah, which is maybe her first name.

Now Ambrose gazes at Miss Cleghorn most severely, and then he speaks:

"The game is up," Ambrose says. "If you wish to confess to me and this party, well and good, otherwise you will tell your story to the gendarmes. I know you kill Mr. Justin Veezee, and," Ambrose says, "while you may have an excellent excuse, it is against the law."

Well, at this Miss Cleghorn turns very pale indeed and begins trembling so she almost forgets to hold on to her veils, and then she sits down in a chair and breathes so hard you will think she just finishes a tough tenth round. Naturally, I am somewhat surprised by Ambrose's statement, because up to this time I am not figuring Miss Cleghorn as such a doll as will harm a flea, although of course I will never lay a price against this proposition on any doll without having something of a line on her.

"Yes," Ambrose says, speaking very severely indeed to Miss Cleghorn, "you make an appointment to go to Mr. Justin Veezee's apartment the other morning after you get through with your Arabian acrobatic dancing here, to look at his etchings. I am surprised you fall for etchings, but I am glad you do, at that, because it gives me my first clue. No guy is hauling out etchings at four o'clock in the morning to look at them by himself," Ambrose says. "It is one of the oldest build-ups of a doll in the world," he says.

"Well," Ambrose goes on, "you look at Mr. Justin Veezee's etchings. They are very bad. In fact, they are terrible. But never mind this. Presently you struggle. You are very strong on account of your Arabian acrobatic dancing. Yes," Ambrose says, "you are very, very, very strong. In this struggle you break Mr. Justin Veezee's neck, and now he is extremely dead. It is all very sad," Ambrose says.

Now, I wish to state that I am greatly mortified at being present at this scene, because if I know what Ambrose Hammer says he knows about Miss Cleghorn, I will keep my trap closed, especially as there is no reward offered for any information leading to the apprehension of the party who gives Mr. Justin Veezee the business, but Ambrose is undoubtedly a very law-abiding guy, and the chances are he feels he is only doing his duty in this manner, and, furthermore, he may get a nice item for his paper out of it.

But when he tells Miss Cleghorn that she is guilty of this un-ladylike conduct toward Mr. Justin Veezee, she gets up out of her chair, still holding on to her veils, and speaks to Ambrose Hammer like this:

"No, Ambrose," she says, "you are wrong. I do not kill Mr. Justin Veezee. I admit I go to his apartment, but not to see his etchings. I go there to have a bite to eat with him, because Mr. Justin Veezee swears to me that his housekeeper will be present, and I do not know he is deceiving me until after I arrive there. Mr. Justin Veezee gets out his etchings later when he can think of nothing else. But even Mr. Justin Veezee is not so old-fashioned as to believe any doll will go to his apartment just to look at etchings nowadays. I admit we struggle, but," Miss Cleghorn says, "I do not kill him."

"Well," Ambrose says, "if you do not think Mr. Justin Veezee is dead, a dollar will win you a trip around the world."

"Yes," Miss Cleghorn says, "I know he is dead. He is dead when I leave the apartment. I am very, very sorry for this, but I tell you again I do not kill him."

"Well," Ambrose says, "then who does kill Mr. Justin Veezee?"

"This I will never, never tell," Miss Cleghorn says.

Now, naturally Ambrose Hammer becomes very indignant at this statement, and he tells Miss Cleghorn that if she will not tell him she will have to tell the gendarmes, and she starts in to cry like I do not know what, when all of a sudden the door of the dressing-room opens, and in comes a big, stout-built, middle-aged-looking guy, who does not seem any too well dressed, and who speaks as follows:

"Pardon the intrusion, gentlemen," the guy says, "but I am waiting in the next room and cannot help overhearing your conversation. I am waiting there because Miss Cleghorn is going to draw enough money off her employers to get me out of this part of the country. My name," the guy says, "is Riggsby. I am the party who kills Mr. Justin Veezee."

Well, naturally Ambrose Hammer is greatly surprised by these remarks, and so am I, but before either of us can express our-selves, the guy goes on like this:

"I am a roomer in the humble home of Mrs. Swanson on Ninth

Avenue," he says. "I learn all about Mr. Justin Veezee from her. I sneak her key to the street door of Mr. Justin Veezee's house, and her key to the door of Mr. Justin Veezee's apartment one day and get copies of them made, and put the originals back before she misses them. I am hiding in Mr. Justin Veezee's apartment the other morning waiting to stick him up.

"Well," the guy says, "Mr. Justin Veezee comes in alone, and I am just about to step out on him and tell him to get them up, when in comes Miss Cleghorn, although of course I do not know at the time who she is. I can hear everything they say, and I see at once from their conversation that Miss Cleghorn is there under false pretenses. She finally wishes to leave, and Mr. Justin Veezee attacks her. She fights valiantly, and in just a straightaway hand-to-hand struggle, I will relish a small bet on her against Mr. Justin Veezee, or any other guy. But Mr. Justin Veezee picks up a bronze statuette and is about to bean her with it, so," the middle-aged guy says, "I step into it.

"Well," he says, "I guess maybe I am a little rougher with Mr. Justin Veezee than I mean to be, because I find myself putting a nice flying-mare hold on him and hurling him across the room. I fear the fall injures him severely. Anyway, when I pick him up he seems to be dead. So I sit him up in a chair, and take a bath towel and wipe out any chance of finger-prints around and about, and then escort Miss Cleghorn to her home.

"I do not intend to kill Mr. Justin Veezee," the middle-aged-looking guy says. "I only intend to rob him, and I am very sorry he is no longer with us, especially as I cannot now return and carry out my original plan. But," he says, "I cannot bear to see you hand Miss Cleghorn over to the law, although I hope and trust she will never be so foolish as to go visiting the apartments of such characters as Mr. Justin Veezee again."

"Yes," Ambrose Hammer says to Miss Cleghorn, "why do you go there in the first place?"

Well, at this Miss Cleghorn begins crying harder than ever, and between sobs she states to Ambrose Hammer as follows:

"Oh, Ambrose," she says, "it is because I love you so. You do not come around to see me for several nights, and I accept Mr. Justin Veezee's invitation hoping you will hear of it, and become jealous."

So of course there is nothing for Ambrose Hammer to do but

take her in his arms and start whispering to her in such terms as guys are bound to whisper under these circumstances, and I motion the middle-aged-looking guy to go outside, as I consider this scene far too sacred for a stranger to witness.

Then about this time, Miss Cleghorn gets a call to go downstairs and do a little Arabian acrobatic dancing for the customers of the Club Soudan, and so she leaves us without ever once forgetting in all this excitement to keep a hold on her veils, although I am watching at all times to remind her in case her memory fails her in this respect.

And then I ask Ambrose Hammer something that is bothering me no little, and this is how he comes to suspect in the first place that Miss Cleghorn may know something about the scragging of Mr. Justin Veezee, even allowing that the etchings give him a clue that a doll is present when the scragging comes off. And I especially wish to know how he can ever figure Miss Cleghorn has even as much as an outside chance of scragging Mr. Justin Veezee in such a manner as to break his neck.

"Why," Ambrose Hammer says, "I will gladly tell you about this, but only in strict confidence. The last time I see Miss Cleghorn up to to-night is the night I invite her to my own apartment to look at etchings, and they are better etchings than Mr. Justin Veezee shows her, at that. And," Ambrose says, "maybe you remember I am around with my neck tied up for a week."

Well, the middle-aged-looking guy is waiting for us outside the Club Soudan when we come out, and Ambrose Hammer stakes him to half a C and tells him to go as far as he can on this, and I shake hands with him, and wish him luck, and as he is turning to go, I say to him like this:

"By the way, Mr. Riggsby," I say, "what is your regular occupation, anyway, if I am not too nosy?"

"Oh," he says, "until the Depression comes on, I am for years rated one of the most efficient persons in my line in this town. In fact, I have many references to prove it. Yes," he says, "I am considered an exceptionally high-class butler."

BROADWAY COMPLEX

It is along towards four o'clock one morning, and I am sitting in Mindy's restaurant on Broadway with Ambrose Hammer, the newspaper scribe, enjoying a sturgeon sandwich, which is wonderful brain food, and listening to Ambrose tell me what is wrong with the world, and I am somewhat discouraged by what he tells me, for Ambrose is such a guy as is always very pessimistic about everything.

He is especially very pessimistic about the show business, as Ambrose is what is called a dramatic critic, and he has to go around nearly every night and look at the new plays that people are always putting in the theaters, and I judge from what Ambrose says that this is a very great hardship, and that he seldom gets much pleasure out of life.

Furthermore, I judge from what Ambrose tells me that there is no little danger in being a dramatic critic, because it seems that only a short time before this he goes to a play that is called *Never-Never*, and Ambrose says it is a very bad play indeed, and he so states in his newspaper, and in fact Ambrose states in his newspaper that the play smells in nine different keys, and that so does the acting of the leading man, a guy by the name of Fergus Appleton.

Well, the next day Ambrose runs into this Fergus Appleton in front of the Hotel Astor, and what does Fergus Appleton do but haul off and belt Ambrose over the noggin with a cane, and ruin a nice new fall derby for Ambrose, and when Ambrose puts in an expense account to his newspaper for this kady they refuse to pay it, so Ambrose is out four bobs.

And anyway, Ambrose says, the theater-going public never appreciates what a dramatic critic does for it, because it seems that even though he tips the public off that *Never-Never* is strictly a turkey, it is a great success, and, moreover Fergus Appleton is now going around with a doll who is nobody but Miss Florentine Fayette, the daughter of old Hannibal Fayette.

And anybody will tell you that old Hannibal Fayette is very, very, very rich, and has a piece of many different propositions, including the newspaper that Ambrose Hammer works for, although of course at the time Ambrose speaks of Fergus Appleton's acting, he has no idea Fergus is going to wind up going around with Miss Florentine Fayette.

So Ambrose says the chances are his newspaper will give him the heave-o as soon as Fergus Appleton gets the opportunity to drop the zing in on him, but Ambrose says he does not care a cuss as he is writing a play himself that will show the theater-going public what a real play is.

Well, Ambrose is writing this play ever since I know him, which is a matter of several years, and he tells me about it so often that I can play any part in it myself with a little practice, and he is just getting around to going over his first act with me again when in comes a guy by the name of Cecil Earl, who is what is called a master of ceremonies at the Golden Slipper night club.

Personally, I never see Cecil Earl but once or twice before in my life, and he always strikes me as a very quiet and modest young guy, for a master of ceremonies, and I am greatly surprised at the way he comes in, as he is acting very bold and aggressive towards one and all, and is speaking out loud in a harsh, disagreeable tone of voice, and in general is acting like a guy who is looking for trouble, which is certainly no way for a master of ceremonies to act.

But of course if a guy is looking for trouble on Broadway along towards four o'clock in the morning, anybody will tell you that the right address is nowhere else but Mindy's, because at such an hour many citizens are gathered there, and are commencing to get a little cross wondering where they are going to make a scratch for the morrow's operations, such as playing the horses.

It is a sure thing that any citizen who makes his scratch before four o'clock in the morning is at home getting his rest, so he will arise fully refreshed for whatever the day may bring forth, and also to avoid the bite he is apt to encounter in Mindy's from citizens who do not make a scratch.

However, the citizens who are present the morning I am speaking of do not pay much attention to Cecil Earl when he comes in, as he is nothing but a tall, skinny young guy, with slick black hair, such as you are apt to see anywhere along Broadway at any time, especially standing in front of theatrical booking offices. In fact, to look at Cecil you will bet he is maybe a saxophone player, as there is something about him that makes you think of a saxophone player right away and, to tell the truth, Cecil can tootle a pretty fair sax, at that, if the play happens to come up.

Well, Cecil sits down at a table where several influential citizens are sitting, including Nathan Detroit, who runs the crap game and Big Nig, the crap shooter, and Regret, the horse player, and Upstate Red, who is one of the best faro bank players in the world whenever he can find a faro bank and something to play it with, and these citizens are discussing some very serious matters, when out of a clear sky Cecil ups and speaks to them as follows:

"Listen," Cecil says, "if youse guys do not stop making so much noise, I may cool you all off."

Well, naturally, this is most repulsive language to use to such influential citizens, and furthermore it is very illiterate to say youse, so without changing the subject Nathan Detroit reaches out and picks up an order for ham and eggs, Southern style, that Charley, the waiter, just puts in front of Upstate Red, and taps Cecil on the onion with same.

It is unfortunate for Cecil that Nathan Detroit does not remove the ham and eggs, Southern style, from the platter before tapping Cecil with the order, because it is a very hard platter, and Cecil is knocked as stiff as a plank, and maybe stiffer, and it becomes necessary to summon old Doctor Moggs to bring him back to life.

Well, of course none of us know that Cecil is at the moment Jack Legs Diamond, or Mad Dog Coll, or some other very tough gorill, and in fact this does not come out until Ambrose Hammer later starts investigating the strange actions of Cecil Earl, and then Nathan Detroit apologizes to Cecil, and also to the chef in Mindy's for treating an order of ham and eggs, Southern style, so disrespectfully.

It comes out that Cecil is subject to spells of being somebody else besides Cecil Earl, and Ambrose Hammer gives us a very long explanation of this situation, only Ambrose finally becomes so scientific that nobody can keep cases on him. But we gather in a general way from what Ambrose says that Cecil Earl is very susceptible to suggestion from anything he reads, or is told.

In fact, Ambrose says he is the most susceptible guy of this kind

he ever meets up with in his life, and it seems that when he is going to Harvard College, which is before he starts in being a dramatic critic, Ambrose makes quite a study of these matters.

Personally, I always claim that Cecil Earl is a little screwy, or if
he is not screwy that he will do very well as a pinch-hitter until a
screwy guy comes to bat, but Ambrose Hammer says no. Ambrose
says it is true that Cecil may be bobbing a trifle, but that he is by
no means entirely off his nut. Ambrose says that Cecil only has
delusions of grandeur, and complexes, and I do not know what all
else, but Ambrose says it is nine to ten and take your pick whether
Cecil is a genius or a daffydill.

Ambrose says that Cecil is like an actor playing a different part
every now and then, only Cecil tries to live every part he plays, and
Ambrose claims that if we have actors with as much sense as Cecil
in playing parts, the show business will be a lot better off. But of
course Ambrose cares very little for actors since Fergus Appleton
ruins his kady.

Well, the next time I see Cecil he comes in Mindy's again, and
this time it seems he is Jack Dempsey, and while ordinarily nobody will mind him being Jack Dempsey, or even Gene Tunney, although he is not the type for Gene Tunney, Cecil takes to throwing
left hooks at citizens' chins, so finally Sam the Singer gets up and
lets a right hand go inside a left hook, and once more Cecil folds
up like an old accordion.

When I speak of this to Ambrose Hammer, he says that being
Jack Dempsey is entirely a false complex for Cecil, brought on
mainly by Cecil taking a few belts at the Golden Slipper liquor during the evening. In fact, Ambrose says this particular complex does
not count. But I notice that after this Cecil is never anybody very
brash when he is around Mindy's.

Sometimes he is somebody else besides Cecil Earl for as long
as a week at a stretch, and in fact once he is Napoleon for two
whole weeks, but Ambrose Hammer says this is nothing. Ambrose says he personally knows guys who are Napoleon all their
lives. But of course Ambrose means that these guys are only
Napoleons in their own minds. He says that the only difference
between Cecil and them is that Cecil's complex breaks out on him
in public, while the other guys are Napoleons only in their own
bedrooms.

Personally, I think such guys are entitled to be locked up in spots with high walls around and about, but Ambrose seems to make nothing much of it, and anyway this Cecil Earl is as harmless as a bag of marshmallows, no matter who he is being.

One thing I must say for Cecil Earl, he is nearly always an interesting guy to talk to, because he nearly always has a different personality, and in fact the only time he is uninteresting is when he is being nobody but Cecil Earl. Then he is a very quiet guy with a sad face and he is so bashful and retiring that you will scarcely believe he is the same guy who goes around all one week being Mussolini in his own mind.

Now I wish to say that Cecil Earl does not often go around making any public display of these spells of his, except when the character calls for a display, such as the time he is George Bernard Shaw, and in fact unless you know him personally you may sometimes figure him just a guy sitting back in a corner somewhere with nothing whatever on his mind, and you will never even suspect that you are in the presence of J. Pierpont Morgan studying out a way to make us all rich.

It gets so that nobody resents Cecil being anything he pleases, except once when he is Senator Huey Long, and once when he is Hitler, and makes the mistake of wandering down on the Lower East Side and saying so. In fact, it gets so everybody along Broadway puts in with him and helps him be whoever he is, as much as possible, although I always claim he has a bad influence on some citizens, for instance Regret, the horse player.

It seems that Regret catches a complex off of Cecil Earl one day, and for twenty-four hours he is Pittsburgh Phil, the race-track plunger, and goes overboard with every bookie down at Belmont Park and has to hide out for some time before he can get himself straightened out.

Now Cecil Earl is a good master of ceremonies in a night club, if you care for masters of ceremonies, a master of ceremonies in a night club being a guy who is supposed to make cute cracks, and to introduce any celebrities who happen to be sitting around the joint, such as actors and prominent merchants, so the other customers can give them a big hand, and this is by no means an easy job, as sometimes a master of ceremonies may overlook a celebrity, and the celebrity becomes terribly insulted.

But it seems that Cecil Earl is smart enough to introduce all the people in the Golden Slipper every night and call for a big hand for them, no matter who they are, so nobody can get insulted, although one night he introduces a new head waiter, thinking he is nothing but a customer, and the head waiter is somewhat insulted, at that, and threatens to quit, because he claims being introduced in a night club is no boost for him.

Anyway, Cecil gets a nice piece of money for being master of ceremonies at the Golden Slipper, and when he is working there his complexes do not seem to bother him very much, and he is never anybody more serious than Harry Richman or Mort Downey. And it is at the Golden Slipper that he meets this guy, Fergus Appleton, and Miss Florentine Fayette.

Now Miss Florentine Fayette is a tall, slim, black-haired doll, and so beautiful she is practically untrue, but she has a kisser that never seems to relax, and furthermore she never seems much interested in anything whatever. In fact, if Miss Florentine Fayette's papa does not have so many cucumbers, I will say she is slightly dumb, but for all I know it may be against the law to say a doll whose papa has all these cucumbers is dumb. So I will only say that she does not strike me as right bright.

She is a great hand for going around night clubs and sitting there practically unconscious for hours at a time, and always this Fergus Appleton is with her, and before long it gets around that Fergus Appleton wishes to make Miss Florentine Fayette his everloving wife, and everybody admits that it will be a very nice score indeed for an actor.

Personally, I see nothing wrong with this situation because, to tell you the truth, I will just naturally love to make Miss Florentine Fayette my own ever-loving wife if her papa's cucumbers go with it, but of course Ambrose Hammer does not approve of the idea of her becoming Fergus Appleton's wife, because Ambrose can see how it may work out to his disadvantage.

This Fergus Appleton is a fine-looking guy of maybe forty, with iron-gray hair that makes him appear very romantic, and he is always well dressed in spats and one thing and another, and he smokes cigarettes in a holder nearly a foot long, and wears a watch on one wrist and a slave bracelet on the other, and a big ring on each hand, and sometimes a monocle in one eye, although Ambrose Hammer claims that this is strictly the old ackamarackuss.

There is no doubt Fergus Appleton is a very chesty guy, and likes to pose around in public places, but I see maybe a million

guys like him in my time on Broadway, and not all of them are actors, so I do not hate him for his posing, or for his slave bracelet
or the monocle either, although naturally I consider him out of
line in busting my friend Ambrose Hammer's new derby, and I
promise Ambrose that the first time Fergus Appleton shows up in
a new derby, or even an old one, I will see that somebody busts it,
if I have to do it myself.

The only thing wrong I see about Fergus Appleton is that he is
a smart-alecky guy, and when he first finds out about Cecil Earl's
complexes he starts working on them to amuse the guys and dolls
who hang out around the Golden Slipper with him and Miss Florentine Fayette.

Moreover, it seems that somehow Cecil Earl is very susceptible
indeed, to Fergus Appleton's suggestions, and for a while Fergus
Appleton makes quite a sucker of Cecil Earl.

Then all of a sudden Fergus Appleton stops making a sucker of
Cecil, and the next thing anybody knows Fergus Appleton is becoming quite pally with Cecil, and I see them around Mindy's and
other late spots after the Golden Slipper closes, and sometimes
Miss Florentine Fayette is with them, although Cecil Earl is such
a guy as does not care much for the society of dolls, and in fact is
very much embarrassed when they are around, which is most surprising conduct for a master of ceremonies in a night club, as such
characters are usually pretty fresh with dolls.

But of course even the freshest master of ceremonies is apt to be
a little bashful when such a doll as Miss Florentine Fayette is around,
on account of her papa having so many cucumbers, and when she
is present Cecil Earl seldom opens his trap, but just sits looking at
her and letting Fergus Appleton do all the gabbing, which suits
Fergus Appleton fine, as he does not mind hearing himself gab,
and in fact loves it.

Sometimes I run into just Cecil Earl and Fergus Appleton, and
generally they have their heads close together, and are talking low
and serious, like two business guys with a large deal coming up
between them.

Furthermore I can see that Cecil Earl is looking very mysterious
and solemn himself, so I figure that maybe they are doping out a
new play together and that Cecil is acting one of the parts, and
whatever it is they are doing I consider it quite big-hearted of Fergus Appleton to take such a friendly interest in Cecil.

But somehow Ambrose Hammer does not like it. In fact, Ambrose Hammer speaks of the matter at some length to me, and says to me like this:

"It is unnatural," he says. "It is unnatural for a guy like Fergus Appleton, who is such a guy as never has a thought in the world for anybody but himself, to be playing the warm for a guy like Cecil Earl. There is something wrong in this business and," Ambrose says, "I am going to find out what it is."

Well, personally I do not see where it is any of Ambrose Hammer's put-in even if there is something wrong, but Ambrose is always poking his beezer into other people's business, and he starts watching Cecil and Fergus Appleton with great interest whenever he happens to run into them.

Finally it comes an early Sunday morning, and Ambrose Hammer and I are in Mindy's as usual, when in comes Cecil Earl all alone, with a book under one arm. He sits down at a table in a corner booth all by himself and orders a western sandwich and starts in to read his book, and nothing will do Ambrose Hammer but for us to go over and talk to Cecil.

When he sees us coming, he closes his book, and drops it in his lap and gives us a very weak hello. It is the first time we see him alone in quite a spell, and finally, Ambrose Hammer asks where is Fergus Appleton, although Ambrose really does not care where he is, unless it happens to turn out that he is in a pesthouse suffering from smallpox.

Cecil says Fergus Appleton has to go over to Philadelphia on business over the weekend, and then Ambrose asks Cecil where Miss Florentine Fayette is, and Cecil says he does not know but supposes she is home.

"Well," Ambrose Hammer says, "Miss Florentine Fayette is certainly a beautiful doll, even if she does look a little bit colder than I like them, but," he says, "what she sees in such a pish-tush as Fergus Appleton I do not know."

Now at this Cecil Earl busts right out crying, and naturally Ambrose Hammer and I are greatly astonished at such an exhibition, because we do not see any occasion for tears, and personally I am figuring on taking it on the Dan O'Leary away from there before somebody gets to thinking we do Cecil some great wrong, when Cecil speaks as follows:

"I love her," Cecil says. "I love her with all my heart and soul.

But she belongs to my best friend. For two cents I will take this dagger that Fergus gives me and end it all, because life is not worth living without Miss Florentine Fayette."

And with this Cecil Earl outs with a big long stabber, which is a spectacle that is most disquieting to me as I know such articles are against the law in this man's town. So I make Cecil put it right back in his pocket and while I am doing this Ambrose Hammer reaches down beside Cecil and grabs the book Cecil is reading, and while Cecil is still sobbing Ambrose looks this volume over.

It turns out to be a book called *The Hundred-Per-Cent-Perfect Crime*, but what interests Ambrose Hammer more than anything else is a lead-pencil drawing on one of the blank pages in the front part of the book. Afterwards Ambrose sketches this drawing out for me as near as he can remember it on the back of one of Mindy's menu cards, and it looks to me like the drawing of the ground floor of a small house, with a line on one side on which is written the word Menahan, and Ambrose says he figures this means a street.

But in the meantime Ambrose tries to soothe Cecil Earl and to get him to stop crying, and when Cecil finally does dry up he sees Ambrose has his book, and he makes a grab for it and creates quite a scene until he gets it back.

Personally, I cannot make head or tail of the sketch that Ambrose draws for me, and I cannot see that there is anything to it anyway, but Ambrose seems to regard it as of some importance.

Well, I do not see Ambrose Hammer for several days, but I am hearing strange stories of him being seen with Cecil Earl in the afternoons when Fergus Appleton is playing matinees in *Never-Never*, and early in the evenings when Fergus Appleton is doing his night performances, and I also hear that Ambrose always seems to be talking very earnestly to Cecil Earl, and sometimes throwing his arms about in a most excited manner.

Then one morning Ambrose Hammer looks me up again in Mindy's, and he is smiling a very large smile, as if he is greatly pleased with something, which is quite surprising as Ambrose Hammer is seldom pleased with anything. Finally he says to me like this:

"Well," Ambrose says, "I learn the meaning of the drawing in Cecil Earl's book. It is the plan of a house on Menahan Street, away over in Brooklyn. And the way I learn this is very, very clever, indeed," Ambrose says. "I stake a chambermaid to let me into Fergus Appleton's joint in the Dazzy apartments, and what do I find there just as I expect but a letter from a certain number on this street?"

"Why," I say to Ambrose Hammer, "I am greatly horrified by your statement. You are nothing but a burglar, and if Fergus Appleton finds this out he will turn you over to the officers of the law, and you will lose your job and everything else."

"No," Ambrose says, "I will not lose my job, because old Hannibal Fayette is around the office yesterday raising an awful row about his daughter wishing to marry an actor, and saying he will give he does not know what if anybody can bust this romance up. The chances are," Ambrose says, "he will make me editor in chief of the paper, and then I will can a lot of guys I do not like. Fergus Appleton is to meet Cecil Earl here this morning, and in the meantime I will relate the story to you."

But before Ambrose can tell me the story, in comes Fergus Appleton, and Miss Florentine Fayette is with him, and they sit down at a table not far from us, and Fergus Appleton looks around and sees Ambrose and gives him a terrible scowl. Furthermore, he says something to Miss Florentine Fayette, and she looks at Ambrose, too, but she does not scowl or anything else, but only looks very dead-pan.

Fergus Appleton is in evening clothes and has on his monocle, and Miss Florentine Fayette is wearing such a gown that anybody can see how beautiful she is, no matter if her face does not have much expression. They are sitting there without much conversation passing between them, when all of a sudden in walks Cecil Earl, full of speed and much excited.

He comes in with such a rush that he almost flattens Regret, the horse player, who is on his way out, and Regret is about to call him a dirty name when he sees a spectacle that will always be remembered in Mindy's, for Cecil Earl walks right over to Miss Florentine Fayette as she is sitting there beside Fergus Appleton, and without saying as much as boo to Fergus Appleton, Cecil grabs Miss Florentine Fayette up in his arms with surprising strength and gives her a big sizzling kiss, and says to her like this:

"Florentine," he says, "I love you."

Then he squeezes her to his bosom so tight that it looks as if he is about to squeeze her right out through the top of her gown like squeezing toothpaste out of a tube, and says to her again, as follows:

"I love you. Oh, how I love you."

Well, at first Fergus Appleton is so astonished at this proposition that he can scarcely stir, and the chances are he cannot believe his eyes. Furthermore, many other citizens who are present partaking of their Bismarck herring, and one thing and another, are also astonished, and they are commencing to think that maybe Cecil Earl is having a complex about being King Kong, when Fergus Appleton finally gets to his feet and speaks in a loud tone of voice as follows:

"Why," Fergus Appleton says, "you are nothing but a scurvy fellow, and unless you unhand my fiancée, the chances are I will annihilate you."

Naturally, Fergus Appleton is somewhat excited, and in fact he is so excited that he drops his monocle to the floor, and it breaks into several pieces. At first he seems to have some idea of dropping a big right hand on Cecil Earl somewhere, but Cecil is pretty well covered by Miss Florentine Fayette, so Fergus Appleton can see that if he lets a right hand go he is bound to strike Miss Florentine Fayette right where she lives.

So he only grabs hold of Miss Florentine Fayette, and tries to pull her loose from Cecil Earl, and Cecil Earl not only holds her tighter, but Miss Florentine Fayette seems to be doing some holding to Cecil herself, so Fergus Appleton cannot peel her off, although he gets one stocking and a piece of elastic strap from somewhere. Then one and all are greatly surprised to hear Miss Florentine Fayette speak to Fergus Appleton like this:

"Go away, you old porous plaster," Miss Florentine Fayette says. "I love only my Cecil. Hold me tighter, Cecil, you great big bear," Miss Florentine Fayette says, although of course Cecil looks about as much like a bear as Ambrose Hammer looks like a porcupine.

Well, of course there is great commotion in Mindy's, because Cecil Earl is putting on a love scene such as makes many citizens very homesick, and Fergus Appleton does not seem to know what to do, when Ambrose Hammer gets to him and whispers a few words in his ear, and all of a sudden Fergus Appleton turns and walks out of Mindy's and disappears, and furthermore nobody ever sees him in these parts again.

By and by Mindy himself comes up and tells Cecil Earl and Miss Florentine Fayette that the chef is complaining because he cannot seem to make ice in his refrigerator while they are in the joint, and will they please go away. So Cecil Earl and Miss Florentine Fayette go, and then Ambrose Hammer comes back to me and finishes his story.

"Well," Ambrose says, "I go over to the certain number on Menahan Street, and what do I find there but a crippled-up, middle-aged doll who is nobody but Fergus Appleton's ever-loving wife, and furthermore she is such for over twenty years. She tells me that Fergus is the meanest guy that ever breathes the breath of life, and that he is persecuting her for a long time in every way he can think of because she will not give him a divorce.

"And," Ambrose says, "the reason she will not give him a divorce is because he knocks her downstairs a long time ago, and makes her a cripple for life, and leaves her to the care of her own people. But of course I do not tell her," Ambrose says, "that she narrowly escapes being murdered through him, for the meaning of the floor plan of the house in Cecil's book, and the meaning of the book itself, and of the dagger, is that Fergus Appleton is working on Cecil Earl until he has him believing that he can be the super-murderer of the age."

"Why," I say to Ambrose Hammer, "I am greatly shocked by these revelations. Why, Fergus Appleton is nothing but a fellow."

"Well," Ambrose says, "he is pretty cute, at that. He has Cecil thinking that it will be a wonderful thing to be the guy who commits the hundred-per-cent-perfect crime, and furthermore Fergus promises to make Cecil rich after he marries Miss Florentine Fayette."

"But," I say, "what I do not understand is what makes Cecil become such a violent lover all of a sudden."

"Why," Ambrose Hammer says, "when Cecil lets it out that he loves Miss Florentine Fayette, it gives me a nice clue to the whole situation. I take Cecil in hand and give him a little coaching and, furthermore, I make him a present of a book myself. He finds it more interesting than anything Fergus Appleton gives him. In fact," Ambrose says, "I recommend it to you. When Cecil comes in here this morning, he is not Cecil Earl, the potential Perfect Murderer. He is nobody but the world's champion heavy lover, old Don Juan."

Well, Ambrose does not get to be editor in chief of his newspaper. In fact, he just misses getting the outdoors, because Cecil Earl and Miss Florentine Fayette elope, and get married, and go out to Hollywood on a honeymoon, and never return, and old Hannibal Fayette claims it is just as bad for his daughter to marry a movie actor as a guy on the stage, even though Cecil turns out to be the greatest drawing card on the screen because he can heat up love scenes so good.

But I always say that Cecil Earl is quite an ingrate, because he refuses a part in Ambrose Hammer's play when Ambrose finally gets it written, and makes his biggest hit in a screen version of *Never-Never*.

THE THREE WISE GUYS

One cold winter afternoon I am standing at the bar in Good Time Charley's little drum on West Forty-ninth Street, partaking of a mixture of rock candy and rye whisky, and this is a most surprising thing for me to be doing, as I am by no means a rumpot, and very seldom indulge in alcoholic beverages in any way, shape, manner, or form.

But when I step into Good Time Charley's on the afternoon in question, I am feeling as if maybe I have a touch of grippe coming on, and Good Time Charley tells me that there is nothing in this world as good for a touch of grippe as rock candy and rye whisky, as it assassinates the germs at once.

It seems that Good Time Charley always keeps a stock of rock candy and rye whisky on hand for touches of the grippe, and he gives me a few doses immediately, and in fact Charley takes a few doses with me, as he says there is no telling but what I am scattering germs of my touch of the grippe all around the joint, and he must safeguard his health. We are both commencing to feel much better when the door opens, and who comes in but a guy by the name of Blondy Swanson.

This Blondy Swanson is a big, six-foot-two guy, with straw-colored hair, and pink cheeks, and he is originally out of Harlem, and it is well known to one and all that in his day he is the largest puller on the Atlantic seaboard. In fact, for upwards of ten years, Blondy is bringing wet goods into New York from Canada, and one place and another, and in all this time he never gets a fall, which is considered a phenomenal record for an operator as extensive as Blondy.

Well, Blondy steps up alongside me at the bar, and I ask him if he cares to have a few doses of rock candy and rye whisky with me and Good Time Charley, and Blondy says he will consider it a privilege and a pleasure, because, he says, he always has something of a sweet tooth. So we have these few doses, and I say to Blondy Swanson that I hope and trust that business is thriving with him.

"I have no business," Blondy Swanson says, "I retire from business."

Well, if J. Pierpont Morgan, or John D. Rockefeller, or Henry Ford step up and tell me they retire from business, I will not be more astonished than I am by this statement from Blondy Swanson, and in fact not as much. I consider Blondy's statement the most important commercial announcement I hear in many years, and naturally I ask him why he makes such a decision, and what is to become of thousands of citizens who are dependent on him for merchandise.

"Well," Blondy says, "I retire from business because I am one hundred per cent American citizen. In fact," he says, "I am a patriot. I serve my country in the late war. I am cited at Château-Thierry. I always vote the straight Democratic ticket, except," he says, "when we figure it better to elect some Republican. I always stand up when the band plays 'The Star Spangled Banner.' One year I even pay an income tax," Blondy says.

And of course I know that many of these things are true, although I remember hearing rumors that if the draft officer is along half an hour later than he is, he will not see Blondy for heel dust, and that what Blondy is cited for at Château-Thierry is for not robbing the dead.

But of course I do not speak of these matters to Blondy Swanson, because Blondy is not such a guy as will care to listen to rumors, and may become indignant, and when Blondy is indignant he is very difficult to get along with.

"Now," Blondy says, "I am a bootie for a long time, and supply very fine merchandise to my trade, as everybody knows, and it is a respectable business, because one and all in this country are in favor of it, except the prohibitionists. But," he says, "I can see into the future, and I can see that one of these days they are going to repeal the prohibition law, and then it will be most unpatriotic to be bringing in wet goods from foreign parts in competition with home industry. So I retire," Blondy says.

"Well, Blondy," I say, "your sentiments certainly do you credit, and if we have more citizens as high-minded as you are, this will be a better country."

"Furthermore," Blondy says, "there is no money in booting any more. All the booties in this country are broke. I am broke myself," he says. "I just lose the last piece of property I own in the world, which is the twenty-five-G home I build in Atlantic City, figuring to spend the rest of my days there with Miss Clarabelle Cobb, before she takes a runout powder on me. Well," Blondy says, "if I only listen to Miss Clarabelle Cobb, I will now be an honest clerk in a gents' furnishing store, with maybe a cute little apartment up around One Hundred and Tenth Street, and children running all around and about."

And with this, Blondy sighs heavily, and I sigh with him, because the romance of Blondy Swanson and Miss Clarabelle Cobb is well known to one and all on Broadway.

It goes back a matter of anyway six years when Blondy Swanson is making money so fast he can scarcely stop to count it, and at this time Miss Clarabelle Cobb is the most beautiful doll in this town, and many citizens almost lose their minds just gazing at her when she is a member of Mr. Georgie White's *Scandals*, including Blondy Swanson.

In fact, after Blondy Swanson sees Miss Clarabelle Cobb in just one performance of Mr. Georgie White's *Scandals*, he is never quite the same guy again. He goes to a lot of bother meeting up with Miss Clarabelle Cobb, and then he takes to hanging out around Mr. Georgie White's stage door, and sending Miss Clarabelle Cobb ten-pound boxes of candy, and floral horseshoes, and wreaths, and also packages of trinkets, including such articles as diamond bracelets, and brooches, and vanity cases, for there is no denying that Blondy is a fast guy with a dollar.

But it seems that Miss Clarabelle Cobb will not accept any of these offerings, except the candy and the flowers, and she goes so far as to return a sable coat that Blondy sends her one very cold day, and she is openly criticized for this action by some of the other dolls in Mr. Georgie White's *Scandals*, for they say that after all there is a limit even to eccentricity.

But Miss Clarabelle Cobb states that she is not accepting valuable offerings from any guy, and especially a guy who is engaged in trafficking in the demon rum, because she says that his money is nothing but blood money that comes from breaking the law of the land, although, as a matter of fact, this is a dead wrong rap against Blondy Swanson, as he never handles a drop of rum in his life, but only Scotch, and furthermore he keeps himself pretty well straightened out with the law.

The idea is, Miss Clarabelle Cobb comes of very religious people back in Akron, Ohio, and she is taught from childhood that rum is a terrible thing, and personally I think it is myself, except in cocktails, and furthermore, the last thing her mamma tells her when she leaves for New York is to beware of any guys who come around offering her diamond bracelets and fur coats, because her mamma says such guys are undoubtedly snakes in the grass, and probably on the make.

But while she will not accept his offerings, Miss Clarabelle Cobb does not object to going out with Blondy Swanson now and then, and putting on the chicken Mexicaine, and the lobster Newburg, and other items of this nature, and anytime you put a good-looking young guy and a beautiful doll together over the chicken Mexicaine and the lobster Newburg often enough, you are apt to have a case of love on your hands.

And this is what happens to Blondy Swanson and Miss Clarabelle Cobb, and in fact they become in love more than somewhat, and Blondy Swanson is wishing to marry Miss Clarabelle Cobb, but one night over a batch of lobster Newburg, she says to him like this:

"Blondy," she says, "I love you, and," she says, "I will marry you in a minute if you get out of trafficking in rum. I will marry you if you are out of the rum business, and do not have a dime, but I will never marry you as long as you are dealing in rum, no matter if you have a hundred million."

Well, Blondy says he will get out of the racket at once, and he keeps saying this every now and then for a year or so, and the chances are that several times he means it, but when a guy is in this business in those days as strong as Blondy Swanson it is not so easy for him to get out, even if he wishes to do so. And then one day Miss Clarabelle Cobb has a talk with Blondy, and says to him as follows:

"Blondy," she says, "I still love you, but you care more for your business than you do for me. So I am going back to Ohio," she says. "I am sick and tired of Broadway, anyhow. Someday when you are really through with the terrible traffic you are now engaged in, come to me."

And with this, Miss Clarabelle Cobb takes plenty of outdoors on Blondy Swanson, and is seen no more in these parts. At first Blondy thinks she is only trying to put a little pressure on him, and will be back, but as the weeks become months, and the months finally count up into years, Blondy can see that she is by no means clowning with him. Furthermore, he never hears from her, and all he knows is she is back in Akron, Ohio.

Well, Blondy is always promising himself that he will soon pack in on hauling wet goods, and go look up Miss Clarabelle Cobb and marry her, but he keeps putting it off, and putting it off, until finally one day he hears that Miss Clarabelle Cobb marries some legitimate guy in Akron, and this is a terrible blow to Blondy indeed, and from this day he never looks at another doll again, or anyway not much.

Naturally, I express my deep sympathy to Blondy about being broke, and I also mention that my heart bleeds for him in his loss of Miss Clarabelle Cobb, and we have a few doses of rock candy and rye whisky on both propositions, and by this time Good Time Charley runs out of rock candy, and anyway it is a lot of bother for him to be mixing it up with the rye whisky, so we have the rye whisky without the rock candy, and personally I do not notice much difference.

Well, while we are standing there at the bar having our rye whisky without the rock candy, who comes in but an old guy by the name of The Dutchman, who is known to one and all as a most illegal character in every respect. In fact, The Dutchman has no standing whatever in the community, and I am somewhat surprised to see him appear in Good Time Charley's, because The Dutchman is generally a lammie from some place, and the gendarmes everywhere are always anxious to have a chat with him. The last I hear of The Dutchman he is in college somewhere out West for highway robbery, although afterwards he tells me it is a case of mistaken identity. It seems he mistakes a copper in plain clothes for a groceryman.

The Dutchman is an old-fashioned-looking guy of maybe fifty-odd, and he has gray hair, and a stubby gray beard, and he is short, and thickset, and always good-natured, even when there is no call for it, and to look at him you will think there is no more harm in him than there is in a preacher, and maybe not as much.

As The Dutchman comes in, he takes a peek all around and about as if he is looking for somebody in particular, and when he sees Blondy Swanson he moves up alongside Blondy and begins whispering to Blondy until Blondy pulls away and tells him to speak freely.

Now The Dutchman has a very interesting story, and it goes like this: It seems that about eight or nine months back The Dutchman is mobbed up with a party of three very classy heavy guys who make quite a good thing of going around knocking off safes in small-town jugs, and post offices, and stores in small towns, and taking the money, or whatever else is valuable in these safes. This is once quite a popular custom in this country, although it dies out to some extent of late years because they improve the brand of safes so much it is a lot of bother knocking them off, but it comes back during the Depression when there is no other way of making money, until it is a very prosperous business again. And of course this is very nice for old-time heavy guys, such as The Dutchman, because it gives them something to do in their old age.

Anyway, it seems that this party The Dutchman is with goes over into Pennsylvania one night on a tip from a friend and knocks off a safe in a factory office, and gets a pay roll amounting to maybe fifty G's. But it seems that while they are making their getaway in an automobile, the gendarmes take out after them, and there is a chase, during which there is considerable blasting back and forth.

Well, finally in this blasting, the three guys with The Dutchman get cooled off, and The Dutchman also gets shot up quite some, and he abandons the automobile out on an open road, taking the money, which is in a gripsack, with him, and he somehow manages to escape the gendarmes by going across country, and hiding here and there.

But The Dutchman gets pretty well petered out, what with his wounds, and trying to lug the gripsack, and one night he comes to an old deserted barn, and he decides to stash the gripsack in this barn, because there is no chance he can keep lugging it around much longer. So he takes up a few boards in the floor of the barn, and digs a nice hole in the ground underneath and plants the gripsack there, figuring to come back someday and pick it up.

Well, The Dutchman gets over into New Jersey one way and another, and lays up in a town by the name of New Brunswick until his wounds are healed, which requires considerable time as The Dutchman cannot take it nowadays as good as he can when he is younger.

Furthermore, even after The Dutchman recovers and gets to thinking of going after the stashed gripsack, he finds he is about half out of confidence, which is what happens to all guys when they commence getting old, and he figures that it may be a good idea to declare somebody else in to help him, and the first guy he thinks of is Blondy Swanson, because he knows Blondy Swanson is a very able citizen in every respect.

"Now, Blondy," The Dutchman says, "if you like my proposition, I am willing to cut you in for fifty per cent, and fifty per cent of fifty G's, is by no means pretzels in these times."

"Well, Dutchman," Blondy says, "I will gladly assist you in this enterprise on the terms you state. It appeals to me as a legitimate proposition, because there is no doubt this dough is coming to you, and from now on I am strictly legit. But in the meantime, let us have some more rock candy and rye whisky, without the rock candy, while we discuss the matter further."

But it seems that The Dutchman does not care for rock candy and rye whisky, even without the rock candy, so Blondy Swanson and me and Good Time Charley continue taking our doses, and Blondy keeps getting more enthusiastic about The Dutchman's proposition until finally I become enthusiastic myself, and I say I think I will go along as it is an opportunity to see new sections of the country, while Good Time Charley states that it will always be the great regret of his life that his business keeps him from going, but that he will provide us with an ample store of rock candy and rye whisky, without the rock candy, in case we run into any touches of the grippe.

Well, anyway, this is how I come to be riding around in an old can belonging to The Dutchman on a very cold Christmas Eve with The Dutchman and Blondy Swanson, although none of us happen to think of it being Christmas Eve until we notice that there seems to be holly wreaths in windows here and there as we go bouncing along the roads, and finally we pass a little church that is all lit up, and somebody opens the door as we are passing, and we see a big Christmas tree inside the church, and it is a very pleasant sight indeed, and in fact it makes me a little homesick, although of course the chances are I will not be seeing any Christmas trees even if I am home.

We leave Good Time Charley's along mid-afternoon, with The Dutchman driving this old can of his, and all I seem to remember about the trip is going through a lot of little towns so fast they seem strung together, because most of the time I am dozing in the back seat.

Blondy Swanson is riding in the front seat with The Dutchman and Blondy also cops a little snooze now and then as we are going along, but whenever he happens to wake up he pokes me awake, too, so we can take a dose of rock candy and rye whisky, without the rock candy. So in many respects it is quite an enjoyable journey.

I recollect the little church because we pass it right after we go busting through a pretty fair-sized town, and I hear The Dutchman say the old barn is now only a short distance away, and by this time it is dark, and colder than a deputy sheriff's heart, and there is snow on the ground, although it is clear overhead, and I am wishing I am back in Mindy's restaurant wrapping myself around a nice T-bone steak, when I hear Blondy Swanson ask The Dutchman if he is sure he knows where he is going, as this seems to be an untraveled road, and The Dutchman states as follows:

"Why," he says, "I know I am on the right road. I am following the big star you see up ahead of us, because I remember seeing this star always in front of me when I am going along the road before."

So we keep following the star, but it turns out that it is not a star at all, but a light shining from the window of a ramshackle old frame building pretty well off to one side of the road and on a rise of ground, and when The Dutchman sees this light, he is greatly nonplussed indeed and speaks as follows:

"Well," he says, "this looks very much like my barn, but my barn does not call for a light in it. Let us investigate this matter before we go any farther."

So The Dutchman gets out of the old can, and slips up to one side of the building and peeks through the window, and then he comes back and motions for Blondy and me to also take a peek through this window, which is nothing but a square hole cut in the side of the building with wooden bars across it, but no window-panes, and what we behold inside by the dim light of a lantern hung on a nail on a post is really most surprising.

There is no doubt whatever that we are looking at the inside of a very old barn, for there are several stalls for horses, or maybe cows, here and there, but somebody seems to be living in the barn, as we can see a table, and a couple of chairs, and a tin stove, in which there is a little fire, and on the floor in one corner is what seems to be a sort of a bed.

Furthermore, there seems to be somebody lying on the bed and making quite a fuss in the way of groaning and crying and carrying on generally in a loud tone of voice, and there is no doubt that it is the voice of a doll, and anybody can tell that this doll is in some distress.

Well, here is a situation indeed and we move away from the barn to talk it over.

The Dutchman is greatly discouraged, because he gets to thinking that if this doll is living in the barn for any length of time, his plant may be discovered. He is willing to go away and wait a while, but Blondy Swanson seems to be doing quite some thinking, and finally Blondy says like this:

"Why," Blondy says, "the doll in this barn seems to be sick, and only a bounder and a cad will walk away from a sick doll, especially," Blondy says, "a sick doll who is a total stranger to him. In fact, it will take a very large heel to do such a thing. The idea is for us to go inside and see if we can do anything for this sick doll," Blondy says.

Well, I say to Blondy Swanson that the chances are the doll's ever-loving husband, or somebody, is in town, or maybe over to the nearest neighbors digging up assistance, and will be back in a jiffy, and that this is no place for us to be found.

"No," Blondy says, "it cannot be as you state. The snow on the ground is anyway a day old. There are no tracks around the door of this old joint, going or coming, and it is a cinch if anybody knows there is a sick doll here, they will have plenty of time to get help before this. I am going inside and look things over," Blondy says.

Naturally, The Dutchman and I go too, because we do not wish to be left alone outside, and it is no trouble whatever to get into the barn, as the door is unlocked, and all we have to do is walk in. And when we walk in with Blondy Swanson leading the way, the doll on the bed on the floor half-raises up to look at us, and although the light of the lantern is none too good, anybody can see that this doll is nobody but Miss Clarabelle Cobb, although personally I see some changes in her since she is in Mr. Georgie White's *Scandals*.

She stays half-raised up on the bed looking at Blondy Swanson for as long as you can count ten, if you count fast, then she falls back and starts crying and carrying on again, and at this The Dutchman kneels down on the floor beside her to find out what is eating her.

All of a sudden The Dutchman jumps up and speaks to us as follows:

"Why," he says, "this is quite a delicate situation, to be sure. In fact," he says, "I must request you guys to step outside. What we really need for this case is a doctor, but it is too late to send for one. However, I will endeavor to do the best I can under the circumstances."

Then The Dutchman starts taking off his overcoat, and Blondy Swanson stands looking at him with such a strange expression on his kisser that The Dutchman laughs out loud, and says like this:

"Do not worry about anything, Blondy," The Dutchman says. "I am maybe a little out of practice since my old lady put her checks back in the rack, but she leaves eight kids alive and kicking, and I bring them all in except one, because we are seldom able to afford a croaker."

So Blondy Swanson and I step out of the barn and after a while The Dutchman calls us and we go back into the barn to find he has a big fire going in the stove, and the place nice and warm.

Miss Clarabelle Cobb is now all quieted down, and is covered with The Dutchman's overcoat, and as we come in The Dutchman tiptoes over to her and pulls back the coat and what do we see but a baby with a noggin no bigger than a crab apple and a face as wrinkled as some old pappy guy's, and The Dutchman states that it is a boy, and a very healthy one, at that.

"Furthermore," The Dutchman says, "the mamma is doing as well as can be expected. She is as strong a doll as ever I see," he says, "and all we have to do now is send out a croaker when we go through town just to make sure there are no complications. But," The Dutchman says, "I guarantee the croaker will not have much to do."

Well, the old Dutchman is as proud of this baby as if it is his own, and I do not wish to hurt his feelings, so I say the baby is a darberoo, and a great credit to him in every respect, and also to Miss Clarabelle Cobb, while Blondy Swanson just stands there looking at it as if he never sees a baby before in his life, and is greatly astonished.

It seems that Miss Clarabelle Cobb is a very strong doll, just as The Dutchman states, and in about an hour she shows signs of being wide awake, and Blondy Swanson sits down on the floor beside her, and she talks to him quite a while in a low voice, and while they are talking The Dutchman pulls up the floor in another corner of the barn, and digs around underneath a few minutes, and finally comes up with a gripsack covered with dirt, and he opens this gripsack and shows me it is filled with lovely, large coarse bank-notes.

Later Blondy Swanson tells The Dutchman and me the story of Miss Clarabelle Cobb, and parts of this story are rather sad. It seems that after Miss Clarabelle Cobb goes back to her old home in Akron, Ohio, she winds up marrying a young guy by the name of Joseph Hatcher, who is a bookkeeper by trade, and has a pretty good job in Akron, so Miss Clarabelle Cobb and this Joseph Hatcher are as happy as anything together for quite a spell.

Then about a year before the night I am telling about Joseph Hatcher is sent by his firm to these parts where we find Miss Clarabelle Cobb, to do the bookkeeping in a factory there, and one night a few months afterwards, when Joseph Hatcher is staying after hours in the factory office working on his books, a mob of wrong gees breaks into the joint, and sticks him up, and blows open the safe, taking away a large sum of money and leaving Joseph Hatcher tied up like a turkey.

When Joseph Hatcher is discovered in this predicament the next morning, what happens but the gendarmes put the sleeve on him, and place him in the pokey, saying the chances are Joseph Hatcher is in and in with the safe-blowers, and that he tips them off the dough is in the safe, and it seems that the guy who is especially fond of this idea is a guy by the name of Ambersham, who is manager of the factory, and a very heard-hearted guy, at that.

And now, although this is eight or nine months back, there is Joseph Hatcher still in the pokey awaiting trial, and it is seven to five anywhere in town that the judge throws the book at him when he finally goes to bat, because it seems from what Miss Clarabelle Cobb tells Blondy Swanson that nearly everybody figures Joseph Hatcher is guilty.

But of course Miss Clarabelle Cobb does not put in with popular opinion about her ever-loving Joe, and she spends the next few months trying to spring him from the pokey, but she has no potatoes, and no way of getting any potatoes, so things go from bad to worse with Miss Clarabelle Cobb.

Finally, she finds herself with no place to live in town, and she happens to run into this old barn, which is on an abandoned property owned by a doctor in town by the name of Kelton, and it seems that he is a kind-hearted guy, and he gives her permission to use it any way she wishes. So Miss Clarabelle moves into the barn, and the chances are there is many a time when she wishes she is back in Mr. Georgie White's *Scandals*.

Now The Dutchman listens to this story with great interest, especially the part about Joseph Hatcher being left tied up in the factory office, and finally The Dutchman states as follows:

"Why, my goodness," The Dutchman says, "there is no doubt but what this is the very same young guy we are compelled to truss up the night we get this gripsack. As I recollect it, he wishes to battle for his employer's dough, and I personally tap him over the coco with a blackjack.

"But," he says, "he is by no means the guy who tips us off about the dough being there. As I remember it now, it is nobody but the guy whose name you mention in Miss Clarabelle Cobb's story. It is this guy Ambersham, the manager of the joint, and come to think of it, he is supposed to get his bit of this dough for his trouble, and it is only fair that I carry out this agreement as the executor of the estate of my late comrades, although," The Dutchman says, "I do not approve of his conduct towards this Joseph Hatcher. But," he says, "the first thing for us to do is to get a doctor out here to Miss Clarabelle Cobb, and I judge the doctor for us to get is this Doc Kelton she speaks of."

So The Dutchman takes the gripsack and we get into the old can and head back the way we come, although before we go I see Blondy Swanson bend down over Miss Clarabelle Cobb, and while I do not wish this to go any further, I will take a paralyzed oath I see him plant a small kiss on the baby's noggin, and I hear Miss Clarabelle Cobb speak as follows:

"I will name him for you, Blondy," she says. "By the way, Blondy, what is your right name?"

"Olaf," Blondy says.

It is now along in the early morning and not many citizens are stirring as we go through town again, with Blondy in the front seat again holding the gripsack on his lap so The Dutchman can drive, but finally we find a guy in an all-night lunch counter who knows where Doc Kelton lives, and this guy stands on the running-board of the old can and guides us to a house in a side street, and after pounding on the door quite a spell, we roust the Doc out and Blondy goes inside to talk with him.

He is in there quite a spell, but when he comes out he says everything is okay, and that Doc Kelton will go at once to look after Miss Clarabelle Cobb, and take her to a hospital, and Blondy states that he leaves a couple of C's with the Doc to make sure Miss Clarabelle Cobb gets the best of care.

"Well," The Dutchman says, "we can afford a couple of C's out of what we have in this gripsack, but," he says, "I am still wondering if it is not my duty to look up this Ambersham, and give him his bit."

"Dutchman," Blondy says, "I fear I have some bad news for you. The gripsack is gone. This Doc Kelton strikes me as a right guy in every respect, especially," Blondy says, "as he states to me that he always half-suspects there is a wrong rap in on Miss Clarabelle Cobb's ever-loving Joe, and that if it is not for this guy Ambersham agitating all the time other citizens may suspect the same thing, and it will not be so tough for Joe.

"So," Blondy says, "I tell Doc Kelton the whole story, about Ambersham and all, and I take the liberty of leaving the gripsack with him to be returned to the rightful owners, and Doc Kelton says if he does not have Miss Clarabelle Cobb's Joe out of the sneezer, and this Ambersham on the run out of town in twenty-four hours, I can call him a liar. But," Blondy says, "let us now proceed on our way, because I only have Doc Kelton's word that he will give us twelve hours' leeway before he does anything except attend to Miss Clarabelle Cobb, as I figure you need this much time to get out of sight, Dutchman."

Well, The Dutchman does not say anything about all this news for a while, and seems to be thinking the situation over, and while he is thinking he is giving his old can a little more gas than he intends, and she is fairly popping along what seems to be the main drag of the town when a gendarme on a motor-cycle comes up alongside us, and motions The Dutchman to pull over to the curb.

He is a nice-looking young gendarme, but he seems somewhat hostile as he gets off his motor-cycle, and walks up to us very slow, and asks us where the fire is.

Naturally, we do not say anything in reply, which is the only thing to say to a gendarme under these circumstances, so he speaks as follows:

"What are you guys carrying in this old skillet, anyway?" he says. "Stand up, and let me look you guys over."

And then as we stand up, he peeks into the front and back of the car, and under our feet, and all he finds is a bottle which once holds some of Good Time Charley's rock candy and rye whisky without the rock candy, but which is now very empty, and he holds this bottle up, and sniffs at the nozzle, and asks what is formerly in this bottle, and I tell him the truth when I tell him it is once full of medicine, and The Dutchman and Blondy Swanson nod their heads in support of my statement. But the gendarme takes another stiff, and then he says like this:

"Oh," he says, very sarcastic, "wise guys, eh? Three wise guys, eh? Trying to kid somebody, eh? Medicine, eh?" he says. "Well, if it is not Christmas Day I will take you in and hold you just on suspicion. But I will be Santa Claus to you, and let you go ahead, wise guys."

And then after we get a few blocks away, The Dutchman speaks as follows:

"Yes," he says, "that is what we are, to be sure. We are wise guys. If we are not wise guys, we will still have the gripsack in this car for the copper to find. And if the copper finds the gripsack, he will wish to take us to the jail house for investigation, and if he wishes to take us there I fear he will not be alive at this time, and we will be in plenty of heat around and about, and personally," The Dutchman says, "I am sick and tired of heat."

And with this The Dutchman puts a large Betsy back in a holster under his left arm, and turns on the gas, and as the old can begins leaving the lights of the town behind, I ask Blondy if he happens to notice the name of this town.

"Yes," Blondy says, "I notice it on a signboard we just pass. It is Bethlehem, Pa."

THE LEMON DROP KID

I am going to take you back a matter of four or five years ago to an August afternoon and the race track at Saratoga, which is a spot in New York State very pleasant to behold, and also to a young guy by the name of The Lemon Drop Kid, who is called The Lemon Drop Kid because he always has a little sack of lemon drops in the side pocket of his coat, and is always munching at same, a lemon drop being a breed of candy that is relished by many, although personally I prefer peppermints.

On this day I am talking about, The Lemon Drop Kid is looking about for business, and not doing so good for himself, at that, as The Lemon Drop Kid's business is telling the tale, and he is finding it very difficult indeed to discover citizens who are willing to listen to him tell the tale.

And of course if a guy whose business is telling the tale cannot find anybody to listen to him, he is greatly handicapped, for the tale such a guy tells is always about how he knows something is doing in a certain race, the idea of the tale being that it may cause the citizen who is listening to it to make a wager on this certain race, and if the race comes out the way the guy who is telling the tale says it will come out, naturally the citizen is bound to be very grateful to the guy, and maybe reward him liberally.

Furthermore, the citizen is bound to listen to more tales, and a guy whose business is telling the tale, such as The Lemon Drop Kid, always has tales to tell until the cows come home, and generally they are long tales, and sometimes they are very interesting and entertaining, according to who is telling them, and it is well known to one and all that nobody can tell the tale any better than The Lemon Drop Kid.

But old Cap Duhaine and his sleuths at the Saratoga track are greatly opposed to guys going around telling the tale, and claim that such guys are nothing but touts, and they are especially opposed to The Lemon Drop Kid, because they say he tells the tale so well that he weakens public confidence in horse racing. So they are casing The Lemon Drop Kid pretty close to see that he does not get some citizen's ear and start telling him the tale, and finally The Lemon Drop Kid is greatly disgusted and walks up the lawn towards the head of the stretch.

And while he is walking, he is eating lemon drops out of his pocket, and thinking about how much better off he will be if he puts in the last ten years of his life at some legitimate dodge, instead of hop-scotching from one end of the country to the other telling the tale, although just off-hand The Lemon Drop Kid cannot think of any legitimate dodge at which he will see as much of life as he sees around the race tracks since he gets out of the orphan asylum in Jersey City where he is raised.

At the time this story starts out, The Lemon Drop Kid is maybe twenty-four years old, and he is a quiet little guy with a low voice, which comes of keeping it confidential when he is telling the tale, and he is nearly always alone. In fact, The Lemon Drop Kid is never known to have a pal as long as he is around telling the tale, although he is by no means an unfriendly guy, and is always speaking to everybody, even when he is in the money.

But it is now a long time since The Lemon Drop Kid is in the money, or seems to have any chance of being in the money, and the landlady of the boarding-house in Saratoga where he is residing is becoming quite hostile, and making derogatory cracks about him, and also about most of her other boarders, too, so The Lemon Drop Kid is unable to really enjoy his meals there, especially as they are very bad meals to start with.

Well, The Lemon Drop Kid goes off by himself up the lawn and stands there looking out across the track, munching a lemon drop from time to time, and thinking what a harsh old world it is, to be sure, and how much better off it will be if there are no sleuths whatever around and about.

It is a day when not many citizens are present at the track, and the only one near The Lemon Drop Kid seems to be an old guy in a wheel chair, with a steamer rug over his knees, and a big, sleepy-looking stove lid who appears to be in charge of the chair.

This old guy has a big white mouser, and big white bristly eyebrows, and he is a very fierce-looking old guy indeed and anybody can tell at once that he is nothing but a curmudgeon, and by no means worthy of attention. But he is a familiar spectacle at the race track at Saratoga, as he comes out nearly every day in a limousine the size of a hearse, and is rolled out of the limousine in his wheel chair on a little runway by the stove lid, and pushed up to this spot where he is sitting now, so he can view the sport of kings without being bothered by the crowds.

It is well known to one and all that his name is Rarus P. Griggsby, and that he has plenty of potatoes, which he makes in Wall Street, and that he is closer than the next second with his potatoes, and furthermore, it is also well known that he hates everybody in the world, including himself, so nobody goes anywhere near him if they can help it.

The Lemon Drop Kid does not realize he is standing so close to Rarus P. Griggsby, until he hears the old guy growling at the stove lid, and then The Lemon Drop Kid looks at Rarus P. Griggsby very sympathetic and speaks to him in his low voice as follows:

"Gout?" he says.

Now of course The Lemon Drop Kid knows who Rarus P. Griggsby is, and under ordinary circumstances The Lemon Drop Kid will not think of speaking to such a character, but afterwards he explains that he is feeling so despondent that he addresses Rarus P. Griggsby just to show he does not care what happens. And under ordinary circumstances, the chances are Rarus P. Griggsby will start hollering for the gendarmes if a stranger has the gall to speak to him, but there is so much sympathy in The Lemon Drop Kid's voice and eyes, that Rarus P. Griggsby seems to be taken by surprise, and he answers like this:

"Arthritis," Rarus P. Griggsby says. "In my knees," he says. "I am not able to walk a step in three years."

"Why," The Lemon Drop Kid says, "I am greatly distressed to hear this. I know just how you feel, because I am troubled from infancy with this same disease."

Now of course this is strictly the old ackamarackus, as The Lemon Drop Kid cannot even spell arthritis, let alone have it, but he makes the above statement just by way of conversation, and furthermore he goes on to state as follows:

"In fact," The Lemon Drop Kid says, "I suffer so I can scarcely think, but one day I find a little remedy that fixes me up as right as rain, and I now have no trouble whatsoever."

And with this, he takes a lemon drop out of his pocket and pops it into his mouth, and then he hands one to Rarus P. Griggsby in a most hospitable manner, and the old guy holds the lemon drop between his thumb and forefinger and looks at it as if he expects it to explode right in his pan, while the stove lid gazes at The Lemon Drop Kid with a threatening expression.

"Well," Rarus P. Griggsby says, "personally I consider all cures fakes. I have a standing offer of five thousand dollars to anybody that can cure me of my pain, and nobody even comes close so far. Doctors are also fakes," he says. "I have seven of them, and they take out my tonsils, and all my teeth, and my appendix, and they keep me from eating anything I enjoy, and I only get worse. The waters here in Saratoga seem to help me some, but," he says, "they do not get me out of this wheel chair, and I am sick and tired of it all."

Then, as if he comes to a quick decision, he pops the lemon drop into his mouth, and begins munching it very slow, and after a while he says it tastes just like a lemon drop to him, and of course it is a lemon drop all along, but The Lemon Drop Kid says this taste is only to disguise the medicine in it.

Now, by and by, The Lemon Drop Kid commences telling Rarus P. Griggsby the tale, and afterwards The Lemon Drop Kid says he has no idea Rarus P. Griggsby will listen to the tale, and that he only starts telling it to him in a spirit of good clean fun, just to see how he will take it, and he is greatly surprised to note that Rarus P. Griggsby is all attention.

Personally, I find nothing unusual in this situation, because I often see citizens around the race tracks as prominent as Rarus P. Griggsby, listening to the tale from guys who do not have as much as a seat in their pants, especially if the tale has any larceny in it, because it is only human nature to be deeply interested in larceny.

And the tale The Lemon Drop Kid tells Rarus P. Griggsby is that he is a brother of Sonny Saunders, the jock, and that Sonny tells him to be sure and be at the track this day to bet on a certain horse in the fifth race, because it is nothing but a boat race, and everything in it is as stiff as a plank, except this certain horse.

Now of course this is all a terrible lie, and The Lemon Drop Kid is taking a great liberty with Sonny Saunders's name, especially as Sonny does not have any brothers, anyway, and even if Sonny knows about a boat race the chances are he will never tell The

Lemon Drop Kid, but then very few guys whose business is telling the tale ever stop to figure they may be committing perjury.

So The Lemon Drop Kid goes on to state that when he arrives at the track he has fifty bobs pinned to his wishbone to bet on this certain horse, but unfortunately he gets a tip on a real good thing in the very first race, and bets his fifty bobs right then and there, figuring to provide himself with a large taw to bet on the certain horse in the fifth, but the real good thing receives practically a criminal ride from a jock who does not know one end of a horse from the other, and is beat a very dirty snoot, and there The Lemon Drop Kid is with the fifth race coming up, and an absolute cinch in it, the way his tale goes, but with no dough left to bet on it.

Well, personally I do not consider this tale as artistic as some The Lemon Drop Kid tells, and in fact The Lemon Drop Kid himself never rates it among his masterpieces, but old Rarus P. Griggsby listens to the tale quite intently without saying a word, and all the time he is munching the lemon drop and smacking his lips under his big white mouser, as if he greatly enjoys this delicacy, but when The Lemon Drop Kid concludes the tale, and is standing there gazing out across the track with a very sad expression on his face, Rarus P. Griggsby speaks as follows:

"I never bet on horse races," Rarus P. Griggsby says. "They are too uncertain. But this proposition you present sounds like finding money, and I love to find money. I will wager one hundred dollars on your assurance that this certain horse cannot miss."

And with this, he outs with a leather so old that The Lemon Drop Kid half expects a cockroach to leap out at him, and produces a C note which he hands to The Lemon Drop Kid, and as he does so, Rarus P. Griggsby inquires:

"What is the name of this certain horse?"

Well, of course this is a fair question, but it happens that The Lemon Drop Kid is so busy all afternoon thinking of the injustice of the sleuths that he never even bothers to look up this particular race beforehand, and afterwards he is quite generally criticized for slovenliness in this matter, for if a guy is around telling the tale about a race, he is entitled to pick out a horse that has at least some kind of chance.

But of course The Lemon Drop Kid is not expecting the opportunity of telling the tale to arise, so the question finds him unprepared, as off-hand he cannot think of the name of a horse in the race, as he never consults the scratches, and he does not wish to mention the name of some plug that may be scratched out, and lose the chance to make the C note. So as he seizes the C note from Rarus P. Griggsby and turns to dash for the bookmakers over in front of the grandstand, all The Lemon Drop Kid can think of to say at this moment is the following:

"Watch Number Two," he says.

And the reason he says No. 2, is he figures there is bound to be a No. 2 in the race, while he cannot be so sure about a No. 7 or a No. 9 until he looks them over, because you understand that all The Lemon Drop Kid states in telling the tale to Rarus P. Griggsby about knowing of something doing in this race is very false.

And of course The Lemon Drop Kid has no idea of betting the C note on anything whatever in the race. In the first place, he does not know of anything to bet on, and in the second place he needs the C note, but he is somewhat relieved when he inquires of the first bookie he comes to, and learns that No. 2 is an old walrus by the name of The Democrat, and anybody knows that The Democrat has no chance of winning even in a field of mud turtles.

So The Lemon Drop Kid puts the C note in his pants pocket, and walks around and about until the horses are going to the post, and you must not think there is anything dishonest in his not betting this money with a bookmaker, as The Lemon Drop Kid is only taking the bet himself, which is by no means unusual, and in fact it is so common that only guys like Cap Duhaine and his sleuths think much about it.

Finally The Lemon Drop Kid goes back to Rarus P. Griggsby, for it will be considered most ungenteel for a guy whose business is telling the tale to be absent when it comes time to explain why the tale does not stand up, and about this time the horses are turning for home, and a few seconds later they go busting past the spot where Rarus P. Griggsby is sitting in his wheel chair, and what is in front to the wire by a Salt Lake City block but The Democrat with No. 2 on his blanket.

Well, old Rarus P. Griggsby starts yelling and waving his hands, and making so much racket that he is soon the center of attention, and when it comes out that he bets a C note on the winner, nobody blames him for cutting up these didoes, for the horse is a twenty to one shot, but all this time The Lemon Drop Kid only stands there looking very, very sad and shaking his head, until finally Rarus P. Griggsby notices his strange attitude.

"Why are you not cheering over our winning this nice bet?" he says. "Of course I expect to declare you in," he says. "In fact I am quite grateful to you."

"But," The Lemon Drop Kid says, "we do not win. Our horse runs a jolly second."

"What do you mean, *second*?" Rarus P. Griggsby says. "Do you not tell me to watch Number Two, and does not Number Two win?"

"Yes," The Lemon Drop Kid says, "what you state is quite true, but what I mean when I say watch Number Two is that Number Two is the only horse I am afraid of in the race, and it seems my fear is well founded."

Now at this, old Rarus P. Griggsby sits looking at The Lemon Drop Kid for as long as you can count up to ten, if you count slow, and his mouser and eyebrows are all twitching at once, and anybody can see that he is very much perturbed, and then all of a sudden he lets out a yell and to the great amazement of one and all he leaps right out of his wheel chair and makes a lunge at The Lemon Drop Kid.

Well, there is no doubt that Rarus P. Griggsby has murder in his heart, and nobody blames The Lemon Drop Kid when he turns and starts running away at great speed, and in fact he has such speed that finally his feet are throwing back little stones off the gravel paths of the race track with such velocity that a couple of spectators who get hit by these stones think they are shot.

For a few yards, old Rarus P. Griggsby is right at The Lemon Drop Kid's heels, and furthermore Rarus P. Griggsby is yelling and swearing in a most revolting manner. Then some of Cap Duhaine's sleuths come running up and they take after The Lemon Drop Kid too, and he has to have plenty of early foot to beat them to the race-track gates, and while Rarus P. Griggsby does not figure much in the running after the first few jumps, The Lemon Drop Kid seems to remember hearing him cry out as follows:

"Stop, there! Please stop!" Rarus P. Griggsby cries. "I wish to see you."

But of course The Lemon Drop Kid is by no means a chump, and he does not even slacken up, let alone stop, until he is well beyond the gates, and the sleuths are turning back, and what is more, The Lemon Drop Kid takes the road leading out of Saratoga instead of going back to the city, because he figures that Saratoga may not be so congenial to him for a while.

In fact, The Lemon Drop Kid finds himself half-regretting that he ever tells the tale to Rarus P. Griggsby as The Lemon Drop Kid likes Saratoga in August, but of course such a thing as happens to him in calling a winner the way he does is just an unfortunate accident, and is not apt to happen again in a lifetime.

Well, The Lemon Drop Kid keeps on walking away from Saratoga for quite some time, and finally he is all tuckered out and wishes to take the load off his feet. So when he comes to a small town by the name of Kibbsville, he sits down on the porch of what seems to be a general store and gas station, and while he is sitting there thinking of how nice and quiet and restful this town seems to be, with pleasant shade trees, and white houses all around and about, he sees standing in the doorway of a very little white house across the street from the store, in a gingham dress, the most beautiful young doll that ever lives, and I know this is true, because The Lemon Drop Kid tells me so afterwards.

This doll has brown hair hanging down her back, and her smile is so wonderful that when an old pappy guy with a goatee comes out of the store to sell a guy in a flivver some gas, The Lemon Drop Kid hauls off and asks him if he can use a clerk.

Well, it seems that the old guy can, at that, because it seems that a former clerk, a guy by the name of Pilloe, recently lays down and dies on the old guy from age and malnutrition, and so this is how The Lemon Drop Kid comes to be planted in Kibbsville, and clerking in Martin Potter's store for the next couple of years, at ten bobs per week.

And furthermore, this is how The Lemon Drop Kid meets up with Miss Alicia Deering, who is nobody but the beautiful little doll that The Lemon Drop Kid sees standing in the doorway of the little house across the street.

She lives in this house with her papa, her mamma being dead a long time, and her papa is really nothing but an old bum who dearly loves his applejack, and who is generally around with a good heat on. His first name is Jonas, and he is a house painter by trade, but he seldom feels like doing any painting, as he claims he never really recovers from a terrible backache he gets when he is in the Spanish-American War with the First New York, so Miss Alicia Deering supports him by dealing them off her arm in the Commercial Hotel.

But although The Lemon Drop Kid now works for a very great old skinflint who even squawks about The Lemon Drop Kid's habit of filling his side pocket now and then with lemon drops out of a jar on the shelf in the store, The Lemon Drop Kid is very happy, for the truth of the matter is he loves Miss Alicia Deering, and it is the first time in his life he ever loves anybody, or anything. And furthermore, it is the first time in his life The Lemon Drop Kid is living quietly, and in peace, and not losing sleep trying to think of ways of cheating somebody.

In fact, The Lemon Drop Kid now looks back on his old life with great repugnance, for he can see that it is by no means the proper life for any guy, and sometimes he has half a mind to write to his former associates who may still be around telling the tale, and request them to mend their ways, only The Lemon Drop Kid does not wish these old associates to know where he is.

He never as much as peeks at a racing sheet nowadays, and he spends all his spare time with Miss Alicia Deering, which is not so much time, at that, as old Martin Potter does not care to see his employees loafing between the hours of 6 A.M. and 10 P.M., and neither does the Commercial Hotel. But one day in the spring, when the apple blossoms are blooming in these parts, and the air is chock-a-block with perfume, and the grass is getting nice and green, The Lemon Drop Kid speaks of his love to Miss Alicia Deering, stating that it is such a love that he can scarcely eat.

Well, Miss Alicia Deering states that she reciprocates this love one hundred per cent, and then The Lemon Drop Kid suggests they get married up immediately, and she says she is in favor of the idea, only she can never think of leaving her papa, who has no one else in all this world but her, and while this is a little more extra weight than The Lemon Drop Kid figures on picking up, he says his love is so terrific he can even stand for her papa, too.

So they are married, and go to live in the little house across the street from Martin Potter's store with Miss Alicia Deering's papa.

When he marries Miss Alicia Deering, The Lemon Drop Kid has a bank roll of one hundred and eighteen dollars, including the C note he takes off of Rarus P. Griggsby, and eighteen bobs that he saves out of his salary from Martin Potter in a year, and three nights after the marriage, Miss Alicia Deering's papa sniffs out where The Lemon Drop Kid plants his roll and sneezes same. Then he goes on a big applejack toot, and spends all the dough.

But in spite of everything, including old man Deering, The Lemon Drop Kid and Miss Alicia Deering are very, very happy in the little house for about a year, especially when it seems that Miss Alicia Deering is going to have a baby, although this incident compels her to stop dealing them off the arm at the Commercial Hotel, and cuts down their resources.

Now one day, Miss Alicia Deering comes down with a great illness, and it is such an illness as causes old Doc Abernathy, the local croaker, to wag his head, and to state that it is beyond him, and that the only chance for her is to send her to a hospital in New York City where the experts can get a crack at her. But by this time, what with all his overhead, The Lemon Drop Kid is as clean as a jaybird, and he has no idea where he can get his dukes on any money in these parts, and it will cost a couple of C's, for low, to do what Doc Abernathy suggests.

Finally, The Lemon Drop Kid asks old Martin Potter if he can see his way clear to making him an advance on his salary, which still remains ten bobs per week, but Martin Potter laughs, and says he not only cannot see his way clear to doing such a thing, but that if conditions do not improve he is going to cut The Lemon Drop Kid off altogether. Furthermore, about this time the guy who owns the little house drops around and reminds The Lemon Drop Kid that he is now in arrears for two months' rent, amounting in all to twelve bobs, and if The Lemon Drop Kid is not able to meet this obligation shortly, he will have to vacate.

So one way and another The Lemon Drop Kid is in quite a quandary, and Miss Alicia Deering is getting worse by the minute, and finally The Lemon Drop Kid hoofs and hitch-hikes a matter of maybe a hundred and fifty miles to New York City, with the idea of going out to Belmont Park, where the giddy-aps are now running, figuring he may be able to make some kind of a scratch around there, but he no sooner lights on Broadway than he runs into a guy he knows by the name of Short Boy, and this Short Boy pulls him into a doorway, and says to him like this:

"Listen, Lemon Drop," Short Boy says, "I do not know what it is you do to old Rarus P. Griggsby, and I do not wish to know, but it must be something terrible indeed, as he has every elbow around the race tracks laying for you for the past couple of years. You know Rarus P. Griggsby has great weight around these tracks, and you must commit murder the way he is after you. Why," Short Boy says, "only last week over in Maryland, Whitey Jordan, the track copper, asks me if ever I hear of you, and I tell him I understand you are in Australia. Keep away from the tracks," Short Boy says, "or you will wind up in the clink."

So The Lemon Drop Kid hoofs and hitch-hikes back to Kibbsville, as he does not wish to become involved in any trouble at this time, and the night he gets back home is the same night a masked guy with a big six pistol in his duke steps into the lobby of the Commercial Hotel and sticks up the night clerk and half a dozen citizens who are sitting around in the lobby, including old Jonas Deering, and robs the damper of over sixty bobs, and it is also the same night that Miss Alicia Deering's baby is born dead, and old Doc Abernathy afterwards claims that it is all because the experts cannot get a crack at Miss Alicia Deering a matter of about twelve hours earlier.

And it is along in the morning after this night, around four bells, that Miss Alicia Deering finally opens her eyes, and sees The Lemon Drop Kid sitting beside her bed in the little house, crying very hard, and it is the first time The Lemon Drop Kid is leveling with his crying since the time one of the attendants in the orphans' asylum in Jersey City gives him a good belting years before.

Then Miss Alicia Deering motions to The Lemon Drop Kid to bend down so she can whisper to him, and what Miss Alicia Deering whispers, soft and low, is the following:

"Do not cry, Kid," she whispers. "Be a good boy after I am gone, Kid, and never forget I love you, and take good care of poor papa."

And then Miss Alicia Deering closes her eyes for good and all, and The Lemon Drop Kid sits there beside her, watching her face until some time later he hears a noise at the front door of the little house, and he opens the door to find old Sheriff Higginbotham waiting there, and after they stand looking at each other a while, the sheriff speaks as follows:

"Well, son," Sheriff Higginbotham says, "I am sorry, but I guess you will have to come along with me. We find the vinegar barrel spigot wrapped in tin foil that you use for a gun in the back yard here where you throw it last night."

"All right," The Lemon Drop Kid says. "All right, Sheriff. But how do you come to think of me in the first place?"

"Well," Sheriff Higginbotham says, "I do not suppose you recall doing it, and the only guy in the hotel lobby that notices it is nobody but your papa-in-law, Jonas Deering, but," he says, "while you are holding your home-made pistol with one hand last night, you reach into the side pocket of your coat with the other hand and take out a lemon drop and pop it into your mouth."

I run into The Lemon Drop Kid out on the lawn at Hialeah in Miami last winter, and I am sorry to see that the twoer he does in Auburn leaves plenty of lines in his face, and a lot of gray in his hair.

But of course I do not refer to this, nor do I mention that he is the subject of considerable criticism from many citizens for turning over to Miss Alicia Deering's papa a purse of three C's that we raise to pay a mouthpiece for his defense.

Furthermore, I do not tell The Lemon Drop Kid that he is also criticized in some quarters for his action while in the sneezer at Auburn in sending the old guy the few bobs he is able to gather in by making and selling knick-knacks of one kind and another to visitors, until finally Jonas Deering saves him any more bother by up and passing away of too much applejack.

The way I look at it, every guy knows his own business best, so I only duke The Lemon Drop Kid, and say I am glad to see him, and we are standing there carving up a few old scores, when all of a sudden there is a great commotion and out of the crowd around us on the lawn comes an old guy with a big white mouser, and bristly white eyebrows, and as he grabs The Lemon Drop Kid by the arm, I am somewhat surprised to see that it is nobody but old Rarus P. Griggsby, without his wheel chair, and to hear him speak as follows:

"Well, well, well, well, well!" Rarus P. Griggsby says to The Lemon Drop Kid. "At last I find you," he says. "Where are you hiding all these years? Do you not know I have detectives looking for you high and low because I wish to pay you the reward I offer for anybody curing me of my arthritis? Yes," Rarus P. Griggsby says, "the medicine you give me at Saratoga which tastes like a lemon drop, works fine, although," he says, "my seven doctors all try to tell me it is nothing but their efforts finally getting in their work, while the city of Saratoga is attempting to cut in and claim credit for its waters.

"But," Rarus P. Griggsby says, "I know it is your medicine, and if it is not your medicine, it is your scallawaggery that makes me so hot that I forget my arthritis, and never remember it since, so it is all one and the same thing. Anyway, you now have forty-nine hundred dollars coming from me, for of course I must hold out the hundred out of which you swindle me," he says.

Well, The Lemon Drop Kid stands looking at Rarus P. Griggsby and listening to him, and finally The Lemon Drop Kid begins to laugh in his low voice, ha-ha-ha-ha-ha, but somehow there does not seem to be any laughter in the laugh, and I cannot bear to hear it, so I move away leaving Rarus P. Griggsby and The Lemon Drop Kid there together.

I look back only once, and I see The Lemon Drop Kid stop laughing long enough to take a lemon drop out of the side pocket of his coat and pop it into his mouth, and then he goes on laughing, ha-ha-ha-ha-ha.

PRINCESS O'HARA

Now of course Princess O'Hara is by no means a regular princess, and in fact she is nothing but a little red-headed doll, with plenty of freckles, from over on Tenth Avenue, and her right name is Maggie, and the only reason she is called Princess O'Hara is as follows:

She is the daughter of King O'Hara, who is hacking along Broadway with one of these old-time victorias for a matter of maybe twenty-five years, and every time King O'Hara gets his pots on, which is practically every night, rain or shine, he is always bragging that he has the royal blood of Ireland in his veins, so somebody starts calling him King, and this is his monicker as long as I can remember, although probably what King O'Hara really has in his veins is about ninety-eight per cent alcohol.

Well, anyway, one night about seven or eight years back, King O'Hara shows up on his stand in front of Mindy's restaurant on Broadway with a spindly-legged, little doll about ten years of age on the seat beside him, and he says that this little doll is nobody but his daughter, and he is taking care of her because his old lady is not feeling so good, and right away Last Card Louie, the gambler, reaches up and dukes the little doll and says to her like this:

"If you are the daughter of the King, you must be the princess," Last Card Louie says. "How are you, Princess?"

So from this time on, she is Princess O'Hara, and afterwards for several years she often rides around in the early evening with the King, and sometimes when the King has his pots on more than somewhat, she personally drives Goldberg, which is the King's horse, although Goldberg does not really need much driving as he knows his way along Broadway better than anybody. In fact, this Goldberg is a most sagacious old pelter indeed, and he is called Goldberg by the King in honor of a Jewish friend by the name of Goldberg, who keeps a delicatessen store on Tenth Avenue.

At this time, Princess O'Hara is as homely as a mud fence, and maybe homelier, what with the freckles, and the skinny gambs, and a few buck teeth, and she does not weigh more than sixty pounds, sopping wet, and her red hair is down her back in pigtails, and she giggles if anybody speaks to her, so finally nobody speaks to her much, but old King O'Hara seems to think well of her, at that.

Then by and by she does not seem to be around with the King anymore, and when somebody happens to ask about her, the King says his old lady claims the Princess is getting too grown-up to be shagging around Broadway, and that she is now going to public school. So after not seeing her for some years, everybody forgets that King O'Hara has a daughter, and in fact nobody cares a cuss.

Now King O'Hara is a little shriveled-up old guy with a very red beezer, and he is a most familiar spectacle to one and all on Broadway as he drives about with a stove-pipe hat tipped so far over to one side of his noggin that it looks as if it is always about to fall off, and in fact the King himself is always tipped so far over to one side that it seems to be a sure thing that he is going to fall off.

The way the King keeps himself on the seat of his victoria is really most surprising, and one time Last Card Louie wins a nice bet off a gambler from St. Louis by the name of Olive Street Oscar, who takes eight to five off of Louis that the King cannot drive them through Central Park without doing a Brodie off the seat. But of course Louie is betting with the best of it, which is the way he always dearly loves to bet, because he often rides through Central Park with King O'Hara, and he knows the King never falls off, no matter how far over he tips.

Personally, I never ride with the King very much, as his victoria is so old I am always afraid the bottom will fall out from under me, and that I will run myself to death trying to keep up, because the King is generally so busy singing Irish come-all-yeez up on his seat that he is not apt to pay much attention to what his passengers are doing.

There are quite a number of these old victorias left in this town, a victoria being a low-neck, four-wheeled carriage with seats for four or five people, and they are very popular in the summer-time with guys and dolls who wish to ride around and about in Central Park taking the air, and especially with guys and dolls who may wish to do a little off-hand guzzling while taking the air.

Personally, I consider a taxicab much more convenient and less expensive than an old-fashioned victoria if you wish to get to some place, but of course guys and dolls engaged in a little off-hand guzzling never wish to get any place in particular, or at least not soon. So these victorias, which generally stand around the entrances to the Park, do a fair business in the summer-time, because it seems that no matter what conditions are, there are always guys and dolls who wish to do a little off-hand guzzling.

But King O'Hara stands in front of Mindy's because he has many regular customers among the citizens of Broadway, who do not go in for guzzling so very much, unless a case of guzzling comes up, but who love to ride around in the Park on hot nights just to cool themselves out, although at the time I am now speaking of, things are so tough with one and all along Broadway that King O'Hara has to depend more on strangers for his trade.

Well, what happens one night, but King O'Hara is seen approaching Mindy's, tipping so far over to one side of his seat that Olive Street Oscar, looking to catch even on the bet he loses before, is offering to take six to five off Last Card Louie that this time the King goes plumb off, and Louis is about to give it to him, when the old King tumbles smack-dab into the street, as dead as last Tuesday, which shows you how lucky Last Card Louie is, because nobody ever figures such a thing to happen to the King, and even Goldberg, the horse, stops and stands looking at him very much surprised, with one hind hoof in the King's stove-pipe hat. The doctors state that King O'Hara's heart just naturally hauls off and quits working on him, and afterwards Regret, the horse player, says the chances are the King probably suddenly remembers refusing a drink somewhere.

A few nights later, many citizens are out in front of Mindy's, and Big Nig, the crap shooter, is saying that things do not look the same around there since King O'Hara puts his checks back in the rack, when all of a sudden up comes a victoria that anybody can see is the King's old rattletrap, especially as it is being pulled by Goldberg.

And who is on the driver's seat, with King O'Hara's bunged-up old stove-pipe hat sitting jack-deuce on her noggin, but a red-headed doll of maybe eighteen or nineteen with freckles all over her pan, and while it is years since I see her, I can tell at once that she is nobody but Princess O'Hara, even though it seems she changes quite some.

In fact, she is now about as pretty a little doll as anybody will wish to see, even with the freckles, because the buck teeth seem to have disappeared, and the gambs are now filled out very nicely, and so has the rest of her. Furthermore, she has a couple of blue eyes that are most delightful to behold, and a smile like six bits, and all in all, she is a pleasing scene.

Well, naturally, her appearance in this manner causes some comment, and in fact some citizens are disposed to criticize her as being unladylike, until Big Nig, the crap shooter, goes around among them very quietly stating that he will knock their ears down if he hears any more cracks from them, because it seems that Big Nig learns that when old King O'Hara dies, all he leaves in this world besides his widow and six kids is Goldberg, the horse, and the victoria, and Princess O'Hara is the eldest of these kids, and the only one old enough to work, and she can think of nothing better to do than to take up her papa's business where he leaves off.

After one peek at Princess O'Hara, Regret, the horse player, climbs right into the victoria, and tells her to ride him around the Park a couple of times, although it is well known to one and all that it costs two bobs per hour to ride in anybody's victoria, and the only dough Regret has in a month is a pound note that he just borrows off of Last Card Louie for eating money. But from this time on, the chances are Regret will be Princess O'Hara's best customer if he can borrow any more pound notes, but the competition gets too keen for him, especially from Last Card Louie, who is by this time quite a prominent character along Broadway, and in the money, although personally I always say you can have him, as Last Card Louie is such a guy as will stoop to very sharp practice, and in fact he often does not wait to stoop.

He is called Last Card Louie because in his youth he is a great hand for riding the tubs back and forth between here and Europe and playing stud poker with other passengers, and the way he always gets much strength from the last card is considered quite abnormal, especially if Last Card Louie is dealing. But of course Last Card Louie no longer rides the tubs as this occupation is now very old-fashioned, and anyway Louie has more profitable interests that require his attention, such as a crap game, and one thing and another.

There is no doubt but what Last Card Louie takes quite a fancy to Princess O'Hara, but naturally he cannot spend all his time riding around in a victoria, so other citizens get a chance to patronize her now and then, and in fact I once take a ride with Princess O'Hara myself, and it is a very pleasant experience indeed as she likes to sing while she is driving, just as old King O'Hara does in his time.

But what Princess O'Hara sings is not Irish come-all-yeez but "Kathleen Mavourneen," and "My Wild Irish Rose," and "Asthore," and other such ditties, and she has a loud contralto voice, and when she lets it out while driving through Central Park in the early hours of the morning, the birds in the trees wake up and go tweet-tweet, and the coppers on duty for blocks around stand still with smiles on their kissers, and the citizens who live in the apartment houses along Central Park West and Central Park South come to their windows to listen.

Then one night in October, Princess O'Hara does not show up in front of Mindy's, and there is much speculation among one and all about this absence, and some alarm, when Big Nig, the crap shooter, comes around and says that what happens is that old Goldberg, the horse, is down with colic, or some such, so there is Princess O'Hara without a horse.

Well, this news is received with great sadness by one and all, and there is some talk of taking up a collection to buy Princess O'Hara another horse, but nobody goes very far with this idea because things are so tough with everybody, and while Big Nig mentions that maybe Last Card Louie will be glad to do something large in this matter, nobody cares for this idea, either, as many citizens are displeased with the way Last Card Louie is pitching to Princess O'Hara, because it is well known that Last Card Louie is nothing but a wolf when it comes to young dolls, and anyway about now Regret, the horse player, speaks up as follows:

"Why," Regret says, "it is great foolishness to talk of wasting money buying a horse, even if we have any money to waste, when the barns up at Empire City are packed at this time with crocodiles of all kinds. Let us send a committee up to the track," Regret says, "and borrow a nice horse for Princess O'Hara to use until Goldberg is back on his feet again."

"But," I say to Regret, "suppose nobody wishes to lend us a horse?"

"Why," Regret says, "I do not mean to ask anybody to lend us a horse. I mean let us borrow one without asking anybody. Most of these horse owners are so very touchy that if we go around asking them to lend us a horse to pull a hack, they may figure we are insulting their horses, so let us just get the horse and say nothing whatever."

Well, I state that this sounds to me like stealing, and stealing is something that is by no means upright and honest, and Regret has to admit that it really is similar to stealing, but he says what of it, and as I do not know what of it, I discontinue the argument. Furthermore, Regret says it is clearly understood that we will return any horse we borrow when Goldberg is hale and hearty again, so I can see that after all there is nothing felonious in the idea, or anyway, not much.

But after much discussion, it comes out that nobody along Broadway seems to know anything about stealing a horse. There are citizens who know all about stealing diamond necklaces, or hot stoves, but when it comes to horses, everybody confesses themselves at a loss. It is really amazing the amount of ignorance there is on Broadway about stealing horses.

Then finally Regret has a bright idea. It seems that a rodeo is going on at Madison Square Garden at this time, a rodeo being a sort of wild west show with bucking broncos, and cowboys, and all this and that, and Regret seems to remember reading when he is a young squirt that stealing horses is a very popular pastime out in the wild west.

So one evening Regret goes around to the Garden and gets to talking to a cowboy in leather pants with hair on them, and he asks this cowboy, whose name seems to be Laramie Pink, if there are any expert horse stealers connected with the rodeo. Moreover, Regret explains to Laramie Pink just why he wants a good horse stealer, and Pink becomes greatly interested and wishes to know if the loan of a nice bucking bronco, or a first-class cow pony will be of any assistance, and when Regret says he is afraid not, Laramie Pink says like this:

"Well," he says, "of course horse stealing is considered a most antique custom out where I come from, and in fact it is no longer practiced in the best circles, but," he says, "come to think of it, there is a guy with this outfit by the name of Frying Pan Joe, who is too old to do anything now except mind the cattle, but who is said to be an excellent horse stealer out in Colorado in his day. Maybe Frying Pan Joe will be interested in your proposition," Laramie Pink says.

So he hunts up Frying Pan Joe, and Frying Pan Joe turns out to be a little old pappy guy with a chin whisker, and a sad expression, and a wide-brimmed cowboy hat, and when they explain to him that they wish him to steal a horse, Frying Pan Joe seems greatly touched, and his eyes fill up with tears, and he speaks as follows:

"Why," Frying Pan Joe says, "your idea brings back many memories to me. It is a matter of over twenty-five years since I steal a horse, and the last time I do this it gets me three years in the calabozo. Why," he says, "this is really a most unexpected order, and it finds me all out of practice, and with no opportunity to get myself in shape. But," he says, "I will put forth my best efforts on this job for ten dollars, as long as I do not personally have to locate the horse I am to steal. I am not acquainted with the ranges hereabouts, and will not know where to go to find a horse."

So Regret, the horse player, and Big Nig, the crap shooter, and Frying Pan Joe go up to Empire this very same night, and it turns out that stealing a horse is so simple that Regret is sorry he does not make the tenner himself, for all Frying Pan Joe does is to go to the barns where the horses live at Empire, and walk along until he comes to a line of stalls that do not seem to have any watchers around in the shape of stable hands at the moment. Then Frying Pan Joe just steps into a stall and comes out leading a horse, and if anybody sees him, they are bound to figure he has a right to do this, because of course not even Sherlock Holmes is apt to think of anybody stealing a horse around this town.

Well, when Regret gets a good peek at the horse, he sees right away it is not just a horse that Frying Pan Joe steals. It is Gallant Godfrey, one of the greatest handicap horses in this country, and the winner of some of the biggest stakes of the year, and Gallant Godfrey is worth twenty-five G's if he is worth a dime, and when Regret speaks of this, Frying Pan Joe says it is undoubtedly the most valuable single piece of horseflesh he ever steals, although he claims that once when he is stealing horses along the Animas River in Colorado, he steals two hundred horses in one batch that will probably total up more.

They take Gallant Godfrey over to Eleventh Avenue, where Princess O'Hara keeps Goldberg in a little stable that is nothing but a shack, and they leave Gallant Godfrey there alongside old Goldberg, who is groaning and carrying on in a most distressing manner, and then Regret and Big Nig shake hands with Frying Pan Joe and wish him good-bye.

So there is Princess O'Hara with Gallant Godfrey hitched up to her victoria the next night, and the chances are it is a good thing for her that Gallant Godfrey is a nice tame old dromedary, and does not mind pulling a victoria at all, and in fact he seems to enjoy it, although he likes to go along at a gallop instead of a slow trot, such as the old skates that pull these victorias usually employ.

And while Princess O'Hara understands that this is a borrowed horse, and is to be returned when Goldberg is well, nobody tells her just what kind of a horse it is, and when she gets Goldberg's harness on Gallant Godfrey his appearance changes so that not even the official starter is apt to recognize him if they come face to face.

Well, I hear afterwards that there is great consternation around Empire when it comes out that Gallant Godfrey is missing, but they keep it quiet as they figure he just wanders away, and as he is engaged in certain large stakes later on, they do not wish it made public that he is absent from his stall. So they have guys looking for him high and low, but of course nobody thinks to look for a high-class race-horse pulling a victoria.

When Princess O'Hara drives the new horse up in front of Mindy's, many citizens are anxious to take the first ride with her, but before anybody has time to think, who steps up but Ambrose Hammer, the newspaper scribe, who has a foreign-looking young guy with him, and Ambrose states as follows:

"Get in, Georges," Ambrose says. "We will take a spin through the Park and wind up at the Casino."

So away they go, and from this moment begins one of the greatest romances ever heard of on Broadway, for it seems that the foreign-looking young guy that Ambrose Hammer calls Georges takes a wonderful liking to Princess O'Hara right from taw, and the following night I learn from Officer Corbett, the motor-cycle cop who is on duty in Central Park, that they pass him with Ambrose Hammer in the back seat of the victoria, but with Georges riding on the driver's seat with Princess O'Hara.

And moreover, Officer Corbett states that Georges is wearing King O'Hara's old stove-pipe hat, while Princess O'Hara is singing "Kathleen Mavourneen" in her loud contralto in such a way as nobody ever hears her sing before.

In fact, this is the way they are riding along a little later in the week, and when it is coming on four bells in the morning. But this time, Princess O'Hara is driving north on the street that is called Central Park West because it borders the Park on the west, and the reason she is taking this street is because she comes up Broadway through Columbus Circle onto Central Park West, figuring to cross over to Fifth Avenue by way of the transverse at Sixty-sixth Street, a transverse being nothing but a roadway cut through the Park from Central Park West to the Avenue.

There are several of these transverses, and why they do not call them roads, or streets, instead of transverses, I do not know, except maybe it is because transverse sounds more fancy. These transverses are really like tunnels without any roofs, especially the one at Sixty-sixth Street, which is maybe a quarter of a mile long and plenty wide enough for automobiles to pass each other going in different directions, but once a car is in the transverse there is no way it can get out except at one end or the other. There is no such thing as turning off to one side anywhere between Central Park West and the Avenue, because the Sixty-sixth Street transverse is a deep cut with high sides, or walls.

Well, just as Princess O'Hara starts to turn Gallant Godfrey into the transverse, with the foreign-looking young guy beside her on the driver's seat, and Ambrose Hammer back in the cushions, and half-asleep, and by no means interested in the conversation that is going on in front of him, a big beer truck comes rolling along Central Park West, going very slow.

And of course there is nothing unusual in the spectacle of a beer truck at this time, as beer is now very legal, but just as this beer truck rolls alongside Princess O'Hara's victoria, a little car with two guys in it pops out of nowhere, and pulls up to the truck, and one of the guys requests the jockey of the beer truck to stop.

Of course Princess O'Hara and her passengers do not know at the time that this is one of the very first cases of heisting a truck-load of legal beer that comes off in this country, and that they are really seeing history made, although it all comes out later. It also comes out later that one of the parties committing this historical deed is nobody but a guy by the name of Fats O'Rourke, who is considered one of the leading characters over on the West Side, and the reason he is heisting this truckload of beer is by no means a plot against the brewing industry, but because it is worth several

C's, and Fats O'Rourke can use several C's very nicely at the moment.

It comes out that the guy with him is a guy by the name of Joe the Blow Fly, but he is really only a fink in every respect, a fink being such a guy as is extra nothing, and many citizens are somewhat surprised when they learn that Fats O'Rourke is going around with finks.

Well, if the jockey of the beer truck does as he is requested without any shilly-shallying, all that will happen is he will lose his beer. But instead of stopping the truck, the jockey tries to keep right on going, and then all of a sudden Fats O'Rourke becomes very impatient and outs with the old thing, and gives it to the jockey, as follows: Bang, bang.

By the time Fats O'Rourke lets go, The Fly is up on the seat of the truck and grabs the wheel just as the jockey turns it loose and falls back on the seat, and Fats O'Rourke follows The Fly up there, and then Fats O'Rourke seems to see Princess O'Hara and her customers for the first time, and he also realizes that these parties witness what comes off with the jockey, although otherwise Central Park West is quite deserted, and if anybody in the apartment houses along there hears the shots the chances are they figure it must be nothing but an automobile backfiring.

And in fact The Fly has the beer truck backfiring quite some at this moment as Fats O'Rourke sees Princess O'Hara and her customers, and only somebody who happens to observe the flashes from Fats O'Rourke's duke, or who hears the same buzzes that Princess O'Hara, and the foreign-looking young guy, and Ambrose Hammer hear, can tell that Fats is emptying that old thing at the victoria.

The chances are Fats O'Rourke will not mind anybody witnessing him heisting a legal beer truck, and in fact he is apt to welcome their testimony in later years when somebody starts disputing his claim to being the first guy to heist such a truck, but naturally Fats does not wish to have spectators spying on him when he is giving it to somebody, as very often spectators are apt to go around gossiping about these matters, and cause dissension.

So he takes four cracks at Princess O'Hara and her customers, and it is a good thing for them that Fats O'Rourke is never much of a shot. Furthermore, it is a good thing for them that he is now out of ammunition because of course Fats O'Rourke never figures that it is going to take more than a few shots to heist a legal beer truck, and afterwards there is little criticism of Fats' judgment, as everybody realizes that it is a most unprecedented situation.

Well, by now, Princess O'Hara is swinging Gallant Godfrey into the transverse, because she comes to the conclusion that it is no time to be loitering in this neighborhood, and she is no sooner inside the walls of the transverse than she knows this is the very worst place she can go, as she hears a rumble behind her, and when she peeks back over her shoulder she sees the beer truck coming lickity-split, and what is more, it is coming right at the victoria.

Now Princess O'Hara is no chump, and she can see that the truck is not coming right at the victoria by accident, when there is plenty of room for it to pass, so she figures that the best thing to do is not to let the truck catch up with the victoria if she can help it, and this is very sound reasoning indeed, because Joe the Blow Fly afterwards says that what Fats O'Rourke requests him to do is to sideswipe the victoria with the truck and squash it against the side of the transverse, Fats O'Rourke's idea being to keep Princess O'Hara and her customers from speaking of the transaction with the jockey of the truck.

Well, Princess O'Hara stands up in her seat, and tells Gallant Godfrey to giddap, and Gallant Godfrey is giddapping very nicely indeed when she looks back and sees the truck right at the rear wheel of the victoria, and coming like a bat out of what-is-this. So she grabs up her whip and gives Gallant Godfrey a good smack across the vestibule, and it seems that if there is one thing Gallant Godfrey hates and despises it is a whip. He makes a lunge that pulls the victoria clear of the truck, just as The Fly drives it up alongside the victoria and is bearing over for the squash, with Fats O'Rourke yelling directions at him, and from this lunge, Gallant Godfrey settles down to running.

While this is going on, the foreign-looking young guy is standing up on the driver's seat of the victoria beside Princess O'Hara, whooping and laughing, as he probably figures it is just a nice, friendly little race. But Princess O'Hara is not laughing, and neither is Ambrose Hammer.

Now inside the next hundred yards, Joe the Blow Fly gets the truck up alongside again, and this time it looks as if they are gone goslings when Princess O'Hara gives Gallant Godfrey another smack with the whip, and the chances are Gallant Godfrey comes to the conclusion that Westrope is working on him in a stretch run, as he turns on such a burst of speed that he almost runs right out of his collar and leaves the truck behind by anyway a length and a half.

And it seems that just as Gallant Godfrey turns on, Fats O'Rourke personally reaches over and gives the steering-wheel of the beer truck a good twist, figuring that the squashing is now a cinch, and the next thing anybody knows the truck goes smack-dab into the wall with a loud kuh-boom, and turns over all mussed up, with beer kegs bouncing around very briskly, and some of them popping open and letting the legal beer leak out.

In the meantime, Gallant Godfrey goes tearing out of the trans-verse onto Fifth Avenue and across Fifth Avenue so fast that the wheels of Princess O'Hara's victoria are scarcely touching the ground, and a copper who sees him go past afterwards states that what Gallant Godfrey is really doing is flying, but personally I al-ways consider this an exaggeration.

Anyway, Gallant Godfrey goes two blocks beyond Fifth Avenue before Princess O'Hara can get him to whoa-up, and there is still plenty of run in him, although by this time Princess O'Hara is plumb worn out, and Ambrose Hammer is greatly fatigued, and only the foreign-looking young guy seems to find any enjoyment in the experience, although he is not so jolly when he learns that the coppers take two dead guys out of the truck, along with Joe the Blow Fly, who lives just long enough to relate the story.

Fats O'Rourke is smothered to death under a stack of kegs of legal beer, which many citizens consider a most gruesome finish indeed, but what kills the jockey of the truck is the bullet in his heart, so the smash-up of the truck does not make any difference to him one way or the other, although of course if he lives, the chances are his employers will take him to task for losing the beer.

I learn most of the details of the race through the transverse from Ambrose Hammer, and I also learn from Ambrose that Prin-cess O'Hara and the foreign-looking young guy are suffering from the worst case of love that Ambrose ever witnesses, and Ambrose Hammer witnesses some tough cases of love in his day. Further-more, Ambrose says they are not only in love but are planning to get themselves married up as quickly as possible.

"Well," I say, "I hope and trust this young guy is all right, be-cause Princess O'Hara deserves the best. In fact," I say, "a Prince is not too good for her."

"Well," Ambrose says, "a Prince is exactly what she is getting.

I do not suppose you can borrow much on it in a hock shop in these times, but the title of Prince Georges Latour is highly respected over in France, although," he says, "I understand the proud old family does not have as many potatoes as formerly. But he is a nice young guy, at that, and anyway, what is money compared to love?"

Naturally, I do not know the answer to this, and neither does Ambrose Hammer, but the very same day I run into Princess O'Hara and the foreign-looking young guy on Broadway, and I can see the old love light shining so brightly in their eyes that I get to thinking that maybe money does not mean so much alongside of love, at that, although personally, I will take a chance on the money.

I stop and say hello to Princess O'Hara, and ask her how things are going with her, and she says they are going first class.

"In fact," she says, "it is a beautiful world in every respect. Georges and I are going to be married in a few days now, and are going to Paris, France, to live. At first I fear we will have a long wait, because of course I cannot leave my mamma and the rest of the children unprovided for. But," Princess O'Hara says, "what happens but Regret sells my horse to Last Card Louie for a thousand dollars, so everything is all right.

"Of course," Princess O'Hara says, "buying my horse is nothing but an act of great kindness on the part of Last Card Louie as my horse is by no means worth a thousand dollars, but I suppose Louie does it out of his old friendship for my papa. I must confess," she says, "that I have a wrong impression of Louie, because the last time I see him I slap his face thinking he is trying to get fresh with me. Now I realize it is probably only his paternal interest in me, and I am very sorry."

Well, I know Last Card Louie is such a guy as will give you a glass of milk for a nice cow, and I am greatly alarmed by Princess O'Hara's statement about the sale, for I figure Regret must sell Gallant Godfrey, not remembering that he is only a borrowed horse and must be returned in good order, so I look Regret up at once and mention my fears, but he laughs and speaks to me as follows:

"Do not worry," he says. "What happens is that Last Card Louie comes around last night and hands me a G note and says to me like this: 'Buy Princess O'Hara's horse off of her for me, and you can keep all under this G that you get it for.'

"Well," Regret says, "of course I know that old Last Card is thinking of Gallant Godfrey, and forgets that the only horse that Princess O'Hara really owns is Goldberg, and the reason he is thinking of Gallant Godfrey is because he learns last night about us borrowing the horse for her. But as long as Last Card Louie refers just to her horse, and does not mention any names, I do not see that it is up to me to go into any details with him. So I get him a bill of sale for Princess O'Hara's horse, and I am waiting ever since to hear what he says when he goes to collect the horse and finds it is nothing but old Goldberg."

"Well," I say to Regret, "it all sounds most confusing to me, because what good is Gallant Godfrey to Last Card Louie when he is only a borrowed horse, and is apt to be recognized anywhere except when he is hitched to a victoria? And I am sure Last Card Louie is not going into the victoria business."

"Oh," Regret says, "this is easy. Last Card Louie undoubtedly sees the same ad in the paper that the rest of us see, offering a reward of ten G's for the return of Gallant Godfrey and no questions asked, but of course Last Card Louie has no way of knowing that Big Nig is taking Gallant Godfrey home long before Louie comes around and buys Princess O'Hara's horse."

Well, this is about all there is to tell, except that a couple of weeks later I hear that Ambrose Hammer is in the Clinic Hospital very ill, and I drop around to see him because I am very fond of Ambrose Hammer no matter if he is a newspaper scribe.

He is sitting up in bed in a nice private room, and he has on blue silk pajamas with his monogram embroidered over his heart, and there is a large vase of roses on the table beside him, and a nice-looking nurse holding his hand, and I can see that Ambrose Hammer is not doing bad, although he smiles very feebly at me when I come in.

Naturally I ask Ambrose Hammer what ails him, and after he takes a sip of water out of a glass that the nice-looking nurse holds up to his lips, Ambrose sighs, and in a very weak voice he states as follows:

"Well," Ambrose says, "one night I get to thinking about what will happen to us in the transverse if we have old Goldberg hitched to Princess O'Hara's victoria instead of one of the fastest race horses in the world, and I am so overcome by the thought that I have what my doctor claims is a nervous breakdown. I feel terrible," Ambrose says.

A NICE PRICE

One hot morning in June, I am standing in front of the Mohican Hotel in the city of New London, Conn., and the reason I am in such a surprising spot is something that makes a long story quite a bit longer.

It goes back to a couple of nights before, when I am walking along Broadway and I run into Sam the Gonoph, the ticket speculator, who seems to have a very sour expression on his puss, although, even when Sam the Gonoph is looking good-natured his puss is nothing much to see.

Now Sam the Gonoph is an old friend of mine, and in fact I sometimes join up with him and his crew to hustle duckets to one thing and another when he is short-handed, so I give him a big hello, and he stops and the following conversation ensues:

"How is it going with you, Sam?" I say to Sam the Gonoph, although of course I do not really care two pins how it is going with him. "You look as if you are all sored up at somebody."

"No," Sam says, "I am not sored up at anybody. I am never sored up at anybody in my life, except maybe Society Max, and of course everybody knows I have a perfect right to be sored up at Society Max, because look at what he does to me."

Well, what Sam the Gonoph says is very true, because what Society Max does to Sam is to steal Sam's fiancée off of him a couple of years before this, and marry her before Sam has time to think. This fiancée is a doll by the name of Sonia, who resides up in the Bronx, and Sam the Gonoph is engaged to her since the year of the Dempsey-Firpo fight, and is contemplating marrying her almost anytime, when Society Max bobs up.

Many citizens afterwards claim that Max does Sam the Gonoph a rare favor, because Sonia is commencing to fat up in spots, but it breaks Sam's heart just the same, especially when he learns that

Sonia's papa gives the happy young couple twenty big G's in old-fashioned folding money that nobody ever knows the papa has, and Sam figures that Max must get an inside tip on this dough and that he takes an unfair advantage of the situation.

"But," Sam the Gonoph says, "I am not looking sored up at this time because of Society Max, although of course it is well known to one and all that I am under oath to knock his ears down the first time I catch up with him. As a matter of fact, I do not as much as think of Society Max for a year or more, although I hear he deserts poor Sonia out in Cincinnati after spending her dough and leading her a dog's life, including a few off-hand pastings—not that I am claiming Sonia may not need a pasting now and them.

"What I am looking sored up about," Sam says, "is because I must get up into Connecticut to-morrow to a spot that is called New London to dispose of a line of merchandise."

"Why, Sam," I say, "what can be doing in such a place?"

"Oh," Sam says, "a large boat race is coming up between the Harvards and the Yales. It comes up at New London every year, and is quite an interesting event from what I read in the papers about it, but the reason I am sored up about going to-morrow is because I wish to spend the weekend on my farm in New Jersey to see how my onions are doing. Since I buy this farm in New Jersey, I can scarcely wait to get over there on weekends to watch my onions grow.

"But," Sam the Gonoph says, "this is an extra large boat race this year, and I am in possession of many choice duckets, and am sure to make plenty of black ink for myself, and business before pleasure is what I always say. By the way," Sam says, "do you ever see a boat race?"

Well, I say that the only boat races I ever see are those that come off around the race tracks, such a race being a race that is all fixed up in advance, and some of them are pretty raw, if you ask me, and I am by no means in favor of things of this kind unless I am in, but Sam the Gonoph says these races are by no manner of means the same thing as the boat races he is talking about.

"I never personally witness one myself," Sam says, "but the way I understand it is a number of the Harvards and the Yales, without any clothes on, get in row boats and row, and row, and row until their tongues hang out, and they are all half-dead. Why they tucker themselves out in this fashion I do not know and,"

Sam says, "I am too old to start trying to find out why these college guys do a lot of things to themselves.

"But," Sam says, "boat racing is a wonderful sport, and I always have a nice trade at New London, Conn., and if you wish to accompany me and Benny South Street and Liverlips and maybe collect a few bobs for yourself, you are as welcome as the flowers in May."

So there I am in front of the Mohican Hotel in New London, Conn., with Sam the Gonoph and Benny South Street and old Liverlips, who are Sam the Gonoph's best hustlers, and all around and about is a very interesting sight, to be sure, as large numbers of the Harvards and the Yales are passing in and out of the hotel and walking up and down and back and forth, and making very merry, one way and another.

Well, after we are hustling our duckets for a couple of hours and it is coming on noon, Benny South Street goes into the hotel lobby to buy some cigarettes, and by and by he comes out looking somewhat excited, and states as follows:

"Say," Benny says, "there's a guy inside with his hands full of money offering to lay three to one that the Yales win the boat race. He says he has fifteen G's cash with him to wager at the price stated."

"Are there any takers?" Sam the Gonoph asks.

"No, not many," Benny says. "From all I hear, the Yales figure. In fact, all the handicappers I speak with have them on top, so the Harvards do not care for any part of the guy's play. But," Benny says, "there he is, offering three to one."

"Three to one?" Sam the Gonoph says, as if he is mentioning these terms to himself. "Three to one, eh? It is a nice price."

"It is a lovely price," old Liverlips puts in.

Well, Sam the Gonoph stands there as if he is thinking, and Benny South Street seems to be thinking, too, and even old Liverlips seems to be thinking, and by and by I even find myself thinking, and finally Sam the Gonoph says like this:

"I do not know anything about boat races," Sam says, "and the Yales may figure as you say, but nothing between human beings is one to three. In fact," Sam the Gonoph says, "I long ago came to the conclusion that all life is six to five against. And anyway," he says, "how can anybody let such odds as these get away from them? I think I will take a small nibble at this proposition. What about you, Benny?"

"I will also nibble," Benny South Street says. "I will never forgive myself in this world if I let this inviting offer go and it turns out the Harvards win."

Well, we all go into the hotel lobby, and there is a big, gray-haired guy in a white cap and white pants standing in the center of a bunch of other guys, and he has money in both hands. I hear somebody say he is one of the real old-time Yales, and he is speaking in a loud voice as follows:

"Why," he says, "what is the matter, Harvards, are you cowards, or are you just broke? If you are broke, I will take your markers and let you pay me on the installment plan. But," he says, "bet me. This is all, just bet me."

Personally, I have a notion to let on I am one of the Harvards and slip the guy a nice marker, but I am afraid he may request some identification and I do not have anything on me to prove I am a college guy, so I stand back and watch Sam the Gonoph shove his way through the crowd with a couple of C notes in his hand, and Benny South Street is right behind him.

"I will take a small portion of the Harvards at the market," Sam the Gonoph says, as he offers the gray-haired guy his dough.

"Thank you, my friend," the guy says, "but I do not think we are acquainted," he says. "Who do you wish to hold the stakes?"

"You hold them yourself, Mr. Campbell," Sam the Gonoph says. "I know you, although you do not know me, and I will gladly trust you with my dough. Furthermore, my friend here, who also wishes a portion of the Harvards, will trust you."

So the gray-haired guy says that both Sam the Gonoph and Benny South Street are on at three to one, and thanks again to them, at that, and when we get outside, Sam explains that he recognizes the guy as nobody but Mr. Hammond Campbell, who is a very important party in every respect and who has more dough than Uncle Sam has bad debts. In fact, Sam the Gonoph seems to feel that he is greatly honored in getting to bet with Mr. Hammond Campbell, although from the way Mr. Campbell takes their dough, I figure he thinks that the pleasure is all his.

Well, we go on hustling our duckets but neither Sam the Gonoph nor Benny South Street seem to have much heart in their work, and every now and then I see one or the other slip into the hotel lobby, and it comes out that they are still nibbling at the three to one, and finally I slip in myself and take a little teensy nibble for twenty bobs myself, because the way I look at it, anything that is good enough for Sam the Gonoph is good enough for me.

Now Sam the Gonoph always carries quite a little ready money on his body, and nobody will deny that Sam will send it along if he likes a proposition, and by and by he is down for a G on the Harvards, and Benny South Street has four C's going for him, and there is my double saw, and even old Liverlips weakens and goes for a pound note, and ordinarily Liverlips will not bet a pound that he is alive.

Furthermore, Mr. Hammond Campbell says we are about the only guys in town that do bet him and that we ought to get degrees off the Harvards for our loyalty to them, but of course what we are really loyal to is the three to one. Finally, Mr. Campbell says he has to go to lunch, but that if we feel like betting him any more we can find him on board his yacht, the *Hibiscus*, out in the river, and maybe he will boost the price up to three-and-a-half to one.

So I go into the hotel and get a little lunch myself, and when I am coming out a nice-looking young doll who is walking along in front of me accidentally drops her poke from under her arm, and keeps right on walking. Naturally, I pick it up, but several parties who are standing around in the lobby see me do it, so I call to the young doll and when she turns around I hand her the poke, and she is very grateful to me, to be sure. In fact, she thanks me several times, though once will do, and then all of a sudden she says to me like this:

"Pardon me," the young doll says, "but are you not one of the gentlemen I see wagering with my papa that the Harvards will win the boat race?"

"Yes," I say, "and what is more, we may keep on wagering him. In fact," I say, "a friend of mine by the name of Sam the Gonoph is just now contemplating wiring home for another G to accept your papa's generous offer of three-and-a-half to one."

"Oh," the young doll says, "do not do it. You are only throwing your money away. The Harvards have no chance whatever of winning the boat race. My papa is never wrong on boat races. I only wish he is to-day."

And with this she sits down in a chair in the lobby and begins crying boo-hoo until her mascara is running down her cheeks, and naturally I am greatly embarrassed by this situation, as I am afraid somebody may come along and think maybe she is my step-child and that I am just after chastising her.

"You see," the young doll says, "a boy I like a very, very great deal belongs to the Harvards' crew and when I tell him a couple of weeks ago that my papa says the Yales are bound to win, he grows very angry and says what does my papa know about it, and who is my papa but an old money-bags, anyway, and to the dickens with my papa. Then when I tell him my papa always knows about these things, Quentin grows still angrier, and we quarrel and he says all right, if the Harvards lose he will never, never, never see me again as long as he lives. And Quentin is a very obstinate and unreasonable boy, and life is very sad for me."

Well, who comes along about now but Sam the Gonoph and naturally he is somewhat surprised by the scene that is presented to his eyes, so I explain to him, and Sam is greatly touched and very sympathetic, for one thing about Sam is he is very tender-hearted when it comes to dolls who are in trouble.

"Well," Sam says, "I will certainly be greatly pleased to see the Harvards win the boat race myself, and in fact," he says, "I am just making a few cautious inquiries around here and there to see if there is any chance of stiffening a couple of the Yales, so we can have a little help in the race.

"But," Sam says, "one great trouble with these college propositions is they are always leveling, though I cannot see why it is necessary. Anyway," he says, "it looks as if we cannot hope to do any business with the Yales, but you dry your eyes, little miss, and maybe old Sam can think up something."

At this the young doll stops her bawling and I am very glad of it, as there is nothing I loathe and despise so much as a doll bawling, and she looks up at Sam with a wet smile and says to him like this:

"Oh, do you really think you can help the Harvards win the boat race?"

Well, naturally Sam the Gonoph is not in a position to make any promises on this point, but he is such a guy as will tell a doll in distress anything whatever if he thinks it will give her a little pleasure for a minute, so he replies as follows:

"Why, who knows?" Sam says. "Who knows, to be sure? But anyway do not bawl anymore, and old Sam will give this matter further consideration."

And with this Sam pats the young doll on the back so hard he pats all the breath out of her and she cannot bawl anymore even if she wishes to, and she gets up and goes away looking very happy, but before she goes she says:

"Well, I hear somebody say that from the way you gentlemen are betting on the Harvards you must know something and," she says, "I am very glad I have the courage to talk to you. It will be a wonderful favor to Quentin and me if you help the Harvards win, even though it costs my papa money. Love is more than gold," she says.

Personally, I consider it very wrong for Sam the Gonoph to be holding out hope to a young doll that he is unable to guarantee, but Sam says he does not really promise anything and that he always figures if he can bring a little joy into any life, no matter how, he is doing a wonderful deed, and that anyway we will never see the young doll again, and furthermore, what of it?

Well, I cannot think what of it just off-hand, and anyway I am glad to be rid of the young doll, so we go back to disposing of the duckets we have left.

Now the large boat race between the Harvards and the Yales takes place in the early evening, and when it comes on time for the race one and all seem to be headed in the direction of the river, including all the young guys with the stir haircuts, and many beautiful young dolls wearing blue and red flowers, and old guys in sports pants and flat straw hats, and old dolls who walk as if their feet hurt them, and the chances are they do, at that.

Well, nothing will do Sam the Gonoph but we must see the boat race, too, so we go down to the railroad station to take the very train for which we are hustling duckets all day, but by the time we get there the race train is pulling out, so Benny South Street says the next best thing for us to do is to go down to the dock and hire a boat to take us out on the river.

But when we get to the dock, it seems that all the boats around are hired and are already out on the river, but there is an old pappy guy with a chin whisker sitting in a rickety-looking little motor-boat at the dock, and this old guy says he will take us out where we can get a good peek at the race for a buck apiece.

Personally, I do not care for the looks of the boat, and neither does Benny South Street nor old Liverlips, but Sam the Gonoph is so anxious to see the race that finally we all get into the boat and the old guy heads her out into the river, which seems to be filled with all kinds of boats decorated with flags and one thing and another, and with guys and dolls walking back and forth on these boats.

Anybody must admit that it is quite a sight, and I am commencing to be glad I am present, especially when Benny South Street tells me that these guys and dolls on the boats are very fine people and worth plenty of money. Furthermore, Benny South Street points out many big white boats that he says are private yachts, and he tells me that what it costs to keep up these private yachts is a sin and a shame when you start to figure out the number of people in the world who are looking for breakfast money. But then Benny South Street is always talking of things of this kind, and sometimes I think maybe he is a dynamiter at heart.

We go putt-putting along under a big bridge and into a sort of lane of boats, and Benny South Street says we are not at the finish line of the large boat race and that the Harvards and the Yales row down this lane from away up the river, and that it is here that they have their tongues hanging out and are nearly all half-dead.

Well, it seems that we are in the way, because guys start yelling at us from different boats and shaking their fists at us, and it is a good thing for some of them that they are not close enough for us to get a pop at them, but the old pappy guy keeps the motor-boat putt-putting and sliding in and out among the boats until we come to a spot that he says is about a hundred years above the finish and a great spot to see the best part of the race.

We are slipping alongside of a big white boat that Benny South Street says is a private yacht and that has a little set of stair steps running down one side almost into the water, when all of a sudden Sam the Gonoph notices his feet are wet, and he looks down and sees that the motor-boat is half-full of water and furthermore that the boat is commencing to sink.

Now this is quite a predicament, and naturally Sam the Gonoph lets out a slight beef and wishes to know what kind of accommodations we are paying for, anyway, and then the old pappy guy notices the water and the sinking, and he seems somewhat put out about the matter, especially as the water is getting up around his chin whiskers.

So he steers the boat up against the stair steps on the yacht and all of us, including the old pappy guy, climb out on to the stairs just as the motor-boat gives a last snort and sinks from sight. The last I see of the motor-boat is the hind end sticking up in the air a second before it disappears, and I remember the name that is painted on the hind end. The name is *Baby Mine*.

Well, Sam the Gonoph leads the way up the stairs to the deck of the yacht, and who meets us at the head of the stairs but Mr. Hammond Campbell in person, and who is right behind him but the young doll I am talking with in the hotel lobby, and at first Mr. Campbell thinks that we come out to his yacht to pick up a little of his three-and-a-half to one, and he is greatly disappointed when he learns that such is by no means our purpose and that we are merely the victims of disaster.

As for the young doll, whose name turns out to be Clarice, she gazes at Sam the Gonoph and me with her eyes full of questions, but we do not get a chance to talk to her as things begin occurring at once.

There are quite a number of guys and dolls on the yacht, and it is a very gay scene to be sure, as they walk around laughing and chatting, when all of a sudden I see Sam the Gonoph staring at a guy and doll who are leaning over the rail talking very earnestly and paying no attention to what is going on around and about them.

The guy is a tall, dark-complected young guy with a little moustache, and he is wearing white flannel pants and a blue coat with brass buttons, and white shoes, and he is a very foreign-looking guy to be sure. The doll is not such a young doll, being maybe around middle age, giving her a few points the best of it, but she is a fine-looking doll, at that, especially if you like dolls with gray hair, which personally I am not so much in favor of.

I am close enough to Sam the Gonoph to hear him breathing heavily as he stares at this guy and doll, and finally the dark-complected young guy looks up and sees Sam and at the same instant Sam starts for him, and as Sam starts the young guy turns and takes to running in the other direction from Sam along the deck, but before he takes to running I can see that it is nobody but Society Max.

Naturally, I am somewhat surprised at seeing Society Max at a boat race between the Harvards and the Yales, because I never figure him such a guy as will be interested in matters of this kind, although I remember that Society Max is once a life guard at Coney Island, and in fact it is at Coney Island that Sonia gets her first peek at his shape and is lost forever to Sam the Gonoph, so I get to thinking that maybe Society Max is fond of all aquatic events.

Now of course the spectacle of Sam the Gonoph pursuing Society Max along the deck is quite surprising to one and all, except Benny South Street and old Liverlips and myself, who are aware of the reason, and Mr. Hammond Campbell wishes to know what kind of game they are playing, especially after they round the deck twice, with Society Max showing much foot, but none of us feel called on to explain. Finally the other guys and dolls on the yacht enter into the spirit of the chase, even though they do not know what it is all about, and they shout encouragement to both Sam the Gonoph and Society Max, although Max is really the favorite.

There is no doubt but what Society Max is easily best in a sprint, especially as Sam the Gonoph's pants legs are wet from the sinking motor-boat and he is carrying extra weight, but Sam is a wonderful doer over a route, and on the third trip around the deck, anybody can see that he is cutting down Max's lead.

Well, every time they pass the gray-haired doll that Society Max is talking to when we come on the yacht she asks what is the matter, Max, and where are you going, Max, and other questions that seem trivial at such a time, but Max never has an opportunity to answer, as he has to save all his breath to keep ahead of Sam the Gonoph, and in fact Sam the Gonoph stops talking, too, and just keeps plugging along with a very determined expression on his puss.

Well, now all the whistles on the boats in the river around us start blowing, and it seems this is because the large boat race between the Harvards and the Yales is now approaching the finish, and one and all on our yacht rush to the side of the yacht to see it, forgetting about everything else, and the side they rush to is the same side the stair steps are on.

But I am too much interested in Sam the Gonoph's pursuit of Society Max to pay any attention to the boat race, and as they come around the deck the fifth or sixth time, I can see that Sam will have Max in the next few jumps, when all of a sudden Society Max runs right down the stairs and dives off into the river, and he does it so fast that nobody seems to notice him except Sam the Gonoph and me and the gray-haired doll, and I am the only one that notices her fall in a big faint on the deck as Max dives.

Naturally, this is not a time to be bothering with fainting dolls, so Sam the Gonoph and me run to the side of the yacht and watch the water to see where Society Max comes up, but he does not appear at once, and I remember hearing he is a wonderful diver when he is a life guard, so I figure he is going to keep under water until he is pretty sure he is too far away from Sam the Gonoph to hit him with anything, such as maybe a slug from a Betsy.

Of course Sam the Gonoph does not happen to have a Betsy on him, but Society Max can scarcely be expected to know this, because the chances are he remembers that Sam often has such an article in his pants pocket when he is around New York, so I suppose Society Max plays it as safe as possible.

Anyway, we do not see hide or hair of him and in the meantime the excitement over the large boat race between the Harvards and the Yales is now so terrific that I forget Society Max and try to get a peek at it.

But all I remember is seeing the young doll, Clarice, kissing Sam the Gonoph smack-dab on his homely puss, and jumping up and down in considerable glee, and stating that she knows all along that Sam will figure out some way for the Harvards to win, although she does not know yet how he does it, and hearing Mr. Hammond Campbell using language even worse than Sam the Gonoph employs when he is pursuing Society Max, and saying he never sees such a this-and-that boat race in all his born days.

Then I get to thinking about the gray-haired doll, and I go over and pick her up and she is still about two-thirds out and is saying to herself, as follows:

"Max, oh, my dear, dear Max."

Well, by and by Mr. Hammond Campbell takes Sam the Gonoph into a room on the yacht and pays him what is coming to all of us on the race, and then he takes to asking about Society Max, and when Sam the Gonoph explains how Max is a terrible fink and what he does to Sonia and all, Mr. Hammond Campbell hands Sam five large G's extra, and states to him as follows:

"This," he says, "is for preventing my sister, Emma, from making a fool of herself. She picks this Max up somewhere in Europe and he puts himself away with her as a Russian nobleman, and she is going to marry him next week, although from what you tell me it will be bigamy on his part. By the way," Mr. Hammond

Campbell says, "not that it makes any difference, but I wonder whatever becomes of the guy?"

I am wondering this somewhat myself, not that I really care what becomes of Society Max, but I do not find out until later in the evening when I am at the Western Union office in New London, Conn., sending a telegram for Sam the Gonoph to the guy who runs his farm in New Jersey telling the guy to be sure and watch the onions, and I hear a newspaper scribe talking about the large boat race.

"Yes," the newspaper scribe says, "the Yales are leading by a boat length up to the last hundred yards and going easy, and they seem to be an absolute cinch to win, when No. 6 man in their boat hits something in the water and breaks his oar, throwing the rest of the crew out of kilter long enough for the Harvards to slip past and win. It is the most terrible upset of the dope in history," he says.

"Now," the scribe says, "of course a broken oar is not unheard of in a boat race, but what No. 6 says he hits is a guy's head which pops out of the water all of a sudden right alongside the Yales' boat, and which disappears again as the oar hits it.

"Personally," the scribe says, "I will say No. 6 is seeing things but for the fact that a Coast Guard boat which is laying away down the river below the finish just reports that it picks up a guy out of the river who seems to be alive and all right except he has a lump on his noggin a foot high."

I do not see Sam the Gonoph again until it comes on fall, when I run into him in Mindy's restaurant on Broadway, and Sam says to me like this:

"Say," he says, "do you remember what a hit I make with the little doll because she thinks I have something to do with the Harvards winning the large boat race? Well," Sam the Gonoph says, "I just get a note from her asking me if I can do anything about a football game that the Harvards have coming up with the Dartmouths next month."

SENSE OF HUMOR

One night I am standing in front of Mindy's restaurant on Broadway, thinking of practically nothing whatever, when all of a sudden I feel a very terrible pain in my left foot.

In fact, this pain is so very terrible that it causes me to leap up and down like a bullfrog, and to let out loud cries of agony, and to speak some very profane language, which is by no means my custom, although of course I recognize the pain as coming from a hot foot, because I often experience this pain before.

Furthermore, I know Joe the Joker must be in the neighborhood, as Joe the Joker has the most wonderful sense of humor of anybody in this town, and is always around giving people the hot foot, and gives it to me more times that I can remember. In fact, I hear Joe the Joker invents the hot foot, and it finally becomes a very popular idea all over the country.

The way you give a hot foot is to sneak up behind some guy who is standing around thinking of not much, and stick a paper match in his shoe between the sole and the upper along about where his little toe ought to be, and then light the match. By and by the guy will feel a terrible pain in his foot, and will start stamping around, and hollering, and carrying on generally, and it is always a most comical sight and a wonderful laugh to one and all to see him suffer.

No one in the world can give a hot foot as good as Joe the Joker, because it takes a guy who can sneak up very quiet on the guy who is to get the hot foot, and Joe can sneak up so quiet many guys on Broadway are willing to lay you odds that he can give a mouse a hot foot if you can find a mouse that wears shoes. Furthermore, Joe the Joker can take plenty of care of himself in case the guy who gets the hot foot feels like taking the matter up, which sometimes happens, especially with guys who get their shoes made to order at forty bobs per copy and do not care to have holes burned in these shoes.

But Joe does not care what kind of shoes the guys are wearing when he feels like giving out hot foots, and furthermore, he does not care who the guys are, although many citizens think he makes a mistake the time he gives a hot foot to Frankie Ferocious. In fact, many citizens are greatly horrified by this action, and go around saying no good will come of it.

This Frankie Ferocious comes from over in Brooklyn, where he is considered a rising citizen in many respects, and by no means a guy to give hot foots to, especially as Frankie Ferocious has no sense of humor whatever. In fact, he is always very solemn, and nobody ever sees him laugh, and he certainly does not laugh when Joe the Joker gives him a hot foot one day on Broadway when Frankie Ferocious is standing talking over a business matter with some guys from the Bronx.

He only scowls at Joe, and says something in Italian, and while I do not understand Italian, it sounds so unpleasant that I guarantee I will leave town inside of the next two hours if he says it to me.

Of course Frankie Ferocious's name is not really Ferocious, but something in Italian like Feroccio, and I hear he originally comes from Sicily, although he lives in Brooklyn for quite some years, and from a modest beginning he builds himself up until he is a very large operator in merchandise of one kind and another, especially alcohol. He is a big guy of maybe thirty-odd, and he has hair blacker than a yard up a chimney, and black eyes, and black eyebrows, and a slow way of looking at people.

Nobody knows a whole lot about Frankie Ferocious, because he never has much to say, and he takes his time saying it, but everybody gives him plenty of room when he comes around, as there are rumors that Frankie never likes to be crowded. As far as I am concerned, I do not care for any part of Frankie Ferocious, because his slow way of looking at people always makes me nervous, and I am always sorry Joe the Joker gives him a hot foot, because I figure Frankie Ferocious is bound to consider it a most disrespectful action, and hold it against everybody that lives on the Island of Manhattan.

But Joe the Joker only laughs when anybody tells him he is out of line in giving Frankie the hot foot, and says it is not his fault if Frankie has no sense of humor. Furthermore, Joe says he will not only give Frankie another hot foot if he gets a chance, but that he will give hot foots to the Prince of Wales or Mussolini, if he catches them in the right spot, although Regret, the horse player, states that Joe can have twenty to one anytime that he will not give Mussolini any hot foots and get away with it.

Anyway, just as I suspect, there is Joe the Joker watching me when I feel the hot foot, and he is laughing very heartily, and furthermore, a large number of other citizens are also laughing heartily, because Joe the Joker never sees any fun in giving people the hot foot unless others are present to enjoy the joke.

Well, naturally when I see who it is gives me the hot foot I join in the laughter, and go over and shake hands with Joe, and when I shake hands with him there is more laughter, because it seems Joe has a hunk of Limburger cheese in his duke, and what I shake hands with is this Limburger. Furthermore, it is some of Mindy's Limburger cheese, and everybody knows Mindy's Limburger is very squashy, and also very loud.

Of course I laugh at this, too, although to tell the truth I will laugh much more heartily if Joe the Joker drops dead in front of me, because I do not like to be made the subject of laughter on Broadway. But my laugh is really quite hearty when Joe takes the rest of the cheese that is not on my fingers and smears it on the steering-wheels of some automobiles parked in front of Mindy's, because I get to thinking of what the drivers will say when they start steering their cars.

Then I get talking to Joe the Joker, and I ask him how things are up in Harlem, where Joe and his younger brother, Freddy, and several other guys have a small organization operating in beer, and Joe says things are as good as can be expected considering business conditions. Then I ask him how Rosa is getting along, this Rosa being Joe the Joker's ever-loving wife, and a personal friend of mine, as I know her when she is Rosa Midnight and is singing in the old Hot Box before Joe hauls off and marries her.

Well, at this question Joe the Joker starts laughing, and I can see that something appeals to his sense of humor, and finally he speaks as follows:

"Why," he says, "do you not hear the news about Rosa? She takes the wind on me a couple of months ago for my friend Frankie Ferocious, and is living in an apartment over in Brooklyn, right near his house, although," Joe says, "of course you understand I am telling you this only to answer your question, and not to holler copper on Rosa."

Then he lets out another large ha-ha, and in fact Joe the Joker keeps laughing until I am afraid he will injure himself internally. Personally, I do not see anything comical in a guy's ever-loving wife taking the wind on him for a guy like Frankie Ferocious, so when Joe the Joker quiets down a bit I ask him what is funny about the proposition.

"Why," Joe says, "I have to laugh every time I think of how the big greaseball is going to feel when he finds out how expensive Rosa is. I do not know how many things Frankie Ferocious has running for him in Brooklyn," Joe says, "but he better try to move himself in on the mint if he wishes to keep Rosa going."

Then he laughs again, and I consider it wonderful the way Joe is able to keep his sense of humor even in such a situation as this, although up to this time I always think Joe is very daffy indeed about Rosa, who is a little doll, weighing maybe ninety pounds with her hat on and quite cute.

Now I judge from what Joe the Joker tells me that Frankie Ferocious knows Rosa before Joe marries her and is always pitching to her when she is singing in the Hot Box, and even after she is Joe's ever-loving wife, Frankie occasionally calls her up, especially when he commences to be a rising citizen of Brooklyn, although of course Joe does not learn about these calls until later. And about the time Frankie Ferocious commences to be a rising citizen of Brooklyn, things begin breaking a little tough for Joe the Joker, what with the Depression and all, and he has to economize on Rosa in spots, and if there is one thing Rosa cannot stand it is being economized on.

Along about now, Joe the Joker gives Frankie Ferocious the hot foot, and just as many citizens state at the time, it is a mistake, for Frankie starts calling Rosa up more than somewhat, and speaking of what a nice place Brooklyn is to live in—which it is, at that—and between these boosts for Brooklyn and Joe the Joker's economy, Rosa hauls off and takes a subway to Borough Hall, leaving Joe a note telling him that if he does not like it he knows what he can do.

"Well, Joe," I say, after listening to his story, "I always hate to hear of these little domestic difficulties among my friends, but maybe this is all for the best. Still, I feel sorry for you, if it will do you any good," I say.

"Do not feel sorry for me," Joe says. "If you wish to feel sorry for anybody, feel sorry for Frankie Ferocious, and," he says, "if you can spare a little more sorrow, give it to Rosa."

And Joe the Joker laughs very hearty again and starts telling me about a little scatter that he has up in Harlem where he keeps a chair fixed up with electric wires so he can give anybody that sits down in it a nice jolt, which sounds very humorous to me, at that, especially when Joe tells me how they turn on too much juice one night and almost kill Commodore Jake.

Finally Joe says he has to get back to Harlem, but first he goes to the telephone in the corner cigar store and calls up Mindy's and imitates a doll's voice, and tells Mindy he is Peggy Joyce, or somebody, and orders fifty dozen sandwiches sent up at once to an apartment on West Seventy-second Street for a birthday party, although of course there is no such number as he gives, and nobody there will wish fifty dozen sandwiches if there is such a number.

Then Joe gets in his car and starts off, and while he is waiting for the traffic lights at Fiftieth Street, I see citizens on the sidewalks making sudden leaps, and looking around very fierce, and I know Joe the Joker is plugging them with pellets made out of tin foil, which he fires from a rubber band hooked between his thumb and forefinger.

Joe the Joker is very expert with this proposition, and it is very funny to see the citizens jump, although once or twice in his life Joe makes a miscue and knocks out somebody's eye. But it is all in fun, and shows you what a wonderful sense of humor Joe has.

Well, a few days later I see by the papers where a couple of Harlem guys Joe the Joker is mobbed up with are found done up in sacks over in Brooklyn, very dead indeed, and the coppers say it is because they are trying to move in on certain business enterprises that belong to nobody but Frankie Ferocious. But of course the coppers do not say Frankie Ferocious puts these guys in the sacks, because in the first place Frankie will report them to Headquarters if the coppers say such a thing about him, and in the second place putting guys in sacks is strictly a St. Louis idea and to have a guy put in a sack properly you have to send to St. Louis for experts in this matter.

Now, putting a guy in a sack is not as easy as it sounds, and in fact it takes quite a lot of practice and experience. To put a guy in a sack properly, you first have to put him to sleep, because naturally no guy is going to walk into a sack wide awake unless he is a plumb sucker. Some people claim the best way to put a guy to sleep is to give him a sleeping powder of some kind in a drink, but the real experts just tap the guy on the noggin with a blackjack, which saves the expense of buying the drink.

Anyway, after the guy is asleep, you double him up like a pocketknife, and tie a cord or a wire around his neck and under his knees. Then you put him in a gunny sack, and leave him someplace, and by and by when the guy wakes up and finds himself in the sack, naturally he wants to get out and the first thing he does is to try to straighten out his knees. This pulls the cord around his neck up so tight that after a while the guy is all out of breath.

So then when somebody comes along and opens the sack they find the guy dead, and nobody is responsible for this unfortunate situation, because after all the guy really commits suicide, because if he does not try to straighten out his knees he may live to a ripe old age, if he recovers from the tap on the noggin.

Well, a couple of days later I see by the papers where three Brooklyn citizens are scragged as they are walking peaceably along Clinton Street, the scragging being done by some parties in an automobile who seem to have a machine gun, and the papers state that the citizens are friends of Frankie Ferocious, and that it is rumored the parties with the machine gun are from Harlem.

I judge by this that there is some trouble in Brooklyn, especially as about a week after the citizens are scragged on Clinton Street, another Harlem guy is found done up in a sack like a Virginia ham near Prospect Park, and now who is it but Joe the Joker's brother, Freddy, and I know Joe is going to be greatly displeased by this.

By and by it gets so nobody in Brooklyn will open as much as a sack of potatoes without first calling in the gendarmes, for fear a pair of No. 8 shoes will jump out at them.

Now one night I see Joe the Joker, and this time he is all alone, and I wish to say I am willing to leave him all alone, because something tells me he is hotter than a stove. But he grabs me as I am going past, so naturally I stop to talk to him, and the first thing I say is how sorry I am about his brother.

"Well," Joe the Joker says, "Freddy is always a kind of a sap. Rosa calls him up and asks him to come over to Brooklyn to see her. She wishes to talk to Freddy about getting me to give her a divorce," Joe says, "so she can marry Frankie Ferocious, I suppose.

Anyway," he says, "Freddy tells Commodore Jake why he is going to see her. Freddy always likes Rosa, and thinks maybe he can patch it up between us. So," Joe says, "he winds up in a sack. They get him after he leaves her apartment. I do not claim Rosa will ask him to come over if she has any idea he will be sacked," Joe says, "but," he says, "she is responsible. She is a bad-luck doll."

Then he starts to laugh, and at first I am greatly horrified, thinking it is because something about Freddy being sacked strikes his sense of humor, when he says to me, like this:

"Say," he says, "I am going to play a wonderful joke on Frankie Ferocious."

"Well, Joe," I say, "you are not asking me for advice, but I am going to give you some free, gratis, and for nothing. Do not play any jokes on Frankie Ferocious, as I hear he has no more sense of humor than a nanny goat. I hear Frankie Ferocious will not laugh if you have Al Jolson, Eddie Cantor, Ed Wynn, and Joe Cook telling him jokes all at once. In fact," I say, "I hear he is a tough audience."

"Oh," Joe the Joker says, "he must have some sense of humor somewhere to stand for Rosa. I hear he is daffy about her. In fact, I understand she is the only person in the world he really likes, and trusts. But I must play a joke on him. I am going to have myself delivered to Frankie Ferocious in a sack."

Well, of course I have to laugh at this myself, and Joe the Joker laughs with me. Personally, I am laughing just at the idea of anybody having themselves delivered to Frankie Ferocious in a sack, and especially Joe the Joker, but of course I have no idea Joe really means what he says.

"Listen," Joe says, finally. "A guy from St. Louis who is a friend of mine is doing most of the sacking for Frankie Ferocious. His name is Ropes McGonnigle. In fact," Joe says, "he is a very dear old pal of mine, and he has a wonderful sense of humor like me. Ropes McGonnigle has nothing whatever to do with sacking Freddy," Joe says, "and he is very indignant about it since he finds out Freddy is my brother, so he is anxious to help me play a joke on Frankie.

"Only last night," Joe says, "Frankie Ferocious sends for Ropes and tells him he will appreciate it as a special favor if Ropes will bring me to him in a sack. I suppose," Joe says, "that Frankie Ferocious hears from Rosa what Freddy is bound to tell her about my ideas on divorce. I have very strict ideas on divorce," Joe says, "especially where Rosa is concerned. I will see her in what's-this before I ever do her and Frankie Ferocious such a favor as giving her a divorce.

"Anyway," Joe the Joker says, "Ropes tells me about Frankie Ferocious propositioning him, so I send Ropes back to Frankie Ferocious to tell him he knows I am to be in Brooklyn to-morrow night, and furthermore, Ropes tells Frankie that he will have me in a sack in no time. And so he will," Joe says.

"Well," I say, "personally, I see no percentage in being delivered to Frankie Ferocious in a sack, because as near as I can make out from what I read in the papers, there is no future for a guy in a sack that goes to Frankie Ferocious. What I cannot figure out," I say, "is where the joke on Frankie comes in."

"Why," Joe the Joker says, "the joke is, I will not be asleep in the sack, and my hands will not be tied, and in each of my hands I will have a John Roscoe, so when the sack is delivered to Frankie Ferocious and I pop out blasting away, can you not imagine his astonishment?"

Well, I can imagine this, all right. In fact when I get to thinking of the look of surprise that is bound to come to Frankie Ferocious's face when Joe the Joker comes out of the sack I have to laugh, and Joe the Joker laughs right along with me.

"Of course," Joe says, "Ropes McGonnigle will be there to start blasting with me, in case Frankie Ferocious happens to have any company."

Then Joe the Joker goes on up the street, leaving me still laughing, from thinking of how amazed Frankie Ferocious will be when Joe bounces out of the sack and starts throwing slugs around and about. I do not hear of Joe from that time to this, but I hear the rest of the story from very reliable parties.

It seems that Ropes McGonnigle does not deliver the sack himself, after all, but sends it by an expressman to Frankie Ferocious's home. Frankie Ferocious receives many sacks such as this in his time, because it seems that it is a sort of passion with him to personally view the contents of the sacks and check up on them before they are distributed about the city, and of course Ropes McGonnigle knows about this passion from doing so much sacking for Frankie.

When the expressman takes the sack into Frankie's house, Frankie personally lugs it down into his basement, and there he

outs with a big John Roscoe and fires six shots into the sack, because it seems Ropes McGonnigle tips him off to Joe the Joker's
plan to pop out of the sack and start blasting.

I hear Frankie Ferocious has a very strange expression on his
pan and is laughing the only laugh anybody ever hears from him
when the gendarmes break in and put the arm on him for murder,
because it seems that when Ropes McGonnigle tells Frankie of Joe
the Joker's plan, Frankie tells Ropes what he is going to do with
his own hands before opening the sack. Naturally, Ropes speaks
to Joe the Joker of Frankie's idea about filling the sack full of
slugs, and Joe's sense of humor comes right out again.

So, bound and gagged, but otherwise as right as rain in the sack
that is delivered to Frankie Ferocious, is by no means Joe the
Joker, but Rosa.

UNDERTAKER SONG

Now this story I am going to tell you is about the game of football, a very healthy pastime for the young, and a great character builder from all I hear, but to get around to this game of football I am compelled to bring in some most obnoxious characters, beginning with a guy by the name of Joey Perhaps, and all I can conscientiously say about Joey is you can have him.

It is a matter of maybe four years since I see this Joey Perhaps until I notice him on a train going to Boston, Mass., one Friday afternoon. He is sitting across from me in the dining-car, where I am enjoying a small portion of baked beans and brown bread, and he looks over to me once, but he does not rap to me.

There is no doubt but what Joey Perhaps is bad company, because the last I hear of him he is hollering copper on a guy by the name of Jack Ortega, and as result of Joey Perhaps hollering copper, this Jack Ortega is taken to the city of Ossining, N.Y., and placed in an electric chair, and given a very, very, very severe shock in the seat of his pants.

It is something about plugging a most legitimate business guy in the city of Rochester, N.Y., when Joey Perhaps and Jack Ortega are engaged together in a little enterprise to shake the guy down, but the details of this transaction are dull, sordid, and quite uninteresting, except that Joey Perhaps turns state's evidence and announces that Jack Ortega fires the shot which cools the legitimate guy off, for which service he is rewarded with only a small stretch.

I must say for Joey Perhaps that he looks good, and he is very well dressed, but then Joey is always particular about clothes, and he is quite a handy guy with the dolls in his day and, to tell the truth, many citizens along Broadway are by no means displeased when Joey is placed in the state institution, because they are generally pretty uneasy about their dolls when he is around.

Naturally, I am wondering why Joey Perhaps is on this train going to Boston, Mass., but for all I know maybe he is wondering the same thing about me, although personally I am making no secret about it. The idea is I am *en route* to Boston, Mass., to see a contest of skill and science that is to take place there this very Friday night between a party by the name of Lefty Ledoux and another party by the name of Pile Driver, who are very prominent middleweights.

Now ordinarily I will not go around the corner to see a contest of skill and science between Lefty Ledoux and Pile Driver, or anybody else, as far as that is concerned, unless they are using blackjacks and promise to hurt each other, but I am the guest on this trip of a party by the name of Meyer Marmalade, and I will go anywhere to see anything if I am a guest.

This Meyer Marmalade is really a most superior character, who is called Meyer Marmalade because nobody can ever think of his last name, which is something like Marmalodowski, and he is known far and wide for the way he likes to make bets on any sporting proposition, such as baseball, or horse races, or ice hockey, or contests of skill and science, and especially contests of skill and science.

So he wishes to be present at this contest in Boston, Mass., between Lefty Ledoux and Pile Driver to have a nice wager on Driver, as he has reliable information that Driver's manager, a party by the name of Koons, has both judges and the referee in the satchel.

If there is one thing Meyer Marmalade dearly loves, it is to have a bet on a contest of skill and science of this nature, and so he is going to Boston, Mass. But Meyer Marmalade is such a guy as loathes and despises traveling all alone, so when he offers to pay my expenses if I will go along to keep him company, naturally I am pleased to accept, as I have nothing on of importance at the moment and, in fact, I do not have anything on of importance for the past ten years.

I warn Meyer Marmalade in advance that if he is looking to take anything off of anybody in Boston, Mass., he may as well remain at home, because everybody knows that statistics show that the percentage of anything being taken off of the citizens of Boston, Mass., is less *per capita* than anywhere else in the United States, especially when it comes to contests of skill and science, but Meyer Marmalade says this is the first time they ever had two judges and a referee running against the statistics, and he is very confident.

Well, by and by I go from the dining-car back to my seat in another car, where Meyer Marmalade is sitting reading a detective magazine, and I speak of seeing Joey Perhaps to him. But Meyer Marmalade does not seem greatly interested, although he says to me like this:

"Joey Perhaps, eh?" he says. "A wrong gee. A dead wrong gee. He must just get out. I run into the late Jack Ortega's brother, young Ollie, in Mindy's restaurant last week," Meyer Marmalade says, "and when we happen to get to talking of wrong gees, naturally Joey Perhaps's name comes up, and Ollie remarks he understands Joey Perhaps is about due out, and that he will be pleased to see him someday. Personally," Meyer Marmalade says, "I do not care for any part of Joey Perhaps at any price."

Now our car is loaded with guys and dolls who are going to Boston, Mass., to witness a large football game between the Harvards and the Yales at Cambridge, Mass., the next day, and the reason I know this is because they are talking of nothing else.

So this is where the football starts getting into this story.

One old guy that I figure must be a Harvard from the way he talks seems to have a party all his own, and he is getting so much attention from one and all in the party that I figure he must be a guy of some importance, because they laugh heartily at his remarks, and although I listen very carefully to everything he says he does not sound so very humorous to me.

He is a heavy-set guy with a bald head and deep voice, and anybody can see that he is such a guy as is accustomed to plenty of authority. I am wondering out loud to Meyer Marmalade who the guy can be, and Meyer Marmalade states as follows:

"Why," he says, "he is nobody but Mr. Phillips Randolph, who makes the automobiles. He is the sixth richest guy in this country," Meyers says, "or maybe it is the seventh. Anyway, he is pretty well up with the front runners. I spot his monicker on his suitcase, and then I ask the porter, to make sure. It is a great honor for us to be traveling with Mr. Phillips Randolph," Meyer says, "because of him being such a public benefactor and having so much dough, especially having so much dough."

Well, naturally everybody knows who Mr. Phillips Randolph is, and I am surprised that I do not recognize his face myself from seeing it so often in the newspapers alongside the latest model automobile his factory turns out, and I am as much pleasured up as Meyer Marmalade over being in the same car with Mr. Phillips Randolph.

He seems to be a good-natured old guy, at that, and he is having a grand time, what with talking, and laughing, and taking a dram now and then out of a bottle, and when old Crip McGonnigle comes gimping through the car selling his football souvenirs, such as red and blue feathers, and little badges and pennants, and one thing and another, as Crip is doing around the large football games since Hickory Slim is a two-year-old, Mr. Phillips Randolph stops him and buys all of Crip's red feathers, which have a little white H on them to show they are for the Harvards.

Then Mr. Phillips Randolph distributes the feathers around among his party, and the guys and dolls stick them in their hats, or pin them on their coats, but he has quite a number of feathers left over, and about this time who comes through the car but Joey Perhaps, and Mr. Phillips Randolph steps out in the aisle and stops Joey and politely offers him a red feather, and speaks as follows:

"Will you honor us by wearing our colors?"

Well, of course Mr. Phillips Randolph is only full of good spirits, and means no harm whatever, and the guys and dolls in his party laugh heartily as if they consider his action very funny, but maybe because they laugh, and maybe because he is just naturally a hostile guy, Joey Perhaps knocks Mr. Phillips Randolph's hand down, and says like this:

"Get out of my way," Joey says. "Are you trying to make a sucker out of somebody?"

Personally, I always claim that Joey Perhaps has a right to reject the red feather, because for all I know he may prefer a blue feather, which means the Yales, but what I say is he does not need to be so impolite to an old guy such as Mr. Phillips Randolph, although of course Joey has no way of knowing at this time about Mr. Phillips Randolph having so much dough.

Anyway, Mr. Phillips Randolph stands staring at Joey as if he is greatly startled, and the chances are he is, at that, for the chances are nobody ever speaks to him in such a manner in all his life, and Joey Perhaps also stands there a minute staring back at Mr. Phillips Randolph, and finally Joey speaks as follows:

"Take a good peek," Joey Perhaps says. "Maybe you will remember me if you ever see me again."

"Yes," Mr. Phillips Randolph says, very quiet. "Maybe I will. They say I have a good memory for faces. I beg your pardon for stopping you, sir. It is all in fun, but I am sorry," he says.

Then Joey Perhaps goes on, and he does not seem to notice Meyer Marmalade and me sitting there in the car, and Mr. Phillips Randolph sits down, and his face is redder than somewhat, and all the joy is gone out of him, and out of his party, too. Personally, I am very sorry Joey Perhaps comes along, because I figure Mr. Phillips Randolph will give me one of his spare feathers, and I will consider it a wonderful keepsake.

But now there is not much more talking, and no laughing whatever in Mr. Phillips Randolph's party, and he just sits there as if he is thinking, and for all I know he may be thinking that there ought to be a law against a guy speaking so disrespectfully to a guy with all his dough as Joey Perhaps speaks to him.

Well, the contest of skill and science between Lefty Ledoux and Pile Driver turns out to be something of a disappointment, and, in fact, it is a stinkeroo, because there is little skill and no science whatever in it, and by the fourth round the customers are scuffling their feet, and saying throw these bums out, and making other derogatory remarks, and furthermore it seems that this Koons does not have either one of the judges, or even as much as the referee, in the satchel, and Ledoux gets the duke by unanimous vote of the officials.

So Meyer Marmalade is out a couple of C's, which is all he can wager at the ringside, because it seems that nobody in Boston, Mass., cares a cuss about who wins the contest, and Meyer is much disgusted with life, and so am I, and we go back to the Copley Plaza Hotel, where we are stopping, and sit down in the lobby to meditate on the injustice of everything.

Well, the lobby is a scene of gaiety, as it seems there are a number of football dinners and dances going on in the hotel, and guys and dolls in evening clothes are all around and about, and the dolls are so young and beautiful that I get to thinking that this is not such a bad old world, after all, and even Meyer Marmalade begins taking notice.

All of a sudden, a very, very beautiful young doll who is about forty per cent in and sixty per cent out of an evening gown walks right up to us sitting there, and holds out her hand to me, and speaks as follows:

"Do you remember me?"

Naturally, I do not remember her, but naturally I am not going to admit it, because it is never my policy to discourage any doll who wishes to strike up an acquaintance with me, which is what I figure this doll is trying to do; then I see that she is nobody but Doria Logan, one of the prettiest dolls that ever hits Broadway, and about the same time Meyer Marmalade also recognizes her.

Doria changes no little since last I see her, which is quite some time back, but there is no doubt the change is for the better, because she is once a very rattle-headed young doll, and now she seems older, and quieter, and even prettier than ever. Naturally, Meyer Marmalade and I are glad to see her looking so well, and we ask her how are tricks, and what is the good word, and all this and that, and finally Doria Logan states to us as follows:

"I am in great trouble," Doria says. "I am in terrible trouble, and you are the first ones I see that I can talk to about it."

Well, at this, Meyer Marmalade begins to tuck in somewhat, because he figures it is the old lug coming up, and Meyer Marmalade is not such a guy as will go for the lug from a doll unless he gets something more than a story. But I can see Doria Logan is in great earnest.

"Do you remember Joey Perhaps?" she says.

"A wrong gee," Meyer Marmalade says. "A dead wrong gee."

"I not only remember Joey Perhaps," I say, "but I see him on the train to-day."

"Yes," Doria says, "he is here in town. He hunts me up only a few hours ago. He is here to do me great harm. He is here to finish ruining my life."

"A wrong gee," Meyer Marmalade puts in again. "Always a hundred per cent wrong gee."

Then Doria Logan gets us to go with her to a quiet corner of the lobby, and she tells us a strange story, as follows, and also to wit:

It seems that she is once tangled up with Joey Perhaps, which is something I never know before, and neither does Meyer Marmalade, and, in fact, the news shocks us quite some. It is back in the days when she is just about sixteen and is in the chorus of Earl

Carroll's *Vanities,* and I remember well what a standout she is for looks, to be sure.

Naturally, at sixteen, Doria is quite a chump doll, and does not know which way is south, or what time it is, which is the way all dolls at sixteen are bound to be, and she has no idea what a wrong gee Joey Perhaps is, as he is good-looking, and young, and seems very romantic, and is always speaking of love and one thing and another.

Well, the upshot of it all is the upshot of thousands of other cases since chump dolls commence coming to Broadway, and the first thing she knows, Doria Logan finds herself mixed up with a very bad character, and does not know what to do about it.

By and by, Joey Perhaps commences mistreating her no little, and finally he tries to use her in some nefarious schemes of his, of course everybody along Broadway knows that most of Joey's schemes are especially nefarious, because Joey is on the shake almost since infancy.

Well, one day Doria says to herself that if this is love, she has all she can stand, and she hauls off and runs away from Joey Perhaps. She goes back to her people, who live in the city of Cambridge, Mass., which is the same place where the Harvards have their college, and she goes there because she does not know of any other place to go.

It seems that Doria's people are poor, and Doria goes to a business school and learns to be a stenographer, and she is working for a guy in the real estate dodge by the name of Poopnoodle, and doing all right for herself, and in the meantime she hears that Joey Perhaps gets sent away, so she figures her troubles are all over as far as he is concerned.

Now Doria Logan goes along quietly through life, working for Mr. Poopnoodle, and never thinking of love, or anything of a similar nature, when she meets up with a young guy who is one of the Harvards, and who is maybe twenty-one years old, and is quite a football player, and where Doria meets up with this guy is in a drug store over a banana split.

Well, the young Harvard takes quite a fancy to Doria and, in fact, he is practically on fire about her, but by this time Doria is going on twenty, and is no longer a chump doll, and she has no wish to get tangled up in love again.

In fact, whenever she thinks of Joey Perhaps, Doria takes to hating guys in general, but somehow she cannot seem to get up a real good hate on the young Harvard, because, to hear her tell it, he is handsome, and noble, and has wonderful ideals.

Now as time goes on, Doria finds she is growing pale, and is losing her appetite, and cannot sleep, and this worries her no little, as she is always a first-class feeder, and finally she comes to the conclusion that what ails her is that she is in love with the young Harvard, and can scarcely live without him, so she admits as much to him one night when the moon is shining on the Charles River, and everything is a dead cold set-up for love.

Well, naturally, after a little off-hand guzzling, which is quite permissible under the circumstances, the young guy wishes her to name the happy day, and Doria has half a notion to make it the following Monday, this being a Sunday night, but then she gets to thinking about her past with Joey Perhaps, and all, and she figures it will be bilking the young Harvard to marry him unless she has a small talk with him first about Joey, because she is well aware that many young guys may have some objection to wedding a doll with a skeleton in her closet, and especially a skeleton such as Joey Perhaps.

But she is so happy she does not wish to run the chance of spoiling everything by these narrations right away, so she keeps her trap closed about Joey, although she promises to marry the young Harvard when he gets out college, which will be the following year, if he still insists, because Doria figures that by then she will be able to break the news to him about Joey very gradually, and gently, and especially gently.

Anyway, Doria says she is bound and determined to tell him before the wedding, even if he takes the wind on her as a consequence, and personally I claim this is very considerate of Doria, because many dolls never tell before the wedding, or even after. So Doria and the young Harvard are engaged, and great happiness prevails, when all of a sudden, in pops Joey Perhaps.

It seems that Joey learns of Doria's engagement as soon as he gets out of the state institution, and he hastens to Boston, Mass., with an inside coat pocket packed with letters that Doria writes him long ago, and also a lot of pictures they have taken together, as young guys and dolls are bound to do, and while there is nothing much out of line about these letters and pictures, put them all together they spell a terrible pain in the neck to Doria at this particular time.

"A wrong gee," Meyer Marmalade says. "But," he says, "he is only going back to his old shakedown dodge, so all you have to do is to buy him off."

Well, at this, Doria Logan laughs one of these little short dry laughs that go "hah," and says like this:

"Of course he is looking to get bought off, but," she says, "where will I get any money to buy him off? I do not have a dime of my own, and Joey is talking large figures, because he knows my fiancé's papa has plenty. He wishes me to go to my fiancé and make him get the money off his papa, or he threatens to personally deliver the letters and pictures to my fiancé's papa.

"You can see the predicament I am in," Doria says, "and you can see what my fiancé's papa will think of me if he learns I am once mixed up with a blackmailer such as Joey Perhaps.

"Besides," Doria says, "it is something besides money with Joey Perhaps, and I am not so sure he will not double-cross me even if I can pay him his price. Joey Perhaps is very angry at me. I think," she says, "if he can spoil my happiness, it will mean more to him than money."

Well, Doria states that all she can think of when she is talking to Joey Perhaps is to stall for time, and she tells Joey that, no matter what, she cannot see her fiancé until after the large football game between the Harvards and the Yales as he has to do a little football playing for the Harvards, and Joey asks her if she is going to see the game, and naturally she is.

And then Joey says he thinks he will look up a ticket speculator, and buy a ticket and attend the game himself, as he is very fond of football, and where will she be sitting, as he hopes and trusts he will be able to see something of her during the game, and this statement alarms Doria Logan no little, for who is she going with but her fiancé's papa, and a party of his friends, and she feels that there is no telling what Joey Perhaps may be up to.

She explains to Joey that she does not know exactly where she will be sitting, except that it will be on the Harvards' side of the field, but Joey is anxious for more details than this.

"In fact," Doria says, "he is most insistent, and he stands at my elbow while I call up Mr. Randolph at this very hotel, and he tells me the exact location of our seats. Then Joey says he will endeavor to get a seat as close to me as possible, and he goes away."

"What Mr. Randolph?" Meyer says. "Which Mr. Randolph?" he says. "You do not mean Mr. Phillips Randolph, by any chance, do you?"

"Why, to be sure," Doria says. "Do you know him?"

Naturally, from now on Meyer Marmalade gazes at Doria Logan with deep respect, and so do I, although by now she is crying a little, and I am by no means in favor of crying dolls. But while she is crying, Meyer Marmalade seems to be doing some more thinking, and finally he speaks as follows:

"Kindly see if you can recall these locations you speak of."

So here is where the football game comes in once more.

Only I regret to state that personally I do not witness this game, and the reason I do not witness it is because nobody wakes me up the next day in time for me to witness it, and the way I look at it, this is all for the best, as I am scarcely a football enthusiast.

So from now on the story belongs to Meyer Marmalade, and I will tell it to you as Meyer tells it to me.

It is a most exciting game (Meyer says). The place is full of people, and there are bands playing, and much cheering, and more lovely dolls than you can shake a stick at, although I do not believe there are any lovelier present than Doria Logan.

It is a good thing she remembers the seat locations, otherwise I will never find her, but there she is surrounded by some very nice-looking people, including Mr. Phillips Randolph, and there I am two rows back of Mr. Phillips Randolph, and the ticket spec I get my seat off of says he cannot understand why everybody wishes to sit near Mr. Phillips Randolph to-day when there are other seats just as good, and maybe better, on the Harvards' side.

So I judge he has other calls similar to mine for this location, and a sweet price he gets for it, too, and I judge that maybe at least one call is from Joey Perhaps, as I see Joey a couple of rows on back up of where I am sitting, but off to my left on an aisle, while I am almost in a direct line with Mr. Phillips Randolph.

To show you that Joey is such a guy as attracts attention, Mr. Phillips Randolph stands up a few minutes before the game starts, peering around and about to see who is present that he knows, and all of a sudden his eyes fall on Joey Perhaps, and then Mr.

Phillips Randolph proves he has a good memory for faces, to be sure, for he states as follows:

"Why," he says, "there is the chap who rebuffs me so churlishly on the train when I offer him our colors. Yes," he says, "I am sure it is the same chap."

Well, what happens in the football game is much pulling and hauling this way and that, and to and fro, between the Harvards and the Yales without a tally right down to the last five minutes of play, and then all of a sudden the Yales shove the football down to within a three-eighths of an inch of the Harvards' goal line.

At this moment quite some excitement prevails. Then the next thing anybody knows, the Yales outshove the Harvards, and now the game is over, and Mr. Phillips Randolph gets up out of his seat, and I hear Mr. Phillips Randolph say like this:

"Well," he says, "the score is not so bad as it might be, and it is a wonderful game, and," he says, "we seem to make one convert to our cause, anyway, for see who is wearing our colors."

And with this he points to Joey Perhaps, who is still sitting down, with people stepping around him and over him, and he is still smiling a little smile, and Mr. Phillips Randolph seems greatly pleased to see that Joey Perhaps has a big, broad crimson ribbon where he once wears his white silk muffler.

But the chances are Mr. Phillips Randolph will be greatly surprised if he knows that the crimson ribbon across Joey's bosom comes of Ollie Ortega planting a short knife in Joey's throat, or do I forget to mention before that Ollie Ortega is among those present?

I send for Ollie after I leave you last night, figuring he may love to see a nice football game. He arrives by 'plane this morning, and I am not wrong in my figuring. Ollie thinks the game is swell.

Well, personally, I will never forget this game, it is so exciting. Just after the tally comes off, all of a sudden, from the Yales in the stand across the field from the Harvards, comes a long-drawn-out wail that sounds so mournful it makes me feel very sad, to be sure. It starts off something like Oh-oh-oh-oh-oh, with all the Yales Oh-oh-oh-oh-oh-ing at once, and I ask a guy next to me what it is all about.

"Why," the guys says, "it is the Yales' 'Undertaker Song.' They will always sing it when they have the other guy licked. I am an old Yale myself, and I will now personally sing this song for you."

And with this the guy throws back his head, and opens his mouth wide and lets out a yowl like a wolf calling to its mate.

Well, I stop the guy, and tell him it is a very lovely song, to be sure, and quite appropriate all the way around, and then I hasten away from the football game without getting a chance to say good-bye to Doria, although afterwards I mail her the package of letters and pictures that Ollie gets out of Joey Perhaps's inside coat pocket during the confusion that prevails when the Yales make their tally, and I hope and trust that she will think the crimson streaks across the package are just a little touch of color in honor of the Harvards.

But the greatest thing about the football game (Meyer Marmalade says) is I win two C's off of one of the Harvards sitting near me, so I am now practically even on my trip.

BREACH OF PROMISE

One day a certain party by the name of Judge Goldfobber, who is a lawyer by trade, sends word to me that he wishes me to call on him at his office on lower Broadway, and while ordinarily I do not care for any part of lawyers, it happens that Judge Goldfobber is a friend of mine, so I go to see him.

Of course Judge Goldfobber is not a judge, and never is a judge, and he is a hundred to one in my line against ever being a judge, but he is called Judge because it pleases him, and everybody always wishes to please Judge Goldfobber, as he is one of the surest-footed lawyers in this town, and beats more tough beefs for different citizens than seems possible. He is a wonderful hand for keeping citizens from getting into the sneezer, and better than Houdini when it comes to getting them out of the sneezer after they are in.

Personally, I never have any use for the professional services of Judge Goldfobber, as I am a law-abiding citizen at all times, and am greatly opposed to guys who violate the law, but I know the Judge from around and about for many years. I know him from around and about the night clubs, and other deadfalls, for Judge Goldfobber is such a guy as loves to mingle with the public in these spots, as he picks up much law business there, and sometimes a nice doll.

Well, when I call on Judge Goldfobber, he takes me into his private office and wishes to know if I can think of a couple of deserving guys who are out of employment, and who will like a job of work, and if so, Judge Goldfobber says, he can offer them a first-class position.

"Of course," Judge Goldfobber says, "it is not steady employment, and in fact it is nothing but piece-work, but the parties must be extremely reliable parties, who can be depended on in a pinch.

This is out-of-town work that requires tact, and," he says, "some nerve."

Well, I am about to tell Judge Goldfobber that I am no employment agent, and go on about my business, because I can tell from the way he says the parties must be parties who can be depended on in a pinch, that a pinch is apt to come up on the job any minute, and I do not care to steer any friends of mine against a pinch.

But as I get up to go, I look out of Judge Goldfobber's window, and I can see Brooklyn in the distance beyond the river, and seeing Brooklyn I get to thinking of certain parties over there that I figure must be suffering terribly from the unemployment situation. I get to thinking of Harry the Horse and Spanish John and Little Isadore, and the reason I figure they must be suffering from the unemployment situation is because if nobody is working and making any money, there is nobody for them to rob, and if there is nobody for them to rob, Harry the Horse and Spanish John and Little Isadore are just naturally bound to be feeling the Depression keenly.

Anyway, I finally mention the names of these parties to Judge Goldfobber, and furthermore I speak well of their reliability in a pinch, and of their nerve, although I cannot conscientiously recommend their tact, and Judge Goldfobber is greatly delighted, as he often hears of Harry the Horse and Spanish John and Little Isadore.

He asks me for their addresses, but of course nobody knows exactly where Harry the Horse and Spanish John and Little Isadore live, because they do not live anywhere in particular. However, I tell him about a certain spot on Clinton Street where he may be able to get track of them, and then I leave Judge Goldfobber for fear he may wish me to take word to these parties, and if there is anybody in this whole world I will not care to take word to, or to have any truck with in any manner, shape, or form, it is Harry the Horse and Spanish John and Little Isadore.

Well, I do not hear anything more of the matter for several weeks, but one evening when I am in Mindy's restaurant on Broadway enjoying a little cold borscht, which is a most refreshing matter in hot weather such as is going on at the time, who bobs up but Harry the Horse and Spanish John and Little Isadore, and I am so surprised to see them that some of my cold borscht goes down the wrong way, and I almost choke to death.

However, they seem quite friendly, and in fact Harry the Horse pounds me on the back to keep me from choking, and while he pounds so hard that he almost caves in my spine, I consider it a most courteous action, and when I am able to talk again, I say to him as follows:

"Well, Harry," I say, "it is a privilege and a pleasure to see you again, and I hope and trust you will all join me in some cold borscht, which you will find very nice indeed."

"No," Harry says, "we do not care for any cold borscht. We are looking for Judge Goldfobber. Do you see Judge Goldfobber round and about lately?"

Well, the idea of Harry the Horse and Spanish John and Little Isadore looking for Judge Goldfobber sounds somewhat alarming to me, and I figure maybe the job Judge Goldfobber gives them turns out bad and they wish to take Judge Goldfobber apart, but the next minute Harry says to me like this:

"By the way," he says, "we wish to thank you for the job of work you throw our way. Maybe someday we will be able to do as much for you. It is a most interesting job," Harry says, "and while you are snuffing your cold borscht I will give you the details, so you will understand why we wish to see Judge Goldfobber."

It turns out (Harry the Horse says) that the job is not for Judge Goldfobber personally, but for a client of his, and who is this client but Mr. Jabez Tuesday, the rich millionaire, who owns the Tuesday string of one-arm joints where many citizens go for food and wait on themselves. Judge Goldfobber comes to see us in Brooklyn in person, and sends me to see Mr. Jabez Tuesday with a letter of introduction, so Mr. Jabez Tuesday can explain what he wishes me to do, because Judge Goldfobber is too smart a guy to be explaining such matters to me himself.

In fact, for all I know maybe Judge Goldfobber is not aware of what Mr. Jabez Tuesday wishes me to do, although I am willing to lay a little six to five that Judge Goldfobber does not think Mr. Jabez Tuesday wishes to hire me as a cashier in any of his one-arm joints.

Anyway, I go to see Mr. Tuesday at a Fifth Avenue hotel where he makes his home, and where he has a very swell layout of rooms, and I am by no means impressed with Mr. Tuesday, as he hems and haws quite a bit before he tells me the nature of the employment he has in mind for me. He is a little guy, somewhat dried out, with a bald head, and a small mouser on his upper lip, and he wears specs, and seems somewhat nervous.

Well, it takes him some time to get down to cases, and tell me what is eating him, and what he wishes to do, and then it all sounds very simple indeed, and in fact it sounds so simple that I think Mr. Jabez Tuesday is a little daffy when he tells me he will give me ten G's for the job.

What Mr. Tuesday wishes me to do is get some letters that he personally writes to a doll by the name of Miss Amelia Bodkin, who lives in a house just outside Tarrytown, because it seems that Mr. Tuesday makes certain cracks in these letters that he is now sorry for, such as speaking of love and marriage and one thing and another to Miss Amelia Bodkin, and he is afraid she is going to sue him for breach of promise.

"Such an idea will be very embarrassing to me," Mr. Jabez Tuesday says, "as I am about to marry a party who is a member of one of the most high-toned families in this country. It is true," Mr. Tuesday says, "that the Scarwater family does not have as much money now as formerly, but there is no doubt about its being very, very high-toned, and my fiancée, Miss Valerie Scarwater, is one of the high-tonedest of them all. In fact," he says, "she is so high-toned that the chances are she will be very huffy about anybody suing me for breach of promise, and cancel everything."

Well, I ask Mr. Tuesday what a breach of promise is, and he explains to me that it is when somebody promises to do something and fails to do this something, although of course we have a different name for a proposition of this nature in Brooklyn, and deal with it accordingly.

"This is a very easy job for a person of your standing," Mr. Tuesday says. "Miss Amelia Bodkin lives all alone in her house the other side of Tarrytown, except for a couple of servants, and they are old and harmless. Now the idea is," he says, "you are not to go to her house as if you are looking for the letters, but as if you are after something else, such as her silverware, which is quite antique and very valuable.

"She keeps the letters in a big inlaid box in her room," Mr. Tuesday says, "and if you just pick up this box and carry it away along with the silverware, no one will ever suspect that you are after the letters, but that you take the box thinking it contains valuables. You bring the letters to me and get your ten G's," Mr. Tuesday says, "and," he says, "you can keep the silverware, too. Be sure you get a Paul Revere teapot with the silverware," he says. "It is worth plenty."

"Well," I say to Mr. Tuesday, "every guy knows his own business best, and I do not wish to knock myself out of a nice soft job, but," I say, "it seems to me the simplest way of carrying on this transaction is to buy the letters off this doll, and be done with it. Personally," I say, "I do not believe there is a doll in the world who is not willing to sell a whole post-office full of letters for ten G's, especially in these times, and throw in a set of Shakespeare with them."

"No, no," Mr. Tuesday says. "Such a course will not do with Miss Amelia Bodkin at all. You see," he says, "Miss Bodkin and I are very, very friendly for a matter of maybe fifteen or sixteen years. In fact, we are very friendly, indeed. She does not have any idea at this time that I wish to break off this friendship with her. Now," he says, "if I try to buy the letters from her, she may become suspicious. The idea," Mr. Tuesday says, "is for me to get the letters first, and then explain to her about breaking off the friendship, and make suitable arrangements with her afterwards.

"Do not get Miss Amelia Bodkin wrong," Mr. Tuesday says. "She is an excellent person, but," he says, "you know the saying 'Hell hath no fury like a woman scorned.' And maybe Miss Amelia Bodkin may figure I am scorning her if she finds out I am going to marry Miss Valerie Scarwater, and furthermore," he says, "if she still has the letters she may fall into the hands of unscrupulous lawyers, and demand a very large sum indeed. But," Mr. Tuesday says, "this does not worry me half as much as the idea that Miss Valerie Scarwater may learn about the letters and get a wrong impression of my friendship with Miss Amelia Bodkin."

Well, I round up Spanish John and Little Isadore the next afternoon, and I find Little Isadore playing klob with a guy by the name of Educated Edmund, who is called Educated Edmund because he once goes to Erasmus High School and is considered a very fine scholar indeed, so I invite Educated Edmund to go along with us. The idea is, I know Educated Edmund makes a fair living playing klob with Little Isadore, and I figure as long as I am depriving Educated Edmund of a living for a while, it is only courteous to toss something else his way. Furthermore, I figure as long as letters are involved in this proposition it may be a good thing to have Educated Edmund handy in case any reading becomes necessary, because Spanish John and Little Isadore do not read at all, and I read only large print.

We borrow a car off a friend of mine on Clinton Street, and with me driving we start for Tarrytown, which is a spot up the Hudson River, and it is a very enjoyable ride for one and all on account of the scenery. It is the first time Educated Edmund and Spanish John and Little Isadore ever see the scenery along the Hudson although they all reside on the banks of this beautiful river for several years at Ossining. Personally, I am never in Ossining, although once I make Auburn, and once Comstock, but the scenery in these localities is nothing to speak of.

We hit Tarrytown about dark, and follow the main drag through this burg, as Mr. Tuesday tells me, until finally we come to the spot I am looking for, which is a little white cottage on a slope of ground above the river, not far off the highway. This little white cottage has quite a piece of ground around it, and a low stone wall, with a driveway from the highway to the house, and when I spot the gate to the driveway I make a quick turn, and what happens but I run the car slap-dab into a stone gatepost, and the car folds up like an accordion.

You see, the idea is we are figuring to make this a fast stick-up job without any foolishness about it, maybe leaving any parties we come across tied up good and tight while we make a getaway, as I am greatly opposed to housebreaking, or sneak jobs, as I do not consider them dignified. Furthermore, they take too much time, so I am going to run the car right up to the front door when this stone post gets in my way.

The next thing I know, I open my eyes to find myself in a strange bed, and also in a strange bedroom, and while I wake up in many a strange bed in my time, I never wake up in such a strange bedroom as this. It is all very soft and dainty, and the only jarring note in my surroundings is Spanish John sitting beside the bed looking at me.

Naturally I wish to know what is what, and Spanish John says I am knocked snoring in the collision with the gatepost, although none of the others are hurt, and that while I am stretched in the driveway with the blood running out of a bad gash in my noggin, who pops out of the house but a doll and an old guy who seems to be a butler, or some such, and the doll insists on them lugging me into the house, and placing me in this bedroom.

Then she washes the blood off of me, Spanish John says, and wraps my head up and personally goes to Tarrytown to get a croaker to see if my wounds are fatal, or what, while Educated Edmund and Little Isadore are trying to patch up the car. So, Spanish John says, he is sitting there to watch me until she comes back, although of course I know what he is really sitting there for is to get first search at me in case I do not recover.

Well, while I am thinking all this over, and wondering what is to be done, in pops a doll of maybe forty-odd, who is built from the ground up, but who has a nice, kind-looking pan, with a large smile, and behind her is a guy I can see at once is a croaker, especially as he is packing a little black bag, and has a gray goatee. I never see a nicer-looking doll if you care for middling-old dolls, although personally I like them young, and when she sees me with my eyes open, she speaks as follows:

"Oh," she says, "I am glad you are not dead, you poor chap. But," she says, "here is Doctor Diffingwell, and he will see how badly you are injured. My name is Miss Amelia Bodkin, and this is my house, and this is my own bedroom, and I am very, very sorry you are hurt."

Well, naturally I consider this a most embarrassing situation, because here I am out to clip Miss Amelia Bodkin of her letters and her silverware, including her Paul Revere teapot, and there she is taking care of me in first-class style, and saying she is sorry for me.

But there seems to be nothing for me to say at this time, so I hold still while the croaker looks me over, and after he peeks at my noggin, and gives me a good feel up and down, he states as follows:

"This is a very bad cut," he says. "I will have to stitch it up, and then he must be very quiet for a few days, otherwise," he says, "complications may set in. It is best to move him to a hospital at once."

But Miss Amelia Bodkin will not listen to such an idea as moving me to a hospital. Miss Amelia Bodkin says I must rest right where I am, and she will take care of me, because she says I am injured on her premises by her gatepost, and it is only fair that she does something for me. In fact, from the way Miss Amelia Bodkin takes on about me being moved, I figure it is the old sex appeal, although afterwards I find out it is only because she is lonesome, and nursing me will give her something to do.

Well, naturally I am not opposing her idea, because the way I look at it, I will be able to handle the situation about the letters, and also the silverware, very nicely as an inside job, so I try to act even worse off than I am, although of course anybody who knows about the time I carry eight slugs in my body from Broadway and Fiftieth Street to Brooklyn will laugh very heartily at the idea of a cut on the noggin keeping me in bed.

After the croaker gets through sewing me up, and goes away, I tell Spanish John to take Educated Edmund and Little Isadore and go back to New York, but to keep in touch with me by telephone, so I can tell them when to come back, and then I go to sleep, because I seem to be very tired. When I wake up later in the night, I seem to have a fever, and am really somewhat sick, and Miss Amelia Bodkin is sitting beside my bed swabbing my noggin with a cool cloth, which feels very pleasant indeed.

I am better in the morning, and am able to knock over a little breakfast which she brings to me on a tray, and I am commencing to see where being an invalid is not so bad, at that, especially when there are no coppers at your bedside every time you open your eyes asking who does it to you.

I can see Miss Amelia Bodkin gets quite a bang out of having somebody to take care of, although of course if she knows who she is taking care of at this time, the chances are she will be running up the road calling for the gendarmes. It is not until after breakfast that I can get her to go and grab herself a little sleep, and while she is away sleeping the old guy who seems to be the butler is in and out of my room every now and then to see how I am getting along.

He is a gabby old guy, and pretty soon he is telling me all about Miss Amelia Bodkin, and what he tells me is that she is the old-time sweetheart of a guy in New York who is at the head of a big business, and very rich, and of course I know this guy is Mr. Jabez Tuesday, although the old guy who seems to be the butler never mentions his name.

"They are together many years," he says to me. "He is very poor when they meet, and she has a little money, and establishes him in business, and by her management of this business, and of him, she makes it a very large business indeed. I know, because I am with them almost from the start," the old guy says. "She is very smart in business, and also very kind, and nice, if anybody asks you.

"Now," the old guy says, "I am never able to figure out why they do not get married, because there is no doubt she loves him, and he loves her, but Miss Amelia Bodkin once tells me that it is because they are too poor at the start, and too busy later on to think of such things as getting married, and so they drift along the way they are, until all of a sudden he is rich. Then," the old guy says, "I can see he is getting away from her, although she never sees it herself, and I am not surprised when a few years ago he convinced her it is best for her to retire from active work, and move out to this spot.

"He comes out here fairly often at first," the old guy says, "but gradually he stretches the time between his visits, and now we do not see him once in a coon's age. Well," the old guy says, "it is just such a case as often comes up in life. In fact, I personally know of some others. But Miss Amelia Bodkin still thinks he loves her, and that only business keeps him away so much, so you can see she either is not as smart as she looks or is kidding herself. Well," the old guy says, "I will now bring you a little orange-juice, although I do not mind saying you do not look to me like a guy who drinks orange-juice as a steady proposition."

Now I am taking many a gander around the bedroom to see if I can case the box of letters that Mr. Jabez Tuesday speaks of, but there is no box such as he describes in sight. Then in the evening, when Miss Amelia Bodkin is in the room, and I seem to be dozing, she pulls out a drawer in the bureau, and hauls out a big inlaid box, and sits down at a table under a reading-lamp, and opens this box and begins reading some old letters. And as she sits there reading those letters, with me watching her through my eyelashes, sometimes she smiles, but once I see little tears rolling down her cheeks.

All of a sudden she looks at me, and catches me with my eyes wide open, and I can see her face turn red, and then she laughs, and speaks to me, as follows:

"Old love-letters," she says, tapping the box. "From my old sweetheart," she says. "I read some of them every night of my life. Am I not foolish and sentimental to do such a thing?"

Well, I tell Miss Amelia Bodkin she is sentimental all right, but I do not tell her just how foolish she is to be letting me in on where she plants these letters, although of course I am greatly pleased to have this information. I tell Miss Amelia Bodkin that personally I never write a love-letter, and never get a love-letter, and in fact, while I hear of these propositions, I never even see a love-letter before, and this is all as true as you are a foot high. Then Miss Amelia Bodkin laughs a little, and says to me as follows:

"Why," she says, "you are a very unusual chap indeed, not to know what a love-letter is like. Why," she says, "I think I will read you a few of the most wonderful love-letters in this world. It will do no harm," she says, "because you do not know the writer, and you must lie there and think of me, not old and ugly, as you see me now, but as young, and maybe a little bit pretty."

So Miss Amelia Bodkin opens a letter and reads it to me, and her voice is soft and low as she reads, but she scarcely ever looks at the letter as she is reading, so I can see she knows it pretty much by heart. Furthermore, I can see that she thinks this letter is quite a masterpiece, but while I am no judge of love-letters, because this is the first one I ever hear, I wish to say I consider it nothing but great nonsense.

"Sweetheart mine," this love-letter says, "I am still thinking of you as I see you yesterday standing in front of the house with the sunlight turning your dark brown hair to wonderful bronze. Darling," it says, "I love the color of your hair. I am so glad you are not a blonde. I hate blondes, they are so empty-headed, and mean, and deceitful. Also they are bad-tempered," the letter says. "I will never trust a blonde any farther than I can throw a bull by the tail. I never see a blonde in my life who is not a plumb washout," it says. "Most of them are nothing but peroxide, anyway. Business is improving," it says. "Sausage is going up. I love you now and always, my baby doll."

Well, there are others worse than this, and all of them speak of her as sweetheart, or baby, or darlingest one, and also as loveykins, and precious, and angel, and I do not know what all else, and several of them speak of how things will be after they marry, and as I judge these are Mr. Jabez Tuesday's letters, all right, I can see where they are full of dynamite for a guy who is figuring on taking a run-out powder on a doll. In fact, I say something to this general effect to Miss Amelia Bodkin, just for something to say.

"Why," she says, "what do you mean?"

"Well," I say, "documents such as these are known to bring large prices under certain conditions."

No Miss Amelia Bodkin looks at me a moment as if wondering what is in my mind, and then she shakes her head as if she gives it up, and laughs and speaks as follows:

"Well," she says, "one thing is certain, my letters will never bring a price, no matter how large, under any conditions, even if anybody ever wants them. Why," she says, "these are my greatest treasure. They are my memories of my happiest days. Why," she says, "I will not part with these letters for a million dollars."

Naturally I can see from this remark that Mr. Jabez Tuesday makes a very economical deal with me at ten G's for the letters, but of course I do not mention this to Miss Amelia Bodkin as I watch her put her love-letters back in the inlaid box, and put the box back in the drawer of the bureau. I thank her for letting me hear the letters, and then I tell her good night, and I go to sleep, the next day I telephone a certain number on Clinton Street and leave word for Educated Edmund and Spanish John and Little Isadore to come and get me, as I am tired of being an invalid.

Now the next day is Saturday, and the day that comes after is bound to be Sunday, and they come to see me on Saturday, and promise to come back for me Sunday, as the car is now unraveled and running all right, although my friend on Clinton Street is beefing no little about the way his fenders are bent. But before they arrive on Sunday morning, who is there ahead of them bright and early but Mr. Jabez Tuesday in a big town car.

Furthermore, as he walks into the house, all dressed up in a cut-away coat, and a high hat, he grabs Miss Amelia Bodkin in his arms, and kisses her ker-plump right on the smush, which information I afterwards receive from the old guy who seems to be the butler. From upstairs I can personally hear Miss Amelia Bodkin crying more than somewhat, and then I hear Mr. Jabez Tuesday speak in a loud, hearty voice as follows:

"Now, now, now, 'Mely," Mr. Tuesday says. "Do not be crying, especially on my new white vest. Cheer up," Mr. Tuesday says, "and listen to the arrangements I make for our wedding to-morrow, and our honeymoon in Montreal. Yes, indeed, 'Mely," Mr. Tuesday says, "you are the only one for me, because you understand me from A to Izzard. Give me another big kiss, 'Mely, and let us sit down and talk things over."

Well, I judge from the sound that he gets his kiss, and it is a very large kiss indeed, with the cut-out open, and then I hear them chewing the rag at great length in the living-room downstairs. Finally I hear Mr. Jabez Tuesday speak as follows:

"You know, 'Mely," he says, "you and I are just plain ordinary folks without any lugs, and," he says, "this is why we fit each other so well. I am sick and tired of people who pretend to be high-toned and mighty, when they do not have a white quarter to their name. They have no manners whatever. Why, only last night," Mr. Jabez Tuesday says, "I am calling on a high-toned family in New York by the name of Scarwater, and out of a clear sky I am grossly insulted by the daughter of the house, and practically turned out in the street. I never receive such treatment in my life," he says. "'Mely," he says, "give me another kiss, and see if you feel a bump here on my head."

Of course, Mr. Jabez Tuesday is somewhat surprised to see me present later on, but he never lets on he knows me, and naturally I do not give Mr. Jabez any tumble whatever at the moment, and by and by Educated Edmund and Spanish John and Little Isadore come for me in the car, and I thank Miss Amelia Bodkin for her kindness to me, and leave her standing on the lawn with Mr. Jabez Tuesday waving us good-bye.

And Miss Amelia Bodkin looks so happy as she snuggles up close to Mr. Jabez Tuesday that I am glad I take the chance, which is always better than an even-money chance these days, that Miss Valerie Scarwater is a blonde and send Educated Edmund to her to read her Mr. Tuesday's letter in which he speaks of blondes. But of course I am sorry that this and other letters that I tell Educated Edmund to read to her heats her up so far as to make her forget she is a lady and causes her to slug Mr. Jabez Tuesday on the bean with an 18-karat vanity case, as she tells him to get out of her life.

So (Harry the Horse says) there is nothing more to the story, except that we are now looking for Judge Goldfobber to get him to take up a legal matter for us with Mr. Jabez Tuesday. It is true Mr. Tuesday pays us the ten G's, but he never lets us take the silverware he speaks of, not even the Paul Revere teapot, which he says is so valuable, and in fact when we drop around to Miss Amelia Bodkin's house to pick up these articles one night not long ago, the old guy who seems to be the butler lets off a double-barreled shotgun at us, and acts very nasty in general.

So (Harry says) we are going to see if we can get Judge Goldfobber to sue Mr. Jabez Tuesday for breach of promise.

A LIGHT IN FRANCE

In the summer of 1936, a personality by the name of Blond Maurice is found buried in a pit of quicklime up in Sullivan County, or, anyway, what is found is all that is left of Maury, consisting of a few odds and ends in the way of bones, and a pair of shoes which have Brown the shoemaker's name in them, and which Brown identifies as a pair of shoes he makes for Maury some months before, when Maury is in the money and is able to have his shoes made to order.

It is common gossip in all circles along Broadway that Maury is placed in this quicklime by certain parties who do not wish him well, and it is also the consensus of opinion that placing him there is by no means a bad idea, at that, as Maury is really quite a scamp and of no great credit to the community. In fact, when it comes out that there is nothing left of him but a pair of shoes, it is agreed by one and all that it is two shoes too many.

Well, knowing that Maury is quicklimed, it is naturally something of a surprise to me to come upon him in Mindy's restaurant one evening in the spring of 1943, partaking of cheese blintzes. At first I think I am seeing a ghost, but, of course, I know that ghosts never come in Mindy's, and if they do, they never eat cheese blintzes, so I realize that it is nobody but Maury himself.

Consequently I step over to his table and give him a medium hello, and he looks up and gives me a medium hello right back, for, to tell the truth, Maury and I are never bosom friends. In fact, I always give him plenty of the back of my neck because I learn long ago that it is best not to associate with such harum-scarum personalities unless, of course, you need them.

But naturally I am eager to hear of his experiences in the quicklime as I never before meet a guy who returns from being buried in this substance, so I draw up a chair and speak to him as follows:

"Well, Maury," I say, "where are you all this time that I do not see you around and about?"

"I am in a place called France," Maury says. "I leave there on account of the war. Perhaps you hear of the war?"

"Yes," I say, "I hear rumors of it from time to time."

"It is a great nuisance," Maury says.

"But, Maury," I say, "how do you come to go to a place where there is a war?"

"Oh," Maury says, "there is no war when I go there. The war is here in New York. This city is very unsettled at the time, what with the unpleasantness between my employer, the late Little Kishke, and Sammy Downtown developing cases for the medical examiner all over the lay-out. I am pleased to find on my return that law and order now prevail."

"But, Maury," I say, "how do you stand with reference to law and order?"

"I am in favor of both," Maury says. "Oh, I am, all right. Immediately upon my return, I call on the D.A. in Manhattan to see if he has anything he wishes me to plead guilty to, and he cannot find a thing, although he seems somewhat regretful, at that."

"Then," Maury says, "I go over to Brooklyn and call on the D.A. there, and he consults the books of Murder, Incorporated, and he states that all he can find entered under my name is that I am deceased, and that he hopes and trusts I will remain so. I am as clean as a whistle, and," Maury says, "maybe cleaner."

"Well," I say, "I am glad to hear this, Maury. I always know you are sound at bottom. By the way, do you run into Girondel on your travels? We hear that he is over there also. At least, he is absent quite a spell. Girondel is always a great one for going around and about in foreign lands."

"No," Maury says, "I do not see him there. But if you care to listen, I will now relate to you my adventures in France."

Well (Maury says), I go to France when things come up that convince me that I am not as popular as formerly with Sammy Downtown and his associates, and, furthermore, I am tired out and feel that I can use a little rest and peace.

And the reason I pick this France as a place to go to is because I take a fancy to the country when I am there once on a pleasure trip all over Europe as a guest of the late Drums Capello, who is in the importing business, and what he imports is such merchandise as morphine and heroin and sometimes a little opium.

But I wish to state that I have no part of Drums' play in this respect and no part of his fall when the Brush finally catches up with him. And, furthermore, I wish to state that I never approve of his enterprise in any way whatever, but I must say he is a fine host and takes me all over England and Germany, and introduces me to many of his friends and business associates, and you can have them.

Now, the exact spot in France to which I go is a sleepy little town on the seacoast, but I cannot reveal the name at this time as it is a military secret and, anyway, I am unable to pronounce it. The main drag of this town faces a small harbor, and you can stand in front of any place of business along the stem and almost flip a dime into the water—if you happen to have a dime to spare.

It is an old fishing spot, and when I first go there, it is infested by fishermen with hay on their chins, and while most of them inhabit dinky little houses in the town, others live on farms about the size of napkins just outside the burg, and they seem to divide their time between chasing fish and cows. But it is quiet and peaceful there, and very restful after you get used to not hearing the Broadway traffic.

I reside in a tiny gaff that is called a hotel on the main street, and this gaff is run by a French bim by the name of Marie. In fact, all bims in France seem to be named Marie when they are not named Yvonne. I occasionally notice an old sack in the background who may be Marie's mamma or her aunt or some such, but Marie is strictly the boss of the trap and operates it in first-class style. She is the chief clerk and the head waiter and she is also the bartender in the little smoky barroom that opens directly on the street, so, if the door is left open, you get herring with your cognac.

I know she makes the beds and dusts up the three tiny bedrooms in the joint, so you can see she is an all-around personality. She is maybe twenty years old, and I will not attempt to describe her except to say that if I am interested in the hugging and kissing department, I will most certainly take my business to Marie, especially as she speaks English, and you will not have to waste time with the sign language.

Well, it is very pleasant, to be sure, strolling around the little town talking to the fishermen or wandering out into the country and observing the agriculturists, who seem to be mostly female personalities who are all built in such a way that they will never be able to sit down in a washtub with comfort, and who really have very little glamor.

It is also very pleasant to nuzzle a dram or two in the cool of the evening at a little table in front of Marie's hotel and it is there I make the acquaintance of the only other roomer in the hotel. He is a fat old guy who is nobody but Thaddeus T. Blackman, a rich zillionaire from the city of New York and a lam-master from the Brush boys back home for over twenty years on an income-tax beef.

It seems that Thaddeus T. is mixed up in a large scandal about oil lands, and a grand jury hands out readers right and left among some of the best people in the U.S.A., although all they do is swindle the government, and it is a great shock to them to learn that this is against the law.

Anyway, Thaddeus T. starts running as soon as he gets wind of the beef and does not pause for breath until he arrives in this little town in France, and there he lives all these years. It seems the Brush cannot touch him there, and why this is I do not know, but I suppose it is because he is smart enough to take his zillions with him, and naturally this kind of moolouw is protection on land or sea.

He discusses his case with me once and gives me to understand that it is a bum beef as far as he is concerned and that he only takes the fall for others, but of course this is by no means an unfamiliar tale to me, and, as he never mentions why he does not try to chill the beef by paying the government the dough, I do not consider it tactful to bring the matter up.

He is up in the paint-cards in age when I meet him, being maybe close to seventy, and he is a fashion plate of the fashion of about 1922. Moreover, he seems to be a lonely old gee, though how anybody can be lonely with all his zillions is a great mystery to me. He always has a short briar pipe in his mouth and is generally lighting it with little wax matches, and, in fact, I never see a pipe man who is not generally lighting his pipe, and if ever I get time I will invent a pipe that stays lit and make a fortune.

Anyway, Thaddeus T. and I become good friends over the little table in front of the hotel, and then one day who shows up but an old pal of mine out of the city of Boston, Mass., who is also an absentee from a small charge of homicide in his home town.

He is called by the name of Mike the Mugger because it seems his occupation is reaching out of doorways on dark nights and taking passers-by by the neck and pulling them in close to him with one hand and examining into their pockets with the other hand, the idea of the hand around the neck being to keep them from complaining aloud until he is through with them.

Personally, I do not consider this occupation at all essential or even strictly ethical, but I always say every guy to his own taste and naturally I have to respect Mike as the very top guy in his profession who never makes a mistake except that one time he clasps a customer too tight and too long and becomes involved in this difficulty I mention.

He is about thirty-odd and is a nifty drifty in his dress and very good company, except that he is seldom holding anything and is generally leaning on me. However, I am personally loaded at this time and I am not only pleased to okay Mike with Marie for the last of her three rooms, but I stake him to walk-about money, which is money for his pocket, and he is grateful to me in every respect.

Naturally, Mike joins out with Thaddeus T. and me in strolling here and there and in sitting at the little table in front of the hotel or in the barroom, talking and playing cards, and what we generally talk about, of course, is the good old U.S.A., which is a subject of great interest to all three of us.

A few fishermen and small merchants of the town are also usually in the barroom, and Marie is always behind the bar, and it is not long before I notice that both Thaddeus T. and Mike the Mugger are paying considerable attention to her. In fact, Mike tells me he is in love with her and is surprised that I am not in the same condition.

"But," Mike says, "of course I will never mention my love to Marie because I am undoubtedly a low-class personality with a tough beef against me and am unfit to associate with a nice lady saloon-keeper."

As far as I can see, Thaddeus T.'s interest in Marie is more fatherly than anything else, which is very nice if you like an old wolf for a father. He tells me he wishes he has her for his daughter because, he says, the one of his own back in the U.S.A. is a dingbat and so is her mamma, and from the way he carries on about them, I can see that Thaddeus T.'s former home life is far from being a plug for matrimony.

Now it comes on 1939 and with it the war, and Thaddeus T., who can gabble the frog language quite fluently and is always around on the Ear-ie finding out what is going on, tells me that the people of the town are pretty much worked up and that some of the guys are going away to join the army, but it makes little difference in our lives, as we seem to be outside the active war zone, and all we know about any actual fighting is what we hear.

We still sit out in front of the hotel in the afternoon and in the barroom at night, though I observe Marie now pays more attention to other customers than she does to us and is always chattering to them in a most excited manner, and Thaddeus T. says it is about the war. He says Marie is taking it to heart no little and quite some.

But it is not until the summer of 1940 that Thaddeus T. and me and even Mike really notice the war, because overnight the little town fills up with German soldiers and other German guys who are not soldiers but seem to be working gees, and it is plain to be seen that something big is doing. Thaddeus T. says he hears they are making a submarine base of the harbor because it is a very handy spot for the subs to sneak out of and knock off the British ships, and in fact after a while we see many subs and other shipping along the quays.

Anyway, the Germans pay very little attention to us at first except to examine our papers, and the officers who come into Marie's bar for drinks are quite polite and nod to us and sometimes talk to Thaddeus T., who speaks German better than he does French. Presently we are practically ignoring the presence of the Germans in our midst, although naturally Marie has no fancy for them whatever and is always making faces at them behind their backs and spitting on the ground when they pass, until I tell her that this is unladylike.

Well, on coming home one night from a little stroll, I hear a commotion in the kitchen, which is just off the barroom, and on entering I observe Marie wrestling with a big blubber in civilian clothes who is wearing a small scrubbly mustache and a derby hat and who has practically no neck whatever.

They are knocking kitchen utensils right and left, including a pot of spaghetti which I know Marie prepares for my dinner and which vexes me no little. Marie is sobbing and I can see that the blubber is out-wrestling her and in fact has a strangle-hold on her that figures to win him the fall very shortly. I am standing there, admiring his technique in spite of my vexation over the spaghetti, when Marie sees me and calls to me as follows:

"Please help me, Chauncey," which, as I forget to tell you before, is at this time my moniker, and I am then in possession of passports and other papers to prove same.

Naturally, I pay no attention to her, as I do not know on what terms she is wrestling the blubber, but finally I see she is in some distress, so I step forward and tap the bloke on the shoulder and say to him like this:

"I beg your pardon," I say, "but the strangle-hold is illegal. If you are going to wrestle, you must obey the rules."

At this, the guy lets go of Marie and steps back and I say to her in English, "Who is this plumber?"

"He is Herr Klauber," Marie says back to me in English. "He is the head of the Gestapo in this district."

Well, then I get a good glaum at the gee and I see that he is nobody but the same Klauber that Drums Capello does business with in Hamburg the time I am Drums' guest, only in those days he is not usually called by the name of Klauber. He is called the Vasserkopf, which is a way of saying "waterhead" in German, because he has an extra large sconce piece that is practically a deformity and as the Vasserkopf he is known far and wide on two continents, and especially here in New York where he once operates, as a very sure-footed merchant in morphine, heroin, opium, and similar commodities.

Naturally, it is a great pleasure to me to behold a familiar puss in a strange place, even if it is only the Vasserkopf's puss, so I give him a sizable hello and speak to him as follows:

"Well, Vasser," I say, "this is an unexpected privilege, to be sure. There you are and here I am, and much water runs over the dam since last we met, and how are you anyway?"

"Who are you?" the Vasserkopf says in English and in a most unfriendly manner.

"Come, come, Vasser," I say. "Let us not waste time in shadow-boxing. Do you know our old pal Drums finally takes a fall in Milwaukee, Wis., for a sixer?"

Then the Vasserkopf comes close to me and speaks to me in a low voice like this: "Listen," he says, "it is in my mind to throw you in the jail house."

"Tut-tut, Vass," I say, "if you throw me in the jail house, I will be compelled to let out a bleat. I will be compelled to remember the time you ship the cargo of Santa Clauses out of Nuremberg and each Santa contains enough of the white to junk up hail of the good old U.S.A. I hear your Fuehrer is a strait-laced gee, and what will he say if he hears one of his big coppers peddles junk and maybe uses it?"

I can see the Vasserkopf turns a little pale around the guzzle at this statement and he says: "Come outside. We will talk."

So I go outside the gaff with him, and we stand in the street in the darkness and have quite a chat and the Vasserkopf becomes more friendly and tells me that he is now a real high-muck-a-muck with the Gestapo and the greatest spy catcher in the racket. Then he wishes to know what I am doing in these parts, and I tell him quite frankly that I am there for my health and explain my ailment to him. I also tell him why Thaddeus T. and Mike the Mugger are there because I know that, as a former underworld personality, the Vasserkopf is apt to be understanding and sympathetic in such situations, especially when he knows my hole card is my knowledge of his background in junk.

"Now, Vass," I say, "all we wish is to be let alone, and if you can assist us in any way, I will personally be much obliged. What is more," I say, "I will see that you are well rewarded, if a member of the Gestapo takes."

"Sure," the Vasserkopf says. "Only let us understand one thing right off the reel. The broad belongs to me. I am crazy about her. But there is talk today at headquarters of closing this place and putting her out of business because of her attitude, and because one of our officers becomes ill after drinking cognac in here last night.

"I will tell the dumb military he probably has a touch of ptomaine," he continues. "I will tell them I need this hotel as a listening post to find out what is going on among the people around here. I will advise them not to molest you, as you are neutrals, and it may make trouble with your government, although," the Vasserkopf says, "I can see that the only trouble your government may make will be for you. But the Reich is not interested in American lammeroos, and neither am I as long as you remember the dame is mine and see that I collect a hundred a week in your money. I can scarcely sleep nights thinking of her."

Now this seems to me to be a very reasonable proposition all the way around, except for the hundred a week. The way I look at it, the Vasserkopf is at least entitled to Marie for all his trouble because, to tell the truth, it will be most inconvenient for Thaddeus T. and Mike the Mugger and me to leave this spot at the moment, as there is no other place we can go and no way of getting there if there is such a place.

So I shave the Vasserkopf to half a C every week, and then I go back into the hotel to find Marie in the bar with Thaddeus T. and Mike, and I can see that she is quite agitated by her recent experience with the Vasserkopf. I also learn from her that it is not his first visit.

"He is here several times before," Marie says. "He comes to me first with news of my brother who is a prisoner in a camp near Hamburg. Herr Klauber tells me he can make things easier for Henri and perhaps get him released. He comes again and again on different excuses. I am frightened because I fear his motive." Then all of a sudden Marie puts her fingers to her lips and says, "Hark!"

We hark, and I hear away off somewhere a sound that I know must come from a lot of planes, and as this sound grows louder and louder, and then dies away again, Marie says:

"English bombers," she says. "Every night they pass over here and go on up the coast to drop their bombs. They do not know what is going on here. Oh, if we can only show a light here to let them know this is a place to strike—this nest of snakes."

"A light?" I say. "Why, if you show a light around here, these squareheads will settle you in no time. Besides," I say, "it may get me and my friends in a jam, and we are Americans and very neutral. Let us not even think of showing a light and, Marie," I say, "kindly cease sizzling every time you serve a German, and, Mike, if you have any more Mickey Finns on your person, please take them yourself instead of dropping them in officers' drinks."

"Who? Me?" Mike the Mugger says.

Well, I see the Vasserkopf in the hotel almost every day after this talking to Marie, and he always gives me an E-flat hello and I give him the same, and, while I can see that Marie is afraid of him, she says he is now very polite to her and does not try to show her any more holds.

Of course, I do not tell Marie about my deal with Vasserkopf and I do not tell Mike either, though I inform Thaddeus T., as I expect him to kick with some of the dough, and he says okay and that he is glad to learn that the Vasserkopf is on the take, only he thinks the half a C is enough without throwing in Marie. But he says a deal is a deal, and I can count on his co-operation.

From now on as far as we are concerned, everything seems to be almost the same as before there is any war whatever, except that we cannot go near the waterfront where the Germans are working and everything has to be blacked out good after dark, and you cannot as much as strike a match in the street, which is a great nuisance to Thaddeus T., as he is always striking matches. In fact, he almost gets his toupee blown off by sentries before he can break himself of the habit of striking matches outdoors at night.

I can see that the Vasserkopf must be keeping his agreement to front for us at headquarters all right, and I am greasing him every week per our arrangement, but I find myself bored by the place, and I have a feeling that it is time for Mike the Mugger and me and maybe Thaddeus T., too, to leave, especially as the Vasserkopf accidentally drops a hint one day that he finds himself impeded in his progress with Marie by our constant presence in the hotel and that he thinks he is getting the short end of the deal. Finally, I have a conference with Thaddeus T. and state my views to him.

"Yes," Thaddeus T. says, "you are a hundred per cent right. But," he says, "leaving here is not a simple matter for us now. I am reliably informed that the military is likely to oppose our departure for the present, because the sub base here is a great secret and they do not care to run the risk of having us noise it about.

"In fact," he says, "I am told that they are sorry they do not chase us when they first come here, but now that they make this mistake, they are not going to make another by letting us depart, and other information that I hesitate to credit is that they may wind up clapping us in a detention camp somewhere."

"Thaddeus T.," I say, "I am an American and so is Mike and so are you, and our country is not concerned in this war. No one can hold us here against our wishes."

Well, at this, Thaddeus T. lets out a large laugh, and I can see his point and laugh with him, and then he informs me that for some days he is personally laying plans for our departure and that he buys a slightly tubercular motor-boat from a certain personality and has it hidden at this very moment in a little cove about a mile up the coast and that all he now needs is a little petrol, which is a way of saying gasoline, to run the boat with the three of us in it out to sea, where we will have the chance of being picked up.

Thaddeus T. explains to me that all the petrol in this vicinity is in the hands of the Germans, but he says that where there is a will, there is a way. Consequently, he makes arrangements with the same personality who sells him the boat for a supply of gasoline, and who is this personality but the Vasserkopf, and Thaddeus is paying him more per gill for the gas than the old Vass ever gets per ounce for his hop, and, as I am personally paying him regularly, I can see that he is getting his coming and going and, naturally, I have to admire his enterprise.

However, Thaddeus states that the Vasserkopf is really most co-operative in every respect, and that he is to deliver the gas at the hotel the following night, and moreover that he is going to escort us to the cove so we will not be molested by any sentries we may encounter in that vicinity, which I say is very nice of the Vasserkopf though I seem to remember that there are never any sentries in that vicinity anyway, as it is part of the coast that does not seem to interest the Germans in any manner.

Then I get to meditating more and more on the Vasserkopf and on what a big heart he has, to be sure, and as I am meditating I am also sauntering late the next evening in a roundabout way up the coast as I wish to confirm the presence of the boat in the cove because, of course, there is the possibility of it getting away after the Vasserkopf has it placed there.

My roundabout saunter carries me across the fields of the little farms beyond the town that in some places run almost down to the sea, and it is a route that the Germans are not apt to suspect as taking me on any considerable journey, even if they notice me sauntering, which I take care they do not.

Finally, I saunter through a field to a slight rise of ground that overlooks the little cove, and there is just enough daylight left by now for me to see a boat floating just offshore, and at this same moment, I am surprised to scent the odor of fresh-turned earth near at hand, and the reason I am surprised is because it is now winter and by no means plowing time.

Consequently, I look around and I am further surprised to observe on this rise a newly made trench on the ground of a size and shape that brings back many memories to me. So I saunter back in a more roundabout way still meditating no little and quite some on the Vasserkopf.

But, sure enough, he shows up this very night around nine o'clock after Marie closes her place, and he brings with him two five-gallon cans of gasoline which he delivers to Thaddeus T. in the bar where Thaddeus and me and Mike the Mugger are waiting to receive the gas. Then, after handing over the cans, the Vass goes looking for Marie, saying he wishes to speak to her before escorting us to the boat.

As soon as he leaves the bar, Mike the Mugger outs with his pocketknife and stabs holes in two corners of the can and speaks as follows: "It smells like gasoline on the outside, but we smear the outside of cans with booze in the old bootleg days for the liquor smell when there is only water inside the cans. I hear the Vasserkopf is an old booter and he may remember the trick, and, besides, I do not trust him on general principles."

Now Mike lifts the can up as if it is no more than a demi-tasse and he holds it to his mouth so he can get a swig of the contents through one of the holes, when all of a sudden who comes into the bar all out of breath but Marie and who is right behind her but the Vasserkopf, and there is no doubt that Marie is greatly flustered, and the Vasserkopf is much perturbed.

"So," he says to me, "you are double-crossing me and are going to take this omelet with you, hey? Well, it is a good thing I walk in on her as she is packing a keister, and I am now arresting her as a dangerous spy."

Marie begins to weep and wail and to carry on as bims will do when they are flustered, and naturally Thaddeus T. and me and Mike the Mugger are quite perplexed by this situation and, in fact, Mike is so perplexed that he is still holding the can in his hands and his cheeks are bulged out on each side from the gasoline in his mouth as if he has the mumps.

I am about to say something to cool the Vasserkopf off, for, to tell the truth, up to this minute I have no idea Marie is going with us, though I can see from the way Thaddeus T. and Mike the Mugger look that it is undoubtedly their idea. And, before I can say anything, Mike steps up to the Vasserkopf and gives a huge ploo-oo-oo and spews his mouthful of gasoline right in the Vasserkopf's kisser and, as he gets his mouth clear, Mike says, "Why, you muzzler, it is somewhat watered, just as I suspect."

Well, naturally, the gasoline runs off the Vasserkopf's face and down over his clothes and he is standing there looking quite nonplussed, and, as Mike the Mugger sees me gazing at him disapprovingly, he becomes embarrassed and self-conscious and, maybe to cover his confusion, he lifts the can of gasoline and holds it over the Vasserkopf's head, and the gas pours out and splashes off the old Vass' derby hat and splatters over his shoulders while he just stands there nonplussed.

Thaddeus T. Blackman is leaning against the bar and, as usual, he is lighting his pipe with a little wax match and watching the Vasserkopf, and Marie has stopped crying and is laughing, and I am just standing there, when we again hear the sound of the planes high overhead and Thaddeus T. speaks as follows:

"A light you say, Marie?" he says. "A light for the English?"

Then he flips the lighted match on the Vasserkopf, whose clothes burst into flames at once and, almost as if they plan it all out beforehand, Mike jumps to the front door and opens it, and Thaddeus T. pushes the Vasserkopf, all ablaze, out the door into the street and yells at him:

"Run for the water!" he yells. "Run, run, run!"

The Vasserkopf seems to see what he means and starts galloping lickity-split towards the waterfront with Thaddeus T. puffing along behind him and giving him a shove whenever he shows signs of lagging, and Mike the Mugger runs up behind the Vasserkopf and keeps throwing little spurts of gasoline on him by jerking the can at him and, from the way it burns on the Vasserkopf, I think Mike's statement of its dilution may be a slight exaggeration.

As he runs and burns, the Vasserkopf is letting out loud cries which bring soldiers from every which way, and presently they start shooting off their rifles in different directions. He is really quite a bonfire there in the darkness, and now I hear once more far overhead the drone of planes and I figure the English bombers see the light and turn back over the town.

All of a sudden there is a whistling sound and then a big *ker-*

bloom, and then more whistling and more *ker-blooms,* and there is no doubt in my mind that it is Katie-bar-the-door for the water-front and the subs lying along the quays.

I can see the Vasserkopf still blazing and I can hear Thaddeus T. still urging him to run, and now the bombs are shellacking the surrounding buildings, and presently I hear, in between the blasts of the bombs, some rifle shots, and I know the soldiers are firing at Thaddeus T. and Mike the Mugger and maybe at the Vasserkopf, too, for making the light.

In fact, by the glow shed by the Vasserkopf, I see old Thaddeus stumble and fall, and Mike the Mugger go down right afterwards with his can of gasoline blazing over him, but the Vasserkopf continues on still in flames until he falls off the quay into the water and, the chances are, goes out with a zizz.

Well, when I think of Marie, I turn from these unusual scenes to the little hotel, but it is no longer there, because a bomb flattens it, too, and it is now nothing but a pile of miscellany. I do not have much time to look for Marie, as the German soldiers are all over the lay-out, trying to learn what happens, but I finally locate her with a big beam across her chest, and I can see that there is nothing I can do for her except kiss her and say good-bye, and when I do this, she murmurs, "Thanks," but I am sure it is only for Thaddeus T. and Mike the Mugger and the light.

You will scarcely believe the difficulty I experience in getting away from this unpleasant situation and out of the country. In fact, I have only a vague recollection of my adventures now, but I will always remember very clearly how neatly I slip past four German soldiers sitting in the new-made trench on the rise of ground above the cove, with a machine gun covering the cove itself, and how I get in the boat and cut it loose and work it, with my hands for paddles, to open water, before they realize what is going on.

And I can never again have any respect for the memory of the Vasserkopf when I take to meditating on his unsportsmanlike conduct in trying to double-cinch a sure thing with a machine gun, although there are times before I am picked up at sea by an English destroyer that I find myself wishing that Mike the Mugger does not waste all the gasoline on the Vass, even if it is watered.

And this is all there is to the story (Maury says).

"But, Maury," I say, "do you not know that some remainders

found in a pit of quicklime up in Sullivan County are supposed to be yours? They have on your shoes, which are identified by Brown the shoemaker. Are you ever in a quicklime pit in Sullivan County and, if so, what is it like?"

"Oh," Maury says, "I am in Sullivan County, all right, but never in a quicklime pit. I go to Sullivan County at the invitation of Girondel, and the purpose of his invitation is to discuss ways and means of getting me straightened out with his chief, Sammy Downtown.

"But one day," Maury says, "Girondel invites me to a stroll in the woods with him and, while we are strolling, he is talking about the beauties of the landscape and calling my attention to the flowers and the birds, which is all very interesting, to be sure, but something tells me that Girondel is by no means the nature lover he seems.

"Finally," Maury says, "he strolls me to a spot in the deep, tangled wildwood, and all of a sudden I catch an odor of something I never scent but once before in my life but will never again forget, and that is the time we lay the late Bugs Wonder to rest in Greenvale Cemetery. It is the odor of the fresh-turned earth from Bugs' last resting place.

"And as I catch this again in the woods," Maury says, "I realize that somebody does some digging around there lately, so I quietly give Girondel a boff over his pimple with a blackjack and flatten him like a Welcome mat. Then I examine my surroundings and, sure enough, there, hidden by the shrubbery, I find a deep fresh-made hole lined with quicklime, and I place Girondel in it and cover him up and leave him with my best wishes.

"But, first," Maury says, "I change shoes with him because my own are badly worn and, besides, I know that if ever he is found the shoes will outlast the quicklime and be traced as mine, and I wish Girondel's connection to think I am no more. By the way," he says, "the odor I mention is the same I notice on the rise of ground at the cove in France which causes me to distrust the Vasserkopf. I guess I am just naturally allergic to the odor of new-made graves."

THE TURPS

A CALL ON THE PRESIDENT

When I got home from work the other night my wife Ethel ses O Joe, an awful thing has happened. Jim the mailman got fired.

I ses who fired him? She ses why, the Government fired him. Somebody told the Government that they saw him take a letter out of his mail sack and burn it. The Government ses Jim, why did you do such a thing, and Jim would not tell so they fired him.

She ses Joe, you go and see some politicians and have them make the Government put Jim the mailman back to work right away because he is too old to do anything else but carry the mail and he would starve to death in no time. It is not justice to fire a man who has carried the mail for over thirty years, she ses.

I ses Ethel sweets, I do not know no politicians that have got anything to do with the Government or justice. I ses anyway we are only little people and they are big people and what is the use of talking to them? I ses they would only give me a pushing around because that is what big people always do to little people.

Well, Ethel ses, who runs the Government? I ses the President of the United States runs the Government and she ses I bet anything the President of the United States would give Jim the mailman back his job if we tell him about it. Lets us go see the President of the United States.

I ses Ethel sugar plum, the President of the United States lives in Washington and he is a busy fellow and I do not think he would have time to see us even if we went there, and she ses now there you go rooting against yourself like you always do. We will go to Washington and see the President of the United States because it is important that Jim the mailman gets his job back. Why, she ses Jim the mailman would simply lay down and die if he could not keep on carrying the mail.

So the next day I got a days layoff and then we climbed in the old bucket and drove to Washington and my wife Ethel wore her best dress and her new hat, and I put on my gray suit and a necktie and when we arrived in Washington about noon, I ses to a cop, look cop, where do you find the President of the United States? He ses I never find him.

O, I ses, a wise guy, hey? I ses cop, I am a citizen of the United States of America and this is my wife Ethel and she is a citizen too and I asked you a question like a gentleman and you have a right to answer me like a gentleman.

Yes, my wife Ethel ses, we are from Brooklyn and we do not like to have hick cops get fresh with us. O, the cop ses, I am a hick am I, and she ses well you look like one to me. I ses pipe down Ethel honey, and let me do the talking will you, and the cop ses Buddy I have got one of those too, and I sympathize with you.

He ses you have to go to the White House to find the President of the United States. You follow this street a ways he ses, and you cannot miss. Give him my regards when you see him, the cop ses. I ses what name will I tell him. The cop ses George, and I ses George what? My wife Ethel ses drive on Joe, that hick cop is just trying to kid people.

So we followed the street like the cop ses and pretty soon we came to a big building in a yard and I ses well, Ethel, I guess that is the White House all right. Then I parked the old bucket up against the curb and we got out and walked into the yard and up to the door of this building and at the door there was another cop.

He ses what do you want? I ses who wants to know? He ses I do. I ses all right, we want to see the President of the United States and he ses so does a hundred million other people. He ses what do you want to see him about anyway? My wife Ethel ses Joe, why do you waste your time talking to the hick cops? I never saw so many hick cops in my life. She ses in Brooklyn people do not have to go around answering questions from cops.

Well, go back to Brooklyn the cop ses. Anyway, get away from here. I do not like to look at you he ses. Your faces make me tired. I ses cop, you are no rose geranium yourself when it comes to looks. I ses I am a citizen of the United States of America and I know my rights. I do not have to take no lip off of cops. I ses it is a good thing for you that you have got that uniform on, and that I have respect of the law or I would show you something.

He ses you and who else? I ses I do not need nobody else and my wife Ethel ses show him something anyway, Joe, and I might have showed him something all right but just then a fellow with striped pants on came out of the door and ses what is the trouble here?

I ses there is no trouble, just a fresh cop. I ses my wife Ethel and me want to see the President of the United States and this jerk here ses we cannot do so. I ses that is always the way it is with cops, when they get that uniform on they want to start pushing people around.

I ses I am a citizen of the United States of America and it is a fine note if a citizen cannot see the President of the United States when he wants to without a lot of cops horning in. I ses it is not justice for cops to treat a citizen that way. I ses what is the President of the United States for if a citizen cannot see him? My wife Ethel ses yes, we are not going to eat him, and I ses Ethel baby, you better let me handle this situation.

The fellow in the striped pants ses what do you want to see the President of the United States about? I ses look Mister, we came all the way from Brooklyn to see the President of the United States and I have got to be back to work on my job tomorrow and if I stop and tell everybody what I want to see him about I won't have no time left. I ses Mister, what is so tough about seeing the President of the United States? When he was after his job he was glad to see any-body. I ses is he like those politicians in Brooklyn now or what?

Wait a minute, the fellow in the striped pants ses, and he went back into the building and after a while he came out again and ses the President of the United States will see you at once. What is your name? I ses my name is Joe Turp and this is my wife Ethel. He ses I am pleased to meet you and I ses the same to you. Then he took us into the building and finally into a big office, and there was the President of the United States all right. I could tell him from his pictures.

He smiled at us and the fellow in the striped pants who took us in ses this is Joe Turp of Brooklyn and his wife Ethel, and the Pres-ident of the United States shook hands with us and ses I am glad to see you, and I ses likewise. He ses how are things in Brooklyn? Rotten, I ses. They always are. The Dodgers are doing better but they need more pitching, I ses. How are things in Washington? He ses not so good. He ses I guess we need more pitching here too.

He told us to set down and then he ses, what is on your mind Joe, but there was some other fellows in the office and I ses Your Honor, what my wife Ethel and me want to see you about is strictly on the q t and he laughed and motioned at the other fellows and they went out of the room laughing too and my wife Ethel ses what is so funny around here anyway? I ses nix Ethel. I ses nix now. Kindly let me handle this situation.

Then I ses to the President of the United States, Your Honor, you do not know me and I do not know you so we start even. I know you are a busy fellow and I will not waste your time any more than I have to so I better come to the point right away, I ses. My wife Ethel and me want to talk to you about Jim the mailman.

Yes, Ethel ses, he got fired from his job. I ses Ethel sugar plum, please do not butt in on this. I will tell the President of the United States all about it. Your Honor, I ses, when women start to tell something they always go about it the wrong end to, and he ses yes but they mean well. Who is Jim the mailman?

I ses Your Honor, Jim the mailman is a fellow over sixty years old and he has been carrying the mail in our neighborhood for thirty some odd years. My wife Ethel and me were little kids when Jim the mailman started carrying the mail. You Honor, I ses, you may not believe it but my wife Ethel was a good-looking little squab when she was a kid. I can believe it, the President of the United States ses.

Well, Your Honor, I ses, you would think Jim the mailman was a grouchy old guy until you got to know him. He is a tall thin fellow with humped over shoulders from carrying that mail sack around and he has long legs like a pair of scissors and gray hair and wears specs. He is nowhere near as grouchy as he looks. The reason he looks grouchy is because his feet always hurt him.

Yes, my wife Ethel ses, I gave him some lard to rub on his feet one day and Jim the mailman ses he never had anything help him so much. My mother used to rub my pop's feet with lard when he came home with them aching. My pops was a track walker in the subway she ses. I ses look Ethel, the President of the United States is not interested in your pop's feet and she ses well that is how I thought of the lard for Jim the mailman.

I ses Your Honor, Jim the mailman was always real nice to the kids. I remember one Christmas he brought me a sack of candy and

a Noahs ark. Yes, my wife Ethel ses, and once he gave me a doll
that ses mamma when you punched it in the stomach. I ses Ethel,
honey, the President of the United States does not care where you
punched it. Well, she ses you punched it in the stomach if you
wanted it to say mamma.

Your Honor, I ses, old Missus Crusper lived a couple of doors
from us and she was about the same age as Jim the mailman. She
was a little off her nut. My wife Ethel ses Your Honor, she was not
so. She was just peculiar. You should not say such things about
Missus Crusper the poor old thing Joe, she ses. You ought to be
ashamed of yourself to say such things.

All right, Ethel baby, I ses. She was peculiar, Your Honor. I
mean Missus Crusper. She was a little old white-haired lady with
a voice like a canary bird and she had not been out of her house in
twenty-five years and most of the time not out of bed. Something
happened to her when her son Johnny was born.

I had to stop my story a minute because I noticed Ethel at the
window acting very strange and I ses Ethel, what is the idea of you
looking out that window and screwing up your face the way you
are doing and she ses I am making snoots at that hick cop. He is right
under this window and I have got him half crazy. I ses Your Honor,
kindly excuse my wife Ethel, but she is getting even with a cop who
tried to keep us from seeing you and the President of the United
States laughed and ses well, what about Missus Crusper?

I ses well, Missus Crusper's name before she got married was
Kitten O'Brien, Your Honor, and her old man ran a gin mill in our
neighborhood but very respectable. She married Henry Crusper
when she was eighteen and the old folks in our neighborhood ses
it broke Jim the mailman's heart. He went to school with her and
Henry Crusper and Jim the mailman used to follow Kitten O'Brien
around like a pup but he never had no chance.

Henry Crusper was a good-looking kid, I ses, and Jim the mailman was as homely as a mule and still is. Besides he was an orphan
and Henry Crusper's old man had a nice grocery store. He gave
the store to Henry when he married Kitten O'Brien. But Jim the
mailman did not get mad about losing Missus Crusper like people
do nowadays. He ses he did not blame her and he ses he certainly
did not blame Henry Crusper. He stayed good friends with them
both and used to be around with them a lot but he never looked
at another broad again.

The President of the United States ses another what? Another broad I ses. Another woman I ses. O, he ses. I see.

Yes, my wife Ethel ses, I bet you would not be the way Jim the mailman was, Joe Turp. I bet you would have been as sore as a goat if I had married Linky Moses but I bet you would have found somebody else in no time. I ses please, Ethel. Please now. Anyway, I ses, look how Linky Moses turned out. How did Lucky Moses turn out, the President of the United States ses, and I ses he turned out a bum.

Your Honor, I ses, Missus Crusper married Henry Crusper when she was about eighteen. Henry was a good steady-going fellow and he made her a fine husband from what everybody ses and in our neighborhood if anybody does not make a fine husband it gets talked around pretty quick.

She was crazy about him but she was crazier still about her son Johnny especially after Henry died. That was when Johnny was five or six years old. Henry got down with pneumonia during a tough winter.

Yes, my wife Ethel ses, my mother ses he never would wear an overcoat no matter how cold it was. My mother ses not wearing overcoats is why lots of people get pneumonia and die. I always try to make Joe to wear his overcoat and a muffler too, Ethel ses. I ses, Ethel, never mind what you make me wear, and she ses well Joe, I only try to keep you healthy.

Missus Crusper must have missed Henry a lot, Your Honor, I ses. Henry used to carry her up and down the stairs in his arms. He waited on her hand and foot. Of course much of this was before my time and what I tell you is what the old people in our neighborhood told me. After Henry died it was Jim the mailman who carried Missus Crusper up and down stairs in his arms until she got so she could not leave her bed at all and then Jim the mailman spent all his spare time setting there talking to her and waiting on her like she was a baby.

I ses I did not know Missus Crusper until I was about ten years old and got to running around with Johnny. He was a tough kid, Your Honor, and I had him marked stinko even then and so did all the other kids in the neighborhood. His mother could not look out after him much and he did about as he pleased. He was a natural-born con artist and he could always salve her into believing whatever he wanted her to believe.

She thought he was the smartest kid in the world and that he was going to grow up to be a big man. She was proud of Johnny and what he was going to be. Nobody in our neighborhood wanted to tell her that he was no good. I can see her now, Your Honor, a little lady with a lace cap on her head leaning out of the window by her bed and calling Johnny so loud you could hear her four blocks away because she always called him like she was singing.

My wife Ethel had quit making snoots at the cop and was sitting in a chair by the window and she jumped out of the chair and ses yes, Your Honor, Missus Crusper sing-sanged O hi, Johnny, and a hey Johnny, and a ho, Johnny, just like that.

The fellow in the striped pants stuck his head in the door but the President of the United States waggled a finger at him and he closed the door again and I ses look Ethel, when you holler like that you remind me of your mother. She ses what is the matter with my mother, and I ses nothing that being deaf and dumb will not cure. I ses Ethel, it is not dignified to holler like that in the presence of the President of the United States.

Why, Ethel ses, I was only showing how Missus Crusper used to call Johnny by sing-sanging O hi, Johnny, and a hey Johnny, and a ho, Johnny. I ses Ethel, that will do. I ses do you want to wake the dead?

Your Honor, I ses, Jim the mailman was around Missus Crusper's house a lot and he was around our neighborhood a good deal too and he knew what Johnny was doing. As Johnny got older Jim the mailman tried to talk to him and make him behave but that only made Johnny take to hating Jim the mailman. The old folks ses Jim the Mailman wanted to marry Missus Crusper after she got over being so sorry about Henry but one day she told him she could never have anything to do with a man who spoke disrespectfully of her late husband and ordered him out of the house.

Afterwards Jim the mailman found out that Johnny had told her Jim had said something bad about Henry Crusper around the neighborhood and nothing would make her believe any different until long later. Your Honor, I ses, Johnny Crusper was one of the best liars in the world even when he was only a little kid.

The fellow in the striped pants came in the room about now and he bent over and said something in a whisper to the President of the United States but the President of the United States waved his hand and ses tell him I am busy with some friends from Brooklyn and the fellow went out again.

Your Honor, I ses, this Johnny Crusper got to running with some real tough guys when he was about seventeen and pretty soon he was in plenty of trouble with the cops but Jim the mailman always managed to get him out without letting his mother know. The old folks ses it used to keep Jim the mailman broke getting Johnny out of trouble.

Finally one day Johnny got in some real bad trouble that Jim the mailman could not square or nobody else and Johnny had to leave town in a big hurry. He did not stop to say good-bye to his mother. The old folks ses Jim the mailman hocked his salary with a loan shark to get Johnny the dough to leave town on and some ses he sent Johnny more dough afterwards to keep going. But Jim the mailman never ses a word himself about it one way or the other so nobody but him and Johnny knew just what happened about that.

Your Honor, I ses, Johnny going away without saying good-bye made Missus Crusper very sick and this was when she commenced being peculiar. Old Doc Steele ses she was worrying herself to death because she never heard from Johnny. He ses he would bet if she knew where Johnny was and if he was all right it would save her life and her mind too but nobody knew where Johnny was so there did not seem to be anything anybody could do about that.

Then one day Jim the mailman stopped at Missus Crusper's house and gave her a letter from Johnny. It was not a long letter and it was from some place like Vancouver and it ses Johnny was working and doing well and that he loved her dearly and thought of her all the time. I know it ses that, Your Honor, because Jim the mailman wrote it all out by himself and read to me and ses how does it sound?

I ses it sounded great. It looked great too because Jim the mailman had fixed up the envelope at the post office so it looked as if it had come through the mail all right and he had got hold of one of Johnny's old school books and made a good stab at imitating Johnny's handwriting. It was not a hard job to do that. Johnny never let himself get past the fourth grade and his handwriting was like a child would do.

Missus Crusper never bothered about the handwriting anyway, Your Honor. She was so glad to hear from Johnny she sent for everybody in the neighborhood and read them the letter. It must have sounded genuine because Jennie Twofer went home and told her old man that Mrs. Crusper had got a letter from Johnny and her old man told his brother Fred who was a plain-clothes cop and Fred went around to see Missus Crusper and find out where Johnny was. Jim the mailman got hold of Fred first and they had a long talk and Fred went away without asking Missus Crusper anything.

Yes, my wife Ethel ses, that Jennie Twofer always was a two-face meddlesome old thing and nobody ever had any use for her. I ses look, Ethel, kindly do not knock our neighbors in public. I ses wait until we get back home and she ses all right but Jennie Two-fer is two face just the same.

Your Honor, I ses, every week for over ten years old Missus Crusper got a letter from Johnny and he was always doing well although he seemed to move around a lot. He was in Arizona California Oregon and everywhere else. Jim the mailman made him a mining engineer so he could have a good excuse for moving around. On Missus Crusper's birthdays and on Christmas she always got a little present from him. Jim the mailman took care of that.

She kept the letters in a box under her bed and she would read them to all her old friends when they called and brag about the way Johnny was doing and what a good boy he was to his mother. Your Honor, old chromos in our neighborhood whose sons were bums and who had a pretty good idea the letters were phony would set and listen to Missus Crusper read them and tell her Johnny surely was a wonderful man.

About a month ago the only legitimate letter that came to Missus Crusper since Johnny went away bobbed up in Jim the mailman's sack, I ses. It was a long thin envelope and Jim the mailman opened it and read it and then he touched a match to it and went on to Missus Crusper's house and delivered a letter to her from Johnny in Australia. This letter ses he was just closing a deal that would make him a millionaire and that he would then come home and bring her a diamond breastpin and never leave her again as long as he lived.

But Your Honor, I ses, Jim the mailman knew that it would be the last letter he would deliver to Missus Crusper because Old

Doc Steele told him the day before that she had only a few hours more to go and she died that night.

Jim the mailman was setting by her bed. He ses that at the very last she tried to lean out the window and call Johnny.

Well I ses, some louse saw Jim the mailman burn that letter and turned him in to the Government and got him fired from his job but Jim could not do anything else but burn it because it was a letter from the warden of the San Quentin prison where Johnny had been a lifer for murder all those years, telling Missus Crusper her son had been killed by the guards when he was trying to escape and saying she could have his body if she wanted it.

Your Honor, I ses, I guess we have got plenty of gall coming to you with a thing like this when you are so busy. I ses my wife Ethel wanted me to go to some politicians about it but I told her the best we would get from politicians would be a pushing around and then she ses we better see you and here we are.

But I ses it is only fair to tell you that if you do anything to help Jim the mailman we cannot do anything for you in return because we are just very little people and all we can do is say much obliged and God bless you and that is what everybody in our neighborhood would say.

Well, my wife Ethel ses, Jim the mailman has got to have his job back because I would hate to have anybody else bring me my mail. I ses Ethel baby, the only mail I ever knew you to get was a Valentine from Linky Moses four years ago and I told him he better not send you any more and she ses yes, that is the mail I mean.

The President of the United States ses Joe and Missus Turp think no more of it. You have come to the right place. I will take good care of the matter of Jim the mailman. Then he pushed a button on his desk and the main in the striped pants came in and the President ses tell them I will have two more for luncheon. The fellow ses who are they and the President ses my friends Joe and Missus Turp of Brooklyn and my wife Ethel ses it is a good job I wore my new hat.

We drove back home in the old bucket after we had something to eat and I got back to work the next day on time all right and a couple of days later I saw Jim the mailman around delivering mail so I knew he was okay too.

I never gave the trip to Washington any more thought and my wife did not say anything about it either for a couple of weeks and then one night she woke me up out of a sound sleep by jabbing me in the back with her elbow and ses Joe, I have been thinking about something. I ses look Ethel, you do your thinking in the day time please and let me sleep.

But she ses no, listen Joe. She ses if ever I go back to Washington again I will give that hick cop a piece of my mind because I have just this minute figured out what he meant when he said he had one of those too and sympathized with you.

EARLY FICTION

THE DEFENSE OF STRIKERVILLE

The squad-room conversation had drifted to the state militia, and everyone had taken a verbal poke at that despised arm of the military resources.

"Onct I belonged to the milish," remarked Private Hanks, curled up luxuriously on his cot and sending long, spiral wreaths of smoke ceiling-ward.

"That's what I thought," said Sergeant Cameron. "I recall the time you first took on—Plattsburg, '97, wasn't it? I had an idea then that you came from the state gravel wallopers."

"I'm kiddin' on the square," said Hanks. "I was an out-and-out snoljer with the milish two years ago out in Colorado. I helped put duwn the turrible rebellion in the Coal Creek district."

This statement was received with obvious disbelief.

"Lemme tell you about that," said Private Hanks, sitting up. "Lemme relate the sad circumstances of J. Wallace Hanks' enlistment in the Colorado State milish, and if you all don't weep, you haven't got no hearts.

"They was a bunch of us discharged from the Fifth, in Denver, in 1904. We all has a good gob of finals, and of course none of us were going back. You all know how that is," and Private Hanks looked suggestively at Private William Casey, who had just reenlisted that day for his fifth "hitch," after a fervid declaration of a week before that he was through with the service forever; Private Casey at that moment being seated disconsolately upon his cot, red-eyed and dispirited.

"It takes me about a week to get ready to back up into the railroad building to hold up my right hand and promise Recruitin' Sergeant Wilson and Uncle Sam to love, honor, and obey, or words to that effect. The rest of the gang was no better off. They was scattered up and down Larimer Street, stallin' for biscuits, and doing the reliever act with them nice new citizens they'd bought in the flush of their prosperity.

"We all see another three-year trick sticking up as conspicuous as a Chinaman in church, but none of us is dead anxious to go back so soon. We don't want the gang out at the fort to give us the big tee-hee after all them solemn swears and rosy air-castles we'd regaled them with when we departed. We'd like to lay off awhile until the novelty of our return wouldn't be so strikin'.

"Most of us is too sick to even think of looking for work. We'd maced about everyone we could think of, from Highlands to the fort, and we're done, that's all. We're about twenty-five strong, take us altogether, and there wasn't forty cents. Mex in the lay-out. Things is certainly looking fierce, and we're all standing around on the corner waiting for the first guy to say the word for a break to the railroad building.

"I happens to pike at one of the signs in front of an employment office to see if someone ain't looking for a private secretary or a good manager, and it reads like this:

"'WANTED!—Able-bodied men for the State militia of Colorado. $2 a day and found.'

"I leaves the rest of these sad-eyed dubs standing around where they are and stalls up into this employment office.

"There's a plug sitting behind the desk looking as chest as a traveling man, and I nails him.

"'What's this gig about militia?' I asks him.

"'Strike-soldiers wanted—two dollars a day and found,' he says, short-like.

"'Well, that's where I live,' I tells him. 'I'm the original soldier; all others are infringements.'

"'You gimme two bucks,' he says, 'and I ships you for a soldier.'

"'Say, mister,' I asks him, 'if I had two bucks, what d'you reckon I'd want to soldier for?'

"'That's my bit,' he says. 'If you ain't got it, of course I can't get it. The noble State of Colorado, she pays me just the same, but when I can get it out of rummies like you, I ketches 'em coming and going. See?'

"I did, all right, and it looks to me like it was a pretty fair graft. This guy explains the milishy business to me. There's a big strike on in the Coal Creek district. The milishy is out, but there ain't enough men, so they gives this employment Guinea orders to pick up all he can. He's just the same as a recruitin' sergeant, only different.

"I tells him about the rest of the bunch, and he agrees to take 'em all. Then I went back and told the gang, and you'd oughta hear the holler they sent up. Milishy! Nix! Not for them! They'd starve first, and a lot more dope like that.

"'Come out o' it!' I tells them. 'Here's a gee hungerin' to slip us two bucks a day and all found, and you hams standing around with wrinkles in your bellies, side-stepping like a bunch of mules in the road. He takes this on while it lasts and gets a stake. The State's good for the money, or ought to be. Come along, children, before the boogie man sloughs you in the skookum for mopery!'

"Course they comes! Why this is duck soup for us all. Think of two cases a shift for snoljering! We're there stronger than father's socks when we lines up in that employment office.

"The gee I talks to sends for an officer from this milish, and he takes charge of us. He ain't a bad feller, only he's a kid and don't sabe the war business much. He asked me if I'd ever seen service, and when I flashes about half a dozen parchments on him, he liked to had a fit. At that, he's a nice little feller and don't mean no harm. Some of the guys were trying to kid him, but I made 'em cut it out.

"This officer shoos us down to the depot and loads us up on a train for Coal Creek. He asks us what we wanted to join, and of course we're all out for the cavalry. It seems that was just what he wanted. They had a troop up there that was away shy of men, and a bunch that can ride fits in mighty nice. And so a slice of the first squadron of the Fifth goes into the milishy business.

"I'd hustled the bunch right through the preliminaries, and they don't get much chanst to ponder over it until they was on the train. And then they was sore at themselves and also me. They breaks up into little squads in the smoker and sits looking gloomy-like out the window. Ever onct in a while some guy would sigh and say:

"'S'posin' ole Bluch would see us now!' meaning Cap. Bluch Baker.

"This kid officer was mighty nice on the train, but he finds everyone but me mighty unconversational. We pulls into Coal Creek late that night, and then he suddenly gets all-fired preemptory.

"'Get out and line up on the platform!' he bawls at us, and seeing we're there, we do it.

"There's a lot of guys in uniform standing around and looking us over some curious, but we're pretty tired and don't mind. This kid officer gives us right forward, and we climbs hills for the next hour or so until we come to a bunch of Sibley tents, and a rooky challenges us.

"'Halt!' he says. 'Who is it?'

"What d'you think o' that? 'Who is it?' But that's what he says, all right.

"The kid officer tells him it's Lieutenant Somebody with a detachment, and the rook yells for the officer of the day. We're finally passed, although all hands looked at us some suspicious, and I don't blame them. Another big gang is standing around rubbering at us as we drills into camp, and they makes a lot of fresh remarks. I'm pretty glad my bunch is tired, or there'd been remains to clean up. We're assigned to tents, and a sergeant comes along and gives us a couple of skinny blankets apiece. The tent has floors, so bunking ain't so bad as it might be, although it was colder'n a banker's heart.

"A kid making a stab at reveille on a trumpet gets us out in the morning, and this same sergeant of blanket fame issues us mess-kits. It had snowed a few feet during the night, and we're none too cheerful when we lines up at the mess-shack for breakfast. We didn't have no roll-call, because we hadn't given in our names. The camp is laid out pretty well, as we see it by daylight. The company streets were laid out in rows on a hillside, and there was a big stable for the cavalry horses at the bottom of the hill. We weighs up our comrades in arms as we sees them at the mess-shack, and they're mostly kids. A few gees with very suggestive-looking shoulders and shame-faced expressions is scattered among them.

"The breakfast ain't so bad, what there is of it, but I could tell by the wise look on the mugs of some of the gang that came with me that there'd likely be a minus in the ranks before long.

"Later in the morning, the captain of the troop lines us up again, swears us in, and takes our pedigrees. I listened mighty intent, but I failed to hear anyone kick in their right name expecting me, and I had to do it because the kid officer had seen my discharge. Then they issues us clothes.

"Say, you orderly-bucking stiffs, I wisht you could see them clothes right now! Most of them was second-hand, and I take it that our predecessors in that troops had put in their time in civil life serving as models for ready-made cigarettes. I never heard such a holler as went up from my gang since the canteen was abolished. They cussed the state milishy, the State of Colorado, the governor, and all his hired hands, and they wound up by cussing me for getting them into it. They was the worst-looking lot of rookies I ever saw in my life, and they was all the madder because I drew a pretty fair outfit myself.

"After clothes, we were sent down to the stables to draw our mounts. I have mentioned that those clothes caused pretty much of a holler, but it was simply a soft guffaw to the muffled roar that the gang let out when they saw them gallant steeds. I think the State of Colorado robbed the hack horse market of Denver when they sent out the milish, and they copped the whole crop of the previous generation of horses at that.

"Skates? Say, they wasn't horses. They were hat-racks! They were shadows of horses—visions—dreams!

"The bunch was sore at first, but the funny side finally struck them, and they commenced picking out the worst mutts they could. There wasn't much choice, but the lay-out my delegation drew was certainly a fright. They had all kinds of fun kidding with them horses and with the rest of the troop. They'd put their saddles on wrong side before, and all such foolishness, to make the troops think they was awful rookies.

"But if the clothes and other things were jokes, that soldiering wasn't. Nix! No play about that. I've monkeyed around in the war business a few days myself, and I never struck anything harder than playing soldier in Colorado. You works right straight through from reveille to taps. Post duty around camp; patrol mounted, and guard down in them mines where they'd drop you in a cage so fast you had to hang on to your hat with both hands to keep your hair from flying off. When you got down a mile or two, they'd throw you off with your little gun and tell you to stick there and shoot anyone that batted an eye. Fine business, that!

"It seems that my bunch was about half of this cavalry troop we belonged to. In addition there was a whole regiment of foot-shakers in camp, a battery with one of them old-time Napoleon fieldpieces and a Gat, and another big troop of cavalry. They called this last lay-out the Denver Light Horse, and it was a bunch of swells. Most of them looked to me like they might be calico rippers in civil life, but they sure laid it on there. They had good horses, and their uniforms fitted them. We looked like a bunch of volunteers fresh from the States, lined up alongside of them.

"The clothes and horses let 'em out. They weren't there with anything else, and most of them had something to say about running the troop. I give it to the guy that had command of us. He was a captain named Pard, and I finds out afterwards that he was a boss machinist or a boiler-maker in Denver when he wasn't working at this tin snoljering business. He was a silent sort of plug, but he was strong on the tactics. He knew what ought to be done, anyway, and when he told you to do anything, you had a hunch he meant what he said.

"This Light Horse outfit weren't for us a-tall. The second night we were in camp, a large delegation comes yelling down to our streets, and when we looks out to see what the trouble was, we finds they had come to toss us in blankets. Get that? Toss them old heads from the Fifth in blankets!

"They didn't toss. Not any to speak of. We turned over four tents coming from under them, and when the hospital corps arrived, there was ghastly bleeding remains scattered about. Naturally, we didn't get popular with the Light Horse.

"This Captain Pard was wise to us in no time. He got hep that he had a crowd of the real things under him, and he didn't try any foolishness with us. The rest of the camp had to drill every day. He gave it to us just once. Then he sorter grinned, said something about us appearing to be pretty well instructed already, and that's the last drill we had. He had to take us out every day for a stall, but we put in our time laying around smoking cigarettes in some shaft house.

"Them strikers we were hired to suppress were already pretty much suppressed, as we found it. They was mighty sore at the milishy, and I don't blame 'em, but our fellers got acquainted with a lot of 'em and found 'em pretty decent at that. There's about 'steen little towns in this Coal Creek district, from one to six miles apart, and our troop did patrol duty on the roads between 'em. The strikers were peaceable enough, although they didn't have no use for scabs. They never started anything with us, so we let 'em alone.

"They was especially sore at this Light Horse outfit. Them guys would go tearing through the streets on their horses, paying mighty little attention to life or limb, and they cut up rough with the strikers whenever they got a chanst. They had a big place downtown called a bull-pen, and these Light Horse snoljers were ever-lasting throwing someone in the pen, and it made the strikers pretty hot.

"When they finds out we're 'tending strictly to our business and not minding theirs, the strikers got sorter friendly with us and told us their grievances.

"The mining companies owned the houses where the strikers lived and when the strike comes on they just naturally throws them strikers out of house and home. So the strikers go to living in tents in regular camps and making out the best way they could. The biggest camp was located about two miles out of town and was on our patrol. We had to stop there every night to see if things was quiet, and it wasn't long before our gang was mighty friendly with them strikers. The women in the camp always had hot coffee for us, and generally a bite, and we got to thinking quite a few of them.

"This camp I'm telling you about is on a hill, and there's only one road to it that's anywhere near decent for traveling. We calls the camp Strikerville.

"We'd been doing this play soldier act for about three weeks and was just sighting for a pay-day to blow, when a striker comes to us one day and tells us that the companies is going to give them the run from where they are camped. He says he has it pretty straight that the deputies will do the job and that this Light Horse outfit is in on the play. The deputies and the milishy are to raid the camp at night and start a row; then the next day the milishy will run the strikers off altogether, on the ground that they are a menace to public peace.

"It seems, according to what this guy tells us, that if the strikers could be chased clean out of the district, scabs could be gotten without any trouble, and the mines put to work again. He says the milishy's part in the deal ain't to be recognized at headquarters, but the snoljers are to go along with the deputies like they was doing it of their own accord; same as the time a bunch of deputies and soldiers wrecked a union newspaper office over at Cadence. The headquarters hollers afterwards about 'disorganized mob,' and making a rigid investigation to discover the guilty parties, but it was always noticed that the guilty parties was never caught, and the office stayed wrecked.

"Well, this feller tells us that the gang was going to pull down the tents and wreck the whole camp. He was mostly worried

about what it might do to the women and children, because there
was a lot of 'em in the camp, and it was colder'n blazes, with two
or three feet of snow on the ground.

"'A girl baby was born to Mrs. McCafferty just to-day,' he says,
'and it will go kinder rough with her and the kid.'

"'Why don't you put up a fight?' asks "Dirty Dick" Carson.

"'Fight? What with?' the feller asks. 'They took up every gun in
the district when martial law was declared. If we could only put
up one scrap, it would put a stop to this thing of sending these disorganized mobs, as they call 'em, around doing the dirty work.'"

"'I got a scheme,' says Dick to me, after the feller left, and he
outlines it with much joy. It made a big hit with me right off the
reel, and in stables that evening C Troop, as represented by the
former members of the Fifth Cavalry, has a quiet meeting, and
Dick and me talks to 'em long and earnest. When we gets through,
we had a hard time keeping them from yelling their heads off just
to show how pleased they are.

"'It's all for that McCafferty kid,' I tells 'em. 'Think how you'd
like it if you was just born and got throwed out of house and
home into the snow. Also think of Mrs. McCafferty's coffee.'

"The bunch got so excited with sympathy, I was afraid they
would tip it off to the rest of the camp. To carry out our scheme,
we had to heave the first sergeant of the troop in. He made up the
night patrols and assigned the other sergeants to command. Dick
and me went to him and has him down to our tent where half a
dozen of the old heads is gathered. It just happens that this top
sergeant was a guy that had been with the volunteers in the Philippines, and he thought he was an old soldier. Along with it, he was
pretty decent, and when he hears our scheme he kind o' grins and
falls for it right away.

"There were two patrols made up of about ten men, each under
a sergeant, and they worked from dark until early morning riding
the roads. At roll-call that evening the top reads off the names of
the men on patrol, and although everyone of my bunch had been
on duty the night before, our names is included in the list. In addition to that, he increases each patrol to eleven men, so as to take
in all us fellers, and he says:

"'There's going to be non-commissioned officers' school this
evening, and I want all my regular non-coms there. I'll appoint

Private Hanks to command Patrol No. 1, and Private Carson to command Patrol No. 2. They'll report to me for instructions.'

"That looked regular enough. The rest of the troop was tickled to death, because they thought the top was throwing it into our gang for double duty. It had commenced to snow again heavy, and no one wanted to ride roads that night.

"'Serves them old stiffs right; they think they know so much,' I heard one of the rooky kids say, as we scattered for our tents.

"In the meantime, I sends one of our fellers through the lines just as soon as we was saddled and ready to start out, with orders to ride to the strikers' camp and put them next. Then Carson and me went to the top for orders.

"I've always had a hunch that when we was talking to him in front of his tent, I saw a pair of eyes gaping through the flap, and that them eyes looked mighty like Captain Pard's, but I couldn't prove it if I had to.

"'Don't let anyone get hurt now,' was what the top had to say, and we falls in our details and rides out of camp.

"As I'm going past No. 1, the sentry hollers at me:

"'More H Troop?' H Troop being the Light Horse.

"'Nope! Cavalry patrols; C Troop,' I told him.

"'I didn't know; most of H Troop seems to be out on mounted pass to-night,' he says, and a sort o' chuckle runs through our bunch.

"It had started in to snow like the dickens, and you could hardly see your file leader. We were all pretty well bundled up, so we didn't mind. The patrols were supposed to take different roads about a mile from camp, but we all headed straight out towards Strikerville. I sent out a couple of scouts to Handley, where the deputies hung out, and told them to hurry up and bring back a report.

"When we climb the road to the strikers' camp, and you had to do it pretty slow on account of the rocks and not being able to see very well through the snow, we finds a big stir going on. There's a light in every tent, and camp-fires are burning all around. The women and kids are huddled over the fires, and the men are scattered about in little bunches, all talking at once.

"This guy I sent ahead had scared the life out of them. The president and half a dozen other leaders of the union who lived in camp met us, and I made 'em get busy right away.

"As I tells you, this camp is on a sort of flat plateau on top of a hill, and there is only one road to it. I made them put the women and kids in the tents furtherest away from the head of the road, leaving the lights and fires burning only where they could be seen from the bottom of the road. Then I gets every man jack and every kid of any size in the camp rolling snowballs. It was a wet, mushy snow and packed fine.

"'Put a few rocks, if you want to,' I suggested, and I guess they did.

"I posts one of the men at the bottom of the hill, and I puts the rest of them to work throwing up breastworks across the top of the road, to avoid accidents. There was a lot of loose rocks laying around, and a fine trench is up in no time.

"Pretty soon my scouts from Handley comes in, their horses dead beat.

"'There's about twenty deputies and twenty-five of them H Troop guys over in Niccoli's saloon,' they tells me. 'They're getting pretty drunk, and someone's liable to get hurt. They won't start until about midnight, and then they're coming a-hellin'.'

"'Any non-coms with the troop?' I asks, and they says 'No.' None of them had their carbines, either; nothing but six-pistols. That was to divert any idea that they was out on anything but mounted pass and a hunt for joy.

"'Them deputies are making a fierce talk about tar and feathering some of your guys,' one of my scouts tells them labor leaders, and it didn't quiet the agitation which was stirring them none.

"I had the snowballs stacked along the front of the trench as fast as they was made, and it wasn't long before there was enough to fill an ore wagon. I kept everyone hard at work just the same, because I didn't want to run shy.

"All we could do was to wait and watch, and it was pretty cold work. The snow stopped along about midnight, but it stayed pretty dark. My fellows loafed around, smoking and talking and visiting the McCafferty kid. None of the women folks went to bed, although they had no notion of what was coming off.

"It must have been about one o'clock when I hears, away off, the pound of the horses' feet on the snow and a jumbled lot of talking and laughing. I hustles my men together and lines 'em up back of the breastworks where them strikers are still rolling snowballs like mad—good hard ones, too. I had ten of the fellers load the carbine magazines, and the rest I bunched with all them strikers, carefully instructed.

"Pretty quick, my outpost comes running up the hill.

"'They're stopped down below,' he says. 'They're going to come with a rush to surprise the camp. All of 'em are half-stewed.'

"I looked over my arrangements with a critical eye and didn't see anything lacking. My friends was lined up back of the breastworks, them with the carbines in the middle, and the strikers and the rest of my bunch on either side with arms full of big snowballs. We could look right down on the roadway, shining like a streak of whitewash across a coal pile. Back of us a few dying camp-fires were sputtering, and lights burned in a few tents. It was as quiet as a graveyard. Then a sudden yell splits the air, and here they comes!

"They was all mounted, and they was trying to run their horses up that steep, slippery road, yelling like crazy people. Some of them starts shooting in the air. They was riding without any kind of formation, and you couldn't tell soldiers from deputies.

"I waits until they are right below us in the road, and then I fires a shot from my carbine and hollers, 'Halt!'

"They stopped right in the middle of a yell for about a minute, but it was long enough. It brings 'em to a stop just below us, and I screeches:

"'Ready! Aim! Fire!'

"My carbine gang tears off a volley, and the rest of the gang behind the breastworks launches about a barrel of snowballs on top of the bench in the road.

"'Fire at will!' I commands, and they does; the fellers with the carbines shooting at the nearest fixed stars, and the others whaling away with the snowballs.

"Say! I've seen crowds suddenly jimmed up in my time; like the old Thirteenth on the Warren the time of the fight, or the gang at Zapote bridge the night the head of Carabao charged us, but that delegation in the road skinned 'em all a Salt Lake City block.

"They was just naturally stood on their heads. They yelled in dead earnest, but they didn't do no shooting; they didn't have time. I hadn't thought about there being any danger until I see that bunch milling around in the road; the horses rearing and snorting and kicking, and everyone trying to go in the same direction at once. I was leary someone was going to get killed. If any one of 'em had gone down in the muddle, it would have been all

day with 'em. The language them men used wasn't scarcely fit
to eat.

"All the time my crowd was slamming big snowballs down on
the heads of the enemy and firing carbines, and some of the yells
that rose out of the cloud of snow in the road sounded real
painful. The firing squad was working them carbines overtime between laughs.

"The women and kids in the camps came running up to the
breastworks to see what was going on, and they gets next to the
game right away and commences to fire snowballs too, screaming
and laughing.

"At what I judges is the psychological moment, I hollers:

"'Charge!'

"Then all of us sets up an awful yell and loads and fires snowballs faster than ever.

"Them in the roadway that had their horses turned right didn't
hesitate. They went down that road with a disregard for their
necks that made me nervous. Them that couldn't get their horses
turned right slipped off and went on foot. Pretty soon all you
could hear was echoes dying away in the distance and the screaming and laughing in the camp.

"We didn't wait for them strikers' thanks. We got our horses
and got out of there almost as fast as the enemy. I separated the
patrols and sent one out one way and took the other direction with
my squad. We rode off a couple of miles and then went racing
back. We got back to the foot of the hill considerably blown, right
after old Major Kelley, Captain Pard, all the headquarters' officers, and some of H Troop came tearing along. Back of them Carson and the other patrol was whooping it up along the road, and
away back a company of infantry and a Gatling squad was kicking up the snow as fast as they could.

"They had heard the shooting at headquarters, and an
H trooper had buzzed into camp with an exciting tale about the
strikers' massacring harmless soldiers and deputies.

"Now, of course, they knew something about this frame-up to
attack the strikers' camp at headquarters but they hadn't figured
on it turning out but one way. Only that lone H trooper had returned, and the major seemed to sort o' expect to find many gory
bodies scattered around.

"I reported having heard some firing, but no signs of excitement. The whole works climbed to the strikers' camp, many hunching up as close to the major as possible. I saw Captain Pard occasionally glancing at me with a funny look, as he took in that mussed-up roadway; but the major didn't seem to notice anything. The camp was as dark as bats, but in answer to our yells some of the strikers came out looking mighty cross and sleepy. No, they hadn't heard anything. No fighting; hadn't heard any disturbance, and it was getting colder all the time, and the major was sleepy himself, it ended in him telling Captain Pard to instruct his patrols to make a thorough investigation. Then they all went back to headquarters.

"On the roads, before daylight, our patrols picked up fifteen H troopers, most of them bunged up about the head or face where them rock-loaded snowballs had landed, and we turned everyone over to the guardhouse for overstaying pass limits. Sore! Oh, no! That's a mistake! I think they had commenced to tumble, because our fellers kidded 'em a good deal.

"When I was turning in that morning, an orderly comes to me and said the major wanted to see me at the officer's mess. I was scared stiff for a minute, thinking the old man was wise, but I went over.

"All the officers of the camp were there eating breakfast. Captain Pard was sitting with an H Troop officer on either side of him, and he looks at me like he wanted to laugh.

"'Private Hanks, did you learn anything about the occurrences of last night?' asks the major, looking stern.

"I saw right away that none of them was on, excepting maybe Captain Pard, and they evidently had been turning it over among 'em and trying to get at the right of it.

"'Sir!' says I, saluting, 'as near as I can make out, a gang of H troopers got gay around the strikers' camp, and the women snowballed them away!'"

TWO MEN NAMED COLLINS

I know some things all right if I could only think of them. These guys say I'm crazy—crazy in the head like a sheep; but I'm as happy as if I had good sense.

I hear 'em talking in the barracks when they think I'm not around, and I know what they say. I'll make some of 'em hard to catch, one of these days. They're afraid of me because I killed a man once. Well, I evened that up, but they don't know it.

When I get out of the army I'm going back to driving hack in Denver like it was before I enlisted. It ain't my fault I'm here. It's the old booze. I gets drunk one day and went out to Petersburg. I met a guy there who belonged to the army, and before I knew what I was about I had on one of these uniforms. I only got six months more, and you bet they won't get me again.

Before I go I'll get good and even with some of these guys. Ever I catch any of them fresh officers down around Arapahoe Street after dark I'll fix 'em.

I've heard 'em say I'm the orneriest white man in the army. I don't know why. I'm big and strong, but that ain't nothing. I can take this Krag and bend it double like it was made of tin; I did it once when I got mad at a sentry because he wouldn't let me be.

I can lift any man in this company waist high with one hand. I can tear open a can of tomatoes with my teeth. But them things don't make a guy ornery, do they?

I used to get drunk whenever I could, and it made me mean. They threw it into me, too. Guardhouse all the time, and hard work. Then one day I heard a non-com tell another they was laying for me with a general guard to give me a bobtail and a dash at Alcatraz next time I come up; so I quit. I haven't touched a drop in over a year.

They's something funny about me, though, and I don't know what it is. Whenever I walk post in front of the officers' quarters them fresh guys and women get out on the porch and watch me. They talk just like I couldn't hear, too. I heard a woman say one day when I was stepping off the post—it's an even hundred of my steps from one end to the other—that I reminded her of a caged lion.

"More like a big bull behind a pasture gate," says an officer.

"Or a battery horse with the weaves," another sticks in.

Stuff like that, you know. Can you blame me for being sore?

About that man I killed. I didn't mean to do it. His name was just the same as mine, Charles Collins, only they called him Pretty Collins. He *was* pretty, too. He had a load of education, and he got into the army accidental, same as me.

I've seen lots of his kind. They're mostly to be found around Torts or at Brown in evening clothes after a show, and they've paid me good money for hauling 'em around in my little old hack. I used to feel like jumping up and saying, "Cab, sir," every time he came past me on the parade ground. He was a private like anyone else, but I've seen sentries half bringing their guns down to salute when they went by. It was the way he wore his clothes maybe.

I've heard some of these guys say he spent a barrel of money going en route, and broke his old lady's heart. His old man give him the run, or something, so he breaks into the army. The officers pitied him a lot, and he used to be something of a pet with them. They didn't holler and growl at him same as they do at me and the rest. I heard the top say once that they offered to get him discharged, but he wouldn't stand for it. Anyway, they used to treat him mighty white.

I had it in for him strong.

I didn't like him from the start because they used to kid us both, changing our names around and calling him Crummy and me Pretty. I know I ain't pretty, and I knew how they meant it.

The top, when he called the roll, used to put it Collins No. 1, which was him, and Collins No. 2, which was me. They ain't anything unusual about that, I've seen companies where they'd have four or five Johnsons, or Browns, or Smiths.

I got so I hated the sight of Collins. I hated his pink and white face, and I hated him because he wasn't supposed to be no better than me, but *was,* somehow.

He didn't know how much I had it in for him, but he did know I didn't like him, because one day he starts to joshing me with the rest, and I took him to the mat. I had my fingers on his throat and his white flesh came out between them like I had grabbed a lump of dough.

They broke me loose, but I told him then that if ever he tried to hand me anything again I'd bust his crust. He looked whiter than ever, but he bowed polite and says:

"All right, Collins; I beg your pardon. It won't happen again."

He offered me his hand, but I spit at it. He never spoke to me again. And I hated him more than ever for it.

They used to rawhide me something fierce in the company. I mean the non-coms did. I got all the extra duty there was doing. I knew I was getting the dirty end, but I couldn't holler. It wouldn't done me any good.

I've seen Pretty Collins come into quarters after taps just spifflicated, and nothing was ever done to him. Do you wonder I was sore on him?

Well, I just laid low and waited. I figured to get to him some day some way, so I laid low.

Finally we goes to Manila and gets sent out on the north line, where they was fighting about every day. That's when I gets next to Pretty Collins.

He was about my height and heft, so was in the same set of fours as me. When we fanned out in open order, that brought him next to me, on my right. The first scrap we went into I watched Pretty, and I was hep in a minute.

His face turned whiter than the time I grabbed him, and his hands trembled so he could hardly hold his gun. I sensed him, all right, all right. He was a coward.

When the bullets commenced to whistle I thought he was going to drop in his tracks. I'm no coward, whatever I am, and you bet I took a lot of satisfaction watching that guy suffer; because they do suffer—all the tortures of hell, I've heard.

I don't think anyone else noticed him, but Pretty knew what I knew—he looked at me once and saw me grinning.

I used to own a pit dog—Sunday Morning. He was beat by Mitchell's Money on the Overland race track one Christmas day. He was nearly all out when I picked him up for his last scratch, and he looked at me out of his eyes like he was trying to tell me not to send him again. Pretty reminded me of Sunday Morning when he looked at me across that rice paddy.

It wasn't much of a fight, but when it was over Pretty was as limp as a rag. The rest thought it was too much sun, but I knew— and Pretty knew I knew—and that was more satisfaction to me than if the whole brigade knew. He never said anything to me; just looked at me out of his eyes like Sunday Morning looked.

It wasn't long after that he was lying in front of a line of trenches which were across a river from us. The general commanding the brigade and his staff was with our outfit. The gugus was slapping a kind of blanket of bullets over our heads, and we was hugging the ground pretty close. The general signs out to our captain:

"Send a man down to Colonel Kelley on the left of the line and tell him to advance at once."

You know what that meant?

A man had to chase across that open field for a quarter of a mile with the gugus pecking at him. It was a two-ace bet that he would get his before he got half-way. Cap looks down the line and says:

"Collins!"

He was looking right at Pretty, over my head, and he meant Pretty. Man! That fellow's face was already white, but it seemed to go dead all at once. I'll bet anything he couldn't have moved if he'd tried, his muscles being sort o' paralyzed.

Cap kept looking at him—over my head. It wasn't three seconds, but it seemed three hours. When I first heard Cap call I felt glad, because it meant all day with Pretty. Then when I looked at Pretty's face I felt sorry, and there's where I made a sucker of myself. I jumped up and started on a run down the line. Cap didn't say anything. It looked like I had made a mistake and thought he meant me, but Cap knew better—and he knew I knew better— and Pretty knew better.

They shot at me considerable and winged me a little once, but I delivered the order and got back in time to go into the charge with my outfit.

I could've gone into the hospital if I'd wanted to, but I wasn't hurt very bad. That night I was sleeping near Cap and the two lieutenants, and I heard Cap say:

"The old man is going to recommend Crummy Collins for a stiffy-cate of merit. He wanted to make him a lieutenant, but I showed him the"—something—"of such a course.

"I meant Pretty Collins all the time, because I knew it was a chance to take him out of the ranks. He could have won his shoulder straps right there, but—"

"Do you think he's—" something I didn't get again, one of the loots asked.

"I fear he is," says Cap, and I went to sleep.

Well, we put in nearly two years on the islands, but Pretty got transferred to special duty, and I didn't see no more of him until we sailed for home. He looked kind of bad in the face, like he'd been going too strong, but he was just as popular as ever in the company. No one knew what Cap and me knew, and I didn't tell, but Pretty kept away from me.

By this time the gang had commenced to treat me a little better, because I'd showed 'em I was a good game guy, but I didn't have no bunkies.

I'd almost forgotten Pretty while he was away, but when he comes back again he made me just as sore as ever at him—just by being around, you know.

He didn't get so much petting from the officers as he used to, but he was still the whole thing with the bucks.

We went to Fort D.A. Russell, just out of Cheyenne, from 'Frisco, and I gets my stiffycate of merit there. It's a big sheet of paper, something like an officer's commission, all engraved, with my name and outfit and telling what I'd done when I carried that order across the firing line. Best of all, it gives me a couple of bucks extra pay every month. I stuck it away in my chest and didn't show it to any of the guys, although they knew I got it. You're supposed to send them things to home to the people, so they can frame 'em and hang 'em up in the parlor, but I didn't have no people or parlor either.

We hadn't been in Russell more'n a month when Pretty shows up one morning missing. They calls his name for ten mornings at roll-call, and then they posts him as a deserter. It like to broke these guys that'd been so friendly to him all up, and you bet I was glad.

They caught him in a couple of weeks up in Rock Springs on a drunk, and they brings him back to Russell and slaps him in the general prison. He's good for about eighteen months at the lowest, because the officers that had been so friendly to him shook him right away.

I was doing guard duty one day over a bunch of prisoners cleaning up quarters, and Pretty was one of 'em. I wasn't paying much attention to any but him, watching him moving around in that brown suit with the big white P on his back, when all of a sudden he makes a break.

He must a-gone nutty. He didn't have a chance in the world to get away. They told me he said before he cashed in that he got wild having my eyes follow him around, but that's rot. All I did, so help me, was just watch him, and I leave it to anyone if that should make him go bugs.

I hollered at him to halt three times. Then I aimed at him, meaning to hit him in the leg. His head kept bobbing in front of my sights, and he was getting further away all the time, so I had to let go. He dropped and laid there kicking around.

The whole barracks come running up, and I don't remember much else, except that they relieved me and sent me to quarters.

None of the fellows would talk to me or tell me what was doing, but I heard someone say he was dead. I stayed in quarters all the next day, and no one came near me. If I'd walk up to some of the fellows they'd get up and move off, like they was afraid of me. The Cap come in towards evening and talked kind to me. He said I'd only done my duty, but that it would be best for me to be transferred, and they was going to send me to Plattsburg to join another regiment. That was all right with me. He told me to get my junk together and get ready to go right away.

It didn't take me no time to pack. While I was throwing my stuff into my chest I came across that stiffycate of merit and shoved it in the inside pocket of my blouse.

I heard some of the fellows talking that night, and they spoke about "him," so I knew they meant Pretty.

"His father and mother are coming in a special train from the East," one of them said. "The top and four non-coms are going to take him to Denver and turn him over to them."

No one even looked at me all this time.

Cap give me my transfer papers and transportation that night, and next morning I went to Cheyenne and got a train for Denver. Only the Cap said good-bye to me.

At Denver I missed the first train I was to take east, and hung around the depot all day. Along towards evening a train of just a baggage car and a Pullman pulled in while I was looking through the fence outside the depot. The Pullman blinds were down, and it looked so mournful and still that I had a hunch right away that it was Pretty's folks. I was right, too. A gray-haired man, who moves around brisk and talks rough to the porters, gets off and helps a little old lady, all dressed in black, to the platform. You couldn't see much of her face on account of a heavy veil, but you could tell by her eyes that she had been crying a lot.

They hadn't more'n got on the platform when the regular Cheyenne train pulls in and the top sergeant and a squad of non-coms from my old company hops off. The old man leads the little old lady up to them, and they shook hands all around and stood talking awhile.

Then they went to the baggage car, and the squad hauls out a long wooden box with a flag across it. Somehow it made me sort o' sick to look at it, because I knew Pretty was inside.

The non-coms put the box on a truck and push it over to the special train and shove the box in the Pullman—not in the baggage car.

The old lady follows it in, and the man stood at the end of the Pullman talking to the top. I couldn't stand it no longer. I wanted to hear what they said, so I sneaks through the gate and around behind a train on the track next to the Pullman.

The old man was saying:

"I'm mighty glad the boy died like a gentleman, anyway. He was always a little wild, but I never believed he was a coward. I was rather pleased when he joined the army, because I felt it would make a man of him."

"Yes, sir," the top says, "he was a man all right. He gave that prisoner a hard fight before he went under, and would have won out if the prisoner hadn't been stronger."

I see the drift all right. They was making this old man believe Pretty had been killed in the performance of his duty; see? I listens to a little more, and I makes out that the top has told him Pretty was guarding prisoners, when one of 'em turns on him and shoots him with his own gun. He was giving Pretty a great send-off.

Maybe you think I wasn't dead sore!

What right had they to tell all them lies? If it'd been me in the box they probably have said I was the worst blackguard in the army and got all that was coming to me.

The top and the other non-coms shake hands all around with the old man again, and then they hikes off. The old man goes into the Pullman, and the engine crew get ready to pull out. I make up my mind in about two seconds, Mex., to go in there and tell them folks all about Pretty and why I had to kill him. I see my chance to get good and even with him more than ever.

I climbed on the rear platform and opens the door. The box was in the aisle, and the old lady was setting in a seat beside it. The old man was with her, holding her hands, and she was crying, soft and easy like. He isn't crying, but he looks old and tired.

They both raise their heads when I come in and looked at me like they was waiting for me to say something.

"I soldiered with him," I says, pointing to the box.

The old lady looked at me out of Pretty's eyes, just as Pretty looked at me that day across the rice paddy. She almost smiled.

"He was all I had," she said. "He was his mother's boy."

The old man didn't say anything—just looked me over.

I don't know what got the matter with me. I couldn't say a thing—just stand there looking at them two like a sad-eye dub. The words I wanted to tell 'em wouldn't come.

"He was a good soldier?" the old man finally asked.

It wasn't what I meant to say, but I just had to tell him yes.

"He was all we had," the old man said. "It is a hard blow, but it is softened by knowing that he served his country well and died in the line of duty."

I tried to shake myself together and tell them that their boy had been a coward and a deserter, and if he'd lived would have put in a year or so in prison, with a yellow bobtail discharge at the end, but I couldn't do it—that's all.

The train commenced to back up, getting ready to start out.

"Do you know any of his companions who have any reminder of my darling boy?" the old lady asked. "They didn't bring anything—but his body."

I felt something crackle in my inside breast-pocket. Ain't I a sucker, though? I stuck my hand in and hauls out that stiffycate of merit.

"Here," I says, handing it to her. "They sent this to you by me."

And then I hikes out of that car, for fear I might get dingey and bust out crying myself.

I know some things, all right, all right.

OTHER FICTION

LOU LOUDER

A Tale of Our Town

Lou Louder was a bartender.

He tended bar in the Greenlight saloon.

He was tending bar there the night Shalimar Duke was killed.

Lou Louder was very tall, and very thin, and very pale. He said he was sent to Our Town by a doctor in Buffalo, N.Y., to die. Lou Louder had tb.

Lots of people used to come to Our Town to die. The doctors in other parts of the country highly recommended the climate.

Shalimar Duke was the owner of the Commercial Hotel. He was a short, fat man. He was one of the most popular citizens of Our Town. His books showed that more than twenty-eight thousand dollars was owing him on old accounts when he got killed.

Shalimar Duke married a Mexican girl half his age, named Pabalita Sanchez. Her people had a big sheep ranch. She had beautiful black eyes and black hair and an awful temper. She was like her mother, Juanita Sanchez. She was like her aunt, Maria Gomez, too.

Pabalita was pretty fly, but how could Shalimar Duke know that? He was forty-seven years of age.

The two Baker boys, Joe and Sid, had a fight about her and quit speaking to each other. This made it inconvenient in their business. They were partners in the B. B. coal yard.

Each thought Pabalita loved him. She told them so.

Shalimar Duke went into the Greenlight saloon one night and was talking to Lou Louder when Sid Baker came in. Sid had a .38-caliber revolver in his left hip pocket. Sid was left-handed.

Shalimar Duke asked Sid to have a drink. About that moment, Joe Baker came in. He had a .44-caliber revolver stuck in the waistband of his pants.

Shalimar Duke asked Joe Baker to have a drink. Shalimar Duke didn't know the Baker boys weren't speaking to each other. Shalimar Duke didn't know about the Baker boys and Pabalita.

He was the only man in Our Town who didn't know.

Joe Baker and Sid Baker were gentlemen. They accepted Shalimar Duke's invitation to have a drink, even though they didn't speak to each other.

Joe Baker stepped up on one side of Shalimar Duke, Sid Baker stepped up on the other side. They were all as close together as your first three fingers. Lou Louder was in front of them behind the bar.

It was a hot night. The side door of the Greenlight, directly opposite the bar, was standing open to let in a little breeze. The breeze brought in the perfume of some roses growing at the side door of the Greenlight.

It was a strange place for roses to grow.

Roses were always growing in strange places in Our Town.

There was no one else in the Greenlight saloon at the time.

Shalimar Duke and Joe and Sid Baker all called for straight bourbon. The Greenlight served good bourbon to its regular customers.

Shalimar Duke stepped up on the foot-rail at the bar, so he was up higher than the Baker boys, and Lou Louder, too. He raised his glass, and said, "Here's now," and they started to drink when Shalimar Duke fell on the floor dead.

A big-bladed knife with a very heavy handle was sticking in the back of his neck at the base of the brain.

His blood ran out in funny little rivulets on the floor.

He never said a word.

Joe Baker was arrested by Sheriff Letch and taken to the county jail. Sid Baker was arrested by Chief of Police Korn and taken to the city jail. The jails were about a mile apart.

They found a .32-caliber revolver in a side pocket of Shalimar Duke's coat. Some said maybe he had learned about Pabalita and the Baker boys, and was out looking for them when they beat him to it.

There was much indignation in Our Town.

Lou Louder was questioned by Coroner Curley. Lou Louder said he had turned to the back bar after serving Shalimar Duke and the Baker boys with their bourbon, so how could he see just what happened?

Coroner Curley said, "That's right, Lou."

A number of citizens went to the county jail and broke down the door and took Joe Baker out and hanged him to a telephone pole. Joe said it was all right with him. Joe said he was the one who stuck the knife in Shalimar Duke. Joe said he wanted to get rid of Shalimar Duke so he could have Pabalita to himself.

Joe said, "Boys, I deserve my fate."

The telephone company afterwards complained because the hanging broke some of its wires.

Joe Baker really thought Sid killed Shalimar Duke. Joe was trying to save Sid by taking the blame on himself. Joe remembered that Sid was his brother.

He didn't know that about the time they were hanging him a different crowd of citizens was taking Sid out of the city jail and stringing him up to a girder on the Union Avenue bridge, and that Sid was confessing that he jabbed the knife into Shalimar Duke.

Sid said he did it so Pabalita would be free to love him alone.

Sid Baker really thought Joe killed Shalimar Duke and was trying to save Joe as Joe was trying to save him. Sid remembered that Joe was his brother. He remembered what fun they had together when they were little kids.

It was all very confusing to the citizens of Our Town when the stories were compared after the funerals.

Some said it showed that blood is thicker than water.

There were many arguments about which of the Baker boys really stuck the knife in Shalimar Duke. Sheriff Letch had a fist fight with Chief of Police Korn about it. Sheriff Letch said his prisoner, Joe Baker, was the more truthful of the Baker boys, and must have done it, because he said he did.

Chief of Police Korn stood up for Sid Baker.

Pabalita Duke ran the Commercial Hotel for six years after Shalimar Duke's death. She died of pneumonia contracted while keeping a date with a traveling man in a snowstorm.

The first thing she did was to try to collect Shalimar Duke's old accounts.

She never was very popular in Our Town.

———

Lou Louder lived thirty years longer. Before he passed away he told Doc Wilcox that when he turned to the back bar after serving Shalimar Duke and the Baker boys with their bourbon, he saw, by the back bar mirror, Pabalita step to the side door of the saloon and throw the knife that killed Shalimar Duke.

The knife wasn't meant for Shalimar Duke. It was meant for Lou Louder. It would have got him, too, if Shalimar Duke hadn't stepped up on the foot-rail of the bar as Pabalita let fly.

If Shalimar Duke had remained standing on the floor, the knife would have cleared his head and hit Lou Louder kerplunk in the back between the shoulders.

Lou Louder said he had quarreled with Pabalita and had written her a note telling her he was through with her. She got awful mad about it. Shalimar Duke found the note and went into the Greenlight saloon to kill Lou Louder.

He was mentioning his intention to Lou Louder when the Baker boys came in, Lou said.

Shalimar Duke stepped on the foot-rail to get up high enough to have a freer crack at Lou Louder, so Lou thought.

The Baker boys had also gone into the Greenlight saloon to kill Lou Louder, so Lou told Doc Wilcox. They didn't know each other's idea because they weren't speaking. Pabalita had told them, separately, that Lou Louder had insulted her, and made each of them promise to kill him. They both mentioned it to friends that they were going to kill Lou Louder, and the friends warned Lou.

Pabalita had no confidence in the Baker boys.

Lou Louder remarked to Doc Wilcox just before he died that he always felt he had rather a narrow escape that night.

He didn't die of tb.

He died of old age.

The Chamber of Commerce of Our Town often pointed to Lou Louder during his life as an example of what our climate will do for a man.

ON THE DEAR DEPARTED

My old man used to say he hated to hear of anybody dying but that it made him tired when people took to boosting some departed citizen who was no account when he was living.

My old man said that he did not think that just the act of dying rounded up a fellow who had been petty and mean. He said the idea that you should say only good of the dead was bosh as far as he was concerned unless the dead was somebody you could say good of in life.

Naturally he came in for some criticisms back in our old home town of Pueblo, because no matter how ornery a chap might have been our people were inclined to forget that side of him when the undertaker dropped around to his house. They then usually tried to think up a few boosts for the departed.

My old man could not see that at all. He said he was always willing to join the boosters if they could show him where the deceased prior to shaking off this mortal coil had made any attempt at reparation for a lifetime of mistreatment of his fellow men in public or private, but that nobody ever presented him with such proof but just said he ought not to talk that way about somebody who was dead.

My old man said he did not see why death should make liars of a lot of the living. He used to make it a point to attend the last sad rites over defunct citizens who had had no popularity in the community to say the least, and were known for traits other than philanthropy or good nature, and he said it astonished him the way even the preachers sometimes tried to make white out of black.

My old man said he thought that set a bad example to the community. He said he did not claim that the preachers ought always to tell the plain unvarnished truth about every departed citizen, unless it could be nice truth, but he did think they should be more noncommittal.

My old man said he could see that the unvarnished truth would often get the preachers in trouble with the surviving heirs of the departed, unless of course, the will had already been read and it had come out that the departed had left all his dough to charity and cut them off with the proverbial shilling.

My old man would have liked the story about the no-good fellow they were burying over in Pennsylvania. A preacher who did not know the departed but had a vague idea that his character was not too hot, read a psalm and, then not altogether at ease over dismissing anybody in this perfunctory fashion, said to the handful of persons assembled at the grave:

"And now perhaps some friend of the departed would like to say something."

There was a long silence and finally a mournful-looking man with a drooping moustache stepped forward, cleared his throat and said:

"Well, if no one else has anything to say, I would like to seize this opportunity to make a few remarks on the iniquities of the New Deal."

My old man said he thought it was downright hypocritical for people to send big bunches of flowers to the funeral of some fellow they knew very well had underpaid his employees, short-changed his customers, oppressed his tenants, and otherwise been pretty much of a heel in life.

He said it was hypocritical to waste time following to some distant burying ground the mortal remains of a chap you disliked and who disliked you when he was alive, and when somebody once told him that it was just a mark of sympathy with the bereaved family my old man laughed right out loud.

He remembered the time he was in Riley's saloon taking exceptions to the liberal boosting by a friend of a lately departed citizen of considerable prominence. The friend said it was a great loss to the community and a greater loss to the man's family.

My old man said that he would give a small cash reward to anybody who could prove to him that the departed had ever done a lick of good for the community. He said he did not know about the man's family but that from what he knew of the man he would bet he had his wife and children scared of him and that he was as stingy and mean with them as he was with everybody else and that they were probably relieved that he had left them.

A good-looking young chap followed my old man out of the saloon and tapped him on the shoulder and drew him into a doorway and said:

"Friend, I am the departed's oldest son and I wish you would not go around knocking his memory—but between you and me, friend, everything you said is true."

DOC BRACKETT

Doc Brackett didn't have black whiskers.

Nonetheless, he was a fine man.

He doctored in Our Town for many years. He doctored more people than any other doctor in Our Town but made less money.

That was because Doc Brackett was always doctoring poor people, who had no money to pay.

He would get up in the middle of the coldest night and ride twenty miles to doctor a sick woman, or child, or to patch up some fellow who got hurt.

Everybody in Our Town knew Doc Brackett's office over Rice's clothing store. It was up a narrow flight of stairs. His office was always filled with people. A sign at the foot of the stairs said: DR. BRACKETT, OFFICE UPSTAIRS.

Doc Brackett was a bachelor. He was once supposed to marry Miss Elvira Cromwell, the daughter of old Junius Cromwell, the banker, but on the day the wedding was supposed to take place Doc Brackett got a call to go out into the country and doctor a Mexican child.

Miss Elvira got sore at him and called off the wedding. She said that a man who would think more of a Mexican child than of his wedding was no good. Many women in Our Town agreed with Miss Elvira Cromwell, but the parents of the Mexican child were very grateful to Doc Brackett when the child recovered.

For forty years, the lame, and the halt, and the blind of Our Town had climbed up and down the stairs to Doc Brackett's office.

He never turned away anybody.

Some said Doc Brackett was a loose character, because he liked to drink whisky and play poker in the back rooms of saloons.

But he lived to be seventy years old, and then one day he keeled over on the sofa in his office and died. By this time his black hair had turned white.

Doc Brackett had one of the biggest funerals ever seen in Our Town. Everybody went to pay their last respects when he was laid out in Gruber's undertaking parlors. He was buried in Riverview Cemetery.

There was talk of raising money to put a nice tombstone on Doc Brackett's grave as a memorial. The talk got as far as arguing about what should be carved on the stone about him. Some thought poetry would be very nice.

Doc Brackett hated poetry.

The matter dragged along and nothing whatever was done.

Then one day George Gruber, the undertaker, said that Doc Brackett's memorial was already over his grave, with an epitaph and all. George Gruber said the Mexican parents of the child Doc Brackett saved years ago had worried about him having no tombstone.

They had no money themselves, so they took the sign from the foot of the stairs at Doc Brackett's office and stuck it over his grave. It read: DR. BRACKETT, OFFICE UPSTAIRS.

JEREMIAH ZORE

Jeremiah Zore was a mean man. He was one of the six meanest men in Our Town.

He stood third on the list.

Jeremiah Zore had a thin body, thin hair, thin lips, and a thin soul.

He got rich through lending money on property, and squeezing every nickel he got hold of. He loved foreclosing mortgages and throwing people out of their homes on Christmas Eve.

He was mean to everybody, and especially to his wife, Mame Zore. She was married to Jeremiah for twenty-nine years, and never laughed once after the first two months of their marriage.

She had one new dress in six years, and she made it herself.

They had one child, a son named Jonathan, and Jeremiah Zore was kind to him on four different occasions in sixteen years. They were the only occasions that Jeremiah was kind to anybody or anything.

Jeremiah Zore was secretly proud of Jonathan, and tried to make friends with him, but he was so mean to Mame Zore that Jonathan hated him, and on his seventeenth birthday he ran away from home.

Some said Jeremiah Zore brooded over Jonathan running away and kept hoping he would return, but Jeremiah never let on to anybody. Meantime, he was getting meaner, and meaner, and richer and richer.

He knew that everybody in Our Town hated him, and one day he said he was going to build a monument to himself that would make Our Town remember him, anyway.

So he built a twenty-four-story building on Commercial Avenue, with a tall tower on top of it.

It was the tallest building in our section of the state, and everybody in Our Town was quite proud of it until it was completed and Jeremiah Zore put his rents so low he almost ruined all the owners of the other downtown office buildings.

He admitted that this was his idea in the first place.

It was a beautiful building by day and would have been beautiful by night if Jeremiah had permitted the tower to be lighted up, but he was too stingy for that.

It shows you what a mean man he was.

Then one day Jeremiah lay dying, and he told Mame Zore his only wish was to see his son once more. He said he had never for a moment ceased thinking of Jonathan, who was a famous aviator, back East.

So Mame sent word to Jonathan and asked him to come as a favor to her and Jonathan sent word back he was flying his own plane to Our Town, and Jeremiah Zore cheered up and became so strong that there was great fear he would recover.

It was a black night, and storming heavily when Jonathan Zore arrived over Our Town in his plane, and flying very low looking for the landing field, he crashed into the tower on the Zore Building and was instantly killed.

He did not know the building had been erected and there was no light on the tower, so Jeremiah Zore died without seeing his son, Jonathan, after all.

POEMS

A HANDY GUY LIKE SANDE

Say, have they turned back the pages
    Back to the past once more?
Back to the racin' ages
    An' a Derby out of the yore?
Say, don't tell me I'm daffy,
    Ain't that the same ol' grin?
    Why it's that handy
    Guy named Sande,
    Bootin' a winner in!

Say, don't tell me I'm batty!
    Say, don't tell me I'm blind!
Look at that seat so natty!
    Look how he drives from behind!
Gone is the white of the Ranco,
    An' the white band under his chin—
    Still's he's that handy
    Guy named Sande,
    Bootin' a winner in!

Maybe he ain't no chicken,
    Maybe he's gettin' along,
But the ol' heart's still a-tickin',
    An' the ol' bean's goin' strong.
Roll back the years! Yea, roll 'em!
    Say, but I'm young agin',
    Watchin' that handy
    Guy named Sande,
    Bootin' a winner in!

(1930)

Sloan, they tell me, could ride 'em,
   Maher, too, was a bird;
Bullman was a guy to guide 'em—
   Never worse than third.
Them was the old-time jockeys;
   Now when I want to win
Gimme a handy
Guy like Sande
   Ridin' them hosses in.

Fuller he was a pippin,
   Loftus one of the best—
Many a time come rippin'
   Down there ahead of the rest.
Shaw was a bear of a rider,
   There with plenty of dome—
But gimme a dandy
Guy like Sande
   Drivin' them hosses home!

Spencer was sure a wonder,
   And Miller was worth his hire.
Seldom he made a blunder
   As he rode 'em down to the wire.
Them was the old-time jockeys;
   Now when I want to win
Gimme a handy
Guy like Sande,
   Bootin' them hosses in!
                 (August 12, 1922)

————

McAtee knows them horses,
   Ensor's a judge of pace;
Johnson kin ride the courses
   In any old kind o' race.
All them guys are good ones,
   But, say, when I want to win—

Gimme a handy
Guy like Sande,
    Bootin' a long-shot in!

(August 27, 1922)

———

Kummer is quite a jockey,
    Maybe as good as the best.
Johnson is not so rocky
    When you bring him down to the test.
But, say, when they carry my gravy—
Say, when I want to win,
    Gimme a handy
    Guy like Sande,
Bootin' them horses in!

(September 22, 1922)

———

Maybe there'll be another,
    Heady an' game, an' true—
Maybe they'll find his brother
    At drivin' them hosses through.
Maybe—but, say, I doubt it.
    Never his like again—
Never a handy
Guy like Sande,
    Bootin' them babies in!

Green an' white at the quarter—
    Say, I can see him now,
Ratin' them just as he orter,
    Workin' them up—an' how!
Green an' white at the home-stretch—
    Who do you think'll win?
Who but a handy
Guy like Sande,
    Kickin' that baby in!

Maybe we'll have another,
    Maybe in ninety years!

Maybe we'll find his brother
  With his brains above his ears.
Maybe—I'll lay agin it—
  A million bucks to a fin—
Never a handy
Guy like Sande,
  Bootin' them babies in!

                              (1924)

A JEW

There's a story in that paper
I just tossed upon the floor
That speaks of prejudice against the Jews.
There's a photo on the table
That's a memory of the war,
And a man who never figured in the news.
There's a cross upon his breast—
That's the D.S.C.,
The Croix de Guerre, the Militaire,
These, too.
And there's a heart beneath the medals
That beats loyal, brave and true—
That's Dreben,
A Jew!

He is short, and fat, and funny,
And the nose upon his face
Is about the size of Bugler Dugan's horn.
But the grin that plays behind it
Is wide, and soft, and sunny,
And he wore it from the day that he was born.
There's a cross upon his chest—
That's the D.S.C.,
The Croix de Guerre, the Militaire,
Mon Dieu!
He's a He-Man out of Texas,
And he's All-Man through and through—
That's Dreben,
A Jew!

Now whenever I read articles
That breathe of racial hate,
Or hear arguments that hold his kind to scorn,
I always see that photo
With the cap upon the pate
And the nose the size of Bugler Dugan's horn.
I see upon his breast
The D.S.C.,
The Croix de Guerre, the Militaire—
These, too.
And I think, Thank God Almighty
We will always have a few
Like Dreben,
A Jew!

TRIAL REPORTING

ARNOLD ROTHSTEIN'S
FINAL PAYOFF

New York City, November 19, 1929

If the ghost of Arnold Rothstein was hanging around the weather-beaten old Criminal Courts Building yesterday—and Arnold always did say he'd come back after he was dead and haunt a lot of people—it took by proxy what would have been a violent shock to the enormous vanity of the dead gambler.

Many citizens, members of the so-called "blue ribbon panel," appeared before Judge Charles C. Nott, Jr., in the trial of George C. McManus, charged with murdering Rothstein, and said they didn't know Rothstein in life and didn't know anybody that did know him.

Arnold would have scarcely believed his ears. He lived in the belief he was widely known. He had spent many years establishing himself as a landmark on old Broadway. It would have hurt his pride like sixty to hear men who lived in the very neighborhood he frequented shake their heads and say they didn't know him.

A couple said they hadn't even read about him being plugged in the stomach with a bullet that early evening of November 4 a year ago, in the Park Central Hotel.

Well, such is fame in the Roaring Forties!

They had accepted two men to sit on the jury that is to hear the evidence against McManus, the first man to pass unchallenged by both sides being Mark H. Simons, a stockbroker, of No. 500 West 111th Street, and the second being Eugene A. Riker, of No. 211 West 21st Street, a traveling salesman.

It seemed to be a pretty fair start anyway, but just as Judge Nott was about to adjourn court at four o'clock, Mark H. Simon presented a complication. He is a dark complexioned, neatly dressed chap, in his early thirties, with black hair slicked back on his head. He hadn't read anything about the case, and seemed to be an ideal juror.

But it appears he is suffering from ulcers of the stomach, and this handicap was presented to Judge Nott late in the day. James D. C. Murray, attorney for McManus, George M. Brothers, assistant prosecuting attorney, in charge of the case for the State, and three other assistants from District Attorney Banton's office, gathered in front of the bench while Mark H. Simon was put back in the witness chair and examined.

The upshot of the examination was his dismissal from service by Judge Nott, which left Riker, a youngish, slightly bald man, with big horn specs riding his nose, as the only occupant of the jury box. Judge Nott let the lonesome-looking Riker go home for the night after instructing him not to do any gabbing about the case.

The great American pastime of jury picking took up all the time from 10:30 yesterday morning until four o'clock in the afternoon, with an hour off for chow at one o'clock. Thirty "blue ribboners," well-dressed, solid-looking chaps for the most part, were examined and of this number Murray challenged a total of fourteen. Each side had thirty peremptory challenges. Attorney Brothers knocked off nine and four were excused.

George McManus, the defendant, sat behind his attorney eyeing each talesman with interest but apparently offering no suggestions. McManus was wearing a well-tailored brown suit, and was neatly groomed, as usual. His big, dark-toned face never lost its smile.

Two of his brothers, Jim and Frank, were in the court room. Frank is a big, fine-looking fellow who has a nifty tenor voice that is the boast of the Roaring Forties, though he can be induced to sing only on special occasions.

Only a very few spectators were permitted in the court, because there wasn't room in the antique hall of justice for spare chairs after the "blue ribboners" were all assembled. A squad of the Hon. Grover Whalen's best and most neatly uniformed cops are spread all around the premises, inside and out, to preserve decorum.

Edgar Wallace, the English novelist and playwright, who is said to bat out a novel or play immediately after his daily marmalade, was given the special privilege of the chair inside the railing and sat there listening to the examination of the talesmen, and doubtless marveling at the paucity of local knowledge of the citizens about a case that he heard of over in England. Mr. Wallace proved to be a fattish, baldish man, and by no means as young as he used to be.

A reflection of the average big towner's mental attitude toward gambling and gamblers was found in the answers to Attorney Murray's inevitable question as to whether the fact the defendant is a gambler and gambled on cards and the horses, would prejudice the talesmen against him. Did they consider a gambler a low character?

Well, not one did. Some admitted playing the races themselves. One mumbled something about there being a lot of gamblers in Wall Street who didn't excite his prejudice.

Attorney Murray was also concerned in ascertaining if the talesmen had read anything that District Attorney Banton had said about the defendant, and if so, had it made any impression on the talesman? It seemed not. One chap said he had read Banton's assertions all right, but figured them in the nature of a bluff.

Do you know anybody who knew Rothstein—pronounced "stine" by Mr. Brothers, and "steen" by Mr. Murray—or George McManus? Do you know anybody who knew either of them?

Do you know anybody who knows anybody connected with (a) the District Attorney's office? (b) the Police Department? Were you interested in the late political campaign? Ever live in the Park Central? Ever dine there? Know anybody connected with the management? Did you ever go to a race track?

Did you ever read anything about the case? (This in a city of over 4,000,000 newspaper readers, me hearties, and every paper carrying column after column of the Rothstein murder for months!) Did you ever hear any discussion of it? Can you? Suppose? Will you? State of mind. Reasonable doubt—

Well, by the time old John Citizen, "blue ribboner" or not, has had about twenty minutes of this he is mighty glad to get out of that place and slink home, wondering if after all it is worthwhile trying to do one's duty by one's city, county, and state.

November 20, 1929

A client—or shall we say a patient—of the late Arnold Rothstein popped up on us in the old Criminal Courts Building in the shank o' the evening yesterday. He came within a couple of aces of being made juror No. 8, in the trial of George C. McManus, charged with the murder of the said Rothstein.

Robert G. McKay, a powerfully built, black-haired broker of No. 244 East 67th Street, a rather swanky neighborhood, was answering the do-yous and the can-yous of James D. C. Murray as amiably as you please, and as he had already passed the State's legal lights apparently in a satisfactory manner, the gents at the press tables were muttering, "Well, we gotta another at last."

Then suddenly Robert G. McKay, who looks as if he might have been a Yale or Princeton lineman of say, ten years back, and who was sitting with his big legs crossed and hugging one knee, remarked in a mild tone to Murray, "I suppose I might say I knew Arnold Rothstein—though none of you have asked me."

"Ah," said Attorney Murray with interest, just as it appeared he was through with his questioning.

"Did you ever have any business transactions with Rothstein?"

"Well, it was business on his part, and folly on mine."

"Might I have the impertinence to ask if you bet with him?"

McKay grinned wryly, and nodded. Apparently he found no relish in his recollection of the transaction with "the master mind," who lies a-mouldering in his grave while the State of New York is trying to prove that George McManus is the man who tossed a slug into his stomach in the Park Central Hotel the night of November 4, a year ago.

Attorney Murray now commenced to delve somewhat into McKay's state of mind concerning the late Rothstein. He wanted to know if it would cause the broker any feeling of embarrassment to sit on a jury that was trying a man for the killing of Rothstein, when Judge Charles C. Nott, Jr., who is presiding in the trial, remarked, "I don't think it necessary to spend any more time on this man."

The late Rothstein's customer hoisted his big frame out of the chair, and departed, a meditative expression on his face, as if he might still be considering whether he would feel any embarrassment under the circumstances.

They wangled out six jurors at the morning session of the McManus trial, which was enlivened to some extent by the appearance of quite a number of witnesses for the State in the hallways of the rusty old red brick Criminal Courts Building.

These witnesses had been instructed to show up yesterday morning with the idea that they might be called, and one of the first to arrive was "Titanic Slim," otherwise Alvin C. Thomas, the golf-playing gambling man, whose illness in Milwaukee caused a postponement of the trial a week ago.

"Titanic Slim" was attended by Sidney Stajer, a rotund young man who was one of Rothstein's closest friends, and who is beneficiary to the tune of $75,000 under the terms of the dead gambler's will. At first the cops didn't want to admit "Titanic Slim" to the portals of justice, as he didn't look like a witness, but he finally got into the building only to learn he was excused.

The photographers took great interest in the drawling-voiced, soft-mannered, high roller from the South, and Sidney Stajer scowled at them fiercely, but Sidney really means no harm by his scowls. Sidney is not a hard man and ordinarily would smile very pleasantly for the photographers, but it makes him cross to get up before noon.

The State's famous material witness, Bridget Farry, chambermaid at the Park Central, put in an appearance with Beatrice Jackson, a telephone operator at the same hotel. Bridget was positively gorgeous in an emerald-green dress and gold-heeled slippers. Also she had silver stockings and a silver band around her blond hair. She wore no hat. A hat would have concealed the band.

Bridget, who was held by the State in durance vile for quite a spell, is just a bit stoutish, but she was certainly all dressed up like Mrs. Astor's horse. She sat with Miss Jackson on a bench just outside the portals of justice and exchanged repartee with the cops, the reporters and the photographers.

Bridget is nobody's sap when it comes to talking back to folks. Finally she left the building, and was galloping lightly along to escape the photographers, when her gold-heeled slippers played her false, and she stumbled and fell.

An ambulance was summoned posthaste, as the lady seemed to be injured, but an enterprising gal reporter from a tab scooped her up into a taxicab, and departed with the witness to unknown parts. It is said Bridget's shinbone was scuffed up by the fall.

Some of the State's witnesses were quite busy at the telephone booths while in the building getting bets down on the Bowie races. It is a severe handicap to summon a man to such a remote quarter as the Criminal Courts Building along toward post time.

November 21, 1929

Twelve good men, and glum, are now hunched up in the jury box, in Judge Nott's court, and they are all ready to start in trying to find out about the murder of Arnold Rothstein.

But the hours are really tough on a lot of folks who will figure more or less prominently in the trial. Some of the boys were wondering if Judge Nott would entertain a motion to switch his hours around and start in at 4 P.M., the usual hour of adjournment, and run to 10:30 A.M., which is a gentleman's bedtime. The consensus is he wouldn't.

George Brothers, one of District Attorney Banton's assistants, who is in charge of the prosecution, will probably open the forensic fury for the State of New York this morning, explaining to the dozen morose inmates of the jury box just what the state expects to prove against the defendant, to wit, that George McManus is the party who shot Arnold Rothstein in the stomach in the Park Central Hotel the night of November 4, a year ago.

You may not recall the circumstances, but McManus is one of four persons indicted for the crime. Another is Hyman Biller, an obscure denizen of the brightlights region of Manhattan Island, who probably wouldn't be recognized by more than two persons if he walked into any joint in town, such is his obscurity.

Then there is good old John Doe and good old Richard Roe, possibly the same Doe and Roe who have been wanted in forty-nine different spots for crimes ranging from bigamy to disorderly conduct for a hundred years past. Tough guys, old John and Richard, and always getting in jams. McManus is the only one on trial for the killing of Rothstein, probably for the reason he is the only one handy.

November 22, 1929

"Give me a deck of cards," said "Red" Martin Bowe plaintively, peering anxiously around Judge Nott's court room in the dim light of yesterday afternoon, as if silently beseeching a friendly volunteer in an emergency.

"Get me a deck of cards, and I'll show you."

You see Red Martin Bowe had suddenly come upon a dilemma

in his forty-odd years of traveling up and down the earth. He had come upon a fellow citizen who didn't seem to savvy the elemental pastime of stud poker, and high spading, which Martin probably thought, if he ever gave the matter any consideration, is taught in the grammar schools of this great nation—or should be.

So he called for a deck of cards. He probably felt the question was fatuous but he was willing to do his best to enlighten this apparently very benighted fellow, Ferdinand Pecora, the chief representative of Old John Law on the premises, and to show the twelve good men, and glum, in the jury box just how that celebrated card game was conducted which the State of New York is trying to show cost Arnold Rothstein his life at the hands of George McManus.

But no deck of cards was immediately forthcoming. So Martin Bowe didn't get to give his ocular demonstration to the assembled citizens, though a man came dashing in a little later with a nice red deck, while even Judge Nott was still snorting over Martin Bowe's request.

Possibly if Mr. Pecora can show a night off later some of the boys who sat in the back room yesterday might be induced to give him a lesson or two in stud poker. Also high spading.

Martin Bowe is a big, picturesque-looking chap, who is getting bald above the ears, and who speaks with slow drawl and very low. In fact all the witnesses displayed a remarkable tendency to pitch their voices low in marked contrast with their natural vocal bent under ordinary circumstances and the attorneys had to keep admonishing them to talk louder.

"Gambler," said Bowe, quietly, and without embarrassment, when asked his business. Then he went on to tell about the card game that will probably be remarked for many years as Broadway's most famous joust. It began on a Saturday night and lasted into the Sunday night following. Martin said he previously played five or six hours at a stretch, and then would lie down and take a rest. He stated:

"It started with bridge, then we got to playing stud. The game got slow, and then some wanted to sport a little so they started betting on the high spade."

"I lose," remarked Bowe calmly, when Pecora asked how he came out. McManus was in the game. Also Rothstein, "Titanic," Meyer Boston, Nate Raymond, "Sol—somebody." A chap named Joe Bernstein was present, and several others he didn't remember, though Sam Boston later testified Bernstein was "doing something and he wasn't playing." It is this Bernstein, a California young man, who "beat" Rothstein for $69,000 though Bernstein was never actually in the play. He bet from the outside.

As near as Bowe could recollect, Raymond, Rothstein, Mc-Manus and Bernstein were bettors on the high card. He heard McManus lost about $50,000. Rothstein was keeping a score on the winnings and losings. McManus paid off partly in cash and partly by check, while Rothstein was putting cash in his pocket, and would give out I.O.Us. Bowe said he heard Rothstein lost over $200,000. The redoubtable "Titanic" won between $20,000 and $25,000 from McManus. Pecora asked: "What about Meyer Boston?"

"He wins."

Under cross-examination by James D. C. Murray, Bowe said he had often known McManus to bet as much as $50,000 on one horse race and never complain if he lost. He said:

"It's an everyday occurrence with him. He always paid with a smile."

After the game, he said, Rothstein and McManus were very friendly; they often ate together at Lindy's. Rothstein won something from McManus in the game, but Bowe didn't know how much.

It was a rather big day for the defense. In his opening address to the jury, George Brothers, assistant district attorney, didn't seem to offer much motive for the possible killing of Rothstein by Mc-Manus other than the ill feeling that might have been engendered over the game in which they both lost.

That, and the fact that McManus fled after the killing, seemed his strongest points, while Attorney Murray quickly made it clear that part of the defense will be that Rothstein wasn't shot in room No. 349 at all, and that he certainly wasn't shot by George McManus.

Murray worked at length on Dr. Charles D. Norris, the city Medical Examiner, trying to bring out from the witness that the nature of the wound sustained by Rothstein and the resultant shock would have prevented Rothstein from walking down three flights of stairs, and pushing open two or three heavy doors to reach the spot in the service entrance of the hotel where he was found, especially without leaving some trace of blood.

During the examination of the doctor, the expensive clothes

that Arnold Rothstein used to wear so jauntily were displayed, now crumpled and soiled. The white silk shirt was among the ghastly exhibits, but the $45 custom-made shoes that were his hobby, and the sox were missing. Dr. Norris didn't know what had become of them.

The jurors, most of them business men on their own hook, or identified in salaried capacities with business, were a study while Martin Bowe and Sam Boston were testifying, especially Bowe, for he spoke as calmly of winning and losing $50,000 as if he were discussing the price of his morning paper.

You could see the jurors bending forward, some of them cupping their hands to their ears, and eyeing the witness with amazement. That stud and high spade game had been mentioned so often in the papers that it had come to be accepted as a Broadway fable. Probably no member of the jury, for none of them indicated in their examination that they are familiar with sporting life, took any stock in the tales of high rolling of the Broadway gamblers.

But here was a man who was in the game, who had lost $5,700 of his own money, and who knew what he was talking about. It was apparent the jurors were astounded by the blasé manner of Bowe as he spoke of McManus dropping $50,000 as "an everyday occurrence," and even the voluble Sam Boston's glib mention of handling hundreds of thousands of dollars yearly in bets on sporting events impresses them.

November 28, 1929

Nothing new having developed in the life and battles of Juror No. 9, or the Man with the Little Moustache, the trial of George McManus for the murder of Arnold Rothstein proceeded with reasonable tranquility yesterday.

Just before adjournment over Thanksgiving, to permit the jurors to restore their waning vitality with turkey and stuffin', the State let it out rather quietly that it hasn't been able to trace very far the pistol which is supposed to have ended the tumultuous life of "the master mind" a year ago.

On a pleasant day in last June—the fifteenth, to be exact—it seems that one Mr. Joe Novotny was standing behind the counter in his place of business at No. 51 West Fourth Street, in the thriving settlement of St. Paul, Minnesota, when in popped a party who was to Mr. Joe Novotny quite unknown, shopping for a rod, as the boys term a smoke-pole.

Mr. Novotny sold the stranger a .38-caliber Colt, which Mr. Novotny himself had but recently acquired from the firm of Janney, Sempler & Hill, of Minneapolis, for $22.85. The factory number of the Colt was 359,946. Mr. Novotny did not inquire the shopper's name, because it seems there is no law requiring such inquisitiveness in Minnesota, and Mr. Novotny perhaps didn't wish to appear nosy.

No doubt Mr. Novotny figures the stranger was a new settler in St. Paul and desired the Colt to protect himself against the wild Indians and wolves that are said to roam the streets of the city. Anyway, that's the last Mr. Novotny saw of pistol No. 359,946, and all he knows about it, according to a stipulation presented by the State of New York to Judge Nott late yesterday afternoon, and agreed to by James D. C. Murray, attorney for George McManus, as Mr. Novotny's testimony.

It may be that some miscreant subsequently stole the gun from the settler's cabin in St. Paul or that he lent it to a pal who was going to New York, and wished to be well dressed, for the next we hear of No. 359,946 is its appearance in the vicinity of Fifty-sixth Street and Seventh Avenue, Manhattan Island, where it was picked up by one Bender, a taxi jockey, after the shooting of Arnold Rothstein. A stipulation with reference to said Bender also was submitted to Judge Nott.

The State of New York would have the jury in the trial of George McManus believe it was with this gun that Rothstein was shot in the stomach in room 349 in the Park Central Hotel, and that the gun was hurled through a window into the street after the shooting. It remains to be seen what the jury thinks about this proposition.

It is not thought it will take any stock in any theory that the gun walked from St. Paul to the corner of Fifty-sixth Street and Seventh Avenue.

If the settler who bought the gun from Mr. Novotny would step forward at this moment, he would be as welcome as the flowers in May. But those Northwestern settlers always are reticent.

It was around three o'clock in the afternoon when Mr. James

McDonald, one of the assistant district attorneys, finished reading the 300 pages of testimony taken in the case to date to Mr. Edmund C. Shotwell, juror No. 2, who replaced Eugene Riker when Mr. Riker's nerves bogged down on him.

It was the consensus that Mr. Shotwell was in better physical condition than Mr. McDonald at the conclusion of the reading, although at the start it looked as if Mr. McDonald would wear his man down with ease before page No. 204.

Juror No. 9, who is Norris Smith, the man with the little moustache, whose adventures have kept this trial from sinking far down into the inside of the public prints long ere this, sat in a chair in the row behind the staunch juror No. 2, which row is slightly elevated above the first row. Juror No. 9, who is slightly built and dapperly dressed, tweaked at his little moustache with his fingers and eyed the press section with baleful orbs.

What juror No. 9 thinks of the inmates of the press section would probably be suppressed by the censors. And yet, without juror No. 9, where would this case be? It would be back next to pure reading matter—that's where.

Juror No. 9 was alleged to have been discovered by newspaper men bouncing around a Greenwich Village shushery and talking about the McManus trial, though he convinced Judge Nott that he hadn't done or said anything that might impair his status as a juror in the case. Finally it was learned juror No. 9 was shot up a bit in his apartment at No. 420 West Twentieth Street on February 20, 1928, by a young man who was first defended by James D. C. Murray, now McManus's counsel.

November 30, 1929

Draw near, friend reader, for a touch of ooh-my-goodness has finally crept into the Roaring Forties' most famous murder trial. Sc-an-dal, no less. Sh-h-h!

And where do you think we had to go to get it?

To Walnut Street, in the pleasant mountain city of Asheville, North Carolina. Folks, that's sin in them hills!

Here we'd been going along quietly for days and days on end with the matter of George McManus, charged with plugging Arnold

Rothstein with a .38, and the testimony had been pure and clean and nothing calculated to give Broadway a bad name, when in come a woman from the ol' Tarheel State speaking of the strangest didoes.

A Mrs. Marian A. Putnam, she was, who runs the Putnam grill in Asheville, a lady of maybe forty-odd, a headliner for the State, who testified she had heard loud voices of men, and a crash coming from the vicinity of room 349 in the Park Central Hotel the night "the master mind" was "settled." And that later she had seen a man wandering along the hallway on the third floor, with his hands pressed to his abdomen and "a terrible look on his face."

Well, there seemed nothing in this narration to mar the peaceful trend of events, or to bring the blush of embarrassment for this city to the cheek of the most loyal Broadwayer. Then James D. C. Murray took charge of the witness and began addressing the lady on the most tender subjects, and developing the weirdest things. Really, you'd be surprised.

Handing the lady a registration card from the Park Central Hotel and assuming a gruff tone of voice several octaves over the perfunctory purr that has been the keynote of the trial to date, Murray asked, "Who are the Mr. and Mrs. Putnam indicated by that card as registered at the Park Central on October 28, 1928?"

"I am Mrs. Putnam."

"Who is Mr. Putnam?"

Mrs. Putnam hesitated briefly, and then replied, "A friend of mine to whom I am engaged."

There were subdued snorts back in the court room as the spectators suddenly came up out of their dozes and turned off their snores to contemplate the lady on the witness stand.

Mrs. Putnam wore a rather smart-looking velvet dress, with a gray caracul coat with a dark squirrel collar, and a few diamonds here and there about her, indicating business is okay at the Putnam grill.

But she didn't have the appearance of one who might insert a hotsy-totsy strain into the staid proceedings. She looked more like somebody's mother, or aunt. She described herself as a widow, and here she was admitting something that savored of social error, especially as the lady subsequently remarked that "Mr. Putnam" had occupied the same boudoir with her.

The spectators sat up to listen and mumbled we were finally getting down to business in this trial.

Murray now produced a death certificate attesting to the demise of one Putnam, who died in 1913, the attorney asking, "The Mr. Putnam who occupied the room with you wasn't the Mr. Putnam who died in 1913, was he?"

At this point Mrs. Putnam seemed deeply affected, possibly by the memory of the late Mr. P. She gulped and applied her handkerchief to her eyes, and the spectators eyed her intently, because they felt it would be a thrill if it transpired that the deceased Putnam had indeed returned to life the very night that "the master mind" was shot.

But it seems it wasn't that Mr. Putnam, and Mr. Murray awoke some very antique echoes in the old court room as he shouted, "Who was it?"

Well, Mrs. Putnam, doubtless restrained by a feeling of delicacy, didn't want to tell, and Judge Nott helpfully remarked that as long as she didn't deny she was registered at the hotel, the name didn't seem important. Murray argued Mrs. Putnam's fiancé might be a material witness for the defense, so Judge Nott let him try to show it.

Finally Mrs. Putnam said the man's name was Perry. He is said to be a citizen of Asheville, and what will be said of Mr. Perry in Asheville when the news reaches the sewing circles down yonder will probably be plenty. Not content with touching on Mr. Perry to Mrs. Putnam, the attorney for the defense asked her about a Mr. Elias, and then about a Mr. Bruce, becoming right personal about Mr. Bruce.

He wanted to know if Mr. Bruce had remained with Mrs. Putnam one night in her room at another New York Hotel, but she said no. Then Murray brought in the name of a Mr. Otis B. Carr, of Hendersonville, N.C., and when Mrs. Putnam said she didn't recall the gentleman, the attorney asked, "Did you steal anything out of a store in Hendersonville?"

Mrs. Putnam said no. Moreover, in reply to questions, she said she didn't steal two dresses from a department store in Asheville and that she hadn't been arrested for disorderly conduct and fined $5. Before Murray got through with her some of the listeners half expected to hear him ask the lady if she had ever personally killed A. Rothstein.

Mrs. Putnam couldn't have made the State very happy, because she admitted under Murray's cross-examination that she had once denied in Asheville, in the presence of Mr. Mara, one of the district attorney's assistants, and County Judge McCrae, of Asheville, that she ever left her room in the Park Central the night of the murder.

She said her current story is the truth. Mr. Murray asked her if she hadn't said thus and so to newspapermen in Asheville. She replied, "I did."

A young man described as Douglas Eller, a reporter of an Asheville paper, was summoned from among the spectators in the court room and brought up to the railing, where Mrs. Putnam could see him. The lady was asked if she knew him, and she eyed him at length before admitting she may have seen him before. Mr. Eller retired, blushing slightly, as if not to be known by Mrs. Putnam argues one unknown in Asheville.

Murray became very curious about the Putnam grill in Asheville. Didn't she have curtained-off booths? She did, but her waitresses could walk in and out of them at any time, a reply that Mrs. Putnam tossed at Murray as if scorning utterly the base insinuation of his question.

Did she sell liquor? She did not. She had been shown pictures of Rothstein and McManus and Biller, but she couldn't recognize any of them. She was mighty reluctant about telling the name of a lady friend with whom she dined in her room the night of the killing, but finally admitted it was a Mrs. Herman Popper. She explained her reluctance by saying, "I don't want to get other people mixed up in this."

December 3, 1929

The most important point to the State in the trial of George McManus yesterday seemed to be the key to room 349 in the Park Central Hotel, which, according to testimony, was found in a pocket of an overcoat hanging in the room.

This overcoat bore the name of McManus on the tailor's label in the pocket.

The prosecution will, perhaps, make much of this as tending to show the occupant of the room left in a very great hurry and didn't lock the door, besides abandoning the overcoat, though Detective

"Paddy" Flood said the door was locked when he went there with a house detective to investigate things.

It was Detective Flood who told of finding the key. He was relating how he entered the room and found, among other things, an overcoat with the name of George McManus on the label. He was asked, "What other objects did you find?"

"A handkerchief in the pocket of the overcoat with the initials 'G. Mc.' There were other handkerchiefs in the drawer in the bedroom and a white shirt."

"Did you find anything else in the coat?"

"A key, in the right-hand pocket, for room 349."

"A door key."

"Yes."

Aside from that, the testimony brought out that "the master mind," as the underworld sometimes called Arnold Rothstein, died "game."

Game as a pebble.

In the haunts of that strange pallid man during his life, you could have had ten to one, and plenty of it, that he would "holler copper," did occasion arise, with his dying gasp.

Indeed he was often heard to remark in times when he knew that sinister shadows hovered near—and these were not infrequent times in his troubled career, living as he chose to live—"If anyone gets me, they'll burn for it."

And cold, hard men, thinking they read his character, believed they knew his meaning. They felt he was just the kind, when cornered by an untoward circumstance, that would squeal like a pig. It shows you how little you really know of a man.

For when the hour came, as the jury in Judge Nott's court room heard yesterday, with the dismal snow slanting past the windows of the grimy old Criminal Courts Building—when Arnold Rothstein lay crumpled up with a bullet through his intestines, knowing he was mortally hurt, and officers of the law bent over him and whispered, "Who did it?"—the pale lips tightened, and Rothstein mumbled, "I won't tell and please don't ask me any more questions."

Then another "sure thing" went wrong on Broadway, where "sure things" are always going wrong—the "sure thing" that Rothstein would tell.

But as the millionaire gambler lay in the Fifty-sixth Street service entrance of the Park Central Hotel that night of November 4, 1928, with the pain of his wound biting at his vitals, and the peering eyes of the cops close to his white countenance, he reverted to type.

He was no longer the money king, with property scattered all over the Greater City, a big apartment house on fashionable Park Avenue, a Rolls-Royce and a Minerva at his beck and call, and secretaries and servants bowing to him. He was a man of the underworld. And as one of the "dice hustlers" of the dingy garage lofts, and the "mobsters" high and low, he muttered, "I won't tell."

A sigh of relief escaped many a chest at those words, you can bet on that.

Detective Flood, who knew Rothstein well, was one of those who bent over the stricken man.

Patrolman William Davis, first to respond to the call of the hotel attendants, also asked Rothstein who shot him, but got no more information than Flood.

The head of the millionaire gambler was pillowed on a wadded-up burlap sack when Davis reached the scene, which was important to the State in trying to show that Rothstein was shot in the hotel, in that it had been said that Rothstein's overcoat was put under his head.

Before the session was completed, the tables in the court room were covered with exhibits of one kind and another taken by Flood and other officers from room 349 in the Park Central.

There was a layout of glasses and a liquor bottle, and ginger ale bottles on a tray. But, alas, the liquor bottle was very empty. Also the State had the dark blue overcoat with the velvet collar that was found in a closet of room 349, said overcoat bearing a tailor's label, with George McManus's name on the label.

Likewise, handkerchiefs found in the room were produced and these handkerchiefs were elegantly monogrammed. One was inscribed "g Mc M.," another like "G. M. A." with the "G" and "A" in small letters, and the "M" big. A third was monogrammed "J. M. W." with the "J" and "W" in small letters on either side of the large "M" while the fourth bore the marking "J. M."

A white shirt with collar attached, some race-track slips, and a window screen with a hole in it were spread out for the jurors to see. Also, the .38-caliber pistol, which one Al Bender, a taxi driver, picked up on Seventh Avenue.

This is supposed to be the pistol with which Rothstein was shot, and the screen is supposed to be the screen through which the pistol was hurled out into the street after the shooting, though the point where the pistol was picked up is quite a hurling distance from room 349.

While Flood and some other officers were in the room Hyman Biller, a cashier at the race track for McManus, and under indictment with McManus for the murder of Rothstein, came in with Frank and Tom McManus, brothers of George, and remained about twenty minutes.

It was the failure to hold Biller on this occasion that brought down much criticism on the heads of the Police Department, for Hymie was never seen in these parts again.

The lights were burning in room 349 when Flood got there. Four glasses stood on the table which is the basis of the indictment returned against McManus, and Biller, and the celebrated John Doe and Richard Roe. The State claims four men were in the room when Rothstein was summoned there by a message sent by McManus to Lindy's restaurant.

Vincent J. Kelly, elevator operator at the Park Central, testified he was working on the service elevator the night Rothstein was shot, and saw Rothstein in the corridor, holding his hands across his stomach, and didn't see him come through the service doorway, through which he must have passed to make good the State's contention he came from upstairs.

He heard Rothstein say, "I'm shot."

Thomas Calhoun, of Corona, Long Island, thirty-two, a watchman on the Fifty-sixth Street side of the hotel at the time of the murder, saw Rothstein at 10:47 standing in front of the time office at the service entrance. Calhoun ran and got Officer Davis.

He heard Rothstein say something to the policeman about taking his money, and it was his impression that Rothstein had his overcoat over his arm and that it was put under his head as he lay on the floor, which impression was not corroborated by other testimony.

Through Calhoun, Attorney Murray tried to develop that Rothstein might have come through the swimming pool by way of Seventh Avenue. While cross-examining Calhoun, Murray suddenly remarked, testily, "I object to the mumbling to the District Attorney."

He apparently had reference to Mr. Brothers, of the State's legal display. Everybody seemed to be a bit testy yesterday, except the ever-smiling defendant, McManus, who just kept on smiling.

Calhoun heard Rothstein say, "Call my lawyer, 9410 Academy."

Thomas W. McGivney, of No. 401 West 47th Street, who was also near the service entrance, testified he had taken Rothstein's overcoat off his arm and placed it under his head. Rothstein's overcoat hasn't been seen since the shooting.

McGivney, a stout-looking young man with a wide smile, and a rich brogue, gave the spectators a few snickers, but by and large it wasn't an exciting day one way or the other.

AL CAPONE

A fragrant whiff of green fields and growing rutabagas and parsnips along with echoes of good old Main Street, crept into the grime-stained Federal Building here today as your Uncle Sam took up the case of Al Capone and gathered a jury in what you might call jigtime.

It is a jury made up mainly of small towners and Michael J. Ahern, chief counsel for Al Capone, frankly admitted dissatisfaction to the Court about it.

He wanted all these persons dismissed but Judge Wilkerson overruled his motion. The jury was sworn in with nine veterans of court room juries among the twelve good men and true, and tomorrow morning at ten o'clock the Government of these United States starts work on Al Capone.

The truly rural atmosphere of the proceedings today was evidenced by horny-handed tillers of the fruitful soil, small town store-keepers, mechanics and clerks, who gazed frankly interested at the burly figure of the moon-faced fellow causing all this excitement and said,

"Why, no: we ain't got no prejudice again Al Capone."

At least most of them said that in effect, as Judge Wilkerson was expediting the business of getting a jury to try Capone on charges of income tax evasion.

Your Uncle Sam says Al Capone owes him $215,000 on an income of $1,038,000 in six years.

Your Uncle Sam hints that Al Capone derived this tidy income from such illegal didoes as bootlegging, gambling, and the like.

"Do you hope the government proves the defendant guilty?" was one question asked a venireman at the request of counsel for the defense.

Apparently none cherished that hope.

"Have you any desire that the defendant be sent to jail?" was another question requested by the defense.

"Well no," was the general reply.

Al Capone sat up straight in his chair and smoothed his rumpled necktie. He felt better. The G-men—as the boys call 'em—want to put Al Capone in a Federal pokey, or jail, for anywhere from two to thirty-two years, to impress upon him the truth of the adage that honesty is the best policy.

As Al Capone sat there with the scent of the new-mown hay oozing at intervals from the jury box, he was a terrific disappointment to the strictly seeing-Chicago tourist who felt that Al should have been vested at least in some of the panoply of his reputed office as Maharajah of the Hoods. Perhaps a cartridge belt. Some strangers felt this Chicago has been misrepresented to them.

The jury as it now stands is as follows: Louis G. Wolfersheim, Chicago; Louis P. Weidling, painter, Wilmington, Ill.; Burr Dugan, farmer, DeKalb County; A. C. Smart, painter and decorator, Libertyville; W. J. Hendricks, lubricating engineer, Cook County; George M. Larsen, wood patenter, Dalton; W. F. McCormick, receiving shop, Maywood; A. G. Maegher, country store-keeper, Prairie View; Ambrose Merchant, real estate agent, Waukegan; Arthur O. Prochno, insurance agent, Edison Park; John A. Walker, abstractor, Yorkville; and Nate C. Brown, retired hardware dealer, St. Charles.

Selection of the jury in one day is regarded as amazingly quick work, and the trial may not be as long drawn out as expected.

Capone arrived for the opening session fifteen minutes ahead of time, which is said to be a record in punctuality for him.

A big crowd was gathered on the Clark Street side of the dingy old building waiting to see him, but Al popped out of an automobile and into the building like a fox going into a hole. Not many of the curiosity-seekers got a good peek at him.

He entered the court room alone and was quickly surrounded by a crowd of reporters, male and female, who began bouncing questions about his ears. They asked him if he was worried, and he replied, logically enough, "Who wouldn't be worried?"

He was scarcely the sartorial spectacle familiar to the winter inmates of Florida, where Al's sport apparel is one of the scenes of interest. In fact, he was quietly dressed this morning, bar a hat of pearly white, emblematic no doubt, of purity.

'Twas a warmish morning and Al, being stout, is susceptible to the heat. Then, too, he was in a hot spot. His soft collar was already crumpled. He frequently mopped his forehead with a white handkerchief. His swarthy jowls had been newly shaved. His black hair now getting quite sparse was plastered back on his skull.

Judge Wilkerson himself is a fine-looking man with iron-gray hair. He is smooth shaven. His eyebrows are black and strong. He wore no flowing robe, like New York judges. He was dressed in a quiet business suit of dark color and wears horn-rimmed glasses.

His voice is clear and very decided. He sits far down in his chair while listening, but when he is doing the talking he leans far forward over his desk, his shoulders hunched up.

Wilkerson made it very clear to the men in the jury box that Capone is being tried on charges of violating the income tax law and nothing else.

Capone's chief counsel, Ahern, a tall, good-looking chap of perhaps middle age, who wore a gray suit and tan shoes, approached the railing in front of the bench as court opened this morning, flanked by his associate in the defense, Albert Fink, a ruddy-faced, baldish man given to easy attitudes.

Ahern's first approach was with a mild protest against the arrangement of the court room by which the thirty or more representatives of the press were crowding defense attorneys out of house and home. He was satisfied when the scribes were shoved off a bit so their hot breath would not beat against the back of Al Capone's neck.

George E. Q. Johnson, the United States district attorney in charge of prosecution, is a forensic-looking man. He has a pink complexion, a rather beaming countenance and a mop of gray hair, all mussed up.

At the request of Ahern, Wilkerson asked the veniremen:

"Do any of you belong to any law enforcement organization? Counsel asks specifically about the Anti-Saloon League?"

None did, it seemed.

"Have any of you ever contributed to a law enforcement organization?"

Well, one man had once chipped in ten dollars to the Crime Commission. His confession didn't seem important to the attorneys at the moment.

None of Capone's so-called bodyguards were in evidence anywhere around the court house, I am reliably informed. Naturally,
I wouldn't know 'em myself. Al goes to his citadel, the Hotel Lexington, out south, as soon as he leaves the court. It used to be a
noted hostelry. The President of the U.S.A. stopped there during the
World's Fair. Now it is Capone's G.H.Q.

October 8, 1931

"What do you do with your money—carry it on your person?"

An income tax examiner asked this question of Al Capone in
September, 1930, when Al was seeking a settlement with your Uncle Sam and could produce no books, bank accounts or anything
else in writing bearing upon his financial transactions.

And, according to a transcript of the examination, Al replied:

"Yes, I carry it on my person."

He must have had plenty of room on his person, judging from
a letter his attorney at that time wrote to the Internal Revenue Bureau, for this letter, the basis of argument lasting most of the day's
sessions, admitted Capone's income was nearly $300,000 in the
years 1926 to 1929, inclusive.

Capone's lawyer at that time was Lawrence B. Mattingly,
Washington income tax expert. In fighting the admission of the
letter, one of Al's present lawyers, Albert Fink, characterized the
letter as a confession by a lawyer in behalf of a client.

He argued that no lawyer has the right or authority to make a
confession for a client.

Judge Wilkerson finally overruled objection to the admission of
the letter, which was undoubtedly a big victory for the government.
Capone seemed deeply concerned when he heard the Court's ruling.

Judge Wilkerson said he believed the weight of authority was in
favor of the admissibility of the document.

The letter was read to Judge Wilkerson, but not to the jury,
which was sent from the room while the lawyers argued. It was
produced by Samuel Clawson, of Washington, one of the attorneys representing the government, as soon as court opened today.

The letter was written by Mattingly when he was endeavoring to
adjust Al Capone's income tax troubles with the government, and
traced Capone's financial rise from a modest $75 per week, prior to

1926, to an income of $26,000 in that year, $40,000 in 1927, "not to exceed $100,000" in 1928, and "not to exceed $100,000" in 1929.

The source of the income was mentioned as an organization, the nature of which was not described, in which a group of employees had a third interest, and Capone and three associates a fourth.

Mattingly wrote:

"Notwithstanding that two of the taxpayer's [Capone's] associates insist that his income never exceeded $50,000 in any one year, I am of the opinion his taxable income for the years 1926 and 1927 might be fairly fixed at not to exceed $26,000 and $40,000 respectively, and for the years 1928 and 1929, not to exceed $100,000."

Capone listened to the letter with keen interest. He seemed in great humor, although it was what you might call a tough day for his side. The letter went on:

"The so-called bodyguards with which he [Capone] is reputed to surround himself, were not as a general rule his personal employees, but were employees of the organization who participated in its profits."

Referring to Capone's assets, the letter said:

"The furniture in the home occupied by the taxpayer while he was in Florida was acquired at a cost not to exceed $20,000. The house and grounds have been thoroughly appraised, and the appraisal has been submitted to you. There is a mortgage against the house and grounds of $30,000. His indebtedness to his associates has rarely ever been less than $75,000 since 1927. It frequently has been much more."

The letter was produced by the government attorneys on the appearance of George E. Slentz, of Washington, D.C., first witness of the day. Slentz is chief of the power-of-attorney section of the Bureau of Internal Revenue, and Attorney Clawson wanted him to identify the letter written by Mattingly.

Helen Alexander, vault clerk at a state bank in Cicero, identified a contract for a vault signed in 1927 by Al Capone and Louis De Cava. She identified Capone's signature and pointed him out in the court room, but she did not recall seeing Capone at the bank in connection with her duties.

Louis H. Wilson, connected with the Internal Revenue Collector's office here, testified to a conference with Mattingly, who said Capone owed income tax, and was willing to pay.

There was another conference at which Capone was present in person, and also C. W. Herrick, Internal Revenue agent. Everything said at the conference was duly set down by a stenographer.

Judging from the transcript of that conference, read in court today, Capone's chief answer to questions about his income was: "I would rather have my lawyer answer that."

He denied having anything to do with a dog track, never owned a race horse and never had a bank account.

After Capone left the conference Mattingly told Wilson he would get some facts together as best he could and make a return. He recommended, Wilson said, that the government get busy at once, as Capone had some money at the moment, and would pay up.

But apparently Mattingly's task was a little difficult. He reported he couldn't get definite records on Al Capone's income. Finally Mattingly produced the letter that caused the excitement today.

At the rate the trial is traveling now, it will take several weeks to conclude it. The defense attorneys are contesting every inch of legal ground. Al is getting a good run for his money, anyway. He came and went today mid the usual excitement outside the court house, but the crowds do not seem able to pick the hole he bobs out of with any degree of success.

Chicago, October 9, 1931

The soft murmur of the blue breakers caressing old Miami shore sort o' sneaked into Judge Wilkerson's court room this afternoon, between shrill snorts of the Chicago traffic coppers' whistles outside, as witnesses from the sunny Southland connected Al Capone up with $125,500 transmitted from Chicago to Miami by wire.

Having shown to the jury in the Federal Court where all those potatoes went, your Uncle Sam was going about the business of trying to prove whence they came when Judge Wilkerson adjourned to a half day session tomorrow.

The last witness of the day, one John Fotre, a sharp-featured citizen, wearing a slightly startled expression, who is manager of the Western Union branch office in the Lexington Hotel here, was identifying a money order showing some of the money went to Capone from Sam Gusick, when Wilkerson called a halt.

The Lexington Hotel is sometimes spoken of as "the Fort," and is said to be the citadel of the Capone forces. Sam Gusick is reputed to be one of Al Capone's business managers. Fotre said he couldn't say if it was Sam Gusick in person who sent the dough per the money order in question, because he didn't know him.

Much of the money was traced to the purchase and improvement of the celebrated winter seat of the Hidalgo of the Hoods on Palm Island, in Biscayne Bay, between Miami proper and Miami Beach.

It was traced through Parker Henderson, Jr., whose testimony indicated he was in Capone's confidence to an amazing degree. He was manager of the Ponce de Leon Hotel in Miami.

It was there Capone stopped when he first went to Florida in 1928, at which time, and later, according to the testimony today, the good burghers of Miami were so perturbed by his presence they held meetings.

How Henderson came to arrive on such terms with Capone did not appear, but it was Henderson who negotiated the purchase of the home, and who handled large sums of money for Capone in improving the place.

Henderson testified to signing numerous Western Union money transfers with the name of Al Costa, turning the money over to Nick Serritela, who worked for Capone, or to Capone himself.

They were generally for sums of $1,000 or $1,500. Other transfers were in the names of Peterson and Serritela. There were over twenty different transfers, amounting in all to $45,000, of which about $15,000 was transmitted to Henderson personally to be spent in improving the Palm Island property.

The rest was for Capone.

These transfers refer only to the telegraph office in Miami. Later witnesses added $30,300 as having gone through the Western Union branch in Miami Beach.

Capone listened with great interest as the witness testified.

Henderson narrated the detail of the purchase of the Palm Island property, which was made in his name. Later he transferred the property to Mrs. Mary Capone, Al's wife.

Henderson came to Chicago, May, 1928, and saw Capone and got money to pay off the men working on the improvements.

He said Al invited him to stay at the Metropole Hotel, then the Capone G.H.Q., and while there he saw such celebrities as Ralph

Capone, Jack Gusick, Charley Fuschetti, Jack McGurn, a party called "Mops" and others.

This was after Capone was living on Palm Island. The money came in batches of from anywhere from $600 to $5,000. Some of the transfers were to Albert Capone, a brother, but the witnesses said Alphonse Capone signed for many of them.

Vernon Hawthorn, a Miami attorney, told of a meeting at which Capone and a number of officials of Miami and Dade County, Florida, were present. It was in 1928; Capone had just appeared in Florida and the good citizens of Dade wanted to find out what the celebrated visitor intended in their startled midst. Al said he was there to rest.

The witness said Capone told him he was in the cleaning and pressing business in Chicago. Finally, the witness said, Al admitted his business was gambling and that he was interested in a Cicero dog track. Furthermore, that he had bought a home in Miami.

The question was asked him at the meeting, "What do you do?" and according to the transcript read this morning, Capone said, "I am a gambler. I bet on horses."

"Are you also a bootlegger?"

"No, I never was a bootlegger in my life."

He said the Palm Island home was in his wife's name. He denied he had received any sums of money from Charles Fuschetti under the name of Costa.

Morrisey Smith, day clerk and cashier at the Metropole Hotel, Chicago, where Capone used to have his headquarters in a suite of five rooms, was examined by Attorney Grossman, who asked, "Who paid for this suite of five rooms?"

"Mr. Capone."

He did not know how much. Grossman handed him the cash sheets of the hotel and Smith picked out a payment of $1,500 for rooms in 1927. No period of time was stated. He was registered as Mr. Ross. The witness testified to numerous other payments, always in cash.

Counsel for the defense could not see what this was all about and spoke to the Court about it. The judge replied, "I presume it's to show he had money. If you pay out something you must have something coming in."

A party for Al's friends who came to the Dempsey-Tunney fight was listed. It cost $1,633. Al gave "small gratuities" to the hotel help now and then, Smith's idea of a "small" gratuity was something surprising. He explained, "He would give five dollars or something like that." Fred S. Avery was manager of the Hotel Metropole when Capone was there. He went to see Capone on one occasion and asked him about a little money and Capone personally paid him the next day. His bills ran around $1,200 to $1,500 a week. Avery said the Dempsey-Tunney entertainment ran two nights.

October 10, 1931

The life of Riley that Al Capone is supposed to live on Palm Island was reflected in testimony brought out by your Uncle Sam before Judge Wilkerson and the jury in the Federal Court this morning.

The butcher, the baker, and the landscape maker from Miami were among the witnesses, not to mention the real estate man, the dock builder, the telephone agent, and the chap who supplied the drapes for 93 Palm Island.

It came out that quite a batch of meat was gnawed up in Al's home in the course of several seasons—a matter of $6,500 worth. Also plenty of bread, and cake, and macaroni was consumed.

The telephoning was terrific. Someone must have been on Al's phone almost constantly. In the course of four Florida seasons there was gabbing, mainly at long distance, to the tune of over $8,000 not counting wrong numbers, but your Uncle Sam contented himself with standing on $4,097.05 in two years in his effort to prove Al must have had plenty of income because he spent plenty.

Your Uncle Sam argues that if a man spends a raft of money he must necessarily have a raft of money to spend, a theory that sounds logical enough unless your Uncle Sam is including horse players.

We had a slight diversion after Wilkerson adjourned court until Monday, with another warning to the jurors not to permit anyone to communicate with them.

The diversion consisted of the seizing of the mysterious Phillip D'Andrea, Capone's bodyguard who has been sitting behind Al since this trial started, by a United States deputy marshal, and the alleged discovery on his person of a .38-caliber John Roscoe, or pistol.

D'Andrea was ordered by Judge Wilkerson to stand trial for carrying a revolver in the court room, and was taken to jail.

D'Andrea is a short, stout bespectacled individual, who dresses well, and looks like a prosperous professional man.

He has been described as a friend of Capone's and Al seemed much perturbed by his seizure. He waited around while D'Andrea was in the marshal's office, with Capone's attorneys, Ahern and Fink, trying to get him out of his trouble.

Al said he didn't know D'Andrea carried a gun, and didn't believe he did.

The twelve men, most of them small towners, and of occupations that would argue a modest scale of living, listened intently to testimony that indicated Al's comparatively elaborate existence, although the reputed magnificence of Al's Palm Island estate dwindled somewhat in the imagination of the urban listeners when expenditures for improvements were related.

These expenditures were not unusually heavy. In fact, Al was depicted in some of the testimony as a householder with a repugnance for being "gypped" in small details.

This morning Capone had on fresh scenery in the form of a dark-colored double-breasted suit of greenish hue, white linen, a green tie and black shoes. He had gone back to his famous white hat.

The attendance at the session today was positively disappointing. Fewer than a dozen persons sat in the seats assigned to spectators when court opened. Can it be that Chicago is losing interest in Al Capone?

William Froelich, of government counsel, read a list of money transfers to the jury showing the transfer of a total of $77,500 to Capone in Florida.

W. C. Harris, office manager of the Southern Bell Telephone Company at Miami, was the first witness. He identified a contract for phone service between the company and Al Capone at 93 Palm Island.

Harris identified company bills for service to the Capone residence amounting to $955.55 in 1928 and $3,141.50 in 1929, a total of $4,097.05, mostly for long distance calls.

Richard Plummer, of Miami, testified to supplying the draperies for Capone's home in 1928 at a cost of $1,000. He said Capone paid him in cash.

George F. Geizer, night clerk at Capone's old G.H.Q., the Metropole Hotel, Chicago, testified to receiving payments in cash to the amount of $2,088.25 from Capone for hotel bills on August 4, 1921.

Louis Karlinch, of Miami, testified he sold meat to Capone to the amount of $6,500 over a period of three years, nearly always getting his money in cash. The bills amounted to around $200 a week. Albert Fink, attorney for Capone, asked, "Do you think Al ate all the meat himself?"

"No. One man couldn't eat it all."

H. F. Ryder, of Miami, built a dock for Capone on Palm Island and worked around the place generally. Ryder, a small, dark-haired fellow, was inclined to be quite chatty about things. He spoke of seeing Capone with a roll of bills that would "choke an ox."

Fink wanted to know how big an ox. He also asked the witness if it couldn't have been a "Western roll," which the attorney explained is a roll of $1 bills with a big bill on top. Ryder said it might have been.

Ryder testified he still has $125 coming to him from Capone for work, but said he wasn't worried about that. He said he expected to get it when he ran into Capone. In fact, Ryder had a boost for Al.

When Ahern asked his opinion of Capone he answered, "A mighty fine man."

Curt Koenitzer, a chunky, red-faced builder and contractor in Miami, testified to building a garage and bathhouse on the Palm Island property. He was paid by one of Capone's brothers.

A swarthy, dapper chap with black hair and a black moustache was expected to turn out at least a duke, but is Al Capone's baker in Miami. His name is Milton Goldstron.

He delivered bakery supplies to Capone's house in 1929, 1930 and 1931 to a total of $1,130 and was paid by Frank Newton, caretaker of the Capone premises.

F. A. Whitehead, hardware merchant, testified to the building of iron gates for the Capone estate.

H. J. Etheritz, who is connected with Burdine's department store in Miami, testified to purchases by Capone of drapes amounting to $800.

Joseph A. Brower, landscape gardener, testified to doing some work on the Capone estate. He was paid $2,100 in checks signed by Jack Gusick. He said Capone described Gusick as his financial secretary.

Frank Gallatt, of Miami, said he was hired in 1929 to put up some buildings on Palm Island. Capone himself did the hiring, he said. Also Capone had paid him personally between $10,000 and $11,000 in cash.

October 12, 1931

A gleaming diamond belt buckle, one of a batch of thirty purchased by Al Capone at $277 apiece, or $8,310 for the lot, was flashed before the astonished eyes of the jury today.

Al bought these buckles for his friends. One of the buckles is said to have been worn by Alfred (Jake) Lingle, Chicago underworld reporter, who was assassinated in June of last year, for which crime Leo V. Brothers is now doing a stretch in the penitentiary.

The jurors peered at the buckle with interest. Each buckle is said to have been engraved with the initials of the recipient, but markings on the buckle displayed today were not revealed, a fact that is doubtless causing someone to heave big sighs of relief.

Judge Wilkerson seemed to think the exhibition of the buckle to the jurors might be with the idea of giving them a line on the quality of the gewgaw, and he remarked, "The quality of the goods makes no difference. It is immaterial whether the defendant got value received or not as long as he spent the money."

In other words, Al may have been "gypped," but that doesn't enter into the case.

Besides diamond buckles, Al passed suits of custom-made clothes around among his friends at $135 per copy, though not so many of these. He also had shirts made at from $22 to 30 apiece, with the monograms $1 each. His ties cost $4 each and handkerchiefs $2.75 apiece. He bought them by the "bunch."

We got right down to Al's skin today.

We found out Al wears silk union-suits at $12 a smash, and athletic "shorts" at $5 a clip. A Mr. J. Banken, of Marshall Field's and who evidently has an abiding artistic interest in his business, told us about that.

Albert Fink, Capone's attorney, who is a fellow you wouldn't think gave much thought to underwear, or other gents furnishings, perked up and interrogated Banken about those union-suits, especially after Banken had described them as a fine silk, "like a lady's glove." Fink leaning forward asked, "Warm?"

"No, not warm. Just a nice suit of underwear."

"How much are they now?"

"Ten dollars."

"Aha," said the attorney, reflectively, "they've gone down?"

"Yes, two dollars," replied Banken, and it looked for a moment as if he had a sale.

The testimony revealed Al as rather a busy and shrewd shopper. While he is usually pictured as a ruthless gang chieftain, he was today presented as a domesticated sort of a chap going around buying furniture, and silverware, and rugs, and knickknacks of one kind and another for his household.

He was shown buying linoleum for the kitchen, and superintending the interior decoration of his home on Palm Island, and personally attending to other details the average citizen is glad to turn over to friend wife.

Moreover Al appears to have been somewhat conservative in big household purchases, considering the amount of plunder he is supposed to have handled.

He spread out more when buying for his own personal adornment in the way of clothing, and neckties, and night shirts.

Oscar De Feo, of Marshall Field's, recalled making over twenty suits for Al and a few topcoats, along with suits for four or five of Al's friends at a total cost of around $3,600.

Samuel J. Steinberg, jeweler, who told of the diamond buckles, also said Al stepped into the store one day and bought twenty-two beaded bags at $22.50 apiece.

During the morning session we furnished Al's Palm Beach home from top to bottom, besides sending some furnishings out to a Prairie Avenue address, where his mother lives.

From Henry E. Keller, an elderly man from Miami, we had a clue to Al Capone's start in life.

Keller was dock foreman for Al on the Palm Island place, at a salary of $550 per month, and one day, when having lunch with Al, Al asked him where he was born. Keller replied, "In the old Tenth Ward, in New York."

"Is that so," said Al, according to the witness, "why, I came from New York. I got my start as a bartender on Long Island."

Al often grinned at the testimony, especially when we got down to his underwear.

October 13, 1931

Your Uncle Sam chucked a sort of Chicago pineapple of surprise under Alphonse Capone's lawyers this afternoon by suddenly announcing these United States of America rested its case against its most conspicuous income tax dodger of the hour.

"What?" ejaculated Mr. Michael J. Ahern, the urbane Irishman, who has been leading the defense.

"Huh," exclaimed Mr. Albert Fink, his bluff and gruff associate.

Then their chairs rattled in chorus as they pushed them aside to step up to Judge Wilkerson's bench in the Federal Court.

Even Al Capone sensed something unusual and leaned forward to listen to the attorneys, his round features set in seriousness, a plump hand rigid before him.

Messrs. Ahern and Fink admitted their astonishment. You gathered they felt your Uncle Sam had sneaked up on them very suddenly from under cover of a day of dry proceedings all along the line of trying to connect Al Capone up with the gambling profits of the Cicero joints.

These profits, the government asserts, amounted to $177,500 in 1927 and $24,800 in 1928, a total for the two years of $202,300.

The startled attorneys argued desperately for the next half hour for a little delay to get their line of defense consolidated, and bring witnesses from New York and other points. But all their conversation did them no good.

It was 2:20 P.M. when the government lawyers concluded with the direct examination of a handwriting expert named Herbert Walters, only witness of the afternoon, who testified certain endorsements on a cashier's check bought with the profits of a Cicero gambling house were in the handwriting of Al Capone.

Indications are the defense will be comparatively brief. Capone's reputed huge gambling losses may be one line. That some of Al's lavish expenditures was on borrowed money may be another.

The government had a short, square-jibbed chap named Bobby Barton walking in and out of the court room every few minutes for identification by different witnesses as the man who handled a large sum of money for Jack Gusick, but Barton was never called to the stand.

The testimony throughout the trial has depicted Gusick as the money man of the Capone combination. He received the money, and apparently cut it up, too, and one witness testified Gusick told him on no occasion to give anyone else any of the money gathered in at Cicero, "not even Al."

Among the things presented by the government which the Capone attorneys say they never heard of before the case opened and against which they have had no time to prepare was the letter from Capone's income tax expert, Lawrence Mattingly, to C. W. Herrick, local revenue collector, offering to compromise Al's indebtedness to the government.

Fred Ries, the man whose testimony is said to have convicted Jack Gusick and Ralph Capone of income tax violations, was today's principal witness.

Ries was the cashier of the Radio and Subway gambling houses in Cicero in 1927 and had charge of all the finances. He identified a cashier's check for $2,500 made payable to J. C. Dunbar, which he cashed and turned over to Bobby Barton. Ries said he was J. C. Dunbar.

He said that as cashier he bought cashier's checks with the profits of the establishment, which he gave to Bobby Barton, who in turn gave them to Jack Gusick. He said he bought over $150,000 worth of checks in 1927. By profits he meant any surplus over the bankroll of $10,000.

There was a long discussion by the attorneys and the Court when Grossman offered the cashier's checks in evidence and Ahern objected.

The jury was sent from the room and Grossman questioned the witness further to show the Court he was going to connect Al up with the checks. Finally Judge Wilkerson decided to admit the checks.

Johnny Torrio, predecessor of Capone as Chicago's gang lord, and now living on Long Island, was not called upon to testify, although he was subpoenaed. The contempt case against Phil D'Andrea, Al's bodyguard, who has been in the coop since Saturday morning when he was grabbed with a pistol on his pudgy person, was postponed until Friday.

October 14, 1931

Your correspondent cheerfully yields the palm he has borne with such distinction for lo these many years as the world's worst horse player to Mr. Alphonse Capone.

Yes sir, and ma'am, Al wins in a common gallop, if we are to believe the testimony brought up in his support today.

Up to closing time this afternoon Al had lost upwards of $217,000 of all that wrong money that your Uncle Sam has been trying to show went into the Capone pockets from gambling operations in Cicero, and what-not, and the end is not yet.

A string of bookmakers testified to clipping Al for his potatoes on the races. He was a high player, betting from $1,000 to $5,000 on a race, according to the testimony, and he must have picked out more lizards, beetles, armadillos, crocodiles, anteaters, polecats, penguins and polar bears than your correspondent on one of his best days.

Al never seemed to win. At least every bookmaker that went to the post today testified to knocking him in for anywhere from $15,000 to $25,000. There were several other bookies in the paddock outside the court room when court adjourned.

Apparently Al didn't believe all horse players must die broke. He was belting away at 'em through 1924 down to 1927.

At the rate the bookies are going now, Al will not have any more of that $266,000 income that your Uncle Sam charges to him by the time court is over tomorrow.

Milton Held, a betting commissioner, testified Al lost between $8,000 and $10,000 at the Hawthorne track in 1924 and about $12,000 in the fall of 1925.

Oscar Gutter, a dark-complexioned little man with a low voice who also described himself as a betting commissioner, said Capone lost about $60,000 in 1927 on bets he handled.

Both Held and Gutter admitted on cross-examination that they had been summoned within the past few days to Capone's headquarters at the Lexington Hotel, where they conferred with Al and his lawyers.

Held said Capone would bet anywhere from $200 to $500 on a horse. Gutter told of bets from $1,000 to $3,000. Once Al bet $6,000 on a nag. He always paid off his losings in cash, either personally or through a "secretary."

The bookmakers say when they paid Capone off on rare occasions when he won they sent checks in the name of "Andy Doyle."

Then came a burly, fat-faced, black-haired chap who described himself as Peter Penovich, Jr. His name has often entered into the case as one of the partners and managers of a Cicero gambling house.

He said he had been subpoenaed by the government. Had appeared before the Federal Grand Jury and had been at the Federal Court House nearly every day for months. He was never called as a witness in this case by your Uncle Sam.

Penovich said he originally had twenty-five per cent of the Cicero place and later his "bit" was cut down to five per cent. Ralph Capone had told him he was to be chopped.

He said Ralph Capone had told him Frankie Pope was the boss of the place.

Ralph Capone is Al's older brother, and stands convicted of income tax violations along with Jack Gusick.

George Leidermann testified he was a café owner and is now a bookmaker. He said he had a book in 1924 with three other partners and that he often booked to Capone. Al would bet from $500 to $1,000 and would sometimes be betting on two or three horses to a race. Sometimes he would make as many as twenty bets a day. He figured Al lost $14,000 or $15,000 with him in 1924. In 1925 he beat Al for $10,000.

Leidermann admitted he now is running a gambling house under the direction of George "Bugs" Moran, seven of whose followers were massacred St. Valentine's Day in 1929.

Sam Rothschild, who said he was in the cigar business, with bookmaking on the side, said Capone had made perhaps ten bets with his books. These bets were all up in the thousands. He didn't recall Capone ever won.

A bald-headed chap named Samuel Gitelson testified he recorded bets for his brother, Ike, a bookmaker, and that Al had lost about $25,000 to the book.

Edward G. Robinson, the movie actor who has given movie characterizations that some believe are Al Capone to the life, was present in the court room peering at Al.

October 16, 1931

That Al Capone is the victim of a wicked plot, conceived in Washington and partly hatched in Miami, was the substance of an utterance by Michael J. Ahern, as he addressed those twelve tired good men and true in Judge Wilkerson's court this afternoon.

Ahern was making the closing address on behalf of Al, whose trial on a charge of beating your Uncle Sam out of his income tax is nearing a close, and ought to be handed over to the jury about noon tomorrow.

Ahern went clear back to the Punic wars and the time of Cato, the censor, whose cry was "Carthage must be destroyed," and said there are a lot of Catos around nowadays, especially around Washington, whose cry is "Capone must be destroyed."

Several years ago when Al first lit in Miami he was summoned before what Mr. Ahern spoke of as a "Spanish Inquisition" of officials and citizens of Miami, and interrogated closely as to his purpose there.

A stenographer took down the testimony at that time, during which Al is said to have admitted he was a gambler, and all this was introduced into the present case.

Ahern insinuated the inquiry was prompted from Washington just before an election and gave it as an idea the thing was the beginning of a plot to undo Al Capone.

Quite a gale of oratory zipped around the corridors of the old Federal Building before the day was done, what with Ahern's remarks, a lengthy outburst by his associate, Albert Fink, and a long lingual drive by Samuel G. Clawson, of your Uncle Sam's team of lawyers.

What Ahern and Fink said, when you boiled it down to a nubbin, was that your Uncle Sam hasn't proved all those things said about Al Capone in the indictments, and that he is entitled to his liberty forthwith.

What Clawson said, reduced to a mere hatful, is that Al had a lot of income and didn't pay tax on said income, and therefore ought to be put in the cooler.

Ahern, who began the closing defense argument at 2:30, said the government had attempted to prove its case by circumstantial evidence. He declared the government was seeking on meager evidence to convict the defendant because his name is Al Capone, "a sort of a mythical Robin Hood."

It was his opinion, Ahern said, that the government might better have diverted the money it has spent proving Al's profligacy to establish free soup kitchens.

October 17, 1931

Those twelve good men and true have gone into a big huddle on Al Capone.

Judge Wilkerson of the Federal Court handed the now famous case over to them with a batch of instructions, which struck the listeners as very fair to Al, at 2:41 this afternoon.

Your Uncle Sam claims Al owes him $215,000 tax on an income of over $1,000,000 derived from illegalities such as Cicero gambling, and one thing and another, in the years 1924 to 1929 inclusive, and wants to clap him in the Leavenworth Penitentiary for anywhere from one to thirty-two years.

Al's claim is that Uncle Sam didn't prove the income alleged, although of course, he entered a plea of guilty last July to the very charges for which he has just been tried, under an arrangement with representatives of your Uncle Sam by which he was to take a jolt of two years and a half in prison.

It was Judge Wilkerson's declaration on hearing of this agreement, "You can't bargain with the Federal Court," that brought on the long trial. It closed with the solemn marching out of the twelve good men and true this afternoon.

Capone was certainly all sharpened up this morning. He has been gradually returning to his old sartorial glory the last few days, and he fairly bloomed today.

He wore a grass-green pinchback suit, reminiscent of Florida. He had on heliotrope socks and tan shoes. Al has meticulously refrained from jewelry during the trial, save for a thin, diamond-studded platinum watch chain.

The judge is rather a thick-set man, of medium height, with a thick shock of iron-gray hair. He told the jury:

"You are the sole judges of the facts of the case. The jury has nothing to do with the question of punishment. That rests with the Court.

"This is a criminal case and I shall give you some general rules applicable to criminal cases. The indictment is not to be considered evidence of the guilt. The defendant is presumed to be innocent until proven guilty beyond a reasonable doubt. He is entitled to the benefit of that presumption."

Judge Wilkerson explained the meaning of a reasonable doubt. If the jurors had a reasonable doubt it was their duty to acquit the defendant. If they believed the evidence proved him guilty beyond a reasonable doubt they should return a verdict accordingly.

In order to convict on circumstantial evidence the jury must be satisfied that the circumstances alleged are true.

Wilkerson told the jury to take up each count and return an opinion on each. He said it was not necessary for the government to show the exact amount of income alleged. The Court explained at length the meaning of income under the law. He quoted the provisions of the income tax law at length.

He said the jury might consider the evidence of the way the defendant had lived and the evidence of the money transmitted to him in determining if Capone had a taxable net income. He added:

"The expenditure of money alone isn't sufficient evidence of taxable income; the possession of money alone isn't sufficient evidence of taxable income. But the expenditure and possession of money may be considered in arriving at a conclusion as to whether the income existed.

"The charges of willful attempt to evade the tax couldn't be sustained unless there were some facts to show the attempt. The jury must first be convinced that the taxable net income of $5,000 existed. The mere failure to file an income tax return doesn't of itself prove an attempt to evade the tax but such failure must be considered with its relations to other actions."

The statement of a duly authorized agent may be considered against a principal, said Judge Wilkerson, dealing with the famous Mattingly letter to the revenue collector admitting Al had had an income of $266,000 for the years charged.

If the jury found that the statement of Mattingly were within the authority of the defendant, he continued, it might be considered in determining the guilt or innocence of the defendant. If they felt Mattingly had exceeded the scope of his authorization, then they should disregard the letter, he said.

On the subject of the corpus delicti or body of the crime, the court said that might be established by the circumstantial evi-

dence. It is not incumbent on a defendant to testify in his own behalf, the judge said.

"This case will determine whether any man is above the law."

So said George E. Q. Johnson, United States attorney, in the final argument on behalf of your Uncle Sam this morning.

"Gentlemen, the United States Government has no more important laws to enforce than the revenue laws. Thousands upon
thousands of persons go to work daily and all of them who earn
more than $1,500 a year must pay income tax.

"If the time ever comes when it has to go out and force the collection of taxes, the Army and the Navy will disband, courts will
be swept aside, civilization will revert to the jungle days when every
man was for himself."

Pointing at Capone, Johnson demanded:

"Who is he, this man? Is he a mythical modern Robin Hood, as
defense counsel has described him?

"The Robin Hood of history robbed the rich to give to the poor.
Did Capone buy thousands of dollars of diamond belt buckles for
the unemployed? Did the $6,500 worth of meat go to the unem-
ployed? No, his purchases went to his mansion on Palm Island.
Did he buy $27 shirts for the men who sleep under Wacker Drive?
No, not he."

Johnson traced the early history of Capone, starting with the
time when the defendant was a bartender at Coney Island. Then
he said he was next heard of at Jim Colosimo's restaurant in Chicago. All the time, he said, the defendant was becoming more af-
fluent. Johnson went on:

"Then we come to 1924, when this gambling establishment in
Cicero was shown to have a profit of $300,000."

"Even if we take the defense statement that he had only an eight
per cent share, his profits would have been $24,000. Let me remind
you that the record shows profits of $215,000 in 1925.

"Then we come to 1926.

"Pete Penovich had a little gambling place of his own, which he
gave up because of Capone's mob. In the parlance of the gentry,
he was 'muscled' out. His successor, Mondi, was also muscled out,
and after this there was no competition in the gambling business
in Cicero."

Johnson drew attention to testimony, by Fred Ries, former associate manager of a Cicero gambling resort. Ries, he said, admitted that after taking out running expenses he bought cashier's checks for Bobby Barton. Johnson went on:

"And Bobby Barton bought money orders transmitting $77,000 to Capone in Florida. Defense counsel was strangely silent about this. Even the master mind who plans the perfect crime—and this was intended to be the perfect tax crime—slips sometimes.

"Capone went to Florida, where he had occasion to spend a lot of money on his home in Palm Island. Again the master mind who attempted the perfect crime slipped when he gave his financial secretary, Jack Gusick, checks to pay his bills."

He scoffed at the testimony of defense witnesses that Capone lost $327,000 betting on the horses. He referred to them as "so shifty they couldn't look you in the eye."

Johnson reminded the jurors the defense lawyers had talked to them for four hours, but made no reference to the money orders sent from Capone's headquarters in the Lexington Hotel in Chicago to Capone in Florida.

He declared the records showed $77,000 was sent and received between Chicago and Florida.

Johnson warned the jury to remember the men and women who pay a tax on incomes over $1,500 a year. He contrasted them with Capone, whom he flayed for evading taxes during "this time of national deficit."

MORGAN THE MIGHTY

Washington, May 23, 1933

Morgan, the mighty, is on the spot!

We wait, anxiously, for the earth to rock.

Nothing happens, except a slight tremor of excitement, as the world gets up on tiptoe to look and listen.

It turns out to be an income tax inquiry, something like Al Capone's or any of the other boys.

Morgan, the mighty, one of the richest men on the face of the globe, pays no income tax in 1931 or 1932. He does not remember about 1930.

His twenty partners in the J. Pierpont Morgan firm, many of them supposed to be very wealthy, pay an aggregated income tax of $48,000 in 1930, and none whatever in 1931 and 1932. That's all of them, understand. Losses, you know, losses, losses, losses.

Morgan, the mighty, appears as he sits at a table with some of our noted Senators in a room foggy with cigar and cigarette smoke, not the fabled giant of world financial history, not the titan who juggles nations like Bill Fields juggles cigar boxes, but a benign old gentleman somewhat harassed by questions popped at him by a person with a jutting jaw and a horribly legal mind, named Ferdinand Pecora.

A nice old gentleman who is trying to make answer to these questions with all the patience that he might exercise in telling a small child just how high is up. A kind old gentleman who seems slightly bewildered at times by the insatiate curiosity of this Pecora person, and whose memory wabbles occasionally, as the memories of old gentlemen will do.

Surely, surely, this is not the Great Morgan who has been pictured as a pirate of the financial high seas, and at whose slightest frown the biggest moguls of the money marts shake and shiver in their boots!

Why, you say, he would make a lovely Santa Claus, with his build and all, if he had white whiskers.

But it is none the less Morgan—Morgan, the Mighty—son of Morgan, the Magnificent, to whom the old gentleman refers with fond intonation in his voice several times during the day.

Master of wealth, and even human destiny. Overlord of commercial realms, and far-flung financial kingdoms—this is undeniably Morgan undergoing a prying into his affairs as a private banker that may yet produce the earthquake we have been anticipating.

This is Morgan, the mighty, being examined by a busy, keen-eyed New York lawyer, and a bunch of eagerly listening country bankers, and merchants, and small business and professional men, representatives of 120,000,000 people.

Slowly, painstakingly, and with a wealth of detail—his lawyers and his business associates banked behind him—he answers Mr. Pecora's questions, telling how his concern has deposits of over $300,000,000 and how it functions in all its personnel and capacity, until Pecora gets down to income tax questions.

Then he does not remember. He knows nothing whatever about income tax matters connected with his firm. But before the Senate committee adjourns to go into executive session, Morgan, the mighty, makes a request that his income tax expert be examined that no suspicion or wrong impression may be left from Pecora's questions and his own answers as to these matters.

So the expert appears, and there is in Pecora's questions to him, over and beyond the questions dealing with the individual returns of Morgan, the mighty, and his partners, the inference that a loss of over $21,000,000 was written into a Morgan House return by the expedient of taking in a new partner.

At times during Morgan's examination you rather feel sorry for him. It is warm. He perspires. He mops his face frequently with a large handkerchief. Toward late afternoon he looks tired. You say to yourself, "That jutty-jawed fellow oughta let this old gentleman be. He's got him plumb worn out."

Possibly Senator Carter Glass, of Virginia, has this humane feeling. He endeavors to spare Morgan some of the Pecoran insistence in asking again and again about income tax matters. It is amazing how curious Pecora is about income tax, but Morgan can give him no help. He says, "I don't know."

Senator Glass says he himself does not know much about his income tax matters, leaving them to experts, and he sees no use in hectoring Morgan.

This develops into a slight spat between Senator Glass and Senator Couzens, of Michigan, who says he resents some one witness being treated any differently from another in the august presence of the committee that is digging into the banking affairs of the community.

Pecora handles Morgan about the same as he would handle a witness in the case of the *People of the State of New York versus Robert Roe*.

He seems cold, implacable. Even when Morgan smiles at him with great geniality Pecora does not smile back, though one good smile always deserves another.

The session ends with the feeling among those who listen that Pecora is trying to clean all the windows in the great House of Morgan so he can get a good peek inside.

When the investigation began this morning we were in a big high-ceilinged room on the third floor of the great white Senate Office Building, where the noble Senators have their offices. The ceiling of the room is tinted a nice baby-blue. There are models of sailing ships on the shelves just under the ceiling at either end of the room.

The walls are of white marble. Three great glass chandeliers that must have cost a pretty penny hang from the ceiling. This is the official hearing room of the Senate Banking and Currency Committee.

The long corridor leading to the doors of the committee room is crowded with men and women unable to gain admittance but waiting there for a peek at the great Morgan. They struggle at the doors, arguing with the door tenders. They are struggling long after the hearing starts. They struggle so audibly that members of the committee complain they cannot hear a word. Streetcars grinding along in the street outside the open windows add to the din.

In a front row sits young Junius Morgan, a fine-looking chap, with all the striking Morgan characteristics in his features. Beside him sits Martin Egan, publicity man of the Morgan forces, and once a famous war correspondent.

Now here comes J. Pierpont Morgan himself through a rear door. He is preceded by his attorney, John W. Davis, Democratic candidate for the Presidency in 1924, a gray, immaculate-looking man. There is great confusion as Morgan advances through the crowd of spectators. It is said he arrived in Washington with a stout bodyguard. This is not in evidence today.

He is a powerful-looking man, easily six feet tall, with much meat on his huge frame. He weighs well over 200 pounds. He is sixty-six years old, but looks older. His face is ruddy, his features heavy. He has a big, predatory-looking nose.

He is dressed in a dark blue suit with a faint pin stripe. His shirt is starched white linen.

His tie is black with white fingers. A huge Oriental pearl adorns the tie. He wears a heavy, old-fashioned watch chain of gold across his vest, the middle hooked in a buttonhole by a crossbar. A green-stone crest ring is on the little finger of his left hand. A pair of eye-glasses dangle by a cord alongside his watch chain.

He is a well-kept, well-groomed-looking man. His head is bald and shiny. He has a huge, bristly moustache now quite white. His eyebrows are black and bushy. He looks like a most benign old gentleman as he enters the court room, carrying a battered Panama hat in one hand, and smiling gently on all the world, but later on you see the lightning behind the brows, and sense the thunder in the voice.

He is surrounded by his partners and aides as he enters. There is Thomas W. Lamont, George Whitney, and other members of the Morgan firm, very rich men, all. Mr. Morgan takes a chair at one end of the room, and the photographers surround him with a temerity they have never before displayed. He poses for them with astounding amiability, his huge hands resting on his knees. He even conjures up a placid beam for the camera men.

Not in the memory of man has a Morgan submitted so tamely to a public photographing. Mr. Morgan gazed about with apparent interest. Indeed, he seemed to be getting something of a kick out of the proceedings, now that he was well into this untoward experience. He posed over and over again for the photographers until somebody in authority came along and said, "That'll do, boys."

He chatted easily with those around him. Then he was asked to take a seat at the committee table, right in the center on one side with Costigan of Colorado to his left and Bulkley of Ohio to his right. He says something to Bulkley as he sits down, and smiles broadly.

Now Pecora enters, swarthy, brisk, and smiling, with a pack of nimble young assistants at his back. Two boys enter lugging a big black trunk between them. This is some of Pecora's evidence. It certainly looks ominous. Pecora wears a suit of "pepper-and-salt" design, and white linen. He has curly iron-gray hair and a jutting jaw and is very clean-looking and business like.

Senator Fletcher, of Florida, in a morning coat with black braid, an elderly man of slow movement and speech, opens the proceedings by calling the committee to order. A number of Senators who are members of the State Banking and Currency Committee but not members of the subcommittee come in and take chairs at the table, including the tall, stately-looking McAdoo of California, his lean neck surrounded by his characteristic white linen collar that would choke the average man. Senator Fletcher asks of Pecora, "Who is your first witness?"

Mr. Pecora, without rising from his chair, replies briefly, "J. P. Morgan."

And the examination is under way.

Pecora does not rise from his chair as he interrogates Morgan. His voice is very calm as he goes through a long preamble of questioning which is designed to establish who Mr. Morgan is. As if everybody didn't know.

Well, it seems that he is senior partner of the firm of J. P. Morgan and Co., of Wall Street, with twenty partners in the New York concern, and that they do a private banking business up in so many millions it makes your head swim to think of them. The Morgan deposits alone are $340,000,000.

As Morgan concludes he leans back in his chair and looks placidly at the committee as much as to say, "There, now boys, I have cleared everything up for you."

Pecora does not look at Morgan while questioning him, but Morgan looks at Pecora in answering and frequently smiles. Perhaps he feels it might be well to conciliate this gentleman until he finds out what is up his sleeve.

When he finally learns this, Morgan ceases to smile. The angry blood comes into his face. The veins in his neck thicken. He is biting his back teeth together so hard the muscles of his neck twitch.

When Pecora finally gets down to the matter nearest and dearest his investigatorial heart, the income tax, Morgan seems to get very nervous. He hauls a white handkerchief out of his breast pocket and mops his face.

An income tax return covering the two days, January 1 and January 2, 1930, inclusive, which return is separate unto itself, is the subject of much inquiry by Pecora. Says Morgan uneasily, "I don't know anything about income tax returns."

Pecora asks, "Do you know that deductions for losses of $21,071,862 are claimed in the returns for those two days?"

Morgan replies, "I don't know."

Then Morgan says he thinks that in view of the fact that the various income tax matters Pecora asked about had been left unexplained and might be wrongly construed, he thinks Mr. Leonard Keyes, his general manager and income tax expert, ought to be heard.

Keyes says he prepares all the returns for J. P. Morgan & Co. and all the individual partners, and in 1930 the aggregate amount paid by the twenty partners was $48,000. In 1931 it was nothing, and ditto 1932.

He says the two returns for 1930 were due to a change in the Morgan partners. S. Parker Gilbert was admitted January 2, 1931, and although no business was transacted on January 1, a holiday, the return showed profits of nearly $2,225,000 for only one day, in brokers' commissions and the like. But it was this two-day return that shows a loss of over $21,000,000.

May 24, 1933

There sit the great J. Pierpont Morgan, proud overlord of the financial world, and his faithful henchmen, all damp with perspiration—the great Morgan who admits he pays Great Britain income taxes in the same years he pays nothing to his own United States.

And there the swarthy Ferdinand Pecora, son of Italian immigrant parents, patiently beats his way through a weird jungle of high finance until the twisting trails around him are alive with all manner of strange things in the form of disclosures that will astound this nation.

Somewhere, close at hand, the dark-browed Pecora believes, lies the lair of the most powerful influences on the public and commercial life of the United States that have existed in all its history, but as he presses on you will read (and perhaps weep), as he shows today how scores of distinguished citizens were "preferred clients" of the House of Morgan.

How they were "given the opportunity" of buying at $20 per share a stock that was sold on the market at all the way from $34 to $50. They were given this "opportunity" before the stock was handed out to the public. They were "on the inside," so to speak, perhaps because in each case it was the same as with William Woodin, to whom a member of the firm of J. P. Morgan & Co. wrote coyly:

"We just want you to know that we are thinking of you."

You will read how Norman H. Davis got a loan, amount unknown, but still unpaid, from the House of Morgan.

You will read, also, how the House of Morgan distributed its deposits of millions over a wide area of banks and trust companies in New York, Boston, Pittsburgh, Philadelphia and Chicago, so that its influence was necessarily woven into the very fabric of the banking system of the country.

Morgan himself sits nearly all day in the witness chair, with a big fat book of typewritten pages in his pudgy hands. It contains records of his firm. When he is asked a question by Pecora he thumbs the pages somewhat helplessly, as if saying to himself, "Now what in Sam Hill is all this I've got here, anyway?"

Then he generally turns and gets a line on the matter in question from those behind him, usually George Whitney. The great Morgan frankly admits he does not know a whole lot about the details of his business, just as he is in the dark on his income tax matters—except those relating to Great Britain.

Only once in the long history of the House of Morgan has there ever been a public statement of its policy and procedures, he says, in the course of his examination. This was made by "father." Morgan never says "my father." Just "father." You can see that this old gentleman, who somehow doesn't look so benign as he did yesterday in the light of the day's revelations, adores the memory of his distinguished sire.

"You refer to the time some twenty years ago when he testified at a public inquiry?" asks Pecora.

"The only time," replies Morgan softly.

He perhaps wishes it still remains the only time there have been disclosures bearing upon the Morgan firm.

It is George Whitney, one of the younger Morgan partners, who is finally pushed forward to bear the brunt of the more startling revelations of the day, when Morgan says he thinks Whitney will know more about the matter of the financing of the Alleghany Corporation by the Morgan company than anyone else.

It is this corporation in which the eminent gentlemen, including Colonel Charles A. Lindbergh, were the favored of the Morgans in the matter of buying stock.

Whitney is said to be called "Icicle" Whitney in Wall Street, because of his cold, dispassionate demeanor, though Pecora has the ice thawing and running all over the premises when he finally gets to examining Whitney about his income tax return, which shows that he netted a nice profit himself on Alleghany.

Whitney is in his early forties, tall, slim, good-looking, pince-nezed, well-groomed and faintly supercilious in his attitude toward Pecora. By the way, Pecora is Italian for "lamb," I am told. This is no lamb, however, this round-headed scion of sunny It'. This is a lion of the law.

He has a curious way of sitting silent in his chair when the members of the committee start asking questions and engaging in windy debates. Pecora lets them exhaust themselves, then goes on quietly with his witness, as if never interrupted.

He asks seemingly irrelevant questions for a time, then, suddenly bang! Out pops a shot that makes you realize he has been aiming at this target all along.

Whitney gets into the proceedings in the morning and becomes spokesman for the Morgan clan when it is expected that next to Morgan himself this role will be filled by Thomas W. Lamont, one of the older members of the crowd, who is present. Whitney rises voluntarily at the morning session to explain something a member of the committee wishes to know, while Morgan is still on the stand, and then he remains standing half an hour while Pecora questions him.

Whitney seems slightly contemptuous in tone as he answers Pecora when he is asked at the morning session if it is not a fact that after paying $11,000,000 in income taxes in 1929 the combined Morgan partners paid an aggregate of only $48,000 the following year, and nothing whatever the next three years.

"So I heard here yesterday," said Whitney.

Pecora thereupon becomes a trifle sharper with the witness than he has been with any other, especially in the afternoon, when Whitney will not positively identify a photostatic copy of his income tax return, saying he prefers to inspect his own record.

"The trouble with these chaps is they have the Bourbon mind," comments Pecora on Whitney's reluctance afterward. "They cannot see that their attitude of wanting to conceal everything serves no purpose."

While Whitney is reluctantly narrating the details of the Alleghany deals and identifying lists bearing the names of our foremost citizens, Morgan sits just behind him, listening intently. It would be interesting to know the thoughts of the old financier at this time when a great democracy has him in hand and is divesting him of so many sacred secrets.

But for all we know, perhaps Morgan privately relishes the pillorying of some of the lads on the list, especially those who still owe him.

May 25, 1933

Mr. Morgan laughs until his stout sides shake today, a jovial old King of Koin, as he listens to disclosures concerning the dealings with his own firm of very, very big shots in the political world—Republican and Democratic.

His demeanor confirms a suspicion that Mr. Morgan now keenly enjoys the predicament in which these recipients of his favors find themselves. Or some of them, at any rate.

He has had his own moments of perspiration before the Senate subcommittee that is investigating his affairs, so perhaps he says to himself, "Well, let the rest of them sweat with me."

Or perhaps some of the boys didn't do right by Mr. Morgan somewhere along the line. Perhaps all of those favors apparently so freely bestowed by Mr. Morgan did not come from his heart.

In any event, Mr. Morgan laughs. And laughs.

Once he just barely suppressed a haw-haw that, if proportionate to Mr. Morgan's size, must shake the Corinthian pillars in the huge caucus room of the Senate Office Building to which the hearing is shifted today. The effort leaves him red-faced and almost apoplectic.

He sputters trying to choke down another outburst. Mr. Morgan probably hasn't so thoroughly enjoyed himself since the last time he took a swing at a photographer's camera, and connected.

A photostatic copy of a letter from John J. Raskob, then chairman of the Democratic National Committee, acknowledging a stock-purchasing courtesy from the House of Morgan (2,000 shares of Alleghany Corporation) is produced and it has one line that seems to give Mr. Morgan a terrific "belt," as the boys say.

Especially as it is declaimed in the ringing tones of Mr. Ferdinand Pecora, who is conducting the investigation for the Senate committee. Mr. Pecora seems to like the line himself.

It runs like this:

"I sincerely hope the future holds an opportunity for me to reciprocate."

He laughs again when Mr. Pecora asks questions as to the identity of Mr. Joseph Nutt, of Cleveland, another gentleman invited to partake of the crumbs from the rich man's board, and is still laughing when it is disclosed that Mr. Nutt is treasurer of the Republican National Committee.

Finally everybody commences laughing with Mr. Morgan. Perhaps it is his idea to leave 'em laughing when he says good-bye, anyway.

Besides the names of Mr. Raskob and Mr. Nutt, we hear from the same list of favored subscribers to Alleghany stock, the names of Mr. Cornelius Bliss, former treasurer of the Republican campaign committee, and Charles D. Hilles, New York Republican leader.

Well, it appears that the only party that has a right to kick about Mr. Morgan's beneficence is the Socialist.

On another list of persons let in on the ground floor, so to speak, in the matter of purchasing Standard Brands, another House of Morgan project, is the name of the late Calvin Coolidge.

Mr. Coolidge was given the opportunity of buying 3,000 shares in July 1929. He left the Presidency in March of the same year.

The name of United States Senator William Gibbs McAdoo also appears on this list. Senator McAdoo reads a statement to the committee immediately upon convening this morning in which he sets forth that his dealings with the House of Morgan were ten years after his resignation as Secretary of the Treasury, and four years before he became Senator, and that they wound up with a net loss of some $3,000 to him.

Mr. Morgan, who appears vestless today in tribute to the local weather, begins laughing almost at the same moment that Mr. McAdoo relates his loss.

John J. Raskob is also on this Standard Brands list. Likewise William H. Woodin, Secretary of the Treasury, Bernard Baruch, Norman H. Davis, our celebrated ambassador-at-large; Charles A. Lindbergh, General John J. Pershing, R. B. Mellon, brother of the former Secretary of the Treasury, and others.

The Lindbergh account is explained by Mr. Whitney with the statement that the House of Morgan generally advises the Colonel about his investments. In answer to a question from Mr. Pecora, Mr. Whitney says he thinks Calvin Coolidge's name must have been suggested by Thomas Cochran, a Morgan partner, though he isn't sure.

These persons, it appears, were all invited by the House of Morgan to buy the stock. Mrs. S. Parker Gilbert, wife of the former agent-general of reparations, is mentioned as an invitee.

Before the session goes into recess over the luncheon hour, Mr. Morgan asks permission to make a statement. He takes the witness chair, and unfurls a crumpled bit of paper that he has evidently had wadded up in his big fist for some time.

He reads this statement aloud. It is about the income tax he paid to England in the years that he did not pay income tax to his Uncle Sammy.

He gazes at Mr. Pecora to see if that gentleman wishes to ask him any questions, and Mr. Pecora shakes his head. Says Mr. Morgan, gratefully, with an extra wide beam, "Thank you, Mr. Attorney, I am very much obliged."

Says Mr. Pecora, "Er-ah, wait a minute, please. If the English system were in vogue here you would be required to pay much more income tax to this country than you do to England?"

Says Mr. Morgan, agreeably, "Oh, yes, but not nearly so much as I paid in 1928 and 1929."

Some of the Senators gather about his bulky figure as the session recesses. Mr. Morgan chats with them a moment and then exits laughingly.

Mr. Will Rogers, the cowpuncher-humorist, another of the world's rich men, arrives for the session to see if Mr. Morgan needs any assistance. The only difference between Mr. Rogers and Mr. Morgan financially is perhaps $8.35. Complains Mr. Rogers, "They are always annoying us rich guys."

The examination of Mr. George Whitney takes up most of the morning. Mr. Morgan sits behind him, one hand on Mr. Whitney's chair. Mr. Whitney reads a long, printed statement.

Mr. Pecora inquires, "Who prepared this statement?"

"Why—"

Demands Mr. Pecora when he finds the preparation is a matter of some doubt, "Well, whose phraseology is it?"

At this point Mr. Will Rogers, who has listened intently to the reading, leans over to this correspondent. He whispers, "I think it's Bugs Baer's."

Nothing is going to happen to Mr. Morgan. Indeed local bookmakers are commencing to offer plenty of two to one that Mr. Morgan winds up out-laughing the subcommittee, despite the efforts of some to laugh with him.

You must not think that because he pays no income taxes to this country that Mr. Morgan has no income at all. I mean you must not start shedding any tears of sympathy for him on that score. He manages to scrape enough together every year to carry on the yacht *Corsair* and the house at Glen Cove, and the one in Lunnon.

And anyway, perhaps Mr. Morgan fears that if he came forward voluntarily and offered to contribute to the support of Uncle Sam, when he doesn't have to, it might increase the mortality rate in this country through heart disease.

But I must suggest it to Mr. Morgan.

It will give him something to keep on laughing about.

May 26, 1933

Blazing mad is Mr. Ferdinand Pecora!

You can hang your hat on his jutting chin as he sticks it out far beyond normal today, and lets fly a verbal blast at a group of United States Senators that almost knocks them out of their chairs.

Irked by petty criticism of his methods in showing how the great House of Morgan manipulates, and perhaps by a disposition that became very evident today on the part of some of the Senators to lend a kindly cloak of secrecy to old Mr. Morgan's business, Mr. Ferdinand Pecora cuts loose with fiery tongue.

And as he concludes a roar of applause sweeps the huge caucus room of the Senate Office Building, in which the examination of the Morgan goings on is being held, and smothers an intended answer to the infuriated Mr. Pecora from his chief heckler, the aged Senator Carter Glass, of Virginia.

The applause, rising with amazing suddenness and continuing some time, spatters over old Mr. Morgan himself, in person, and in the flesh, as he sits among his personal entourage smoking a huge cigar.

It startles the Senators. Some of those who have been only lukewarm in their enthusiasm toward Mr. Pecora's efforts to spade up all the financial skeletons in the House of Morgan that he can locate, begin running to the cover of declarations of confidence in Mr. Pecora.

He has just let them know, in effect, that he does not care a tinker's cuss about them, and the resultant applause gives the Senators a faint sniff of the public attitude toward this investigation. The Senators know that a mere roomful of applause may possibly be elaborated into fearful thunder as it goes out over the land.

The moral of all this is: never get an Italian mad.

Mr. Pecora arrives for the session looking quite moody. He has been in attendance on an executive session of the committee which decides that it isn't going to permit Mr. Pecora to make public certain matters that he considers positively vital to this investigation into the House of Morgan.

It is plain that he is seething inwardly as he takes his seat and calls for his first witness, Mr. George H. Howard, a New York lawyer, who is president of the United Corporation and the New York United Corporation.

These are light and power concerns. Mr. Pecora's intention is to show that the House of Morgan made colossal sums through stock operations in United. He is proceeding slowly with Mr. Howard, a somewhat hesitant witness, when old Senator Glass, who has been something of an obstructionist throughout the inquiry, starts growling.

He wants to know where the inquiry is leading. He wants to know why Mr. Pecora is asking all these questions. He asks the witness himself if the United Corporation has ever violated any Federal statute in its business dealing; Mr. Howard very promptly says no.

Mr. Pecora, his face pale, his teeth gritted, sits silent while the old Virginian talks. He has often had to endure Senator Glass' interruptions and objections. The Senator is given to little witticisms and irrelevancies that sound strange in an inquiry of this nature.

Senator Kean, of New Jersey, a placid-looking man with a large gray moustache, asks Mr. Howard if it isn't customary for railroads and other corporations to do thus and so with their stocks and securities. You may hear of Senator Kean again before the inquiry is over. Other Senators gabble somewhat aimlessly. Says Mr. Pecora, suddenly, "All right! I'll tell you what it's all about!"

He picks up and reads the Senate resolution directing this inquiry, the terms of which are so sweeping that they give the Senate committee power to do just about anything it desires, and adds that he is proceeding under this resolution.

Now Senator Couzens, of Michigan, a ruddy, strong-featured citizen who has been the bulwark of the Pecoran efforts throughout, rises to his feet and says, "I ask the chair to rule whether the examination is proceeding under the terms of that resolution?"

Old Senator Fletcher, of Florida, another staunch supporter of Mr. Pecora and the inquiry, says it does. Senator Couzens says, "I now ask if that is a complete answer to the gentleman from Virginia?"

Senator Glass starts roaring. He says he does not consider it a complete answer.

He says no one informed the subcommittee as to what Mr. Pecora expected to bring out. He even goes so far as to say that he does not recall seeing anything in the minutes of the subcommittee authorizing Mr. Pecora to conduct the examination.

At this, Mr. Pecora flares out, "I did not solicit this assignment; it was offered to me; I accepted, and I have done the best I can do to fulfill it. I have worked day and night at it. But it would be impossible for me, in New York, to call up the committee every time I thought I had a lead and ask instructions how to proceed. If the committee thinks it is any pleasure to do all this work, it is mistaken, and if it thinks that the compensation of $255 per month that I receive is any incentive, it is also badly mistaken."

There is in his tone and manner the inference that if they do not like what he is doing he will withdraw, although later on Mr. Pecora takes pains to deny for the record a statement appearing in print that he would resign unless the committee does as he desires about admitting certain evidence.

Senator Glass starts to reply but you cannot hear him for the applause. It is difficult to hear Senator Glass at any time, as he throws his words out of one corner of his mouth. The Senators try to ignore the applause. When it dies away, Mr. Pecora then states the purpose of his examination of Mr. Howard. Senator Glass wants to know why all this wasn't brought forward before, and he insists he is still not satisfied with the method of procedure.

He also complains about the publicity some of the executive sessions have received, and says he doesn't care about the House of Morgan, or any other house but that he is not going to see any injustice done it. Then Senator Glass closes with a self-eulogy to the effect that he is the only man who has done anything about the banking laws, anyway.

Mr. Morgan appears today in a gray suit with a single-breasted three-button coat. The old boy has an excellent tailor. His clothes fit him well despite a large "bay window." His linen is purest white, and starched. His shoes are low tans.

As he sits down the photographers close in around him and Mr. Morgan submits to his daily ordeal with a grace that continues to amaze the boys.

"Smile now," one of them orders, and the great financier beams.

"That's great!" he remarks as the camera men let fly with a raft of flash bulbs. "Shoot a lot of them. I own stock in the General Electric."

Young Junius Morgan is asked by one of the photographers to pose with his father and he immediately takes a chair alongside his distinguished sire and they smile together.

Young Junius is tall, good-looking, neatly groomed. He has black hair, slightly gray.

Young Junius displays great curiosity about the flash bulbs and a photographer explains them to him in detail, with the elder Morgan also listening intently.

The old gentleman even goes so far as to chat pleasantly with a newspaperman. Let this newspaperman try to get in at 23 Wall next week and see what happens to him.

The observers are somewhat surprised to see that these very rich people are rather human after all. If the inquiry continues much longer it will wind up with everybody being just like this with the Morgan crowd.

Senator Fletcher lauds Mr. Pecora at length, and says that the attorney often consulted with him as chairman of the subcommittee, and that he is proud of Mr. Pecora, and that he deems him thorough and efficient. Senator Barkley, of Kentucky, also put in a boost for the now somewhat surprised Pecora, and added it is too bad he isn't getting more money. Indeed, the session winds up as a general plug for Mr. Pecora, though he remains somewhat moody-looking when the committee recesses until next Wednesday.

May 26, 1933

I presume you really might call the inquiry into the petty affairs of Mr. J. Pierpont Morgan, "The Revenge of the Photo Grabbers."

For years, it has been Mr. M.'s favorite pastime to play ring-around-a-rosy with the Photo Grabbers, most faithful, and conscientious, and hardest working of all the newspaper tribes. Why, I once knew a Photo Grabber—but never mind.

In playing with Mr. M. the Photo Grabbers were always "It." He loved to chase them, and tag them. If he could get a camera away from one of the Photo Grabbers and tag his man with the lens box, the game was a big success for Mr. M. Of all our public characters, only Mr. Gene Tunney came close to Mr. M. as an adept chaser of Photo Grabbers.

And of course, at best, Mr. Tunney was only an amateur. He never had Mr. M.'s wind, or depth. Especially depth. This is evidenced by the fact that Mr. Tunney has abandoned the pastime altogether. He is a retired Photo Grabber chaser.

Now, for the first time in his long career, at the game, Mr. M. is "It."

When he enters the august presence of the Senate committee which is delving (as we say) into his goings-on, the Photo Grabbers swarm all over him and take his picture with impunity, and also with all kinds of cameras.

The first day of the inquiry, when Mr. M. looked up and found himself surrounded by lenses, he seemed somewhat startled, and I thought he was going to pick a few of the boys up and start throwing 'em about. But I suppose he reflected on the danger of hitting a United States Senator with a Photo Grabber, which would be high treason beyond a doubt, and so dismissed the idea.

Instead, he gathered a great big broad smile together, and spread it over his countenance, and beamed at the Photo Grabbers with such cordiality that several of them seized their mills and retreated some distance.

They felt that a smile on Mr. M.'s face, especially in the presence of Photo Grabbers, augured no good to them. But I am inclined to give Mr. M. the benefit of the doubt and suggest that he smiled merely because he wished to look beautiful in the pictures.

Day in and day out, since then, the Photo Grabbers have been blasting away at Mr. M.'s rugged features, and never once has he rebuffed them. Flashlights, stills, movies—they were all one to him.

Occasionally one of his aides tried to shoo the Photo Grabbers away, but Mr. M. never requested it. He even went so far as to chat with Photo Grabbers while they were taking his picture, although I am bound to say that some of the Photo Grabbers considered this an unwarranted liberty on Mr. M.'s part.

He was docile, tranquil, and wholly peaceable. So much so, in fact, that one of the Photo Grabbers privately confided to me that he thinks the old boy is going back. He didn't say back where. Not back to the Senate committee's room after this inquiry, if he can help it, you can bet on that.

Today there were only a few Photo Grabbers present in the inquiry room. Satiated with pictures of Mr. M., most of the boys had gone on to fresher subjects. They've got enough pictures of him now to last them for years to come.

I thought Mr. M. glanced around with real regret for the missing ones. He had on a new pair of tan shoes, too. I fear that Mr. M. has succumbed at last to an old complaint among our public characters. It is known as Camera-itis.

That's the trouble with the Photo Grabbers centering their attention on one character for several days at a stretch. It makes the subject utterly lens-conscious. Thus when the Photo Grabbers suddenly let him alone, he develops a yennion for them. I mean he wants to see them around.

I suppose the next time Mr. M. comes back from a trip abroad and looks around and sees no Photo Grabbers waiting for him on the dock, he will be right peeved about it. Still, he will be peeved if they are there, so it's all even.

May 31, 1933

It is getting so you are practically nobody unless you are on the kind Mr. Morgan's preferred list.

Only don't call it "preferred" list. The House of Morgan does not care for the term.

"It gags," says Mr. George Whitney, "the icicle," handsome, debonair—a movie director's idea in the flesh of a big Wall Streeter, which Mr. Whitney certainly is.

Mr. Whitney means that the term "preferred list" gags him and, doubtless, his associates in the House of Morgan. Nobody bothers to tell Mr. Whitney how the "preferred list" itself is gagging a large number of American citizens.

And yet it is conceivable that in the years to come, when some scion of an old American family is claiming proud heritage, and is asked, "Did your folks come over on the *Mayflower*?" they will haughtily reply, "No, but you will find our name on Mr. J. Pierpont Morgan's list."

Let us see, now, how the "list" that may determine future blue-bloodedness in America shapes up at this time. We have so far:

Four or five candidates for President of the United States of America.

A Justice of the Supreme Court of the United States.

A Secretary of the Treasury of the United States of America.

Two Senators of the United States of America.

An Ambassador-at-large of the United States of America.

One parcel of small-time judges.

One job lot consisting of a chairman and treasurers of political parties.

One large batch of millionaires.

Another large batch of ex-millionaires.

One lot of bush-league political bosses, bank directors, business men and lawyers.

One large barrel of parties not yet sorted and identified.

Even one of our celebrated war correspondents and radio broadcasters almost gets on the list this morning.

Senator Reynolds, of North Carolina, perusing a string of names longer than a hack driver's dream, finds the monicker "F. Gibbons" staring him in the face, and inquires, "Does this mean Floyd Gibbons?"

Nineteen necks along the press bench crack audibly as the boys lean forward, breathless, and I may say, somewhat envious, to catch the reply.

Mr. Whitney looks blank, then confers with some of his assistants behind him before he answers, "I think it's one of our clerks."

The press bench falls back indignant. The list remains palpably discriminatory against newspapermen.

Old Senator Carter Glass, of Virginia, whose waspish buzzing about the ears of Mr. Pecora, and whose declamation that he will not stand by and see any injustice done the House of Morgan, featured the inquiry last week, waves a large portfolio of telegrams and letters at the committee today.

He says some of these are missives calling him a no-gooder in various terms, and threatening his life, while others are big boosts for him as an American patriot, and a Southern gentleman, suh.

Senator Glass' threat to read these contributions strikes terror to every heart, for much of the morning session has already been given over to senatorial digressions, with Mr. Pecora sitting idly by unable to ask a question for half an hour, hand running, but it comes out that Senator Glass does not mean at once.

He puts in much of the noon recess being photographed alongside his portfolio of knocks and boosts, and his gray felt hat sitting jack-deuce on his head, as the faro bank players would say. Presently along comes Mr. Pecora, and the two pose together with big smiles on their faces, though the spectators are offering eight to five that neither means a single wrinkle of their smiles.

Mr. Pecora keeps burrowing into the transactions of the House of Morgan, throwing behind him as he delves, plenty of financial dirt. He begins with Mr. George H. Howard, president of the United Corporation as a witness, but presently Mr. Whitney steps up voluntarily to answer some questions that Mr. Howard seems dubious about, and Mr. Pecora always welcomes Mr. Whitney.

Mr. Pecora realizes that Mr. Whitney is one man who knows more about the House of Morgan than all the rest put together, so every time Mr. Whitney bobs up, Mr. Pecora says, "Why, sit right down, Mr. Whitney."

Then Mr. Whitney sits down and they keep him sitting. However, it must be said for Mr. Whitney that he doesn't just sit. He also thinks; Mr. Whitney is no dumbbell. He is extremely intelligent, suave, and sure of his ground.

Not far behind him sits old Mr. Morgan, gazing at the witness in admiration and probably wondering how Mr. Whitney can remember so many details of the Morgan business when Mr. Morgan himself can remember so few.

June 1, 1933

Our little inquisition into the doings of Mr. J. Pierpont Morgan opens today with sideshow features.

A female midget about knee high to a grasshopper, from the Ringling Circus now playing in Washington, is brought into the Senate caucus room and Mr. Morgan obligingly holds the wee lady on his knee while the photographers get busy and the spectators giggle.

It looks like a ventriloquist act.

I mean you half expect to hear the small figure on Mr. J. Pierpont Morgan's knee, pipe, "Now, Uncle John, tell me the story of the Bad Old Bear."

And Mr. Morgan to reply, "I don't know any story about a bear, Melissy, but I'll tell you one about the Great Big Bull."

Mr. Morgan seems to enjoy the experience for a spell, and handles the midget as gently as if she were a costly doll. Indeed, the midget isn't much bigger than a doll such as Santa Claus might bring any good little gal at Noel. And by the way, Santa Claus also gets into the inquiry today when Senator Bob Reynolds, of No'th Ca'lina, finally hits upon a name for those famous lists heretofore designated, to the distress of the House of Morgan, as "preferred."

Senator Bob speaks of them as "Santa Claus lists."

It seems a happy compromise.

It is just as well Senator Carter Glass is not present to see the performance with the midget. It might tend to confirm the aged Virginian's contention that the investigation is mainly a circus.

In fact, it is only just the other day while supplying some of the clowning that the Senator is remarking that all we need to make the thing complete is peanuts and red lemonade. Of course, he didn't think of midgets.

But the philosopher may see something else in this picture of Mr. Morgan, sitting there with a benign expression on his face, and a midget on his knee. The philosopher may see the midget as occupying toward Mr. Morgan the same relative position now occupied by the proletariat of these United States of America.

That is to say, we are all more or less on Mr. Morgan's financial knee.

There is this difference between us and the midget, however: Mr. Morgan occasionally bends us over his financial knee, south side uppermost.

While the midget is roosting on Mr. Morgan's knee, a scout reports the sinister figure of Mr. Dexter Fellowes, the Ringling press-agent, lurking in the corridors. He is afraid to enter in person and sends the midget in with a proxy.

The proxy finally overdoes himself and shifts the midget to Mr. Morgan's other knee, and crushes into the picture himself, at which Mr. Morgan looks irked, and mutters, as if to say, "Just for that you've all got to get off."

But he puts the midget down on the floor tenderly enough, and turns to beam at his immediate following, the members of which are utterly aghast at the proceeding. No one can think up out of his experience in Wall Street a precedent for a great financier posing with a midget on his knee.

The members of the Senate committee are not in the room when this incident takes place. They hear of it later and are greatly annoyed, possibly because there are no midgets left to pose on their knees. The sergeants-at-arms are instructed to guard against similar invasions of Mr. Morgan's privacy. Some of the committee fear that Mr. Fellowes may return with an elephant and try to put him on Mr. Morgan's knee.

The photographers are barred from the caucus room, after enjoying a long field day, although they are scarcely to blame for littering up the place with midgets.

Senator Fletcher, of Florida, chairman of the committee, denounces the incident with some vociferousness, as he calls the session to order and asks the newspapers not to print the pictures.

The crowd applauds Senator Fletcher's statement that he considers the midgeting of Mr. Morgan an outrage. The first thing we know, we will all commence to feel sorry for poor Mr. Morgan, and forget the bewildering financial sleight-of-hand that Mr. Ferdinand Pecora is exposing in the manner of the tobacco ads.

Mr. Morgan does not appear to take the business of the midget seriously. Perhaps he thinks he may have brought the midget in himself in one of his pockets by accident.

A man never knows when he may find a midget on his person.

Anyway, as soon as we are relieved of the sinister presence of Mr. Leif and his midget we feel greatly relieved and the inquiry proceeds.

The opening of the morning session is long delayed. This because of the rule adopted by the skittish members of the committee that Mr. Ferdinand Pecora must reveal to them in advance what he expects to bring out during the inquiry. It is old Senator Glass' idea, but some of the others fell in with surprising alacrity.

The senatorial committee has the inquiry slowed down to a walk and seems to love the pace. At the beginning Mr. Pecora was going through the mass of evidence like water through a tin horn. He was bringing out the high spots one after the other with bewildering rapidity.

Now the members of the senatorial committee spend much time mumbling. The mumbles leave Mr. Pecora sitting silent at the head of a long table at which the Senators are assembled. He gets in a question just now and then. But Mr. Pecora remains sweetly patient with the gentlemen. After all, it is their inquiry and Mr. Pecora is getting the terrific sum of $255 per month for sitting around.

Mr. George Whitney is again on the stand most of the day. Mr. Whitney is our only sex appeal in this inquiry. The ladies enjoy gazing at Mr. Whitney. In fact we hear that if it wasn't for Mr. Whitney, the female attendance at the inquiry would fall to low ebb. As it is, the ladies continue to occupy the best seats.

Mr. Whitney today wears a dark blue sack suit with a starched white linen collar against a colored shirt. A crest ring and a wrist watch are his only jewelry. His iron-gray hair is combed to a gloss. His nose glasses are delicately balanced on his patrician beezer.

Toward the close of the morning session Mr. Whitney seems to grow somewhat Wall Streetish toward Mr. Pecora who is cheerfully trying to show how the House of Morgan lends millions of dollars without collateral and far beyond the limits permitted a public bank.

Mr. Whitney refers to a matter of $30,000,000 as "a relatively small amount." I am inclined to think that it is this supercilious, not to say blasé attitude toward money on Mr. Whitney's part that impresses the ladies. They can see what a handy thing around the house a man must be who considers $30,000,000 "a relatively small amount."

Mr. Morgan seems to start slightly, as Mr. Whitney speaks of the thirty million in this offhand way and to gaze keenly at Mr. Whitney. You know Mr. Morgan got his start by carefully saving all his thirty millions, and perhaps it alarms him to hear a young man speak so casually of them.

The inquiry drags on toward six o'clock reminding many of the spectators that it is supper-time in Washington. Dinner time to you swells, perhaps, but supper-time in Washington. The folks began going home. All Senators except Senator Fletcher, the chairman, and Alva Adams, of Colorado, had departed.

Senator Adams is a banker in Pueblo, Colorado. He is sticking to the inquiry in the hope that he may learn some new ideas for Pueblo. I doubt if Senator Adams will ever persuade the Puebloans to Mr. Whitney's idea that $30,000,000 is a "relatively small amount" of money.

If the attendance keeps falling off we may have to take this show on the road.

June 2, 1933

If Mr. J. Pierpont Morgan should fall into a barrel of onion soup—may the fates forfend!—the chances are he would come up with a rose in his hand. At least you gather this impression from the testimony today in the Senate inquiry into the private financial life of Mr. Morgan.

In one of the darkest hours of the long, long night of Wall Street, Mr. Morgan—or rather one of Mr. Morgan's bright young blades—joined with other financiers in an attempt to prop the market, at the moment aslant, like the Leaning Tower of Pisa.

They bought a job lot of those checks that seemed to be most afflicted with what the deep sea divers call the "bends," and wound up making over $1,000,000 for the rescue mission. Which brings us to the thought that to him who hath shall be given. Also a stitch in time saves nine. Likewise you can't keep a squirrel on the ground.

Mr. George Whitney, that cool, calm, suave, impeccably arrayed gentleman who comes out the most limelighted of all the members of the House of Morgan, tells the story today. Give Mr. Whitney a question, and a few quotations, and he is one of the finest financial raconteurs in the world. I spoke yesterday of Mr. Whitney being our only sex appeal in this inquiry. I said the ladies enjoyed gazing at him. A committee of ladies waits on me this morning to inform me that I am all wrong in my impression that Mr. Whitney is entirely responsible for the feminine attendance at the inquiry. They say:

"We really like Mr. Morgan better than anyone else. Mr. Whitney is very nice, but his answers to Mr. Pecora's questions indicate that he may be a man very handy with excuses when he comes home. Anyway, he can undoubtedly out-talk any woman. Mr. Morgan is our candidate."

Well anyway, Mr. Whitney gives a thrilling word picture of that black hour in Wall Street in 1929, when you couldn't find another drying towel on the rack, and when in fact, to use Mr. Whitney's own language, all was chaos. Or do you remember it yourself?

In this hour, a little group of intrepid souls gathered in Mr. Morgan's office and said to each other, "Well, boys, what will we do?"

Mr. Whitney recalls the names of the members of this devoted band: his brother, Dick Whitney, now president of the New York Stock Exchange, the Messrs. Potter Williams, Mitchell and George F. Baker, Jr., all representing big financial institutions.

"Well, boys, what will we do?"

So they do it.

They pool their resources, and buy up Alleghany, Allied Chemical, American Can, Anaconda, F. & O., American Telephone, Columbia Gas, Bethlehem Steel, and others. ("Vas you dere, Sharlie?") The liquidation some months later finds them winner, off of $37,000,000 worth of buying, to the tune of $1,067,000.

Your correspondent, grown calloused to anything short of $90,000,000, whispers disdainfully to the brilliant young Mr. Julius Berens, financial editor of the New York *American,* "It doesn't sound like much profit."

Mr. Berens pauses in his voluminous note-making and whispers back, "You may sneeze at it, but it makes a big noise to me."

History does not record that the errand of mercy embarked on by these philanthropists put the market back on an even keel, although it is only fair to say it had its beneficial effects at the time.

Mr. Morgan, who enters the inquiry room rather cautiously this morning, perhaps fearful that some miscreant may be lurking about to slip a midget into his pocket, listens to Mr. Whitney's recitation quite enthralled.

Indeed, Mr. Whitney, in his many hours on the witness stand, must have been a liberal education to Mr. Morgan, especially in the matter of the affairs of the House of Morgan, which Mr. Morgan frankly confessed early in the inquiry are somewhat of a mystery to him.

He hasn't muffed a word uttered by Mr. Whitney, and he has been watching Mr. Whitney with an approving gaze, and many head-noddings, as if saying to himself, "I think I'll have to raise this young man's salary."

Mr. Ferdinand Pecora, who says Mr. Whitney is about as clever a witness as he ever tackled, concludes his examination of the gentleman shortly before noon today, and is starting in on young Mr. Thomas Stillwell Lamont, son of old Thomas W. Lamont, of the Morgan firm, when the Morgan attorney, John W. Davis, once a candidate for President of these United States, ups with objections.

Finally the inquiry adjourns until Monday morning when it will be resumed with young Lamont on the stand. Mr. Pecora expects to get through with the House of Morgan by Tuesday. He will then start taking up other more or less celebrated houses of Wall Street.

The one touch of tone, or class, needed to make our inquiry the high-tonedest affair from top to bottom on record, is provided this morning by Senator Bob Reynolds, of North Carolina, who works in a couple of real kings.

Senator Bob, a husky, ruddy-faced gentleman, who omits all "r's" from his conversation, is the chap who tagged the Morgan favor rolls as "Santa Claus" lists.

He opens the inquiry this morning with a series of questions directed at Mr. Whitney. He wants to know a few names on the foreign lists of the House of Morgan.

Senator Bob has a large voice. You can imagine him singing "Carolina Sunshine" most effectively.

Senator Bob asks Mr. Whitney if he has ever heard that a member of royalty was asked to subscribe to the Morgan units at the inside figure. Mr. Whitney looks somewhat perplexed. The crowd in the inquiry room leans forward expectantly.

Senator Bob becomes specific. He wants to know if Mr. Whitney has ever heard that King Albert of Belgium was ever offered the privilege that so far seems to have been allotted only to members of our best families.

Mr. Whitney replied, "I not only never heard of it, but I am sure it isn't true."

Then Senator Bob asks him about members of the French government, and King George of England, and members of King George's family.

Mr. Whitney insists, "I am sure that it is not true."

Then Senator Bob says, "Now there is another chap I want to ask you about, I can't pronounce his name. Sometimes I call him Moose-oo-leeny, and sometimes Muss-a-lon-ey. Well, anyway, whatever it is, did he ever participate in these units?"

Mr. Whitney thinks not, but he says he will supply the committee with copies of the foreign lists of the House of Morgan.

Mr. Pecora bows politely and with respect to Mr. Whitney as he excuses him from the stand, and Mr. Whitney bows in return. They have the measure of each other's steel, these two gentlemen, one the scion of Italian immigrant parents, the other of a proud old American family.

OCCASIONAL PROSE

WHY ME?

When physical calamity befalls, the toughest thing for the victim to overcome is the feeling of resentment that it should have happened to him.

"Why me?" he keeps asking himself, dazedly. "Of all the millions of people around, why me?"

It becomes like a pulse beat—"Why me? Why me? Why me?"

Sometimes he reviews his whole life step by step to see if he can put his finger on some circumstance in which he may have been at such grievous fault as to merit disaster.

Did he commit some black sin somewhere back down the years? Did he betray the sacred trust of some fellow human being? Is he being punished for some special wrongdoing? "Why me?"

He wakes suddenly at night from a sound sleep to consciousness of his affliction and to the clock-like ticking in his brain— "Why me? Why me? Why me?"

He reflects, "Why not that stinker Smith? Why not that louse Jones? Why not that bum Brown? Why me? Why me? Why me?"

Was he guilty of carelessness or error in judgment? "Why me? Why? Why? Why?"

It is a question that has been asked by afflicted mortals through the ages. It is being asked more than ever just now as the maimed men come back from war broken in body and spirit and completely bewildered, asking "Why me?"

I do not have the answer, of course. Not for myself nor for anyone else. I, too, am just a poor mug groping in the dark, though sometimes I think of the words of young Elihu reproving Job and his three pals: "Look into the heavens, and see; and behold the clouds which are higher than thou."

The Book of Job may have been an attempt to solve the problem why the righteous suffer and to point out that such suffering is often permitted as a test of faith and a means of grace. They sure put old Job over the hurdles as an illustration.

He was a character who lived in the land of Uz, 'way back in the times recorded in the Old Testament. He had more money than most folks have hay and he was also of great piety. He stood good with the Lord, who took occasion to comment favorably on Job one day to Satan, who had appeared before Him.

"There is no one like Job," remarked the Lord to Satan. "He is a perfect and upright man. He fears God and eschews evil."

"Well, why not?" said Satan. "You have fixed him up so he is sitting pretty in every way. But you just let a spell of bad luck hit him and see what happens. He will curse you to your face."

"You think so?" said the Lord. "All right, I will put all his belongings in your power to do with as you please. Only don't touch Job himself."

Not long afterwards, the Sabeans copped all of Job's oxen and asses and killed his servants and his sheep were burned up and the Chaldeans grabbed his camels and slaughtered more of his servants and a big wind blew down a house and destroyed his sons.

But so far from getting sore at the Lord as Satan had figured would happen after these little incidents, Job rent his mantle and shaved his head and fell down upon the ground and worshipped and said:

"Naked I came out of my mother's womb, and naked shall I return thither; the Lord gave, and the Lord hath taken away; blessed be the name of the Lord."

Now had I been Satan I would have given Job up then and there, but lo, and behold, the next time the Lord held a meeting Satan again appeared and when the Lord started boosting Job for holding fast to his integrity, Satan sniffed disdainfully and said:

"Skin for skin, yea, all that a man has he will give for his life, but just you touch his bone and his flesh and see what your Mr. Job does."

"All right," the Lord said, "I will put him in your hands, only save his life."

———

Then Satan smote poor Job with boils from the soles of his feet to the crown of his head. I reckon that was the worst case of boils anyone ever heard of, and Job's wife remarked:

"Do you still retain your integrity? Curse God, and die."

"Woman," Job said, "you are a fool. Shall we receive good at the hands of God and not evil?"

But when those pals of Job's, Eliphaz, Bildad and Zophar, came to see him he let out quite a beef to them and in fact cursed the day he was born. In the end, however, after listening to discourses from his pals of a length that must have made him as tired as the boils, Job humbly confessed that God is omnipotent and omnipresent and repented his former utterances and demeanor "in dust and ashes" and the Lord made him more prosperous than ever before.

"Why me?"

"—*Therefore have I uttered that I understood not; things too wonderful for me, which I knew not.*"

SWEET DREAMS

We think the greatest institution ever devised for human comfort is the bed. Let us talk about beds.

A man is usually born in bed, and spends at least half his life in bed. If he is lucky, he dies in bed. We used to think that the best place to die was on the battlefield, face to the foe, etc., but that was when we were much younger and more casual about dying.

Now we know that a battlefield is likely to be an untidy sort of place and much more lonesome for the purpose of dying than a nice clean bed, with the doctors and the sorrowing relatives clustered about, all wondering how soon they are going to get paid off.

However, let us not pursue those morbid reflections about beds. We prefer thinking of beds in their more cheerful aspects. We like to think of a bed as a place of refuge and rest—as a sanctuary against the outside world with its troubles and woes, where sometimes in beautiful dreams, a fellow can live a few hours in ecstasy.

Of course there may be a few bad dreams, too, but we always figured they are stood off by the pleasure derived from awakening to a realization that they are not true. Only the other night a bloke shoved us off a twenty-story building, but we woke up just before we hit the ground and our joy on discovering that we were still safe in bed completely canceled the few sweaty seconds we suffered while falling.

We claim to be one of the greatest authorities in the United States on beds—that is, on the sleeping qualities of beds. We have slept in beds in every State in the Union, and we must say good beds are fairly common in these days when the construction of springs and mattresses has reached a degree approaching perfection, and American housewives, in furnishing their homes, are properly placing more importance on beds than on any other items of household equipment.

We can remember when some hotel beds, and a lot in private homes, too, were pretty hard to take. Even now I occasionally run across a survivor of the times when a bed was commonly just a sort of rack with a lumpy mattress and creaky springs and skimpy coverings for a fellow to toss around on between suns, though in general Americans have become educated to the idea of complete comfort in beds.

The trouble with Americans about beds in the past was their theory that a bed typified indolence. They apparently did not realize that the better a fellow rested in bed, the livelier he was likely to be when he got up, and that the better the bed, the better his rest. It is our opinion that the energy of Americans generally has greatly increased since the improvement in beds.

We hold that many Americans owe their lack of appreciation in beds to faulty education in youth. Some parents send their children to bed as punishment. If they would reverse this procedure and send them to bed only as a reward, and keep them out of bed as a penalty, it would inspire in the kids a respect and appreciation for beds for which they would thank their fathers and mothers in later years.

It might be a good idea, too, to teach the youngsters right from taw that they should never take any worries to bed with them— that they should regard bed as a secure nest in which they should rest without giving a thought to worldly concerns. If you started on them early enough maybe they would grow up with the knack of disregarding the winds of worry rattling at the window-panes, or the rain of adversity pattering on the roofs that disturbs so much adult peace of mind in bed.

We never cared much for that Spartan simplicity in beds that some fellows profess to fancy. A cot in the corner, or a crude pallet on the ground 'neath the stars is not for us. We went through all that in our army days, and you can have it.

We will take all the luxury with which a bed can possibly be surrounded—a gentle, yielding mattress, and quiet, cushiony springs, and soft, downy pillows, and snowy linen and the richest of coverings. A fellow gets little enough out of life under any circumstances without making his hours of rest too tough.

We like a bed wide and long that we can kick around in without falling out or stubbing our toes. As we have said, good beds are common enough, but a truly great bed—one that fits perfectly, and that sleeps good, is a rarity that a fellow should cherish above all other possessions. We have a bed in New York City that we think is the sleepingest bed in the whole world and would not part with it for anything, but of course another fellow might not like it. It might not just fit him. That is the thing—to get a bed that fits.

I realize, of course, that my appreciation of a bed is due largely to the fact that I am one of those fortunate chaps who sleeps fairly well, for which I am grateful to a kind providence. I can imagine nothing worse than insomnia. I am lucky enough to be able to sleep after a fashion standing up, or hanging on a hook, but in a good bed—say, that is when I really saw wood!

PASSING THE WORD ALONG

Since I lost my voice or about ninety per cent of its once bell-like timbre, I have discovered many inconveniences as well as some striking conveniences.

The greatest inconvenience is that it involved explanations to friends on meeting them for the first time since the vocal abatement and they are grieved by the absence of my former thunderous salutations.

You see in my set warmth of greeting is rated by the size of the hellos you give and receive and I was always noted for issuing the hood rive, or top size, the good old "Hello, hello, hello, hello," the old "well, well, well, hello, hello, hello."

Now that I am perforce down to the 6⅞ size hello for one and all which is just a nubbin of a hello and the brush-off kind you give a gee you do not like, my friends are inclined to huffiness towards me until I explain about the voice.

This is a bit of strain in itself but fortunately they soon start telling me about remedies that cure other blokes they know so all I have to do is to stand there and nod my head at intervals.

I find the nod wonderfully non-committal, especially when someone is delivering a big knock against someone else because word cannot be carried to the knockee that Runyon was a party to the knock. At least they cannot quote a nod.

I am occasionally distressed by strangers to whom I address myself in my low murmur answering me in imitative whisper, possibly inadvertently, possibly because they think I am kidding and possibly just because they have no sense. Sometimes even my friends do the same thing in that gentle spirit of mockery of human affliction from which many actors and others have long drawn their humor.

You have undoubtedly heard some of our public performers discoursing humorously on cross-eyed persons, on bald heads, on the deaf and the dumb and the lame and the halt. You have perhaps seen them simulate limps and other distortions of the body to point up their jokes. It is a common practice for us to apply nicknames suggestive of affliction such as "Gimp," "Frip," "Humpty," "Deafy," "Blinky," "Baldy" and the like.

False teeth and glass eyes and the toupee have long been standard items of jest among our jokesters. A person who is compelled to resort to a hearing device, one of the greatest boons to afflicted humanity ever invented, is said to be "wired for sound" which is supposed to be good for a hearty laugh.

And not only is infirmity one of our leading topics of humor but it is often brought up by men in moments of anger against the infirm, as when they say things like "That one-legged so-and-so," as if the infirmity itself was a reproach.

Of course the humor that deals with infirmities is in bad taste. Most American humor is in bad taste and growing worse under the present vogue for the suggestive and downright obscene in the spoken and written word. But even the suggestive and the obscene is not as unkind as the humor dealing with bodily affliction.

The hale and hearty shun the afflicted and I cannot say I blame them much. I can well imagine that I am a great trial to my friends who have to bend their ears close to my kisser to hear what I am saying. Maybe it would be better for all concerned if I did not try to talk at all because everybody else is talking these days and I would not be missed.

I carry a pad of paper in my pocket and when conversation is indicated I jot down my end of the gabbling on paper and pass it on to my vis-à-vis who takes a glaum at the chirography, crumples up the slip of paper and casts it aside, nodding his head or muttering a non-committal um-hah because he cannot read it any more than I can after it is two hours cold.

The forced practice has produced a headache for me as this morning I was waited on by four guys who were all mighty belligerent. I mean they all wanted to place the sluggola on me. They wanted to bash out my brains, if any. I mean they were sizzling.

The first one to appear we will call Pat, though his name is really Pete. He had a piece of paper in his hand that he handed to me, saying, truculently:

"What does this mean?"

The paper had obviously been wadded up and smoothed out again and I could not decipher the writing, though it looked familiar.

"Who wrote this?" I asked Pat (in writing).

"You did," he said, fiercely.

Then it dawned on me that it was indeed my own writing and I read it better.

"Pat is a louse," the writing said.

I tried to remember when I had written it. It could scarcely have been at the editorial council in Joe Connolly's office because insects were not discussed, only a few heels. As a matter of fact I did less talking in Joe Connolly's office than anywhere else in town because when I walked in he had a great big pad of foolscap lying on his desk and I felt insulted. It was a hint that I talk a heap.

It might have been in Lindy's late at night when I had a meeting with Oscar Levant and Leonard Lyons, but it comes to my mind that we did not get as far down in the alphabet as the P's. We quit at the O's because I ran out of pad paper and Lindy commenced to get sore at the way I was working on the backs of his menu cards.

I was busy writing out a denial for Pat when Joe and Ike and Spike, as we will call them, came barging in and each of them had a crumpled slip, and were so hot that taken jointly you could have barbecued a steer on them. I read one slip that said Mike would rob a church, another stated that Ike would guzzle his grandmamma if he thought it would help him, while there was still another that I would not think of putting in a public print. I did not realize that I knew some of the words.

I think if there had been only one present he would have belted me but the four being there at the same time complicated matters because each one knew the others are copper hollerers or stool pigeons, which is what I had in mind in my writing, and would belch to the bulls if a murder or mayhem came off.

So they finally left muttering they would see me later and I was taught a lesson about leaving written testimony scattered around. However, I think that there is a plot for a great crime story in all this by my favorite mystery writer of the moment Raymond Chandler of Los Angeles. I mean he could have the real killer going about dropping notes that finally land him in the gas chamber at Quentin because Chandler puts all his mysteries in California as if we do not have them in Florida, too.

I notice that whipping out the pad sends most of my acquaintances to searching themselves for their specs and they invariably have some fatuous remark to make about getting old as if I did not know by just looking at them or remembering how long I have known them.

I do not pull the pad and pencil on the dames. I just shake hands and grin idiotically. Most women are near-sighted since infancy and too vain to wear cheaters but why should I embarrass them. Besides not all of them can read.

YOUR NEIGHBOR—
THE GAMBLER

"One day it's milk an' honey,
Next day haven't got no money;
Every gamblin' man he knows
Easy comes and easy goes.
One day you're a great big winner,
Next day hustlin' around for dinner—
An' when you die there's few will sigh
For a gamblin' man!"
   —Old Song

One hot summer night, two young gentlemen in their shirt-sleeves faced each other across a table in a hotel room in the heart of Manhattan's Roaring Forties. The Roaring Forties encompass what is left of New York's night life.

On the table between them, crisscrossed and crumply, like a pile of soiled handkerchiefs, stood a tall stack of loose currency.

Meantime, the Roaring Forties throbbed with commotion. My friend, "Smitty," a lean-faced man with a babbling tongue, who always knows everything that is going on, stood on a corner hard by the hotel explaining why.

"That big gambler from Chicago's come to town," he said, breathlessly. "That Nick the Greek. Him and Arnold Rothstein's tied up in a crap game, and last I hear he's got Arnold hooked for $96,000. Man, that's a dude of a game! Them's two gamblin' fools, them are!"

His news was important to the Roaring Forties.

Out of the West had been coming at intervals, word of a new and spectacular figure in the world of chance, a man familiar as "Nick the Greek," a strange, mysterious fellow who quoted Socrates and Plato, and who would gamble you high and gamble you wide on any proposition under the sun.

In the East had arisen one Arnold Rothstein, a young chap whose gambling ventures were making the best traditions of "Dick" Canfield and other notable gamesters of another day seem trifling. He owned a couple of gambling houses, but on the side he played any other man's game that offered.

The Eastern gambling men said his gambling like had never before been seen. The Western gamblers listened to tales of his prowess, and laughed, and said:

"Well, wait'll he runs up against Nick the Greek!"

And here they were.

Seeing Mr. Rothstein across the table from the Greek, and seeing the Greek, too, you might have realized that Bret Harte once described both very accurately before either was born. Only, of course, Bret Harte did not have Mr. Rothstein or Nick the Greek in mind when he wrote the description. He was speaking of Mr. Jack Hamlin, the famous gambler of his fiction, when he spoke of him "with his pale Greek face, and Homeric gravity."

That is both Mr. Rothstein and Nick the Greek to a *T*. Perhaps pale Greek faces and Homeric gravity run in the gambling family. However, Nick comes honestly by his pale Greek face, because he is Grecian by birth. Mr. Rothstein is a Hebrew, New York born.

The money on the table was at the moment the property of the Greek, by virtue of a happy turn of a pair of dice. He had Mr. Rothstein "hooked," as Smitty related, for $96,000. There it lay, in cash. And now the Greek, tall, slender, and darkly handsome, spoke as follows:

"You can have any part of it!"

Meaning that Mr. Rothstein, if he desired, could "shoot" with the chance of getting even, or of losing $192,000 at one roll, a sporting offer indeed. History is not clear as to Mr. Rothstein's exact words in replying, but in speaking of the matter to me afterwards, he remarked, casually:

"I wiggled out."

The translation being that he lost no money, and the inference that he rolled for "the chunk."

A fairish crap game, you may say, yet but a passing incident in the lives of Mr. Rothstein and the Greek, merely a step toward their better acquaintance, in fact. Afterwards they met in other social sessions of this nature, until it is estimated that upwards of a million dollars has passed back and forth between them.

I introduce these two men with a definite purpose. I present neither as an heroic or romantic figure. I introduce them because they are representative cases of an epidemic which has been sweeping America for some years—because they are peculiar to, and their little dice transaction typical of, a singular period in the history of the country, a period of high rolling in a gambling way such as the land has never before known.

That period is partly the present.

I say partly, because after about six years of a frenzy of gambling, during which the butcher, the baker, and the candlestick maker were flipping thousand-dollar notes around in wagers as carelessly as mere words, the inevitable has set in.

They are still gambling with all the old frenzy, but with not so much of the old money. That is being gradually gathered up by the few.

Gambling men, including Mr. Rothstein, tell me that the "biggest" gambler proportionately to his means that the world has ever seen is this strange Nick the Greek. He is not as "big" a gambler as Rothstein in point of operations, because he hasn't Rothstein's means with which to operate.

But Nick the Greek will gamble you with all he has at any time, at any game, asking nothing more than an even break, and a man can gamble no higher or more desperately than that. No one seems to know much about his life. It is believed he came to this country from Greece some fifteen years ago, and that he is of good family. In his mid thirties, suave, polished, well dressed, and well mannered, quoting his Socrates and his Plato, he roams the country restlessly, always gambling, and always gambling "big."

The gambling world, which is the underworld, keeps track of its children and their financial condition by word of mouth, which travels more swiftly than the telegraph. Now Nick the Greek is in Los Angeles, losing $150,000 to the "Kansas City Kid" and the Kid's associates; the Kid being a lofty roller from the Missouri River, and the game at which the Greek loses, "low poker." This diversion is ordinary draw poker, with the exception that the low instead of the high hand wins.

Now he is in New Orleans, playing the races. Now he is in Chicago, broke, but rapidly digging up a new bank roll. Now he is back in New York again with plenty of money, and the Roaring Forties simmer with tales of his activities.

In one crap game involving a number of players, Nick the Greek is said to have won $185,000. On another occasion he lost $105,000 which is believed to have represented his entire bank roll at the time. It was early in the morning when the game broke up, and Nick arose with his stock remark after a losing, and which probably sums up his gambling philosophy.

"Well," he said, "it's all even."

Then he returned to his hotel with a friend, and got out a deck of cards.

"I can't sleep now," he said. "Let's play pinochle."

So until noon, the loser of what most persons would regard as a comfortable fortune sat there sedately playing pinochle, and the stakes were a penny a point!

Rothstein started his gambling career by betting a few dollars at a time on the horse races. He was then quite young. Presently he was knocking around with the professional gambling element, playing pool for high stakes, cards, craps—anything that involved gambling.

Inside of a few years, and before he was thirty, Rothstein ran his bank roll into a considerable fortune. Some rate him several times a millionaire. Unlike Nick the Greek, he does not move around. He stays in New York, and has fixed haunts. He is now thirty-eight years old, small, dapper, and as nervous as a cat.

I had a talk with Rothstein not long ago, and found him somewhat depressed, not to say despondent about the gambling situation. A gambler, he said, is misunderstood.

And misrepresented. For instance the name of Rothstein had been dragged into the baseball bribery scandal, which at that time flared across the sport pages in furious headlines. Mr. Rothstein seemed downright pained by this publicity.

"Why," he said: "I only had one small bet on the World Series they say was fixed and I lost that. I lost $6,000."

Because of misunderstandings, and misrepresentations, Mr. Rothstein explained to me, he has retired from gambling, and is in real estate, with a racing stable as a mere source of amusement. I subsequently noted in the newspapers tales of a glowing victory of one of the Rothstein horses, with the report that the owner has won well into six figures on the result.

If you can explain Nick the Greek, and if you can explain Arnold Rothstein, you may be able to explain the disease of gambling.

I asked Rothstein why he gambled, and found him a bit inarticulate.

"Why," he said, "it's exciting. I get a thrill out of a big bet."

Perhaps the thrill is the life of the germ of the disease which has had such a hold on the country the past few years.

It began with the War. It followed the convulsion of buying in the days when, as it was said and, as it seemed, "everybody had money." Finally satiated with the novelty of buying, men with their fists full of fat bills turned to gambling for new excitement.

The whole world seemed quite mad about them, but none so mad as the Americans at their gambling. With our entry into the great conflict, there was a slight cessation. The war over, it began again with renewed frenzy.

New millionaires, home grown, or imported from South America, Cuba, Spain and the other countries that had grown fat on the war, were on every hand with fresh-laid bank rolls, seeking action for their money. Men and women had become accustomed to big prices, in everything, and they gambled big. Some played the market. Some went to the races. Some shot craps. Others played cards.

Forty-five years ago, oil was struck on the premises of one John W. Steele, a poor farmer in Pennsylvania, and a thousand dollars a day, and more, began popping in on the astonished Steele. Before he had fully recovered from his amazement, he had $100,000 in the bank, and set about spending it.

As "Coal Oil Johnny," with a loose and careless way of tossing bank-notes to the public, buying saloons and opening them to one and all free of charge, and acting the part of a "nut" generally, he gained much notoriety. For many years his name represented bogie in the spending line in America. He was considered the highest of all high rollers.

Coal Oil Johnny died in January 1921, seventy-seven years old, and broke. He was a station agent for the Burlington railroad at Fort Crook, Nebraska. His wife estimated the amount he tossed off during his career at $150,000.

Coal Oil Johnny's total expenditure was not the price of one of the late "Diamond Jim" Brady's jewelry sets, and was $50,000 short of a losing at roulette made by a modern oil man at a single sitting the night after the echoes of Coal Oil Johnny had been stirred up in the newspapers by his death. The player himself remarked on the circumstance, laughingly.

"And it wasn't a button off his vest," he added, with some pride, meaning his departed $200,000.

The losing was made in an exclusive "club" at one of the Florida winter resorts, a club being a gambling house, polished up some.

In the old days, a gambling house was a public institution, not infrequently fronting on a street, with tables efficiently tended by bulky, gruffish men with bristling moustaches and soft black felt hats. Anyone could walk right in and play the whirring roulette wheels, the crap game, faro bank, or chuck-aluck, and no questions asked.

With progress have come the "clubs," swagger, softly carpeted places indigenous to the playgrounds of the rich. Only English hazard and roulette are played in these clubs; and one must be properly introduced to get in. If one is not well known to the management, one is led aside and politely questioned as to antecedents, connections, intentions, and bank roll, especially bank roll.

With the dealers, who have suddenly become croupiers, in evening attire, and gentlemen players similarly arrayed, and with the bare shoulders of the beautiful women present gleaming beneath the subdued lights, such a "club" presents an impressive scene, and the financial losses there are sometimes equally impressive.

The reason is simple enough. A person will invariably lose more, when he is losing, than he will win when he is winning. The gambling fever runs higher when one is on the losing side. The night before the oil man lost his $200,000, he won $8,000 and was content to quit.

These new oil men came bobbing up out of the mesquite of Texas and the undergrowth of Oklahoma in numbers a few years ago, heavy with money. They bought town houses, country landscapes, motor cars and yachts, and meanwhile they gambled.

The race tracks of the East are the real padded cells of the gambling insanity, with thousands of men and women rattling furiously at the bars of fortune. I have before me an estimate of the amount of money handled by the pari-mutuel or betting machines during the hundred days of racing at the four tracks in Maryland in 1920, and this estimate is $70,000,000! The average was $700,000 per day.

No one knows how much money is wagered daily at the New York tracks. Betting is supposed to be illegal on these tracks, but it goes on just the same, and it is on a bigger scale than in Maryland. It is believed that if they had the pari-mutuel machines in New York state, the "iron men," as the machines are called, would be handling an average of $2,000,000 per day of the public's money at one track.

The betting system employed at the New York tracks just now is called "oral betting." You can find a bookmaker without any trouble at the tracks, in fact you might have difficulty avoiding them, for they are all over the premises, and if the "bookie" knows you, or you are properly vouched for by someone he knows, you can make a wager with him.

This is accomplished by the simple expedient of writing down the bet you desire on a slip of paper and handing it to him. You settle after the race, or the following day. Naturally there has to be a good deal of trust to this system, and when a bettor fails to meet his obligations, the bookmaker has no recourse. He simply has to forget it.

The result has been to make thousand-dollar bettors out of normally two-dollar men. The return to normalcy is now setting in to some extent, but in the meantime the bookmakers are holding worthless slips of paper supposed to represent millions.

For a spell, waiters, and newsboys and bootblacks were betting hundred-dollar bills with such frequency that one old bookmaker was moved to remark:

"I think everybody must have a private printing press nowadays."

The immutable law of the races is that you can't beat 'em. Only one man ever made a lasting success of the beating process, and he died to make it lasting. The shade of "Pittsburgh Phil" Smith must have been stirring uneasily in the Valhalla of plungers during these many mad months of play at the tracks.

Prohibition has become an established fact, and some persons claim that Americans, denied the excitement of drinking, have gone in for gambling more strongly than ever as an outlet to their excess energy.

I doubt that theory. America has always gambled, if only in a comparatively small way. Thirty years ago every town of any size in the country had its wide-open gambling houses. The stories of the steamboat gamblers of the Mississippi, and of the golden days of California and the Rocky Mountain West, when the mining kings and the cattle barons played poker for huge amounts, are part of American literature. Once every cigar store had slot machines in front and policy shops in the rear.

The average American seems to be born with germs of the gambling fever in his blood. Sometimes the germs remain dormant throughout a lifetime. Again they take on early manifestations in the reprehensible form of marbles for "keeps." Most of us, I think, have experienced moments when the germs were stirring violently.

An ingenious inventor, recognizing the national trait, recently put out so simple a device as a top, converted into a gambling instrument by a little lettering on the sides. This top, called "put-and-take," has been eagerly purchased by millions of persons, and millions of dollars have changed hands on its gyrations.

The spinning of the top took too much time for some players, so another inventor promptly put out a pair of dice which answer the same purpose. The American gambler wants speedy action, which is one reason why craps is so popular.

Long ago reformers said gambling was worse than drink, so they set about making bonfires of the gambling apparatus and outlaws of the gamblers who once had definite business status in every community. Presently open gambling disappeared, though of course it merely hid out. You can still find it, I regret to state, in almost any town in the country, if you look long enough.

Men gamble when they have the money to gamble with. It is one pastime that requires above all things money. After the money goes, they sometimes toss in their honor, and even their lives.

Prohibition did not produce gambling, but oddly enough prohibition is the source of the money that produces one of the biggest gambling games that goes on anywhere in this country. It is a crap game in New York in which the participants are mainly bootleggers from the Lower East Side.

They all have plenty of money. Whisky is now an article dealt in only for cash, and so the crap shooters come with big, coarse notes in their pockets. Two men, heavily armed, guard the door and escort each player, who must be known to them, to the gambling room. About this room are eight other men, with guns not unostentatiously displayed.

It is not uncommon to see as much as $100,000 in cash in sight on the table, and in the hands of the players. If a man makes a big winning, say $20,000, and desires to quit, he is escorted in a taxicab to the place where he wishes to go by two armed men. All this display of force is to avoid a holdup. Holding up crap games was long a popular amusement with the gorillas of Manhattan.

My friend, Smitty, who plays in these games, once owned a gambling house, and had $200,000 to his name. He was of the old regime, and went broke when the murder of Herman Rosenthal, the gambler, played hob with the business in New York, and sent Becker, and "Lefty Louie," and "Gyp the Blood," and the rest to the electric chair.

Now Smitty occasionally has money, but more often he hasn't. An old gambler, once broke, rarely comes back. Youth, with its nerve and verve, is a tremendous asset in a game requiring exactly these things, the gambling men say. They point to a young Chicagoan, for example.

They call him "Slats." He is a quiet little fellow, about twenty-five, and one of the big bettors of the land just now. Occasionally he hooks up with Nick the Greek in terrific tilts. Once, it is said, he beat Nick out of $97,000. A few years ago Slats was penniless, bustling around Chicago, and doing the best he could.

"Now you can't stop him," says Smitty. "It's his youth. When you're young you've got the courage to do anything. When you get old you lose your nerve. You can't win because you're afraid of losing. Youth is a wonderful thing in gambling."

So I asked him a question.

"If a young man should come to you," I said, "and told you he wanted to start out as a professional gambler, what would be your advice to him?"

Smitty never hesitated.

"I'd tell him to hang himself first," he answered.

MR. "B" AND HIS
STORK CLUB

The only night-club owner listed in *Who's Who in America* is Sherman Billingsley. The fine type following his last and first name in the July supplement to the 1943 edition of that collection of big-shot biographies begins with ". . . owner, Stork Club. Born in Enid, Oklahoma, March 10, 1900. Educated in grade schools in Oklahoma . . ."

Now I have nothing against *Who's Who in America,* but that seems to be a mighty dull way to make a reader acquainted with the proprietor and host of a colorful and glamorous institution on Fifty-third Street, Manhattan, U.S.A., which future historians may refer to as the Mermaid Tavern of our time. A Mermaid Tavern complete with debutantes.

I don't see how anybody can start a Billingsley biography by merely saying that he is owner of the Stork Club and letting it go at that. After all, there is a great deal of difference between the Stork Club and every other night club in the world. It has no floor show, no line of undraped girls and no excruciatingly witty master of ceremonies. The absence of that last attraction may be one reason why so many customers are always trying to beat their way through the front door every Saturday night. It also has no melancholy French blues singer who speaks no English. That seems to be all right with the customers, too. Why, bless your hearts, I could make out a case stronger than the nuts, as the saying is, meaning the three shell game, against any form of entertainment in night clubs whatsoever, and cite the Stork as proof of my contention.

Instead Mr. Billingsley concentrates on nice furniture and interior decoration and good food. He is not afraid to keep the lights on so that you can see what you are eating. I am told that he also serves fine liquor which will not remove the enamel from the teeth. And, unlike other night-club owners, he keeps his peppy and pleasant dance music toned down so that you do not have to shout at the top of your lungs to make the punch line of the story heard above the roar of the brass and the crash of the cymbals.

But the best attraction in the house is the kind of people you see and meet there. The Stork Club is swanky but not snooty. Its clientele is always an interesting mixture of the more bearable members of the Social Register set, the well-mannered politicians, sports people, show people, writers, businessmen, scientists, artists, doctors and lawyers. Seen there frequently are such different types as Ann Sheridan, J. Edgar Hoover, Morton Downey, Ambassador James W. Gerard (he prefers the secluded Table Fifty-seven in the Cub Room), Alfred Vanderbilt, Lucius Beebe, Beth Leary, George Jean Nathan and Julie Haydon, Bernard Baruch, Drew Pearson, James A. Farley, Gypsy Rose Lee, Winthrop Rockefeller, Leon Henderson, Merle Oberon, Dorothy Kilgallen, Peter Arno, Gene Tunney, Helen Hayes, David O. Selznick, Mayor Ed Kelly of Chicago, Dorothy Lamour, Garson Kanin, Paul Gallico, Leonard Lyons, Mrs. Harrison Williams and, of course, Walter Winchell. But the trade at the Stork consists mainly of nice people from the big and small towns of America whose names you never see in the Broadway columns. And, last but hardly least, those beautiful debutantes and their undergraduate escorts. What I am trying to point out is this: the Stork Club, unlike most other night clubs and restaurants I know, is not a hangout for any particular kind of mob.

A lot of people who have never been there have the mistaken notion that you cannot get by the plush rope on the front door unless you are an established movie star. The man who has charge of the rope, a fellow named Frank Harris, who knows the names and faces of more than twenty-five thousand people, tries to keep out the characters who are inclined to tap dance on top of the tables and fight waiters. On a busy night he has to turn away as many as five hundred people, but only because they lack reservations and there is no room for them. These people can never understand why there is no room. It is a simple matter of arithmetic.

The Stork Club can hold only five hundred people comfortably, and Billingsley feels that it is smarter business to seat five hundred comfortably than eight hundred uncomfortably. The turnover of customers is not frequent. Between eleven in the morning until four the following morning, the club serves about twenty-five hundred persons. The Stork, by the way, is one of the few big clubs in the world that keeps its doors open for three hundred and sixty-five days a year. It is quite a lively place at noon on Sundays. People go there from church for a big Sunday breakfast, bringing their children with them. The dance floor is usually filled with fox-trotting couples eight or nine years of age.

When you enter the door of the club, after checking your coat in the small reception hall, you pass first through a bar and cocktail lounge which seats sixty people. Twelve hundred drinks are consumed at the bar daily, in case you are interested. Adjoining the bar are the main ballroom—large and square, with enough space for three hundred—and, off to left, the Cub Room, a small quiet place holding one hundred people. It is designed for quiet conversation. There is no orchestra in the Cub Room and no dance floor. A customer in the Cub Room who is overcome with the urge to rumba gets up and leads his lady outside into the main ballroom. Upstairs from the Cub Room is the Blessed Event Room, an even smaller chamber with room for forty people, although sometimes sixty squeeze in there. It is used for small private parties and, occasionally, for the overflow from downstairs. The exclusiveness that is often mistakenly attributed to the whole Stork Club is really confined to the Cub Room. At lunchtime only men eat there. It is usually reserved at night for celebrities and for established and respected customers. One of the few celebrities who shuns the Cub Room is Tommy Manville. He prefers the main ballroom where more people can see him.

In order to reach the powder room at the Stork Club, ladies from the bar and the main ballroom must pass the door of the Cub Room. Billingsley sees to it that the choicest available celebrity is seated in the Cub Room at Table Fifty, directly opposite the door. Then the lady who returns from the powder room will sit down breathlessly at her table in the main ballroom and announce that she has just seen Tyrone Power. It helps business.

Through these rooms every day at lunch and all evening long, wanders the landlord, nodding here and waving to somebody over there and sitting down for a few moments of conversation at this table while he scribbles initials on an order which sends a free bottle of champagne to that table. Sherman Billingsley is a soft-spoken man with a cherubic smile and an easygoing air of Oklahoma informality about him.

He is American to the core. He refuses, like many American males, to wear formal evening dress. While his assistants and many of his customers wear a stiff shirt and black tie, Mr. B always makes his appointed rounds in a conservative business suit and a rather loud and flowery cravat. He forbids his employees to wear moustaches on the ground that they look unsanitary. There is one exception to this rule—the Stork Club chef, Gabriel Beaumont, who used to preside over the kitchen of Louis Rothschild in Vienna. "Oh, well," Sherman shrugs, "he has to be different."

As he passes through the Stork Club, Mr. Billingsley is constantly followed. Fred Hahn, a former waiter, stays near him and watches every move he makes from seven o'clock in the evening until closing time. He even accompanies Mr. B to the theater and to prize fights. Hahn rarely speaks to his boss. Every few minutes he passes him a slip of paper with a message on it. "Doris Duke has just come in," the message may read. Or, "Do you want the music to stop at three fifteen?" Mr. B will glance at it without interrupting his conversation and shake his head or nod. "Governor Green of Illinois and Bing Crosby are here; both want Table Sixty-one." He scribbles a solution and hands it to Hahn while he asks Leon Henderson about the stock market. He passes another table and stops to say hello, rubbing his right index finger against the side of his nose. Hahn knows this means a gift of perfume for each lady at the table, just as the adjustment of his handkerchief in the Billingsley coat pocket means free champagne and a turn of the ring on his little right finger means no check for this party.

Hahn has held his job for two and a half years. His predecessor was a former waiter who operated smoothly with Mr. Billingsley until a photographer from *Life* magazine did a picture story about their teamwork. The pictures showed the Billingsley shadow taking notes with a pad and pencil and receiving hand signals from his boss. "Fame ruined him," Mr. Billingsley said. "He began to strike picture poses all over the club every night."

Mr. B's hand signals give away three hundred thousand dollars' worth of gifts to the customer every year. Mr. B belittles the cost of his generosity. "You must remember," he says, "that I don't spend as much on gifts as other night clubs do on floor shows. And I spend nothing on newspaper advertising." The Stork Club gifts range from automobiles, wrist watches, expensive jewelry and solid-gold cigarette lighters to dice and cigarette holders. He specializes in perfume—which is free to every lady in the powder room—and lipstick, which comes in three shades named after his three daughters, Jacqueline, Barbara and Shermane. He gives dolls to the little girls at lunchtime and official major-league baseballs to the boys. He used to send Franklin D. Roosevelt bow ties. On Sunday night before the war, he staged balloon parties which he hopes to resume again soon. At these parties the patrons would scramble for hundreds of floating balloons to which were attached one-hundred-dollar bills, tickets for free parties at the Stork Club and coupons which entitled the bearer to receive silver cocktail sets, pedigreed dogs, and even horses.

Sherman says that he began to give away perfume years ago when he found a seaman who was bringing the stuff by the suit-caseful from the British West Indies where the expensive French brands can be picked up cheaply. It seems that there were two kinds of bottles in the seaman's bags. One bottle was large and fancy and the other was small and plain.

"I never knew anything about perfume," Mr. B recalls. "I naturally gave the large, fancy bottles to the important ladies and the little ones to the kids."

One evening Mr. B had the finger put on him in a nice way by his friend, Beth Leary. "Now don't misunderstand me, Sherman," she said. "I appreciate these big bottles of perfume you've been giving me. But the kind of perfume I like best—and it's very expensive and hard to get—is the kind in the little bottle you just gave that child at the next table."

Quite often, of course, an expensive gift ends up by mistake on the table of somebody Billingsley hates and never wants in the club again. And then there was the time he asked his people to find out the latest married name of a society lady and to send something to her home. A few weeks later he saw her in the Cub Room. "That was a nice case of champagne you sent to my maid," she said.

Although Mr. B does not believe in advertising, he knows the value of publicity. When a public figure arrives in town, he receives a gift from Mr. B and an invitation to the Stork Club, where, he is casually reminded, the seclusion of the Cub Room will protect him from autograph hunters and drunks. When he arrives, Don Arden, the Stork's publicity man, takes his picture and sends it to the wire services and to his home-town newspapers. The club's file of pictures is larger than that of most newspapers. Many an editor finds in it a desperately needed photograph when every other source has failed him. On November 28, 1940, Arden noticed Jesse Livermore, the Wall Street tycoon, dining in the Cub Room with his wife. Arden asked if he might snap a picture. "Go ahead," said Livermore. "This will be the last picture made of me because I am going away for a long time." Two hours later a wire service called Arden and asked if he had any recent pictures of Livermore. The financier had just committed suicide in an East Side hotel. The picture of Mr. and Mrs. Livermore, with a Stork Club ash tray prominently in the foreground, ran in practically every big paper in the nation.

Once upon a time a Stork Club photograph showing two men sitting at a table full of liquor was published in the home town of one of the men in the Middle West. A few days later, Mr. Billingsley heard from him. "You've ruined me," he said. "I own the dry paper here, and I'm the campaign manager for a politician who is running for office on a dry program. You sent that picture to the wet paper in town, and they are running it on the front page every day."

A few weeks later the same man entered the Stork Club. "I don't like the way you run your publicity," he told Billingsley, "but I like the way you run your club. So I'm back." He is still a regular customer.

It is no accident, of course, that Mr. B has encouraged such nationally published columnists as Winchell, Lyons, and Louis Sobol and Dorothy Kilgallen to use his club as a headquarters. On the other hand, the number of important people who frequent the premises make it advisable for the columnists to spend time there. It is a wonderful place for news. Stories of the marriages and divorces of celebrities are always being revealed by Stork Club communiqués. The marriages of Sonja Henie and Dan Topping, Gloria Vanderbilt and Pat di Cicco, Brenda Frazier and John "Shipwreck" Kelly, and Victor Mature and Martha Kemp were all announced there. So was the divorce of Lana Turner and Artie Shaw.

Anything can happen in that house on Fifty-third Street. Leonard Lyons tells, for example, about the evening in November 1941 when American-Japanese relations were strained to the breaking point. A reporter, sitting in the Cub Room, heard for the first time about an important statement on foreign policy made by Prince Konoye in Tokyo that afternoon. He asked for a telephone. The call went through quickly and Table Fifty talked at length with the Japanese governmental official.

Spending most of his waking hours in such an atmosphere, Mr. B has quite naturally developed a rather startling store of strange information beneath his slightly receding hairline. He knows at a glance that the red-faced man at the corner table is now cheating on the lady with whom he had previously been cheating on his wife. He hears some things about the stork market and the stock market long before the rest of us. He also knows that the favorite dish of Annie Sheridan is not caviar or filet mignon or lobster thermidor. It is canned salmon, served with chopped onions and vinegar. He knows that Amon G. Carter and Larry Fisher of the Fisher Body Fishers bring their own steaks with them from Fort Worth and Detroit, respectively, and have them cooked in the Stork Club kitchen. He knows that Carole Landis adores a half grapefruit with flaming cognac in its center and that Beatrice Lillie likes a drink which consists of one-half lime, one teaspoon of sugar, two jiggers of crème de menthe, one white of egg and one scoop of vanilla ice cream, shaken well and poured in a Tom Collins glass. He is glad that the war is over because during it the amateur generals were always drawing maps on his table cloths, adding twenty-five per cent to his laundry bill which runs around thirty thousand dollars in normal years. He knows that there is a girl somewhere in Texas who thinks that she is married to his son. Mr. B has talked to her on the phone and assured her that he never had a son. But she knows better because she is sure that her husband would never lie to her. "Why don't you two make up?" she asks Mr. B. "Why do you keep up this silly quarrel?"

Incidentally, Mr. B is accustomed to having strangers pose as his relatives. During the war he received a letter from a sailor named Billingsley who had been telling everybody on his ship that Sherman was his brother. Now the ship was unexpectedly heading for New York, the sailor explained with a red face, and his shipmates were demanding that he take them to the Stork Club to be wined and dined. If they found out the truth, his life would be miserable. Would Mr. B be a good sport and help him out by putting on a brother act? Mr. B did just that and earned the sailor's lifelong gratitude.

As Sherman elbows his way through the bar and the ballroom and the Cub Room, one of his problems is to avoid the bores who want him to sit down and spend the whole evening at their table. If he imbibed alcohol, the quantity of drinks he would be forced to accept out of politeness might double the Stork Club's annual liquor consumption. (As it is, he sells and gives away thirty-three thousand six hundred bottles of Scotch and fourteen thousand and four hundred bottles of champagne each year.) But fortunately for his health he has not touched the stuff in years. He does not smoke, either.

One especially busy Saturday night, when the place was filled with people he wanted to talk with, a headwaiter told him about a customer who was extremely anxious to see him. Mr. B recognized the name as that of a gentleman who had owed him nine hundred dollars for several months. "Tell him I'm busy," he told the headwaiter. In twenty minutes the headwaiter was back again. The gentleman said it was urgent. "Oh, all right," Sherman grumbled. "Tell him I'll talk to him in the pantry." The pantry is a very noisy spot. Mr. B calculated that an interview taking place there, amid the clatter of dishes, could not possibly last long. The guest waited in the pantry almost ten minutes before Mr. B arrived.

"Sherman," he said, "I just had a good week in the market. I want to pay you that nine hundred dollars I owe you."

Such incidents and his experience with customers in general lead him to believe that most people are fundamentally honest. Considering the great number of checks he cashes in a day, remarkably few of them bounce. If Sherman knows you, he'll cash a check for almost any amount. And he will cash a check for anybody if it isn't over twenty-five dollars. If one of them turns out to be made of rubber, he figures that the money is well spent. "Those guys never come back to the club," he says. "And it is worth twenty-five dollars to me to get rid of such people." When a big check comes back to him unpaid, it is usually due to an honest oversight on the customer's part; he forgot to cash in some coupons that month or there was a mix-up in his bookkeeping. "You can tell about business conditions from the number of bad checks we get," Mr. B observes. "Very few of them during the war. Nowadays there are more."

One of the rubber checks he took during the war came from a second lieutenant. A few days later he mentioned it to a friend. A major who was sitting with the friend proceeded to give Sherman a long lecture on how to check on the identity of Army officers. "Ask for their AGO card," he said, showing his and explaining how the identification system worked. The next day Mr. B read in a newspaper that the major had been arrested for impersonating an Army officer.

The Stork Club's law firm, Goldwater and Flynn (Ed Flynn, the Democratic boss of the Bronx), finds that most of Mr. B's legal work consists in bringing suits against night clubs in other cities who use the Stork Club name. They have won such battles in Buffalo and Philadelphia, and now they are waging similar ones in San Francisco, Denver, Boston, Baltimore and Chicago. Mr. B does not ask damages. He merely tries to stop the use of the name and recover court costs. His argument is a long column of figures showing the amount of money he has spent building up the identity of the name since he opened his club at 132 West Fifty-eighth Street in New York, back in 1929. Mr. B today has not the vaguest idea how that place happened to get called "Stork Club."

Besides protecting the name of his business, one of the main problems in Mr. B's life is trying to get enough sleep. He maintains that he once went a whole week without closing his eyes. "A shower and a change of clothes is just as refreshing as sleep," he says. But still he wishes he could have more slumber. He blames the lack of it on Leonard Lyons who always appears at the Stork Club when the doors are closing at four in the morning, and demands another round of the continuous gin-rummy game which Lyons and Billingsley have been playing for years. This means that Mr. B gets home at five-thirty instead of four-thirty.

Still he manages to be on the premises at lunch-time, bright and cheerful. In the afternoon he either goes home again to spend a few hours relaxing with his family or gets involved in business discussions. At five he is sitting at the table nearest the front door, reading the stock prices. After the dinner crowd begins to thin, he usually retires to his three-and-a-half-room apartment above the club for a shower, a rubdown and a nap, reappearing downstairs around ten-thirty or eleven. Sometimes it is hard to wake him from these evening naps. One Saturday the waiter who was supposed to arouse him shook him vigorously and, hearing a muffled response, left the room. When Mr. B finally did come to, he looked at the clock and discovered to his horror that it was seven-thirty Sunday morning.

"Can you imagine a character like me being wide awake at that hour on that day in New York?" he says. "I went for a walk. I met a few people who knew me and they pointed at me and began to laugh. When I went home, the neighbors were thunderstruck. They thought I'd lost my job. I felt like a fish out of water."

Mr. B compensates for his meager sleep by taking very good care of his health in other respects. He eats generously but never sits down to a big meal. He has snacks several times a day. He is extremely partial to Canadian bacon and green vegetables. He often walks from the Stork Club to his Park Avenue apartment, a distance of more than two miles. In the summer he spends his mornings in the sun at the Atlantic Beach Club.

While he rests in his apartment upstairs, Mr. B keeps in touch with everything that is going on downstairs in the Stork Club by means of a two-way telephone system. By snapping a switch he can listen to the conversation in the service bar, at the telephone switchboard, in the lobby and in the kitchen. Knowing that the boss may be overhearing their words, employees are careful to ask the price before ordering tomatoes from the grocer. The telephone system enables Mr. B to prevent bus boys being persecuted by waiters or captains and also enables him to give orders to the entire staff at one time without taking the time to assemble them in one room.

The success of the Stork Club is largely due to the kind of relationship that exists between Mr. B and his help. The boss, as every employee in the club calls him, makes it a point to know everything about everybody who works for him. No one is allowed to quit or to be fired without talking to Mr. B.

Several of his twenty-seven captains—those gents in black suits who take your order and supervise the service of the white-coated waiters—started working for him as bus boys and were fired as bus boys. After talking to the boss, they decided to give the job another try. Mr. B follows a policy of filling vacancies by promoting somebody within his organization. This makes for loyalty and general contentment. A few years ago a private detective, hired by the Stork Club to pose as a bartender in order to check on the cash register, liked it so well he quit the detective racket and stayed there.

There are three hundred people working in the Stork Club on a payroll that runs around $600,000 a year. There are fifty-three in the kitchen alone—one head chef, one night chef, one *saucier*, two assistant *sauciers*, two roast cooks, eleven cooks, two *garde-manger* (that baffled me, too: it means the men who store and cure the meat), two assistant *garde-manger*, two oystermen, four pantrymen, four vegetable men, four silvermen, eight dishwashers, two porters, three food checkers and four stewards. I won't even attempt to guess at the earnings of the Stork Club waiters because a lot of their income is derived from tips, and waiters do not like to broadcast how much they make a week from tips. Stork Club customers, however, are pretty good tippers.

The largest tip in the history of the Stork Club was twenty-five hundred dollars which a wealthy advertising man from Michigan gave to Arthur Brown, a former day manager. On another occasion the same man asked Frank Harris, the guardian of the velvet rope at the main entrance, what was the biggest tip he had ever received. "One hundred dollars," said Harris. Our friend promptly handed him two hundred and then asked who had given him the one-hundred-dollar tip. "You did, sir," Harris replied.

Because he has to say no to so many people, Harris holds probably the most unenviable job in the house. He lives in constant fear of saying no to the wrong people. There was the evening, for instance, when he found himself faced by a large party with no reservation. He explained that there was no room. The leader of the party, a Paramount executive on his first trip to the Stork, said to Harris, "You tell Billingsley that if we are not in the Cub Room within five minutes, there will never be a movie called 'The Stork Club.'" Naturally, they got in.

Then there was the time when Mr. B was engaged in a feud with Fiorello H. LaGuardia, who, as mayor of the City of New York was threatening to have the ABC Board revoke the Stork Club liquor license. That would have meant Mr. B's ruination. One night Sherman received word that two ABC men were at the front door and wanted to see him as soon as possible. This, thought Mr. B, mopping his brow, is the end of everything. He approached them with nervousness. "Can I do something for you?" he asked them.

"Yes," one of the ABC men said, pointing at Harris. "Can you fix it so this guy will let us go inside and have a drink?"

Not long ago a well-known killer, formerly employed by the Luciano mob, found himself on the wrong side of the velvet rope. He informed everybody present that he was planning to come back again and that, if he could not get in, there would be a dead doorman in the Stork Club. Mr. Billingsley walked up to the mobster and said to him, "If you think you're so tough, let's see you stand where you are for the next five minutes."

"What do you think you're going to do?" the gangster demanded.

"I'm going to call your bluff by calling the cops."

The character beat a sullen retreat.

As it said in *Who's Who*, Sherman Billingsley was born in Enid, Oklahoma, on March 10, 1900. One of his biographers, trying to tie him up in some way with the Abe Lincoln tradition, uncovered a tattered photograph of a tacky frontier dwelling and announced that it was Mr. Billingsley's birthplace. Sherman showed it to his mother. "Law, no honey," she exclaimed. "You weren't born in that house. You were born in the back room of a little old grocery store."

Sherman's father, a Kentucky mountaineer by origin, was a jack-of-all-trades, and he happened to be running a grocery store in Enid that month. There were nine Billingsley children in all. Six of them are now living. He has three brothers—Logan, Ora, and Fred—in New York. One sister, Lottie, is married and living in Oklahoma. The other sister, Pearl, lives in New York. She makes the sensationally good Stork Club pies.

Soon after his birth, Sherman and the Billingsley family moved from Enid to the Oklahoma town of Anadarko, where at a tender age Mr. B made his first business contact with Demon Rum. There were a number of Indians living near Anadarko. The sale of alcoholic beverages to Indians was then and is now forbidden by law. When he was seven, one of Sherman's older brothers brought joy to his childish heart by presenting him with a little red wagon. Then his brother carefully placed in the wagon one dozen bottles of beer. On top of the beer he put a blanket, and on top of the blanket he put Sherman's nephew, aged two.

"Now, Sherman," he said. "You just pull your wagon down by the Indian village and you just stand there. When an Indian takes a bottle of beer out of the wagon, you take fifty cents off him."

Thus Sherman was introduced to that phase of the liquor traffic known as rumrunning. In fact, it may be that Sherman was the
youngest rumrunner in history. The baby nephew can scarcely be
considered as a contender for the title because he was not actually
an active participant in the transactions. He was asleep during
most of the business hours. The Indians removed the beer bottles
from under him with great care so as not to wake him up.

At the tender age of sixteen Mr. B was already embarked on a
modified form of his present business. He and his brother Fred
had opened the Lyric Drugstore at First and Robinson Streets in
Oklahoma City. In a dry territory, such as Oklahoma was in those
pre-Prohibition days, certain angles of the drugstore business bore
a family resemblance to certain angles of the night-club business
today. Not everybody bellied up to the soda fountain in dry territory drugstores calling for a strawberry ice cream or a nut sundae.
The majority of applicants for refreshment called for a shot in the
arm, as a jolt of redeye was then known. The drugstores could get
whisky from the warehouses on government withdrawal permits.
The government assumed the whisky was for medicinal purposes.
And who should say, when a man called for a slug, that he wanted
it to make the drunk come, not to relieve the pains and aches
aforesaid? I mean, was the drugstore clerk or soda puller to make
a mere call for a dram a case for the D.A.?

No one seemed to think so in those good old days. We used to
have drugstores like that in Colorado Springs which was dry territory many years ago, and I always thought the whisky tasted
rather funny. It was one reason why I quit drinking whisky. Anyway, the Lyric ran for two years under the firm of Billingsley and
Billingsley and did fine.

There were similar ventures in other parts of the country. Then
Sherman became a wholesaler of legitimate liquor in St. Joseph,
Missouri. This was still pre-Prohibition, and Missouri was a wet
state, though hard by was Nebraska which was dry. The dryness
thereof Sherman made it his business to alleviate.

He began riding the bleak Western roads through the dark of
night with loads of liquor for the relief of thirst in such towns as
Omaha. It was what they called rumrunning. He was young, and
it was the high excitement that youth craves. I would not be surprised if today, as he sits in the lush elegance of his Stork Club, ab-
sently nodding to passing celebrities, there are times when he sees

beyond the lights and the gay crowds the lone reaches of some black and muddy road in the back country of Nebraska and hears above the oompah of the rumba number only the steady hum of his motor as he drives furiously through the night. I find it almost impossible to reconcile these facts of his early career with his shrinking and gentle personality, but of course every man changes when responsibility takes him by the elbow and starts guiding his steps.

Afterwards, Sherman worked in the equally dry sections around Des Moines. Then he became owner of three grocery stores in Detroit. There, Fred Armour, an Oklahoma schoolmate, worked with Mr. B. He has worked with him ever since. Today Fred is day manager of the Stork Club and runs its concessions.

In the early 'twenties, Sherman came to New York and invested his Detroit earnings in a Bronx drugstore, which soon expanded into a string of drugstores in the Bronx and Westchester County, Harlem, Staten Island and Brooklyn. He also delved into real estate, and built a four-block residential district known as Billingsley Terrace. In 1925, he married Hazel Donnelly. Their oldest daughter, Jacqueline, who is now nineteen, drops into the Stork quite frequently. Barbara, ten years old, often throws a luncheon party for her schoolmates. Shermane, the youngest Billingsley girl, does not pay much attention to her father's business. She is only two.

The first Stork Club, which opened in 1929 on a site on West Fifty-eighth Street where a Western Union office now stands, looked not unlike the current establishment. And like 21, El Morocco, and the Colony in those Prohibition days, it was a speakeasy.

The management of a speakeasy had its headaches. On the one hand there was the law. The Federal agents who raided the Stork Club had to use a member's card to get by the door. When they completed the raid, they would hand the card to Mr. B with a smile. The name and number were carefully obliterated, of course. Mr. B went frantic trying to figure which of his customers was in cahoots with the Department of Internal Revenue.

Finally he designed a membership card which was really two cards; the second one, bearing the same number, was glued tightly to the first one. After the next raid, Mr. B accepted the telltale document from Federal agents and split it in two. Inside he found the number of the guilty member, who, to this day, remains on his blacklist.

On the other hand, when the speakeasy proprietor was not worrying about the law, he pondered about the underworld. When the Stork Club became popular, Mr. B was visited one evening by two notorious racketeers who inquired politely what valuation the owner placed on his business. Sherman, whose original investment amounted to something like six thousand dollars, allowed it might be around thirty thousand.

The more repulsive member of the team licked his thumb and placed ten one-thousand-dollar bills on the table.

"We now own one third," he announced.

The owner of a speakeasy in that era could hardly turn down such a proposition. The gangland powers had too much influence with the sources of liquor supplies. There was also the possibility of being put out of business in a manner that might leave you somewhat maimed for the rest of your time on this earth.

Sherman, to put it mildly, did not care for the arrangement. He found himself owning pieces of other speakeasies in which he had no particular interest. He was forced to do business with certain friends of his new partners. These same friends often appeared in the Stork Club at inopportune moments, frightening the regular customers. But Mr. B was advised strongly by acquaintances whose judgment he respected to do nothing about it.

Finally there was a meeting of the partners in the Stork Club cellar at which Sherman attempted to buy back the one third of the stock. "We don't own one third of the club," he was informed coldly. "We own one third of *you*."

But after a year Mr. B got out of the alliance rather easily. He merely paid thirty thousand dollars to regain full ownership of his own business, three times more than he had received under the original shakedown.

The underworld was not pleased. At that point, however, Mr. B was a good friend of several very influential people. One of them, highly placed in New York politics, let it be known around town that if anything happened to Sherman there might well be a general crackdown on rackets and several mobsters would find themselves forthwith in the pokey, or as the British prefer to call it, the gaol.

In the meantime, the Stork Club became famous. It started to attract the Social Register trade. The free champagne and perfume and the free publicity really paid off after Sherman moved to Fifty-first Street, near Park Avenue. The Vanderbilts and the Astors were followed by the Washington politicians and the Hollywood glamour girls. Now, in the Fifty-third Street location, where he has been since 1934, Mr. B does a two-million-dollar business annually.

The present headwaiter of the Stork Club is a short, fat and bald little man named Victor Crotta. When Mr. B opened the original institution in 1929, he hired Victor as headwaiter. Victor stuck it out for a few months. Then he handed Sherman his resignation. "I don't think you are going to be a success," he said.

Victor opened a restaurant of his own on Fifty-second Street and later gave that up to go into the liquor-importing business. In October 1942 he dropped in to see Mr. B and asked if he could go to work for him again. "I think you are going to be a success," he said.

Victor's second guess was undoubtedly correct.

ESSAY AND ANNOTATIONS

by Daniel R Schwarz

We have arranged the Broadway stories in chronological order because subsequent stories are on occasion dependent on knowledge
of earlier plots or themes and because characters often recur.

RUNYON'S WORLD

Manhattan is both island and seaport, and the geographic limits
of the port area did not allow much room for expansion. Yet New
York took off in the 1890s and, stimulated in 1898 by the consol-
idation of its five boroughs into one city, gradually grew into
America's leading urban center. By 1900, electrification had made
New York a city of bright lights. Glamorously lit, Broadway began to flourish as out-of-town tourism and business visits vastly
increased, in part because public transportation improved. The
subway was an image of speed and dynamism, of nervous energy
and accelerating stimulation. Its opening in 1904 was an important event, bringing hordes to Times Square—the hub of New
York's mass transit system—and its immediate surrounding area.

By 1913, vaudeville houses had opened. Legitimate theater and
movie theaters and nightclubs concentrated in the Times Square
area; by the late 1930s nightlife spread northward from Times
Square to Fifty-second Street. The peak theatrical season was
1927–28 when 264 shows opened in the district.[1] And the theatrical stars had an influence on public behavior. In his columns Damon Runyon would exploit the public fascination with celebrity
lives, including stars of New York theater. Songs like James W.
Blake and Charles E. Lawlor's "The Sidewalks of New York"
(1894) and Charles B. Ward and John E. Palmer's "The Band
Played On" (1895) kept New York life in America's aural con-

sciousness. People living outside New York City wanted to learn more about the exotic megalopolis, and in particular about its amusements and entertainments; they eagerly devoured the daily columns of Runyon, Walter Winchell, and their compatriots.

With its underground transportation nexus, its grid of streets, and Frederick Law Olmsted's ingeniously planned Central Park, New York had a seeming underpinning of order. Runyon's idiosyncratic yet highly structured plots are a kind of metaphor for New York's orderly grid of streets, but like that apparent order, they hide—as he shows—a subversive demimonde where economic relationships are oftentimes illegal or morally suspect.

With few public buildings and its elaborate billboard displays, Times Square became the heart of the "informational" city. The Times Square area was named after the *New York Times*'s new office building in that area. Advertising and entertainment joined to create a center of consumer culture. As Eric Lampard writes, "[A] symbiosis of commercial advertising and commercial entertainment prophetically juxtaposed . . . the glittering theater marquees and extravagant electrical billboards of Times Square."[2]

Broadway became the brightest star in New York's firmament. Runyon defined "Broadway" as extending from Fifty-second Street on the West Side to Times Square as its center at Broadway and Forty-second Street. In addition to the newspaper, theater, and music business, Broadway also included the new version of Madison Square Garden—completed in 1925—between Forty-ninth and Fiftieth Streets on Eighth Avenue. Madison Square Garden was central to the boxing industry, one of Runyon's interests, as well as to a diversity of other popular entertainments from circuses to horse shows.

The sidewalk in front of Madison Square Garden was called Jacobs Beach after the fight impresario Mike Jacobs, and it extended to the front of Lindy's. Runyon's fictional restaurant Mindy's is based on Lindy's—an eatery and center of nocturnal life named for its owner-manager, Leo Lindemann—that was located between Forty-ninth and Fiftieth on Broadway. Jack Dempsey, the former heavyweight champ and a Runyon friend, owned two restaurants in the area where sports figures and sportswriters hung out. Until Prohibition ended, the lower Fifties were heavily populated by speakeasies. This is where Runyon locates Missouri Martin's establishment, based on the one Texas Guinan ran at 151 West 54th

Street, and the establishment of Good Time Charley Bernstein, based on Charlie Desserich's Pioneer Club.

Broadway was the quintessence of the melting pot, and Runyon reveled in its variety. Broadway welcomed ethnic diversity more than other sections of the city, and the road to prosperity for Lower East Side Jews and others often went through Times Square.

The onset of the Depression; the increasing costs of live theater; and the coming of popular, accessible, and inexpensive cinema affected the legitimate theater. (Runyon loved films and went to about ten a week.) Many of the legitimate theaters became motion picture houses and theaters for radio shows. Vaudeville departed by the late 1930s. Burlesque theaters flourished in the mid-1930s until the license commissioner of New York, Paul Moss, closed them in May 1937. Despite occasional reprieves via court victories, the heyday of burlesque theater was over. Even the Fifty-second Street strip clubs finally were closed. The theater district narrowed to West Forty-fourth and Forty-fifth between Times Square and Eighth Avenue. By the 1940s, the Times Square area had become raffish and something of a cross between a carnival and an amusement park.

Runyon published his first four Broadway stories in 1929. As the prosperity of the 1920s gave way to the Depression, Runyon created a world that is far different from the fantasy world of Fred Astaire and Ginger Rogers films, where the right girl and guy get paired up and which the Depression seems not to have touched. In the Astaire-Rogers world everyone wears elegant clothes and lives in expensive hotel rooms, and characters open their mouths and sing Irving Berlin and George and Ira Gershwin tunes. Berlin, in particular, as Stephen Holden insists, "could touch on a common chord of feeling . . . Often wistful but never bitter, his lyrics embodied a bedrock faith in hearth, home, and country that transcended sentimentality."[3]

By striking contrast, in Runyon's world, selfishness often prevails, no matter the consequences, even if those consequences cause physical harm to others. Here grinding poverty and economic humiliation are prevailing facts of everyday life. The rich are treated radically differently from the poor. Within the horse-racing world, the difference between a tout and a handicapper is whether or not one is broke; if he is not broke, then the tout becomes a handicapper. Runyon's denizens expectantly await the smile of lady luck, but luck rarely smiles. What gets respect is the perception that a person has some money; even the doormen at nightclubs give "a very large hello" to those who have money and "a very small hello" to those who don't ("The Big Umbrella").*

For women, life is often hardscrabble. A woman awaits a man who will take her away from the humiliation of the chorus line to "a little white house with green shutters and vines all around and about" ("Pick the Winner"). While marriage is the one bridge from poverty to economic comfort, more often than not interminable engagements end finally in disappointment. Runyon's stories include quite a few destitute teenagers who become chorus girls and are promised marriage by unscrupulous characters who may even beat them. Yet some of his fictional women take advantage of and even betray gullible men. In "That Ever-Loving Wife of Hymie's"), even though Hymie gives his wife every nickel he has to support her in style, she cheats on him.

Let us take a further look at Runyon's New York during the Depression. Runyon's imagined world wears the scars of a broken economic system. Jobless men haunt the streets at four in the morning in the hopes of borrowing a few dollars for rent at shabby hotels—or, more often, for gambling—and often awaken in the afternoon. While the musical comedy *Guys and Dolls* generally makes his Broadway citizens lovable characters, some of Runyon's ruthless and desperate characters are murderers and use their revolvers and machine guns without compunction. In Runyon's macho world violence is never far from the surface, and people are not infrequently shot.

The criminal justice system is often helpless in the face of gamblers, whiskey runners during Prohibition, and ruthless gangsters. Bank failures hurt little people. In "Broadway Financier," Silk is a tiny seventeen-year-old orphan who has to work as a showgirl; her mother died heartbroken after losing her life's savings earned from scrubbing floors. People don't bathe every day or use deodorants and often have smells carried over from what they eat or do. Thus in "It Comes Up Mud," the Runyon narrator says of Little Alfie, "what with hanging out with his horses most of the time, he never smells like any rose geranium." A schizophrenic such as Cecil Earl

---

* "The Big Umbrella" and a few other stories mentioned below—"Pick the Winner," "That Ever-Loving Wife of Hymie's," "Situation Wanted," and "Baseball Hattie"—do not appear in this collection.

"is subject to spells of being somebody else besides Cecil Earl," while psychopaths roam the streets ("Broadway Complex").

Runyon writes in the present tense as if to capture the immediacy of every conversation and the life of every story. He has a wonderful capacity for rendering the sounds, smells, and tastes of New York. His eye is the eye of a camera—the camera of tabloid newspapers for which he wrote—and his imagination is a visual one. No wonder that twenty of his stories became motion pictures and two, *Little Miss Marker* and *Lady for a Day* (based on "Madame La Gimp") were major successes. His ear hears and renders gossip, street lingo, and the cacophony of city sounds. Perhaps Runyon's most fantastic fiction is that his retrospective narrator seems to have the capacity to accurately remember every word he hears.

In Runyon's world corruption is rife. The police and even the racing authorities are far more concerned with protecting the wealthy than the class of citizens who are just trying to get by. The police are alternately unwilling or unable to intervene to prevent public or private mayhem. The police are often complicit with the gangsters. Not infrequently, mobsters seem to make the rules rather than the police. Thus if someone complains about how a mobster puts his enemies in sacks in such a way that the victim strangles himself when he awakes, the mobster will report the complainant to police headquarters ("Sense of Humor").

Runyon sympathized with the dispossessed, yet admired those who excelled even if it was in gambling, manipulating the outcome of sports events, and crime. Thus he held in high regard Arnold Rothstein and Al Capone. The Broadway stories depict gangsters as merely another part of a complex socioeconomic system. They provide for those seeking liquor, speakeasies, gambling opportunities, showgirls, and sought-after sports tickets.

Runyon defined the image we hold of New York as the commercial and entertainment capital of American culture. Yet he portrayed its success as inextricably related to its aggressive, materialistic, and clandestine darker side. He not only helped invent the double image of New York as a romantic, exciting, glamorous city that was at the same time an unwholesome, edgy, dangerous place, but he also strongly suggested that this weird duality existed nowhere else.

He also understood the appeal of gangster chic. Do we not see the interest in the ruthless behavior and cynical speech of gangsters continuing in the popularity of Mario Puzo's novels (the source of Francis Ford Coppola's flamboyant *Godfather* films) and Martin Scorsese's nihilistic portrayal of secondary mob figures in *Goodfellas?* One could also cite the blood-soaked *Gangs of New York,* Barry Levinson's rough *Bugsy,* the chic toughness of the HBO series *The Sopranos,* and the hard-edged John Kander and Fred Ebb Jazz Age musical *Chicago.* Indebted to Runyon's depiction of speakeasy culture during Prohibition, *Chicago* takes a similarly cynical and bemused attitude to the underworld and its complicit relation to the respectable world, even while stressing how the media create reality as a kind of theater for a voyeuristic audience.

RUNYON'S STYLE

Runyon invented a special language to render the variety, commotion, and speed of the modern city. Like Piet Mondrian's painting *Broadway Boogie Woogie* (1942–43), Runyon's style is dynamic, colorful, and exuberant. For his locutions, he borrowed and combined terms from vaudeville, jazz, newspaper headlines, gangster argot, sports, and diverse ethnic discourses, especially Yiddish and Italian. His sentences teem with life, move in several directions at once, and overflow with intensity. Without sacrificing the manic comic energy that he borrowed from vaudeville, he wrote with the loquacity of the New York culture that loved talk for its own sake. Like jazz musicians, his narrators relentlessly play on a central theme, but take off on solo flights or riffs that are oblique variations of that theme. Runyon does not often refer to jazz, but his expressive style, his verbal riffs, and his improvisation certainly owe something to it.

As a journalist, Runyon was taught to put the essential information in the first paragraph, and his fictional beginnings reflect that training by presenting the essential facts. The stories depend on a crisp slang that quickly reveals crucial information. He eschews glittery phrases.

His use of vernacular, slangy, often boozily accented Broadway speech inverted the expectations of high art and expressed his underlying skepticism about wealth, social position, and respectability in a world where money and power prevailed. If a passage is read aloud, it is evident how the sound of his language—tumultuous, cacophonous, brassy, and shrill—represents the world of Broadway. Sentences seem to wander away, as if they've had a drink or two at four in the morning, but eventually recover their bearings.

Runyon not only listened with his magnificent ear to the grammatically lax conversational speech that was characteristic of working-class New York, but also embroidered and transformed it into his own inimitable voice. He heard New York City talking—its sounds, its conflicts, its history, and its culture—and offered the rest of the English-speaking world his complex take on it.

The hardboiled, heavily stressed, consonant-loaded style of Runyon owed as much to the sounds of American entertainment as it did to gangster argot and popular journalism. In the New York accent of Runyon's characters, the consonants are always articulated and the final ones are enunciated fully; the speech slows down as the sentence ends and the final consonant is orated as if a long closing note.

New York culture emphasizes talk as performance and is often accompanied by head and hand gestures almost as a jazz pianist plays with flourishes of his hands, head, and feet. New York conversation is often restless, with the participants intermittently looking around, glancing at their watches, making eye contact and looking away, moving away from the person to whom they are talking as they think of their next destination—or their next conversational opportunity within a room or at a dining table—as their fellow conversationalist finishes. To some outsiders this is rude, but this is the essence of the style in Runyon's stories.

Just as the stories often end with surprises and reversals, so do the sentences. Indeed Runyon often inverts grammatical expectations, or uses a sequence of clauses to gradually undermine the original premise of a sentence's first independent clause. The last sentences of a story are memorable for their twists and turns, their wheedling and seduction of the reader into accepting as logical what is in fact outrageous. Take the last sentence of "Situation Wanted": "Well, afterward I hear that the first lot Asleep sells is to the family of the late Benny Barker, the bookie, who passes away during the race meeting in Miami, Florida, of pneumonia, superinduced by lying out all night in a ditch of water near the home of Miss Anna Lark, although I understand that the fact that Benny is tied up in a sack in the ditch is considered a slight contributing cause of his last illness." All the apparent circumlocutions at the outset are, upon a second reading, informative and without fluff. Perhaps Asleep found Benny Barker with his fiancée. Indeed, are not many sentences like dances in burlesque and even vaudeville with their playful teasing, arousing of expectations, and surprise reversals? And entire stories bear some relation to the stories of comic burlesque entertainers, stories that depend on punch lines. The rhythms of delivery owe something to stage comedians, often Jewish, whose stories are almost always narrated in the present tense.

The unity of Runyon's stories as a collective corpus derives in part from the consistency of the Broadway narrator's hardbitten ironic style and in part from recurring characters like Ambrose Hammer, the drama critic, who is an amateur detective (and may owe something to Raymond Chandler and Dashiell Hammett) and is always falling in love; Waldo Winchester, another scribe, whose name suggests Walter Winchell; Dave the Dude; the Brooklyn hoodlum Harry the Horse and his friends Spanish John and Little Isadore; Sam the Gonoph, the ticket broker; Hot Horse Herbie; John Brannigan, the cop who comes from the same neighborhood as Big Jule and who has his own code in enforcing the law; and Spider McCoy, the fight manager who is always searching for the next heavyweight champion of the world.

ANNOTATIONS FOR RUNYON'S
BROADWAY STORIES

"Romance in the Roaring Forties" (July 1929, *Cosmopolitan*) refers to the West Forties in Manhattan, not to the 1940s. Waldo Winchester is a comic version of Runyon's tabloid rival Walter Winchell before they became close friends in Runyon's final years. The two were the most important tabloid voices in America between the 1920s and Runyon's death in 1946.

Dave the Dude may be based, as Pete Hamill suggests, on Frank Costello, whom Runyon knew quite well and who used brains more than brawn, but I think he is more likely an amalgam of colorful bookmakers and bootleggers with whom Runyon was familiar.

Billy Perry works as a tap dancer for Missouri Martin at the Sixteen Hundred Club; Martin is based on a ribald New York speakeasy manager who called herself Texas Guinan and ran the

Three Hundred Club with sexy hostesses; her real name was Mary Louise Cecilia.

"A Very Honorable Guy" (August 1929, *Cosmopolitan*), Runyon's second story, introduces Armand Rosenthal, known as The Brain. He is based on the gambler and loan shark Arnold Rothstein, who fixed the 1919 World Series and with whom Runyon consorted at Lindy's and whom Runyon considered a friend. (Runyon may also have had in mind Herman Rosenthal, a gambler who was murdered by corrupt police in 1912.) In "Baseball Hattie," Runyon uses the name Arnold Fibleman for a character who tries to fix a baseball game.

"Madame La Gimp" (October 1929, *Cosmopolitan*) is the source of Frank Capra's 1933 film *Lady for a Day* and his upbeat remake in 1961, *A Pocketful of Miracles*. The latter film fuses the nameless apple lady who takes care of The Brain in "The Brain Goes Home" (see below) with Madame La Gimp, an alcoholic street person who sells old newspapers and faded flowers.

"Dark Dolores" (November 1929, *Cosmopolitan*) is the first of Runyon's noir stories and the last and darkest of the first four stories that appeared in 1929. Dave the Dude plays an important role, as he does in three of the first four stories. He presides over a major gangster gathering in Atlantic City. When Waldo Winchester complains there are no longer dolls around killing guys, he is referring to the Edward Hall–Eleanor Mills and the Ruth Snyder–Judd Gray murder cases, which Runyon covered in all their lurid details in 1926 and 1927 and which are anthologized in Runyon's *Trials and Other Tribulations* (Philadelphia: J.B. Lippincott, 1947).

"Lillian" (February 1, 1930, *Collier's*) is one of a group of early stories (others include "A Very Honorable Guy," "Madame La Gimp," and "Social Error") where Runyon uses fairy-tale endings to transform lonely, isolated, alienated, rejected, and powerless figures into people living comfortable domestic lives. Illegal drinking during Prohibition, which lasted from 1920 to 1933, played a large role in Runyon's early stories.

"Social Error" (March 22, 1930, *Collier's*) features Waldo Winchester, the Winchell surrogate, who, like Winchell, uses the term "underworld complex" to convey romantic fascination with the criminal world—a fascination held by no one more than Runyon and Winchell. Florenz Ziegfeld was the impresario of Ziegfeld's *Follies*, vaudeville revues featuring beautiful women and more than a touch of burlesque; the *Follies* outlasted Ziegfeld, who died in 1932.

"Blood Pressure" (April 3, 1930, *Saturday Evening Post*) is the basis for the dice game in *Guys and Dolls,* in the posthumous musical derived from Runyon's stories that was written by Jo Swerling and Abe Burrows with songs by Frank Loesser. In the musical Big Jule (not, as in this story, Rusty Charley) intimidates his fellow players.

"Butch Minds the Baby" (September 13, 1930, *Collier's*) was the source of a 1942 film of that name that Runyon produced during his Hollywood days. In this story he introduced the recurring Brooklyn-based gangster Harry the Horse and his accomplices, Spanish John and Little Isadore.

"The Hottest Guy in the World" (November 8, 1930, *Collier's*) introduces the detective Johnny Brannigan, who grew up in the same neighborhood as Big Jule and who loves the same woman. Big Jule is foregrounded in *Guys and Dolls*.

"The Lily of St. Pierre" (December 20, 1930, *Collier's*) is one of a series of Christmas stories—along with "Dancing Dan's Christmas" (1932) "Three Wise Guys" (1933), and "Palm Beach Santa Claus" (1938)—that were published in *Collier's* in December and that sentimentally evoke domestic values in juxtaposition to gangster violence and cynicism.

"The Bloodhounds of Broadway" (May 16, 1931, *Collier's*) is a story in which Runyon uses the high-spirited farcical technique of the early western tales that he wrote before he arrived from Colorado in 1910. But the central point is Runyon's resentment of old money and inherited wealth, personified by the exploitative Marvin Clay. Runyon is typically sympathetic to women as victims and to such powerless and poor women as Lovey Lou as well as her sister (a dancer for Missouri Martin at what now is called the Three Hundred Club rather than the Sixteen Hundred Club as in "Romance in the Roaring Forties") and John Wangles.

"Gentlemen, the King!" (April 25, 1931, *Collier's*) shows Runyon's characteristic soft spot for children, especially orphans. Here violent hoodlums—Izzy Cheesecake, Kitty Quick, and Jo-jo from Chicago—are captivated by a child who reminds them of their youth. Al Capone was the Chicago gangster whom Runyon treated sympathetically in a series of columns later in 1931, when he was on trial for income tax evasion (see "Al Capone" on pages 527–48 in this book). These columns were originally collected in *Trials and Other Tribulations*.

"The Brain Goes Home" (May 1931, *Cosmopolitan*) depicts The Brain's murder, which closely resembled actual events in Arnold Rothstein's demise. Rothstein was shot at the Park Central Hotel on November 4, 1928, by George McManus in what seemed an underworld execution. McManus had lost a large sum of money in a poker game in which they had both participated. Runyon covered that trial. (See "Arnold Rothstein's Final Payoff" on pages 509–26 in this book. Some of these columns are collected in *Trials and Other Tribulations*.) The judge, before jury deliberations, exonerated McManus; the state lacked the evidence to prove its case, in large part because Rothstein, while still alive, had refused to identify his assailant.

"The Snatching of Bookie Bob" (September 26, 1931, *Collier's*) is a noir story whose opening paragraphs refer to the desperation caused by the Depression, which began in earnest in 1930. Waldo Winchester, who had been kidnapped in the earlier story "Romance in the Roaring Forties," takes a dim view of snatching. We also have a reprise of the Brooklyn-based gangsters Harry the Horse, Spanish John, and Little Isadore from "Butch Minds the Baby."

"Hold 'em Yale" (November 14, 1931, *Collier's*) is one of three stories (the others being "Undertaker Song" and "A Nice Price") that juxtapose the elite Harvard-Yale-Princeton upper-class social world with Broadway's demimonde. Runyon loved the ethnic variety of New York. Sam the Gonoph—his name is based on the Yiddish word for "thief" (also spelled *gonif, ganef,* or *ganof*)—is from Essex Street on the Jewish Lower East Side. He and his crew scalp tickets for major sports events; that is, they buy them at cost and sell them well above cost.

"For a Pal" (January 9, 1932, *Collier's*) is a touching story about homosocial male bonding among lonely men. It is also one of the few in which the self-dramatizing narrator doesn't explain how he knows the principals.

"Broadway Financier" (January 30, 1932, *Collier's*) captures the hum and buzz of the overpopulated Lower East Side during the Depression. In 1900 that section was more populous than Bombay. It focuses on the event that nearly all people feared before the New Deal rescue operation began in March 1933: namely, the collapse of their bank. Between the 1929 stock market crash and the 1933 legislation, five thousand banks failed, costing depositors $7 billion. For those living outside the New York region, Runyon's stories helped establish the Lower East Side as a Jewish area in the popular imagination.

"Little Miss Marker" (March 26, 1932, Collier's) is a parable about the restorative power of love and the depressive blight of loss. One of Runyon's signature stories, it is the source of three separate films: the 1934 Little Miss Marker—in black and white like all movies of that time—with Shirley Temple and Charles Bickford, which was rereleased in color in 1961; Sorrowful Jones, a 1949 Bob Hope vehicle; and a star-studded 1980 Little Miss Marker with Walter Matthau, Tony Curtis, Bob Newhart, and Julie Andrews.

"Dream Street Rose" (June 11, 1932, Collier's) takes place on West Forty-seventh Street between Sixth and Seventh Avenues, where Rosie lives. A grim area during the Depression, it was known as Dream Street because the theater magazine Billboard was located there and Actors Equity was nearby on Sixth Avenue and West Forty-seventh Street.

"Tobias the Terrible" (December 10, 1932, Collier's) illustrates what Winchell called the "underworld complex," in which the world of criminal violence and shady dealings seems more exciting and attractive than the pedestrian world of ordinary citizens. This is another Runyon story in the mode of what I call gangster chic, where the gangster demimonde is more admirable than the respectable world.

"Dancing Dan's Christmas" (December 31, 1932, Collier's). See my comments above on "The Lily of St. Pierre."

"Earthquake" (January 1933, Cosmopolitan) focuses on the pursuit by the recurring police figure Johnny Brannigan of a cop killer named Earthquake.

"The Idyll of Miss Sarah Brown" (January 28, 1933, Collier's) is the principal source for the musical comedy Guys and Dolls and the successful film version in which Marlon Brando played Sky Masterson and Frank Sinatra played Nathan Detroit. The drama and film character Nathan Detriot is based as much or more on Runyon's Dave the Dude than on any of his other fictional characters, including Nathan Detroit.

Toward the end of the nineteenth century the Salvation Army began to play a proselytizing role in New York among the urban immigrant poor. They used the hoopla and chutzpah of Broadway performance—with religious texts set to popular melodies, minstrel tunes, vaudeville songs, and even drinking ballads—and advertising to convey their orthodox Wesleyan message of temperance, grace, and forgiveness.

"The Old Doll's House" (May 13, 1933, *Collier's*) features a recurring Runyon theme: the corruption and ineffectuality of the legal system. The trial of Lance McGowan, who executed two gangsters at Good Time Charley's speakeasy, recalls that of the aforementioned George McManus. Here Judge Goldstein, "one of the surest-footed lawyers in town" (who helps Silk make restitution for money that her sugar daddy Israel Ib stole in "Broadway Financier") manipulates the legal system to get his client, McGowan, off.

"It Comes Up Mud" (June 10, 1933, *Collier's*) is a hilarious satire of the culture of materialism where wealth matters and where people adopt whatever names and identities suit them. Beulah is one of Runyon's many gold-digging women.

"The Brakeman's Daughter" (July 8, 1933, *Collier's*) is a noir story dealing with the period immediately after the lifting of Prohibition, when the once-illegal distributors of alcohol fought over control of the now legal manufacture and distribution of alcoholic beverages. It is one of Runyon's most tightly and intricately plotted stories. When we are told that Big False Face "comes from the Lower East Side," Runyon's readers would have known this as code for his being Jewish.

"What, No Butler?" (August 5, 1933, *Collier's*) is the first of the five Ambrose Hammer stories—the others are "Broadway Complex" (1933), "So You Won't Talk!" (1937), "Broadway Incident" (1941), and "The Melancholy Dane" (1944)—and Hammer also makes a cameo appearance in a sixth story, "Princess O'Hara" (1934). A journalist, Hammer is a kind of fictional comic surrogate for Runyon. Hammer has Runyon's dandyish appearance, short stature, obsessive curiosity, and fascination with crime, iconoclastic cynicism, and strong attraction to sexy younger women with weak intellects. Like Runyon, Hammer uses his knowledge of other people to manipulate events. His name has the same number of syllables as Runyon's, and each begins with a stressed syllable—in other words, each name is a double trochee. With the story's implausible plot reversals, Runyon is poking fun at the crime stories of Dashiell Hammett and Raymond Chandler.

"Broadway Complex" (October 28, 1933, *Collier's*) focuses on Hammer, who has been writing a play for years. Writing a Broadway play was one of Runyon's fantasies, which he fulfilled in 1935 when he collaborated with Howard Lindsay on *A Slight Case of Murder*. Hammer, as a Harvard graduate, has the credentials Runyon earned in the school of hard knocks.

"The Three Wise Guys" (December 23, 1933, *Collier's*), one of the aforementioned Christmas stories, is an exceptionally rich and well-crafted story that plays with the name of an actual place, Bethlehem, Pennsylvania. The populist Runyon satirically compares the gangster Blondy to business moguls like John D. Rockefeller, Henry Ford, and J. P. Morgan, who he felt were not ethically superior to some of his criminal friends such as Rothstein and Capone.

"The Lemon Drop Kid" (February 3, 1934, *Collier's*), a poignant, dark tale, is one of Runyon's best race-track stories. It tells of the toll taken by the Depression. Because the title character lacks funds for proper medical care, his wife and child die in childbirth. The 1951 film *The Lemon Drop Kid* was a Bob Hope vehicle.

"Princess O'Hara" (March 3, 1934, *Collier's*) foregrounds the world of horse-drawn carriages that even today take people through Central Park, including the 66th Street transverse mentioned in the story. The 1943 Abbott and Costello slapstick film *It Ain't Hay* is loosely derived from the story.

"A Nice Price" (September 8, 1934, *Collier's*) owes much to the prior and more deftly plotted "Hold 'em Yale." It focuses on class distinctions between marginalized characters of Jewish heritage, trying to make a buck in the Depression any way they can, and the WASP establishment. Benny South Street's class resentment has a Marxist tinge.

"Sense of Humor" (September 1934, *Cosmopolitan*) is a noir story about committing murder by putting the victim into a sack trussed up in a bundle with a cord or wire around his neck, which will strangle him when he tries to escape. Strewn with corpses, this is one of Runyon's darkest stories.

"Undertaker Song" (November 24, 1934, *Collier's*) includes Ivy League characters, and as in all stories with Ivy League characters, the principal figure from the Broadway demimonde is Jewish—here he is called Meyer Marmalade.

"Breach of Promise" (January 1935, *Cosmopolitan*) portrays Judge Goldfobber (who is not a judge) as probably an amalgam of greedy lawyers who defend and consort with criminals. As with some Mafia lawyers today, the line between advocacy and a lawyer's participation in criminal activity is not always clear.

"A Light in France" (January 15, 1944, *Collier's*) takes place in the summer of 1940, when Americans were regarded as neutrals even though their strong sympathies lay with the British whom they were supplying. On the Nazi-occupied Atlantic coast of France, German U-boats (a term taken from the German word for submarine, *Unterseeboot*) were sinking British ships five times faster than new ships could be constructed. Rarely has Runyon written such a grim and cynical tale with so little humor as the ironically titled "A Light in France." Devoid of sentiment, the story combines the senseless violence of war with the perfidious behavior of every figure except the innocent Marie. Runyon gave this noir story a patriotic reversal appropriate for a wartime story in an American popular magazine. Marie is the bold and proud resistance figure who won't submit to German occupation.

THE TURPS

"A Call on the President" (August 13, 1937, *Saturday Evening Post*) is about a middle-class couple living in Brooklyn, Ethel and Joe Turp. In the Turp stories, most of which are imaginary letters that Joe Turp writes to an editor about his working and married life, Runyon demonstrates his understanding that New York reached beyond Manhattan and that he had to date given the customs and conventions of greater New York, and in particular Brooklyn, scant attention. These stories show us that Runyon was more of a divided self than has been recognized. One part of his psyche envied the conventional middle-class marriage, where the working male lived on a daytime schedule. Runyon was fascinated by what he called "little people" of modest means, semi-educated people who were trying to make their dreams come true and who enjoyed the pleasures of decent meals, new clothes, movies, and companionship.

The Turps are the kind of people for whom Runyon wrote, the people he imagined reading his columns. He often extols their simple lives and stresses their separation from the cultural elite. In these mostly epistolary stories he shows an awareness of social mobility and social stratification within America. The Turps have a strong sense that they belong to Brooklyn, not New York.

It is worth remembering that until January 1, 1898, Brooklyn was a city separate from Manhattan, and that Runyon arrived in New York in 1910, only twelve years later. Living in Brooklyn, the Turps are recused from the Broadway world and from some of the razzle-dazzle of Manhattan. Runyon neither condescends to the Turps, nor does he step back to moralize. While he does not completely restrain his characteristic cynicism, the dominant tone is a boundless American optimism that, no matter what happens this time, next time everything will work out.

"A Call on the President" did not appear in any version of the Turp columns but, along with the 1938 "Nothing Happens in Brooklyn," does appear in the collection *More Guys and Dolls* (Garden City Books, 1951). Nor does Runyon use the convention of writing to an editor that he used in all the other Turp stories except "Nothing Happens in Brooklyn."

In some ways "A Call on the President" is a paean to Franklin D. Roosevelt. It shows the Turps' ingenuous but well-founded faith in democracy. The story is told in Joe Turp's usual digressive manner, one that is taken further off track by his wife's even more digressive comments; the narrative decision to include those comments results from Joe's respect for—and even awe of—his wife.

The Turps protest what they feel is the unfair firing of their mailman and go down to Washington in their car to straighten things out. When Joe arrives, he speaks for everyone who is a citizen, and thus has the right to speak up, when he says to the man in striped pants in front of the White House: "I am a citizen of the United States of America and know my rights. . . . I ses Mister, what is so tough about seeing the President of the United States? When he was after his job he was glad to see anybody. I ses is he like those politicians in Brooklyn now or what?" Joe is an innocent, expecting the Bill of Rights and the Constitution to work for him. Runyon—perhaps as a vestige from his wilder western days, perhaps from his intimacy with criminals in his newspaper career— has Joe express suspicion if not outright disdain for the police.

The Turps meet the president, who is not identified by name as Roosevelt but is Runyon's version of a president who cares about the average American or "little fellow." The president personifies a caring paternal government to which little people like the Turps can look for recourse. He represents security in the face of the vicissitudes of life. He is able to set things right when they go wrong and restores the mailman to his position. In the story the president is a metaphor for interventional government that can overturn arbitrary decisions made in the interests of predatory capitalism. Runyon depicts the federal government as the ultimate refuge for citizens from the travail brought on by the Depression, a travail that hit New York City harder than most cities.

Public employment in the postal service and in elaborate public works projects, along with such New Deal programs as Social Security and unemployment insurance, turned the U.S. government from an indifferent distant relative into a paternal figure personified by Roosevelt in his fireside chats, the very kind of figure portrayed in "A Call on the President." That Roosevelt was a former governor of New York and had taken a hand in the removal of corrupt Mayor Jimmy Walker accentuated the link between New York City residents and the president.

EARLY FICTION

"The Defense of Strikerville" (February 1907, *McClure's*) displays the beginnings of Runyon's lifelong attraction to society's outcasts; old soldiers take the side of the strikers they were sent to suppress. The story is basically told by Private Hanks, one of the strikebreakers who sides with the strikers; he is introduced somewhat awkwardly by a nameless narrator. As if Runyon were searching for ways to attain the immediacy of the present—and anticipating the characteristic present-tense technique of his New York stories—Hanks moves into the present tense for a time but returns to the past.

"Two Men Named Collins" (September 1907, *Reader*) anticipates the Broadway stories by using a self-dramatizing first-person narrator who is often verbally aggressive. Here is a narrative of male camaraderie in which violence takes a backseat to male bonding. The paranoid narrator begins with puzzling present-tense nonsequiturs reminiscent of the sociopathic behavior of Edgar Allan Poe's self-deluded narrator in "The Tell-Tale Heart": "I know some things all right if I could only think of them. These guys say I'm crazy—crazy in the head like a sheep." The narrator's name and character are inextricably intertwined with those of another man, perhaps reflecting Runyon's fear that no matter what he achieves, a shadow of his dissolute Pueblo past will expose him as a drunken Runyan, which was his original name and identity. This early story of a double in which both characters have a dark, subversive side—one a coward deserter, the other seeking personal vengeance in the guise of doing his duty—may reveal not only Runyon's fascination with the criminal mind but also his fear that, like Crummy Collins, he will always be regarded as an outsider.

OTHER FICTION

"Lou Louder" (August 8, 1936, *Collier's*), like two other *Collier's* sketches of 1936, "Joe Terrace" and "Burge McCall," drew upon the popularity in urban areas of dime-novel westerns, where rugged individualists—sometimes desperadoes—were in control of their lives.

All three have the hard-edged cynical humor of the "In Our Town" sketches. Perhaps because they were slightly longer than the pieces in "In Our Town," Runyon could sell them to *Collier's*. Among other things, they reveal that during the Depression a popular magazine like *Collier's* was willing to cater to gallows humor with sketches that are far less funny to us than Runyon's usual stories.

"My Old Man" (columns collected in *My Old Man*, Stackpole and Sons, New York, 1938) is the closest Runyon comes to the myth of the American pastoral, the notion of the West as a simpler world of—to recall "America the Beautiful"—"spacious skies and amber waves of grain." The concept of "homespun" represented a mythic version of an orderly premodern way of life based on household production: the farmer in his field, his wife at her spinning wheel or in her kitchen, craftsmen like cobblers and blacksmiths in their small shops, and children in little red schoolhouses. But Runyon also realized that this pastoral myth ignored the poverty and harshness of much rural life in the West.

"In Our Town" (columns collected *In Our Town*, Creative Age Press, New York, 1946) is a series of brief caricatures of small-town life that recall the world of Norman Rockwell. Runyon looks back nostalgically to a simpler world, but—following a tradition in American literature that included Twain, Faulkner, and

Sherwood Anderson—his nostalgia is qualified by a hard-edged and cynical perspective. Runyon is amused by but not unsympathetic to the way that dreams provide sustaining fictions in a difficult world and the way that dreams are manufactured on the thinnest thread of evidence that a horse will come in or a scheme will come to fruition.

With its simpler world, Runyon's nostalgic evocation of the American frontier at first seems to give his readers a pastoral myth. Like the Turp stories, the western stories depend upon an implicit juxtaposition to the world of sophisticates in New York. Yet Runyon reveals that underneath people are similar, some decent, some predatory, and many a mixture of both. Based on a fictional version of Pueblo, Colorado, which he evokes with neither New York hype nor his characteristic sardonic hyperbole, Runyon focuses on the small virtues, idiosyncrasies, and vices of the title figures of his anecdotes. While many of these figures maintain their integrity in the face of trying circumstances, others act meanspiritedly after they reach their breaking point.

POEMS

Written primarily for his working-class and middle-class audience, Runyon's poems were basically part of his journalism. His intended audience, as with much of his writing, seems to be more male than female, and his poems in particular take up male subjects of sports and gambling. Often written in dialect, they belong to an oral tradition of tale-telling and ballads. He not infrequently incorporated his verse into his newspaper columns. He dashed off poems with little literary merit, but because of the Runyon name and their accessibility in newspapers and magazines, they found an enthusiastic and large readership. Their wisdom and folk humor appealed to a readership that turned to Runyon each day for a moment's pleasure and wisdom.

Runyon was editing *Poems for Men* (1947) at his death, and it was published posthumously. He did not even list in his collected works his early books of poetry, *The Tents of Trouble* (1911) and *Rhymes of the Firing Line* (1912). But in *Poems for Men* he and Clark Kinnaird, who completed the volume after Runyon's death, acknowledged and reprinted some of the earlier poems. The best known is his paean to the jockey Earl Sande, entitled "A Handy Guy Like Sande," wherein the speaker, undoubtedly a Runyon surrogate, nostalgically recaptures a feeling for his own youth in writing about Sande's comeback in 1930 to ride Gallant Fox to victory in the Triple Crown. The poem, a composite of various stanzas that Runyon published in his columns in response to Sande's racing exploits, including riding Flying Ebony to victory in the 1925 Kentucky Derby after what seemed to be Sande's career-ending injury, evolved into the version reprinted here. Sande won five Belmonts and three Kentucky Derbys in addition to the one Preakness.

Runyon often used his poems to impart the wisdom of his life experience. But in a poem entitled "A Jew" in the November 1922 *Cosmopolitan*—a poem not included in *Poems for Men*—he is a teacher reminding his readers of the folly of anti-Semitism. Making little effort to create a dramatized persona, Runyon presents a speaker who is more like Runyon himself than usual. It is a poem in praise of a real hero, Sam Dreben, a Jewish soldier who emigrated from Russia and was much decorated for his World War I service by France and the United States. When the poem was originally published, underneath it in italics was a brief description, presumably written by Runyon, that concludes: "Sam Dreben, patriot, soldier and gentleman known throughout the army as 'The Fighting Jew,'" an epithet we might find less appealing than Runyon meant it to be.

TRIAL REPORTING

By the 1920s modern urban life had created a spectator culture, where the morning newspaper reported on sensational events, especially crime scenes and trials. As part of this culture, Runyon's reporting of major trials affected the public's response to these crystallizing media events. What distinguishes the modern spectator culture is its focus on not only the act of observing but also the interchange between those looking and those being looked at. In thinking about how spectator culture evolved, we need to examine not only the evolution of penny newspapers and tabloids but also the invention of photography.

In 1903, wireless telegraphy not only enabled messages to reach ships, but also enabled political leaders to communicate across the ocean. When Archduke Franz Ferdinand was assassinated at the outset of World War I, the shot was heard round the world because of telegraphic communications and the resulting newspaper stories. The age of electronic communication not only reflected but created events. The reporter as spectator became not merely the person who detachedly observes the effects of events but the person whose perspective helps create those effects.

"Arnold Rothstein's Final Payoff": Runyon covered the trial of George C. McManus, who was charged with shooting Arnold Rothstein at the Park Central Hotel on November 4, 1928, after Rothstein lost a large sum in a poker game in which they both participated. It was assumed—perhaps correctly—that Rothstein couldn't or wouldn't pay McManus the money he owed him. Because the state could not prove that McManus was the gunman, the judge ordered a verdict of not guilty and did not allow the jury to deliberate.

"Al Capone": In the columns collected under the title "Al Capone," we see Runyon's sympathy with the gangster on trial in 1931 for income tax evasion. Runyon never reveals that he knew Capone quite well or that he was taken with the splendor of Capone's lifestyle, including Capone's Palm Island house. If in the Rothstein piece Runyon at times emphasizes the distance between himself and a gangster he knew well, here he somewhat bridges the distance by humanizing Capone as "Al," a victim of big government. He implies that citizens of America might expect more from their government, whom he refers to as "your Uncle Sam," than the pursuit of Capone for $215,000. Runyon's calling Capone "Al" has the effect of making him into a regular guy being pursued by a predatory government that wants to imprison him.

"Morgan the Mighty": When Runyon covered the Senate Committee on Banking and Currency's 1933 investigation of Morgan's business empire, he showed no mercy to J. Pierpont Morgan. Runyon's scathing portrayal of Morgan's arrogance and of the favoritism shown to insiders, who accumulated stock at a special price before others could purchase it, helped create the political environment needed for the establishment of the Securities and Exchange Commission. Ultimately, the Securities and Exchange Commission was empowered to regulate how stocks were issued and sold.

Writing during the high tide of the Depression, Runyon the populist underscored the revelation that Morgan himself paid no taxes in 1931 and 1932 and that the Morgan partners paid a mere $48,000 in 1930 and nothing in 1931 and 1932. Using his characteristic technique of iteration to create caricatures, Runyon repeats the ironic epithet "the mighty" after Morgan's name as if Morgan—the despot of Mammon—were conquering royalty descended from an ancient line of kings and emperors.

Lindbergh Trial

After the March 1, 1932, kidnapping of the Lindbergh baby, the story dominated the media. Even the elite *New York Times* devoted thirteen columns of its March 2 issue to news and photographs. Finally on May 12, the baby was found in a shallow grave near the Lindbergh home. Bruno Richard Hauptmann, the alleged kidnapper and murderer, was arrested on September 19, 1934. The guilty verdict came in on February 13, 1935, and Hauptmann was sentenced to die in the electric chair on March 18, 1935.

The Lindbergh kidnapping immediately captured the attention of the nation. One of America's heroes had been plagued by tragedy, and a whirlwind of drama surrounded the case as it developed. With themes of celebrity, suspense, ransom money, and murder, this case truly was to become the trial of the century. Thus it was not surprising that on January 2, 1935, such famous reporters as Damon Runyon and Walter Winchell descended upon the small town of Flemington, New Jersey, to observe and report on the trial. Although Runyon's articles on the Lindbergh trial are not included in this collection, his reports on the case are an important part of his oeuvre.

The Lindbergh case was a litmus test of the power of the media and gives an idea of the world in which Runyon was working. Using techniques that had boosted the importance of major sporting events and employing reporters like Runyon, who had made his mark in sports writing, the media created a spectacle that captured the imagination of the American public.

While Winchell never wavered in zealously advocating Bruno Hauptmann's guilt, Runyon became increasingly detached and thoughtful. Yet early in the Lindbergh trial he had milked the event for its sensationalism, beginning his report of January 3,

1935, the day after the trial began, with a characteristically precise description in terms that would arouse the sympathy and anger of his readers: "They hand slender, gentle, little Anne Morrow Lindbergh the stained, torn garments that her baby wore the last night she saw him alive in the crib, as she sits on the witness stand this afternoon, bravely fighting back tears." And in the same piece he juxtaposes the woman on the witness stand to Hauptmann's wife—sitting with the Hauptmanns' "own little son"—while telling us that "Hauptmann himself stares at the lovely figure on the witness stand out of his deep-sunken eyes, his face impassive." In this story of the trial's opening, he organizes his story around the mother's testimony rather than the father's, whom he calls Colonel Lindbergh; he speaks of the "day of drama which reaches its peak when his wife is on the witness stand facing the staring eyes of the spectators, with half the women in the courtroom sobbing in sympathy with her." However, in his contribution to the 1935 *Cosmopolitan* article "Why They'll Never Forget the Trial of the Century," Runyon wrote movingly in favor of abolishing the death sentence.

OCCASIONAL PROSE

"Why Me?" "Sweet Dreams," and "Passing the Word Along" (*Short Takes*, 1946). After Runyon's April 1944 operations removing his malignant larynx, he could no longer speak. His frankness about disability takes place in a world where such infirmities were either not discussed or were discussed only in whispers behind the victim's back: "Since I lost my voice or about 90 percent of its once bell-like timbre, I have discovered many inconveniences as well as some striking conveniences." A man who had once had the cachet of a movie star, Runyon was reduced to virtual silence. He took the position of one who is handicapped: "The hale and hearty shun the afflicted and I cannot say I blame them much." We hear Runyon's irrepressible spirit as well as his resilient attitude; he insists that we can't feel sorry for ourselves and that we all start where we are. But we also hear some self-pity and bitterness: "Maybe it would be better for all concerned if I did not try to talk at all because everybody else is talking these days and I would not be missed." He poignantly describes how he communicates by notepad and how his friends begin searching for their spectacles.

Runyon's illness revealed a poignant yet attractive vulnerability. His columns on his illness, some of which are collected in *Runyon First and Last* as "Written in Sickness" and in *Short Takes* as "On Being Sick," are excruciatingly honest and moving. He is every-man asking for sympathy, even while knowing it will not help. Indeed, Runyon's eloquence and directness as his life slowly ebbed would have been particularly striking to an audience that was, as many of us born in the 1930s and 1940s recall, culturally educated not to speak about such things.

"Your Neighbor—The Gambler" (November 1921, *Cosmopolitan*) embodies what I call gangster chic. Runyon himself was a gambler and was fascinated by those whose commercial dealings were on the edge of legality or crossed over into criminality. Just as the demimonde within his fiction has an attraction for supposedly respectable people who are quite pleased to consort with gangsters, so too, Runyon realized, does the demimonde have an attraction for readers. Respectable middle-class people enjoyed reading about those who don't work nine-to-five jobs before returning to their family lives at the end of the day.

"Mr. 'B' and His Stork Club" (May 1947, *Cosmopolitan*), Runyon's last magazine article, is a hagiographic piece about Sherman Billingsley and the Stork Club, a nightclub where he spent a great deal of time in his final year.

Notes

1 *Inventing Times Square: Commerce and Culture at the Crossroads of the World,* ed. William Taylor (New York: Russell Sage Foundation, 1991), 179.
2 Lampard, Eric, "Introductory Essay," in Taylor, 16.
3 Holden, Stephen, "Books of the Times: Not for Just an Hour, Not for Just a Day ... but Always," *New York Times,* October 31, 2001, E10.

THE STORY OF PENGUIN CLASSICS

Before 1946 . . . "Classics" are mainly the domain of academics and students; readable editions for everyone else are almost unheard of. This all changes when a little-known classicist, E. V. Rieu, presents Penguin founder Allen Lane with the translation of Homer's *Odyssey* that he has been working on in his spare time.

1946 Penguin Classics debuts with *The Odyssey*, which promptly sells three million copies. Suddenly, classics are no longer for the privileged few.

1950s Rieu, now series editor, turns to professional writers for the best modern, readable translations, including Dorothy L. Sayers's *Inferno* and Robert Graves's unexpurgated *Twelve Caesars*.

1960s The Classics are given the distinctive black covers that have remained a constant throughout the life of the series. Rieu retires in 1964, hailing the Penguin Classics list as "the greatest educative force of the twentieth century."

1970s A new generation of translators swells the Penguin Classics ranks, introducing readers of English to classics of world literature from more than twenty languages. The list grows to encompass more history, philosophy, science, religion, and politics.

1980s The Penguin American Library launches with titles such as *Uncle Tom's Cabin,* and joins forces with Penguin Classics to provide the most comprehensive library of world literature available from any paperback publisher.

1990s The launch of Penguin Audiobooks brings the classics to a listening audience for the first time, and in 1999 the worldwide launch of the Penguin Classics website extends their reach to the global online community.

The 21st Century Penguin Classics are completely redesigned for the first time in nearly twenty years. This world-famous series now consists of more than 1300 titles, making the widest range of the best books ever written available to millions—and constantly redefining what makes a "classic."

The Odyssey continues . . .

The best books ever written

PENGUIN CLASSICS

SINCE 1946